Preaching Through the Bible

BY
JOSEPH PARKER

Vol. 5

Joshua—Judges V

BAKER BOOK HOUSE
Grand Rapids, Michigan

Standard Book Number: 8010-6876-2

Library of Congress Catalog Card Number: 59-10860

Reprinted 1971 by
Baker Book House Company

Originally printed
under the title,
The People's Bible

CONTENTS.

THE PENTATEUCH

(Continued).

"HANDFULS OF PURPOSE,"

FOR ALL GLEANERS.

" Yet in this thing ye did not believe the Lord your God."—DEUT. i. 32.

Note the possibility of partial faith. —There may be very considerable credence in divine promises, yet there may be one weak point.—In this as in other respects the law holds good : he that offends in one point offends in all. —Faith is no stronger than its weakest point.—We must not expect to realise divine blessings if we bring a crippled faith to the exercise.—It is sometimes supposed that faith is one act, and that as such it is either strong or weak. —All consciousness and all spiritual history distinctly disprove this theory. —We may have a general faith in the inspiration of the Scriptures, and yet encounter with strong doubt some particular injunction or promise which appeals to our self-sacrifice.—We may believe in other men praying and have doubts about our own prayers.—We may have general faith in Christian doctrine and yet be lacking in the particular faith which applies that doctrine to actual life.—We should examine the whole line of faith day by day to see which points are weak and to amend them accordingly.—What if we believe God and do not practise godliness ?— Where is faith then ?

" Your little ones . . . shall go in thither."—DEUT. i. 39.

God's purposes are not to be broken off. — Wherever they appear to be broken off it is only in detail and momentarily : the great line still stretches onward towards the completion of the eternal decree.—It is not in the power of man to frustrate the purposes of heaven.—Why do the heathen rage ?—The generations are one as to the divine intention, though multitudinous in their particular details ; the divine thought, therefore, cannot be judged here and now or at any particular break in history, it must be judged when all is completed and sealed.—The first shall be last and the last shall be first.—Those who are little now may be great hereafter. —The little are not condemned because of the sins of their ancestors.— Our fathers have failed, but that is no reason why we should not succeed. —God's regard is continually fixed upon character, and never upon mere personality.—Heaven is for the good and for none else, so all wealth, power, fame go for nothing in view of that grand realisation.—There is always a promise laid up for humanity. Better things are yet to grow upon the earth, and fairer lights are yet to shine on human history.—The future has a continual influence upon the present. —Posterity ought to do something for contemporaries, where the mind is alive to the influence of actions and the certainty of harvest coming after seed-time.

" There was not one city too strong for us."—DEUT. ii. 36.

This is a human testimony to divine promise.—Every city appeared to be too strong, yet in the strength of the Almighty the most powerful cities were as straw before fire.—What is true of cities is true of temptations.—There need not be one temptation that can distress the tried Christian.—If left to himself every temptation would be too much for him ; but he is never left to himself ; he is fighting God's battle ; he is not at the war at his own charges, but at the cost of God, and under the security of heaven.—When we reach the better land we shall be enabled to repeat this testimony according to the variety of the circumstances through which we have come.—It will apply to difficulties of every kind,—personal, social, spiritual : the testimony will be that throughout the whole scheme of life he that was for us was more than all they that were against us.— My soul, hope thou in God !

" Thou hast begun to shew thy servant thy greatness."—DEUT. iii. 24.

This is what is always happening.

—The broadest revelation is but a beginning of the disclosure of divine riches.—Even if there be no more seed given, the possibilities of growth and development are infinite.—At the last we shall feel that we have but begun to see the greatness of God.—This is the glory of the Bible : no man can read it through with the feeling that he has exhausted its whole meaning. —The Bible grows by being read.— Without doing any violence to words or to historical forms it is felt that again and again new meanings surprise the soul like unexpected light.— The same rule holds good with regard to providence, or the daily ministry of life.—There comes a day in every man's history when he sees the beginning of the greatness of God in the outlining and direction of his own life.—Looking back to his fancy, his weakness, his poverty, his friendlessness it may be, he is surprised to find how out of the very dust of the earth God has made a man.—It is a singular testimony but universal in the Christian Church that God is never regarded as a dwindling quantity or as a contracting revelation ; he is always represented as surprising students, believers, worshippers, with new resources.—He is able to do exceeding abundantly above all that we ask or think.—When man has overtaken God he will himself be God. —It is of the very essence of God that he should be unsearchable and his wisdom past finding out.—This should be an encouragement to us in our spiritual education. — Progress should be the law and the motto of every process of spiritual inquiry.— There is always some unattained height, some unmeasured orb, some untraversed ocean.—" I count not myself to have apprehended."—Grow in grace and in the knowledge of our Lord Jesus Christ.—All human education is but a series of beginnings.—Finality in religious progress is impossible, and where it is supposed to have been attained the supposition risks the destiny of the soul.

" Behold . . . not go."—DEUT. iii. 27.

This was what was to occur in the case of Moses. He was to have a sight of the promised land, but he was not to go into it.—This was no exceptional act on the part of God ; on the contrary it is what he is always doing as the ages move onwards.—There are men who see what they will never personally enjoy; and however much their impatience may wish to turn sight into still closer uses, they are filled with ecstatic joy even by the vision of the good things which are yet to come.—In this way we should live in one another and for one another. —Moses could return from the mountain and say that he had seen the good land ; even that message would be a comfort to those who were weary, and in whom wonder was fast turning into doubt.—There must always be men in a progressive age who see further than others.—As some see the time when men shall learn war no more.—Others see the time when there will be no need for any man to say to his brother, "Know the Lord," for all shall know him from the least unto the greatest. — This method of divine providence is educational, inasmuch as it shows that not to go does not prevent the enjoyment of the soul in the prospect of realised promises. It is something to submit gracefully to a subordination of the individual, and to accept gladly benefits which are intended for the whole commonwealth.—There is no tone of impatience in the statement of Moses when he hears the Lord's proposition.—We must accept our place

whether we are seers or literal travellers.—It is no small pleasure to see even in dream or in assured hope the beautiful summer which is yet to spread its glories over the whole land. —The enjoyment is, indeed, intensely spiritual, but not, for that reason, the less real.—Moses may have had a fuller realisation of the promised land than the children of Israel ; they had to endure the battle and the fatigue, and to win their way inch by inch : Moses saw the land, and knew that every foot of it would be given to the people whom he had led. —Aged Christians must take this standpoint.—Exhausted ministers must content themselves with the view that is before them, and leave others to secure that view in all its detail and literal value.—The oldest man should have the keenest sight into the beautiful future.—He uses his old age mischievously who uses it as a period of languor or sleep : the oldest man should have the most cheerful voice in the church.

" So we abode in the valley."—DEUT. iii. 29.

Places have moral interest.—Sometimes the valley is in the highland, and is therefore only a valley relatively: as compared with valleys far away down it may actually be a very high mountain.—The lesson we have to learn is to abide in the place assigned by Providence.—There is a subtle tone of submission and patience in the text. There is no complaining as to the lot. —The valley is accepted as a sanctuary. It was a valley of God's making, and therefore was to be regarded as a place on which he had expended special care.—In the valley we may have *shelter.*—In the valley we may have *harvests.*—In the valley we may have *security.*—It is the business of the Christian to discover the advantages of his position rather than to moan over its disadvantages.—There is another valley in which we shall not abide, but shall pass through it under the comfort of the rod and the staff of the divine Shepherd.—Some persons seem never to get out of the valley; they literally abide in it as men abide in a home.—Who are we that we should chide the Providence which has made such appointments? How do we know how much the dwellers in the valley are saved from? Who can tell what compensations fall to their lot?—The text is not supposed to teach the kind of contentment which it is almost impossible to distinguish from indifference. Such contentment is no virtue. The true contentment is that which accepts the hard lot without repining, knowing that God has some good purpose in its appointment, and assured that even the hardest position may be turned to noble uses. —When our superiors attempt to keep us in the valley we may well inquire as to their authority: when God means us to abide in the valley we may be sure that he will not forsake us in our lowest estate.

" The Lord hath brought you forth . . . out of the iron furnace."—Deut. iv. 20.

Imagery is sometimes the most real method of representation. There was neither furnace nor iron in the case in any literal sense, and yet the moral experience of the people could not better be represented than that of having spent no small portion of their life in a burning fiery furnace.—Sorrow creates its own imagery.—What is exaggeration to one man is literal truth to another.—We are indebted to sorrow for the sublimest imagery.—

The Psalms are full of proof that such is the case.—The divine power is always magnified by spiritual worshippers.—They do not look upon history as a series of chances, but as a line along which the divine Being moves with dignity and beneficence.— He allows men to be thrown into the iron furnace, and has profound reasons for so doing; it is not his pleasure that they should be there, but it is certainly for their good that they should know the ministry of fire: the Lord knows exactly how long we have been in the furnace: he knows precisely what benefit has arisen from our being there: he knows when to liberate us from distress and despair.—There is no furnace too deep for the Lord to penetrate.—Though the furnace be of iron he can melt it and lead forth the captive with a new song in his mouth. —Do not regard furnaces as of men's construction, or as expressing the triumph of evil principles.—There hath no temptation happened unto you that is not directly sent of God, in the sense of trial and discipline.—He who has come out of the furnace can speak most tenderly of the power and compassion of God.—Not to have been in the furnace is not to have been in one of the most fruitful schools appointed by Providence for the education of mankind.—To have been in the furnace is to have learned the holy art of sympathy. To have been comforted ourselves is to be qualified to give comfort to others.—He who has dug most graves can speak most tenderly to the bereaved.—He who has stood in the midst of desolated acres without losing his confidence in God is by so much qualified to preach the duty and the joy of resignation.—The whole human race will one day be led out of the furnace, but not until the lessons of that tremendous discipline have been fully learned and applied in all the progress and duty of life.—Throughout the whole of the Scriptures it is the Lord who is magnified and not man who is praised for having found out some secret way of escape.—To know the Lord as a Deliverer in great crises and straits is to be assured that, in all the minor difficulties and trials of life, his presence shall be our protection and our hope.

" I must not go . . . but ye shall go."— DEUT. iv. 22.

This is a brave speech on the part of an old man. Such speeches ought to be uttered by the most advanced Christians to-day.—This man utters his speech without complaint.—It seems impossible to reconcile the imperfect revelation granted to some men with the goodness of God.—They come so near seeing the perfect light, and yet die without beholding the noontide glory.—It would have been very different with the people had Moses been a man of another spirit; querulous, discontented, complaining against God. —The spirit of progress rejoices in the progress of others.—We are not to limit the revelation of God by that which we see ourselves.—We must look to the future of the race and see in that future something brighter than has yet shone upon our own vision.— That thought may be applied to theological thinkers.—There is nothing final in theological investigation.— Interpretation will show the progressiveness even of the Bible itself.— The greatest students of the book die exclaiming to the younger men, " Ye shall go over, and possess the good land."—The thought should also be applied to Christian workers as well as to Christian students.—Though we die without reaping the harvest, the harvest will surely be reaped by others.

—We should so live that when we come to die our last speech may be one of encouragement to the men who are following.—The man who dies thus does not die at all, in any degrading sense.—Moses, though dead according to the flesh, lived in all the power of the spirit, and was a continual inspiration to the people whom he had led so many years in the wilderness.—There is always a good land to be possessed ; a land of larger liberty ; a land of larger knowledge ; a land of surer trust in divine realities. —The spirit of the Church must be a spirit of conquest; when it drops from this noble elevation it inflicts upon itself a most humiliating disability.

" The Lord made not this covenant with our fathers, but with us, even us, who are all of us here alive this day."—DEUT. v. 3.

There is a general revelation intended for all men through all time.— There is also a special revelation given to individuals, and limited by precise periods of duration.—All moral revelation—that is, revelation dealing with righteousness, truth, duty—is universal and everlasting.—Jesus Christ answered the lawyer who temptingly questioned him, " What is written in the law ? how readest thou ?"—Whilst it is true that some portions of the Bible were written for individuals, and were limited by local circumstances, it is surprising how many of these apparently merely local texts assume a relation to our individual necessities. —Wherever this is the case we have been mistaken in calling such passages local and limited.—The heart often creates its own Scripture. When the true soul reads the Bible and sees in it an anticipation of his distresses and a remedy for his sufferings, he is entitled to believe that the passage was written for himself as if he had been the only individual in the world.—We are not to go in quest of these passages as if with an intention to force them into new meanings, but when they open naturally to the touch of necessity and pain we are certainly entitled to accept their doctrine and their solace. —It is beyond all doubt that every law bearing upon purity of spirit and goodness of conduct was written for the benefit of the whole race throughout every age of its development.— This is at once the glory and the defence of the Bible.—It abides through all time; the Word of the Lord endureth for ever.—The Bible is a book addressed to humanity, and therefore it is at home in every land and in every language.—It has been remarked upon as a notable and suggestive circumstance that no book is so available for purposes of translation into all tongues as is the Bible.—Every man whose soul is hungry has, by virtue of his hunger, a right to this tree of life.—Let every one beware, however, how he takes the consolations and omits the commandments.— This would be a felonious use of the Scriptures.—The Bible is not to be read as a compliment to our feelings, but as a stimulus to our whole nature, that the man of God may be thoroughly instructed and perfected in all holiness. —Many men are particular about having the covenants confirmed who do not appear to be quite so particular about having the commandments obeyed.

" The Lord loved you."—Deut. vii. 8.

The word love is an Old Testament word.—It would not be difficult to show that the tenderest expressions ever used by heaven to earth are reported not in the New Testament but in the Old.—It is not enough for the people to know that their Lord is almighty, because power may become a terror.—Not only power belongeth unto God but also mercy: this is the complete aspect of the divine nature. —That the Lord loved Israel was shown by long-suffering, by hopeful patience, by pouring down blessing upon blessing, notwithstanding the ingratitude of the people ; it would seem as if even sin itself was hardly allowed to block out the light of heaven.—The love of God is the true interpretation of the history of man in all its movement towards nobility and spiritual sovereignty and rest.—Nothing but love could account for the continuance of the world under all its sinfulness and ingratitude.—It is love that explains the greatest revelations of God.—It is love that explains the Cross of Jesus Christ.—It is love that explains the assured progress of redeemed and sanctified souls.—The love of God excludes all other claims to his attention and interest : thus we are not allowed to say that God's favours come to us on account of our merit, or ancestry, or excellence above others ; whatever we have is of the free mercy and love of God.—The love which explains all the past is the surest guarantee of all the future.—Love never changes.—What is true of divine love in the soul is true of that same love in God himself; it hopeth all things, endureth all things, believeth all things, it never faileth.—It is our joy to believe in a God of love; nay, in our highest moods we do not regard love as an attribute of God, but we say God himself is love.—Love does not exclude discipline.—Love does not exclude anger.—But on the other side, neither discipline nor anger changes or diminishes the love of God. —"Good when he gives, supremely good ; not less when he denies."

"*The faithful God.*"—Deut. vii. 9.

Considerable instruction is supplied by noting the qualifying terms which are often attached to the divine name. —We read of the living God, the mighty God, the glorious Lord God, and in the text of the faithful God.— Sometimes the qualifying terms are rather repellent than attractive, as, for example, "the great and terrible God," and in Daniel we read of the "great and dreadful God."—These terms do not occur in the New Testament, yet even in the later books of revelation God is described as "a consuming fire," and in the Apocalypse we read of "the wrath of the Lamb," so that there is a line of consistency in the Old Testament and the New as regards the description of the character of God. —Perhaps there is no word which is more profoundly comfortable than the word "faithful" as applied to the divine Being.—It would appear as if "love" were more attractive and soothing, but this is an appearance only. Faithfulness is love; without faithfulness love itself would be impossible, because it would become a mere sentiment, liable to be cooled and changed by passing circumstances. It should be observed that even in the Old Testament, in the very text in which the divine Being is described as the great and terrible God, he is further described as "keeping covenant and mercy for evermore with them that love him and observe his commandments."—God is not the less loving because he is "great and terrible." —The Apostle Paul is very fond of applying the word "faithful" to God and to Jesus Christ, thus: "Faithful is he that calleth you, who also will do it."—"The Lord is faithful, who shall stablish you, and keep you from evil."—"God is faithful, who will not suffer you to be tempted

above that ye are able."—"God is faithful, by whom ye were called unto the fellowship of his Son Jesus Christ our Lord."—The Apostle John, too, in a remarkable passage, avails himself of the same descriptive term: "If we confess our sins, he is faithful and just to forgive us our sins."—Thus forgiveness itself is an expression of faithfulness and justice, and therefore may be accepted as essential and everlasting.—If God is faithful himself, he expects faithfulness in others.—He praises faithfulness in those who have completed their course of life honourably: "Well done, good and faithful servant."—He would see himself in others.—Faithfulness means consistency, permanency, reality of thought and service, and is absolutely intolerant of all fickleness, self-regard, menpleasing, and time-serving.—"Be thou faithful unto death."

———

"... *to possess nations greater and mightier than thyself.*"—Deut. ix. 1.

This would seem to be an inversion of the doctrine of proportion.—We forget, however, that there is a proportion of quality as well as a proportion of quantity.—Force is not to be measured by bulk.—The helm is very small compared to the whole ship, yet it turns the vessel's course. The man is very small physically in relation to the mountain which is thousands of feet high, yet the man is master of the mountain. The rider is small in strength compared with the horse he rides, yet the steed obeys the touch of his hand.—We constantly see how apparently little things rule obviously great bulks and quantities.—The true sovereignty is in the spirit.—This is the seat of the highest miracles that are wrought; such miracles simply illustrate the sovereign influence of mind over matter.—How little is man as to mere arithmetical measurement compared with the great globe; yet God has put all things under the hands of man: "All sheep and oxen, yea, and the beasts of the field; the fowl of the air, and the fish of the sea, and whatsoever passeth through the paths of the seas."—Let us reason upwards towards moral power: the power of ideas, impulses, sympathies, convictions.—The time will come when moral forces will be regarded as the true sovereignties. Towards this consummation Christ has been working from the beginning. The sword shall be beaten into a ploughshare, and all violence shall be deposed by the quietness of power.—Carry this a step higher into the religious region, and draw from the whole reasoning the inference that the religious nature is the most influential of all.—Truth shall take captive all the superstitions, idolatries, misconceptions, and false worships of the world.—We must admit what may be called even the smallest truth; let it have free course, and it will overturn the most ancient thrones and dominions which have been claimed by the powers of darkness.—Even the light of a candle will break up the darkness which fills the largest building.—In the strength of these thoughts and hopes every Christian should toil gladly, delighting himself with the pleasures of expectancy, knowing that the whole earth shall be filled with the knowledge of God.

"*The Lord hearkened unto me at that time also.*"—DEUT. ix. 19.

The memorable prayers of life.— Times of conscious conquest.—Who cannot recall periods in which the Lord by consent allowed himself to be overthrown, as if in war and wrestling, by the tender violence of love?— These great memories stimulate us to renewed endeavours in prayer and service.—We date our best endeavours from our latest conquests.—Only the good man can say whether prayer can be answered or not.—Moses here pledges his word as to the reality of answered prayer. — To destroy this answer we must first discredit Moses. —This is the real reply to those who would discuss the virtue of prayer.— This is not a question which can be settled in controversial terms, or within the narrow grounds of verbal definition; the inquiry must be addressed to the praying soul itself; the praying soul has never feared to say that its supplications have been rewarded with great answers.—Family history may be inquired into to bear evidence upon this matter. What of sickness? What of deliverance in the time of vital perplexity? What about the dispersion of clouds that hung like an infinite night over the whole life? What of sudden and unexpected answers to questions which we expected would cut us like swords?—A man must be very wise who can answer all such questions offhandedly, and dispense with the idea of the personality and intervention of God in the shaping and direction of human affairs.

"*Circumcise therefore the foreskin of your heart.*"—DEUT. x. 16.

What God wants is moral purity.— We cannot live in rites and ceremonies. —It was well to begin with the outward, but the meaning was that we should go forward to the inward and spiritual.—Nor was this revelation of the spiritual purpose long delayed; even in the Old Testament we read, "Circumcise yourselves to the Lord, and take away the foreskins of your heart, ye men of Judah."—Nothing would be more convenient or more pleasant to the carnal man than to merely observe some outward laws and regulations; but the word of the Lord is sharper than any two-edged sword, and its business is done in the innermost heart of man. "He is not a Jew, which is one outwardly; neither is that circumcision, which is outward in the flesh. . . . Circumcision is that of the heart, in the spirit, and not in the letter."—There is, therefore, an evangelical or spiritual circumcision. —"In whom also ye are circumcised with the circumcision made without hands, in putting off the body of the sins of the flesh by the circumcision of Christ."—If we have escaped that which is physically painful, we have come into that which is spiritually disciplinary.—"Rend your heart, and not your garments."—Man himself is called upon to do this, not that he has the ability to complete the circumcision, but any desire which he shows to begin it will call the almightiness of God to his aid.

"For ye are not as yet come to the rest."
—DEUT. xii. 9.

Still, it is of infinite value to the soul to know that there is a rest.—A man is helped through the week by knowing that he is coming to a period when labour will be suspended, and quietness will be at least rendered possible.—If we are stimulated by beginnings, we are comforted by promised endings.—To be told that there is no termination to the road we are upon, discourages us for advancing even the next few yards; but to be told that every few yards traversed will bring us nearer the end, where we may expect home and rest and security, is really to nerve us for service and danger.—Heaven is not promised as an appeal to our selfishness, but as a comfort to our weakness and a sure reward of all obedience and excellence in human life.—Even the Apostle looked forward to the close with the highest gratification and thankfulness, seeing, as he did, the crown of righteousness which was laid up for him, and knowing that he should join the general assembly and church of the firstborn.—A man need not work the less energetically on Monday because he sees in the distance the quiet Sabbath-day offering him harbour and refuge.—There is a period of strife which is to be succeeded by a period of rest. But what rest can he have who has never known the strife? Is not all pleasure, in some degree, by contrast? The sleep of the labouring man is sweet, simply because he is a labouring man and has earned the repose which his exhaustion needs.—What heaven can they have who have made earth into a mere sleeping-place or garden of delights, having walled out, so far as it is possible to human wealth and vanity to do so, all darkness and necessity and trouble?—What a home-coming must the true soldier have who is conscious of having fought patriotically and daringly in the interests he went out to serve!—A beautiful picture is given of the ending from all toil and strife in the good cause.—"And the Lord gave them rest round about, according to all that he sware unto their fathers: and there stood not a man of all their enemies before them; the Lord delivered all their enemies into their hand."—Christ himself was encouraged by the disclosed termination of his toil and suffering.—He knew that he must reign until he had put all enemies under his feet.—For the joy that was set before him, he endured the Cross, despising the shame. Here every good worker may be comforted and stimulated: if the work were to go on for ever, it seems as if our poor strength would regard its continuity with despair; but not knowing how soon it may end, and knowing that all faithfulness will end in heaven, the soul is encouraged to put on its strength, and to do with its whole might whatsoever it may find to do.—"There remaineth therefore a rest to the people of God."

"... when he giveth you rest from all your enemies round about. . . . Then there shall be a place."—DEUT. xii. 10, 11.

There are temporary rests on the road of life.—The battle is sometimes suspended, and we know not when it may be resumed.—Some spiritual use is to be made even of temporary cessations of difficulty.—The religious use which was to be made in ancient times of periods of rest expressed itself in the building of altars and the offering of sacrifices.—Ancient life seemed to be divided between war and worship.—In reality that distribution would seem to be continued throughout all time.—The Christian is either in the field of battle or in the house of prayer.—Even rest is not to be spent slothfully, but is to be enjoyed with a religious purpose as well as to be inspired by religious thankfulness. —When Jesus Christ offered his disciples rest, it was only for a limited time. His words were, " Come ye into a desert place, and rest a while,"—not rest a long time, and certainly not rest for the remainder of your days, but rest a while—take a breath, stand still for a moment, and then resume with energy the pursuits of life.—The holiday is only to make the subsequent labour more energetic and hopeful.—We are not to use rest as a confection which would give us distaste for labour.—

Nor are we to use rest as a kind of opiate which would disable the very powers it affects to renew.—Even rest may be a form of labour, or, at least, it may be so enjoyed as to give the soul promise of renewed endeavour to redeem human life and bless the human lot, now so full of sadness, and now so enfeebled by weariness.—It is but cowardice for men to run away from labour that they may enjoy inglorious ease.—When merchant-men succeed in laying by sufficient to maintain themselves in comfort, they should be planning some new sphere of activity, so that they may better serve their day and generation when they are released from the wear and tear of the drudgery of life.—No man is to say to his soul, Take thine ease, eat, drink, and be merry; he is rather to say, I have no further care about the body; now shall my soul have full swing in the highest and best activity. —This is the true preparation before the Sabbath—the Sabbath of heaven.

"... as he is able."—DEUT. xvi. 17.

This is the law of giving in the Old Testament, and it is the law of giving in the New Testament.—It is a just and equitable law.—It devolves a supreme responsibility upon the giver.— It makes him an accountant in the sight of God.—He has to add up his resources and diligently to consider their sum, and then to give as he may be able.—This law does not relate to money only, but to time, influence, and sympathy.—Nothing would be so easy for many men as to buy themselves off, by the gifts of money, from all further service. Simply because of the abundance of their wealth, money is as nothing to them, and the giving of it is not felt.—It is only when the giving is touched with the pain of sacrifice that it becomes of any value in the sanctuary.—Still, most of us have to begin with the donation of money, but no man has to end with it.—There is no niggardliness in the promises of God in relation to the true giver, of whatever nature his gifts may be.—"Every man according as he purposeth in his heart, so let him give; not grudgingly, or of necessity: for God loveth a cheerful giver."—"He which soweth sparingly shall reap also sparingly; and he which soweth bountifully shall reap also bountifully."—Jesus Christ noticed what gifts were thrown into the treasury, and he regarded them all in the light of proportion.—"God is not unrighteous to forget your work of faith and labour of love."—Not a cup of cold water is to go unrewarded if given to a disciple in the name of Christ.—These grand moral standards of gift and service constitute a powerful defence of the heavenly origin of the Bible.

. . . then thy brother should seem vile unto thee."—Deut. xxv. 3.

This was the law of punishment as laid down by Moses.—The stripes were to be not more than forty, because if there were more—that is to say, if they were given at random—the man who received them would become "vile" in the sight of the man who inflicted them.—A measure of punishment is rendered necessary by the quality of the man who is punished.—Man is not to be regarded as a beast of burden. Even when he has done wrong he is a man still, and a man capable of restoration and re-adoption into good citizenship.—Thus mercy is wonderfully mingled with law even in the Old Testament.—When God corrected his people he said he would "correct them in measure."—Where the punishment ends hope is to begin.—This is really the meaning of all controversial chastisements, losses, and difficulties of every kind.—They do not come with overwhelming and destructive force; they come "in measure," and with a purpose of mercy; and as to how we receive such visitations, that will depend upon the spirit in which we view them; if we view them as chastisements only, or the expressions of an arbitrary will, we shall quail under them and be driven into despair; but if we look aside from the chastisement into the purpose it was meant to elucidate or enforce, then we shall kiss the hand which lifts the rod.—When the sufferings of Bildad seemed to be intolerable, the exclamation was: "Wherefore are we counted as beasts, and reputed vile in your sight?" The Apostles, too, when apparently left without regard either from God or man, betook themselves to the same line of reasoning: "We are made as the filth of the world, and are the offscouring of all things unto this day."—Parents should take notice of this law of measured correction.—So should all magistrates and judges.—God himself regulates his discipline by it, and expects that every man on whom the rod falls will bethink himself and turn and repent.—Man should never be so treated as to cause his manhood to be ignored.—Contempt should never be either the reason or the result of any course of punishment.—When penalty ceases to be connected with hope, it ceases to be righteous.—Behold the goodness and the sovereignty of the Lord.—Blessed are they who have accepted the chastisement and have turned it into a renewal of hope and an assurance of ultimate purification.

SELECTED NOTE.

" We find that in the guidance of the human race, from the earliest ages downwards, more especially in the lives of the three patriarchs, God prepared the way by revelations for the covenant which he made at Sinai with the people of Israel. But in these preparations we can discover no sign of any legendary and unhistorical transference of later circumstances and institutions, either Mosaic or post-Mosaic, to the patriarchal age ; and they are sufficiently justified by the facts themselves, since the Mosaic economy cannot possibly have been brought into the world, like a *deus ex machina*, without the slightest previous preparation. The natural simplicity of the patriarchal life, which shines out in every narrative, is another thing that produces on every unprejudiced reader the impression of a genuine historical tradition, This tradition, therefore, even though for the most part transmitted from generation to generation by word of mouth alone, has every title to credibility, since it was perpetuated within the patriarchal family, "in which, according to divine command (Gen. xviii. 19), the manifestations of God in the lives of our fathers were handed down as an heirloom, and that with all the greater ease, in proportion to the longevity of the patriarchs, the simplicity of their life, and the closeness of their seclusion from foreign and discordant influences. Such a tradition would undoubtedly be guarded with the greatest care. It was the foundation of the very existence of the chosen family, the bond of its unity, the mirror of its duties, the pledge of its future history, and therefore its dearest inheritance " (*Delitzsch*). But we are by no means to suppose that all the accounts and incidents in the book of Genesis were dependent upon oral tradition ; on the contrary, there is much which was simply copied from written documents handed down from the earliest times. Not only the ancient genealogies, which may be distinguished at once from the historical narratives by their antique style, with its repetitions of almost .stereotyped formularies, and by the peculiar forms of the names which they contain, but certain historical sections—such, for example. as the account of the war in Gen. xiv., with its superabundance of genuine and exact accounts of a primitive age, both historical and geographical, and its old words, which had disappeared from the living language before the time of Moses, as well as many others—were unquestionably copied by Moses from ancient documents."

GENERAL REVIEW.

PRAYER.

ALMIGHTY GOD, let there be in our hearts a light brighter than noonday. We would that the Son of man might live within us his life of light, and cause all our life to burn with his glory, so that men passing by may take knowledge of us that we have lived with Jesus, and that we no longer live ourselves but that Christ liveth in us. For this miracle we pray. We ask for no change in thy great creation which we cannot follow because of our littleness and dimness of sight; but we ask for a miracle within, a transformation which we can realise as to its results, though quite unable to tell whence it cometh or whither it goeth. We would be born again. We would see with new eyes and hear with new hearing, and answer all the appeals of thy providence with new voices. We would be startled by our new selves; we would wonder at the music of the new voice; we would be soothed by the tones of the new intercession. Withhold not this sign from us! Grant this token from heaven! We shall know it well, for there is none like it, nor can it be simulated with perfectness. We bless thee for any love of light we have. Once we loved darkness rather than light. Thou hast brought us out of darkness not only into light, but into a marvellous light—like light upon light, day upon day, until shamed darkness has fled away, and all heaven burns with glory. Help us evermore to walk as children of the day and not of the night, to speak the language of light, and to be found always amongst those who are not afraid or ashamed of the Gospel of Christ. We owe ourselves unto that Gospel: we were dead, and are alive again; we were lost, and are found; and now, in possession of this immortal life, we stand up before thee a ransomed host, our hearts kindling with gratitude, our lives prepared for sacrifice. We will not think of the troubles thou hast caused us to pass through, for the joy is greater because of the sorrow. Men forget the night in the morning; the reaper forgets the seed-time in the golden harvest, when his barns are too small, when his fields are rich with corn; so do we forget our trouble in our gladness. The trouble was but for a moment; the joy is an exceeding great and eternal weight of glory. This thou hast taught us by divine ministry; for hast thou not taught thy servant to say that where sin abounded grace did much more abound? so that even sinners began to sing; their crime had vanished like a black, windy night, and their adoption had excited within them the spirit of worship and the angel of music. We forget our hunger at the feast; we soon forget the cold in which we shivered when we stand at our Father's board, and are under the light of our Father's blessing. Make us rich with wisdom, wealthy in understanding; give us the unsearchable riches of Christ as our treasure; then when the drought cometh we shall not see it, and when the springs are dried up there shall be a secret fountain in the sanctuary. We bless thee for all the way along which thou hast led us—now in the deep valleys, now full of sunshine and summer gladness; here an inviolable palace, there a grave-stone rich with memories, and yonder a bright place where we feasted well, and sang loudly, and wished the day were twice as long. For all the road we thank thee. It has been educational; we have been receiving stimulus by all the progress we have made; and now that we are here, putting up another Sabbath milestone, we will say,—Hitherto hath the Lord helped us, and as for the rest of the road, we shall run and not be weary, we shall walk and not faint. Keep us as the apple of thine eye. Receive special thanks and blessings, from all who have special thanks and acknowledgments to make to thee—for individual blessings, for family life, for business prosperity, for direction, guidance, sympathy, and hope. The Lord look upon the country; it is ours, and we love it, and pray for it. But all lands are thine. We pray continually that the glory of the Lord may cover the whole earth. We stand here, but we live everywhere: we touch a point, but pray for a whole circumference—the entire family of man. Liberate the slave; break the arm of the tyrant; cause sudden night to fall upon those who are in eager quest of things forbidden, and prosper every good man and upright cause and true purpose; and bring all into the great millennial light, the grand era of Christian reign, when the Lord shall be enthroned, and all men shall know in their hearts that the night is gone and the morning has come. Amen.

THE GREAT QUESTIONS OF THE PENTATEUCH.

IT is instructive to notice the exact position of the first question in the Bible. It has come to be quite a common and simple thing for us to ask questions. We think nothing of it. Some men hardly think of anything. Many suppose that they have a perfect right to ask questions. There is a morality in question-asking, and, therefore, a limit. Persons will say, with assumed or sincere feeling, Surely we have a right to ask a question? The answer to that innocent suggestion is a broad and emphatic denial. Persons are accustomed to call certain questions "harmless." There is no harmless question that has an unavowed motive behind it, or that seeks to serve an ulterior but undiscovered purpose. The most "harmless" questions and suggestions to be found in the whole range of the Bible are the utterances of the devil! He was perfectly "harmless"! The mark of interrogation he softened into a dying cadence; the evil suggestion he conveyed with armfuls of flowers, rich with colour and fragrance. When the devil spoke to Jesus the words were of the most "harmless" nature; when he accosted our first parents it was with the civility of a " Good-morning," with the calculated courtesy of a spirit that has an object. But the words are without stain or suggestion of evil. At first they were but an inquiry; and to ask a question of a human being in a human voice is surely the very first element of civility.

Where is the first mark of interrogation in the Bible? Who instituted that punctuation? Up to that time we had been content with comma and semicolon and period : who introduces this crooked mark? You will find that the first question is in the very first book of the Bible :—"And he said unto the woman, Yea, hath God said, Ye shall not eat of every tree of the garden?" (Gen. iii. 1). Question-asking has been the ruin of the world. Yet it is so simple that every man thinks he has a right to it. He reflects not that to ask a question is to put out boundaries, to seek intellectual enlargement at some possible moral cost. Question-asking either begets discontentment or fosters it. Men would be better if they asked no questions, except those that obviously limit themselves as to their moral purpose, or that indicate the urgency and sanctity of a prayer. One question begets another. Questions can never be answered. The mischief is that question-asking is considered a sign of intellectual progress; within given limits it may be justly so regarded, but there is a limitation to interrogative inquiry, and we should be careful about the limit before we put the question. There comes to be quite a trick of question-asking, which is often mistaken for genius; so men become proud of it: having put one difficult question, and seen how the interlocutor is utterly puzzled, another is invented, because the cheapest of all cleverness consists in asking questions and composedly waiting for replies that can never be given. By asking a question you may ruffle a mind: by putting an inquiry you may poison a life; the question may be harmless in words, but most fruitful of baleful issue in the outworking of all the processes which it begins. Here is a new form of human conversation. Up to this point we have had next to no conversation; the man and woman have been created, but as to what passed between them we know next to nothing; it is the third party who excites new intellectual ferment or disquietude, or who quietly troubles the life with an inquiry, and then vanishes. We may ask questions of ourselves, sharp, penetrating, accusatory questions; we may stimulate ourselves by inquiries keen as double-edged swords; but there is a question-asking that is profanity, because it touches upon the impossible and vexes the mind by chafing against the infinite limitation, the eternal boundary, on which is written, Hitherto shalt thou come, but no further. Let a man encounter that utterance with *Why ?* and he is lost. The moment he says *Why ?* he has overleaped himself; he has passed the altar-line; he is no longer safe. If he did say *Why ?* he should say it timidly, reverentially, with the awe and the wonder akin to prayer; but he should not put the word as a question to which he demands an answer before he will believe, or adore, or serve the Spirit of creation. Nor is this intellectual timidity : it is intellectual self-restraint, which is the highest intellectual courage; it is the very heroism of faith. It says, The world is larger than I comprehend. I have not time to settle all the questions which vex even the surface of life; I must therefore live a day at a time, and take one step at a time, and not turn over a page until I have read the page preceding; and thus I will be led and educated from point to point. The devil often comes into the mind in the form of a question, and comes in with some civility, because of the frankness and perfect courtesy of the inquiry. He asks questions about the books we read, the prayers we pray, the events we endeavour to construe into moral significance. Upon the altar, where we have been since child-hood, he simply writes with black finger a mark of interrogation; not a word is said, but the query looks us in the face and makes us afraid, because our hearts are greater than our heads, our moral emotion and desire in excess of our intellectual education : and this must always be so, because feeling is the universal language, and is not within the sphere of debate, controversy, or intellectual contention. Search into the origin of question-asking. Be suspicious of all inquiries that are "absolutely harmless." Nothing is so easily disturbed as the angel of faith —not disturbed through fear ; but, because of a sensitiveness akin to the sensibility of God, the fall of a leaf in the night-wind is heard, a sound of a distant step is detected. A sigh may take an interrogative form; a prayer may be but an aspect of scepticism. Watch the question-gate! It is an element in the bad renown of the devil that he began the battle by asking a "harmless question."

Who put the next inquiry? You will find that the next question was put by Jehovah himself:—"And the Lord God called unto Adam, and said unto him, Where art thou?"— (Gen. iii. 9)—an extraordinary inquiry when searched into; an impossible inquiry from certain points of view. Is Omniscience blind? Did he who formed the eye not see? "Where" does not always relate to locality; it is a wide word, full of solemn and tender suggestion. A man may be standing face to face with you, but be separated from you in heart by the diameter of creation. "Where art thou?' is not a mere inquiry of position, or relating to measurable points, but where art thou morally, sympathetically? where art thou in purpose, in supreme desire, in settled and chastened motive? A man may be in the sanctuary, and yet far from the altar. This is a novel question. Where art thou?—yesterday at the gate meeting me, waiting for me; here, as it were, first, longing for the light to come back again; why this change? what has occurred? Who told thee thou wast naked? A man is not naked until he is told that he is naked. It is the ear that makes the sound which is struck and elicited in the infinite wilderness. Now question-asking introduces a new element into human intercourse and human responsibility. Already here is a great white throne; the judgment is set, and the question is asked which will determine the destiny of the world. Everything depends upon our answer to this simple inquiry. Does human liberty begin here—at least in some new phase? or is human liberty bounded by this inquiry? Has not a man a right to be either here or there, outside the garden or inside, on the right hand or on the left? May he not walk east or west, as he pleases? Why this Voice that asks as to locality, or purpose, or sympathy, or moral attitude and relation? Temptation had not long been in the world when judgment followed it. Where men will ask questions, or allow questions to be received into the mind, they have begun a criticism which

God will continue. The question-asking cannot be all on one side. God may not ask for information : he asks that in answering his inquiry man may accuse and confound himself. Remember how true it is that men realise certain positions upon being told of them. Happily, this tells in both ways. Say to some poor soul who is blind, and groping, and wondering, "Behold, he prayeth,"—and he may actually pray. You have supplied him with a form of words which exactly expresses his feeling. He knew not what he was doing; he was upon a border-line; he seemed to see men as trees walking, and to see new lights and gleams in the sky—a mystic writing in the clouds—and he felt his hands rising upwards as if to seize some nearing blessing; but he knew not what he did until an angel said, "Behold, he prayeth." Say to some earnest student, who dare not so much as lift his eyes unto heaven, but who, closing them, looks on high with inward vision alight with the tender gleam of hope—say to him, "Thou art also a Christian : thy speech betrayeth thee, thy look identifies thee; thou art also a follower of the Son of man," and the very suggestion may be the one spark that was needed to cause his courage to flame up in testimony and holy avowal and witness. Yesterday the man knew not that he was naked. Some one must have told him.

So we have the first question directly traceable to the enemy, and the second question directly falling from the lips of Jehovah. Is there any more question-asking? Who asks another great question?—the angels. We may call them angels : we cannot tell who they were; they were mysterious personalities; they were representative of those mystic influences which are continually playing around human life, exciting wonder, or fear, or joy—persons without names, influences without nameable bounds, ministries that allure, or deter, or sway, or repel; and we cannot tell by what authority they speak; yet they work miracles, they feed multitudes, they quiet the sea. Three of these mysterious personalities are before us. They ask a question in reply to human unbelief:—"Is anything too hard for the Lord?"—(Gen. xviii. 14)—the thing we always forget. Having learned it to-day, to-morrow we shall forget the solemn lesson. We follow our eyes, and call it faith; we believe

mightily concerning things which are already in our clutch, but
such belief is not accredited to us as faith. What we have to
consider in the difficult circumstances of life is—the Lord's power.
It is perfectly clear that we may be in a deadlock; the walls
are thick, the doors are of iron, the key is lost, and we cannot
escape; but the question is not for us at all. Therein is our
mistake—that we suppose the circumstances to be bounded
by our personality. Through all the winds of time, all the
currents of the centuries, there comes this all-exciting yet
all-quieting inquiry—"Is anything too hard for the Lord?"
He gives, he takes away; he shakes the prison; he conducts
the ministries of life: the Lord reigneth. Christians will say
so in theory: they would dispute with any man who offered
to deny it: but who believes it? Not only have we come
to the last loaf, but we have come to the last little piece of
the loaf, and we are all an hungered; that is the time when the
question is to come to us with the power and sanction of a faith
—"Is anything too hard for the Lord?" So to say, we
disappoint God of his opportunities: we will persist in outrunning him; and thus he allows our weakness to go first
in many instances. The thing to be done is to leave him a
clear field, bounded east, west, north, and south by absolute
necessity: there is the divine sphere; but whilst we are
looking around and exciting our poor ignorance and weakness,
and persisting in doing something, God may not work. He
often waits until we are asleep, and takes our sleep as a kind
of faith. He says, in effect,—I must not be too hard with
them: they are question-askers; they were early serpent-
bitten: bitten through an interrogation, and the poison has been
awful in effect; they cannot believe: I must wait until they
are dead asleep, and at midnight I will work some wonder
for them; even then, when they begin to rub their eyes in
a new wakefulness, they will ask questions, and wonder who
did it, as if they were in a dream; and they will attribute
the whole incident to a species of somnambulism;—still, they
were made yesterday: they dwell in dust, in clay of the earth;
their breath is in their nostrils; I must account sleep as a
kind of faith, and unconsciousness as a species of trust; I
will not forsake them, I will set a miracle at their bedside,

so that when they awake they may begin to believe. Thus
we are drawn on little by little, line by line. Blessed be God,
we have come a long way from the first point in many instances.
Some are now, in mid-life, beginning to pray; they say they
see it now. It has taken them full fifty years to begin to see
men as trees walking, but they now do so begin; and they attest
their faith by a new tone in the voice, by a new aspect of
kindness, by a new gait in the world as they pass along; they
are more upright, their very stature seems to have increased,
there is a fearlessness of a subtle kind about their down-
sitting and their up-rising; they say they see it now! Will
they use their sight to-morrow under a new set of circumstances? No; they will be as blind as ever then. But the Lord
knoweth we are dust—a wind that cometh for a little time,
and then passeth away—question-askers, who mistake interrogation for revelation, and a power of scepticism as a sign of
intellectual progress.

Thus we have had three interrogators—the serpent, Jehovah,
angels. Will not man ask some question little or great? Shall
there be no human element in all this interrogation? There
are human questions in the Bible, as for example :—"Wilt thou
also destroy the righteous with the wicked?"—(Gen. xviii. 23)
—the first time we have heard so solemn a question from
human lips. The question is being asked to-day. It does seem
as if Providence were marked by indiscriminateness. A man
is killed at the altar: if so, does not that destroy the theory
of particular providence? A man has fallen down dead in
church. Impossible! if God be so careful of his loving ones.
The righteous have been thrown down in the streets, and the
wicked have plundered them, and passed on and enjoyed the
booty with a fool's laugh; virtue has been pinched with poverty,
vice has multiplied its balance at the usurer's :—"Wilt thou also
destroy the righteous with the wicked?" It looks so. The one
soul in the house that prayed is dead, and they who laughed at
the supplicant live to turn the memory into jesting. "Wilt thou
destroy the righteous *and not* the wicked?" would seem to be
a question justified by some limited aspects of Providence.
These are mysteries—not created by the Bible, but found outside
the Bible and independently of the Bible, and are to be adjudged

and determined apart altogether from Christian faith, if we will have it so. Blessed be God, they can be otherwise adjudged within the sanctuary, by the help of Christian faith ; and then there comes a light upon all the gloom, and if the midnight is not sunny, it is so full of stars that it cannot be called darkness.

Let us now turn to some questions which were put directly to Almighty God Himself. Since question-asking has begun, who can tell to what lengths it may go ? We have just seen that the devil put the first question, and began that dangerous method of intellectual development, and that he is in no wise less guilty because the first question was, from an outside point of view, perfectly harmless as to words. One of the great questions put by man to God was this: "Am I my brother's keeper?" (Gen. iv. 9). There are two tones in that inquiry. The one is a tone of amazement. God's investigation into the destiny of Abel seems to have amazed with unutterable astonishment the murderer of his brother. The inquiry came upon Cain like a revelation. He did not comprehend the fact that society is one, that humanity is one, that we are responsible socially for one another to a very high degree—for one another's strength, progress, honour, and specially responsible for one another's life. So the inquiry may be taken as an expression of astonishment, meaning—"If I had known that I was my brother's keeper and had to be called to account because of my brother, I should have looked after him ; I should have been careful about him ; nothing should have been keener than my criticism of my own spirit and action towards him ; I am wonderstruck ; I knew not that I was my brother's keeper." But that is not the natural tone of the inquiry; that only constitutes one of those mean excuses of which inventive minds may take advantage in the hour of accusation and judgment. We must not practise the unworthy trick of amazement too much. Even astonishment may cease to be a miracle. We may be far too much amazed, and in astonishment we may fritter away any supposed claim we had to frankness and innocence and simplicity of mind. There is an amazement that is self-condemnatory. What is the natural tone of the inquiry? It is one of peevish reproach. The question ought to be asked with great keenness and poignancy of voice. It is the inquiry of an offending man who is conscious of guilt and afraid of punishment, and who yet wishes, with an apparent defiance, to keep back the arm that would smite him in return. All sin leads to peevishness of manner. The bad man is never profoundly serene. He knows not the poetry or the order of fully-rounded composure and contentment—the fall of a leaf frightens him out of his simulated propriety; the closing of a door, the opening of a window, the touch of a child, an unexpected question,—these continually alarm and extort from him fretful inquiries, petulant remarks, impetuous criticism. Thus sin riddles the character through and through, punctuates it, makes it full of holes, takes away all its solidity, continuity, strength, and nobleness. A peevish voice may mark the course of sin, avowed or unavowed. It is singular how character comes out in vocal tones, in menial attitudes, in exclamations of surprise or petulance. That was the natural tone of Cain's inquiry. He asks, "Am I my brother's keeper?" in a tone which means, "What have I to do with him? He is capable of taking care of himself; I cannot always be going about after my brother; he is a man as well as I am; he must beware of all dangers and of all surprises, and bring himself home again after the journeying of the day,"—a speech too independent to be candid, too defiant to be religious, too hurriedly spoken with hot lips to express the conviction of a solid affection, or the desire of fraternal solicitude. Cain will not plead guilty, nor will he avow innocence in so many words; he will avail himself of a question—a question so large as to be an open gate through which he may escape the judgment of God. Understand that this question was put to the Almighty as the result of an inquiry of his own. God made inquest for blood. The first speech was made by the Almighty himself. Instead of being met frankly and lovingly it was met by an inquiry. This is the method of sin in all time: it seeks to put the judge off the scent; it attempts to divert the mind, to distract the attention, to suggest a new possibility; and, with some claim of a haughty kind to independence, it seeks to enclose the soul within walls which must not be violated even by the Judge of the whole earth. Let us read our own character in this kind of questioning. We have lost the straight line: we have ourselves become as crooked as the interrogation with which we punctuate our utterances. God meant us to be upright, plain of speech, real in soul and heart, sound in motive, having nothing to hide ; and we have resorted to the cunning of a question, to the evasion of an " innocent " inquiry.

Another question put directly to the Almighty himself was propounded by the astounded Abraham :—" Shall not the Judge of all the earth do right ? " (Gen. xviii. 25.) This question was indeed put to three men who visited him ; but it is our joy to believe that one of those personalities represented the Lord God himself. There was a mystery about the Third Man which none could understand. The same Man comes up again and again in Biblical history, and works wonders in the lives of men —now by dreams, now by mental visions, now by disturbing impressions, and anon by events which man did not begin and which man cannot perfectly control. For this reason we hesitate not to say that the question was addressed to the Eternal himself. A wonderful word occurs in this question. Wonderful words are startled out of men by marvellous ministries of a supernatural kind. Here is one of the grandest words in all human speech. That little word is " right." What is " right " ? Who can define it ? All men can define it within, in the court of conscience, and receive the sanction of judgment and reason ; but who can define it outwardly and to another so as to bind that other by his definition ? We must not escape from the pressure of this inquiry by taking refuge in the impossibility of one man defining right for another. Every man knows what right is. When he begins to quibble about the etymological definition he begins to show that he knows himself to be wrong. This is a marvellous fact in the constitution of men who have lived under Christianising influences—and it has often appeared in nations to which the name of Christ was utterly unknown—that there should be a spirit in man that knows right from wrong, that feels it, that, how poor soever may be the faculty and use of speech, yet in the soul there is a sense that says, This is right, that is wrong ; Thou shalt, thou shalt not. Herein the commandments have their supreme hold upon our moral attention. They are indisputable. The moment we hear them, we hear, so to say, our mother-tongue. We know it, arise to it, and say, That is right ; whatever may be said upon the other side is of the nature of a quibble, a fool's criticism; it is without solidity and reality, it will not bear the pressure of life all round ; these great commandments thundered from the mountain are right : we affirm them, and confirm them, and answer back again, This is right. Abraham knew from observation, from experience, that the Judge of the whole earth would do right. Some have discovered a tone of doubt in this inquiry. There may be such a tone, for who can altogether escape the plaguing action of doubt within the mind ? He would be a bold man who would say that there was no doubt in this inquiry, who would affirm that conscience was not alarmed in the case of Abraham. Yet there is surely another tone in it. Abraham has life enough behind him to justify complete confidence in God. By such life alone can such confidence be established. We cannot have theoretical confidences, metaphysical trusts and dependencies ; we are not sufficiently trained and chastened to seize such filmy supports and insubstantial claims and guarantees. The time will come when we shall value the spiritual and be able to see it and penetrate to its real meaning ; but now we want fact, history, things that have really occurred under our eyes, within our touch, that we can affirm beyond all disputation, to which we can call witnesses whose word is an oath, whose affirmation is a bond. Thus has God trained us, and we ourselves ought to have a lifetime to fall back upon in the presence of all great doubts and all startling wonders or new phases of providence. When the heavens are black, and not a star struggles through the gloom ; when the sea is in infinite trouble, and the rocks crack under our feet, giving way because of some sudden shock, we should be able to say, reading the Bible of our life,—This is right, this will be justified ; at present all is mystery, but suddenly the Lord will come to his temple, and where there is darkness there shall sit the morning—the queen of light—the very benediction of God. What is our lifetime worth if we cannot talk so ? We must not refer even to the Bible itself, solely, for proofs of this ; we must refer to our own experience in addition. Our own experience will confirm the Bible, will annotate it with vivid comment ; but to read the Bible only in the presence of stupendous events and crises may be but to vex inquiring minds. The Bible may come better afterwards. Christians should be able to say, Fear not : be ca.m ; the God whose I am and whom I serve will bring this storm to peace, will overrule these events, and out of tumult will bring solemn and heavenly harmony. Then may come the ancient testimony, the witness of patriarchs and sages long dead ; but all such testimony must be accentuated by personal experience, must live because of the speaker's own energy. We cannot live upon dead men : we cannot always be quoting their words and simply resting upon their authority ; we must be able to confirm it, and explain it, and repeat it in modern tone and expression, and so make the Bible the newest of books, by lifting up its mysteries into newness of expression and reality. We have said that wonderful words are startled out of men. Probably Abraham, when he began his question, did not know how it would end ; but how sorrow makes men eloquent ; how great occasions change the countenances of men and make them shine with light, and express eagerness, expectancy, or devoutness, as the case may be ; how little we knew what we should say until the great storm drove around us in mighty whirl and tempest and rain ! It was then that our heart found its tongue ; then that our understanding became as a flame ; and then that our lips were as a rock from which streams of eloquence flowed. Men must be trained by severe trials and great crises, and have their questions verified by the very stress of the circumstances which tried their faith. We learn a new language in new circumstances. The climate changes the customs of a people. Let a change take place in the temperature, and that change repeats itself in all the action of civilisation : men address themselves to the altered temperature whether in an access of heat or an increase of cold. Civilisation repeats the sun. Modern living human nature practically recites what is passing in great nature ; it may be without speech, but the reproduction is certainly accomplished So it is in all the breadth of human education. Let God burn upon a man's life like a hot sun, and the man answers the blistering heat by an attitude or an exclamation. Let the Lord's cold smite man in the face—great morsels of ice, great showers of snow—and man shudders back his reply to the inclement heavens. Let a man's life be assailed, and great judgments be brought to his knowledge, and he will ask questions, and introduce into those questions words of the noblest and solidest kind. Thus are we trained ; thus are we vexed into new progress ; thus are we driven up many a hill and along many a valley. "This is the Lord's doing; it is marvellous in our eyes!"

One more question will satisfy our inquiry as to the kind of interrogation that may be addressed directly to the Almighty. Said Moses: When I go to Egypt and speak to the children of Israel, they will say to me, Who sent thee ? what is his name ? What shall I say ? (Exod. iii. 13). That is a grand historical picture !—a man about to be sent, but who will not go until he has his credentials : a strong man conscious of weakness, not unwilling to plead infirmity, somewhat inventive, it may be, in the multiplication of excuses ; but all this must be made up by a name, a password, a secret masonry :— How shall I shake hands with the strangers ? What shall I give them to show that I am no common man or mere adventurer? When they ask me quietly, What is his name ? what shall I say ? I could invent names, but must not ; give me a name they will know at once : if they have never heard it before, yet it shall be so grand, rich, complete, that the moment they hear it they will say—Never did man invent that appellation. What is thy name ? We know things and persons by names. Names may be only momentary conveniences ; still, they *are* conveniences, and cannot be dispensed with. Entrust me with thy name ! And what a name it was !—"I AM THAT I AM !" Say that to the children of Israel, and they will hear in it the boom of a sea over which they have sailed ; whisper that name to them—if such a name will accommodate itself to a whisper—and the host will answer, "That is verily the name of our God." We are at liberty to ask such questions as Moses. They must be marked by reverence ; we must mean what we say. There is a flippant interrogation that gets no reply. Sometimes we ask questions without putting them into an interrogative form. A question may be suggested as well as plainly put. A prayer may be a great inquiry without the mark of interrogation ever occurring in the solemn speech. Man can be in an attitude of groping, lighting a candle, and sweeping the house diligently for a piece that is lost. Man can be uttering words, and leaving God to punctuate them. The heart can hurry through a speech which may be incoherent to ears that cannot hear the inner music, but which is perfectly continuous and complete to the ear of listening heaven. Yet are we forbidden to ask questions? That depends upon the nature of the inquiry, as we have just seen. Men may ask certain questions in a certain way, if they do not hinder divine progress. Never make a question an excuse. Never turn a question into a mystery, and say, This is the end, and advance is therefore impossible. There are questions which the heart will dictate, and which the judgment will know to be right. He is evasive in mind, he is ignoble in temper, who supposes that he does not know when he is asking a right question. Do not attempt to puzzle God, to multiply mysteries, to invent or create them. If we ask God for a clean heart and a right spirit, we know we are asking a question that is proper, and that God waits to answer. Beware of merely intellectual inventiveness in the sanctuary. Beware of that busy faculty which can always excite doubt and disturb the mind, and lead away the attention, or fasten it upon false issues. There is a spirit in man, and the inspiration of the Almighty giveth him understanding ; and let no soul attempt to do itself the infinite dishonour of putting questions which it does not want to have answered, or of raising inquiries the reply to which it can never understand. There is enough to be done. Life is too solemn, because too short, to be frittered away in vain interrogation. If we search the Scriptures, and ask the Holy Spirit to be with us, ruling our temper into quietude, and creating within us a spirit of docility, we shall understand as we read : light will come up out of the Word—down upon the Word. In God's light we shall see light, and our one question will be—" Lord, what wilt thou have me to do ? "

PRAYER.

ALMIGHTY GOD, thou hast given a wonderful setting to our life. Even the poorest man may behold thy heavens and look upon all the host thereof, and wonder concerning their meaning and their destiny. Thou hast filled the earth with beauty and the air with music, so that we stand in the midst of revelation, and if we be not blind and deaf we must hear messages from God. We bless thee for all this setting of our life · it is helpful. We hear speech from many an unexpected quarter; we listen, and, lo, it is as if angels sung to us in the dark night-time; and even in the mighty wind there is a tone of tenderness, which means health and purity, renewed life and invigorated hope. Help us to read the symbols, to understand somewhat of the meaning of the types; then shall our mind be stored with sacred wisdom, and our heart shall be as an instrument of music on which divine fingers shall discourse. Enable us to see beyond nature to nature's God; give us that penetrating look which sees beyond the veil of the visible and beholds somewhat of the mystery and glory of that which is unseen. Thus may we be drawn upward by a gracious compulsion; thus may we be unwilling to tarry in a place too small for us. May we accept the hospitality of God, and move upward to the larger, brighter spaces, the wider liberties, the service without weariness, the worship without tedium. That we have such thoughts as these is of thy goodness; their very presence in the soul shows that we are not forsaken of Heaven; we are still in the land of the living and in the sphere of religious hope. Touch us as thou wilt and in what measure thou wilt, but let thy touch bring us nearer to thyself. May we be among those who grow upward and heavenward, from beholding external and natural beauties to beholding the mystic splendours of the inner heavens; and not of those who having looked upon thine handiwork are by reason of manifold and aggravated sin condemned to outer darkness. Let our lives continue to be precious to thee. Still think it worth thy while to water the earth and to send the warmth of the sun upon its smoking soil; still care for us, and send the seed-time and the summer and the harvest and the restful and nourishing winter with its blessed sleep; and thus help us by outward ministries, by natural appeals, by sustenance for the body and suggestions for the mind, to attain to higher heights and worship at the highest altar; and through all the way of the world, and sin and danger and death, may we be led to the Cross—the great Cross of sacrifice, the mystery of redemption, the problem of atonement by the shedding of blood. Lead us into this mystery it appals us it affrights us, and then it grows upon our attention and confidence and love, until we are enabled to say to the dying Christ,—my Lord and my God ! Amen.

THE PENTATEUCH AS A WHOLE.

HAVING studied the Pentateuch in detail, beginning at the beginning and concluding with the final word, it may be profitable to inquire somewhat into the teaching of the books in their unity. The five books of Moses—often called the Pentateuch—are placed in our hands, and if we have read them through we are at liberty to inquire into the meaning of the Pentateuch as a whole: to ask what impression it has made upon the mind; how far it has established any claim to be considered an inspired book; what are its supreme qualities and characteristics—qualities and characteristics which separate it from all other books and give it a unique place in the library of the world.

We cannot have run through the Pentateuch even hurriedly without having been in some measure struck by the simplicity of its theology. The Pentateuch is full of God. The Deity overflows the wondrous writing. God is so near his creatures : he speaks to them, as it were, face to face ; he is familiar with them though always retaining the augustness of his Deity, and never relaxing the majesty proper to his being and duration; he comes down to earth, walks upon it, talks to men, tells them what his will is, elects them to service, enriches them with promises, points out their respective destinies. In the Pentateuch God is a God nigh at hand, and not afar off. The Pentateuch is a kind of nursery book : everything is written in such large letters ; the pictures are innumerable, most vividly coloured, appealing to the eye with very broad claims to attention. Everything is upon a great scale, most vivid, most graphic ; it is impossible to pass by without being arrested by noble figures, by marked events, by startling claims and appeals. We say sometimes that there are no children in the Pentateuch. Let us consider the thought and see whether in reality there were any thing but children in the five books of Moses. What else could there be ? Adam was a child. The world was begun with a child-man ; not with an infant, so far as the beginning of biblical history enables us to judge. When man comes upon the page, he comes on in full stature, with the breath of God living in him, and so affecting his features as to make them shine with the subdued majesty of God. The book is adapted to the earliest ages of manhood. We repeat, it is a species of nursery-book, full of capitals, full of pictures, eventful, short in its statements, striking in its representations. Yet there is nothing shallow in all the matchless simplicity. It takes the sun in heaven and all the chemistry of earth to grow the tiniest flower that lifts up its head in the green mead. Nothing is thrown in as make-weight and as of no consideration. Were there only one little flower promised to grow upon the earth to the end of time, that very promise would involve the maintenance of the astronomy of the universe as we know it; so when even simplicity seems to be simplest in the striking records of Moses, the simplicity is the last expression of eternal power, eternal wisdom, eternal beneficence. It required God to take hold of the historian's hand when he wrote the very first verse in Genesis. No human fingers unaided by divine energy ever penned that most startling and bewildering of all sentences. Nor is mystery wanting in connection with simplicity. The word "God" assumes plural forms. It creates a kind of grammar all its own. Who can number the plural "US" as we find it in the expression, "Let us make man"? The word will stand for all energies; it will stand for all the creatures ever created through all the endless ages of eternal duration. An angel is promised—the Angel of the Covenant—the angel of the Lord. Anonymous ministries are operating all through and through the book. Mystery shadows simplicity. Great marvels are closely related to simple events. So the simplicity is not shallowness. The darkness is not without atmosphere, mediation, interception between the essential Deity and the creature of a day, unable to bear upon his eyeballs the unclouded splendour of essential flame.

Nor can we read the Pentateuch as a whole without being struck by the very close way in which it reproduces human nature as we know it. The Man of the Pentateuch stands next in mystery to its God. He is a wondrous man. He comes upon us suddenly; he comes straight from the hand of God. Yet his coming is not without mystery. He was made of "the dust of the ground." But what is the dust of the ground? We read that expression as if we understood it—as if any child could give a sufficient reply. How was the dust made? Of what is it compounded? Who can read the stony and mouldering record? What is dust? Is it suspended life? Is it a new mode of being? When did it begin? Is it a symbolical or a literal term? The dust carries in it all the ages preceding. So we must not narrow or vulgarise the words by imagining that any one knows the meaning of the expression, "dust of the ground." When God took of that dust, he took of his own handiwork: he made the dust before he made the man. We are not to suppose that the dust is something wholly independent of God—something which God himself found in the world and made use of. The dust is his; the dust has a theology; the dust has a magnificent history. But we begin with the historian; and though we begin with the historian, we are not excluded from the society and inspiration of the poet. We cannot have even the dust of the ground treated with contempt; the augustness of its history must be acknowledged by every diligent student. But the "Man" stands before us historically upright, physically complete, responsible at once, beginning the very next day to obey or disobey. How did he act? His reproduction of human nature as we know it is perfect in its likeness. Man soon wanted more. He was told by an insidious and seductive voice that if he would adopt a certain course he would become "as God." Who ever resisted that temptation? It is the one temptation that besieges human life as an army might besiege a citadel. Examine life, and say if this be not the religious expression of the temptation that is supreme. It means: you shall have more, you shall have pleasure, you shall have delights heaped up; you shall advance: make progress your motto, write it upon your life-banner, and be not ashamed of the legend. This is what human nature is doing to-day. No sooner did humanity become social and assume family forms than family feuds succeeded. Cain murdered Abel—and Cain will murder Abel unto the end of time. It will require a redeeming rather than a creating God to stop the murder of Abel. Then came social deceptions: one man overreaching another; man telling lies to man, smiling with the lips, cursing with the heart;

offering friendship with the hand, vowing vengeance in a spirit dumb with determination. Is this human nature as we know it? We speak of old records, and primitive man, and pre-historic times, and times incalculably ancient;—where is all this antiquity? That it exists we cannot doubt; and we doubt it the less that we ourselves repeat and confirm it in every beating pulse we tell. So in the Pentateuch we have a marvellous theology—simple, profound, graphic, yet mystic; and in the Pentateuch we have human nature in its broadest lines and aspects, with a singular and incalculable origin—an origin so described that science can never either overtake it or outwit it: the terms that are there are awaiting final interpretation; and human life—individual, social, national—discloses itself before us as if reproducing our own experiences. Sometimes men say, on hearing startling statements,—Where did we hear these words before? Did we dream them? Is this the second time of hearing such terms? What is the meaning of this? So when we read the Pentateuch we seem to read our own biography. We take out proper names, we put in our own appellations, and still the history rolls on as if we were perfectly familiar with it and could ourselves annotate it with facts which have occurred within our own experience. This, as we have seen again and again is the great hold which the Bible gets upon human attention and confidence. It knows man; it explains man to himself: man brings the riddle, the Bible supplies the answer. We are not following in the lines of an unknown human nature—a nature that lived in other time and in other space, and of which we know nothing except by revelation; we know the man so well that what the book says of God would be made just as clear and positive could we follow that mystery to the inner places now invisible.

We cannot peruse the Pentateuch as a whole without remarking the fearlessness with which it sets forth the otherwise incredible circumstance of divine disappointment. Can disappointment follow Omniscience? Can God be surprised? Did he not see the end from the beginning? Is not the whole plan, in all its development and purpose, the outcome of his own mind? in a sense, the answer must be—Certainly, unquestionably. All things express in some way the intent of the moral will, or the regal will: God will have it so for a time, or he will have it so for ever, either in the form of moral purpose or of a sovereign fiat. All things must be traced to God. "Can there be evil in a city, and the Lord have not done it?" Can there be a hell in the universe, and God not have dug it? Can there be any devil in creation who cannot trace his origin to God? "The Lord reigneth." We must take this larger view, for by it alone are certain moral mysteries lifted into adequate light, that they may receive at least tips of illumination, glints of glory, which help us to believe that the full enlightenment will come by-and-by. God was disappointed:—"It repented the Lord that he had made man on the earth." He wept over the Jerusalem of the ancient world, as his Son wept over another Jerusalem. The speech of the heavenly Father was, in effect:—"O Jerusalem, Jerusalem, . . . how often would I have gathered thy children together, as a hen doth gather her brood under her wings, and ye would not!" How otherwise could he have sent a flood upon the earth? Make of the flood what we may—universal, partial, literal, symbolic—there remains the fact of a flood—a display of judgment, in other words, a display of disappointment: because whenever God punishes he must have been disappointed before he could inflict the penalty. He made the world for virtue, uprightness, innocence, holiness; so when criminal blackness came before him he must have felt the pang of disappointment, which he has never failed to express:—"Hear, O heavens, and give ear, O earth: for the Lord hath spoken, I have nourished and brought up children, and they have rebelled against me." How otherwise could he have sent fire upon cities splendidly situated, well-watered, in fruitful plains, beautiful for situation? Why the fire? Why the brimstone? Why these smoking, smouldering heaps? The answer is—Sin, apostasy, wickedness, disobedience; and could God look upon these forms or expressions of evil without corresponding disappointment? The words, "It repented the Lord that he had made man," express a real not a dramatic emotion. The disappointment continues. There is nothing surprising in flood and fire being sent down in judgment; the surprise is that they are withheld to-day. Sodom and Gomorrah could not have been so wicked as the cities of the present time can be. Modern cities have larger opportunities, broader civilisations, multiplied resources; and the devil never alters, never repents, never prays: he will fight out the battle so long as one glint of light remains in the western sky; he will not die unless by compulsion. The cities of to-day are more wicked than the cities of any other time. The wickedness is more varied in form; it is often perpetrated with greater boldness; it is turned to commercial account. It so grows upon the wicked man himself that he loses all feeling, all sense of dignity, all consciousness of shame; nothing is sacred to him: the grave has no protection from his violation; childhood is not too young for his defilement, nothing too fair to be smitten and wrecked by his violent hand. We know this as matter of fact, not as matter of poetry; and it is matter of fact not outside us but within us. Other men do the deeds of which we conceive the thoughts: other men may be but the executioners, whilst all men may be the thinkers and dreamers. Herein divine judgment alone can be right. He who made us must judge us. We must not suppose that all things of an evil kind are open and known and avowed; nor must any man attempt to sit in judgment beyond a given point. There is a line within which society may judge, ought to judge, and must judge; but there is a further line towards which human judgment cannot even move: God only can be Judge there. When the prophet was ordered to dig down he found a wall going very deeply into the ground; he was told to dig more deeply still: he dug, and at length came to a door; he was told to open the door and pass in; and there, under the roots of things, under the foundations of cities, he found what is called the chamber of imagery, and there in that hidden place he saw the symbols of indescribable dissolution. It is so with the human mind. There is an aspect in which all is public and open and about which there can be no doubt; but there is a chamber of imagery—a mind with painted walls, an inner life full of unholy symbolism, and crowded with secret worship—a hole within a hole, concerning which God must be Judge.

So then, we have a simple theology, a human nature which we can recognise, and a divine government that is stung by disappointment; these things we have in the book called the Pentateuch, or, in other words, the five books of Moses. We

ought to beware lest in discussing the comparatively trivial
question—Who wrote the Pentateuch? that we miss the
purpose of the fivefold writing. Comparatively unimportant—
what, then, is the supremely important point? Evidently it is
to know what is written rather than who wrote it. That there
may have been more hands.than one in the composition of the
Pentateuch is perfectly possible; in some few instances indeed,
it cannot be otherwise than real and indisputable. That the
books of the Pentateuch might be.differently arranged is not
beyond the bounds of possibility. That the supposed dates of
the five books might be modified or readjusted is also within the
limits of possibility. But we are not called to the consideration
of such questions. The one inquiry we have to make is—What
is the moral purpose of the book? What is its spiritual tone?
What is its religious claim? What are its great theological and
anthropological doctrines? What is its God, and what is its
man? Mythology presents us with innumerable impossibilities :
we know them to exceed all likelihood and to offend every conception of order and probability; but the Pentateuch presents us
with nothing that is improbable, so far as our own experience
extends. We can comprehend most of it, and where we do touch
it we feel how firm is the association between the ancient writing
and the modern experience. Coming upon antiquities in this
fashion, corroborating them one after another, we feel that where
one or two may seem to fall out of the line of corroboration in
other instances the coincidence is so striking and so vital that we
need have no fear as to an explanation coming by-and-by even
in reference to mysteries at present hidden in sevenfold darkness.
We must stand by Moses. Our study of his character has given
us profound confidence in his spirit and in his purpose. He has
suffered for his convictions. What critic ever suffered for his
sneers? What annotator of to-day ever lost position or
opportunity of advancement of so broad a kind as that which
Moses lost when he " refused to be called the son of Pharaoh's
daughter ; choosing rather to suffer affliction with the people of
God, than to enjoy the pleasures of sin for a season ? " When
men confirm their theology by acts of sacrifice so plain, clear, and
complete, they deserve consideration ; they appeal, though unconsciously, to the reverence of mankind. In what sense, then

is the Pentateuch old ? Only in a temporal sense. There is
nothing that is old in the Pentateuch if we regard it spiritually,
symbolically, alphabetically. The root is not old so long as there
is fruit on the uppermost branches. The New Testament is the outcome of the Old : the Gospels are the Pentateuch in full bloom—
in all its spiritual culmination and sublimest meaning. Read the
Pentateuch thus, straight through, without asking minor questions,
without pausing intermediately ; read it as a whole, from end
to end, and then ask what are the impressions it makes upon the
mind ; and first will be the impression that God is near, direct in
his communication, interested in every action, holding every man
of value ; that God is Critic of all time, Judge of all action, never
afraid after having blessed the world to drown it, to burn it, for
human wickedness may be greater than divine blessing. The
impression made upon the mind will be that human nature is a
mystery, not to be judged here and now, not to be summed up
and valued within given and measurable limits, but to be regarded
as a continual mystery, a profound and insoluble problem,
awaiting the judgment of God. Nor can we read the Pentateuch
without being struck with the fact that though hand join in hand
the wicked shall not go unpunished. " Be sure your sin will
find you out." There is more water in the clouds, there is
more fire in the throne of God ; and God will not hesitate to
drown the world or to burn the universe, if so be that man's sin
exceed God's grace.

We cannot read the Pentateuch as a whole without being
struck with the way in which it all grows up into the fortune of
one man. At first there is quite a number of men. The number
grows and multiplies exceedingly, so that the whole earth seems
to be covered with an active population. Page by page we turn
over the record, and one name comes up above another ; then
we come to a period when a special name takes precedence and
stands royally aloft above all other names, as if the whole history
had been evolved and consolidated for the manifestation of that
one name. The one name is that of Moses. Having concluded
the Pentateuch, the mind seems to have before it but that
resplendent name. It is the name of ruler, leader, shepherd,
and friend of unnumbered hosts. The name is a symbol of

strength, light, leading, sustenance of a spiritual and moral kind.
True leadership seems to begin with Moses. He is a kind of
father-mother, a shepherd-friend, a legislator with a Gospel voice,
—a man accustomed to interpret thunders and lightnings, and to
pluck from the midst of the tempest the still small Voice of
divine solicitude and divine commandment, and to interpret that
Voice to all the host in a language which they can understand.
Is not this like all human history? Are there not even in the
annals of common civilisation names that gather up into themselves all that was typical of the age, all that was purest in its
morality, ripest in its wisdom, and most benign in its influence?
Do these things stand for nothing in history? Is there not
behind them a suggestion? Is there coming a Name that shall
be above every name? Shall even Moses be forgotten in the
splendours of a nobler title? As the Pentateuch has led up to the
coronation of Moses, do not all the books of both Testaments lead
up to the enthronement of him who is King of kings and Lord
of lords, and before whom all living powers bow in profoundest
homage, and to whom they look with most expectant hope?
There is a genius in history of this kind. This is not a novel
arrangement on the part of the Bible—that a name here and
there shall be a dominant name of that particular time and place.
We find the same idea through all history. There is a king
everywhere, in all society a leader, in all organisation a throbbing
heart, a beating pulse, an eye with accent in it, a point of light;
and to that man, that influence, that eye, all other men for the
time being look for sustenance, guidance, stimulus, and inspiration. So the pages are turned over; so history rises, falls,
recombines, and amplifies, and at the last there is one Name
that swallows up all other names—JESUS, the Name to sinners
dear. And Jesus is not ashamed to be associated with Moses.
When the great song rolls in the heavenly places, like thunder
upon thunder, it is the song of Moses and the Lamb—as if these
two names touched the extreme points of history and gathered
up into themselves all the elements of human education, human
progress, and human salvation. See if this be not so. This
cannot be seen unless the revelation is read from beginning to
end—so read that the mind is cleared of every other thought
and recollection, and the grand Biblical purpose engraves itself

upon the intellect and the heart, the understanding and the imagination. To believe in the Bible, read it. No man who ever *read* the Bible, with body, soul, and spirit, disbelieved it. Readers have come in here and there in a violent and wanton way that would be rebuked as indecent were they treating a human poem so, and have said severe and foolish things about the Bible; but wherever the Bible has been fairly treated, read as a whole, understood in its parts and relations, apprehended in all its moral relations and all its moral issues, it has been received and adopted and worshipped as the book of God.

We cannot read the Pentateuch as a whole without being struck with the fact that all the human movement in it is a movement towards one land. After a certain time we are conscious that a great procession is taking place. There is a loud trampling of feet, there is a tumultuous sensation everywhere: men are moving, standards are pitched, tents are struck, and travelling begins on a mighty and unprecedented scale. Whither goes the host? What is the name of your country, O pilgrims in the desert? Know ye to what destination ye hasten?—tell us the name. To the land flowing with milk and honey, to the land sworn to be given to Abraham, and Isaac, and Jacob, to a land of green things and plentifulness, and singing birds; to that land we go, and every night we pitch our camp a day's march nearer home. Are you all bound for one land? All—men, women, and children, the mightiest and the feeblest. Is it a hospitable land? It flows with milk and honey. Do you take any people up with you on the road? Yes: "Come thou with us, and we will do thee good: for the Lord hath spoken good concerning Israel." So everything is forgotten in the presence of the all-constraining Canaan. It is the magnet-land; it is the all-drawing cord. Men must have something ahead. You cannot destroy this element of purpose and hope, without making a tremendous reduction in the volume, and deterioration in the quality, of the human mind. All men are travelling to *some* land. Many a poet who has never written rhymed lines sings to himself of some fair country where he will have Sabbath a week long—rest, peace, reconciliation, health, and the power of enjoying every point of accessible and visible nature. Then there is nothing startlingly novel or simply romantic about all these people moving to a common country? Nothing whatever. This is the programme of all human life; this is purpose of every intelligent soul. To what land are we journeying? To a land flowing with milk and honey. Has any description of the land been handed to any traveller who can give us some notion of the country to which we are moving? Yes: the country has been discovered, and it is called a city—a city where they have no need of the sun, or of the moon; a land in which there is no night, no sin, no death, no sea. The describers of that land have often to portray it in striking negatives. Wherever we find any thing that is repellent, undesirable, uncomely—anything that is feared, avoided, disliked, the describers say,—The city to which you are going has nothing of that kind in it; cleanse your mind of all such fears: it is morning-land, it is summer-land; the light never fades, and the service is never accompanied by tedium or weariness. It is right to ask one another, To what country are you going? For what place are you bound? We are to that extent our brother's keeper; and it never can be an impertinent question, if not impertinently put, Brother, to what land do you hasten? We have been so trained by the Moses of the new covenant—the Son of God—that there is no land upon earth we could tolerate for a moment as a final resting-place. We could not tolerate the grave, if it were the end. We speak about it poetically as the end; sometimes the weary traveller longs for it : he says,—Oh that I could lay me down under the sod and enter into the peace of a long dreamless sleep!—but we are so trained to the estimation of values, to the estimation of time and space and all resource adapted to human necessity, that we despise time, space,—Lebanon, Bashan, and all the vineyards of the earth, and all the cattle upon a thousand hills, with the silver and the gold hidden there. When we are asked our destination, we say,—We seek a country out of sight, a city that hath foundations whose builder and maker is God. A romantic reply to the untrained mind, but prose-poetry to the soul that has been educated, chastened, purified, and made meet for the inheritance of the saints in light. Poor is the life—poor to contemptibleness—that lives in any other direction, that goes downwards in its desires, and that trains itself to dispositions that are grovelling. Herein is the glory and the joy of the Christian inspiration, that it fills the soul with discontent with regard to everything time and space can give as final medicaments and benedictions, and stirs in the soul that lofty desire which can only be satisfied with all that we know by the sweet name of heaven. So long as Christianity thus creates larger desires, nobler aspirations, discontentment with all things finite, it will maintain its place in human history and in human education. If it excited discontent only, men would become weary of it, and shake it off as a burden; but it only creates discontent that it may bring in a larger capacity and a more profound contentment.

We cannot read the Pentateuch as a whole without being struck as to the way by which that land is to be reached. We cannot reach it by desiring it, by talking about it merely, by dreaming of it in periods of sleep, or even in day-dreams of intellectual recreation. It is a land that must be walked to— a long, long walk, over stony places, up great hills, through winding and perilous valleys, where beasts of prey roam, and where pits are dug, and where dangers lie thick as the travellers' footprints; the way must be walked step by step, it is a way regulated by law. Men do not make paths for themselves. "Thou shalt," "Thou shalt not,"—are the words which continually ring in the ear of the traveller. The wanderer sees a way he would like to take; it seems to be a way of greensward, and on the greensward there seem to be little quiet flowers, and the traveller says,—May I not walk by that green road?—and a voice says, "Thou shalt not." The way is over stony places; for days together there may be no water to drink, for weeks together no green thing can be seen;—this is the way: walk ye in it. Human life is based upon divine discipline. Human life is not a clever trick, a conjuror's art, an opportunity for displaying invention as to the discovery of roads. The roads were made before we were born; the paths have been laid from before the foundation of the world: the Lamb of God was slain before human sin was committed. We must therefore build back upon eternity, and look forward to eternity, and accept the chastisement, and say,—The thong is heavy and cuts often to the bone, but it is wielded by a Father's hand : even so, for so it seemeth good in thy sight. We want to take near courses, short cuts ; and God will not allow us to do so. The true life is a life of obedience. He cannot rule who cannot obey. What every man has to ask is this : What wilt thou have me to do, thou Father of spirits ? Show me the way, tell me the law, keep me with thy right hand, guide me with thine eye, and afterward receive me to glory. This is not the surrender of reason, this is not the subjugation of intellect ; this is the finite accepting the infinite, this is ignorance asking for wisdom, this is the lamb pleading to be carried in the shepherd's arms. Such is the philosophy of revelation in the matter of human progress. No little suffering accompanies that progress : —" Whom the Lord loveth he chasteneth." He beats us back sometimes. Now and then we would move too soon, and the Lord says we have yet to remain in the same place a day or two, or more. Thus is patience tried, thus is temper tested, thus is character consolidated, mellowed, ennobled. We should have been poor but for our suffering ; we should have been mere talkers of human dreams, if we had not lived in tragedy all the pain of this life. " Though he slay me, yet will I trust in him." He has been with me in six troubles, and in the seventh he will not forsake me. As to the weapon that is being formed against me, it shall not prosper : it shall rust in the night-time, and in the morning have no handle, and shall only cut the man who seizes it. O rest in the Lord, and wait patiently for him ; and he shall give thee thine heart's desire.

Then, again, the whole Pentateuch is marked by its persistent religiousness. It is an intensely religious book. The religious service never ceases ; there is no intermission, no lifting away of the hand that presses : the sacrifice never ends, the fire is never put out, the blood never ceases to flow. There is no time for play, for privilege, for self-indulgence : one service is scarcely ended before another begins ; and so the ceremony rolls on in impetuous determination to subdue the human will and exhaust all that is poorest and meanest in human life. So must human life itself be. To be really grand, it must be supremely religious to be really useful, it must be continually active in the service of God. We cease to live when we cease to pray. We cease to give when we cease to love. We lose the Sabbath day when we lose the resurrection. We can only lose Christian doctrine when we lose the Cross out of which it flows. We cannot do good from a motive that is not equal to the occasion without showing how shallow is the well out of which we have drawn. There is but one motive that will stand all weathers, all strains and tests: "the love of Christ constraineth us."

JOSHUA.

PRAYER

ALMIGHTY GOD, thou art always thinking of us: all thirgs are for our sake. Thy providence is the proof of thy redemption; they are one and the same great thought of love. Thou didst make man in thine own image and likeness, and thou art continuing so to make him; and thy great labour shall not cease until the similitude be perfected. This is thy work amongst us. We weary thee, and try thee, and bring the warm tears to thine eyes because of perverseness and self-will; but thou dost not release thyself from the great task: the purpose of God standeth sure; it is an eternal thought; thou wilt not be wearied out. Yea, thou hast burned the world, or drowned it with great tempests of water; yet thou hast preserved a root, a germ, so that thy process may go on and thy will may be made known; and, behold, who can set himself so much against the purpose of heaven as finally to destroy the decree of the Almighty? It is thine to work through all the ages. Eternity is thine. We know nothing of duration: we are a wind that cometh for a little time and bloweth away into forgetfulness; we are a light quickly blown out; we are a fading flower; there is none that abideth: but the throne of the glorious God is for ever. We rejoice in this thought: it makes us steadfast and calm in the midst of storms and threats that would render our lives intolerable. Things are shaken that are meant to be shaken, that those things which cannot be shaken may reveal their solidity the more. We rest in God; we would be one with God; we would know no will but thine; and thus ordering our life according to the music of thy commands, thy statutes shall become songs, and the darkest night but a time to sing in most loudly, sweetly, tenderly. We give one another to thee in continual prayer. To be in God is to be in one another; to be in Christ Jesus the Lord is to have fellowship of soul one with another and to enter into the preliminary joy of blessed heaven. We come to the Cross of Christ; we glory in that alone. We do not comprehend all its mystery: we cannot tell why the blood is so red, why it was poured out from an innocent, holy heart; we can say nothing in words of all the great emotion which moves our hearts, but we believe that is thy revelation, thy way of saving the world; Lord, we believe, help thou our unbelief! We are the better for this look towards the Cross. It is a look away from ourselves, away into eternity and heaven and mystery divine. We rejoice that thou hast appointed times when we may specially commune with thee, in o en terms, in a common language, when the old, and the young, and the asy, and the suffering may all commune in open fellowship under the open sky of heaven, praising God with a common voice and with a loud song.   We own our sinfulness, but we own thy might to destroy it.   Thou wilt not forsake thine own seed, the work of thine own hands, the heart in which the Son of God is born.   Reveal thy Son within us day by day. May we see his beauty, may we feel his touch, may we be assured of his love, and may we live and move in his eternal strength.   Help us to live this little life wisely and well; may we not invent methods of our own whereby to make our life better, but, reading thy law, meditating on thy truth, we shall be enabled to deal wisely, to subdue every enemy and opposition, and to enter into the prepared rest.   Hear us in these things, and let thy love be continued toward us as thou dost continue the light of the sun to warm and cheer the earth.   Leave none unblessed!   May the worst heart lift itself up in new strength; may the soul in which there has been desolation like the darkness of night know that the light of hope is shining upon it, and that the music of heavenly welcomes is addressed to its despair.   Spoil every evil plan; thwart every mischievous purpose; sweeten every sour disposition, and make straight the will that is perverse.   May we now enter into an oath of consecration, a solemn, noble vow to be better, to do better, to work more diligently, and construe each other's action more charitably, and all this in Christ, and by Christ, without whom we can do nothing.   Continue thy pity toward us, for we are not yet strong enough to do without it: we still come to thy compassionate side; we dare not face thy righteousness, or challenge the burning light of thine honour and thy law, but we may come and say, at the Cross, and through its power, God be merciful to me a sinner! Amen.

Joshua i. 1-9.

1. Now after the death of Moses the servant of the Lord it came to pass, that the Lord spake unto Joshua the son of Nun, Moses' minister, saying,

2. Moses my servant is dead; now therefore arise, go over this Jordan, thou, and all this people, unto the land which I do give to them, even to the children of Israel.

3. Every place that the sole of your foot shall tread upon, that have I given unto you, as I said unto Moses.

4. From the wilderness and this Lebanon, even unto the great river, the river Euphrates, all the land of the Hittites, and unto the great sea toward the going down of the sun, shall be your coast.

5. There shall not any man be able to stand before thee all the days of thy life: as I was with Moses, so I will be with thee: I will not fail thee nor forsake thee.

6. Be strong and of good courage: for unto this people shalt thou divide for an inheritance the land, which I sware unto their fathers to give them.

7. Only be thou strong and very courageous, that thou mayest observe to do according to all the law, which Moses my servant commanded thee: turn not from it to the right hand or to the left, that thou mayest prosper whithersoever thou goest.

8. This book of the law shall not depart out of thy mouth; but thou shalt meditate therein day and night, that thou mayest observe to do according to all that is written therein: for then thou shalt make thy way prosperous, and then thou shalt have good success.

9. Have not I commanded thee? Be strong and of a good courage; be not afraid, neither be thou dismayed: for the Lord thy God is with thee whithersoever thou goest.

THE MAN AND HIS CALL.

THE book of Joshua has been divided into three sections— namely, the conquest of Canaan, chapters i.–xii.; the division of the land, chapters xiii.–xxii.; while chapters xxiii., xxiv., are devoted to a statement concerning the closing days of the soldier Joshua. The main action of the book comprises a period of twenty-five years. The pedigree of Joshua is illustrious; it may be seen in 1 Chronicles vii. 20-27, reaching back through generations to Joseph. His grandfather, Elishama, marched through the wilderness of Sinai at the head of his tribe, and probably he had special charge of the embalmed body of Joseph. The book is indirectly referred to in many places both in the Old Testament and the New; for example in Judges xviii. 31; 1 Samuel i. 24; iii. 21; Isaiah xxviii. 21; Psalm xliv. 2-3; lxviii. 12-14; lxxviii. 54-58; cxiv. 1-8; Habakkuk iii. 8-13; Acts vii. 45; Hebrews iv. 8; xi. 31; xiii. 5; James ii. 25. These passages are collated to show that the references to the book of Joshua are not merely incidental or occasional, but that the book is certified by reference and endorsed by application throughout the most of the remainder of the sacred records. Joshua was a prince of the tribe of Ephraim, born in the land of Goshen, and trained as a soldier,—kept in repression during many years, because there was really nothing for a soldier-prophet to do. He was appointed to repel the attack of Amalek. He was honoured to accompany the great minister partly up his solitary way which lay towards the meeting-place on the summit of mount Sinai. He was one of the two spies who came back with a good heart and an inspiring word, saying that the work could be done and was worth doing. For a long time he was in the background: nothing was known of him during the years of weary wandering in the Arabian desert. A weird character altogether!—Speaking of his

house, but with a limitation ; without wife, or child, or heir ; standing, as it were, midway between Moses and Samuel—a period
of four hundred years. A soldier always,—prompt, obedient,
decisive, sharp in expression ; his attitude a challenge or a
benediction. Great was his honour, too : into his much-mean-
ing name there was inserted part of the name of the Eternal ; and
Joshua in its Greek form is Jesus—the captain of our salvation—
the name which is above every name. So may our names grow
and blossom and fructify into great meanings ; they are trusts :
we hold them as stewards ;—shall they vanish like blanks that can
never be missed, or live on day after day,—a memory, a blessing,
an inspiration ? Each man must answer the inquiry for himself.

Now let us turn to the book with religious attentiveness.
" Now after the death of Moses—" (v. 1). Can there be any
" after " under such a circumstance ? Does not all time seem
to breathe for certain men ? And does it not seem as if there
would be no need of time if their great figures and generous
influence were removed ? Does not time seem to focus itself
in some noble characters—as if all other life were tributary to
those eminent personalities, as if all other influence circulated
around them and had heaven enough in a subordinate relationship ? But God can bury any one of us, and continue the history
as though we had never lived. We cannot make great
gaps in God's providence. His thoughts are not our thoughts,
neither his ways our ways. He toucheth the mountains, and
they smoke ; he taketh up the isles as a very little thing, and
the nations are as a drop of a bucket—a poor trembling eye
of dew—before Him. We cry over this opening line as if
some great chasm had been dug in our little heaven. We
forget that the man spoken of is only dead to us, not dead
to the universe, or dead to God, or dead in any sense equivalent to extinction or destruction. The word is a cold one, and
full of hideousness in some aspects ; we must use it ; no
other term touches the reality of things so significantly, but we
must, by living in a right course so look down upon all
things as to account death as only a word—a mere term of
expediency, a mark of punctuation, rather than an articulate
term,—a point a printer might use, but really without any terror
or sting or dread. Death is dead to every man who is himself

alive with the immortality of his soul. And some great names must be removed to make way for lesser names that have growing sap in them and real capability of beneficent expansion. Some great trees must be cut down to make room for lesser trees that mean to be great ones in their time. We owe much to the cutting-down power of death, the clearing power of the cruel scythe or axe. Death makes history as well as life. Of life death is the servant. The great thing to know about the dead is their character. That character in the case of Moses is indicated here explicitly—" the servant of the Lord." Is the term so definite as almost to amount to an indication or singularity —as if the Lord had but one servant ? The expression is not " one of the servants," or " a " servant, but " the " servant. Nor is this an ancient term only ; it is part of the speech of our day. There are men who are pre-eminently primates. We do not contest their primacy. It is not official. The greater the man the readier he is to own that Moses is above him : for in no domineering or tyrannous sense is the higher above the lower, but in the sense of wisdom, graciousness, fraternity of feeling, willingness to serve,—for what child is there, how naked and poor soever, that the sun will disdain to light him home ? The greater man is the lesser man in proper form. The least brother has a right to look at the greatest and say—that is myself enlarged and glorified ; that shining face is mine ; that eloquent tongue is uttering my speech ; that mighty form is carrying my burdens ; so, then, there is no contentious rivalry, or clamour for place or honour. God makes every appointment, and makes it with infinite wisdom.

Whilst all this is true in regard to Moses, surely there is some painfulness of preference with regard to the man who must follow him ? Yet who can tell how good God is even here ? Men are prepared almost unconsciously : it is but one step that has to be taken. The men did not know all the time that they were waiting to take that upward step. The announcement of elevation may have come suddenly, but then there is an answering voice which says—I have heard this before ; this but reads the riddle of a dream ; now I feel that God is calling me. Let every man, therefore, be faithful in his own place ; let every man watch, do his duty, carry his burdens, be ready for enlarging opportunities and new disclosures of gracious providence. Do not force the gate that is closed : there is plenty to do upon this side of the way; in due time the gate will fall back as if an angel invisible had touched it, and by the falling back of the gate know of a surety your opportunity has come.

What is the duty of the Church when the announcement is made, " Moses my servant is dead " ?　The answer is sublime ! The Lord addresses himself to the soldier-spirit of Joshua :— " Now, therefore "—stopping there for one moment and wondering what the next word can be—we think it must be : Bow down your heads in sorrow; weep all your tears, for the loss is irreparable.　What *is* the following word ?　Take the sentence altogether :—" Now therefore arise " !　Who can extinguish the animation of the divine word, or throw a shadow upon the divine hope, or discourage the heart of Heaven ?　Moses is dead : therefore—stand up ! gird on thy sword, put on thy strength ; be thy best self and noblest, for the sphere is large, and to follow Moses is to be created a new and greater man.　What is Joshua to do ?　An epoch opens in reply to that inquiry.　We turn over a new page in the world's history at this moment : we come upon words we have not seen before—words which abide in all their energy through the ages.　Joshua is referred to written orders.　Up to this time there has been no reference to writing in the sense in which that reference is made now. Behold, in all the outgoing of providence there is a book amongst us—a written thing—a silent scroll, burning with messages from heaven.　Moses had no Bible ; Moses lived on the spoken word : he heard the tone and translated it into the speech of the people, but there was nothing written in the sense in which the word is used in the eighth verse of this first chapter of Joshua. A new responsibility is imposed upon the Church.　This is the difficulty with many men—namely, that there is a Book.　The Book is so often in the way.　We might build a thousand airy churches, and make their glittering pinnacles prick the clouds, but for the Book.　There is a written law, a declared testimony, a quotable word,—something requiring attention, intelligence, sympathy, grammar.　Thus liberty itself passes under the yoke. When there was no king in Israel, every man did that which was good in his own eyes : if there were no book, every one of us might have his dream, his prophecy, his saying, his little pastoral staff and crook. But Joshua is told to begin to read :—" This book of the law shall not depart out of thy mouth ; but thou shalt meditate therein day and night, that thou mayest observe to do according to all that is written therein " (v. 8). An excellent thing this, too,—namely, to have a book ! The question admits of being put from two opposite points of view. An excellent reflection that there is a writing which may be consulted, and which must be perused if life is to seize the very highest treasures of wisdom. To the law and to the testimony then,—not that they are to be interpreted hardly, in some tone of domination that oppresses the soul, but a written word that is to be a living seed, growing its fruits in every clime, answering all the influences of heaven as revealed in civilisation, education, and progress of the broadest and noblest kind. The eighth verse is, however, noticeable in view of the fact that it puts a book into the hand of men. The book has never been changed. Jesus Christ did not change it : he said not a jot or tittle of it should be changed or taken away, unless by fulfilment, completion of purpose, when the meaning intended by the Almighty had been carried out,—then there might be a passing away of literal form, but even then veneration would bow down before pillars at which the ages had halted and refreshed themselves in prayer. Where then is liberty ? Again and again there comes upon the imagination the wondrous possibility of things under a liberty in which every man might write his own Bible. How we would change its spirit to suit the circumstances ! How we would temper its tone to meet the occasion ! A little manipulation would give its moralities release from their severest claims: a retrimming of the lamp would throw light in an unfamiliar direction ; but man is only allowed to interpret the law—to meditate therein day and night, to find out its meaning—for though it be so clear, so simple, it is the simplicity that is unfathomable, the simplicity that expresses the last result of divine processes in human education. So, then, we are called to be law students, Bible readers, inquirers into written revelation. Here comes in a great popular liberty. The law is published in our mother tongue : every man may take his own copy into his own sick-chamber, and there peruse it in the light of other history and personal consciousness and experience, and test the book by individual necessities. This is the great answer to the tumult of the day. On the one hand we hear of men who long to resuscitate and reimpose stately theologies, formal creeds, endorsed by illustrious names,—and the age will not have them; it says that such theologies and creeds and men served their purpose in their own time, and within the limits of their operation they were good and useful, but the ages grow : the sun has not been sowing all this light upon the earth without an accompanying sowing of light having taken place in the fields of human inquiry and intelligence. On the other hand there are those who say—Our refuge must be in science, new discovery, in broad, generous progress;—and the age cannot receive that testimony either. The great human heart says—That of which you speak is good and noble and most useful, and we thank God for every discovery that makes life brighter, happier, easier to live; but you have not touched the innermost wound—the secret pulse of the soul,—that seems to lie beyond the reach of your finger. What then is our position in relation to these rival claims? Our position is : let the Bible speak for itself. We want Biblical teaching, thorough exposition, a reading of the word in the light of the present day;—not by theology of a formal kind, not by science of a domineering sort, but by the Bible itself is the kingdom of heaven to be advanced. Use Bible words. Do not be ashamed of Bible images and Bible doctrines. Do not make the Bible part of a library, but make it a library by itself. "Let the word of Christ dwell in you richly." If you are controverting, arguing, disputing, setting one opinion against another, what can come of it but dust and noise? Our position as Christian thinkers and teachers is only strong in proportion to our intelligent and reverent study and appropriation of the law—meaning by that the whole written revelation of God. Here, again, we must beware of interpreters, and only accept them as friendly helpers. No man is authorised to say, to the exclusion of the opinion and learning of every other man,—This is the meaning, and there is none other. The Bible will bear looking at from every point of view. It rises to every occasion. Not a word of it need be changed. The word simply asks for a right utterance, a profound and appropriate exposition. It is wonderful that men can talk about theology and about science, and never say a word about the Bible. Nor will it do to say, "Of course the existence of the Bible is assumed." The Bible asks for no such recognition : it asks to be *read*. Its voice would seem to be : Read me night and day ; read me aloud ; read me in tones appropriate to the occasion : whisper me to the sick and the dying ; utter me with tunefulness and fascination of tone to little children and persons who are in the age of wonder or curiosity ; read me rudely, stormily, if you will, in the hearing of tumult and the rage of the heathen and the people ;—I only ask to be read— to be all read—to be read night and day, until there can be no mistake as to my purpose ;—do this, and live ! Surely this is the meaning of the divine promise made to Joshua : "for then thou shalt make thy way prosperous, and then thou shalt have good success." The word "prosperous" is not a literal translation. The word would read better thus : for then shalt thou deal wisely —or act wisely —in the spirit of wisdom, having understanding of the times, making allowances for the varieties of human mind and human character, and adapting me to the state of education which may be disclosed from time to time. He acts wisely who lives in the wise God—the only wise God, and our Saviour. We are not referred to our own wit, mental agility, intellectual brilliance or genius : the word in answer to temptation is in the law ; the word explanatory of righteousness is in the law ; the word which will keep us right in business is in the law ; the word which will save us from sin is in the written book of God. So, whilst on the one hand men ask you to accept some great scroll of theology, and on the other ask you to accept some great scroll of science, whilst you are reverent and grateful to both of them according to their obvious merits, stand you upon the written law : it grows whilst we read it ; it takes upon itself all the colour of the times ; it has in it a central constancy and yet an eternal adaptation and variation. The Bible is never obsolete : when all other voices have ceased, its noble majestic tone creates attention for itself,—yea, men who do not bow down before it as a spiritual ministry refer us to it as to the noblest English that can be written,—the purest, simplest, grandest specimen of our mother tongue. It is so in every language. Wherever it undertakes to represent itself in any language it makes itself the chief specimen of that language. It speaks all the tongues of the world with equal familiarity, grace, and dignity. It only asks to be translated into your mother tongue to lift that tongue up into unknown and unprecedented dignity. A book that asks no other favour can do without our patronage better than we can do without its counsel. Without changing a word, only asking for a broad and just interpretation, we stand upon the Bible, and to the Bible we go when the devil tempts us, when life is a heavy burden, when death is the last foe ; and so going we go to victory.

The following is another treatment of the same passage :—

"Now, after the death of Moses . . . ." Yes, what after that ? Can there be any " after " in such an event ? Are there no great gaping vacancies in life which seem to foreclose history and to turn present events into an anticlimax and a humiliation ? After the death of Moses—there can be no after. After the sun has gone down has God a lap of stars he can shower upon the darkness to alleviate it a little ? Doth after vision seem to enlarge it and to mock our memory of a brighter present ? Are there not some men who have no successors ? Does not the poet say, " Only himself can be his parallel ? " Why then do we come upon these mocking words in histories sacred and profane, " after the death of . . . " as if the road were a common plain, an ordinary level, one milestone and another milestone ahead, the monotony of common-place, the common-place itself occasionally vigorous enough, yet still to-morrow shall be as this day, and more abundant in the way of human life and human power and human exaltation and majesty ? Does history stand still because of the death of any one man ? Are we not always reminded that God can do without the strongest and wisest of us ? We remain here just long enough to think that we are needful to God, and when our pride has filled its little goblet, and made itself drunk with its own poison, he removes us, and history rolls on like a wave over a forgotten tomb. We are told that all the great men have gone, the age of miracles has gone, so has the age of inspiration, so has the age of speaking many and divers tongues in the Church, all healings, and marvels of signs and wonders have vanished from the sphere ecclesiastical.

You who make the objection are in your departments of life fellow-sufferers with ourselves. Your Shakespeare is dead, as well as our Moses—your Goethe and Dante are dead as well as our Isaiah and Ezekiel. All your great things have been done, your little miraculous *rôle* has been played out and shelved as well as ours—so let there be no mocking or undue and foolish triumphing the one over the other, but let there rather be sober and earnest meditation upon this question, whether all these things that appear so great in the past have not been displaced by things greater, only less sensuous and demonstrative. Why, the poorest of all time is always the present. When am I richest? When I go back upon my yesterdays, when I retrace my journeys without all the inconvenience of detail which is found in all voyagings and travellings. Seated in my quiet chair, in my pleasant solitude, with closed eyes I look back over all the yesterdays, reclimb the mountains and sail again on the silvery lakes, and move again with might and quiet serenity to the great sea. When I blow the trumpet of resurrection in the churchyard, and call up the dear lost ones, the old and the young, the bright and the sweet, the strong and the patient, then am I very rich. When are you, dear little one, richest? When you are telling me what you are *going* to do, *going* to see, *going* to be. It is the doll you are going to have that is to be the queen of all other dolls. It is the sight you are going to see that is to eclipse all other gaieties. Just now—nothing—a mere cobble-stone in a brook that may topple over. But all my wealth lies in the past, or glows in anticipation, and "just now" is always the poorest time in any history that is worth living.

"Now after the death of Moses, the servant of the Lord." Does God let his servants die? Was it the blame of Moses that he died, or is his death to be credited to his Lord? Is there an appointed time to men upon the earth—is there just a little length of thread that is long enough for the very strongest and wisest of us, and if an inch were added our past would be put in peril as well as our future? Are things set—are there fixed quantities in time, age, wealth, talent, power? Everything is weighed out and measured by the balances and standards of the Lord. He weighed the gold dust of the stars, and not a speck can be lost upon the wind. The very hairs of your head are all numbered. Not a sparrow falleth to the ground without your Father. He is a severe economist : like all great givers he is severely critical in his balances and results. Only the spend-thrift keeps no note-book of his outgoings. God hath a book, yea, many a book hath God, for when he had opened book after book, the Apocalyptic writer says then he opened another book wherein was set down everything. Your time is known ; you are his servant, yet he will call you into rest. He doth not let us die, he permits us to live. Blessed are the dead which die in the Lord, for they rest from their labours, and their works do follow them. I heard this in no whisper ; it was not a confidential communication made to me : I heard a great voice behind me, saying, "Blessed are the dead which die in the Lord, . . . that they may rest ;" I knew that word "rest," I had heard it before, it was one of Christ's very earliest, sweetest notes, for he said, "Come unto me, all ye that labour and are heavy laden, and I will give you rest." Dying ones, in his name, accept his hospitality, and go forward into his banqueting-house, quiet, at peace for evermore.

What will the Lord do, now that Moses has gone ? He will be put to sore straits. What will Omnipotence do now that the staff in his hand is broken—can he make another, or find one more ? Does he create a Moses ? No, he elevates a Joshua. He means to elevate you next : be ready ; do not be in the field when he calls for you in the house.

"The Lord spake unto Joshua, the son of Nun, Moses' minister," Moses' servant. Moses was the servant of the Lord, Joshua was the servant of Moses, and thus we belong to one another. He has no higher title to give. Paul and Timotheus, slaves of the Lord Jesus Christ. Paul, the servant of our Lord Jesus Christ. Joshua then had served well, and he was called to promotion. "Thou hast been faithful over few things, I will make thee ruler over many things," is God's rule. Thou hast been faithful at Jerusalem, thou shalt see Rome also. No metropolis shall shut its gates in thy face : if thou hast been faithful in the little villages and provincial towns and minor capitals, thou shalt surely see the greatest cities and the loftiest places. The first Napoleon was wont to say no man could rule well who could not serve well. If you are unable to serve, you

are unable to rule. We know nothing about service in some of
its severer senses in our common civil life. Some of you have
been under masters and tutors and governors: you know what
discipline is—you have overgotten the infantile period of controversy and questioning and reasoning: you have learned not
to reason why, but to do, and, if need be, die. You are going
to make an excellent person, I believe, in the course of about
seven years. I tell you you will not. Shall I explain my
reason for that discouraging prediction? It is that you were
never an obedient child. You cannot, therefore, unless God
repeat his miracle of making you over again, be a good husband,
or wife, or head of a business. There is a philosophy in these
things that you cannot wriggle out of. To be unused to service,
unaccustomed to obedience, is to be utterly unprepared for the
responsibilities of the house, or of the place of commerce, the
legislature, or the church.

Not a word is said in praise of Joshua. How then do we
know that he was so excellent a man? Because of his promotion
to succeed Moses. God studieth, to use a human phrase for
the sake of our littleness, the proportion, measurement, relation,
of one thing to another. He who put the stars in their places
knows whom to call to high succession. To have called Joshua
to this place is to have endorsed and accredited him as no
merely formal testimonial could have done. My friend, young
and wondering, anxious, impetuous—wait: there cannot be two
men of the name of Moses, and of the weight and influence of
Moses, at the same time. Give the first man his full opportunity
—thy day will come by-and-by; be ready for it, enlarged with
all the nobleness of divine inspiration and qualified by all the
patience that comes of obedience to the discipline of Almighty
love and wisdom.

"The Lord spake unto Joshua, the son of Nun, saying, Moses
my servant is dead. Now therefore . . ." Why say, in so
many words, that look cold in this dry ink, that Moses is dead?
It needed to be said. Sometimes we need to have told us the
very plainest things in life in simple strong prose. In the case of
Moses, a declaration of this kind was particularly needful. Who
knows what wonderings and speculations, what rash conjectures,
foolish imaginings and vain hopings and dreamings, might have

come out of the disappearance of Moses, but for this plain and undeniable declaration of his decease? No man saw him die, no man closed those weary eyes with gentle fingers, no tender hand stretched out those poor worn limbs, no gentle woman or loving child planted a flower on that high mountain grave. God who took him comes back from Nebo to say, "He is dead; it is over, he is gone. Now therefore. . . ." At this point one's interest becomes intense. We say, "After Niagara?" Then do we put a huge mark of interrogation, as if we had put to the world a question which has no answer. So when I began by saying, "After the death of Moses, what?" I felt as if any reply given to that inquiry would be unworthy of the occasion, would fall flatly, and would utterly disappoint and discourage us. We have now come to the place wherein the answer is found. "Moses my servant is dead; now there-fore—sit down; bemoan yourselves, take it so deeply to heart as utterly to disqualify your energies for making even the feeblest effort; it is no use your endeavouring to propagate a race of men after the withdrawal by death of that majestic leader who is now but a memory "—does the history read so? God says, "Moses my servant is dead, now therefore, arise "— in every sense of the word, arise—to nobler manhood, to diviner power, to higher conception, to nobler endeavour, to more devoted and solemn and holy attempt to do God's will.

That is what you have to do now that your dear little child is dead. I found you with handkerchief pressed to streaming eyes, sitting down as if your bones had melted like heated wax, and you could do no more, and I came to say to you, "Arise, the Master is come, and calleth for thee." That is what you have to do after your great loss in business. You thought to settle down into nobody. That is not God's law: the disaster has come, now arise. The loss has taken place, the table is clean swept, not a shadow of the golden coin can be found on the tessellated table—now therefore, arise. It is God's Gospel to the dejected, it is God's medicine for those who suppose them-selves to be wounded incurably. Again and again God says, "Look up, arise, go forward." And he always does this in the presence of great loss, whether of life or property. This he always says. When poor Jacob called himself a worm, and took up what he thought his appropriate place in the dust; when Zion stripped herself of her white mantle and sat down under the shady tree, and said, "God hath forgotten to be gracious"— when she held her fair head far down into the dust which she thought too good for one so dispossessed and disennobled, God found her so, and what said he? "Lift up your eyes on high, and behold who hath created these things." The straightening of the neck will do thee good—a walk out into the living air will help to heal thee. Looking down does no man good. Looking up and looking abroad, arising and going forward, elevating and arousing exertions, are God's answers to the dejection, the self-limitation of man.

"Arise and go over this Jordan." How seldom we are allowed to finish our work. It seems as if we could die more happily upon the other side of the river than upon this side. Only let me build my church, finish my house, complete my plan, lay out my grounds, see the youngest trees flourishing into maturity—only let me see my children all attaining the age of manhood and womanhood and settled in life, and then I can, I think, die comfortably. This our weak speech, this our staggering eloquence, this our halting argument, before him who carrieth us in his arms, who sets us down and takes us up as it pleaseth him, and who is unrestrained in the high heavens and in the deep places where the lake of fire is and where all darkness dwells.

"As I was with Moses, so I will be with thee." God quotes himself: whom else can he quote? As—so. History repeats itself, God repeats himself. I know not of any clearer and fuller vindication of himself as to his providential care and dealing than is to be found in this very expression. Observe to whom it was addressed. To a man who had actually seen God's way with Moses. He is not invited to meet a providence unde-clared and mysterious, he is asked to accept a repetition of that which has passed before his own eyes, and impinged most closely upon his own consciousness and experience. Does God say, "I was but a little with Moses, I will be much with thee— I will do much more for Joshua than ever I did for Moses"? Does he tempt him by some unmeasured and enormous bribe? The expression is, "As—so." As was the past, so will be the future. God's repetitions are creations. Miracles of providence never lose their fascination and their value. This is God's voice to us to-day—as he was with the fathers, so will he be with the children. Hear, O Israel, the Lord our God is one Lord. He is the same yesterday, and to-day, and for ever. The heavens become aged, and the stars stagger in their journeys, yea, the Lord doth fold up that great blue firmament like a garment outworn, and put it away, but he is the same, and his years fail not. A thousand years are in his sight as one day, and one day is as a thousand years. He says, "I am the Lord, I change not." So when he comes to speak to us he repeats himself. He quotes no other authority; he signs the same sign manual, stamps the book with the same great seal; his promises are yea and amen, repeating themselves like the seasons, constant, yet ever new; old as eternity, yet fresh as the morning just being born in the flush and hope of a new dawn.

We have then God's Book to guide us and show us precisely what he has for us, and what he can do for our life. Why dost thou dream, O poor mystic, why dost thou wonder what God will do on the morrow? Thou hast all his yesterdays in human history to go back upon, and his expression to thee is, "As—so. As I was with Moses, so will I be with thee: I will not fail thee nor forsake thee." See him giving his omnipotence in pledge to a poor startled secretarial servant of the dead Moses; see him taking up in his great arms the garment of his own almightiness and covering with it the shoulders of this newly-appointed leader. That garment is large enough for us, that almightiness is sufficient to our daily distresses and perpetual wants. What time I am afraid I will trust in God, yea, when the enemy secretly pursueth me I will run into God's almightiness as into a great tower, and there will I sit down till the pursuer weary himself with beating the air. All God's promises are before men: he writes in no new ink: he asks for no new hand that he may dictate a new and ampler revelation. It is "As—so." Moses—Joshua. John—Paul. A repetition without weariness, a reduplication that startles by its originality.

That is all? No. "Be strong and of a good courage. . . . Only be thou strong and very courageous." There is something for man to do. God's almightiness is sent to us as a pledge, not that it may do everything for us, but that it may awaken our

strength and call up every energy we possess, and consecrate it
to the high and solemn service of the great Lord. Awake,
awake, put on thy strength, O Zion, put on thy beautiful
garments, O thou beloved of the Lord. Only be thou strong
and very courageous : do thy little best; if thou canst not fly,
flutter ; if thou canst not run, crawl. He will make it all up to
thee, only do thy little share. It hath pleased God to adopt the
great principle of co-operation in administering the affairs of the
lower courts of his universe. This book of the law shall not
depart out of thy mouth, but thou shalt meditate therein day and
night. Man is not to trust to his own genius, nor is he thrown
back upon his own resources in the high vocations of life. We
are not allowed to live upon the empty pittance and miserable
inheritance of our own wit. There is written for us a Word,
deep, large, loving, clear, accessible, and we must continually
meditate therein. Beautiful words, and full of meaning. Some
of the print in God's book I can see best by day, other of the
book I can read most clearly by night. Can I tell how this
is? It is utterly impossible for me to explain it, but I see
angels at night : they do not come out in the garish white light
of the mid-day, but I have seen troops of them in the dusk—I
have heard many a voice not otherwise articulate in the deep
watches of the night. God does great wonders in the darkness : the darkness and the light are both alike unto him. You
never knew the meaning of " Suffer little children to come unto
me, and forbid them not, for of such is the kingdom of God "
until you read those words in the night of your great loneliness.
Then you saw what priest and presbyter never could explain,
what had eluded the touch of the most diligent annotator : you
saw God's meaning, yea, you saw his great outstretched gentle
arms taking up the very thing he was blessing.

So it is through and through life. Every heart must make its
own application of this great lesson : some part of the book is best
read by day, some is most clearly seen by night. God's book is
a book that cannot be exhausted either in the day or in the
night. It needs the sun and the moon and every star of the
firmament, candles of glory lighted by hands divine to see its
deep, its infinite meaning. Poor, poor fool, thou didst say thou

hadst read the Bible through and through : rather thou didst
mean, if thou wilt let wisdom speak and love interpret, that thou
hast begun to read, and that thou art still stumbling over the first
lines; or if thou art at all restful, it is with a great amaze, a
solemn and glad wonder, because the Paradise grows upon thee,
and thou canst not move yet, because of the ever-deepening
fascination of the immortal beauty.

Now, faint-hearted ones, let us repent and believe. If all the
great men, as we think, are dead, it is that others may take
their places. Whose place are you going to take ? Who will
be baptised for the dead ? This may be an awakening time for
aught I know : it is a solemn hour ; there is a stillness in it
which may prelude a great resurrection of intellectual and
spiritual energy and a great solemn consecration of personal
powers and possessions to the service of the God of Moses.
The great merchant in the city is dead : arise ! The great
political leader is dead : arise ! The great preacher is dead :
arise ! Whose place will you take ? There are a thousand
vacancies to-day in the great gallery historical ; which of the
places will you take ? Are you waiting until God has spoken
to you ? He speaks to you now. What are you ready for ?
Anything ? That is the right spirit. Any time ? That is the
right answer. In whose strength will you come—in Christ's ?
It is sufficient, even to redundance and infinite overflow. Hast
thou set thyself to some part of God's work ?—only be strong
and very courageous : keep close to the book : by day read it,
by night spell it—close, close, close to the book ; and as for
those who would stand before thee, they shall be melted like
wax in the fire ; yea, as fences of stubble before the conflagration of the presence of God in the life.

Oh for a Church alive, with its beautiful garments on its
shoulders, and all its powers throbbing like an eternal pulse !
Then our presence would be felt in the city, in the village,
everywhere, and our presence would not be seen, because of
the lustre of Him whose we are and whom we serve.

PRAYER.

OH, how patient is the Lord ! how tender is his mercy ! how loving is his kindness ! We are amazed with a great amazement, and our hearts are filled with thankfulness. Our steps are guided by the Lord, and our hairs are numbered by him, and there is nothing that concerns us too little for his notice and his care. This is the faith in which we live, and it makes us strong and glad, and gives us brightness of hope and fulness of resort in all the difficulties and perils of life. This faith we have proved. We are ourselves living witnesses of this nearness of the divine hand and this interest of the divine eye. We have been low down, and we have been lifted up ; we have been in great distress and have not known which way to turn, but the Lord hath held a light before, and come close to us and said, This is the way : walk ye in it. We cannot contradict ourselves : we cannot put down the testimony of a lifetime ; the writing is thine, the voice is thine,—the praise be thine, thou glorious Christ ! We look back and see thee now as we did not see thee once. The cloud became a night, and in the night no star trembled : the burden was very heavy, and our eyes poured out rivers of tears, and in all the agony we caught the mocker's tone gibing us about our God and our faith ; but we see all now : it was well, it was best ; the grave was right, the burden was none too heavy, and the way, though often crooked and invisible, was leading on to Canaan, to rest, to mother-land, where there is no night, no death. We delight to look back, for the prophets are there, and the minstrels who cheered us in the night-time. Our life, too, has its Old Testament,—its Pentateuch, its moving histories, its painful tragedies, its psalms so noble, its songs so tender, and its prophecy— the outlook and the forecast of faith ;—behold, we cannot give up these : they are thine, and the book is sealed by thine hand. So, too, has our life its New Testament : its birth in Bethlehem, its wondrous teacher, its worker of great miracles, its marvellous speaker—we wonder at the gracious words which proceed out of his mouth—and its cross, its priest, its redemption ;—wondrous is this life, and it is the writing of God. Help us to read well, to think deeply, to answer thee instantaneously with all the swiftness of eager love ; then when what we call the end comes, it shall be no end but a beginning, bright as morning, warm as summer. Amen.

Joshua i. 10-15.

10. Then Joshua commanded the officers of the people, saying,

11. Pass through the host, and command the people, saying, Prepare you victuals ; for within three days ye shall pass over this Jordan, to go in to possess the land, which the Lord your God giveth you to possess it.

12. And to the Reubenites, and to the Gadites, and to half the tribe of Manasseh, spake Joshua, saying,

13. Remember the word which Moses the servant of the Lord commanded you, saying, The Lord your God hath given you rest, and hath given you this land.

14. Your wives, your little ones, and your cattle, shall remain in the land which Moses gave you on this side Jordan; but ye shall pass before your brethren armed, all the mighty men of valour and help them;

15. Until the Lord have given your brethren rest, as he hath given you, and they also have possessed the land which the Lord your God giveth them: then ye shall return unto the land of your possession, and enjoy it, which Moses the Lord's servant gave you on this side Jordan toward the sunrising.

ASPECTS OF HUMAN CHARACTER.

THESE opening paragraphs present Joshua in several interesting aspects, which we may profitably consider and personally apply: for there is nothing old in them, in the sense of outwornness; what is old in them is old in the sense of venerableness, ascertained reality, enduring energy and virtue. In that sense we must never give up what is old. Whatever is effete, exhausted, evidently done, you may shake off into forgetfulness, because however good it once was, it has served its time, and the age longs for some new inspiration, and clearer, broader, direction and guidance.

First of all, Joshua comes before us as a man with great official antecedents. He does not succeed a little man: he begins what, from the human point of view, is a rivalry that will strain his energy and test his quality. Men cannot go from a leader like Moses and follow some inferior personage, as if he filled up all the space and represented what was necessary to satisfy the heart's hunger. This web cannot be continued, as to the weaving of it, by an apprenticed and unskilled hand. Our call is precisely the same.

Every age succeeds an age marked by greatness peculiarly its own. We are born now into a grand civilisation; it admits of no indolence, or reluctance as to work, and it cannot be satisfied by what is petty, perfunctory, and inexpensive as to the strength which is laid out upon it. History brings its responsibilities. To be born immediately after such and such leaders have played their part in the world's theatre is itself to have a cross of no mean weight laid upon the shoulder. We may close our eyes and think nothing about these things, but we do not thereby make them the less realities, nor do we thereby destroy the standard of judgment which they force upon us and by which our life will be tested. To close the eyes is to play a foolish part. Every man should say, Whom do I succeed? Whose are these footprints near the place whereon I stand? Has a giant been here —a great leader, a noble sufferer, a patient student, a father great in love, a mother greater still?—then my responsibility begins with their greatness and goodness; what I have to do —the soliloquist should say—is to go on: where they have been great, I must try to be greater still,—or if not along their line, along some line of my own,—so that the ages may not stagger backwards but with steadiness and majesty of strength advance from one degree to another as the light increases to the perfect day. Thus we honour our ancestors; thus we bury Moses—not in the grave of forgetfulness, but by turning his strength, wisdom, patience, foresight, and energy into elements which contribute to the sustenance and ennobling of our manhood. Now it has come to pass that every man is in a great historical succession. That succession may not localise itself in his particular family, but we do not live within the four corners of a measurable house: we are citizens of the world; whatever was done in the past was done for our sakes, upon whom the end of time has come—for every age has an end of time to itself: every age must look for the Lord and say—He will be here present at midnight—at the crowing of the cock, ere the dawn has time to whiten the east and purple the mist-shrouded hills. Be ready! watch! Let those who have wives be as if they had none; let those who have fields ready for reaping be as if they had none; his chariot-wheels are sounding: he will be here to-day—to-morrow: in that expectation we should live! It is in vain to say it is not realised in what we call localisation, or narrow fact: he comes when he moves our heart to an expectation of his coming; he descends upon us when he so ennobles our prayer as to make us feel more in heaven than on earth. So we have a great past; and that great past creates a solemn present, and forecasts a brilliant future, and clothes all life with responsibility and honour.   So far, there is nothing old in the story of the soldier-prophet : he followed a great man; we follow men also great.

In the next place, we find Joshua as a man with a definite purpose,—a purpose which Moses could not have carried out. One man completes the work of another.   Moses was a legislator : Joshua was a soldier,—in every line of his story the soldier is evident.   How he listens ; how acute his attention ; look at him—he is all ear !   Nothing can miss the observation of a man who looks like that when a voice from heaven speaks to him. He asks no questions, raises no difficulties ; he receives hi marching-orders, and rises.   The soldier is born in the man— not the petty fighter, not the pugnacious aggressor and self-promoter, but the valiant man, the heroic man, the man who sees only the purpose and hears only the command, who has no ear for objection, but a great capacity for inspiration.   This is the secret of strength.   Joshua did not attempt a hundred things : he concentrated his strength, for he had for the time being only one thing to do.   What is there old in this state of affairs ? Nothing that need awaken our contempt, or content us in our disregard.   Why do not men succeed to-day ?   Often because they have no purpose, and not seldom because they have more purposes than one.   To have a hundred purposes may be to have no purpose at all.   Some men run away in multiplicity of vocation : they diffuse themselves, and by unwise attenuation their strength is gone, and when they strike they miss the object of their blow or smite it with a feeble hand.   Every man should ask himself, what is my purpose in life ?   What have I to do ? Am I prophet or soldier or minstrel ?   Am I commander or servant ?   Is it mine to create new heavens and a new earth, or mine to be diligent in heaven's light and make some corner of the earth greener and happier than it was before ?   That question may be put by every one, by the simplest and obscurest.   Blessed is that servant who is found waiting, watching, doing the work of the moment, and satisfied with it because it is preparing him for some larger duty yet to be disclosed.   How criminal it is to fritter away strength ; how often we hear the moan of old age to the effect : Had I but pursued one definite line for the last twenty years, had I but been constant to the thing I could do, without making experiments in things I could not do, how different would have been my lot to-day; but I was here and there and yonder; I ran with the crowd, I scattered my power, and to-day I have nothing to show ; I have been a truant,—a runner after bubbles that gleamed in the air and which, had I caught them, would have fallen to nothingness in my grasp. Why not learn from that moan? Why not vow to be some one thing, to pursue that one thing steadily? And why not vow especially to keep within the line of your obvious talent?—along that line you will find honour and restfulness and gladness of heart: it is enough for you. Few are the men that can take up more lines than one. He who is faithful in the least shall be promoted to rulership, and shall be surprised that steady regard for one object in life has secretly and unconsciously prepared the industrious servant for the rulership of five cities, or ten. Power grows, capacity enlarges ; thou knowest not how.

In the third place, Joshua comes before us as a man with a divine qualification. God " spake " to him. God promises not to " fail " him :—" As I was with Moses, so I will be with thee: I will not fail thee nor forsake thee" (v. 5). What did God want in return? Cheerfulness :—" Be strong and of a good courage. . . . Only be thou strong and very courageous . . . turn not . . . to the right hand or to the left,"—be strong and of a good heart. So Joshua did not go to war at his own charges. Is there anything old and outworn in that happy reflection? Inspiration cannot cease until the Holy Ghost expires. It is the very function of the Holy Ghost to inspire ; without that function he has, so to say, no mission amongst men ; the very fact of his being the Spirit of God invests him with the continual prerogative to inspire and qualify his Church. We may all be divinely qualified ; and unless we are so qualified our work ends in a cloud blown away by the veering wind. " If any of you lack wisdom, let him ask of God, that giveth to all men liberally, and upbraideth not." " If ye being evil "—broken-minded, dim of eye, and feeble altogether— " know how to give good gifts unto your children, how much more "—what a challenge to the contemplation and measurement of magnitude !—" how much more shall your Father which is in heaven give the Holy Spirit unto them that ask him." " Ye have not because ye ask not, or because ye ask amiss." There is nothing that a man can do of his own strength. Inspiration must not be confined to what is too narrowly called the Church. No man can go forth to his labour to do it with real skill and with pureness of motive without being divinely qualified. He who handles the graving-tool handles it with fingers God made, and uses metal which God created in the earth. We must not have a Church God, a Sabbath deity, an altar available only one day in the week : we must live and move and have our being in God. The Lord inspires the letter-writer, the reader, the father, the merchant, the poorest labourer in the poorest sphere. Are the insects not regarded ? Does a worm move in the mould apart from the eternal throne ? "The earth is the Lord's, and the fulness thereof ;" and if any man has arisen to mark off the world into " sacred " and "secular," " religious " and " profane," he has not studied geography in God's sanctuary. Let us, then, seek divine qualification that we may do our poorest work well and treat our one talent as if it were a thousand, for if the talents be few in number they determine the consequent responsibility, —only " be strong and of a good courage ;" " only be thou strong "—we read again—" and very courageous,"—rise to the work, take pleasure in it ; if you do the work as an addition to something else of a different quality, what wonder if it be a joyless task and if the reluctant heart has only one prayer— prayer for eventide and release from toil ? The Church is lacking in courage : she allows every one who pleases to arise and insult her ; she soon loses heart ; she says—The enemy is too strong for me : I will keep within doors. So saying, what has she lost ? A comprehensive and just sense of her mission ; —she has lost God !

What does all this issue in but in divinely-promised and divinely-guaranteed success. " Thou shalt make thy way pros- perous. . . . Thou shalt have good success. . . . Be not afraid, neither be thou dismayed." . . . "Only be thou strong and very courageous." Let the youngest student hear this word and obey it. Take heart again. If you are weary for the moment, rest awhile. Do not abandon the study: to-morrow you will come to it with a conqueror's heart; the pages will almost turn over of themselves, and he who wrote the difficult lines will annotate them and turn them into gracious simplicity,—"only be thou strong and very courageous." The meaning is that you may rest, sit down awhile, recover strength: but whilst expending your energy you need not surrender your courage. Hope wins; gladness conquers; confidence in God beats down the mountains and lifts up the places that are below the valley. These are the guarantees of success. The issue will be good. Virtue, it is proverbially known, is its own reward. There is a mystery about this which the heart knows full well. Being busy in the right way, how the time flies! There is no time to the truly-inspired worker; he has but one complaint which he translates in some such words as—How short the day is! It is no sooner dawn than it is evening! How have the hours flown away! What is the voice of the sluggard in regard to this same matter of time? —a voice of complaint: the hours are leaden-footed: they will not move, they are a burden; and the heart dies for want of what is called excitement. True work brings its own heaven with it. The true toiler lifts up his head from his task, saying—I began it in God's strength, I have carried it on in divine energy, and I am only sorry that I cannot do more of it and do it better,—God permit that to-morrow may be as this day and more abundant. Christian workers all bear this testimony; there is no break or flaw in the massive and noble witness. All history testifies that to serve God is already to enter into rest.

Whilst Joshua comes before us so, there is an aspect or two in which the divine Being presents himself worthy of our notice. He comes before us in this record as removing men. He said unto Moses—Your work is done. It is for him to say when the tale has been completed. Is there not an appointed time to man upon earth? Is there not a dial by which the shadow makes known to men when the evening approacheth? We are all immortal until our work is done. Do not fret yourselves about the latter end,—let it come in God's time. To die now in the fulness of your strength and hope would be indeed a species of murder, but you will be led gently down the easy slope, step by step, little by little, until you say, " Lord, now lettest thou thy servant depart in peace ; I have a desire to depart and to be with Christ ; I want to sleep,—I long to see the upper world." Do not be in bondage all your lifetime through fear of death. When death does come to the true Christian worker and waiter, it will come as a veiled angel ; and when you are shut up together in the chamber you will have sweet converse and call the interview the beginning of heaven.

God comes before us as explaining his own method towards man. Canaan was promised as a gift,—and now it must be fought for ! Long ago we heard that this land was to be presented,—and now as the history evolves we find that it is to be conquered ! This is the divine method in all things. " I will give thee," is the one word ; " rise and do battle," is the completing word. We value what we labour for; we treat with contemptuous disregard that which costs us nothing. We enter into rest by the gate of labour. We enjoy Canaan because we have toiled after a divine manner for it. So with heaven : it will come as a kind of reward for industry and labour, faith and love, prayer and patience. " Well done, thou good and faithful servant : thou hast been faithful over a few things, I will make thee ruler over many things." It will seem as if the Lord had permitted us to fight our way to heaven and to have won it by dint of valour. Nor do we claim any merit herein, or look upon heaven as a prize for superior strength. It pleases the Lord to accommodate himself to our modes of expression : so we shall have as a reward what we could not have obtained as the result of labour : our faith will be credited with the miracles which were wrought solely by divine grace ; rulership will be given as a prize when it never could have been won as a reward. We need have no fear of corrupting the mind upon these questions, and so bedimming our vision as to lose full, clear sight of the divine glory. What we have to remember is this : God is king ; God is the source of inspiration ; God calls whom he will to such and such offices : the distribution of honour and place is with God, but he called all Israel to the land, to its possession and enjoyment ; they were not all equal to Moses, they were not all equal to Joshua, they were not all commanders and mighty men, but the wise wife and the little ones and the whole host were all regarded by the divine love. So it is in the greater scheme of things divine which we call Providence, or by the nobler name of Redemption. We are not all called to bear the mantle of Elijah, or to play upon the harp of David, or to sing in the lofty strains of Isaiah, or to see the mystic symbolism of Ezekiel ; we cannot argue like Paul, or love like John, or pray like Peter. Some are called to high places and to great honour, and are clothed with responsibility as with a garment, but, blessed be God, whilst there can be but few leaders, few commanders, few prophets and poets and legislators, the great call of God is to every man under heaven :—" He that believeth shall be saved ; " " Come unto me, all ye that labour and are heavy laden, and I will give you rest ; " " Look unto me, and be ye saved, all the ends of the earth." So, whilst we speak of sovereignty and appointment, and distribution of place and honour, we are not speaking of the great matter of human salvation,—for the Gospel is to be sounded unto all nations and kindreds and peoples and tongues. Wherever the Gospel is preached it is to signify love, welcome, offered pardon, offered heaven. For such a Gospel praise be to God the Father, God the Son, and God the Holy Ghost.

SELECTED NOTE.

All the after life of Joshua is the carrying out with a remarkable simplicity of unquestioning faith this first charge of his God. His obedience is immediate. . . . At once he assumes in all its breadth the office so committed to his hands, and as God's vicegerent " commands the officers of the people " (i. 10).

The first command was one which showed his great faith, and tested strongly the obedience of the people. The river Jordan lay between the camp and the land of their promised inheritance, and it must be passed over by them at the very outset of their march. But how could this be accomplished ? Even if it were possible, with difficulty and risk, to transport over it a chosen handful of warriors, how could he possibly carry over the mixed multitude—the women and the children, and the flocks and the herds ? Even over the fords of Jordan, under the most favourable circumstances of the river, this would have been almost impossible ; and at this season of the year, when, from the melting of the snow upon the highlands, Jordan was greatly flooded (for Jordan overfloweth all his banks all the time of harvest), it was more than ever impossible (iii. 15). Yet down to these threatening floods, on the hopeless errand of passing over them, all the people are ordered to march. Surely, it must have been a sore strain upon the simple faith of the young commander to issue such an order. But his faith was strong, and he commanded, and was obeyed.—SAMUEL WILBERFORCE, D.D

PRAYER.

Thy word is exceedingly comfortable to our souls, thou Father of spirits, thou God of eternity ! We know thy words are good and full of power : they fill the necessity of our heart to overflow, yea, even to abundance, as of fulness upon fulness, until there is not room enough to receive thy gift. Thou dost speak from the sanctuary of eternity, and thy words come with all the infinite power of thy majesty; yet are they gentle, gracious, like the soft rain upon the tender herb : they come from a great height, but thou dost cause them to fall without burdensomeness, and they refresh and cheer and satisfy us as no other words have done. We bless thee for any measure of constancy in thy kingdom which we have been enabled to realise and to manifest. There have been many who have said, Turn to the right-hand; and others have said, Turn to the left-hand ;—but because thou hast been with us, an abiding inspiration and a daily light, we find ourselves still in the sanctuary, standing upon the rock, clinging to the blessed Cross, looking to the Son of God for redemption and all the mystery of pardon. This is the Lord's doing, and it is marvellous in our eyes. We would have no other delight; all other joys would we know in this lofty passion—to love the Saviour, to know him more intelligently, and to serve him with a profounder obedience. Thou wilt not decline our prayer, or cause a cloud to come between thy throne and this poor earth : when we so cry we know that we have the answer even whilst we are breathing the prayer : for this is the will of God, even our perfectness,—the completeness of our manhood, the subjugation of our will to right and truth and love. So we know that we have thy reply,—may we know it still more confidently, and rejoice in deepening peace, and in ever-increasing strength, and in continual delight which makes the heart young and the hand strong. As for our sin, take it up in thy mighty power and love, and bury it where no man can find it, and thou thyself forget where the burden has been laid. Amen.

Joshua i. 16-18.

16. And they answered Joshua, saying, All that thou commandest us we will do, and whithersoever thou sendest us, we will go.

17. According as we hearkened unto Moses in all things, so will we hearken unto thee : only the Lord thy God be with thee, as he was with Moses.

18. Whosoever he be that doth rebel against thy commandment, and will not hearken unto thy words in all that thou commandest him, he shall be put to death : only be strong and of a good courage.

UNANIMITY.

JOSHUA had commanded the officers of the people to pass through the host, saying, "Prepare you victuals; for within three days ye shall pass over this Jordan, to go in to possess the land, which the Lord your God giveth you to possess it." A charge was delivered to the people, interpreting the divine will, and promising great blessedness, possession, and rest. The people having heard the appeal answered Joshua saying, "All that thou commandest us we will do, and whithersoever thou sendest us, we will go." We see men occasionally at their best, and then the revelation of human nature is not without enchantment and great comfortableness. Men like to speak in crowds, to multiply their voices by a thousand and ten thousand ; and then they imagine that they are revealing the strength and enjoying the confidence of what is termed unanimity. It is a beautiful thing to see forty thousand men all intent upon one purpose, and to hear them uttering one cry, and to know that their utterance is expressive of an obedient spirit. This is the answer which ought to have been given, and which ought now to be given to every divine appeal. We should answer love by love ; we should answer music by music ; when heaven descends to earth with some unusual blessing, earth should become almost heaven in its grateful appreciation and response. We see this sometimes in the sanctuary. A sublime revelation of divine care, providence, grace is made, and hearts are melted into one, and the final hymn becomes a pledge, a solemn vow, a great musical consecration of the heart. It is beautiful now and again to see what ought to be, —occasionally to see the ideal, now and again to hear a common sentiment uttered by an inspired heart ;—surely such are sights and sounds which might do us good evermore ! Herein is part of the benefit of the sanctuary : we become our best selves under its holy inspiration. We did not know altogether what was in us whilst we were outside the sanctuary, walking solitarily, brooding upon our own thoughts, and heaping up reproaches against society ; when we came into the house of God and heard the universal language, something moved in us which claimed kinship with the speech, and we longed to spring with a thousand men to our feet to sing our convictions and to utter our vow in solemn music. You do not see a man at any one moment; you see some aspect of him, but what he is as to his true spiritual bulk, value, scope, force, you do not see at any one observation: but you see most of him when under the sway of inexpressible emotion, when his prayer is interrupted with praise, when his supplication sobs itself into confession and humiliation, and when his hope rises into song and expresses itself in exclamations of loyalty and thankfulness to God. We never could have known human nature in its wholeness but for religious influences and Christian appeals. The divine appeal is a resurrection-trumpet: it awakes the dead within us, it makes the churchyard of the heart throb with new life. You lose inexpressibly by cutting off religious connections, by interrupting channels through which religious communications flow. It seems to be an easy thing to leave the church and to allow great voices and appeals to waste themselves upon the empty wind, but we cannot tell how much we lose by ceasing to mingle in the common emotion and reciprocate the universal sentiment of the church. To leave the altar is to forego the touch which connects us in a mysterious but wonderfully sensible manner with the eternal throne, the infinite power, the ineffable grace. So do not put away the blessing of an ideal answer. The people meant every word of it. They did not know what they said; still, they were excited to a nobler selfhood than perhaps they had ever realised before; and we do say things in prayer and hymn and religious speech the full scope of which we do not apprehend; —do not be literal with us and say that we lied in the hymn, that we committed treason in the prayer, and spoke falsely in the noble excitement; it is not so: another self, larger, better than we have ever known before, rose up within us and sang that grand hymn, uttered that heaven-moving prayer, and ennobled that sublime excitement.

This is an answer which experience has uniformly discredited. We have never lived this reply. The words are still ringing in the air, and the air seems to have a kind of pleasure in

retaining the tones and reproducing them, until they become
not reminders only but reproaches and criticisms and appalling
judgments. We remem! er the altar : we need no mocking
spirit to remind us how far we have wandered from it. We
remember the wedding-day when Christ and we became one,
—and what a feast there was on that radiant morning; what
vows were exchanged ; what love was pledged; how the future
was enriched with all the hospitality of inexhaustible bountifulness so that we would for ever dwell in the banqueting-house
and for ever hear the flapping of the banner bearing the
divinest name ! We know what we said when we were young.
Youth has a speech all its own—a flower language, a garden
rhetoric, a beautiful efflorescence and poesy. Every word was
meant, and by the help of God the soul now says, every
word shall yet be redeemed ! But what wandering we seem to
have had; how wayward we are; how subtle are the influences which bear upon memory, and becloud the imagination,
and pervert the heart, and enfeeble the will ! Did Adam fall ?
—Certainly. There ought to be no more fully-attested truth
in all the range of the theological judgment and imagination
than the fall of every living man. Compare the speech of
promise and its attempted excuses ; compare yesterday and to-
day ; contrast the morning prayer with the evening recollection.
No other man could fall for us. We seem to think there
is a kind of substitutionary action in the Adamic apostasy,—as
if Adam had mysteriously consented to fall on our account,
or to represent us in a great tragedy. The truth is, every
man falls himself, in himself, and for himself; and the
experience of the world is lost upon every one of us : were it
not so, the first two chapters of Ecclesiastes would save the
world from all further practical mistake. But nobody believes
those two chapters ; they read fluently, the style is copious
and urgent, the experience is full of colour, and it beats with a
very strong pulse, and we would not like to give up the
chapters as part of a literary treasure,—but who believes
them ? No living soul ! Every man builds his own Jerusalem,
gets around him his garden of delights, yields to his own
serpent, and is damned on his own account. It is not for
us to become the censors of antiquity, saying that Israel

failed to carry out in literal exactness the pledge which was made almost in song. Let us keep to our own experience; stand upon the facts which make up our own daily life, and through them we shall see how it was that antiquity sinned and that the first man fell. Were we to close here we should close under a great cold cloud; but this is not the stopping-place: there are points beyond.

This was an answer given without full consciousness of the motive which dictated it. We are not rapid, as we certainly are not exact, in the analysis of motive: we take the first explanation which comes to hand, and are content if other people will receive it. A mysterious action is this, which we have come to know by the name of motive,—that is to say, why we do certain things, or say them, fear them, or hope for them. It is not always convenient to descend into the secret place where motive lives and reigns. It is better sometimes not to know the deeper psychological reality. What was the case in this particualr history? A great promise had been made; land was to be given; rest was to be assured: Sabbath was to dawn upon the world, and the desert was to be as a fruitful field; under this promise the command was given, and whilst the command and the promise mingled together in a common music, the people said—We are ready! Nor did they speak untrustfully or insincerely. We do not surely know by what motives we are moved. Motives are not simple, they are complex, mixed up with one another, now coinciding, now separating, again approaching,—and not to be expressed fitly in words. How far did the promise of the land tell upon the obedience of the men who answered Joshua? Who can tell how subtly the word "rest," which occurs so often in this opening chapter, entered into weary lives, distracted hearts, and made men ready to say anything that lay in the direction of its immediate and complete realisation? Who can take himself out of himself? Who can die unto God? This is a miracle which lies beyond us just now; yet it is well to keep our eyes upon a plan—a position that must be attained—if we are to grow up into the measure of the stature of men in Christ Jesus; we are to have no self: when asked where our life is, we are to point to the Cross on which it has been nailed and on which it has expired.

Do we not find the operation of the same motive now in our spiritual experience? What is it that has been promised?—rest, release from the torment of conscience, the destruction of accusing recollection;—another promise has been made under a sweet name which no man has ever been able to define : we are to have heaven. We have placed heaven above the blue sky : we would not have it in the east or in the west, but straight up in the zenith of the visible firmament. We have thought of heaven as a place of pureness, rest, joy, song, recognition of one another, riddance of all evil, escape from death in every form ; and whilst godly men have been making the soul these promises, what if the soul said—We accept the conditions; we will obey; for such a prize we are prepared to serve and suffer until life's last day? Having uttered the pledge, we have another step to go to get back to old lines, and perhaps the interposition of that one step may happily deter us from returning to our old pursuits. A prayer should be a thick wall through which it is difficult to get back to the old non-praying state; a day in church should separate us by a practical eternity from all evil and irreligious propensity and act. Are not many men Christians because they want to go to heaven? It is a poor reason, yet it may be better than none at all. It is full of selfishness : it is a little, narrow, unworthy reason. What we should aim to be enabled to say is this : If this life were all, it is better to live in the spirit of Christ than in any other spirit;—if so be God will it that we are but contributaries to a greater humanity and an enduring civilisation, it is enough that we have ever prayed and ever loved. Who can attain that spiritual sublimity? We cling to the promised Canaan ; we long to escape the threatened perdition. Our reasoning may be in all such respects narrow, superficial, and selfish,—still, it is something to begin with : for the literary truth of Christianity cannot be urged upon us all at once : we have to grow in grace and in the knowledge of our Lord Jesus Christ, so that every day brings not its new Bible but its new interpretation, its larger claim, its ennobled and brightened outlook.

This was an answer given before battle. The idea of the battle was not fully recognised. The Lord said, "I will give you,"—and scarcely, as we have seen, had "I will give you" been uttered than the other words were, "Fight for it!" What land were they to possess?—the land whereon their feet trod. You must go the land to claim it: your footprint must be your title. We are not called to some land that lies in the unmeasured region of the fancy; the land shall be yours whereon soever you set the sole of your foot. Hence we read in the third verse,— "Every place that the sole of your foot shall tread upon, that have I given unto you, as I said unto Moses." That is the true idea of possession. Do not live in the imagination but in the realisation of spiritual truths. What have we fought for. Is there now a man who can stand up and say, "I have fought for my faith, and I hold it with a hand that has bled"? What wonder that we change our faiths easily if we took them into possession easily? We simply heard of them, and we desire to hear no more about them. Who has studied, pondered, prayed, corrected himself, modified his conclusions—readjusted them, and gone on from point to point as from conquest to conquest,—now and again chargeable with inconsistency, but only with the inconsistency of self-correction, profounder criticism, and using a broader light than was available yesterday? We want sturdy soldiers in the Church—men who say,—Though all is given to us, yet it has to be fought for, and our answer before battle shall be quiet, modest, religious. "Let not him that girdeth on his harness boast himself as he that putteth it off." "Let him that thinketh he standeth take heed lest he fall." Do not force us to answer just now. We have heard the sublime appeal; we know it has come down from infinite heights, it has about it the fragrance of other worlds,—thank God for it!—for its broad words, its grand challenges: they move the soul, they shake the spirit out of prison;—but as for the full reply, we ourselves will wait: every day we will add a syllable to the answer, secretly hoping that by the grace and comfort of the Holy Ghost we may be able at the end of the days to present a complete word, steady as a planet, bright as the sun, glorious with the purity of a good conscience; just now our answer must be hesitant, broken, confused, but, believe us, our meaning is right: we will pray ourselves into greater prayers, and transfer ourselves through the medium of action into higher sacrifice and higher expositions of holy mysteries. Do not judge any one by the one day. We are aware that he replied ecstatically—" I will !"—and he meant it in the very secret places of his soul. We know that the day after he faltered and fell, but his faltering and falling did not destroy the purpose of his soul : the seed of God was in him ; and he in whomsoever that seed is found must win Canaan, with all its light and rest, its everlasting morning and its surprising joys. Do not fix your mind upon your failures and slips and apostasies ; they are a thousand in number and they are without defence, but you can say, " Lord, thou knowest all things : thou knowest that I love thee." If you can say so honestly, the battle is won before it has begun ; if you can say so sincerely, you need have no fear of the end ;—only be strong and very courageous, and there shall not a man be able to stand before thee all the days of thy life. What are the appeals addressed us ?—not to take a Jericho measurable, but to advance to positions remote but glorious. " What doth the Lord require of thee, but to do justly, and to love mercy, and to walk humbly with thy God." " Come out from among them, and be ye separate, saith the Lord, . . . and I will receive you." " If any man come to me, and hate not his father and mother . . . he cannot be my disciple." Who is on the Lord's side—side of righteousness, side of truth, side of pureness ? These are the questions and propositions that are thundered upon our ears. Let us reply saying,—God helping us, we will endeavor to be true, constant, loyal.

PRAYER.

How many there are whose life is a battle thou knowest, O Father of all living! They wonder why they should exist; all things are hard to them: the night is dark, every road is difficult of passage, every door is shut, every man is a foe. They wonder and can hardly pray; they are amazed, and struck down with astonishment. Yet sometimes a little shining of light makes them glad; then they foretell the time of peace and rest and joy. Thou hast set in the midst of the week a day on which there shall be proclamation from time to time of thy mercy and sympathy, and on which some hint of life's great meaning shall be given to the sons of men. Thou dost show us that all thy way is full of goodness, though we cannot now realise the significance of every event. When the grave is dug, thy meaning is pitiful and merciful and most compassionate; when thou dost send sorrow upon our life it is to chasten and refine that life and cleanse it of all defilement. Thou dost cause all things to work together for good to them that love thee; and thou dost surprise thy children by newness of revelation. We set to our seal that God is true; we will stand up and say in the hearing of men—God is good, and his mercy endureth for ever; he abideth through all the ages, and his love is an unchanging light. We are enabled to say this notwithstanding the battle, the bereavement, the great loss, the mortal disappointment; when we recover ourselves a little we say, Thou hast done all things well; thy will not mine be done; lead kindly Light. So we feel it worth while to fight all the battle and endure all the sorrow, that at the end we may see light as we never saw it before, and feel the very peacefulness of peace, the very restfulness of rest. We come to thee by a way that is living, the eternal way, the only way. We look unto Jesus, and are saved: we behold the Lamb of God, and in beholding him with the eyes of our faith we see our sins carried away. Was ever love like his? Scarcely for a righteous man will one die: for a good man peradventure some would die; but thou dost magnify thy love towards us in that while we were yet sinners—neither righteous nor good—Christ died for us, —amazing love! Oh the depth of the wisdom and grace! We are amazed; we are made glad; we feel we are forgiven. Amen.

Joshua ii.

1 And Joshua the son of Nun sent out of Shittim two men to spy secretly, saying Go view the land, even Jericho. And they went, and came into an harlot's house, named Rahab, and lodged there.

2. And it was told the king of Jericho, saying, Behold, there came men in hither to night of the children of Israel to search out the country.

3. And the king of Jericho sent unto Rahab, saying, Bring forth the men that are come to thee, which are entered into thine house : for they be come to search out all the country.

4. And the woman took the two men, and hid them, and said thus, There came men unto me, but I wist not whence they were :

5. And it came to pass about the time of shutting of the gate, when it was dark, that the men went out : whither the men went I wot not : pursue after them quickly; for ye shall overtake them.

6. But she had brought them up to the roof of the house, and hid them with the stalks of flax, which she had laid in order upon the roof.

7. And the men pursued after them the way to Jordan unto the fords : and as soon as they which pursued after them were gone out, they shut the gate.

8. And before they were laid down, she came up unto them upon the roof;

9. And she said unto the men, I know that the Lord hath given you the land, and that your terror is fallen upon us, and that all the inhabitants of the land faint because of you.

10. For we have heard how the Lord dried up the water of the Red sea for you, when ye came out of Egypt ; and what ye did unto the two kings of the Amorites, that were on the other side Jordan, Sihon and Og, whom ye utterly destroyed.

11. And as soon as we had heard these things, our hearts did melt, neither did there remain any more courage in any man, because of you : for the Lord your God, he is God in heaven above, and in earth beneath.

12. Now therefore, I pray you, swear unto me by the Lord, since I have shewed you kindness, that ye will also shew kindness unto my father's house, and give me a true token :

13. And that ye will save alive my father, and my mother, and my brethren, and my sisters, and all that they have, and deliver our lives from death.

14. And the men answered her, Our life for yours, if ye utter not this our business. And it shall be, when the Lord hath given us the land, that we will deal kindly and truly with thee.

15. Then she let them down by a cord through the window : for her house was upon the town wall, and she dwelt upon the wall.

16. And she said unto them, Get you to the mountain, lest the pursuers meet you ; and hide yourselves there three days, until the pursuers be returned : and afterward may ye go your way.

17. And the men said unto her, We will be blameless of this thine oath which thou hast made us swear.

18. Behold, when we come into the land, thou shalt bind this line of scarlet thread in the window which thou didst let us down by : and thou shalt bring thy father, and thy mother, and thy brethren, and all thy father's household, home unto thee.

19. And it shall be, that whosoever shall go out of the doors of thy house into the street, his blood shall be upon his head, and we will be guiltless : and whosoever shall be with thee in the house, his blood shall be on our head if any hand be upon him.

20. And if thou utter this our business, then we will be quit of thine oath which thou hast made us to swear.

21. And she said, According unto your words, so be it. And she sent them away, and they departed: and she bound the scarlet line in the window.

22. And they went, and came unto the mountain, and abode there three days, until the pursuers were returned: and the pursuers sought them throughout all the way, but found them not.

23. So the two men returned, and descended from the mountain, and passed over, and came to Joshua the son of Nun, and told him all things that befell them.

24. And they said unto Joshua, Truly the Lord hath delivered into our hands all the land; for even all the inhabitants of the country do faint because of us.

THE SPIRIT AND PURPOSE OF DIVINE PROVIDENCE.

RAHAB was a woman without social repute. She became, however, a considerable figure in history. She was the wife of Salmon, the son of Naason, by whom she became the mother of Boaz, the grandfather of Jesse, the father of David. in proof of this see Matthew i. 6; Ruth iv. 20, 21: and I Chronicles ii. 11, 54, 55. Thus there was Gentile blood in the lineage of the Son of man. These points, apparently incidental and even trivial, are not to be passed by without eager and devout attention. Jesus Christ was not what is commonly known as a Jew only: he was in very deed what he called himself —the Son of man. All the ages seemed to conspire and breathe in him. The city of Jericho was the key of Palestine. It lay about seven miles west of the Jordan and commanded the entrance of the main passes into the land of promise. The city was very old and strongly walled. On the west side it was shut in by craggy and inhospitable mountains; yet even in Jericho there were springs of water, and not far off, toward the river, lay a great grove of palm trees. How to take that city was the military problem of the time. I propose to regard the narrative given in this chapter as illustrating the spirit and purpose of divine Providence. By studying it with this view we may see the continuity of history, which, indeed, is the continuity of human nature, which also in one aspect is the continuity of God. Ancient Jericho is gone,—not a vestige of it remains;

why, then, should we turn our telescope in the direction of extinct planets? Why seek a river which no longer flows? Why drop our bucket into a well dried up? These inquiries show how superficial our thinking may be. There is an eternal spirit in history; we should always be in quest of that spirit: it carries with it the whole meaning of God.

From military wisdom we may learn the moral wisdom of always striking first at the right point. Everything turns upon the first stroke in many a controversy and in many an arduous battle. Why are there so many fruitless efforts in life? Simply because the beginning was wrong. Why do men come home at eventide, saying, the day has been wasted? Because their very first step in the morning was in the wrong direction, or the very first word they spoke was the word they ought not to have uttered. Why do ye spend your strength for nought? Why beat with your poor feeble hands at points which never can be taken, which are not the right points at all to begin at? With all thy getting, get understanding of how to begin life, where to strike first, what to do and when to do it, and exactly how much of it to do within given time. If you strike the wrong place you will waste your strength, and the walls of the city will remain unshaken. A blow delivered at the right place and at the right time will have tenfold effect over blows that are struck in the dark and at random : however energetic they may be, and however well-delivered, they fall upon the wrong place, and the result is nothing. That is what is meant by wasted lives. Men have been industrious, painstaking, even anxious in thoughtfulness, and the night has been encroached upon so that the time of rest might be turned into a time of labour ; yet all has come to nothing : no city has been taken, no position has been established, no progress has been made. Why? Simply because they did not begin at the right point. In every place in which we may be situated there is one opportunity, and unless that be seized all other occasions will be but empty promises, fruitless and mocking chances. God hath set us thus in very critical positions. We are called upon to keenest vigilance : we are to watch night and day. When the chance may come none can tell with certainty. Watch always : it may come now :—" What I say unto you I say unto all," said Christ, "Watch." It is in vain to tell how we toiled and laboured, and begrudged our sleep, and tried again and again, if we are working at the wrong point, walking in the wrong direction, or failing to seize the divinely-created opportunity. If any man lack wisdom herein, let him ask of God. Great courage may be required in extricating yourself from wrong positions. Great nobleness of mind may be required on the part of a man to say—I have begun at the wrong point : I ought not to have begun here at all ; I renounce this effort and begin anew. Blessed be God, every day is a new opportunity to the man whose eyes are in his head, and whose heart has as its determining purpose a desire to obey the will of God.

We cannot deny the marvellous coincidences which occur in life, nor the wonderful opportunities which such coincidences create. As the men went, they "came into an harlot's house, named Rahab, and lodged there." Perhaps the only house they could have got into without exciting suspicion. The woman was in the way : the opportunity was created. We cannot understand how these things should be. We see how history has many a time been in great peril,—yes, the whole substance of what is known as human history has sometimes been within one thread of breaking up altogether. Sometimes that marvellous quantity of life—event, purpose, which we call history, has gone so close to the fire as nearly to be consumed. From great depths God has rescued history ; in infinite perils God has appeared to save the race alive. Into these matters none may enter with words ; they are to be dealt upon by the spiritual imagination, and they admit of being sanctified by the spiritual reason and faith of man. Who can follow the way of the Almighty, or find out to perfection the counsel of Heaven ? Along this same line what victories Christ himself has won ; the noblest things he ever said and did were in connection with the lineage of Rahab ! The story of the woman taken in adultery will stand above all our stories whilst the sun shall last. The answer made to Simon the Pharisee, when in his cruel heart he destroyed the Messiahship of Christ, will convert the world from its despair, when the maxims of moralists and the dreams of reason have been forgotten. "Simon, I have somewhat to say unto thee—" then came the proposition about the two creditors, and then the story of forgiveness, and then the benediction upon the heart-broken, weeping woman. How the pulses of Rahab made his blood tingle! We cannot tell who it is in us that speaks now, or then, at this or that particular moment. No one man is one man only. Every man represents the whole line along which he has come. Who knows the inspiration of the tender speeches of Christ in relation to the very class which we have now particularly in view? Who has sounded all the mystery and subtlety of heredity? Now some honest, sturdy old ancestor speaks in us the firm, stern word—an answer like a bolt of iron, by which the approach of the enemy is driven away; now some poor, timid, halting soul that took part in our lineage speaks in us: our words are pithless, our tones are without soul, our life has in it no spark of fire; now arises some demon within us, opening a throat that can swallow rivers and not be cooled;—who can tell who it is that thus assumes the momentary domination of our life? We must not be superficial in our view of these things. One man is many men. Jesus was the Son of MAN, representing all humanity, knowing all its temptations and burdens and stresses : feeling in himself every fire that ever burned within the human breast, and every sigh of peace that ever lulled the tumult of life into momentary tranquillity. "We have not an high priest which cannot be touched with the feeling of our infirmities ; but was in all points tempted like as we are." What, therefore, is the grand conclusion?—"Let us therefore come boldly unto the throne of grace, that we may obtain mercy, and find grace to help in time of need."

Nor can we deny the beginnings of new life in unexpected places. In conversation the woman appeared to have received very considerable spiritual enlightenment. But there is a woman within the woman—a man within the man. We are not made up altogether of mere circumstances a moment old, coming to-day, going to-morrow,—a shifting, fleeting environment ; we are spiritual beings with a spiritual instinct and a spiritual history and outlook. Rahab was not a "harlot" only : she was really a student of history, and had pondered many serious things in her heart, and had put events together and construed their meaning, and the meaning which revealed itself to her was this :

A new age is coming; the night is far spent; I do not know what it is, but the air is moved by a new trouble; I hear in it footfalls as of advancing men; presently some great event will supervene; what it is I know not,—I will hasten to my house and lie down to sleep. News had come to the city : people were hearing of an advancing host who never struck but to slay, whose progress nothing could stop; expectation had been excited : events might occur at any moment which would give new direction and momentum to human history and social energy. So it is spiritually; so it is to-day, and every day. There are always men who hear the signs of the coming age, who observe tokens and omens, and who, putting things together, say—The summer draweth nigh, the harvest cannot be long in whitening; we hear footfalls, and they are firm yet soft, and we interpret the method of their coming peacefully and hopefully :—he is coming whose right it is to reign : new thought is coming, new speech, new prayer, new life :—even so, Lord Jesus, come quickly ! Human history is not all past and all future : there is a middle quantity—a period of transition, wonder, expectation, uncertainty : we know not what the meaning of signs may be. Persons who are caught in the enthusiasm of that transitional period may be called heretics, unorthodox, unsound, peculiar, or eccentric. They cannot help it : the spirit of the enlarging and descending heavens is upon them; to-morrow they will be like ancient history. So quickly does time come and go that the men who are heretics to-day are called effete and behind the times to-morrow. Here, however, in this particular instance we see the working of this side of Providence. Even in Jericho the name of Israel has been heard;—even within the walled city fear of Israel has been created.

The part which Rahab played in the transaction is not easy of explanation. She was plainly guilty of treachery and falsehood. Two or three things should be clearly remembered about this circumstance. Nowhere is the treachery or falsehood of Rahab commended in all the holy books. It has been sometimes thought that the falsehood of Rahab had been made matter of divine eulogium. Nothing of the kind ! We cannot too persistently urge this truth upon the minds of inquirers. Nowhere, from end to end of the history, is treachery commended or is lying approved. Still, what marvellous faith the woman had ! Her faith is spoken of with almost veneration. There are moments in life when we do not seem to belong to present things or things past: we talk as in a dream; some greater self rises within us, and we speak in the spirit and power of prophecy. We have seen already that the woman was at least *two* women. She was indeed a sinner, but she was endowed with great spiritual enlightenment, and like another historical woman she "pondered" human events and divine providences in her heart. Why not from her some great speech? Does not God proceed constantly by this plan ? It is the *unexpected* voice that charms us; it is from quarters unlooked for that messages arise that cheer the heart;—it is in Bethlehem that Christ is born; it is from Nazareth that some . " good thing " cometh. Life is not a straight line : it is a perplexity and a complexity which does not admit of being disentangled. We cannot tell all we say, all we are ; nor can we give account of ourselves at the bar of man. Great is the mystery of humanity !

An appalling doctrine, however, has been founded upon such circumstances as are represented in the history of Rahab. Of that doctrine we ought to beware. It has been said again and again that there are circumstances under which people may tell lies and yet preserve a good conscience,—nay, but may even be regarded as doing the will of Heaven. I reply : God never said so, Christ never said so, Christ's apostles never said so ; we cannot find our authority in the Bible, and any authority outside of it is not worthy an instant's consideration. It is worth while, however, to dwell upon the matter one moment, because there is a tendency in the human mind to create casuistical difficulty. The mind will ask, What ought to be done under such and such circumstances ? The mind enfeebles itself by creating such foolish and almost impossible and romantic riddles. We ought not to try our ingenuity too far in inventing possibilities under which it may be right to tell lies. Casuistry may be the beginning of falsehood. A man may so engage his mind in the proposition and solution of riddles as to do fatal injury to his conscience. What we have to consider is the reality of life, the circumstances under which we ourselves are placed. There is romance enough in real life without inventing romances of a merely speculative kind. Now the teaching of the Bible is this : that there are no possible circumstances in life in which it is right to do wrong, in which it is right to tell lies, in which it is right to be double-minded and double-tongued. On the other hand, whilst laying down this doctrine with all clearness and definiteness and absolutely without reserve, we cannot overlook the fact that some men are placed in real circumstances of great peril and difficulty. When a man is told that if he will not act so and so, either religiously or politically, his daily bread will be taken from him ; and when he is asked to give a definite answer upon the matter, and when he knows that his answer would dispossess him of house and business and bread, and when he knows that he is not the only sufferer, but that wife and children and infirm and aged dependents are all involved in the issue, that man's position is not an easy one ; nor is it to be treated flippantly : we are rather to gather around him sympathetically, prayerfully, and acknowledge that he is now about to make the decision of a lifetime. Say to him—The crisis is upon you : you are at the stake, the head is down upon the block, the axe is gleaming in the air,—God help you ! The man may say, Had I but myself to consider, I would drive off with defiance and scorn all who assail my integrity, but the innocent will suffer : the little children will be brought under the pinch of hunger, and the old folks who live upon my bounty will have no bed to lay their weariness upon ;—my God ! what shall I do ? Personally I have no patience with the flippant people who fling easy answers to such men—people who have never had to suffer under that tremendous wheel themselves. What, then, is the message from the sanctuary upon such a crisis ? It is still : Fear God, and have no other fear ; if ye suffer for well-doing, great is your reward in heaven ; whether it be right in the sight of God to hearken unto men more than unto God, judge ye ; "herein do I exercise myself, to have always a conscience void of offence toward God, and toward men ;" you threaten me : I cannot reply to you in your own terms ; you have the upper hand of me now, and you intend to use your position

tyrannously, but they that be for me are more than all that
can be against me;—I will not lie: I will, in God's name and
fear and strength, tell the truth! So the sanctuary sends no
mitigated message, sets up no question of casuistry; nor does
it deliver that message alone: it says—Taking all history into
account, and judging the future by the past, they that do so
shall have a crown of glory, which the Lord, the righteous judge,
himself will give. Meanwhile, the case is a difficult one—that
is to say, it is a hard and trying one, but the other side is not
the side I dare adopt. Given that I have personally to choose
to be on the one side or the other—on the side of the tyrant
or on the side of the oppressed—it is better to be on the side
of the suffering than on the side of those who inflict the pain.
The tyrant seems to have it all his own way to-day: he quaffs
his wine, sits down to his banquet, and laughs the loud laugh
of folly, and all things seem to be under the manipulation of his
skilful fingers; but the candle of the hypocrite is blown out,
the day of the wicked is short:—"I have seen the wicked in
great power, and spreading himself like a green bay tree. Yet
he passed away, and, lo, he was not: yea, I sought him, but
he could not be found,"—his roots were torn up and burned with
unquenchable fire. We shall never be truly influential, and
never have real peace of heart, until we put ourselves under the
inspiration of the Spirit of Truth. We must not trifle with words;
we must not stain them with forbidden colours; nor must we
impart into them suggestive tones. Who, then, can live?

SELECTED NOTE.

Some commentators, following Josephus, and the Chaldæan interpreters
have endeavoured to make Rahab only a keeper of a house of entertainment
for travellers; translating thus:—"The house of a woman an innkeeper."
But in the face of the parallel passages (*e.g.* Lev. xxi. 7; Jer. v. 7), this
rendering cannot be maintained: and it is a gloss in striking contrast with
the simple straightforwardness of the writer of this book of Joshua, and
inconsistent with the Apostolic phraseology (Heb. xi. 31; James ii. 25).
Rahab had hitherto been, probably, but a common type of heathen morality,
but she was faithful to the dawning convictions of a nobler creed, and hence
is commended by Christ's Apostles for that which was meritorious in her
conduct.

PRAYER.

ALMIGHTY GOD, thou art always doing wonders. This is the day of thy miracles more abundantly than any other day in all the history of man. Thou hast not ceased to work thy wonders before us : we know them, and cannot mistake them, for they bear thy signature, and are radiant with thy presence. Thou doest mighty wonders in every land every day, according as the people are able to bear thy revelation. Thy wonders are spiritual : thou dost regenerate the heart that was dead ; thou dost give light to them that sit in darkness, and as for those who were afar off, they have been brought nigh by the work of thy Son. We rejoice, therefore, that we live in daily expectation that to-morrow shall be greater than this day, and in the assurance that thou art able to do exceeding abundantly above all that we ask or think. This is our joy, our inspiration, our daily comfort and rest. The Lord's arm is not shortened that it cannot save ; thy hand is still mighty, and it is outstretched in sign of blessing. Lord Jesus, come quickly ! Pardon our impatience. We know it takes away from the faith of our prayer, but thou knowest the yearning of our heart, the desire of our spirit, that the east may dawn with a new light, that the whole sky may be filled with glory, and that the western lands may dwell in the blessing of thy glorious truth. Comfort us whilst we gather around thy word : give it meanings suitable to our immediate necessities ; show us what Jordan we must cross, what cities we must take, and how we must wait for the Lord, and wait patiently for him, and confidently hope for his salvation. Thus do thou give us rest, give us assurance of thy presence, care, power, and beneficence of purpose ; and as we have seen all this realised in thy Son our Saviour, may we have in him the assurance that all lands shall be God's, all time shall be sanctified, and earth itself shall be, as it were, part of heaven. Amen.

Joshua iii.

" And Joshua rose early in the morning ; and they removed from Shittim, and came to Jordan, he and all the children of Israel, and lodged there before they passed over " (v. 1).

THE NEW SYMBOL.

IN this first verse we have a vivid and beautiful illustration of the method of Providence. The people were called upon to undertake a great and historical task. It is comforting to note how gently and graciously they are led to their work. There is no sign of precipitateness; there is no urgency indicative of impatience. A great and historical city is about to be thrown down to the very foundations, and a new page of human history is about to be turned over; yet the Lord leads up the people to a lodging-place. " God's mill grinds slowly." We are impatient because we are little and ignorant. We have not the completeness of character which means calmness of disposition. We must hasten, we must be noisy; we do not understand how it is that the planets burn without fury or rush or sign of tumult: it is their very speed that brings them to rest. God will, therefore, have no demonstration of impatience in the carrying out of his purposes. Sometimes the Church rests, as if afflicted with indifference. We are too much urged in some circumstances; we have mistaken the place and happy effect of tranquillity. It is quite true that some may misunderstand this and sink into indifference, but they turn God's water of life into poison, and probably nothing that wisdom could say would restrain them in their infatuation. We must speak to the wise and the thoughtful and understanding, and reflect that there are times when we do most by doing nothing, and that we advance with the greatest pace when we stand still. Happy indeed, and often timely, is the exhortation which pricks us forward; but we are not saved by works. This human urgency is often a misapplication of divine teaching and purpose.

"And it came to pass after three days, that the officers went through the host " (v. 2).

In this verse we learn that something came to pass after " three days." A wonderful place that period of time occupies in history! There seems to be some spiritual magic in that number. The words ought not to be read hastily, as if they but indicated an accidental period of time. There are no such periods as can be described as merely accidental or fortuitous. The whole feast of time is measured out; every man has his portion in due season; every life is started with a foreknown and fore-regulated dowry of days. There is an appointed time to man upon the earth in the deepest sense of the terms—a little period within which he may labour—the longest life but a flying shuttle. " Whatsoever thy hand findeth to do, do it with thy might." One thing is certain, amid all the dubitation and change of this earthly scene : that life at its best is brief, and that no man can calculate its duration with a view to fixing its termination. " In such an hour as ye think not the Son of man cometh," to call up his servants to account, to hold judgment in his household. The great principle of individualism has not been surrendered by the Bible ; still it is true that every one of us must given an account of himself to God. Whilst, therefore, we are not unwilling to have the individual sometimes merged in the social, whilst it may be pleasant and profitable and useful that the unit should realise its relation to the whole number, it should never be forgotten that individuality is to be the law of responsibility and the law of judgment. We cannot rub ourselves out as individuals, or so merge ourselves into the common life as to cease to have a personal pulse and a personal destiny. The " three days" are passed with some of us : we ought now to be at work ; the rest was only for three days,— the work is of an immeasurable duration. Do not expend the rest thoughtlessly or unworthily, but make it a time of recruital of strength, so that youth may be renewed and every faculty may be reinvigorated.

In the third verse we find a command given :—

" And they commanded the people, saying, When ye see the ark of the Covenant of the Lord your God, and the priests the Levites bearing, it, then ye shall remove from your place, and go after it."

We must live by command. Even gentleness must often take upon itself the imperative tone. Whether the commandments be ten, or one, or ten thousand, there is the great principle that we are moving religiously in obedience to command. If we were moving in obedience to instinct, our movement would be irregular, and without pith or certainty ; but we are soldiers, we are under military discipline, we call our Saviour our captain, and we ask that we may fall into rank and order, and move together on many occasions, to show how individuality may become socialism, and yet how socialism does not impair the integrity and the responsibility of the individual soldier. What is to be seen now according to the command of the officers ? In what direction are the people to look ? We know how they have been looking these many years gone, and now the object of vision is changed in the third verse. It is most important and instructive to note all points of departure ; to see exactly where things become new in their relations, though not in their substance and highest purpose. Up to this time we, as readers of the Holy Book, have been looking for the cloud. When we wished to know whether it was time to move, we looked for the rising of the cloud, and for its hovering ; at night we looked for a pillar of fire that divided the sovereignty of the darkness. Has the cloud gone ? Yes. Is the fire put out ? Not in the sense of extinction, but in the sense of withdrawment. Thus we close the pages of history and thus we open the pages of prophecy. It seems as if, in our poor blind reading, we were always coming to some new place. God has come variously into the human movement, and touched in a thousand different ways the springs of thought and the fountains of life. Now the people are to look for the ark of the covenant. The cloud is taken up, the fire is withdrawn, the great cloud of the wilderness—so much like a spectre or a spirit—is no more to be looked for ; the fire that burned like judgment against Egypt, the eye that smote off the iron wheels from the chariots of the oppressor, the fire that accommodated itself to the frailty of the bush,—these are no longer amongst us in the outworking of human history. What has taken their place ? The Covenant, the written Book. We are coming thus nearer to Incarnation. This is the method of Providence—the Cloud, the Book, the Man, the Holy Ghost ! The very development of Providence is a sublime argument in support of the history which records it. Fix the mind attentively upon this evolution, and see in it shape, meaning, beneficent purpose. First, nature will contribute her symbolism : the cloud, the fire, will be beautiful images of the mysterious, the energetic, the uncontrollable, the eternal ; the Lord will build himself a house of cloud, the Lord will show that the universe is set upon pillars of flame. It is enough : it is adapted to the wilderness ; such beauty will make us forget that we are in a desert ;—let us steadily follow the cloud. But the Lord interferes with a monotony which might become oppressive. He will have a scroll written—a holy book—a statement that can be read, published, translated into every language,—a companion of every fireside, and a chart for every sea. Then will come the Man of whom the writing speaks ; he will say : I am here that the Scriptures may be fulfilled ; this is the meaning of the ark, this the meaning of the law hidden in it, this is the

meaning of the lid which set forth the divine conception of mercy
—"Beginning at Moses and all the prophets, he expounded unto
them in all the Scriptures the things concerning himself." Will
he abide? No:—"It is expedient for you that I go away,"—
but I will send the Paraclete, the Comforter—that living Cloud,
that living Fire; and he shall abide with you for ever; being
immeasurable, he can never become wearisome; being infinite,
there can be in him no monotony; he will settle upon every
man according to that man's psychology, and out of the individuality of man he will write all the meaning of God's love : the
writing shall be manifold in colour and in shape, but the meaning
shall be one. Thus let us always mark points of departure,
critical junctures; and not hasten through history as if it were
an unmapped desert—a sea without a shore.

The religious element was to prevail in that great military
plan. We do not read altogether about soldiership, schemes and
plans and maps, which indicate the warrior's genius. The controversy is religious; at the head of it goes the Covenant. Let
us see to it that we take no part in any history that is not headed
by the Book of God. Nothing is worth fighting for that is not
symbolised by that book, and it will comfort us in days and
nights of stress and hard weather to know that wherever we are,
we have come up to that position on account of the leadership of
the book. This is what we want : more Bible—the Bible in the
people's tongue, the Bible open to every old man and every little
child; we want to speak of Bible things in Bible terms; we
require now to follow the Covenant. If the Book of God is not
at the head of the procession in which we are moving, the
procession is moving into darkness, disaster, and humiliation.

A space was to be between the marching host and the advancing ark. For what purpose? That every man in the
procession might know his relation to the holy ark :—

"Yet there shall be a space between you and it, about two thousand
cubits by measure: come not near unto it, that ye may know the way by
which ye must go" (v. 4).

There was to be order even in this arrangement. God has
always been consulting the necessities of his believers and
followers and children. He has fixed positions of every kind so

ns to suit the army he has been leading. It is not enough that
a few men at the head of the host should see the Covenant;
it was needful that all the host should see the sacred symbol.
So it should ever be. The poorest soul born into the world,
without a single advantage of a social kind, should not be left
without sight of the ark. Every man must look for himself. It
is not enough to be looking where the next man is going to,
and to be following him. Here the great principle of individuality again asserts itself. Every wounded man must give his
own attention to the uplifted serpent,—every man must read the
Bible for himself. And yet here comes the sublime possibility
that every man may be looking in the same direction and the
host, therefore, moving like an undivided and indissoluble phalanx.
If the individual is right, the host will be right. You cannot deal
with the host as a whole number; you must deal with the
individual. When individuals are right nations cannot be wrong.
    The reason given for this arrangement and this observance of
the covenant is—

    "... for ye have not passed this way heretofore" (**v. 4**).

This passage is often misunderstood, and therefore misapplied.
It cannot simply mean, This is an unfamiliar path; or, This is
new ground; or, This is a position which you have never
occupied before; for then the same observation would apply to
the whole course which the Israelites had been pursuing for
many years. This is not a provision against the dangers that
may arise from unfamiliar scenes. We have here indicated a
new point of history. "Ye have not passed this way heretofore"
means: Up to this time you have had cloud by day and fire
by night; now there will be no cloud, there will be no fire; now
you pass as obedient to a written and treasured Word; you have
now become a great Bible school, a great army following a
written inspiration. A great light shines upon the instruction
now. Up to this time we have felt the words which conclude
the fourth verse to be but a commonplace, which might have
been applied to the history of Israel any time during almost
half a century before; but now we see that a new method of
travelling is adopted—a new object of vision is let down from
heaven; and although the method of revelation may change,

nothing ever changes the Bible itself in the substance of its
meaning. A revised version is not a new revelation. A
new Bible is not a new testimony. It is because of the scholar-
ship which has been lavished upon it a more sure word of
prophecy, but the prophecy itself abideth for ever. What can
we understand of this Covenant in the way in which it is too
often read? Some men are calling for the restoration of theological systems, and others are calling for obedience to scientific
discovery and law ; without saying one word of deprecation in
reference to either of the parties, we may again and again put in
a word for Bible reading, Bible study ; for giving the Bible an
opportunity of speaking continuously, and thus argumentatively
and persuasively. He would not be unjust to his age who
charged it as a Bible-neglecting age. The Church itself does not
always read the Bible aright. The Bible is read in texts. He
would not be too bold a man who affirmed that isolated texts had
done more to hinder the progress of truth than any assault that
was ever made upon Christianity from the outside. Men should
humble themselves in crying penitence before God because they
have torn the seamless robe and given it away in rags The
Bible is one ; the Bible is a stupendous whole. Could we hear
its cry it would be, Read me ; read me all ; read me through in
every page, line, word, and syllable. O earth, earth, earth! hear
the word of the Lord! What is at the head of the armies of
the day ? What new programmes! what exciting propositions!
what criminal promises! The Christian should insist that the
Church at least should follow no leadership but the ark of the
eternal testimony. Every college should rise up in the morning
to do one thing—read the Bible. Every congress and conference
should meet to do one thing—read the Bible. Every congregation should come together for one purpose—to read the Bible.
This would absorb all the little rods of necromancers and wonder-
workers, and would end in such practical mediums of expression
as would suit the new life ; and though many mistakes of an
external and temporary kind might be made, the outcome would
be as the flowing of the river of God. How can the Bible be
read alone ? This inquiry points to a sophism which is working great mischief in the Christian Church. A man will say,
in some unworthy mood of sullenness or resentment, that he

will remain at home and read his Bible. He may remain at
home, but he cannot read his Bible in that temper. Compelled
to remain at home by stress of circumstances, by infirmity, by
ill-health in himself or in others, he may read the Bible alone,
and God will treat him as if he were the whole assembly of the
blessed, withholding nothing from his loving attention and gentle
touch. But there is a public reading of the Book—a common
reading. Noble is the term—the Book of Common Prayer.
That phrase is full of sacred import. There is common prayer,
there is common reading, there is a public emphasis, there is a
contagion of sympathy; there is given to the united perusal of
the Bible answers which cannot be given to any solitary recluse
who shuts himself away from the Church as if the Church were
unworthy of his presence. Would we have the world cleansed,
disinfected of all evil literature? Let the Bible be read in-
terestingly, lovingly, with sympathy and with delight. Would
we have great thoughts, noble purposes, sublime expectations
which put out the little trials of the day? We must let the
word of Christ dwell in us richly—an answer to every temptation, a light regularly as the night descends, a spring of water
in a thirsty land. Stand up for the Bible! Do not stand up for
it without first reading it and becoming imbued with its spirit.
Defend the Bible in the spirit of the Bible, which is a spirit of
sovereign power and redeeming love. Punctuate your reading
with your tears, and then when you preach even the terror of the
law, it will be to persuade men—fire used, not to burn but to
enlighten, not to destroy but to cheer. My hope for the future
of history is in the continuous, connected, and massive study of
the Holy Scriptures.

PRAYER.

ALMIGHTY GOD, thou art round about us and within us, and thy nearness is an encouragement and a joy. Surely it is not wholly a judgment, a piercing and destructive criticism, but a help, a comfort, a sustenance infinite. So will we regard it in Jesus Christ thy Son our Saviour. We will not be afraid of thee: God is love; we will draw near unto thee, yea, with boldness we will come to the throne of grace, not that we may plead our righteousness, but that we may obtain thy mercy and grace to help in every time of need. We would live the wise life; we would that ours might be the life that is rooted in God, by consent as well as by necessity. We are in God, all things are embraced by thine infinity—all evil, all hell, all good, all heaven— the Lord reigneth. But we do not want it so wholly; we want to be in God by consent; we would fix our love upon God, and our faith and our hope should trim its daily lamp at the flame of thy glory. Thus would we live and move and have our being in God, returning to him, going out from him to speak his word, and coming again to him to hear his word that we may speak it still more simply and gladly. We have heard thy word, and we know it: it is no stranger's voice that speaks to us therein; we know the music. Imitators there can be none; we know the music of thy grace and the tunefulness of thy comfort. We cannot be deceived; for there is no voice like the eternal. May we hear it, receive it, and answer it with all loving obedience; then shall our joy be full, and our day shall have no night. Thou hast sent us into a mysterious life. Sometimes, by reason of our ignorance, it looks nothing: it is a mere trifle, a spasm, a flutter for one little moment, followed by eternal silence; but this is the fool's reasoning: whilst we look upon our life and muse upon it and study the divine purpose which lies under it, how solemn is life, how grand; how majestic in mystery; how glorious in possibility! Thou dost tear our hearts that our hearts may know themselves. When thou dost tantalise us it is that we may be taught the mystery of prayer; when thou dost disappoint us, it is not to mock us but to show us that things are larger than we thought—more mysterious, more awful. May we no longer live as those who have no centre, no altar, no God; but live the deep life and the true, feeding ourselves upon the bread sent down from heaven, lost in wonder, love, and praise as we gaze upon the truth of God; and thus may our life, being divinely nourished, express itself in human beneficence: may we go about doing good, knocking at doors that are shut upon us, that in opening them we may find an opportunity of preaching Christ and exemplifying the light of heaven. Pity us in our distresses— so acute, so many, so difficult to bear; save us from looking at those who seem to have no distresses, lest our faith be swallowed up in despair: may we not look upon such, may we turn our eyes to the hills whence cometh our help; show us that every heart knoweth its own bitterness, that there may be no mourning or complaining against the supposed partiality of heaven. Thou dost give every day a night, every summer a winter, every life a burden to carry; thou hast thrown a shadow upon the sunniest way. Help us to know that these things are of God, and are under God's control, being meant in love, and at last will be shown to be parts of a divine and beneficent purpose. Look upon us according to our need: it is a great necessity, but thy fulness is more than our hunger, the riches of God are unsearchable, the river of God is full of water. We bless thee for all we have seen of thy hand: we still commit ourselves wholly to its protection and guidance; they win who fight under thy banner, thou Saviour-God; they that be for us are more than all that can be against us, and when thou dost press upon the enemy with the weight of thine eternity, behold he is crushed and cannot rise. Follow us about all the day as if thou hadst no other concern. We are so foolish, so unutterably inexperienced in all the deepest mysteries and ways of life: our record every eventide is full of crossing and blundering; still have patience with us, for by thy grace we will to-morrow do better. Pity the broken heart; give enlargement of thought and brightening of hope to the soul that repents and longs to do thy will more obediently and perfectly; establish, strengthen, settle every good word, thought, and purpose; and as for the counsel of the wicked one, turn it upside down, and by pouring darkness of sudden night upon him may he never be able to find his way again. The Lord pardon our sin. Come over our guilt as over a mountain, and by the touch of the mystery of the Cross may that mountain be dissolved and the union between God and the soul be for ever completed. Send upon us the Holy Spirit, the Paraclete, the Comforter; may he abide with us for ever; teach us with infinite patience, and sustain us with tenderest, sweetest solaces. Amen.

Joshua iii.

"And the Lord said unto Joshua, this day will I begin to magnify thee in the sight of all Israel, that they may know that, as I was with Moses, so I will be with thee" (v. 7).

UP TO THE BRINK.

"THIS DAY." It is pleasant to come upon the definite time. We are to be so blessed "to-morrow," but to-morrow never yet came to any human life: it is always the next day; no man has seen it; its shape no man can tell, its messages no man has heard;—it is the unborn time. In the instance before us we have the day and the blessing assigned to it, so that, as it were, the soul leaps into the immediate heaven, saying, Behold, that heaven is here and now! There are days of enlargement, intellectual and spiritual and moral, in human life,—days that dawn upon the mind like an infinite summer; days in which we see the meaning of words, the relation of scattered things, the unity of what we supposed was but chaos. These are days of liberty; there falls from us, almost consciously and audibly, manacles and fetters that bound us in humiliating slavery, and we spring into great enlargement and are conscious of divine communion. Call these days birthdays! When were you born? is a limited question. Any birthday of the flesh is no birthday; it but gives a man a *chance* to be born. He is not born who is not conscious of the advent within him, bringing with it sense of responsibility and willingness to submit to sacrifice, and the hope that no sacrifice can kill him for more than three days. We may pray for the day of enlargement and ennoblement, but the best way of praying for that day is to work for it. If we work well to-day we may get the enlargement to-morrow. Work *is* prayer: hence the grand Lutheran motto— "to labour is to pray."

"This day will I begin to magnify thee." We can almost see the beginning of the magnifying of some lives. Although things do grow very subtly and all but invisibly, and often altogether invisibly as to process, yet we sometimes feel as if we saw the child become a man. It was in the darkness we saw it—the darkness of a trouble that seemed to come too soon. The boy was playing, laughing loudly, running merrily round the little circles of opening life,—a boy all laughter; and a great distress fell upon him, new responsibilities were instituted, he began to see the situation, and as it came upon him in great volumes of darkness, see how he stood up in a new stature and a new strength, and put out his arm as if he might tackle, with valour and hopefulness, the hardest task of time. There are times when we are magnified by the possession of conscious intellectual strength. At these times we can do anything. We hover above the world, and descend upon it, and rise again, and touch it with more than adequate strength, and retire from it in ease and majesty, and return with redoubled energy. So then, labour is rest, and endurance is the counterpart of heroism. Woe unto that life that is unconscious of being magnified, that does not go in the upward direction. Are there not men who are no larger to-day, in mind, purpose, and outlook, than they were five-and-twenty years ago? They have had no dream, no vision; they have heard nothing unusual; they have not seen heaven opened and the Son of man standing at the right hand of God. How dull that life, if not criminal! how monotonous, if not guilty!—pitiful everywhere—in the common school pitiful—but how infinitely more pitiful in the Christian Church than anywhere else! No burning bush, no startling voice, no conscious call to nobler service, no seizure of inheritances infinite in wealth; still the old life, the old monotony, repeating the old phrases and not knowing their meaning. All true magnifying, however, is from God. A man cannot make himself really great:—this is the Lord's doing, and it is marvellous in our eyes. But this we can do: we can be prepared for larger magnitude of personality and influence; we can be found waiting, watching, looking; we can use the one talent as if it were a thousand, and be as industrious about the little plot of ground as if it were an estate of countless acres. Whom does God magnify? The humble, the contrite, the broken-hearted, the faithful, the industrious. Does he grant the magnifying all at once? Not according to the observation of the text. He begins to magnify; he shows a new aspect of the mind: persons are surprised at a new development of power, a new tone in the voice, a new expression in the attitude; they say, something has occurred here—what is it? and by the end it will be discovered whether the magnifying is an inflation or a divine call and investiture.

Wonderful, too, is the way in which the word of chastening mingles with the word of encouragement:—"As I was with Moses, so I will be with thee"—not more so. Moses is not dishonoured or thrown into any secondary place: he will abide until he comes whose right it is to reign. So Joshua must still peruse the life of Moses, look upon himself as a continuation of a grand beginning. He does not detach himself from his official ancestry and found a house of his own: he is but a golden link in a golden chain; and because we are but links none must magnify himself unduly, or suppose that he will start a new humanity in his vain and frail personality. And again, and still more subtly, does the Lord show that all his manifestations in and through his officers are meant to reveal his own glory. Human greatness is a revelation of God's presence. Moses is not great except as God is with him; Joshua would be a little and unknown name if God did not burn in it and cause it to radiate throughout the whole circumference of immediate history: the Church is not great except for the purpose of showing that the great God is within her walls. We are to look through Moses to Jehovah; through Joshua to the great, all-inspiring, all-construing God; and through the Church, with all its ministries and instrumentalities, its white lights and glorious stars and great inheritances, to the all-giving God. From him is every donation. There is but one donor: we are the instruments in his hands. Do not look at Moses, do not look at Joshua, do not look at the institutions of the Church, except as mediums through which we may see the spiritual glory of the eternal God.

What was Joshua to do? You find the answer in the eighth verse :—

"And thou shalt command the priests that bear the ark of the covenant, saying, When ye are come to the brink of the water of Jordan, ye shall stand still in Jordan."

Go up "to the brink,"—that is the point we shrink from. Many will stay by the meadows, and under the shadowing trees, and in the gardens of flowers, but they will risk nothing. Jordan is pouring down from the north: it is the time of the swelling of the waters,—what are the priests to do?—To go up as if there were no waters, as if the bed of Jordan were dry :—go up to the brink, let your very feet touch the water, and then—stand still! This is difficult, and is not to be lightly esteemed by any who would hurriedly read the lines of providence and come to superficial conclusions regarding the mystery of life. This is divine boldness; this is religious prudence. We are to go up to every Jordan as if it had no existence. Everything will one day be under spiritual direction. All things shall obey the spiritual voice in the day of true glory. The day of miracles has only gone for a moment: it will return when faith returns :—if ye had faith as a grain of mustard seed, ye would say to this mountain, Be ye cast into the depths of the sea,—and it would fly from you like a thing affrighted. This is the great possi-bility, the daily and continual miracle of faith. We are content with small things; we are shut out by a door: we return saying, The door was shut,—as if any door ever made by finite skill and strength could stand against the sovereign will of the man who is one with God. We complain that there is danger coming down upon us—a great, rushing, flying, lightning train,—as if we could not split it in two and bury it by a word if we were in right relations to the Infinite. We are the children of fear; we say, There is a lion in the way,—as if the very glance of faith could not destroy it in every limb. To speak so is to speak to the ear of timidity that which is foolish and even absurd, but the Bible means this or it means nothing. Believe me, all things are or shall be under spiritual control: we shall command the beasts of the field to come to us; we shall call the fish of the sea to the shore or to the boat when we want them: we shall be like the Lord. It is in this direction we must grow; nor can we grow to it in one day, or perhaps in any measurable period of time; it is enough, meanwhile, to have the sublime ideal and the confident hope, and to be moving quietly in that direction. We are not called unto the spirit of bondage and fear, but unto the spirit of liberty and power and a sound mind.

What effect had this interview upon Joshua? Was he so magnified as to forget himself? You have the answer in the ninth verse :—

"And Joshua said unto the children of Israel, Come hither, and hear the words of the Lord your God."

So he is "but minister." He does not attempt any crude originality. He will simply repeat what he has heard, but he will repeat it as a believer. The believer has an emphasis incommunicable to the hypocrite. There is about truth some-thing that endures so well, that stands all friction so strongly, that responds to all necessity so abundantly, that it cannot long be counterfeited: there are masks sold for pence which seem to reproduce it with skill, but the masks become weather-stained, their very skin peels off, and their expression is lost.

Truth stands for ever, night and day, the same when the
morsels of ice strike it in the face, or the sun blesses it
with mid-day glory.　Joshua would but repeat what he had
heard.　So must every preacher simply read the Bible.　If he
does not quote texts he must speak biblically—that is, in the
spirit of the Bible; and he must never wander one inch from
the Book : it is his shield and buckler; it is a strong tower to
which he may continually resort; it is his authority and
warrant.

Joshua thus pledges God to what he is about to say.　We
must not hesitate to risk the divine name.　Joshua said :—

"Hereby ye shall know that the living God is among you, and that he
will without fail drive out from before you the Canaanites, and the
Hittites, and the Hivites, and the Perizzites, and Girgashites, and the
Amorites, and the Jebusites" (v. 10).

Joshua would make the march a religious one.　The Christian
Church ought to make every department of life a department
of itself.

"Let us have no suggestion of possible divine help under
such and such circumstances,"—that is the language of timidity,
and timidity is sin in all such relations as are indicated by
this history.　We do not simply hope that God will be with
us, or trust that God may in due time appear for us, or express
the dubious desire that all things may turn out better than
we might have ventured to expect.　That is not religious talk,
or if it is talk it is without soul, without emphasis.　Risk the
divine name,—that is to say, pledge it.　This was the strength
of the old prophets.　If such and such things do not befall
thee, then God hath not spoken by my mouth; "thus saith
the Lord."　The prophets thus put God in the foreground, and
made him true or false ; they pledged his name : with reverent
familiarity they put his signature upon every great promise
and every grand prediction; they exposed God to criticism, so
much so that the mocker availed himself of the opportunity
and said, Ha, ha, where is now thy God? he called God his
father, let him save him, if he will have him;—and the fool
wagged his head, and the sneerer laughed over his own gibe.
We have omitted the divine name from our speech; we have
risked nothing; we have but contributed one more to the

endless number of suggestions made for the benefit and progress of the world. Let the good man not hesitate to say to the good-doer—God shall be with thee, and deliver thee in six troubles and in seven; and when the day is as the night and the night is sevenfold in blackness, his hand shall find thee and his counsel shall be thy strength. These are the great speeches,—not words that mothers might speak to children or fathers might whisper to sons, but the great speeches that pledge eternity, which, if not carried out, would sweep all the stars from heaven and make the universe an empty temple. To what are we now pledging God the Father, God the Son, and God the Holy Ghost? it is possible whilst professing a religious faith to ignore it in its practical applications.

A very beautiful expression occurs in the twelfth verse :—

"Now therefore take you twelve men out of the tribes of Israel, out of every tribe a man."

It was typical that the whole people were interested in this movement. What was typical then ought to be typical now. We want "out of every tribe a man." Into how many tribes are we divided? We want the rich man's representative; we do not want his gold only, but himself—his life, as pledged in some representative name. The poor man's delegate, where is he? Let him stand up in his poor clothing, in his weather-worn and travelled-stained weakness, and say with bold timidity—Behold, I am here and ready to serve. And the young men's tribe, where is the David sent by that multitudinous host as pledge and hostage? Let him stand up,—sunny-faced, bright-eyed, full of strength and hope, and it may be with a dash of imprudence in his chivalrous nature; and let him say—Behold, I am here in the city of God, and if there be stones to carry, or foes to fight, make what use you can of me. "Of every tribe a man,"—not that the whole tribe is to be satisfied with the one man, but the one man is to represent the unity and consecration of the tribe. Who then will be baptised for the dead? Who will come and take the place occupied by the rich deceased leader? Who will come forward and say—Poverty is not ashamed of God or Christ or the Bible, and it will do what its two little weak hands can do, and do it with hearty good-will,

and the Cross itself shall not deter it in its passion and
enthusiasm ? " Of every tribe a man." That must be the
motto of the Church ; that must be the motto of the family,—not
any wicked theory of substitution or proxy, but the sublime
theory of representative and symbolic service.

What was to come to pass when the whole instruction had
been obeyed ?

> "And it shall come to pass, as soon as the soles of the feet of the priests
> that bear the ark of the Lord, the Lord of all the earth, shall rest in the
> waters of Jordan, that the waters of Jordan shall be cut off from the waters
> that come down from above; and they shall stand upon an heap" (v. 13).

Mark the period : " As soon as the soles of the feet of the priests
. . . shall rest in the waters of Jordan." The priests should go
forward. We cannot have the priests—men of bright mind,
daring courage, simple faith—lagging behind, or their practice will
contradict their preaching. The preachers must be at the front,
wherever there is danger challenging courage, wherever there is
risk defying confidence. The preachers should be the great
believers : they should be all faith. Whoever else is wanting,
the Bible-teacher should be present ; wherever there is peril,
difficulty, hardship, the preacher should subscribe more than
any other man in the whole Church. It is an infinite
blasphemy for the preacher to write his name second on the list
of endurance or in the records of hardship and sacrifice. There
is no irony bitterer or guiltier than that the priests should send
the people first to test the promises of God. He is not a priest
who is anywhere behind. Listen not to his plea: he is a
hireling and careth not for the sheep. When Christians of the
highest type advance the rest will follow. What I have thus
said must, of course, be regarded as a matter of proportion. The
widow gave more than all the rich men, though she gave nothing
in comparison. Let no man attempt to escape on arithmetical
grounds, setting so much on the one side and so much on the other.
There is no such law. How hateful is the cant which says : I
am waiting to see what other people will do. What right have
you to wait ? How long are you going to wait ? On what
authority are you about to wait ? To wait !—why that is to
usurp the prerogative of God ! as if you had one moment of

time in which you could wait or could use! and by what right
does any man, in the pulpit or out of it, stand up to say that he
is waiting to see what other people will do?   He is not bound
by what they do; he is not the custodian of their consciences;
he has nothing whatever to do in relation to them: he must obey
the voice of God in the voice of conscience.   When those—let it
be repeated—who are Christians of the highest type are found
at the front, others will follow.   There is a contagion about
example, there is a subtle influence about high courage.   Without saying a word to the coward, you may shame him into
action by the magnanimity of your own bravery.   So then, this
is the order of the divine movement: God calling the leading
man; the leading man expressing the divine will to others; every
tribe contributing its man, so that in symbol the whole tribe is
pledged to the holy march.   Are the priests going at the head,
the preachers answering their own prayers, responding to their
own challenges, living the results of their own appeals?   And
if any lag behind, who dare pray that God may have any pity
upon them?   There is a lagging behind which cannot be helped,
but let us be careful how we claim its exemption from criticism:
that must be left to the judgment of God.   Some are "faint,
yet pursuing;" some would go fast, but they cannot; in some
instances "the spirit indeed is willing, but the flesh is weak;"
where such is found to be the case, then God's pity is hardly
large enough for such frailty: God will "have compassion,
making a difference."   But how can he waste compassion upon
any truly Christian man who for a moment wavers when he
ought to be at the head of the great procession, with nothing
in front of him but Jordan, and Jordan not in the subsidence
of its flow, but in the very anger and pride and scorn of its
strength?

PRAYER.

ALMIGHTY God, we will think now of thy redemption wrought out for us in Christ Jesus thy Son, and for the moment we will not be cast down but lifted up as upon a great wave of gladness. We have been told that we are polluted and unholy, until the story has thrown us into despair : we know it to be true ; but now we would turn our eyes unto the Cross set up for sinners, the mystery of eternity, the enigma of time : the angels cannot understand it, we are unable to comprehend all the wonders of its love and pity, but our hearts are glad whilst they gaze upon it : they see beyond the pain and the sorrow and the darkness, they behold great lights, opening heavens, expanding and assured liberties, and they are glad with a great joy. Sorrow endureth for a night ; joy cometh in the morning. The night cannot be so long as the day. The night of sin is not thine ; the bow of peace is thine, and high noon, all the firmament glowing with light-seeds, and is some faint type of thine infinite glory. The night shall be lost ; it shall never come again ; that cloud shall be broken up and dissolved and for ever forgotten. But the light of thy countenance shall be heaven, the glory of thy presence shall make the whole home of the saints. We will therefore be glad and rejoice, and find in thine house a place of banqueting and feasting, so that the soul may be made fat with the promises of God and our life be made strong by divine encouragement. We have come from many places into one house : is not this a hint of what shall be in the great future of promise and prediction ? Shall we not come from the east and from the west, from the north and from the south, and sit down in our father's house ? Shall not all alienations be forgotten, and all differences be absorbed, and all hearts be united in one commmon and everlasting loyalty ? This is our prospect in Christ Jesus ; to this end he came and taught and suffered and died and rose again ; nor can he rest whilst one shadow of sin rests on the fair universe : behold, he is pledged to receive unto himself the very ends of the earth : all the heathen shall be his, all kings shall bow down before him, and gold and incense bring. May we enter into the spirit of this joy ; may we feel that the slavery of the past is forgiven, forgotten, and that a great future of light and growth and liberty challenges and encourages the soul. Wherever a burden is too heavy for the strength, Lord, increase the power of endurance ; wherever the tears cannot be explained, do thou speak a message to the heart in secret ; wherever the perplexity is thick and defiant, persisting in its stubbornness notwithstanding all that human skill can do, come from thy sanctuary and help the perplexed ; wherever sin is a spectre in the air, a touch in the darkness, a flash of fire in the conscience, show thy Cross, thou Saviour of the world, and save the creation of God. Thus come to us every one now and at all times, and thy coming shall be like the dawning of the day, and like the opening of a great door which leads us into home and peace and plentifulness. Amen.

Joshua iv.

1. And it came to pass, when all the people were clean passed over Jordan, that the Lord spake unto Joshua, saying,

2. Take you twelve men out of the people, out of every tribe a man.

3. And command ye them, saying, Take you hence out of the midst of Jordan, out of the place where the priests' feet stood firm, twelve stones, and ye shall carry them over with you, and leave them in the lodging place, where ye shall lodge this night.

MEMORIAL STONES.

THUS a memorial was to be set up, commemorating the power and goodness of God. The way of life should be full of such cairns. But is it not early in the history to be setting up stones of memory? The battle has not begun. Israel did not march forth to cross a river but to overthrow a city wellwalled and hoary with antiquity. Is it not, then, rather early in the day to be building altars and to be setting up signs of triumph? It is in putting such questions as these that we show the littleness of our faith. In all great spiritual controversy the beginning is the end. The whole history is in one sentence. The entire history of the human race is in the first few chapters of Genesis; all the rest has been translation, variation, rearrangement of particles and individualities and colours; but the soul of the history is all there. With God the end and the beginning are one. To have crossed Jordan is to have torn down all the Jerichos that opposed us. One step is the pledge of another. The first miracle is the pledge of the last. He who turns water into wine at the beginning will raise himself from the dead at the end. The miracles are one. One miracle carries with it all the host of wonders. So it is in all the departments of properly-regulated and disciplined life. It is so in any properly-graduated system of education. He who has conquered one book has conquered all books. The reason why men do not conquer the third book is that they have not conquered the first. No student can set himself heart and soul to the mastery of the First Book of Euclid without therein and thereby mastering the next and the next, until the very end. There must be no paltering, no half

and half work, no touching the labour with reluctant and dainty
fingers, but a real tussle, a tremendous wrestling, at the first.
Jordan passed, Jericho shall totter and fall. Why is the Church
so hesitant and uncertain in its movement? Perhaps because it
does nothing firmly and completely; it may not have mastered
its first principles; it may have considered itself altogether too
advanced in life to trouble itself with elementary theologies and
considerations, but so considering it will never take any Jericho.
The place of evil will have faces at every window smiling upon
its furious feebleness. The devil will open his idol-temples
shoulder by shoulder with any cathedral or minster we can
build; he says—These people did not perform the first miracle:
they never got through Jordan; they are still splashing in the
waters that lave the brink of the channel; they are not complete
students, they are not well-equipped thinkers; they have nothing
in their hearts they are quite sure about; they are changing all
the time,—now it is a great argument which none can comprehend,
now it is a radiant cloud on which no man can satisfy his hunger,
now it is an elaborate and pompous programme without a
beginning and without an end and without any reason for its
existence at all;—these people will never fight me; if they could
but get hold of one thing and be perfectly certain of that my days
would be numbered, but they have nothing in the possession of
certitude; they call themselves "honest doubters" and "patient
inquirers," and whilst they are doubting and inquiring I am
digging hell miles deeper. Could we but really read one book of
the Bible, could we but hold one Gospel in our hearts, could we
but get hold of something and say, This one thing I have and
know and use,—all the rest would come in happy sequence. So
it was not too early to set up a cairn on the one side of the bank
and on the other side of the bank. We must have memorials
in life. If we do not set up stony memorials we shall still leave
footprints. Every man has his history, and every man has had
his opportunity and has left behind him a record as to its use or
abuse. Blessed is the life that is full of memorial stones! It
ought never to be far back to the last one; and if whilst we are
building the next one the enemy should suddenly come down
upon us in some black suggestion, in some terrific temptation, we
should flee back to the memorial last put up, and, under the

shadow of that Ebenezer, calmly await the future. Why this unbuilt life ? Why this life without any pillar of stone or temple behind it ? What wonder if in turning round and seeing nothing a great fear should seize us, and we should suppose that we had been given over to the enemy of souls ? There should hardly be one step between one memorial stone and another, so that we may instantly retire for a moment to recruit our strength and renew our hope and confidence in God. How mean are some lives in this matter of erecting no memorial ; no diary is kept, no journal is posted up, no entry written, it may be in a trembling hand, but yet setting forth the formula : The true God was with me to-day ; he helped me to cross the river, he enabled me to run through a troop and to leap over a wall ; and though I can scarcely read the words yet I will inscribe them every one and come back to them as to a Bible and to a revelation. Men who live in times of haste say they have no leisure for such enterings. The enterings need not be literal : we need not be talking about material paper and ink, but about the tablets of the heart, the records of the memory, always having a vivid recollection of the last deliverance, the last vision, the last mighty prayer, the last sublime victory. There is no other way in which to make life rich and thoughtful. When accused, we should be able to flee back to God's last record ; when tempted to disbelieve him, we should go back to the last fact. Our life should not be a mysterious argument, in the processes of which we may be vexed and troubled by subtler intellects than our own : life should be its own fact, its own confirmation of spiritual truths, its own sanctuary, its own refuge. Have the witness in yourselves. Do not wait for posterity to build the cairns ; build your own memorials. Posterity will come and read them, but we might build our own altars, set up our own standards and unfurl our own banners, and accept the responsibility, as we have received the reward, of our own religion. So building we should crowd out all unworthy houses. We should want every inch of land. The whole earth would be filled with the divine presence and glory. Every room in the house would be a church ; every window in the dwelling would look towards the Jerusalem that is above ; every chair would be an altar ;—the whole dwelling would burn with unconsuming fire. We cannot, then, begin too soon. The

moment the first conviction is wrought in the mind, build a
stone memorial; the moment you are conscious of having taken
the first real step in advance, build; vow never to retire behind
that building, for it begins your best history, it points towards
your broadest, brightest future.

We have spoken of posterity. The cairn was to be a sign
among the Israelites :—

"That this may be a sign among you, that when your children ask their
fathers in time to come, saying, What mean ye by these stones? Then ye
shall answer them, That the waters of Jordan were cut off before the ark of
the covenant of the Lord; when it passed over Jordan, the waters of Jordan
were cut off: and these stones shall be for a memorial unto the children of
Israel for ever " (vv. 6, 7)

Blessed indeed is he to whom such inquiries are put; they
create for him a splendid opportunity of usefulness. What was
the answer to be ?—argumentative, controversial, suggestive?
Was it to be a guess attached to a riddle very profound and
difficult? Nothing of the kind: it was to be a recital of history :
—This was done; on such and such a day this was accomplished. Are there questions and facts in our lives? Do we
live in a troubled cloud, or in a house which hath foundations
whose builder and maker is God? When children ask you
questions about grey hairs, and wrinkles in the face, and sighs
that have no words, and smiles too bright to be carved upon
the radiant face by the hands of hypocrisy,—when they ask
you about kneeling at the altar, speaking into the vacant air,
and uttering words to an unseen and invisible Presence,—when
they interrogate you about your great psalms and hymns and
anthem-bursts of thankfulness, what is your reply to these? Do
not be ashamed of the history. Keep steadily along the line
of fact. Say what happened to *you*, and magnify God in the
hearing of the inquirer. This every man can do. He may
not be able to have a philosophy of history conceived and
evolved by his own genius, but every man must know his
own story, and be able to speak about his own experience,
and to explain in some degree his indebtedness to the infinite
power and goodness of God. Thus we shall have a building
Church, a speaking Church, an explaining Church,—every man

keeping upon the rock of his own experience, and uttering the music of his own consciousness, and staggering the inquirer whose flippancy had supposed it had overflowed the mysteries of spiritual communion. More personality of reference, a deeper individuality of experience, perfectly consistent with the most beautiful modesty, is what we want in the affirmation of great truths and the illustration of great precepts. The children would ask, "What mean ye by these stones?" The stones were so shaped that they could not have put themselves into their positions. Walking along the common road we have stones enough, the desert is full of stones; nobody thinks of asking about the quality of the stones, who put them there, or what is meant by their being there; they are dumb stones, stones without sermons; they are stones astray; they are not in line, they are without related shape and colour; so they are passed by without heed on the part of the traveller. But when stones have actually taken shape, when one stone is upon another, and stone is added to stone until a wall is built, and when the wall turns the angle and becomes another wall on the other side, and again reverts and so completes the square, people know that the stones could not have put themselves in that relation. Here questioning becomes intelligent; here questioning may become necessary to every man who would master somewhat of human history and the significance of the great tragedy of human life. Is it so with us? Are the stones which we might have used still lying about the road, without being put together, related, or built up into any intelligible and useful shape?— stones enough, building material enough, but all lying without plan—a hideous chaos. Who would ask questions about such shapelessness, except as suggestive of amazement that men could have been so indolent, or unwise, or so insane? The very life-building should be so well put together that men ought and must ask questions about it, saying thus: What a character that is; what a noble life; what copious accommodation for all kinds of poverty, weakness, distress, friendlessness! what a summer outlook—how large, and how truly built for hospitality rather than for selfishness! Who built that house? Who owns it? What is the meaning of that life-edifice? It is possible, on the other hand, so to live that no man will ever ask a question

about us,—so commonplace, so poor, so wanting in all the
higher suggestiveness, so selfish, isolated, and so utterly destitute of sweet philanthropies, that men pass us by as they
might pass by ruins which have not even the advantage of
antiquity. How shall it be with us? Blessed are they whose
lives suggest questions !—more blessed still they whose explanations magnify the glory of God !

History should be matter of interest to all men, and in all
history we should be able to identify Providence with the past
and to speak of the wonders of the days of old. Here there
ought to be no mystery and no doubt. The wonders of
redemption may lie far from our intellectual grasp, but the
goodness of providence should lie quite handy to every man.
Every intelligent man should be able to say—Be the mysteries
what they may, it is perfectly certain that this life of ours is
bound, limited, directed : its ambitions are checked, its blood-
thirstiness cannot go beyond a certain range ; it is watched ;—
at all events that is the best explanation of life which we have
yet discovered ; it is so near being almighty, and yet so near
being powerless : now it stands upon some eminence as if it
would be lord of all, and presently it overreaches itself and
falls down in utterest humiliation ; we are watched, barred in,
shut up. We go certain lengths as if we could go ten times
farther, and, lo, in a moment, a great wall of darkness asserts
the limit and defines the prison. On this matter of Providence
there ought to be no uncertain sound. It is not supposable
that any life amongst us has not within itself elements sufficient for the construction of a practical argument on behalf of a
living, loving Providence. But are there not many broken lives,
sad hearts, perplexed souls ? Unquestionably there are ; but
there are men who have seen God even in darkness and have
acknowledged his hand even amid the chastening of affliction ;
there are men who have said, "Though he slay me, yet will
I trust in him." There was one singer so valiant in spiritual
music that when all nature seemed to be given up to silence
and despair he said, "Although the fig tree shall not blossom
. . . I will joy in the God of my salvation ;"—my religion

is not an affair of abundant herbs and plentiful harvests and green meadows : I live in the sanctuary of God's love, and as a child adopted into his family I will sing as loudly in winter as in summer : I will make up for the inhospitableness of the desert by the loudness and sweetness of my song. So we must not retire upon our desertions, difficulties, broken-heartednesses, and say, Whoever may have arguments, we have none. It is possible for ruins to be so shaped and so left as to excite inquiry, touch commiseration, and awaken reverence.

Thus miracles were to be brought within the lines of history : the time was to come when men would speak about miracles as they would speak about the commonplaces of life. The miracle is very startling at first, but there comes a time when men can write about the miracles with hands that do not tremble, with a certitude in which there is no flutter. At first they amazed and stupefied : we questioned their possibility ; but by living along that line, moving steadily step by step along that course, we come to a period when we can write about a miracle as if it were a common occurrence, when we can sing the sublimest poetry as if it were glorified prose, when our prayer gradually ascends into praise. Do not, therefore, be deterred by men who ask questions about the miracles, and especially by those men who have proved to their own satisfaction that miracles are impossible. There is nothing so impossible to my imagination as the existence of a man who can deny miracles. He indeed is an enigma in the course of my reading. How he can have unmade himself, choked the angel within him, suffocated the infant spirit, —how he can have been guilty of this infanticide I cannot tell : I must leave him to be expounded by-and-by. Meanwhile, my own life springs up into a daily miracle—a miracle every moment, a day crowned with wonders ; and the time comes when we speak about these things as if they were commonplaces —not in the sense of being unsuggestive or unworthy of heed, but in the sense of being so abundant that we have come to regard them with reverent familiarity, and to expect them as men expect the miracle of the harvest. Yes, the miracle of the harvest ! The seed is sown and left in the cold earth, but the whole chemic ministry of nature works upon it : the dew and the rain ; the morning does its work, and the evening continues its labour; and by-and-by the seed springs up some thirty, some sixty, some an hundredfold, without a stain of earth upon it, pure as if it had grown downwards from the sky, —a great golden answer to the prayer of industry. Miracles! The air is full of them, life throbs with them. We have been so blind that we have not seen them, or so fond of doubt that we have questioned their possibility. If we were to live in God we would live *as* God, and the coming and the going of nature—the perpetual miracle—would be the perpetual rest. O that men were wise, that they understood these things! This was the Church of sacred romance. We have left romance out of the history of the Church now. It is a question of surface, of bulk, of statistics, of movable figures. Would God the day of sacred romance would return when great things were attempted and great things done in the name of the Almighty God!

There is a Jordan before every one of us. That Jordan must be passed. We call it Death. We speak of it as the black last river. We talk of it sometimes as in swelling indignation and fury, and ask what shall we do in the swellings of Jordan? To the Christian, Jordan is already past. In a material, physical, and limited sense the little conquest has yet to be won, but in all its spiritual significance and glory Jordan is dried up, and they who are in Christ Jesus, the great priest of the everlasting covenant, walk through the bed of the river as upon dry ground. This is our Christian confidence, this is our spiritual hope, this is our standing in life. Death is abolished. The miracles have been completed in the resurrection of our Lord Jesus Christ. All that follows will follow like a cadence, without effort,—a sweet necessity, the logic of poetry.

PRAYER.

ALMIGHTY GOD, thou art always drying up rivers before us, or Red Seas, or beating down mountains, or making straight that which is crooked. Thy love is a daily concern for us, leaving nothing untouched and unblessed, but covering the whole sphere of our life as with summer sunshine. We bless thee for thy love, for we live in it. Thy love encourages us, inspires and sustains us, and makes the wilderness into a fruitful field. We know thy love in providence: we see it everywhere every day; but we see thy love most of all in the Cross of Jesus Christ, thy Son, and looking upon the Cross we say, Herein is love; and we hear thy voice saying thou didst so love the world as to create and glorify this Cross. At the Cross we bow; at the Cross we wait; here is forgiveness and here alone. This is the beginning of a new life, this is a gate opening upon eternal blessedness. We therefore glory in the Cross of Christ, and have no other glory, by reason of its celestial majesty. It is the voice of God to the pleading of man, the answer of mercy to the demand of law. May we love the Cross more and more, dying upon it with Christ, with Christ buried, with Christ rising, crowned, and sharing his throne. May this be our life-word; may this be the speech of our tongue and the testimony of our conduct, that we live, yet not we, but that Christ liveth in us, and that the life which we now live in the flesh we live by faith on the Son of God, who loved us and gave himself for us. As for rivers, thou didst make them flow, and thou canst make them cease; as for the desert, it is of thine own ordination, and thou canst turn it into a garden more beautiful than paradise. About these things we have no fear; we are in God's hands and God's love. What fear we have relates to sin, guiltiness of soul, forfeiture of sonship and standing in the family of God; and herein where our fear abounds, the glory of thy love abounds still more, so that we have yet hope in the prison-house, and are assured that our sins, which are many, are all forgiven us. In this faith we live; in this faith we serve; in this faith we would die. Amen.

Joshua iv. 15-24.

15. And the Lord spake unto Joshua, saying,

16. Command the priests that bear the ark of the testimony, that they come up out of Jordan.

17. Joshua therefore commanded the priests, saying, Come ye up out of Jordan.

18. And it came to pass, when the priests that bare the ark of the covenant of the Lord were come up out of the midst of Jordan, and the soles

of the priests' feet were lifted up unto the dry land, that the waters of Jordan returned unto their place, and flowed over all his banks, as they did before.

19. And the people came up out of Jordan on the tenth day of the first month, and encamped in Gilgal, in the east border of Jericho.

20. And those twelve stones, which they took out of Jordan, did Joshua pitch in Gilgal.

21. And he spake unto the children of Israel, saying, When your children shall ask their fathers in time to come, saying, What mean these stones?

22. Then ye shall let your children know, saying, Israel came over this Jordan on dry land.

23. For the Lord your God dried up the waters of Jordan from before you, until ye were passed over, as the Lord your God did to the Red sea, which he dried up from before us, until we were gone over:

24. That all the people of the earth might know the hand of the Lord, that it is mighty: that ye might fear the Lord your God for ever.

COMING UP OUT OF JORDAN.

THE Canaanites might reasonably have looked upon the Jordan as one of their natural defences. This it was at all times, but it was to all human appearance more so at this season than at other periods of the year. Springing among the spurs of the Lebanon, at a great height above the level of the sea, becoming first Lake Merom, and then expanding into the Lake Tiberias, so large and important that it was called the Sea of Galilee, its impetuous course terminated in the Dead Sea. It would seem to have been made to roll just where it did that it might be a natural protection or defence for the people upon the side of the Canaanites. The time of this history was April or May. We know from another passage that it was the harvest of flax and barley; all the snow upon Hermon had melted, and was pouring down into the valley through which the swollen torrent plunged and roared on its way to the Dead Sea. The time of the year is thus worth noticing; it was a time at which the Jordan was in the very pride of its fulness and strength. It has been pointed out as a striking contrast that "when the Goths, in the fifth century, nearly a million of people, crossed the Danube to seek a home in the south of Europe, they had a fleet of vessels at their command; yet the crossing of the Goths occupied many days, and many lives were lost in the passage." Be it observed, then, that the writers make no doubt as to the reality of this miracle. Fifty days later the wheat harvest would have set in, and at the time of the wheat harvest Jordan had considerably subsided. Sceptical critics might therefore have said that the Israelites crossed at low water; there were many shallow places in the channel, and no doubt they took advantage of the subsidence of the river in order to cross. But the sacred historian makes it very clear that the Jordan was at its height: there was no mistake about its fulness and urgency; so we have to deal with the facts as we find them stated in the record. There is happily confirmatory evidence as to the time at which the Israelites passed, and that evidence tends to show that the river must have been at its fullest. Nature only *apparently* protects doomed men. We can imagine the Canaanites on their side of the river thinking that nature was in their interest, that nature was concerned for them, and had provided a defence inviolable; but nature is never on the side of the doomed man; certainly nature is never on the side of the bad man; even if apparently so, it is in appearance only, and not in reality; there is not a stone in the field that is not at enmity with him; there is not a beast browsing on any hill that does not count him a foe. This is the deep interpretation of things. Appearances notwithstanding, let us set it down as a very clear line in our book of serious reflection that the whole earth casts out the bad man, and would not give him accommodation or offer him hospitality, and at best would consent to the humiliation of providing him a grave. The strongest defences are worthless if our character be not sound and righteous in the sight of God; inroads can be made upon all securities, and will be made; and we shall be overthrown just in proportion to our guilt and corruptness. " I have seen the wicked in great power, and spreading himself like a green bay tree." There is no doubt about the appearance; the security was to all human vision ample and complete, but when God is against a man what wall can build him out? When character is wrong and judgment is coming, what hand dare hold itself up to keep back the lightning of just penalty? It is in the time of fancied security that we are often overthrown. God delights to stain the pride of all glory. He would seem almost in his providence to wait until we have reached the very culmination of our strength; and when we say, Now we are safely lodged within walls which cannot be shaken or burned, then he shows the greatness of his strength, and puts forth his arm to find us in our hidden securities. We cannot build out the lightning; we cannot build out God when he comes in judgment. We may withhold our consent when he makes propositions; we may reject his mercy and slay his Son; but in the time of judgment we have no will, no power, no answer to the infinite challenges of God.

Why dwell upon the merely local incidents connected with this narration when we know that there are crossings in life which our power did not accomplish? Strip the record of everything that appears to be romantic or unduly excited—all that touches what we may believe to be the incredible; yet there remains in our own history the fact that we have accomplished transitions and passages which we never completed in our own strength or by our own wisdom. We cannot tell how the difficulty was crossed, but that it is crossed we know well. Did we cross it in our sleep? Was it a dream-bridge that spanned the chasm? How did we get upon this side, where all is fertility and hopefulness and contentment? How did we come into this estate? We remember confusedly opposition, battle, natural difficulty—the natural difficulty being the worst of all: the disadvantage of birth, early life, a thousand oppositions that crowded upon us—far, far back in the morning of memory; yet here we are this day in a fruitful place, under a blue sky, and the morning comes without threatening, and the whole heaven seems to make way for the sun that he may show his splendours in unusual fulness. How was this transference completed? We cannot tell the process in detail, but that we are here is the supreme fact in our life. Why, then, send the memory back upon some critical but fruitless errand, to find fault with the process, to ask questions about the detail? Better and wiser to begin our life from this conscious deliverance, and date everything from this side the river. Thus the past may chasten the present: from the long-gone years there may come some voice of warning; but all our dating of experience and vowing and service is from this side the river—is from the stones which memorialise the deliverance. This is called the religious life and the religious construction of life; and this delivers us from memories which become tumultuous and confounding when not barred back by the boundary of definite consciousness of divine deliverance.

Are there not opportunities for crossing all rivers ? And are not those opportunities of very brief duration ? It is wonderful to mark how the door of opportunity swings back in life : it is even more wonderful to notice how it swings back again, as if to declare that mercy is not to be trifled with, and the hospitality of God is not an indiscriminate beneficence or munificence. Have not the poets told us that " there is a tide in the affairs of men " ? Whilst we are reading words which we declare to be inspired and sacred, these very words are confirmed by experiences within our own knowledge, and they do but express in sacred colour what we ourselves have known to be true in daily life. The Gospel is itself a great opportunity ; written upon it are the words, " Now is the accepted time ; behold now is the day of salva-tion." Who can utter that word " Now " with tone sufficient in expressiveness and pathos ? When is " now " ?—always a dying term, always a new projection ; a time limited by a moment, and yet true of every moment coming. " Seek ye the Lord while he may be found, call ye upon him while he is near." These words define periods of time, exactness of opportunity ; and we know them to be true by the broad facts and the daily experiences of life.

Reading of this passage of the river we find one great omission. The omission was purposed. *There was no way of retreat pro-vided.* The river did not stand back until the Israelites saw what they could do with Jericho ; no sooner were they over than the river came down as before, and Israel was locked up to his work. Thus God brings us into face-to-face conflicts ; thus divine providence drives us into close quarters with the enemy. It is supposable that a host advancing to conquer a walled and ancient city might have had to bear the pressure of some sudden terror and might have desired to retire ; but the river was rolling on to the Dead Sea, and there was no promise made that it should be cut in two again for the accommodation of timid or cowardly men. Some of us must be forced up to our work. We do not know what is in us or what we can do until there is no escape—battle, or death ; battle, or victory. Let us bless God, I would again say, that we are sometimes scourged up to our work. To retreat is to be drowned : to advance is to achieve at least possible victory. There must be no going back again. We are bound to this holy work—taking the devil's citadel. There can be no reconstruction as to the terms of service and loyalty. We are committed to the overthrow of this city or kingdom, this evil or corruption, as the case may be. If we do not advance we shall be slain; if we try to run away we shall be drowned. "Quit you like men." Better fight and die honourably than run away and be as drowned dogs in the sullen stream. We are men who are committed, and cannot go back.

"And the people came up out of Jordan on the tenth day of the first month, and encamped in Gilgal, in the east border of Jericho" (v. 19).

What is that to us? These are forgotten dates? No, there is nothing forgotten. Great things took place upon this date long ago, and it ought to be familiar to us. In Exodus xii. 5, the people had been commanded to take them a lamb for an house that they might eat the Passover. When was that? "*On the tenth day of the first month.*" That was exactly to a moment forty years before. Coincidences of time are full of suggestion. History repeats itself in many ways in very subtle colourings and suggestions. So we seem to have been here before, and to have read this discourse, or to have heard this speech somewhere, long ago. Did we dream this scene? Who told us of it? There is a strange and even weird familiarity about the place, the man, the whole vision—what is it? It is but the revival of a date; it is but time set in a new relation, the old and the new strangely mingled; for God has always worked upon the plan of continuity, the continuity sometimes apparently lost, but suddenly reappearing and projecting itself through the ages. "Hear, O Israel: The Lord our God is one Lord;" "I am the Lord, I change not." Jesus Christ is the same yesterday, and to-day, and for ever. To-morrow will bring up the memory of to-day. The world has lived long enough now to allow its days to double back upon one another, and to take from the impression some of the ink with which ancient history was written. The days are repetitions. Time is full of history. Forty years taken in the passage of the distance between the crossing of the Red Sea and entering into Canaan? Yes! Make of it what we may, here is the fact of the present time, that men are hindered by their wickedness. The Israelites might have been sooner in Canaan but for their rebellion. We, ourselves, know that our sins have kept good things from us. Sin keeps back the millennium. Evil-doing keeps us digging in the earth when we might have been serving in heaven. There are men who are to-day suffering from what they did forty years ago. Things do not die. " Everlasting punishment" is written upon the whole scroll of life. Punishment has no end, except it be ended by some mysterious but loving action on the part of God. A man sentenced to prison for one day for an evil deed is in prison the remainder of his life ; when he has left the jail he has not left the prison. Long ago we got wrong somehow, and we cannot get back into the right line. It was a mistake, or a misadventure, or an evil purpose, or a settled treason ; it was a piece of selfishness, or miscalculation, or wrong-doing ; we said the wrong word, we were too late by one day, we mistook the right hand for the left—something it was ; and the consequence is that we have been forty years in doing what might have been accomplished in one. See if this be not so by examining life carefully. It seems impossible to disentangle the knot; it is weary work at the best. We know we might have been so much further on, and yet to-day we are baffled and hindered and mocked by some spirit of the air which is without shape or name. The interference with the river is nothing compared with the subtle spiritual interferences which are always changing the route of life. We have set out upon a certain course, and said in specific terms,—this shall be our route towards the goal. Without any action upon our part which we can recall, and without any conscious relation to the action, the route has been changed, the course has been turned to the right hand or to the left. These interferences with life-routes are taking place every day. The young soul has its plan, and having mapped out the future with a hand that knew no trembling, and with a pencil incapable of feeling, the boy joyfully says: "I will go; and thus I will travel; here halt, and there remain a year, and buy and sell and get gain, and then proceed according to the record." This is the boast of folly. This is the utterance of men who have not the key of to-morrow. The Lord suddenly changes the course, and they who thought they were going westwards at a rapid pace are awakened to the consciousness that they have been hastening eastwards, and knew it not. Why will not men consider these things and put facts together, so patiently and inductively as to find a law at the end of them ? the law being that it is not in man that liveth to direct his way, and that it is the Lord who presides over the battle and directs the pace of the going of the world, and that there is but one God, reigning over all things and for ever blessed.

Israel might have penetrated into the Land of Promise when they were on the frontier at Kadesh-Barnea in the second year of the exodus. Think of it ! they might have been in Canaan long ago—a generation since ! What happened to prevent this penetration into the Land of Promise ? Sin happened. Let us call it commonplace if we are prepared to lose the richest cream of historical instruction ; but there is the fact : it was sin that hindered the early penetration into the Land of Promise. Say Edom was obstinate, and the king thereof said : " No, you shall not go through this land ; you must find some other way ; " the king of Edom did not speak words of his own, the descendant of Esau had a mission from God. Men do not always know whose ministers they are. We speak words that have upon them and around them the texture of eternity, and we say we knew not why we spoke them, but we could not resist the speech : the words flew to our lips and burned upon our tongue, and we must needs utter them. We cannot allow Israel to assume the character of an ill-used traveller, who, having suddenly come upon inhospitable provinces, was put to very serious inconvenience. Israel was not a white-robed saint in the wilderness—the pure, the patient, holy traveller ; Israel had defied God, and murmured against his captain, and resisted the law ; and rebellion must always be punished. It is not always punished in the same way, but punished it always is. Men think they have secured their purpose ; they say that this time at all events they have been victorious ; and now they will handle life just as they please—and behold, their very victory is the cruellest defeat ! They may have had their desire granted, but leanness has been sent into their souls. There is only one way of living rightly, and that is living in the sanctuary of God,—that is, in obedience to the eternal law which facts, as well as revelation, have established. If you are unwilling to believe that the eternal law has been revealed, and has been written down with pen and ink, and is to be referred to as an ancient document, then take some other course. Let this be your course: call for quietness in the mind; silence all tumult of thought; read history—centuries of it at a time; take in breadth and scope enough or you will be the victims of details; seize as with the mental vision great periods of time; and this you will find to be the law of fact, as well as the law of revelation, that only he who falls into the rhythm of the universe, who is part of the great whole, who is so individual as not to lose his sense of responsibility, and yet so social as to know that he is one of a great host—only they who have moved rhythmically to the beat of righteousness and the throb of justice have come into ultimate rest, and peace, and dignity. Revelation looks to facts for its commentary. It is willing to rest until history has had its say; and revelation and history are to be one in their final testimony. Observe what has been required in this contention: that sufficient time should be taken within the purview. These arbitraments are not to be settled by what occurred this day, or within the limits of that one hour. We must take in field enough if we could realise all the teaching of historical perspective and colour. So judged, the Bible has nothing to fear; it is a prophecy of facts, the forecasting of what we know ourselves has occurred and is evermore transpiring.

What, then, was the purpose of this memorialising of the crossing of Jordan? Why these stones? Why this religious consideration? The answer is given in the twenty-fourth verse:—

"That all the people of the earth might know the hand of the Lord, that it is mighty: that ye might fear the Lord your God for ever."

All providences are to have a religious effect upon others, even upon nations far away. We cannot put an end to this species of judgment. Observers look upon us and say: He lives well; there must be a force in that character we have underestimated; he prays even now, notwithstanding the storm which has fallen upon him, the tempest which has desolated his fields, the scepticism which has assailed his faith; he has dug a dozen graves, yet he has made of them a dozen altars—how is this? Surely the hand of the Almighty is with him, and the Spirit of the Eternal is within his soul. It is the same also in nations. Mark how they stand in the world's esteem. One nation makes a proposition, and the proposal is hailed with universal derision, because the nation has lived itself into the infamy of a known liar. Another nation makes a proposal, and all the other nations of the world hasten to accept the terms. Why? The nation has acquired fame for honesty, uprightness, integrity; for being right in its supreme purpose, often making mistakes, often returning to correct its own miscalculations—yet, the soul of it is healthy; its word is its bond; it is a nation honourably known. So what we do as individuals and as nations has an effect upon observers near and far away. It is possible for us to live so that the atheist will be obliged to say: After all, there is a mystery about this I cannot make out. It is possible so to live that the mocker shall let the gibe die on his reluctant lips, saying even in his bad heart: It is a cruel thing to mock consistency so noble and beneficence so generous. It is possible for any nation under the influence of Christ so to live that other nations, whilst disputing Christian doctrine and contending against Christian metaphysics, shall say: The soul of that nation is honest, righteous, just; and what if in this concession there should be hidden an unexpressed avowal that the Lord is God, and Christ, his Son, come whence he may, mysteriously makes man better, sounder, grander? The critics who would be glad to discrown the Messiah may stop and wonder and think when they note the quality of character which his grace creates and sustains.

PRAYER.

OH that we knew where we might find him! We would come even unto his seat and plead with him mightily and long. We bless thee that we need not repeat the words of thy servant of old, for we know where thou art: thou art not a God afar off but nigh at hand. Thou hast, in Christ Jesus thy Son, reconciled the world unto thyself. We meet thee at Bethlehem. We hear thee speaking to us in the wind. We watch thee in all thy daily course of humiliation and pain and redeeming love. We see thee in the Cross of Jesus Christ; we recognise in that Cross the highest revelation of thy righteousness and love. God forbid that we should glory save in the Cross! It touches our life when no other power can come near it; it charms our solitude without intrusion; it speaks to us when we could hear no other voice. It is the hope of the world; it is the way to pardon; it is the gate of heaven. Blessed Cross; infinite Cross; tender Cross! May we ourselves be daily crucified upon it, that, dying daily, we may know daily the power of Christ's resurrection, and become so accustomed to death that when the death of the flesh comes we shall not know it. We thank thee for all Christian hope and confidence, for all spiritual consolation, for all voices which address us from the skies; we need these in dark times, on cloudy days, when the sun is quite shut out; then do we know how great is thy love, how tender thy pity, how precious the dew of thy tears. Thou hast made our life so that no voice can truly speak to it but thine own. Other voices address us in parts, and upon given days, and under special circumstances; but thy voice is the same by night and by day, in winter and in summer; thou comest near us, and our weakness thou dost lift up by thine own almightiness; there is no touch like thine. Other hands hurt us even in their endeavours to help, but thy hands, omnipotent One, are full of mercy; they express thine heart. We thank thee for all love which makes life's burdens sit less heavily upon us; we thank thee for all home delights which make the world more bearable, we thank thee for all spiritual comfort which enables us to overcome material distresses; these are the gifts of God, these are messages from the eternal spheres, these are voices which the soul knows and which the heart lovingly answers. We cannot understand this religious nature with which thou hast endowed us; it is a great pain oftentimes,—eager to look into things which are at present sealed, and impetuous in inquiry rather than patient, troubling God with violent addresses rather than waiting patiently for his coming. Yet it is our life's highest life; it enables us to touch heaven, eternity, things infinite; by it we realise thy purpose in making all things that are round about us, so stupendous, so minute,—the great heavens, the dying flowers. Thou hast made all these things, and filled them with meaning; if we were wise we could read that meaning easily and lovingly, and be comforted by the tender solaces of unspoken gospels. Anoint our eyes that we may see! Circumcise our ears that we may hear. Give us the understanding heart; and every place shall be the house of God, and every delight shall be as a gate of heaven. We bless thee for a sense of thy nearness: we can whisper to thee; we can call upon thee instantaneously, and thy reply can come before our friend can see we have prayed or have received answers from God. Direct us in all our way: it is sometimes so difficult: we shrink from it: we cannot bear the deep places and the rough; we do not know what may befall us along the perilous line: some ravenous beast may destroy us, some hidden pit may engulf us, some sudden wind may be charged with death. But this is our ignorance: thou wilt pity it and forgive it. We would rather say, in our Christian faith— Father, let our hand be in thine, then nothing can come but peace and light and heaven. We mourn our sin: it is bitterer to thee than it can be to us; because thou art all holy; but thou hast grappled with this difficulty; thou didst meet sin before sin arose: the Cross is older than the crime, the grace more venerable than the sin. We trust in the living God; we cast ourselves upon Jesus Christ thy Son; we will not reason or understand in words this mystery of love, for who can grasp in his little palm all that is above him? Now we fall into thy hands, and evermore abide there, growing in wisdom, in confidence, in charity, in holiness, knowing Christ more thoroughly, comprehending him by our sympathy where we cannot follow him by our reason; and do thou enable us to die with him that with him we may rise again. Amen.

Joshua v.

MEMORABLE EVENTS.

THIS chapter is remarkable for two or three points which happily combine the miraculous and the experimental. Here and there we cannot touch the genius of the chapter at all, and then suddenly it descends upon familiar lines, so that we can interrogate it, and in a measure understand it, because it confirms our own personal experience. The foot of this ladder is upon the earth: the head of it is in the sky.

Take the first verse :—

"And it came to pass, when all the kings of the Amorites, which were on the side of Jordan westward, and all the kings of the Canaanites, which were by the sea, heard that the Lord had dried up the waters of Jordan from before the children of Israel, until we were passed over, that their heart melted, neither was there spirit in them any more, because of the children of Israel."

The heathen kings did not disbelieve in miracles. It seems as if we had lost a good deal by our civilisation. We have come into a very complicated state of existence, and are so fretted by questions and scepticisms as to be almost divested at once of our dignity and our peace. It must have been wonderful living in the days when miracles seemed to be quite credible, quite near at hand, topics of common converse, instances which men had seen with their own eyes. We have lost *something* by this cessation of the outward miracle. What we have lost is faith—faith in human history, faith in the processes of human evolution and education : we have lived ourselves into the commonplace pointless. Lord Lytton says : " The man who has no faith in religion is often the man who has faith in a nightmare. Julius Cæsar publicly denounced a belief in hereafter, and rejected the idea of a soul and a deity, yet muttered a charm when he entered a chariot, and did not cross the Rubicon until he had consulted the omens. Lord Herbert, of Cherbourg, writes a book against revelation, and asks a sign from heaven to tell him if his book is approved by his Maker. The man who cannot believe in the miracles performed by the Saviour, gravely tells us of a miracle vouchsafed to himself." Thus we measure everything by our own experience and consciousness. We have lost the power of projecting ourselves into the universal consciousness of ancient and contemporary spiritual history. The heathen kings drew inferences from what had occurred around them. They said—If the river has been crossed, the city is gone. They were not unreasoning or infantile minds. They saw somewhat of the logical issue of things. The power of following the seed to its fructification is what we have lost. Otherwise, we should all be prophets : we should know that as certainly as a man has told a lie he has dug a hell. We think the law will be modified, or turned aside, and that the thunderbolt of judgment will somehow be averted. We are not morally logical. We peddle about verbal sequences and account it cleverness to trace literary consequences, but what about moral concatenation and issue ? Were we as bold in the matter of inference as were the heathen kings, we should know that the moment a man has given up self-control he is damned. It seems to be a great leap from the first step to the last, but

that is moral logic, that is spiritual sequence; as a question
of logic there is no way of getting out of it. What then can
be done? All men have surely been false, and all men have
surely done that which is wrong. There comes the sublimity
of divine revelation. God takes up the case: the great miracle
is performed from above. There is no halting between falsehood
and perdition; so far as the man is concerned, his first lie
killed him. The first act of disobedience "brought death into
our world and all our woe." Death is not the result of a
series of actions; it is the result of a thought, a purpose, a
deed. Whilst thus we contemplate with a kind of inexcusable
dignity the kings and mighty men who lived long ages ago,
and even begin to question whether they lived at all or not,
they seized the great idea of process, development, and culmination: they knew that one miracle meant all miracles. They
did not ask for another sign from heaven as the unbelieving
Jews were always asking. Therein was the sophistry of the
Jewish reasoning and the folly of the Jewish relation to the
great Man of their day: they did not know that one miracle
meant all miracles, one lie meant all the fire of eternity burning
the liar. We, too, seem to suppose that only at the end of
a series of offences can certain penal consequences arise. That
may be well for mere social convenience, that may be a proper
limit for human magistracy and imperfect power; but looking
at things in the light of heaven and the light of eternity, to tell
one lie is to go into everlasting punishment. Who, then, can
be saved? None by himself. No man has the power to rub
out a lie. You cannot expunge a falsehood; once done, it is
done for ever, so far as the doer is concerned. If there be any
balm in Gilead, if there be any physician there, if there be any
undreamed of love and power in heaven, if it lie within the
circuit of Almighty power and infinite wisdom to meet the case,
so be it; but within the limits of the man's own life and
responsibility and power, the lie means hell. Blessed be God,
there is a gospel in relation to this—a Cross, a Saviour, a way
out of it all,—not to be understood or reduced to words which
always exactly fit the occasion, but to be seized by faith and
appropriated by the hunger of the helpless heart. Heathen
kings lo~t spiritual conviction, and therefore their arms fell

right down by their sides. It is when the heart "melts" that
the arm gives in. Men fight with the heart; men live with
the heart; men return to the battle because of the inspiration
of the heart. What wonder, then, if the Christian teacher
should come forward and say, "With the heart man believeth
unto righteousness"? Man does not lay a withered hand upon
heaven's pillars and draw himself up by that palsied grasp.
It is with the heart we live and suffer and return to the battle;
it is the heart which says—To-morrow shall see victory;
to-morrow we bury the enemy in the grave. The walls of
Jericho were still standing; all the kings of the Amorites and
all the kings of the Canaanites had their armies intact and all
their resources at hand, but "their heart melted, neither was
there spirit in them any more." And what is a man without
heart, without spirit, without moral confidence? To know
that righteousness is not with us is to have all the pith taken
out of our muscles; to know that we are going into the garden
to kiss an innocent Christ and thus betray him is, when we see
him, to fall right back, blanched and dead. Be right in spiritual
conviction. Know that the thing proposed to be done is right,
wise, good; and then the rest will be peace, victory,—enduring,
untainted honour.

Another interesting point occurs in the sixth verse :—

"For the children of Israel walked forty years in the wilderness, till all
the people that were men of war, which came out of Egypt, were consumed,
because they obeyed not the voice of the Lord : unto whom the Lord sware
that he would not shew them the land, which the Lord sware unto their
fathers that he would give us, a land that floweth with milk and honey."

Here we find what we are constantly seeing : a new generation
but a permanent humanity. According to this statement all the
people that were men of war which came out of Egypt were
consumed. The Israel that entered Canaan was not the Israel
that left Egypt, so far as detail was concerned. This is the
mystery of human development or human progress. Men die
—man lives. The generation passes away—humanity abides.
God thus raises up a Church to himself. Much is apparently
lost by the way : the leaves of a thousand years ago are all dead
and buried, or have entered into chemic relations with the
universe which we cannot follow, but the tree on which they grew

still stands, lifting itself up to the blue heavens, and waiting next
year's inspiration and fruitfulness. Here lies a truth which
many men dare not really put into words, which cannot be so
put into words as to explain itself to everybody. We must
grow up into some mysteries, pass into them subtly and come to
their realisation suddenly; they are not to be explained or made
matters of controversy; they are to be seized by the expanding and strengthening mind; they are to be appropriated by the
refined and sanctified consciousness. The mocker might step in
here and say, Where are they who left Egypt to come to a land
of promise? They are dead; their carcases are in the wilderness.
That is historically, and as a matter of detail, true; but humanity
is in man. The great human quantity is within the individual
detail. The Church is within the sinner. Here are men who, like
ourselves, were born in the wilderness but destined for Canaan.
That is human life in a sentence. All these people were children
of the wilderness, yet they were not meant for the wilderness
as a final settlement; they knew it: the spirit of marching was
in them; the angel of battle moved them to arms. Is it not so in
our own consciousness? We were born in poverty, but never
meant to remain there; we were born under great disadvantages,
but had a soul given to us which said—We will beat them all
down, stand upon them, and make use of them to heighten the
very honour and dignity the Lord has enabled us to win. We
are all wilderness-born: we have no right to remain in the
wilderness or to die in it. The men died in the wilderness,
" because they obeyed not the voice of the Lord "—and
there cannot be two Lords, two Masters, two Sovereigns, two
thrones. "Hear, O Israel,"—O humanity,—"the Lord our God
is one Lord." Do not let us set up our little will and whim and
idea as against the eternal purpose, but fall down and resolutely
and tenderly pray that we may know God's will and do it every
syllable. That is "the whole duty of man." God is disappointed
with the individuals, but he will be pleased with the race. When
God made Adam he did not make *an* Adam; he made what
"Adam" signifies—man. The judgment of God does not lie as
between himself and the one little creature we call a man. God
is not set up as the centre of innumerable details any one of
which may crush his purpose and render his decree a nullity.

God takes another view of man :—As I live, saith the Lord, the whole earth shall be filled with my glory. What part or lot are we about to play in this matter ? Fool is he who thinks he can rule back the purpose of God or tear in twain the covenant of Heaven. It is one of two things : we fall upon the stone and are broken, or the stone falls upon us and we are ground to powder. Do not let us contend about terms or technicalities, or avail ourselves of all the suggestions offered by a crudely-formed and crudely-expressed theology. Here lies the infinite truth, confirmed by all life, that there can be but one will that is right, one God blessed for evermore. He will carry out his purpose. He has vowed as it were by his life, his eternity, that his word shall not return unto him void. He may be cast out, reviled, killed ; but he will still have the whole earth for his inheritance and humanity for a gem in his crown. "It is hard for thee to kick against the pricks." Every man has within himself the power— not the right—of self-damnation ; but God's word shall be fulfilled, though it take innumerable ages to accomplish it, that *man* shall stand in his image and likeness. He will never cease to work until the image is perfected. Whoever comes, whoever goes, though the wilderness be one infinite cemetery, God shall have a seed to serve him and to call Jesus blessed. We *can* fight, we *can* disobey, we *can* have our own poor way,—all that lies within the possibility of sin ; but it comes to nothing, except dishonour and ruin and death.

The most interesting point of all is found in verses 11, 12 :—

"And they did eat of the old corn of the land on the morrow after the passover, unleavened cakes, and parched corn in the selfsame day. And the manna ceased on the morrow after they had eaten of the old corn of the land ; neither had the children of Israel manna any more ; but they did eat of the fruit of the land of Canaan that year."

The manna had fallen in the wilderness thirty-nine years and eleven months, excepting on the Sabbath-day. A modern commentator says :—"The manna finally ceased or kept Sabbath on the very day afterwards marked by our Lord's resurrection, which became the Lord's day." Now this is matter of simple arithmetical calculation. There is no possibility of so using figures and dates as to mislead the mind upon this particular ; and here, by a process of rigid arithmetical demonstration, it is made clear that the manna finally kept Sabbath on the very day afterwards marked by our Lord's resurrection; and our Lord replaced the manna of ancient teachers by himself saying:—I am the true Bread sent down from heaven: eat of me—eat of this old corn; other means of sustenance are done away, and I am the Bread sent down from heaven. Some very striking inferences immediately follow the perusal of this state of things. For example, here we have the reason for the cessation of miracles. When did the manna cease to fall?—Immediately that there was corn to be eaten. No sooner was it possible to live, as we should say naturally, than the supernatural method of existence was ended. This is God's method all through. There is no further need for manna, the manna will cease to be rained upon the wilderness. When we can find food for ourselves God will not find it for us otherwise than primarily, otherwise than by showing us how to discover and appropriate it. This is the beauty of righteousness: this is the very centre and soul of the divine discipline of mankind. When we are in the wilderness and cannot grow corn, we shall not die of hunger, for God will intervene and sustain the life of his servants. Have no fear; let your courage abide in God. When the times are so hard and cruel and difficult that it is impossible for any honest man to live by natural methods and ordinary customs, God will not see him lost for want of sustenance. No man can say how that sustenance will be found, but it will be supplied. We may speak sometimes of the method of its production almost flippantly, or regard it with some measure of indifference, but in our most serious moods we shall come to the conclusion that after all there is a hand, infinite in power and in tenderness, working amid the affairs of men. But the other lesson is just as true. When the times are not so hard and impracticable and inhospitable, when men can dig and sow and cut down and grind and bake their bread, God will allow natural processes to be resumed, and he will so far throw us upon them as to withdraw what may be termed the supernatural or unimaginable. This is the very way of life. It is the right way in the house; it is the right way in the culture and upbringing of little children; it is the very secret of Providence:—God always near to us if there is no meat in the wilderness; God always ready to train by labour when labour is possible. So we are called to duty, to diligence. We are not to look for the supernatural so long as the natural is available. What do we want with the miracles when the whole land simply waits to be cultivated in order to answer our industry with abundant harvest? If any thing unrighteously stand in the way of this it must go down: it will inevitably go down, for God is with humanity—the whole, the sum-total quantity, with man, and for man all things shall be smoothed, and man shall pass on to the fulfilment of the divine idea. Not one word here can be spoken for indolence; not a single excuse can be set up for reluctance to labour. The light was made to work in. He who invented a jet that should break up the darkness invented a method of extending the sphere of industry. We are not to look to fathers and mothers to do for us what we can do for ourselves; it is unmanly, ignoble, unworthy. Depend upon it the fatherly and motherly spirit will see that the wilderness be turned into a fruitful field, if it be impossible for us to do anything by ourselves; but when that possibility is an open fact it is right that fatherly and motherly care should be withdrawn, and if not withdrawn its continuance becomes a crime.

A wonderful process we have seen in all these readings. We have seen the cloud by day displaced, giving way to the ark of the covenant. Hence the words, "Ye have not passed this way heretofore,"—that is, as we have seen, Ye have not heretofore had the ark of the covenant ahead of you, but only a symbolic cloud—now the cloud goes and you follow a written document. We have seen the manna displaced by the corn of Canaan: there is no more manna because the corn is plentiful, and nature will not do the work of the supernatural: the work of the supernatural is not indeed amid the bountifulness of nature. And, further than this, let us remind ourselves again and again, we know Christ no more after the flesh. Paul says, "He is risen." He is vanished. There is no fleshly Christ now. The great dispensation of the Spirit has opened. Under that dispensation we live. How wondrously we have returned to the cloud period and the fire-by-night method of guiding the world!—for what is the Spirit but as it were a cloud without measure, impalpable,—a fire we cannot touch, yet whose radiance and warmth are always available? We live under the dispensation of the Spirit, under the dispensation of new influences, new movements of the soul, daily inspirations from Heaven ; and so living, it is not for this man or that man in his individuality to arise and set up any Church in his own name, saying, *I* have a special revelation from God. To-day it is humanity that is inspired, the whole Church that is a sacred priesthood. This, from my point of view, is the true philosophy of succession. It is folly to dispute that great principle. Whoever disputes it dissociates himself from organic history and from organic humanity. From the first the principle of succession has been asserted in the Scriptures ; to the last things were committed from man to man—put in trust, so that they have been handed on from one generation to another. The only thing to insist upon now is this : that the Church is the great individual—the whole Church, not as broken up into communions, one having the partiality of Heaven and another living under the disapprobation of the skies, but the whole redeemed Church. There is a common sentiment, a common cry—a great, grand faith common to every soul in all the uncounted host. It is when we introduce our petty opinions, and one man sets up his inferences as against the inferences of some other man, that we lose touch and lose the altar, and lose God. From these verbal controversies we must retire, and know that the kingdom of heaven is not in contentions, in philosophies, in vain representations of self-will and self-opinion ; but under all forms of worship, under all ecclesiasticisms, there is a spirit common to the whole redeemed Church. To realise the presence of that spirit is to enter into the very mystery of the work of Christ and to understand what he meant when he prayed that we might all be one, as he was in the Father and the Father in him.

PRAYER.

ALMIGHTY GOD, thou art writing thy signs upon the heavens and upon the earth, and upon all the flying days of time. Blessed is he who can read them and apply their lessons to his heart, and walk according to their meaning. We can discern the signs of the weather—how is it we cannot discern the signs of the times? We have quick vision in some directions, and yet we are quite blind in others. We are double men,—eloquent, yet dumb; bright of eye, yet dull of perception. We cannot tell what we are, we are so confused and bewildered within our own consciousness. Sometimes we think we see the dawning light: then we sing like birds that are glad; then the whole sky is a great cloud, unbroken, unblessed with a single star; and then we sink into silence and despair. We have no constancy of life, no steadfastness of faith; our souls as to their moods veer about like the incalculable wind. We pray that our faith may be established, that it may be broad, massive, not to be shaken, strong in the Lord and in the power of his might. Lord, increase our faith—especially in solidity, that we may be the same to-morrow as to-day, confidently hoping in God. We know what thy word is: we are ennobled as we read it; no man can utter such words as thou hast written without being enlarged by their very perusal: they are sublime, they are full of God. Still, we cannot see the application of thy words; we look upon life within some one day and say— Behold, the purpose of Heaven is frustrated, and the counsel of the Most High is turned upside down. We are impatient, because ignorant; we are furious, because weak. We would be calm with the peace of God. Help us to live every moment as if it were the last. May the spirit of solemnity touch our whole life; yet may we feel that the highest solemnity is consistent with the purest joy. The Lord grant unto us clear shining after rain. The Lord bless us with the sound of the turtle when the winter is over and gone. We love the summer: we long for things that are verdant and beauteously coloured, and we long to hear all nature sing. If the winter days must come, give us a brave heart, a true faith, and may we so live in Christ, God the Son, that the winter itself shall be but a variation of summer. We can do all things through Christ which strengtheneth us. He is the mighty Saviour, he is the infinite Redeemer; there is none other who can save. He died for us, the just for the unjust, that he might bring us to God. We know that we are the unjust; we would flee unto the living Christ and ask him to give us all he has; the very asking shall express a divine inspiration, the very desire shall bring its own answer and comfort: thou dost not excite such passions in the soul without gratifying them with a great content. Amen.

Joshua v. 13-15.

"And it came to pass, when Joshua was by Jericho, that he lifted up his eyes and looked, and, behold, there stood a man over against him with his sword drawn in his hand : and Joshua went unto him, and said unto him, Art thou for us, or for our adversaries ? And he said, Nay ; but as captain of the host of the Lord am I now come. And Joshua fell on his face to the earth, and did worship, and said unto him, What saith my lord unto his servant ? And the captain of the Lord's host said unto Joshua, Loose thy shoe from off thy foot ; for the place whereon thou standest is holy. And Joshua did so."

SIGNS OF THE TIMES.

"WE have no such visions now" may be the easy comment of men who walk by sight and not by faith. Everything depends upon what you mean by "vision." Jesus Christ said— How is it that ye cannot discern the signs of the times ? Jesus Christ saw signs. All men whose eyes are set in their head see tokens, omens, and prefigurations of many kinds and full of urgent suggestion. We should see more if we looked more. He who looks sees. But there is a looking which is not seeing—a casual inspection, a hurried glance, a superficial regard scarcely to be distinguished from utter unconcern. We should put things together ; we should follow facts until they become laws. This indeed is the only way of finding out laws—namely, to gather facts together from every quarter, facts of every quality and every degree ; fearlessly bring together whatever has been established in the way of fact, and then when the evidence is thus as nearly complete as our time can make it, the inference which we draw from this collation will have of necessity the authority and force of a law. We must not judge by one fact, nor must we betake ourselves to any special field and say—all the facts we require are to be found within the four corners of this particular plot. All facts must be recognised, admitted into the great composition, and from the whole of them we must bring those inductions which settle themselves into law, until still larger facts are brought in to displace them or give them newness of accent and value. The "man" is still standing over against us. Nothing has been lost of all that is morally significant in this apocalypse. We have been looking in the wrong direction, or we have not been looking with sufficient eagerness, or we have failed before the spirit of languor, having succumbed to its lull ; and so we have lost our hold upon the age and all its forces. There is a man (visible to the spiritual eye) standing in this day or in that day over the whole continent with a drawn sword. It is the day of war. We shall hear presently, when we see such signs, the clash of battle. All the uneasiness, restlessness, discontent, unholy ambition with which we are made familiar from time to time, being interpreted means that the war spirit is ahead, is animating the sentiment of nations, is troubling the peace of the world. Thus we can find out from the journals of the day what figure it is that presides over the fortunes of the hour ; but we must bring, let us repeat, steadily and fearlessly, facts from every quarter, and shape them into this man, that we may through facts know his name, his figure, and his purpose. Account for it as we may, " coming events cast their shadows before." There is a spirit regulating and directing all things, and we may see with considerable clearness of vision what the spirit of the age is if we will only open our eyes and look at events and chasten our hearts, and study them with religious constancy. Sometimes the figure changes into quite another expression. The man is the same, but he is bent on other work. The sword has gone. What has he in his hand now ?—a plomb, square, balances, weights,—what means he? He says he will rectify things ; he will reform, and he will reconstruct ; he will have justice done ; he will apportion things on another principle : he will carry up justice to generosity, and regulate generosity by justice ; he counts the flock and says, There is one wanting, and that one must be found. He audits the accounts of the day and he says, Every man has not had his due ; some have worked and have not reaped the reward of their labour, and the cry of the labourer has entered into the ears of the Lord of Sabaoth, That is the image of reform, which has displaced the spectre of war We can easily see that figure through all the agitations and sudden movements and violent and even spasmodic and disastrous efforts of the times. We must not construe such events too harshly or too narrowly. Within themselves and within easily given limits they are bad and they are only to be condemned ; but all these upheavals have a history, and we cannot judge of the immediate event except in the atmosphere which is historical. We must know what happened generations ago. There is no event which belongs merely to the passing twenty-four hours: hence the rashness and imperfectness of our judgment. Now this spirit which is in the air from time to time, standing over against doomed cities and doomed institutions, can easily be distinguished if we ask the meaning of the things that are going on round about us. It will not do to shut our ears and say, We hear nothing; to close our eyes and to say, Behold, all is in peace. We must face the spectre; we must look at the image of the time; we must not fear the form which is standing over against a nation, or a continent, or the world. Blessed is he who can fearlessly ask the meaning of that presence and interrogate it as to its purpose. They are short-sighted men who hurry to their own houses, enclose themselves within their own quarters, and say, every fire is as bright as their own, every table is well-laden, and every house is well-cared for. How is it ye cannot discern the signs of the times? Rightly discerning them, you will be patient with many of their features. They are irritating, exasperating; they have about them at first sight an aspect of injustice, and in their assertion there may be more clamour than music; but we must see the reality within the appearance; we must penetrate the environment if we would understand the soul of the age. Now another spirit comes over the times. What is the man like who now holds dominion over the current thought of the age? He has no sword; he has in his hand,—books, written leaves, scrolls; his eyes are deeply set in his head, his head is bent in an attitude of study, perusal, meditation akin to worship. What means that man? He says —I will have all the people well-informed: every child on the face of the earth shall be taught to read and write and think; knowledge is power, knowledge is self-control,—I will not rest until the institution of ignorance is thrown down and the Jericho of superstition is destroyed; the people shall be taught, and when they are taught—well-taught and fully taught—all tyrannies will go down—priestly, social, imperial; and the Son of man shall come—the glorious and complete humanity: the very Christ of God shall be realised in the newly-constructed race. Are there not times when this is perfectly evident? We say, the day is given up to the work of education. That is too short and superficial a way of accounting for things. The spirits do not come and go by some rule of mere whim or fancy. There is a purpose in the ages, a method in the infinite government of things. Now the man has a sword; now he weighs with the balances of the sanctuary; now he cries, Come, and be taught; come, and read and think, and chasten your life by the spirit of knowledge :—how long, ye simple ones, will ye love simplicity, and ye fools hate knowledge? We must accept the spirit of the times, and work according to its inspirations. We cannot double one age over another, or turn the ages backward to catch some ancient spirit; every day has its dawn, its own particular meaning, its own special and definite opportunity; and blessed is he who can read the spectres in the air so as to make out the purpose of their coming and the end of their revelation. Who does not see in our own day another attitude and expression of the same spirit? What is the man doing now? He has no sword, no balance, no book, we can see : they are still within his reach; but now what does he? He weeps: he is in sorrow. He does not shed tears for himself but for others :—" Jesus wept." What spirit is it that rules the age? A spirit of pity, compassion, tenderness; a spirit that has heard the sighing and crying of all earth's weary trouble, and that bends over the suffering creation with infinite compassion. Now every one is trying to alleviate distress, to make homes glad, to bring in the erring and far-straying one. The great question is, What can be done to chase away poverty, to make the sad happy, to dry the tears of sorrow, to plant flowers on the tomb of mortality? " Can ye not discern the signs of the times ?" Why should we attempt to change those signs when they are providential writing, every day having its own duty, and its own vocation, and its own opportunity? Blessed is that servant who can hear the footfall of his Lord's coming, and understand somewhat of the signs of the times, and who is not trying to do something that was quite in place five hundred years ago, but who is answering the call of this very morning with instancy of obedience and with absolute consecration of love. Live in your own day; express the spirit of your own time; be fearless; " Quit you like men."

The right reading of these signs brings us into a sure and blessed consciousness of a spiritual presence. We begin to feel that things are ghostly, rather than material. There is matter enough on which the broad hand can lay itself, and about which there can be no dispute; but the more we put history together into shape and form, and watch it assuming its true colour, the more we begin to say, Surely God is in this history and I knew it not; this is none other than the house of God, and this is the gate of heaven. We have missed the spirit. We have thought things were all living according to some rule of their own, without relation, without responsibility one to the other; we looked upon things as constituting a kind of seething chaos; but the more patient, the more highly chastened we are in mind, the more sober in understanding, and the more fearless, the more do we see that—account for it as we may, or not account for it at all— there is a spirit that rules, and guides, and directs everything. The chariots of God are twenty thousand in number. In what chariot he will come to-morrow, none can tell. It is not for us to say whether this or that chariot is God's. The number baffles us; we cannot read a record of the whole. God will come into his own universe as it pleases him.

When we are in great religious moods, in sublime spiritual ecstasies, in immediate and vital touch with God, we are not afraid to adopt apparently impracticable measures in carrying out the purposes of righteousness and wisdom. What could be more ridiculous, from a purely military point of view, than the directions given for the capture and overthrow of Jericho? They had no relation to the event. On the face of them, from a military point of view, they were absurd:—the carrying an ark around the walls of the city, walking round the city day by day for seven days, blowing a loud blast of trumpets,— and the wall should fall, and the city should surrender! We are quite prepared for the mocker to enjoy himself over such an absurd proposition. But what is absurdity? The foolishness of God is wiser than the wisdom of men. We cannot always judge things by appearances. We ourselves are often startled by the want—apparent, at least—of adaptation of means to ends. Life is carried by surprises; the whole scheme of things is made remarkable by sudden incomings and new interpretations and positions. To describe great historical events as in any measure absurd, is to approach the danger of self-idolatry by exalting personal judgment above the occurrences of ancient or modern times. The religious method may always be called impracticable. It is very slow; it does not seem to work with any immediate effect. What can be duller, slower, than what is generally understood as teaching? Yet it is by teaching that the kingdom of heaven is to be prepared for,—sitting down with men and communicating ideas to them, endeavouring to touch their higher natures, to move their mental springs, to bring their whole mental life into relation to other and unfamiliar truths. It is a very slow method. One gleam from heaven's own midday would startle the world more surely! Why not this sudden outburst of intolerable glory? Because there is no lasting in it, no power of duration and sustenance. Men cannot live upon such visions. Men are so constituted that they can only live upon knowledge, truth, conviction, moral persuasions, ideas that vitalise and ennoble their whole nature. The apostle is said to have spoken of "the foolishness of preaching." That is a sentence very often misunderstood. The apostle was not speaking of the foolishness of preaching as an art and practice, because he was addressing himself to men who valued eloquence above all other gifts; he was speaking of the foolishness of *the thing that was preached*—the foolishness of the Cross : the idea that a dying man was to be king of the universe ; that a slain victim was to sit upon the eternal throne, judging and directing all things in righteousness and love. The apostle represents in his epistle to the Corinthians the very picture which we have in relation to the capture of Jericho. Things that are not, are employed to bring to nought things that are. Foolish things, little things, contemptible things, are used by the hand almighty to shake down towers and walls and temples and capitals, and bring them to nought before the throne of righteousness. Thus religion is not afraid of the impracticable—at least, of what may appear to be impracticable to those who look only upon the surface. Religion has never been afraid to claim prayer as one of its very pillars—the signature of its very power. What can, from the outside, be more futile and ridiculous than to be speaking into the vacant air—to exclude all living things upon

the earth, and to speak to one we have never seen, and pour
our heart's penitence, woe, hope, into an ear we cannot detect
amid all the clouds which float through the heavens ?   Yet religion,
says, "Continue instant in prayer;" you have no other hope;
there is a throne accessible; heed not the voices that mock
you; you cannot pray without being the purer for the prayer;
the words of prayer cleanse the mouth that uses them; the
desire expressed in prayer purges the heart in which it burns,—
"pray without ceasing."   So religious men ought not to be
deterred by apparent impracticableness; by the mocker, who
has but two hands, and wants to use them both in great
impetuosity; by the giber and sneerer, who wants all things
done to-day.   We are content to follow in the wake of Jesus
Christ.   If we had faith as a grain of mustard seed, we would
exercise great sovereignties; we would kill the wolf of hunger
long before he came to our door; we would be full of wealth
within, without a coal in the grate, or a crust in the cupboard;
we would have triumphed over death ere yet we had seen
his ghostly figure.   Besides, processes may be long, and results
may be brought about in startling suddenness.   We have read
of a place not far from the city of New York which was
called Hell's Gate, a dangerous place for navigators,—in fact,
practically an impassable gate.   What was to be done ?   It was
to be attacked with the slowness of wisdom, with the calmness
of science; men must go down into that great rocky region nine
acres in extent; they must pierce the rock, and fill the cavities
with dynamite.   Month by month they must work at that
and come slowly up, and still Hell's Gate defies the navigator.
The year passed, and another year, and still the process goes on.
Science says, Be calm, industrious; the process is very
tedious; we do not wonder that men are weary with waiting;
but continue the work, stroke by stroke, day by day.   Now you
are within a month of closing your labours,—now but one little
week remains,—now to-morrow all you can do in that prepara-
tory direction will be done.   A strange hush falls upon the
interested public.   What is to be the issue ?   See, the rocky
gate still remains; there it abides to mock the scientific engineer;
facts are against him : the rock has been hammered, tunnelled,
pierced, charged with dynamite; but it is still there, and not

a ship dare come near. The scientific engineer knows more than
the ignorant public. He says, I think we are ready now, and
tells his own little girl, far off, to touch a tiny knob and communicate an electric spark according to his directions. The spark
is communicated, and the nine acres of rock, and all the water
floating over them, are heaved two hundred feet into the air in
the twinkling of an eye,—rent, torn, never to be put together
again; and it will require some two years or more to take away
the rent stones. So there is a period of waiting, a period of
preparation, a period of clearing out; but who can tell what
sudden things may occur anywhere—in cities, in states, in doomed
laws? What we are doing now, if we are wise servants of
the King, is to go down morning by morning to our work—
preaching the gospel, teaching the young, standing up in living
testimony for righteousness: and the Lord will suddenly come
to his temple. Blessed is that servant who shall be found
waiting, watching, working. We have nothing to do with the
communication of the electric spark; that is in the hands of
God. Hope on, work on; who can tell when the end may be?
Yet now and again on the road we are blessed with visions
which give us comfort and encouragement. In 1832 the most
celebrated naturalist in the world, our illustrious countryman
Charles Darwin, went round the world in a ship called the *Beagle.*
The diary of that circumnavigation is full of abiding interest.
The great naturalist called at Tierra del Fuego on the South
American coast. His description of the people of that part
of the world is full of horror; he says he never saw such people.
They represented the very lowest type he had ever seen of
humanity. They were savages of the worst degree and quality.
No civilised man dare approach that awful place; the figures
of the people were shocking to behold; their habits were not
to be described in language. The naturalist left them, supposing
them to be beyond the reach of civilisation. This is the testimony,
not of a *missionary*, but of a *naturalist*—a man supposed to be
without religious emotion. One day a little babe was found
lying on the streets of Bristol, in very deed a foundling, without
known father or mother, or friends, a little crying thing in
all the wilderness of life—" Oh, it was pitiful!—near a whole city-
ful, home it had none." The day on which it was found, by
a constable, was St. Thomas's Day; so the infant was called

by the name of the dead Thomas. The child was found in a
place which lay between two bridges of the city, so was
called Thomas Bridges. The little foundling was lodged in
the workhouse, and brought up on the public bounty. Years
came and went, and the boy, now a young man, longed to be
a missionary. He offered his services to the Church Missionary
Society; having special work in that part of the world which we
have just described in the language of Darwin, he went out, not
fearing what might befall him. The gospel is heroic; it has
never been terrified. He went amongst the people, lived
amongst them, heard their curious vocal tones, put them into
shape, created a language for the people, interested them in
these forms which he had traced with his own hand, taught
them to read the forms and understand them,—every day living
in peril of his life. He translated part of the story of the
Saviour's life, and got the people to read it in the Yah-gan tongue.
They read it, understood a little of it, were melted by it, and
they wanted to read still further; and the missionary translated
more of the Blessed Word into the tongue which he may be said
to have created, and the people read, and were subdued and
civilised and christianised; and the facts were brought before
the great English naturalist, and he—honest, fearless soul,
pure and noble in every instinct—instantly subscribed to the
Missionary Society, one of whose agents had wrought, under God,
this stupendous change. The English Admiralty had issued
orders that that part of the coast was not to be approached
by their ships; hearing of the change that had taken place,
the orders were recalled, ships were allowed to go to visit
and to trade there. What wrought that mighty, wondrous
change? Let us be honest; let us be fearless. It was the
Gospel of Christ. Agnosticism did not do it; Secularism did
not do it; Rationalism did not do it: the heroic Cross did it;
Christ did it. It was impracticable as to its mechanical arrangements, laughable, absurd, contemptible; but it was done.

> "Fly abroad, thou mighty gospel,
>   Win and conquer, never cease;
> May thy lasting, wide dominion
>   Multiply and still increase.
>   Sway thy sceptre,
>   Saviour, all the world around."

Amen, amen!

The following is an extract from a graphic account of the destruction of Hell Gate Rock, which appeared in the *New York Times* the day after the explosion :—

Over nine acres of obstructing rock formed the barrier which was yesterday destroyed. Just 21,670 feet of tunnelling, in galleries whose floors lay from 50 to 64 feet below mean low tide, with walls from 10 to 24 feet thick between them, and supported by 467 columns of rock, each 15 feet square, had been charged with cartridges filled with explosives. In an instant the tremendous convulsion of an explosion reaching through those four miles of galleries tore the solid rocks asunder, and hurled them in broken masses into the waters of the river. And when those shattered pieces have been gathered up and taken away by the dredgers, Hell Gate will have lost its dangers, and the wrinkled front of navigation through the Sound will have been smoothed into an inviting smile. Ocean steamers will find 26 feet of good, clear water over the once treacherous bottom, and a new highway will be open for the commerce of the world.

People held their breath. Eyes were strained and riveted on the bare brown rock. There was a death-like silence. No one saw her, but over on the Astoria shore a young girl, the daughter of General Newton, was preparing to free the imprisoned forces. Nine years ago, when but a prattling babe, her tiny finger had performed the same office. Then she could not know what she did. But yesterday what did she think?

Away it flew, that viewless spark, to loose three hundred thousand chained demons buried in darkness and the cold, salt waves under the iron rocks. A deep rumble, then a dull boom, like the smothered bursting of a hundred mighty guns far away beyond the blue horizon, rolled across the yellow river. Up, up, and still up into the frightened air soared a great, ghastly, writhing wall of white and silver and grey. Fifty gigantic geysers, linked together by shivering, twisting masses of spray, soared upward, their shining pinnacles, with dome-like summits, looming like shattered floods of molten silver against the azure sky. Three magnificent monuments of solid water sprang far above the rest of the mass, the most westerly of them still rising after all else had begun to fall, till it towered nearly 200 feet in air. To east and west the waters rose, a long blinding sheet of white. Far and wide the great wall spread, defying the human eye to take in its breadth and height and thickness. The contortion of the wreathed waters was like the dumb agony of some stricken thing.

For a trembling moment the sublime spectacle stood sharp against the sky, like a mighty vision of distant snow-capped mountains. Then down, down, and still down the enormous mass rushed with a wild hissing, as if ten thousand huge steam valves had been opened. The yellow waters of the river were riven and torn into immense boiling masses of white foam. Great waves, ten feet high, rolled outward. Big streaks and spots of deep brown mingled with the white and made ominous shadows under the silver lights. All around the rocks the river swirled and rolled and leaped upward, like the whirlpool of Niagara. A dazzling yellow cloud—the pent-up gases of that subterrene convulsion—spread over the spot. Then it widened and turned to a brilliant green, then to a faint blue, and floated slowly away toward Astoria. Showers of spray fell like summer rain through the air, and returned to the river. The big hoisting apparatus over the shaft had toppled over and lay broken and smashed on its side. It had not risen into the air. Not a stone was seen to go upward. The wall of ghost-like waters was unbroken. And when the spray had sunk down, and the waters of the river, filled with brown mud, lay boiling around the site of the great explosion, there lay the old rock, torn into myriads of pieces and scattered with débris —a ragged, smoking, dun-brown mass. *Troja fuit* (Flood Rock was).

A hundred steam whistles broke into a shriek of triumph, and cheers were heard on every side. Then the oarsmen in the rowboats bowed their backs, and the steamers opened up their valves, and all hands on the water hastened to the scene of the explosion. All around the place the water was turned to a dirty brown by the upheaval of the bottom of the river. The foam was still bubbling, nearly ten minutes after the explosion. Thousands of pieces of wood, mingled with marine weeds and myriads of dead fish, killed by the shock, were floating down into the East River. Wide sheets of feathery scum, such as may be seen along the sea-shore after a gale, were lying on the surface of the water. It was all a dingy brown, tinted with the colour of the riven rock and earth. Among the foam and scum floated quantities of fine, yellowish powder, which looked like sawdust. It was the material of which the covering of the cartridges was made. As more than 75,000 of them had exploded, the quantity of this powder was not surprising.

"The survey," says General John Newton, the engineer, "will occupy two or three weeks, and when that is completed, and the necessary advertisements can be published, the work of removing the broken rock will begin. This will occupy two or three years . . . . and will probably cost $500,000. . . . . The channel is, to all intents and purposes, practically doubled, and, when the rock is removed, will be fully 1200 feet in width, as compared with 600 feet, its present dimensions. New York can get along very well without the removal of the other rocks and reefs in the Hell Gate basin, and, if necessary, a new entrance for ocean steamers is afforded. At certain stages of the tide they can come in through the new channel without any trouble whatever, and with very little trouble at any stage of the tide. The principal difficulty of Hell Gate Channel will hereafter not be on account of its width or depth, but will be due to the crowded nature of the thoroughfare. There will be fully 26 feet of water, and, when all the débris is removed, probably more."

I reprint this account because of its suggestiveness in many spiritual directions.

PRAYER.

ALMIGHTY GOD, we would do everything according to thy will. Do thou settle everything for us, and simply entrust us with thy commandment. Not our will, but thine, be done. We would have no concern except with the dignity and sacredness of thy purpose, our hearts' desire being that thy will should be done on earth as it is done in heaven. To this end do thou grant unto us daily the comforting ministry of thy Holy Spirit, that the spirit of disobedience may be cast out of us, and the spirit of loyalty may be established within us. Without thee we can do nothing; without thy Spirit we are blind, selfish, utterly ignorant, as well as helpless. We therefore cast ourselves upon God, and would be God's chosen servants, instruments in his hands, vessels to be used as he may direct or wish. This is the Lord's doing, and it is marvellous in our eyes. Whilst we were perverse and self-willed, we knew not what was right and what was best, and would listen to no voice, but would repel every advancing teacher. Now we have returned to the Shepherd and Bishop of our souls; we have seen our folly; we mourn our sin; we would now, through Jesus Christ, the Priest of the everlasting Covenant, be made one with the living God. We come always by the Cross of Christ; there we find the loving, compassionate, forgiving God; there we find law satisfied, righteousness exalted, compassion made possible, and pardon offered to the sons of guilt. Hear us, then, as we pray for more light, more truth, for deeper peace, for a sweeter consent to all the will of God. May we be enabled to say, by day and by night, in summer and in winter, on the birthday and the day of death, It is well, it is best, for God's holy will is done. Dry the tears of our sorrow, comfort us in our unspoken distresses, enter into our hearts and see what is wrong there, and if there be in us any wicked way, cast it out and make our hearts beautiful as thine own temples, holy as thine own sanctuaries. Direct us amid all perplexity, show us what is right, wise, just, and good; keep down within us all evil temper, all rebelliousness, all self-will; fill us with the spirit of charity, which is the Spirit of Christ, and under its blessed inspiration may we do our day's work and await the issue of the toil. Amen.

Joshua vi.

DISCIPLINE.

WE have seen how, from a certain point of view, all the arrangements made for the capture of the walled city were obviously impracticable—from a military point of view, simply absurd. We are now prepared to advance a step, and look at one or two of the almost hidden points of the narrative with a view to its illumination from incidental lights and references. Our object will be to find out how far these points are confirmed by our own experience and observation, how far they commend themselves as probably historical to our religious consciousness. The subject before us may well be described as the subject of Discipline. The men were held in severe check. The laws laid down for their marching and general conduct were laws marked by great rigour. Let us inquire whether those laws were merely arbitrary, expressing the will of one man, and limited as to their action to one locality or to one event. If we find that they were simply arbitrary, thus local, and thus limited, they can have no deep moral concern for us; if we find that they were not arbitrary, but were part of the gracious necessity of things, we may read another lesson on that sublime doctrine the continuity of man, the oneness of God, the infiniteness and unchangeableness of law.

Was it not of the nature of discipline that the men were to have arms, and yet were not to use them? Was not that a great lesson in the most difficult of all arts—the art of self-control? That the men were armed is clear from the ninth verse, which opens with the words, " And the armed men went before the priests." Yet no arm was to be used. Had the men been without arms, they would not have felt the pressure of the discipline. Is it not a continual lesson in life that, having certain things capable of executing immediate effects, we are yet to let them fall as it were by our side, and to look in other directions, and to adopt other methods in view of deliverance and victory? It is hard to have the weapon, to see the thing that is to be done, and to know that the proposed thing could be done by the use of the weapon, and yet to allow it to remain in disuse. This is part of the continual discipline of life; this is what we are all called upon to do to-day. We do not use all our faculties; sometimes we have almost to strip ourselves of our distinctive faculties, or to let them lie in disuse, and to be doing everything by doing nothing. This is part of a deeply-planned scheme of education. The government that

has established this law in the great school of human culture
moves in wide ranges, is apparently not careful about immediate
effects, has contemplated the acquisition of issues upon a scheme
and upon lines which transcend the impatient imagination of
man. To see the stone which could be thrown at the enemy,
and to know that our right hand has the power and skill to
throw that stone, yet to walk past it, as if it were not discerned,
is a lesson worth learning. To know that it lies easily within
your power to blast an opponent with satire or bitterness which
he could not endure, and yet to treat him with all courtesy and
deference, is no small attainment in Christian education. To
have the power, and yet not to use it—that is how we stand in
the school of Christ. This is how Jes s Christ himself conducted his own life in the sight of men. He did not use all
his faculties; he did not call into requisition all his resources;
he was quiet when he might have been restless, calm when he
might have excited a tumult which would have had all the effect
of an unexpected and irresistible storm. When one offered to
defend him, he said, Nay, not thus; thou dost not understand
the spirit of the kingdom; thinkest thou that I could not now pray
unto my Father, and he would send twelve legions of angels,
which would look all these petty enemies into dismay? We
must not use all our resources. We have the strength, but do
not resort to the tyranny of using it. Some things are to be
accomplished by submission, patience, meekness; knowing the
righteousness of the cause, we await the issue with imperturbable
calm. But what a lesson this is to those who are impatient!
We want things done at once, and when asked as to the prac-
ticability of their accomplishment, we point to arms, and weapons,
and stones, and faculties, and say, Why not put all these things
instantaneously into action, and the issue is a matter of easy
calculation? We admit all this with regard to military arrangements; and, so far as the proposition is kept within what may
be termed abstract limits, we have no hesitation whatever in
adopting it in some measure; but it is a proposition which touches
every life. To be armed, and yet to be peaceful; to have
weapons, and not to use them; to stand with a hand upon a gun,
one discharge of which might shatter the walls of the enemy,
and yet to fall down before that gun as if it were a sacred

altar, and there wait with bowed head and clasped hands the revelation of the divine will—that is religion. Anything short of that is vanity, self-will, impatience ; the kind of thing which is valued by men who mistake the bubble for the river, the thunder for the lightning. Life without discipline is life without dignity.

Was it not, further, of the nature of discipline for the men to be in the midst of plenty, and yet not to touch it ? Verses 18, 19 are very clear upon this point :—

"And ye, in any wise keep yourselves from the accursed thing, lest ye make yourselves accursed, when ye take of the accursed thing, and make the camp of Israel a curse, and trouble it. But all the silver, and gold, and vessels of brass and iron, are consecrated unto the Lord : they shall come into the treasury of the Lord."

This is the continual difficulty of life. To walk past bread that we could eat, and that we feel we need, and yet to say, We must not touch it, is a lesson not learned easily. Are we not all exposed to this very trial ? Things we want lie so near. But a pane of glass between the needy man and the thing which is coveted ! *Mine* and *thine* touch one another ; which is mine ?—which is thine ? To keep men back from things which they could so easily use and so naturally appropriate, and to remain in comparative poverty in the very midst of abundance, is not easy. It cannot be a pleasant thing for the man who has not one foot of soil to be passing over acres to which he can lay no claim, and to be begging a brother of the earth to " give him leave to toil," and for that brother to dismiss his petition with a sneer. It is at this point that our quality is tested. When we do not want the things, it is no trouble to let them alone ; but when they are round about us, urging themselves upon us, and are almost clamorous in their appeal that we should appropriate them ; to stand in their presence as with folded arms, and look upon them, not with contempt, but with a judgment that values them, yet with a conscience that will not appropriate them, is an attainment in religious manhood which we must not expect to secure without long training. This is part of the mystery of Providence. It enters into the whole history of human life. The person next door to you has all you want—but he *is* next door ; and a deal partition an inch thick is an infinite separation where morality is concerned. What relates to property, relates to pleasure, enjoyment, gratification,—everything. When soldiers enter the city, and have the whole place at their command, and yet behave themselves like honest men, they are greater soldiers in their abstinence than they were in their successful assault. Here it is that character discovers its quality. We are in reality what we are in critical circumstances. It is the exceptional hour that is the key to the lifetime. "Let him that thinketh he standeth take heed lest he fall." We may be good in ninety-nine points in the hundred, but it is the hundredth point that tests the quality of the whole man. Herein we should be gracious and charitable in mutual judgment. Men "compound for sins they are inclined to, by damning things they have no mind to," we know well. It is easy religion ; it is a game that needs no learning : the small skill of it seems to be born with us. When we see men falling before great temptations, we should sometimes reflect that they would not be temptations to us, and that therefore our virtue in their presence adds but another layer to the thick hypocrisy under which we conceal our real character. It may be better in some circumstances to be poor than to be rich ; the wealth may be with poverty, and the poverty may be with wealth. There is a law of "Touch not, taste not, handle not," and in the not doing of some things, we do other things most worthily. Nor must any man take comfort from this. Who can boast that he does not care about things that partake of the nature of property and dignity, ease and honour ? The careless man has no right to any comfort derived from this doctrine, but the man who is pressed by the fiend of covetousness, the man who is poisoned by the virus of that bite, the man who says in his soul, "I want it : I am almost afraid to be in its presence for fear I should seize it ; God keep my fingers off it ! God pity me ! God save me !"—is the man who in his weakness is really strong ; he has right to this comfort ; abstention in his case is positive virtue ; not to do, is to do. May God comfort him, and beat back the pursuing fiend, and give his child rest from torment !

Is it not in the nature of discipline to be in great excitement, and yet not to express it ? Read verse 10 :—

"And Joshua had commanded the people, saying, Ye shall not shout, nor make any noise with your voice, neither shall any word proceed out of your mouth, until the day I bid you shout ; then shall ye shout."

The instruction seems easy. Obedience under such circumstances
would be most difficult. Who can keep down excitement—
honest and honourable excitement? Who can say to his very
voice, Be still? To shout under such circumstances as are
described in the text is natural. We must not drag nature into
the witness-box to testify for us when we are committing outrages
upon her. People suppose that if a thing is natural, it is proper.
It is proper under some circumstances, but we must have critical
regard to those circumstances, because even nature may be
outraged. Inborn instincts may be profaned, and the very voice
of God within the soul may be mistaken, or have its touch
perverted. Progress is kept back by shouting men. The whole
kingdom of heaven is hindered in some instances because people
will not hold their tongues. They are people who see a little
part of a case, and rush out into the war as if they were
fully-equipped soldiers; they are excitable, vehement, quick;
they call themselves sensitive, but they are extremely disagree-
able and hindersome. Silence in the midst of great crises is
simply invaluable, and there is a silence which is often misunderstood and attributed to timidity. People will say to public men,
Why do you not speak on such and such subjects? The persons
making the inquiry would speak! Of that we have no doubt!
There is a time for silence. Then there is a speaking which
really expresses silence. That may appear to be paradoxical,
but we know it to be true. A man has spoken an hour, and
yet he has in that one hour only shown how much more he
could have said but for self-control, for regard of broader, deeper
interests than are apparent to many who look on. We cannot
have two captains in the army. There can only be one leader,
if the discipline is to be complete, if the organisation is to move
with the effect and precision of one soul. God knows when his
children should shout, speak, pray, work; the distribution of
parts, functions, duties, is with God. The one thing every
Christian man has to do, is to say, Lord, I am in thine hands:
make me a hewer of wood, drawer of water, captain, lowest man
in the whole army; I have no voice in the matter, no wish; thy
will, my God, thy will be done.

Here we clearly see that much detail must go before great
results. The men must go out one day, and another day, and

even to six days, and on the seventh day rising early, " about the dawning of the day." Their impatience seems to betray itself a little. Things cannot go beyond the " seventh " day. There is no mention made of an eighth day. " Three days "—there may be a resurrection : " seven days "—Sabbath ! Now the " seventh day " has come, and some very early risers are abroad. There is a faint whitening in the far east : the full day is coming :—

"And it came to pass on the seventh day, that they rose early about the dawning of the day, and compassed the city after the same manner seven times : only on that day they compassed the city seven times. And it came to pass at the seventh time, when the priests blew with the trumpets, Joshua said unto the people, Shout ; for the Lord hath given you the city " (vv. 15, 16).

The order came and could not be mistaken. A soldier's blood was in its sacred fury. The critical moment had come, and Jericho must fall. So it shall be with all corruptions, all doomed institutions, all unholy adventures and enterprises, all causes that may have been useful in their day, but whose day is at an end : there must be walking round about them by armed men who will not use their weapons ; there may be great excitement, but the very greatness of it necessitates its repression ; there may be great loot and bounty, and much that might be appropriated, but it must be left for divine appropriation or divine distribution. It is not for us to take this work out of the Lord's hand. Be patient in the detail. It seems a long time since we began going round this awful hell. It seems to be encroaching upon us, rather than we seem to be encroaching upon its heat. Travel on ! It is the fifth day ; to-morrow is the sixth day ; the day after is the seventh day. " The Lord shall suddenly come to his temple." " I beheld Satan as lightning fall from heaven." How quickly he falls ! How useless is arithmetic in the computation of that velocity ! What we have to do, is to hold on in prayer, keep to duty, and be Christ-like. As for the violent man : Put up thy sword into its sheath ; we do not want such rude assistance as thine. As for those who are in great excitement, appear not unto men to fast ; hide your turbulence in your heart ; be cool in the very midst of tremendous excitement of soul ; anoint thine head and wash thy face, that thou appear not unto men to be excited. Let it be a religious excitement, a chastened excitement, an excitement

not inspired by selfishness or the realisation of individual imagi-
nations and proposals, but sweet, yet glowing, acquiescence in
the divine will, the infinite purpose that broods over the ages
and makes them in the end what it will.   As for those who are
longing for plunder, and booty, and prize : Seek first the kingdom
of God and his righteousness, and forsake the contemplated spoil.
Better be righteous than be rich ; better be morally noble than
surrounded by things which were confiscated, and which you
never worked for.   But who can do the will of Christ ?   Who
can put up his sword into its sheath ?   Who can refrain from
appearing unto men to fast when the hunger is biting the very
soul ?   Who can seek first the invisible, the impalpable, the
infinite, when things concrete are lying close at hand ?   " Who is
sufficient for these things ? "   This man,—namely, who has the
Spirit of Christ.   Only he who has the Spirit of Christ can do the
will of Christ.   Such a man is called to the miracle of having
arms, and yet not using them ; of being in the midst of plenty,
and yet not touching it; of being under intolerable excitement,
and yet not expressing it.   He has the Spirit of Christ who
puts his sword into its sheath, saying, This is not a battle of
steel ; this is not a question of one sword against another ; it is a
question of eternal decree, divine righteousness, ineffable morality ;
it must be left to the decision of God.   Blessed be Heaven, a
" seventh day " is promised !   It will not all be walking, waiting,
toiling, suffering—only for a little while, quite a little space of
time ; it will appear to be as nothing when it is all over, and the
kingdom of God has come in all its white radiance and glowing
summer.   We shall forget the night in the joy of the morning,
the cold seed-time in the joy of the harvest.   Blessed Messiah,
thou shalt reign !   Thou shalt have the heathen for an inheritance
and the uttermost parts of the earth for a possession ; kings shall
bow down before thee, and gold and incense bring.   In our
impatience we say, Even so, Lord Jesus, come quickly.   Forgive
the word *quickly !*   We have no ill-meaning in it ; it expresses
our impatience : we pray that our impatience may never be used
as a weapon with which to attack the solidity of thy throne and
the beneficence of thy purpose.

PRAYER.

WE have come to hear thy voice, O thou Saviour of the world! Thou art full of compassion. We live upon thy mercy, and therefore we are the witnesses of thy love. Jesus wept! Thou hast sanctified the tears of sorrow, and made sorrow itself a piety by thy shedding of sympathetic tears. Thou art always compassionating us. Thou dost not burn with anger against human weakness or human want; thou dost burn with anger only against human sin; and dost thou not treat human sin as it was never treated before? Dost thou not go far back into things, and show us darkness centuries old, and wickedness nearly as old as time? And dost thou not trace the progress of evil, and point out to us somewhat of the mystery of guilt? We are not individuals; we are links in a long chain. No man liveth unto himself; no man is himself alone: he is his father and his mother; he is in one life all the lives that went before him. Herein is mystery; herein is sorrow; herein is sin manifold and aggravated. We know not what to say. We ourselves are double men: when we do good, evil is present with us; the spirit says yes to God, and the flesh says no. Sometimes we wonder which answer will be uppermost at the last! The Lord help us, sending us strength daily from his sanctuary, and comforting us as he alone can comfort the struggling and weary sons of men. We bless thee for the ends we see, as well as for the beginnings we enjoy. We should be killed by an infinite monotony; but thou hast made the morning a beginning and the night a close, and by this symbol thou hast marked off all time and all the ways of men, so that no man knoweth even the day of his birth or the day of his death: he can but say, Born—died; and between these two points, what tumult urges itself, what sin defiles the little space, what prayer seeks to redeem it, and what divine love seeks to turn it into spiritual fruitfulness! Behold, we find ourselves pressed upon by mysteries, mocked by spectres, pursued by enemies; and yet, amid all this uproar and assault, we find the altar, the revelation of heaven, the Son of God, the Cross of Christ. Help us to be patient, careful, reverent; keep us steadfast in all holy faith, and may we cling to that which is good, that, having such in our hands, the rest will come, or such revelations will be granted as will cheer the desponding life. Thou hast appointed men to places as thou wilt; so far, all is good, for thou knowest what space each spirit wants, and what room each life can take up. But some men have appointed themselves to their own places, and brought disorder into the great social poem. Thou dost not crush their self-will and greed by violence, thou dost rather train men by long processes, showing light in new directions, sending deliverers from unexpected quarters, so that shepherds become captains, and mean men lead the army, and those who were not known stand up in the infinite fame of manhood. We will put everything into tl ine hands; we will do nothing of ourselves; we will await the voice within, the light of the soul, the face at heaven's window beckoning us to further progress and service. We will talk of our sins to ourselves, and we only name them to thee that they may be destroyed in the confession : for Jesus Christ hath tasted death for every man. Help us to seize the truth as it is in Christ; give us clearness of vision to see horizons and not the arbitrary boundaries set up by men ; give us a clear view into heaven's own blue arch, lest we mistake the roofs built by human hands for the heavens of God. The Lord grant unto us the quietness of heart which is essential to true education, the comfort of soul which enables the spirit to seize the prizes of God ; and thus may we grow in grace and in the knowledge of our Lord Jesus Christ, and without knowing it of ourselves, as a merit due to ourselves, may we come into a great estate of wisdom and power. Be with all our loved ones who cannot be with us in the public sanctuary; they are with us in sympathy, in eager wonder as to what we are doing; they think they know the time of the song and of the prayer, of the sweet reading and the speech to the minds and souls of men; and they accompany us along the living line ; the Lord give them comfort in solitude, hope in darkness, and a healing of soul in the time of bodily frailty. The Lord look upon the little child as if there were but one in all the universe, and so pet him with infinite love as to make him strong and wise. The Lord save young life from those who would devour it; the Lord save it from the jaws of hell. Help us to esteem one another very highly in love for Christ's sake—to live in confidence and affection, and in such union as will make the weakest feel that he enjoys the protection of the whole. God be merciful unto us, and bless us, and cause his face to shine upon us; and in the shining of that look we shall forget the sun. Amen

Joshua vii.

HINDERED BY SIN.

AS a matter of fact, there are unexplained checks in human progress. We wonder why we do not advance more surely and quickly. Mystery comes upon us in great clouds. Every appointment is right, the direction unquestionably true, and all the conditions seem to be as they ought to be ; but somehow there is an invisible wall through which we cannot pass, and over which we cannot climb : so progress comes to a standstill. Men are troubled, and can give no reason for their sorrow; they feel that they ought to be advancing, and yet progress is impossible. It is so in business. For months together the business goes swingingly; customers throng the threshold; everything that is done bears upon it the sign of prosperity. It was so easily done, that business became a kind

of play. Suddenly there is a dead stop in the machine. How
is it to be accounted for? It cannot be accounted for at first
sight. What a wonderful change has taken place!—everything
has fallen off. The sun used to blister the windows with light,
and now for days together not a gleam is seen. It is so in
social honour. Men used to be able to go up and down social
lines amid applause, and cordial recognition, and every symptom
of genuine friendliness. What a change has taken place! Men
look coldly; the very exchange of civilities is sobered down
to the lowest possible point. No open fault can be found
with anything, but still there is the fact that a change of
social atmosphere has taken place; the climate is by no means
so warm as it used to be; and men who had but a step to
take to the very throne are unable to move a limb in the
direction indicated by their ambition. It is also the same even
in lawful enterprise. The business is morally sound, thoroughly
respectable, honourable, useful; and yet it brings in no return:
the principal is disheartened, the followers are all cowed, the
whole organisation is out of gear and will not respond to the
friendliest touch; the enterprise is practically dead. These are
not matters of ancient history; they are matters of modern
and immediate experience.

Such checks bring divine providence under criticism and
suspicion. Even Joshua, hearing of the defeat of his people,
"rent his clothes, and fell to the earth upon his face before
the ark of the Lord until the eventide, he and the elders of
Israel, and put dust upon their heads," and complained heavily
against God (verses 6-9). This is an easy refuge for men.
Providence has had to sustain many a slander. It seems the
handiest of all things to blame the mysteriousness of the divine
way. Who ever says, "The fault must be within the house
itself; let every man in the house be examined, right away
down to the youngest child in the whole home; somebody is
to blame for this mystery—who is it? By inquiry, or by lot,
or by some exhaustive process, let us find out the criminal and
exculpate eternal Providence"? But it is easier to sit down
under the supposedly comforting doctrine that all this is meant
for our good; it is chastisement; it is part of the mysterious
process of human education; it is God who arbitrarily says to

gold, Do not enter that house; to friends, Do not be so cordial to-day as you were yesterday; to lawful enterprise, Sit down, and terminate your progress disappointingly. That would be religious, if it were true; but whatever truth there may be in the mysteriousness of the divine action—and undoubtedly there is truth in it—we must not imagine that we ourselves are poor, innocent, guileless creatures who have done nothing to deserve the cloud or the famine. At the same time it must be remembered that the sufferer himself may not be personally guilty. Certainly Joshua was no criminal in this case; yet Joshua suffered more than any other man. *Here* we may find the mysteriousness of the divine action. Joshua had a larger capacity for suffering; he was spiritually sensitive, he was intimately allied with God, he felt as if he were representing the divinity of heaven to the heathen nations of his time; and that which others might hardly feel, would penetrate to his very soul, and throw a shadow upon the altar of his life. We suffer indirectly, yet not always so indirectly as we suppose. What is "indirectness" in this matter of suffering? Who can occupy an indirect relation to the human race? Again and again we are taught how true it is that we are one. Humanity is not a concourse of individual atoms; there is a solidarity of humanity—a holy and indissoluble unity: whether one member suffer, all the members suffer with it. This is the doctrine which has yet to be realised on the largest possible scale; and not until this doctrine is recognised shall we have the great problem of social inequality and hostility, struggle and suffering, permanently adjusted and determined. Human nature was never intended by its Creator to represent a battle as between the strong and the weak; humanity was meant to be a great commonwealth, a great family, a whole commune—not in some vulgar and debasing or selfish sense which may have been conceived here and there, but on a scale and according to an inspiration truly and eternally divine. The leader was hindered by the follower; in other words, Joshua was kept back by Achan—a man whose name had to be sought out; reference had to be made to the register to find who the man was, and not until after considerable searching was it found that he was " Achan, the son of Carmi, the son of Zabdi, the

son of Zerah, of the tribe of Judah." Our hindrances are often
in obscurity, among the shadows of the hardly-remembered
past. In every sense is this true. Many an appetite for
which we are blamed was set burning within us by a man
who has been dead five hundred years. We must view this
whole subject therefore in high light and within broad spaces.
Christ is hindered by his followers. The Son of God is kept
back by some criminal unknown to fame. That criminal mis-
represents Christ, travesties the holy character, plays impiously
with the ineffable morality; and thus Christ in the very heavens
is kept out of his throne by men who have no name, by obscure
Achans, by sinners who within their own circle are exposing the
Saviour to continual shame.

What, then, was to be done? Divine partiality was to be
shown. Here comes a great problem in theology, What direction
does the partiality of God always take? The doctrine is that
the partiality of God is not for persons, but for character.
"Therefore," reads the twelfth verse, which sums up the logic
of the divine argument :—

"Therefore the children of Israel could not stand before their enemies,
but turned their backs before their enemies, because they were accursed:
neither will I be with you any more, except ye destroy the accursed from
among you."

This is righteous partiality. We must universally approve it.
We are not affronted by this partiality as if it were arbitrary—the
mere action of spiritual taste directed to a discrimination of
persons on account of some incidental feature or hue of colour.
The universe, hearing this judgment, must say, Content. This is
necessary partiality, as well as righteous. The necessity comes
out of the nature of God : the holy One will not identify himself
with unholy people and unholy purposes. This is not an action
of mere virtue, as it is socially understood and limited; it is the
very necessity of God : he cannot touch "the accursed thing;"
he cannot smile upon fraud; he will not even audit the books
which are written by a thievish hand; he will only burn them
with unquenchable fire. Having confidence in God, we are at
peace. The army does not move because of human inspiration
or military ambition : the army moves because God reigns, and
God knows every soldier and the action of the whole army, and

from the heavens he troubles the earth when anything occurs that offends his purity. O, thou little, sin-loving earth! God's eye is upon thee, and he will pain thee, and vex thee, and hinder thee, until exasperation becomes agony, unless thou repent and forsake thy sins.

A new light is thus thrown upon sovereignty and God's elective laws. God elects righteousness, pureness, simplicity, nobleness. He will forsake Israel, if Israel forsake him. He will tear the covenant into pieces, and put the rags of it into heathen hands, that pagans may laugh at Israel dispossessed, rather than associate himself with a mere name, or carry out any covenant that is supposed to be conventionally binding. There is nothing binding upon God but character. Love God, and all the rest will follow; and by "the rest," we mean beauty of character, sweetness of soul, nobleness of conduct. The Lord gives the reason why we are stopped. We must go to Heaven to find out why we are not making more money, more progress, more solidity of position. We must ask heaven to explain how it is that it is not with us as it used to be in the olden time—the sweet, bright days of old, when roses sprang up in our footprints, and when rivers of water refreshed the desert; days when, before we began to pray in words, we had the answer stored in our hearts; brave days of old, memorable days of the Son of man upon the earth—Sabbath days. So rigid inquiry must be made into the cause or origin of failure.

Joshua, accepting the divine direction, arranged for this inquiry :—

"In the morning therefore ye shall be brought according to your tribes : [in the morning of scrutiny, that long-delayed day, to-morrow morning] and it shall be, that the tribe which the Lord taketh shall come according to the families thereof ; and the family which the Lord shall take shall come by households; and the household which the Lord shall take shall come man by man" (v. 14).

We must not attempt to teach the Lord how to scrutinise. All our examinations and inquests are modelled upon divine lines. There can be no escape. Whilst the whole tribe is in judgment, we may hope not to be detected ; whilst the household is all there, we may think one will be nothing in a multitude : but when it comes to a question of "man by man," the quarters are very close, and the result is inevitable. Why should we not anticipate the divine judgment by a sober and faithful judgment of our own? We can begin the scrutiny. We can write out a list of questions by which to cross-examine ourselves. Our eloquence would be punctuated by many an accusation. The questions would become spears; the words would be sharp as darts that strike through the liver. Have I broken a vow? My arm, once so strong, can hardly extend itself so as to allow its shadow to be thrown. Why? I have not violated any laws of health, yet my very muscle is flaccid and the bones are melted. Have I broken a vow? Let me read the past. I will remind myself of myself. Have all the lines been carried out? Who can stand before the burning question? Dare I then lift a face of simulated innocence to heaven and say, This is thy rod, this is thy chastisement, this is thy doing, O God of the universe, and I must bear thy discipline as best thy grace may sustain me? That would be hypocrisy. Better keep to the truth known by the consciousness within. Have I kept back part of the price? It is so hard to give the whole,—can I not be let off by giving, say, most of what I sold the land for? To a certain extent I may, if I say it is only so much and only a large proportion. But have I not given it as if I were giving it all? If so, I must not turn eyes to heaven that counterfeit the aspect of injured innocence or delayed and affrighted righteousness. The money that I have kept back will burn my hand, and the seething of the blood shall be heard as an accusation against me. "When thou vowest a vow unto the Lord, defer not to pay it." Have I fallen before a lower motive? Once the motive approached purity: the thought was good, the intention was healthy; there was a genuineness about the whole action of the soul that almost challenged scrutiny and criticism. Has the motive changed? If the spiritual motive has changed, the spiritual ambition has gone down along with it, and the whole quality of the life-work partakes of the deterioration. When a man searches himself with questions in this way, he renders unnecessary the formal judgment of God, as if that judgment were required to dissolve a mystery. Let a man examine himself. Let every one be unsparing with his own life. When a man tells lies to himself, he cannot speak the truth to anybody else. There must be scrutiny and there must be penalty.

Achan was detected. Achan told the tale of fraud, and Joshua executed the judgment of Heaven. In those days the law maintained its sovereignty. Joshua himself would have been ground to pieces by it as certainly as the obscurest man in all the host. " God spared not the angels that sinned." He would grind the stars to powder, were they conscious, and did they sin against his throne. Not a planet but God can spare, if the planet has stained the universe. Do not imagine that men are held up because they are great, distinguished, sons of the morning, and have high social stewardship to maintain and justify. Be the man who he may, he goes down before the divine judgment. Achan, the son of Zerah, was taken, "and the silver, and the garment, and the wedge of gold, and his sons, and his daughters, and his oxen, and his asses, and his sheep, and his tent, and all that he had," and judgment fell upon him : " all Israel stoned him with stones, and burned them with fire . . . and they raised over him a great heap of stones unto this day " (vv. 24-26). There is no heap big enough to hide the hinderer of the kingdom of heaven. It is a fearful thing to fall into the hands of the living God ! Sin is not to be apologised for, excused, compromised, allowed for; it must be extirpated, dragged out—every root and fibre ; and not until that eradication has been completed can the kingdom go on, fair as the heavenly lights and terrible as a bannered arn y.

PRAYER.

ALMIGHTY GOD, thou hast set the day and the night closely together; the summer and the winter follow quickly. Behold, thou art always teaching us by things which differ from one another, so that by their contrast we may be brought to thoughtfulness and religious wonder. Life and death seem to go hand in hand: the tomb is in the garden. We are shocked by these conjunctions; we do not understand these contrasts: but thou wilt give unto us wisdom: then we shall see all their meaning and be thankful for their instruction, and shall be the better for looking into things contrary to all beauty and light and loveliness. What must thine own eyes behold! We ourselves see things so contrary to one another; yet we see hardly anything: what we look at is a transient vision. We do not know what thou seest, thou who knowest where the chamber of imagery is, thou who seest all heaven and all hell. Enable us to know that, notwithstanding these things, there is but one throne, one Lord, one Eternal Sovereign, righteous, wise, full of compassion, accepting the death of the Cross, rising to the throne of the universe. May we fix our minds upon these ultimate truths, which yet are first truths, embracing all other truths and making life noble even to sublimity. Reign thou whose right it is! reign, O Christ, until thine enemies are made thy footstool! Thou shalt have the heathen for thine inheritance and the uttermost parts of the earth for thy possession. We long to behold the light of that glad day. Others have been yearning to see it. If thou hast inflicted disappointment upon the generations, it is because thou seest what they could not behold, and understandest what was beyond their comprehension. We leave everything in thy hands: thou knowest what is right and best; thou dost keep the time of the universe; thou wilt come in thine own way and at thine own hour, and when we see thy coming and know thy presence, we shall bless thee even for the delay. Let thy mercy multiply itself towards us: let it be tender mercy; let thy kindness be loving kindness, so that it may not press upon us unduly, but may have sympathy with us, and patience with us, the very mercy of mercy, the very kindness of kindness. Amid all visions show us the blessed Cross of Christ, full of deepest meaning, pregnant with infinite love, the very door of pardon and of heaven. Amen.

Joshua vii.

CURIOUS CONJUNCTIONS.

A PART from the main course of this narrative, there are some conjunctions of names which are full of interest, and full also of spiritual instruction and comfort. We have to go in search of some beautiful things : they do not always lie upon the broad and open surface. The loveliest parts of a country are not always seen by travellers who keep on the highway : they lie apart, they have to be sought for ; there are little dells, waterfalls, tarns, and natural gardens which only the pedestrian can see, and he only as the result of patient inquiry. It is so with the Scriptures. Almost every verse has its hidden jewel. We read perhaps too rapidly, or we have come under the mischievous operation of a familiarity which supposes it knows all about the Bible. "All about the Bible" it is impossible for any finite intellect to know. The deepest and most continuous readers of the holy record rise from their last perusal to assure us that they have hardly begun to spell out the initial meaning of God's written revelation.

What conjunction, then, strikes us first in reading this exciting narrative ? There is a remarkable one in the second verse : —"Joshua sent men from Jericho to Ai"—where is that ?— "which is beside Beth-aven, on the east side of Bethel." The striking conjunction is in these two names—"Beth-aven" and "Bethel." For a long time they were supposed to be different names of the same place, but the latest and highest authorities have determined them to be two distinct places. Coming before us in these strange syllables, many may not be able to see the contrast or feel its force. "Beth-aven" means, "house of vanity," "house of idols ; " "Bethel" means, "house of God." Now read :—"Ai, which is beside Beth-aven, the house of vanity, on the east side of Bethel, the house of God." So we find it all through life. Contrarieties face us every day, and make us wonder why they should be. It is possible to draw two totally different pictures of society, each of which shall be exactly done, and neither of which shall represent the reality of the whole case. There are people so constituted that they can see but in one direction : they can see only that which is good ; they multiply the sanctuary into a church which covers the whole earth, and they say, The millennium has come, if not in its fulness of splendour, yet in a dawn about which there can be no mistake ; they listen to the reports of gracious charity ; they hear the song of the worshipping multitude ; they see what is being done on the right hand and on the left—all of which is good, beneficent, beautiful; and they say, looking at these things alone, This is the Sabbath of the world, the great rest-period of time; now is the day of God's salvation. There are others who can see only the darkness, the misery, the sin, and the sorrow—the fatal wound; and they say, Churches have failed, ministries have come to nothing, evangels have sounded their silver trumpets and delivered their sweet messages, and all their sounding has died upon the air and nothing is left but emptiness. Neither of these statements, taken as a whole statement, is correct; we must put them together if we would really understand the exact position of the world. But there are people who will not look upon Beth-aven—the house of vanity, the house of idols. They are singularly constituted—at least, in the sense that they will not look upon evil or believe in its existence. When evil is described, they follow the description with the criticism that it is an exaggeration. They are hopeful, buoyant, generous themselves, and most pure, and therefore they will not believe in the so-called revelations of the perdition of modern civilisation. There are others who will only look upon that side. The point to be kept in view is that there *are* two sides, and they must both be looked at fearlessly in a spirit of righteousness, with an intention to ascertain the truth, abide by righteous consequences, and make life-long reparation for life-long unrighteousness. The timid people who will not look upon Beth-aven are often most exasperating. Nothing can persuade them to look into certain cases: they prefer not to be shocked; they pass Beth-aven in haste, and speed to the house of God. We recognise their goodness in a measure, and the sweetness of their disposition generally, but we must not take the key-note of progress and administration from people who are oppressed with such timidity. Beth-aven exists in every age, in every civilised land; it stands next door to the house of God, and we must face the fact and all its consequences. Enter into what city we may, there is the house of wealth, and there is the hovel of poverty just behind. The city has its great thoroughfares aflare with gas, brilliant with decoration, astir with all the signs of modern activity and progress; but, alas! the city has its back streets, its out-of-the-way places;—some of us dare not go through such portions of the city,—what wonder if we only see thoroughfare life; and say,

Behold the signs of wealth, and splendour, and power; this is the culmination of civilising influence? Who reflects that there are quarters in every metropolis in Europe into which decency dare not enter, and purity itself, except associated with the highest moral strength, shudders to think of? We find also in this city the house of piety and the house of profanity. How we deprive ourselves of many a stimulus to fuller labour by concealing from ourselves that there is a house of profanity! We do not destroy the house by ignoring it. We bless God that there are some brave spirits who do not ignore the existence of the house of profanity, but who go boldly up to it, and ask to walk through it, and leave a message to its owner, and ask its inhabitants to discuss great questions and submit themselves to the influence of new atmospheres. These are the apostles of the time—the brave pioneers of heaven's own King; they should be supported, honoured, and sustained by persons who have not their moral nerve or their spiritual dauntlessness. All this we may admit and yet forget that Beth-aven and Bethel are in the same man. Every man would seem to be two men. What contrasts there are in our own personal character! On one side how generous, noble, trustful, philanthropic; almost grand to a heroic point in our impulses and propositions and activities; and yet presently we come upon a vein of the purest selfishness that ever debased a character. We have public benevolence and private self-will: we will do anything for the masses, we begrudge everything expended upon our own family. Or contrariwise: the little personal house may have everything—every door-panel a picture, every window a garden, every floor a bed of flowers; but we care nothing for those who are outside, wasting, suffering, dying, hastening, for aught we know, to all the horrors of perdition. Let every man examine his own character, and he will be struck with the contrasts which it presents—the singular and instructive conjunctions which come together even in the individual spirit. One self speaks up in the name of right; another self says, Do not speak so loudly. Everything depends upon the self which is uppermost at the time. It is perfectly possible in a moral sense for the same fountain to pour sweet waters and bitter. The apostle asks the question in a sense which was not intended to exclude that possibility. There does not live a Christian man who is not conscious of this dual movement in his own soul : within himself he says, I know not what to do ; when I would do good, evil is present with me ; when I would pray, the evil spirit will not allow me ; when I would sing, I am suddenly choked ; when I would give, my hand seems smitten and it falls by my side in helplessness. So everywhere the seeing eye beholds Beth-aven, the house of vanity, Bethel, the house of God ; and the Christian teacher wants in some way to bring the influence of the latter to bear upon the action of the former.

What a curious conjunction is found in verse 24 :—" Achan the son of Zerah." This does not strike us as a conjunction or contrast in English reading. " Achan" means " trouble ; " " Zerah " means " the rising of light." " Achan the son of Zerah "—not immediately, for Achan was " the son of Carmi, the son of Zabdi, the son of Zerah." But the division is most startling as seen in this twenty-fourth verse :—Achan—trouble ; Zerah—the rising of light ! How family histories vary ! A praying father has a blaspheming son. The honestest man in the city lives to see his first-born expatriated as a felon. Heredity in virtue is exploded. Good men have not good sons by necessity. It is easy and pleasant talking to say, Given a good stock, and the branches will all be right ; given an excellent father and mother, and the children need not be much looked after ; they will come up in the way of righteousness and be ornaments in society. That sophism has been exploded in countless tragical instances. Zerah, representing the rising of light—quite a poetical name ; the horizon widens as he gazes upon it, all heaven heightens as he looks the prayerful look towards its sublimity ; how little he thinks that presently there will arise in his family a man who will be stoned to death as a thief ! He could not help that. Abel is not responsible for Cain. We do not understand the working of many a mystery in Providence. Things are not to be explained by one reference, or two : the explanation lies far back in history. The dead live. Reproduction accompanies development. We cannot tell what virus stained our blood. But, on the other hand, heredity in vice is not fatal. The blaspheming father has a praying son. The man who was never known for his goodness has a child who is a philanthropist, a missionary,—who dies with Christ

upon the cross, and counts the crucifixion coronation. So the
law does not operate in one direction only : it is an impartial
and comprehensive law. Let no man say, I am fated to do
thus, and so. It would be a wicked criticism upon Providence.
The answer is in every man's soul ; and who does not know that
he could if he chose be a better man, a larger man altogether ?
Let the soul itself answer the question in its own identity and
in the solemnity of its own oath.

What a beautiful conjunction is found in verse 26, when connected with another passage of Scripture in a later book! In the
twenty-sixth verse are these words :—" Wherefore the name of
that place was called, the valley of Achor, unto this day "—that
is, the " valley of trouble." The valley of Achor is said to be
a pass leading from Gilgal towards the centre of the country,
or, as it might be represented, from Jericho to Jerusalem,—
that is, from the city of destruction to the city of God. Remember
that " Achor " means what Achan also means, namely, *trouble.*
Now read Hosea ii. 15, and see what is meant by the beauty
of the conjunction :—" And I will give her . . . the valley
of Achor for a door of hope "—I will make the valley of
trouble the door of hope. See the great power of God ! He
can accomplish even this miracle. " Thy dead men shall live."
The desert shall blossom as the rose, and the wilderness shall
become as a fruitful field. Where thou didst weep, thou shalt
laugh in godly triumph ; where thou didst fall, thou shalt rise :
affliction shall become an altar ; tears shall be turned into tele-
scopes through which thou shalt see still further into the heights
of God's astronomy—the mystery of heaven's blazing glories.
God will not have valleys of trouble left in his earth. It is
the purpose of Heaven to cleanse out all the stains and taints
of sin and all the footprints of misery, and to grow a flower
where poison grew before. " I will give her the valley of
Achor for a door of hope ; " she will hope the more when she
remembers the trouble. Our afflictions add to our enjoyments
when sanctified and turned to their highest uses. Chastening
lifts up victory to higher, if soberer, triumph. It is the contrast
that arrests the soul. Had all been garden-land flowers, singing
birds, summer air, we should not have know want or pain,

nor should we have been surprised by new revelations of God's goodness. We see the stars in the darkness. We know where home is, and think of it as the evening closes in. We left the house in the morning, it may have been thoughtlessly or carelessly, without highly-accented recognition of its security and plentifulness; but as the shadows gathered, and the wind grew colder, and people rose from labour and went away from the field, we too thought of home. The light scattered us, the darkness brought us together! "I will give her the valley of Achor for a door of hope;" the background shall be adapted to the picture: she shall see the light thrown upon the darkness, and be astonished with great amazement when she beholds what can be done in unexpected or forsaken places. Our own experience confirms this. We know this sweet passage to be quite true. We are the better for the visit to the churchyard. We are the richer for the grave; it is to us a freehold worth more than a thousand acres, nay, it consecrates all other acres: it touches the whole land with religious suggestiveness and solemnity. Now we are the better and richer for the loss. Now we feel that we would not forego the advantages of the great sorrow. Let us find in our own experience a commentary upon Holy Scripture. If the Bible is a book far outside of us, without any vital relation to what we know and feel and handle, what wonder if it should fall into desuetude or become almost contemptuously neglected? But finding in the Bible our own history, a mirror in which we can see ourselves, reading in the Bible the universal language and not a provincial dialect, feeling that it touches life at every point, who can wonder if it should be the man of our counsel, the chief book in the house, our chart at sea, our confidence on land? Let us say again and again to ourselves, as if reciting heaven's own poetry, "I will make the valley of Achor a door of hope." The very repetition of such words discovers their music. Say it in your distresses, repeat it in the snowy winter-time, rehearse it when the fig tree doth not blossom, whisper it to your souls on the way to the graveyard; and in the time of personal despondency, of which you can only speak with reluctance even to your dearest friend, hold this soliloquy, "Why art thou cast down, O my soul? and why art thou disquieted within me? hope thou in God: for I shall yet praise him, who is the health of my countenance and my God." The utterance of that word will break the spell of misery. To speak such a sentence to the soul will be to break the fetters which bind it in unholy and humiliating bondage. I will make the valley of Achor a door of hope. So though to-day we be in trouble and darkness and distress, wait awhile, and the valley shall be a door, and the door when it springs back will open heaven.

SELECTED NOTES.

"*The valley of Achor for a door of hope*" (Hosea ii. 15).—The Easterns prefer a figure that is suggestive but at the same time hazy and indistinct, and this passage belongs to such a class. The Valley of Achor runs up from Gilgal towards Bethel. There Achan was stoned, and the divine indignation removed. The word *Achor* means *trouble, affliction;* and it is just possible that from it we get our word *ache.* Thus the valley of affliction was the door through which Israel first entered the land of Canaan. And so again, by Hosea, the Lord promised to lead Israel to peace and rest through the valley of trouble. The very indistinctness makes this mode of speaking the more suggestive.

"*Achan . . . was taken*" (v. 18).—When Jericho was taken and devoted to destruction, Achan fell under the temptation of secreting an ingot of gold, a quantity of silver, and a costly Babylonish garment, which he buried in his tent, deeming that his sin was hid. For this which, as a violation of a vow made by the nation as one body, had involved the whole nation in his guilt, the Israelites were defeated with serious loss, in their first attack upon Ai; and as Joshua was well assured that this humiliation was designed as the punishment of a crime which had inculpated the whole people, he took immediate measures to discover the criminal. As in other cases, the matter was referred to the Lord by the lot, and the lot ultimately indicated the actual criminal. The conscience-stricken offender then confessed his crime to Joshua; and his confession being verified by the production of his ill-gotten treasure, the people, actuated by the strong impulse with which men tear up, root and branch, a polluted thing, hurried away not only Achan but his tent, his goods, his spoil, his cattle, his children, to the valley (afterwards called) of Achor, north of Jericho, where they stoned him, and all that belonged to him; after which the whole was consumed with fire, and a cairn of stones raised over the ashes. The severity of this act, as regards the *family* of Achan, has provoked some remark. Instead of vindicating it, as is generally done, by the allegation that the members of Achan's family were probably accessories to his crime after the fact, we prefer the supposition that they were included in the doom by one of those sudden impulses of indiscriminate popular vengeance to which the Jewish people were exceedingly prone, and which, in this case, it would not have been in the power of Joshua to control by any authority which he could under such circumstances exercise. It is admitted that this is no more than a conjecture: but as such it is at least worth as much as, and assumes considerably less than, the conje 'ures which have been offered by others.

PRAYER.

ALMIGHTY GOD, we ask for a clean heart and a right spirit, an obedient will, an unquestioning, restful faith. We would say the Lord's prayer, Not my will, but thine, be done. Who but the Lord could say this to thee? We can repeat the words; we can feel after the sentiment as blind men grope for what they want, but we cannot pray the prayer in all the fulness of its meaning, because of the infirmities which disable us, and because of the temptations which assail and weaken the soul. What we do not understand is God's will. If we knew that, we should wish it to be done. But we do not know it; we misunderstand it; we make it narrow, and empty it of all divinest thought and meaning: so how can we pray that it should be done? But even this miracle thou canst work within us; thou canst reveal thy will to our hearts, and make us know how good it is, how necessarily wise and beneficent, righteous and pitiful. Lord, do this great thing for us, and so deliver us from ourselves, and lead us into thy personality, that we may live and move and have our being in God, and be conscious of no other life, but have all the triumph and sense of security rising from the sure consciousness that we are in the Living One. We are blind, and would see afar off. Thou seest the end from the beginning. We mistake all things; we misplace them; we cannot follow all the drift of their meaning, or appreciate all the colour of their suggestion; we are poor, inapt scholars in the great school. Give us rest from ourselves by giving us deeper peace in God. Thus would we come to the Lord's prayer, which lay so near the Lord's Cross. If we can pray this prayer, the bitterness of death will be past, and the Cross we shall despise as to its shame. Help us to carry life's burdens with some measure of cheerfulness, and enable us to say, This also cometh forth from the Lord, even this great cross, this dark cloud, this large loss, this weakening infirmity. Thus we shall count the stones upon the road as jewels; the Cross will be a way to the crown; and all the discipline of life will have as its promise an exceeding great reward. As for our sin, we remember it only to mourn it, and we bring it to the Cross, and we nail it there: there it is borne away by the Lamb of God, in whom is our heart's trust, and from whom is our daily expectation. Love us every one, throw thine arms more closely and tenderly around us, give us a feeling of security, work within us a godly discontent with everything that is less than ourselves, and create in us that fierce hunger which only the infinite can satisfy. Pity us in our weaknesses and reckon not our infirmities against us until they aggravate thy righteousness and provoke thy law, and come over the mountain of our sin as one who travelleth in haste, and destroy the mountain as thou dost touch it in the passage. We pray this in the name of Jesus Christ, who taught us to pray. Until he came, our prayers were poor, and narrow, and selfish; but he being in our hearts, by the Spirit, we can pray to have no will: we can say, Thy will be done on earth as it is in heaven. Amen.

Joshua vii. 18.

"And Achan . . . was taken."

ACHAN A REPRESENTATIVE MAN.

THERE is nothing old in these words. Achan is "taken" every day. Achan is sure to be "taken." If we are practising the policy of Achan, the fate of Achan we can never avert; the detail will be different—the mere map and plan— but the issue will be the same, because God's throne is the same, and there is no change in his righteousness. So this is not ancient history, but a line taken out of this day's record—a line we would gladly not read; but why should we spoil our school- ing because we are eclectic, reading a line here and there just as it may please us, instead of reading straight through, solemnly, minutely, and fearlessly? We do not like to look into perdition —we are afraid of being scorched! But whatever we find upon the way of life and in the discipline of life, it will be well to look at steadfastly and reverently, and ask God for that apt mind and interpreting faculty which can seize meanings and secure them and hold them as spiritual riches.

What a representative man is Achan! Does he not represent those, for example, who are continually taking great risks? What a life some men lead! They are always on the brink; an unforeseen pebble might topple them over in a moment. There is a kind of moral speculativeness about them. Their psychology is difficult to understand. They will take chances, they will run into dangerous places; their happiness appears to consist in the number and the quality of the risks they accept. It was very unlikely that any man would escape who took such a risk as Achan took. But we must not lightly dismiss the people who are taking risks. It would be easy to blame them, easy to chastise them with stinging words and bitter and just re- proaches; but there is something in the making of a man : we cannot account for it; there is a tincture in the blood. Some men would seem to be almost born to risks and dangers, every laugh a concealment, every joke a new hypocrisy, every appear- ance of guilelessness an attainment in infernal skill. There is but a step between them and death. The partition which keeps them from the prison and the gallows is almost transparent ; a wind of the gentlest kind might blow it down.   What an excited life ! and not the less excited that it appears to be measured and quiet ; every tone is a calculation ; the whole life is constructed upon dramatic and poetic lines ; not a posture that is not also a confession, or an evasion, or a suggestion, if we had those keen eyes which can see below surfaces into meanings and purposes.

But the mystery of it is that Achan represents also men who have no need to take risks.   They have plenty ; they have sweet homes ; they have gardens rich with all kinds of flowers ; and the very air is made musical by the birds which sing in it. They need not go out of their own doors for a single pleasure : their table is bounteously spread ; every corner of the house is built upon a rock, and every voice in the house is charged with some musical message.   Yet they covet just a little more : it is only one acre to complete the estate ; it is only one thousand pounds more to make the odd figure into an even one—then all will go rhythmically in the matter of finance and property ; it is only one more slave that is needed, and then the enjoyment will be sphered off into completeness, and will roll and shine among a thousand globes, and be a source of daily joy.   If they had need, there would be some excuse.   When David ate the shewbread he was excused because of his hunger.   So men may do many desperate things, and be excused in some degree for doing them, because of biting hunger and void necessity and tremendous urgency of circumstances.   These are not defences, complete replies to righteous impeachments, but they may be construed into extenuations, and the just magistrate may take note of them when he has to pronounce his sentence ; they may throw a sob into the judge's speech ; they may be the means of suggesting even to the criminal that his punishment has mercy mingled with it.   But when men have no need to take risks, and yet take them, it becomes a wonder whether they are so fated, crushed down by Heaven to do this thing, or whether they have attained a mental and moral perversity absolutely beyond the range of any chaste imagination.   These things show us the critical nature of life, the awful difficulty of living, and the tremendous pressure that is put upon some men in certain directions.   We must be charitable in all our judgments, especially

charitable towards those who are young and inexperienced,
who do not understand the mischief they are beginning; and
something must be set down to an imagination too buoyant to
bow before the sober dictates of reason. Then allowance must
also be made for men of a certain descent. We carry our fathers
with us. We have seen again and again in these studies that no
man liveth unto himself, and that no man is himself only. What
can some men do who were born in darkness, born in slavery,
born just outside hell; who have had no friends, no education,
no chance in life, and who seem to think—and not unreasonably
—that life is a battle in which the strongest wins, a race which
is given to the swiftest, and that sometimes strength must be
outwitted by cunning, and sometimes swiftness must be deceived
by putting the time forward or backward so as to baffle calculation? Thank God we are not judges. We stand in the same
dock: let God be judge.

Achan committed a sin which is common to us all, in so far
that he felt it extremely difficult to subordinate the personal to
the communal. He might have said—and in so saying he would
have talked good, round English,—What can a wedge of gold
matter in all this great heap of wealth? What is the difference
one Babylonish garment more or less? Who will be the worse
for my taking it? Nobody need know. I want a relic of this
event, I want a keepsake; this has been a very wonderful
miracle, and I want to keep in my house some memorial of it;
I could turn these things into good, moral uses: I could preach
sermons upon them, I could derive lessons from them. It cannot
make any difference where thousands of men are concerned if
I take one wedge of gold, two hundred shekels of silver, and a
goodly Babylonish garment—they are all but a handful, and who
will miss them? In fact, there will be no reckoning; things in
connection with a battle are done so tumultuously and so irregu-
larly that none will ever think of looking up such a handful of
spoil as I may seize. That is the exaggeration of individualism;
that is the lie which man is always telling to himself. It is the
falsehood which enables him to cheat the body politic :—What
can it matter if I do not vote? There are thousands of people
who want to vote, let them enjoy themselves, and I will take
mine ease. What can it matter if I do not keep the laws of the

company—the municipal or other company? The great majority of the neighbours will keep them, and as for any little infraction of them of which I may be guilty, it is mere pedantry to remark upon it. Who cares for the body politic—the body corporate? We are being taught to respect that so-called abstraction; but the lesson is a very difficult one to learn. What seems to belong to everybody, belongs to nobody. When shall we come to understand fully that there is a corporate humanity, a public virtue, a body politic, with its responsibilities, laws, duties,—a great training-school in which individualism is subordinated to the commonwealth? We talk to-day in this matter the language of Achan. Let him who is not guilty say so to himself, for no other hearer could well believe him.

Does not Achan represent those who create unnecessary mysteries in the course of divine Providence? It is the concealed man who could explain everything. It is the thief behind the screen who could relieve all our wonder, perplexity, and distress. We have to search him out by circumstantial evidence. If he would stand up and say, "Guilty!" he would relieve our minds of many a distressing thought even about the divine government. We wonder why the people are delayed, why the battle goes the wrong way, why the heathen pursues the chosen man, and beats him down, and scorns his assaults. We speak of God's mysterious way. It is a mistake on our part. The silent man, skulking behind the arras, could explain the whole affair, and relieve divine Providence of many a wonder which grows quickly into suspicion or distrust. There is such a thing, however, as circumstantial evidence: point after point is established, link after link is forged and added, and we watch the chain getting round a man, closing in upon him, beginning at the foot and coiling upwards until it strangles him! That is not a picture in romance; that is the reallest thing in all human affairs. There is a providence of time, circumstance, and the relation of the one to the other. Now the man escapes, and now he is swiftly brought back; at this moment circumstances favour him, and presently they close in upon him with tremendous certainty and awful pressure. So we have bye-circumstances, often so difficult to piece together and put into any meaning shape, to discover crimes which should be confessed openly, and the confession of which would relieve the religious consciousness of men from many an unhappy and unwelcome thought about divine Providence. There can be no escape! The very stones of the field will fight against the criminal; the light will shine at the wrong time. The detection of God is unerring. We say this, but do not realise it. If we could realise it we should begin to consider, and repent, and return.

Look at the case in one or two remarkable aspects. Consider Achan, for example, as a *solitary* sinner. He was the only man in the host who had disobeyed the orders that were given. Only one! It is therefore incredible. It cannot be that one man would stand apart from the whole host, the solitary criminal. It is excusable, if not incredible. He was the only one. Why judge him? Why arrest a whole army on account of one traitor? Or if it is neither incredible nor excusable, it is trifling. Nothing smaller could have occurred. Let the host go on. So man would say. God will not have it so. He does not measure by our scale. One sin is a thousand. One uplifted arm is a universe in rebellion. How many sins has a man to commit before he is a sinner? God will not allow us to alter the relation of things. It is SIN that is abominable to him—not a thousand sins; it is the spirit—not the number of actions. This is the rule of the divine judgment, and this is the explanation of the divine movement in a redemptive and judicial direction.

Think of Achan as a *detected* sinner. For a time there was no prospect of the man being found out. But God has methods of sifting which we do not know of. He himself will say how the sifting process is to be conducted : the tribe, the house, the family, the man ! To see the judgment coming, to see it a day nearer, to see it within an hour, to feel the inward fire burning into unquenchable self-accusation, to know that any one moment the arresting hand may fall,—that is punishment, that is everlasting punishment. Why this discussion about everlasting punishment? All punishment is everlasting. We have made the word "everlasting" the principal word in the argument, whereas it is merely incidental. The abiding word is *punishment.* And no punishment is for a day. A man once condemned has to bear the results of that condemnation for ever. The young man commits a crime, and is punished fifty years after; a stone will be thrown at him on that very account. Only God can deal with this great mystery. The great ,evangelical theology says that it is possible now for God to be just, and yet the Justifier of the ungodly by the great mystery of sacrifice—the shedding of atoning blood. But it needed God to work the miracle. Nature never worked it. Conscience never worked it. Law never thought of it. This is God's doing, in love, in pity, in the justice which is inspired by compassion.

Then look at Achan as a *confessing* sinner. He did confess his sin, but not until he was discovered. And the confession was as selfish as the sin. That is a difficulty we must face. A man's religion may be the only thing really against him. Beware of irreligious religion! That is the explanation of your imprecatory psalms. That is the explanation of Pharisaism. That is the explanation of narrow and unworthy views of Providence and heaven. Men may pray selfishly, believe selfishly, attend to religious ordinances selfishly, confess their sin selfishly,—make an investment of their tears, and aggravate their original offence by an awful hypocrisy.

The picture of Achan as a *punished* sinner is appalling. Who punished the sinful man? The answer to that inquiry is given in the twenty-fifth verse, and is full of saddest, yet noblest meaning. Who punished the thief? "All Israel stoned him with stones,"—not one infuriated man, not one particularly interested individual, but "all Israel." The punishment is social. It is the universe that digs hell—the all rising against the one. A great mystery is here, yet a most holy and beautiful point. Society punishes the bad man. When the magistrate pronounces sentence, he does not speak in his own name: he is a representative man; he is Society delivering sentence upon the evildoer. So it will be at last. There will be no one to arise and vindicate the sinner, no volunteer advocate, no man so left to himself as to stand up and say, "I defend the prisoner at the bar." Then things will be seen in their reality. Sin will be measured by the righteous standard, judgment will be meted by the righteous Ruler; and the sinner shall be stoned by the universe, buried by the universe, forgotten by the universe. My soul, come not thou into that secret!

PRAYER.

ALMIGHTY GOD, feed us with the bread sent down from heaven! This is the true bread, even thy Son Jesus Christ. He called himself the Bread of Life. He gave his flesh for us, and his blood, in mysterious and most holy sacrifice. He could not tell us all he had to tell because of our want of capacity and sympathy and nurture in the Lord; but we begin now to see somewhat of his deep meaning. He laid up words which time would explain: he gave hints which the ages would bring to perfectness of meaning. Now we hear the rising music; it sounds far off, a distant bell, but the sound thereof will grow, and all nature shall answer it, and all hearts shall be made glad by it, and heaven and earth shall melt into one another. We draw around thy Son Jesus, for he has the words of eternal life, and he speaks them as thou thyself wouldst speak them, with such fulness and depth and tenderness that our hearts know them to be true, and say, Of a truth this is a voice from heaven, a gospel from eternity. If we say otherwise, we condemn ourselves, and the truth is not in us. When we are under proper exultation of spirit we answer Christ in his own tongue: for we are taught of God, and being under the direction of the Spirit we understand Christ's language and speak it like our mother-tongue. Reveal to us the unsearchable riches of thy Son. Show us that if we are poor, it is not because the wealth of heaven has not been offered to us. If we are sitting in darkness, it is because we have wilfully shut our eyes. If our souls are not alive with God, it is because we have chosen death. Multiply thy grace unto us according to the need of the hour. Sometimes it is an hour of blackness, yea, of sevenfold night, of darkness gathered and heaped up into gloom that cannot be borne. Sometimes it is an hour of delight, of genial sunshine, of summer hopefulness; and then we think we shall never die, and wonder why we were ever sad. Save us even in hours of exultation, lest we become heedless and forget the littleness of our own strength. Visit us in the house and make the four corners thereof as four lamps, and the table thereof as a board of sacrament, and the fire thereof like an altar kindled from above; thus shall the house be a delightsome place, full of holiest memories, enriched with noblest associations, every footprint marking a progress, every night a rest, every morning a grander vow. The Lord comfort us in sorrow, in affliction, in loss, in trial. Visit our dear ones in the sick-room and in the places of waiting, in the sanctuary of distress and in the places of wonder, sore expectancy, that kills the heart's life because of long and mocking delay. Lift up those who are bowed down, yea, straighten them into their first uprightness, and give them the joy of returning youth. The Lord be our strength when our poor life totters under some tremendous blow. The Lord clothe us for the battle, and bring us home after the war more than conquerors. Amen.

Joshua viii.

THE TAKING OF AI SPIRITUALISED.

THE details of this chapter are certainly not in keeping with the spirit of the later revelations of the mind of God. We have nothing to do with the chapter locally and incidentally; in that respect it is a forgotten thing. Revelations are unquestionably matters of time. This is the solution of many difficulties which are supposed to be found in the Bible, where there are really no difficulties at all when the whole is measured by the right scale and examined in the true light. It must not be thought that the events recorded in the Bible took place one after another, just as quickly as they could occur. There may be ages between one book and another. The first chapter of Genesis may be a chapter stretching over countless epochs, rising and falling myriads of years. Between Malachi and Matthew there is but a page in the printed book, but between Malachi and Matthew as a matter of historical literature there is a span of four hundred years; in other words, Malachi having laid down his pen, that pen is not taken up in continuous history for four centuries. Keep this in view, and very much that is cloudy and perplexing will be dissolved and made luminous. What, therefore, shall we do with a chapter like this, so full of cunning, stratagem, military surprises, and what would be called sharp practice upon the unsuspecting inhabitants of Ai? We can spiritualise it in the best sense. There is a legitimate way of spiritualising ancient history, and this is the only way in which a history of this kind can be treated with modern pertinence, comfort, and edification.

With this precaution then, how does the striking story appear to us? It appears, in the first place, that in going out to battle with anything that is doomed we must have a right character and a right cause. This was insisted upon in the case of Ai. The Lord would not allow a blow to be struck at the city by a wicked hand; he will have judgment executed by righteousness; he will have the law proclaimed by lips that have been circumcised and anointed. Israel was all but innumerable in force.

In relation to the city of Ai, Israel was a torrent that could not
be withstood. But Israel had committed sin. A goodly Babylonish garment and two hundred shekels of silver and a wedge
of gold fifty shekels in weight had been stolen by an Israelitish
soldier. The Lord will not have such warriors. His purpose
has ever been to prove that right is might, that without character
we cannot do his work—not spotless character, which may be
impossible under present conditions, but character that is intensely in earnest, set in the right direction, aspiring after continual perfectness. Do not go to battle with a wrong cause,
or your weakness will be assured before you begin. No man
can be really eloquent upon a bad cause. He may be fluent,
and may use many highly-coloured words, and use them with
great skill ; but earnestness of conviction is absolutely necessary
to all-persuasive and all-enduring eloquence. So, before going
to war, there must be an inquiry instituted into the character
and into the quality of the thing that is proposed to be done.
The first great inquiry of man is a moral inquiry, not an inquest
about numbers, places, and possible issues—but, is this thing
right? and am I right who attempt to do the work ? That being
the case, go forward. Do not be deterred by any man, by any
man's threatening, or any man's inexcusable folly, but proceed
steadily, prayerfully, confidently. This is the rule of the chapter.
This is the rule of all ages. Do not take a step until that rule
has been observed and realised. Nor must the term "r'ght"
be construed narrowly. There is a spirit in man, and th: inspiration of the Almighty giveth him understanding about
right. We have murdered right, or divided it into opinions and
enumerated them, and accounted our individual opinions the
sum-total of right. Let the spirit commune with the Spirit of
God, and inspiration will not be withheld. It will be difficult
to keep down selfishness, vanity, ambition, and all that brood,
but it lies within the compass of the power of God even to crush
the serpent's head.

The next great lesson of this incident is that we must *all*
advance upon the doomed institution. When the idea of taking
Ai was first broached, there were clever men in Israel who said,
Let two or three thousand of us go up and take the city; the
whole army has been perambulating round about the walls of

Jericho; it is quite needless to put the entire army to this
expense of time and strength; depute some two or three thousand
of us, and we will go up and smite Ai and burn it to ashes;
it is a pity to weary all the people when a handful of them
might execute the design. There are always such meddle-
some people in God's army, who will divide, and distribute,
and cultivate what they call opinions. They will not allow the
great laws of God to move on in massiveness and majesty;
they will meddle with God. Two or three thousand of the
people of Israel went up against Ai, and we have seen the result.
Now we must return, says the historian, in effect, to God's
own appointed law in this matter: "I, and all the people that
are with me, will approach unto the city" (v. 5). That must
be the rule of the Church in all its great moral wars. The
battle is not to be handed over to a few persons, however
skilful and zealous. The work of teaching the world and
saving the world is a work committed to the whole Christian
body. There are to be no laymen in this war. We must
obliterate the official distinction between clergy and laity, pulpit
and pew. The living Church of the living God is one. Forgetting this rule, what has come to pass?—that destructive
work and constructive work, acts of benevolence and charity,
have devolved upon handfuls of men, and they have been left
to do all that was needful in battle and in charity. They have
been favoured with the *criticism* of those who have stayed at
home. Criticism has never been a scarce article in human history!
Persons who have done nothing, sacrificed nothing, given nothing,
are the very people who are able, by some vicious inspiration,
to find fault with everybody else. When the Church realises
its totality, when every man is part of an army and not an
isolated warrior, then every Ai doomed of heaven shall reel under
the battering-ram which the Church will employ. When all
the people are at work, there can be no criticism: they are
involved in the same strife and issue; they are common patriots,
fellow-soldiers, parts of the same great multitude, and there
is no time for mutual exasperation and folly. The clever men,
therefore, were in the second instance displaced. They supposed
that they had realised quite a clever idea, that all the great
body of Israel might remain at home and two or three thousand

young, sharp, clever, active men might go up and do all the work, and come galloping home at night conquerors rich with spoil. The Lord will not have it so. Joshua must himself go up, and all the people must go up with him. There are to be no mere critics; there are to be thousands of active soldiers.

This being so, the incident brings before us in a very suggestive and picturesque manner the fact that we must excel the enemy in shrewdness. A perusal of the chapter will show what military cunning was expended upon this particular situation. The idea is not to be taken in its literal sense as applicable to-day to anything with which the Church has to deal; but this is the eternal thought: that the Church is to be shrewder than the world, believers are to be keener of mind and more active in every energy than unbelievers. Who was to be "wise as serpents," "harmless as doves"? Who was called to realise that startling paradox? It is the law of true advancement and conquest in things moral and divine. But the Church can never learn this lesson. "Harmless as doves," in the sense of doing nothing, the Church is superhumanly able to be; but "wise as serpents"—silent, thoughtful, shrewd, far-sighted, patient,—who can realise this idea? Whatever the world does, the Church should show a nobler strength. The Church should buy up every institution which it cannot burn up. The Church should have all the thoroughfares and crowd back the evil—back, and further back still, till it reels into the river! The Church has not done this, but has taken up positions in quiet corners, and out-of-the-way places, and has lived a very inoffensive and peacefully obscure life. The Salvation Army is right, or Christianity is a mistake. Respectability, conventionally understood, in Christian service may be blasphemy. So long as men remain in obscure positions and show themselves to be so infantile that they would not even injure the devil if they saw him, the devil is perfectly willing that chapels without end should be put up; but where men are burning with godliness, mad with earnestness,—where the universe divides itself into heaven and hell, right and wrong, there can be no peace, there can be no truce, there can be no hand-shaking over the chasm. Would Heaven that all the quiet people were on the other side of this question! They could be well spared! Christianity in a fallen world is not quietness. Herein is that wonderful word true :—"Think not that I came to send peace on earth : I came not to send peace, but a sword"—I came to kindle a fire upon the earth, and to set a man against his fellow-man, and to make war in the house. We call these expressions "figurative" and escape the awful discipline !

It is evident, moreover, that if we are to do any real work in the world in the name of God and in the cause of Christ, we must be about our business night and day. In the tenth verse we read :—"And Joshua rose up early in the morning ;" in the thirteenth verse we read :—"Joshua went that night into the midst of the valley." That was a soldier's life ! We are, as Christians, supposed to be soldiers. How reads the old story? "And Joshua rose up early in the morning . . . . Joshua went that night into the midst of the valley." It is sad that we can appease our consciences by telling them that this is a piece of ancient history and related to very obscure incidents. It is not so. If men will subject themselves, the apostle says, to such processes of discipline to obtain a corruptible crown, what should we do whose aim is to secure an incorruptible ? The argument is a cumulative one, aggravating itself even into agony. If any will so discipline themselves to obtain an ivy or a parsley chaplet, what shall we do whose prize is the crown of life ? If we cannot attain this sublimity of heroism, we can at least set it before us, keep it as the continual idea of life. We need not upbraid ourselves unreasonably if we do not attain it, for the apostle himself said he counted not himself to have apprehended, but he pressed toward the mark,—that is to say, he was always found pressing in one direction, never vacillating, halting, returning, but eternally set, like the needle to the pole. Who will join this great army ? How useful some men might be if they had the spirit of consecration : what time they have on hand ! They can rise early and sit up late, and order their affairs with comparative freedom. Would they give themselves to the Cross, would they be slaves of Christ, would they make up their minds to be either infidels or Christians ! The difficulty is with the tepid man, with the man who wants to walk upon both sides of the road,—to keep sacrament once a month and visit the devil between whiles.

We should miss one great lesson of this story if we did not note that we are bound to set fire to every devoted abomination. Ai was burned. The smoke of the city ascended up to heaven, and Ai became, not *a* heap, but *the* heap,—as if it were the only heap. That was complete work. Is our work complete? Have we added fire to the sword? Is ignorance burned, or is it only labelled " wisdom "? Is slavery burned with unquenchable fire, or has it only changed its relation and its colour? We are called to a work of extirpation. We are not called to compromise, to paltering, to arranging, to expediency where ignorance is concerned, or slavery, or vice, or wrong. We must not omit the fire. Things must be so burned down that they can never grow again. Otherwise we shall have all the work to do over again, and the ages will be hindered in their highest progress.

And after destruction, what then? Positive religion comes next :—" Then Joshua built an altar unto the Lord God of Israel in mount Ebal " (v. 30). It is no use building your altar until you have burned the abomination. A great destructive work is to be done first, and in the doing of it, there will be great outcry about change, and novelty, and reprisal, and revolution, and confiscation, and a number of terms very imperfectly understood. But we must not build where the altar itself will be burned down. Be sure about the foundation before you put up the building ; know where you are going to set the altar. If you have not been faithful in the work of destruction, you cannot be faithful in the work of construction. It is lying unto the Holy Ghost to build an altar upon the basis of a rotten life. So we are called to thoroughness of work. There is to be no superficial action here. In doing this we may give great offence ; we may have to part with friends. But our fathers did more than that. Read their history—indeed, read the history of all progress, and you will find it to be a history of loss on the one side and of gain on the other. Blessed are those workers in the field to whom no favour can be shown, because they want none, whom it would be impossible to patronise. They, having done the destructive work, may and will erect the altar.

And after the altar, what? The law—the law of righteousness, the law of God. Verse 32 reads :—" And Joshua wrote there upon the stones a copy of the law of Moses, which he wrote in the presence of the children of Israel." This is complete work—destruction, the erected altar, the inscribed law. This is healthy work. The surgeon has done his duty, and now nature will proceed to heal and comfort and bless. The enemy has been driven off the field! Now the altar is put up and the law is promulgated. Society without law is chaos. An altar without righteousness is evaporative sentiment. Prayer without duty may be a detachment of the wings from the bird they were intended to assist.

The picture is a right noble one. Omitting all that was local, incidental, and temporary, here stands the great law of spiritual conflict :—a right character, a right cause, a unanimous advance, a super-excellent shrewdness, a business that touches the early morning and the late night, fire set to the devoted abomination, an altar built upon the ashes, the law written upon the altar,— that is the programme ; and any programme whose lines are not covered by this sublime delineation may be a clever invention, but it is not a revelation from heaven. We are thus called to energy, called to labour, called to sacrifice. We are *all* called. Merely to hear what the army has been doing is not patriotism. In the Church there is no place for indolence, there is no place for criticism, there is no place for mere sentiment. Has the world to be captured for Jesus Christ, or has it not ? If you say it has not, then abandon the standard altogether ; if you say it has, then never forsake the standard. Seek ye first the kingdom of God and his righteousness. Strive to enter in at the strait gate. Take unto you the whole armour of God. Stand against the wiles of the devil. Never leave it an open question as to which side you are upon. Having done the destructive work, do not imagine that the whole programme is complete ; now begin the construction of the altar. And having made a place for prayer, do not suppose that the whole duty of man has been perfected ; next put up the law :—battle, prayer, law ; law, prayer, battle. If there is aught else, it has not yet been to me revealed.

ALMIGHTY GOD, the bitterness of death is past: the world's worst history has been lived; and now the latter days have come upon us—days of morning, beauteous and rich with light; the glory of hope is round about us, and heaven is near at hand. We will not sorrow as men who have no hope; this would be to offend thee grievously, for thy providence was never so near our life as it is at this moment. All things teach us the divine nearness. Our own life is a witness that the whole world has become a sanctuary because of the Cross of Christ, and the whole priesthood of the Son of God. We bless thee that the future is lighted up with ineffable glory: now we speak of abolished death, of descending heaven, of immortality, of life all purity, service all music, and hope that cannot fade away. This is the realisation of the gospel of Jesus Christ,—the very perfectness of love, the bringing to maturity of thine eternal thought concerning man. We will therefore dry our tears, and assure our hearts, and go forward like men inspired and made strong. May all tone of mourning be taken out of our voices, all colour suggestive of dismay and fear be wholly removed from the whole course of our being; may our life be a daily witness to the power and goodness of God. For thine open book we bless thee; for its most ancient history we thank thee; for everything that shows the unity of manhood and the human heart we cannot but be grateful to God. The earth is the Lord's and the fulness thereof. All time is thy clothing; yea, thou hast made a garment of the universe, and thou standest amongst us clothed with that glittering humiliation. Behold, for God to be, is to make all other being possible, and yet to distress it with a sense of infinite distance. Thou chargest the angels with folly; the heavens are not clean in thy sight;— what can compare with the infinite pureness of God? Still, thou comest near to us, and thou diest upon a cross; thou settest forth a great mystery of sacrificial blood: we understand it not, but we know it to be the gospel which the heart most needs. Amen.

Joshua ix. 2-27.

THE GIBEONITES.

IT would seem on reading this narrative that it can have no possible relation to our time and our circumstances. But God would never write a Bible which was to obliterate itself as the ages come and go. If he could have written such a Bible, surely some instruction might have been given as to the excision of the parts whose meaning has been exhausted. But the book remains in its entirety. It must therefore contain meanings which were not merely local. All that can be required of us is to search the Scripture even in its oldest forms of history and parable; to penetrate it, to take it reverently to pieces, and examine it with devoutest scrutiny. We have undertaken to show that such an examination may be conducted with great profitableness. Again and again we have seen that the Bible is *within* the Bible,—that all letters, forms, representations are symbolic, or are so many doors through which we may pass into the inmost places, the awful sanctuaries, in which may be found eternal truth, celestial purity, supernal music. Flowers grow along the road traversed by the Bible story. The old wells are worth opening; water comes from deep rocks, and is refreshing to men and fertilising to the whole Church. Let us not be beguiled by the easy thought that the Bible is a self-exhausted book, that time obliterates its revelation, that the days impoverish it of heavenly energy. Be it ours rather to believe that it is the book which is daily inspired, daily written, and continually applicable to every variety of human circumstance and need.

The proof of this is upon the very face of the exciting narrative now before us. Do we not see here, first and foremost, the pitiable shifts to which all spiritual fear is driven? The fear of Israel came upon the Gibeonites, and the result was an invention, a false arrangement, an attempt to escape the inevitable. This is the story of to-day. Volumes might be written upon this one thought—namely, that spiritual fear is always and of necessity driven to the most pitiable shifts. Spiritual fear says, What can I do? I will undertake long pilgrimages; I will discharge severe and exhausting penances; I will set apart certain days for self-distress; I will pay great fines willingly; I will draw a mask over my face and obliterate my identity; I will create a system of lucky days and fortunate numbers, and enter into complex speculations and arrangements; I will build churches, and seem to worship; I will commingle with the people of God as if I were one of them when my heart is a thousand leagues away from the very poorest soul in all the sacred number. This is the very philosophy of

superstition. Great and solemn histories find their foun: and
origin in this one circumstance—how to baffle God, how to pray
without praying, how to succeed by trick and lie and mean
pretence. Who will say that the Bible is exhausted as to its
inner meanings and its profound revelations? The trick of the
Gibeonites is the game of to-day. Spiritual fear knows not the
spirit of truth, and cannot of course know the spirit of joy. So
long as we are in fear, we are not in God, we are not in love :
" perfect love casteth out fear ; " we are not in truth, for truth
blinks not in the presence of the mid-day light,—it goes forth to a
thousand lions, leaps over a wall, and runs through a troop as if
through a film of air. Are we not always cursed by this spirit of
fear? It leads us to misconstructions of God. He ceases to be
God when he is looked at through the medium and under
the base inspiration of servile fear. The man in whom the
spirit of fear is, cannot read the Bible. It is a mere idol to
him. He looks at it, pronounces its words, accepts its partial
perusal as a task ; but he never enters into the inner meaning,
the divine thought, the eternal affection and redemptiveness
of the book. What is the consequence? The consequence is
that he can be frightened away from the book by any man
who has a larger mind than his own, and who has a more
inventive faculty in the region of destructive criticism and
embarrassing remark. Hold the Bible with the timid hand
of fear, and any thief may take it from our yielding grasp;
hold it in our love and read it in the sunshine of joy derived
from conscious sonship with God, and no man can pluck it
out of our hand : it then becomes the *Bible* to us,—not a
collection of letters, forms, but a breathing spirit, the Holy
Ghost, proving its inspiration by inspiring others. We may
make the house of God an idol temple. We may make the
Bible itself a mere idol. We may dispossess the heart of love
by almost welcoming the spirit of fear. Being under bondage
to fear, we are always inventing religions, inventing methods
of escape, trying to impose upon the world and the Church,
and even upon God. We have therefore to pray that the
spirit of fear may be cast out of us as an evil spirit darkening the soul, weaving impenetrable clouds around the horizon
of the divine revelation, and making the stars—bright globes

of heaven—dim and murky, divesting them of all poetry and
all religious suggestion. The spirit of fear must be driven
out of the Church, or the young will not come near us. The
spirit of the Church is a spirit of joy, truth, love, poetry,
music,—these are the fruits of the Spirit !

The application of this narrative to modern states and needs is
made evident by the very fact that the best of men are powerless without the divine Spirit. This is proved by the fourteenth
verse :—

"And the men took of their victuals, and asked not counsel at the mouth
of the Lord."

We know what came of it. We are beguiled and befooled by
appearances. Some circumstances appear to be so very simple as
not to require consideration. That is the moment of danger !
Men say to themselves, Here is a case in which there is no complexity ; the proof of the innocence of these men is patent ; there
cannot be two opinions about that ; they are travel-stained, they are
way-worn ; the bread they carry is mouldy, the bottles in which
they brought their wine are old and rent and useless ; the evidence
is perfectly complete ; there can be no reason whatever for making
this a religious problem or an occasion of prayer ;—let us honour
our own common-sense, pay tribute to our own reason, and act
according to circumstances about which there can be no dispute.
Thus the Church has always been ruined in some degree by its
clever men ! Except ye be converted and become as little
children, ye cannot manage the Church of the living God, even
in the lowest ranges of its affairs. Do not attempt to lock the
church door except as a religious act. When you light up the
sanctuary for worship, do it as if it were a solemn act of prayer
and sacrifice. In everything, the smallest and apparently clearest,
consult God. This is the religious life, the joy life, the free life, to
do nothing without the spirit of prayer. There need not be any
affectation of mere posture and form of prayer : there is a spirit
of fellowship, a continual realisation of the divine presence, a
feeling after God ; and then the uplifting of a hand is prayer, as
is the falling of a tear. When our reason seems to be equal to the
occasion, the temptation of the Evil One is heavy upon us. We
practically dismiss God. We do not mean to do so. If the
charge were made in words, we should repel it. But we are not

always right simply because of our willingness to repel charges that are made against us. Men do not always know when they are the subjects of envy, jealousy, evil passion; in the very paroxysms of jealousy of another man's repute or good position, men have denied that there is any burning of envy in their hearts. How is this? Because envy has a way of coming in disguise; it says, "I have come a long way; I am no enemy of yours, I am no enemy of any man's; I am really not envy or jealousy at all; I will do you good: I will prompt your righteousness to high indignation, but in all the flame of its wrath there shall be nothing that is not akin to the very fire of God's own feeling." Let us beware how we receive disguised spirits into the heart. "Brethren, believe not every spirit, but try the spirits whether they be of God;" and most try those spirits that look so perfectly simple and bring with them credentials written in large letters and signed by very conspicuous names. Truth requires no such introduction. Truth is fearless. Sometimes literally it may be discrepant and inconsistent with itself, so much so that a clever reader could mass all the discrepancies and make a case against the witness; but truth can afford to stumble, stammer, correct itself in the matter of mere memory; truth can apologise with dignity; truth can retract with candour. The great difficulty is that people will not make their reason a religious power; in other words, identify its action with religious prostration and inquiry of God. They say the case is so perfectly simple. Such simplicity is not to be found anywhere. God is in the smallest flower he ever made. Every atom that requires even a microscope to discover its existence has a distinct relation to the eternal throne; and reason in its proudest moments loses nothing, but gains everything by the prayer that ennobles its understanding and whets its penetration. Joshua and his men were beguiled by appearances, by a most evident and obvious case. They took not counsel at the mouth of the Lord, and what came of it is revealed in the narrative. How pitiful is the issue! How short is the life of the schemer!

"And it came to pass at the end of three days" (v. 16).

That is the life of a lie. It cannot go any longer practically; it may do so arithmetically, but "three days" is the measure of its duration. The third sunset—the appointed time—sees the mask fall off and the liar stand—stand only to fall. When will men learn this? When will we lay this lesson to heart? Everything looks so successful, and the whole business is just approaching completion, or has actually passed the point of mechanical maturity, and the Gibeonites are about to settle down as men who have successfully perfected a trick; and, lo, at the end of "three days" their whole purpose is exposed and their cleverness is exhausted and at an end! Possibly some may be pursuing precisely the same policy. The circumstances are wholly different; but do not delude yourselves with the notion that circumstances make the reality of the case. What are we about now in commerce, in family life, in all the relations, personal and social, which we sustain? What about the trick, the mean device, the covered lie, the well-painted mask, the falsehood well got up? He would be no prophet of the Lord who did not ask the question so burningly as almost to force an answer from the perpetrator of the imposition. But men will not learn from history: every man must commit suicide. We see a thousand men before us in the very line we are taking, all dead, and yet we think *we* can pass the heap of ruin and successfully reach the final point of the line! It cannot be done. God is against it; and when God is against a man his reason is like a candle blown out, and his cleverness but adds to the aggravation of his guilt. Nothing will stand but truth, honour; truth will stand when all things fail. It lives in the open air all the days of the year; it can go out at midnight as safely as at midday; it speaks to a king, to a child, to a peasant, with all the simplicity of innocence and the beauteousness of a high and noble and valiant courage. But the man who is imposing upon others skulks, listens, wonders, is astonished at little sentences which people drop as if they were dropping them on purpose, is excited by an inquiry, is affrighted by an unexpected letter. He is a liar, and the liar has a bad time of it. O that men were wise, that they understood these things!

But the Gibeonites were spared. Yes, they were spared, but were made bondmen—servants for ever :—

"And Joshua made them that day hewers of wood and drawers of water for the congregation, and for the altar of the Lord, even unto this day, in the place which he should choose" (v. 27).

The liar comes to humiliation. He cannot come to honour. If he came to honour, he dare not touch it. Everything turns to ashes in the bad man's hand. His children are not his : they disown him; without being able to explain it, they hate him; they represent to him the wrath of an indignant God ; they would not touch him : his kiss blasts their young lips ;—he is a liar, and should be kept a universe off virtue and beauty. Do not suppose a lie can be made permanently successful. Better eat the bread of poverty than the bread of falsehood. Better have the very lowest social position, hardly a foothold in the world at all, yet maintain it like an honest man, than have all the surface of the globe, and know that the air is full of anger, and that the judgment is gathering and will presently explode and destroy the victim. No counsel can prosper against God. The escape from one form of punishment is not an escape from all. A covenant had been made, and according to Eastern custom, when men had eaten salt with one another, the salt was to be as a perpetual protection between them. We have already seen how men spread salt upon a sword and took the salt, each of them : hence-forth that sword was sheathed. So it was in this instance. The covenant had been made, and therefore was to be literally respected. So far as that covenant was concerned, it stood ; but God has always one other thing he can do that we never imagined or suspected. We cannot escape God. It is a fearful thing to fall into the hands of the living God. Our God is a consuming fire. He never consumed that which was good : he has no fire that would burn it. Men have tried to burn the good, and have failed. Men have guillotined noble reformers and patriots, but the reform and the patriotism came up sevenfold greater than before. Great tyrants have issued orders that rebels should be slain and crushed, and crushed and slain they have been, but in so far as the rebels represented righteousness, justice, fair play, the guillotine failed, not the men who were decapitated by it. So there is honour reserved for the good man and the true, however much he may suffer ; and there is judgment reserved for the bad man, how-ever much he may succeed. Set it down as part of your very life's programme : God is with truth, God is with right, God is against falsehood, God is against wrong ; and at the end of " three days " —that is, at the end of some measurable period—the liar shall stand convicted, the bad man who carried his head so high shall find that head falling upon his breast, and the man whose cause was bad and who succeeded for a considerable period will be brought short up, God will look at him, and in that look there will be hell enough !

What is the cure for all this ? What is the great answer of Heaven to all this falsehood and suffering upon earth ? The answer of Heaven is the answer of the Cross. Always we come back to the Cross of Christ—the blood shed for the sins of the world. We have all been liars in the sight of God, though not to one another mayhap. " If we say that we have no sin, we deceive ourselves, and the truth is not in us ; but if we confess our sins, he is faithful and just to forgive us our sins, and to cleanse us from all unrighteousness." It comes to one of two things : to detection or confession. Detection means perdition. Confession means pardon !

SELECTED NOTE.

Gibeon is a town celebrated in the Old Testament, but not mentioned in the New. It was "a great city," as one of the royal cities ; and to its jurisdiction originally belonged Beeroth, Chephirah, and Kirjath-jearim (Josh. ix. 17; x. 2). It is first mentioned in connection with the deception practised by the inhabitants upon Joshua, by which, although Canaanites (Hivites), they induced the Jewish leader not only to make a league with them, and to spare their lives and cities, but also, in their defence, to make war upon the five kings by whom they were besieged. It was in the great battle which followed, that " the sun stood still upon Gibeon " (Josh. x. 12, 1-14). The place afterwards fell to the lot of Benjamin, and became a Levitical city (Josh. xviii. 25; xxi. 17), where the tabernacle was set up for many years under David and Solomon (1 Chron. xvi. 39; xxi. 29; 2 Chron. i. 3), the ark being at the same time at Jerusalem (2 Chron. i. 4). It was here, as being the place of the altar, that the young Solomon offered a thousand burnt-offerings, and was rewarded by the vision which left him the wisest of men (1 Kings iii. 4-15; 2 Chron. i. 3-13). This was the place where Abner's challenge to Joab brought defeat upon himself, and death upon his brother, Asahel (2 Sam. ii. 12-32), and where Amasa was afterwards slain by Joab (2 Sam. xx. 8-12). None of these passages mark the site of Gibeon ; but there are indications of it in Josephus (*De Bell. Jud.* ii. 19, 1), who places it fifty stadia north-west from Jerusalem ; and in Jerome (*Ep.* 86 *ad Eustoch.*) : which leave little doubt that Gibeon is to be identified with the place which still bears the name of El-Jib ; for Jib, in Arabic, is merely a contraction of the Hebrew Gibeon. The name *Gabaon* is indeed mentioned by writers of the time of the Crusades as existing at this spot, and among the Arabs it then already bore the name of El-Jib, under which it is mentioned by Bohaedin (*Vita Saladin,* p. 243). Afterwards it was overlooked by most travellers till the last century, when the attention of Pococke was again directed to it.

PRAYER.

ALMIGHTY GOD, we are exceedingly afraid of thy power: we dare not come nigh it; we may not provoke it. Our God is a consuming fire. It is a fearful thing to fall into the hands of the living God. So we speak of thee, and so we feel that verily this is true. Yet, God is love; God is our Father in heaven; like as a father pitieth his children, so the Lord pitieth them that fear him. This also is true; this is the joy of our life, and its brightest hope; this is the glorious gospel of the blessed God. This view have we of thee in Christ Jesus thy Son; he revealed the Father unto us, and by him we have received the Spirit of adoption, whereby we are able to say, Abba, Father, with a new meaning and a new music in our voice, for the love of God is shed abroad in our hearts by the Holy Ghost, which is given unto us. Thou hast great resources of wrath, yet thy mercy endureth for ever. In wrath thou dost remember mercy. Power belongeth unto thee, and to thee also, O Lord, belongeth mercy. It is unto thy mercy that we come: God be merciful unto us, sinners! Let thy mercy prevail, that our iniquities strike us not with the great hailstones from heaven, killing the creatures whom thou hast redeemed. Spare the lightning, and the hailstones, and the great rains, and the devastating tempests. Be pitiful unto us. We are as bruised reeds and smoking flax; as a vapour that cometh for a little time and then passeth away. The Lord be pitiful unto us; look upon us through the tears of his love and not through the anger of his righteousness. Comfort us according to our mourning: fill up the great vacancy in the heart; establish that which is wanting in our faith, so that it may be long, constant, strong, quite majestic and noble because of its amplitude and its power. Lord, increase our faith! Then we shall rejoice in tribulation also, finding in tribulation the beginning of patience and the pledge of final refinement and sanctification. The Lord send none unblessed away. If it please thee to send upon us first a great fear, let thy love afterwards reveal itself unto us, and may we see the brightness the brighter because of the darkness which made us afraid. Carry on our little life a little longer. Desert us not when the day gets towards eventide and far-spent. Thou hast not brought us thus far along to cast us away into the pit or leave us in desert places. We will think of all thy goodness in the past, and out of it we will bring a holy confidence, through the Lord Jesus Christ, our blessed and only Saviour, that thou wilt surely complete what thou hast begun. This is our strength in Christ; this is our hope as we stand near the Cross. We know our sin is great, but where sin abounds, grace doth much more abound. We will say this to our hearts; the Lord repeat the music to our listening expectancy and hope, and we shall yet be filled with a great gladness, and the eventide shall be brighter than the morning. Amen.

Joshua x. 11.

"They were more which died with hailstones than they whom the children of Israel slew with the sword."

THE LORD'S ARTILLERY.

WE have seen how Gibeon made peace with Joshua. Adoni-zedec, king of Jerusalem, was exceedingly displeased with the men of Gibeon for making peace with the enemy. He sent, therefore, unto the mountain kings of the Amorites, inviting them to smite Gibeon, saying, " It hath made peace with Joshua and with the children of Israel." So the five kings of the Amorites went up ; and the Lord said unto Joshua, " Fear them not . . . . there shall not a man of them stand before thee." " So Joshua ascended from Gilgal, he, and all the people of war with him, and all the mighty men of valour." And Joshua smote the enemy " with a great slaughter at Gibeon, and chased them along the way that goeth up to Beth-horon, and smote them to Azekah, and unto Makkedah ; " and when Joshua had done all that lay in his power, the Lord took up the case, and he hailed out of heaven upon the enemy, and " they were more which died with hailstones than they whom the children of Israel slew with the sword." The Lord never loses a battle. The picture of that fight is most vivid. It gleams with many colours, and as it stands in the gallery of ancient history, it seems to say, This is how it always is ; study me, and see the providence of the Lord. We accept the invitation.

The divine cause has enemies. The miracle is upon our side. Why complain or utter wonders equal to complaints about miracles divine ? The miracle is on the human side, and is expressed in the incredible fact that the divine cause has human enemies. Reason seems to be offended by the statement. A voice within us protests against the possibility of an anomaly so glaring and so violent. We should listen to the protest if we could shut our eyes to the facts. Show us something divine, and we will worship it. Men would say in certain moods, Show us the truly beautiful, and we will fall down before it in an attitude of adoration. Thus we exclaim. The common doctrine would seem to be : we have only to see the good, and we will accept it ; to behold the beautiful, and we will worship it ; to know the right, and we will do it. It would be pleasant to believe this. We want to believe it for our own creed's sake. But facts are dead against us. We are witnesses against ourselves. We see the right, and yet the wrong pursue. We say openly, with frankness that will be turned against us some day, This is the right road. But we are going in an opposite direction, that is the miracle! When you have settled and determined that anomaly, then you may begin to challenge the possibility of miracles upon the upper or divine side. "Hear, O heavens, and give ear, O earth : I have nourished and brought up children, and they have rebelled against me." What do you make of facts? We sentimentalise, or dream, or speculate,—what is your answer to the awful mystery that a man, not only can say, but does say, This is right, but I decline to do it? If this were matter of speculation, you would put the speculation from your mind as unworthy of the dignity of human reason. If this were a charge laid against a distant nation, we should make some trifling remark upon the incident, describing it as romantic, if not impossible ; but it is the great line of our own life, the broad line which marks our whole experience, action, and attitude ; and we are continually face to face with the solemn charge, that we know the Lord's way and the Lord's cause, and we set ourselves in distinct disobedience to his law and claim.

But the enemies of the divine cause have both earth and heaven against them :—the sword of Israel, and the hail of God. The living God has two great forces ; if you escape one, you fall under the power of the other. Men cannot do with the earth as they please. They think they can, but that is a deadly mistake. What can they do with the earth? Consider the case, and learn how little is human power in relation to those very things which seem to come easily within its sway. What can men do with the earth, which is under their feet, as if in sign of humiliation and unworthiness? Can they stop it? Can they reverse its motion? Can they illuminate it? What can these masters do with their nominal slave? They can smite it with iron, and make it grow what they please. No, they cannot! The dull earth, hoed into grooves, will not obey the iron pick, will not turn to the pluck of the bit and bridle given by violent hands. What, then, can we do with the earth? We are obliged to study it,—to find out all its moods and whims and tempers. We are compelled to humour the old earth. We have to treat it very delicately and very kindly. At first we think we have only to smite it with iron, and it will be only too glad to respond in harvests : but the earth is a mystery ; the earth will not do what we want it to do. It openly says, I will not grow this crop ; this year you must change my food ; I am tired of this monotony, and I will not move again. We form associations to consider the earth, to report upon it, to take measurements and temperatures, and to arrange means to ends ; and there the old earth swings on in the darkness, now night, now day, and must be humoured like a living thing. How dreadful is this place ! This is none other but the house of God, and this is the gate of heaven. The stones of the field seem to have a mind, and the winds and the stars to be under a purpose, and to be expressing a design. Then the upper earth—if I may so call the atmosphere —for what is it but an upper and enlarged earth ? We may be able to do some little thing with spade and mattock, with plough and harrow, but what can we do up in the clouds ? There is a minister of wrath called the weather. We have never been able to bribe him, propitiate him, bring him within the circle of our influence. The weather has come down upon our navies, and broken them into wet chips. The weather has stopped our great steam-horses, and said, No further on this road just now ! It an earthquake had done it, there would have been some harmony between the process and the result ; but little flakes of snow have done it—white little wings, things that lock like beautiful insects,—down they have come, and down, until that which in detail weighed nothing accumulated itself into millions of tons, and great steam-horses, challenging and thundering and roaring, have had to stand still before the white opponent, unable to move one inch. Why, our power is quite a nominal thing after all. We thought we were so great, and yet the earth beats us, or if we win a little success in the soil and report it, we can do nothing in the clouds ; we have no ladder a hundred feet long, or two hundred feet long, or five hundred feet long, and if we had, there is nothing to set it against. After all, our pride is shaken down, our vanity is cut in two ; and men who have discovered a new variety of crop for the soil have to say parenthetically, almost religiously, "weather permitting"! When Christian men charge reformers and empirics with inability to touch the heart's deadly sore, they can illustrate their position and vindicate their fear by the littleness of the limit which binds in the power of all men even in matters terrestrial and confessedly material. Mend the weather before you mend human manners. Stop the rain before you attempt by merely human means to stop the torrent of human iniquity. When you have won triumphs in your own world, we will accept them as proofs that you may be able to do some mightier thing on broader lines.

All things fight for God. The hailstones are his friends and allies; the stars in their courses beat and throb according to his purpose and express his intent. The bad cause has no friends; it comes to an ignominious end; it is overwhelmed by hailstones. It is so humbling! If men could have shown on the forehead a great scar made by a gleaming sword swung by the arms of a Hercules—a very giant in stature and strength—we should have said, Well, you had a foeman worthy of your steel; it is equal to a victory to have been felled by that man. You come in under stress of weather. Hailstones! you beaten back by hailstones? Yes! Why then there is no glory in it, not a whit. Come back because of the weather? Yes. Well, that is very crushing. Exceedingly so. But you are a man; why didn't you "stand up like a man"? I did, but the hailstones knocked me down! Why is it so? All the world over. You cannot lock the hail up. You cannot find a shutter that will certainly keep the lightning on the outside: God takes the hasp off after we have shut up the front-door. Consider the ignominy of the end! To be slain with a sword is to meet a soldier's fate; to be killed with hailstones is to be treated as an inferior creature—is to feel the contempt of an invisible and infinite enemy.

These are the strongholds and grounds of the Christian attack. We are not speaking to men, you see, who can walk as if with the wings of the wind, and make the clouds the dust of their feet, and bring in the spring when they please, and detain the summer as long as they have a mind to detain that shining guest; we are speaking to men, however great or little,—to men who have to make careful parentheses and reservations in their boldest talk; to men whose triumphant essays are wetted through and

drenched by God's snow, so that they cannot read their own
writing. "Acquaint now thyself with him, and be at peace."
There is only one safe motion, only one astronomic rhythm, and
if you get out of beat and harmony with that, you are at war
with God. A short fight is his who encounters gravitation. For
a moment he may leap, but he will soon lie down ; for a little
while he may seem as if master of the situation, but the great
serene law moves on and flattens whatever opposes its tranquil
operation. " Acquaint now thyself with him, and be at peace."
The bad cause perishes in contempt. The five kings ran away
and hid themselves in a cave, and Joshua said, Bring them out !
and to the men of Israel, Put your feet upon their necks ; and the
men of Israel put their feet upon the necks of the kings ; and he
said, Now hang them upon trees ; and the men of Israel hanged
the five kings upon five trees, and at the evening hour cut them
down and threw them into the very cave in which they had
hidden themselves, and laid great stones against the mouth of the
cave, and there they are until this day. The great life-lesson
running out of all this ancient history is : it is a fearful thing to
fall into the hands of the living God. " Acquaint now thyself
with him, and be at peace." No hailstone ever ranked itself on
the bad side. No rain ever offered itself to help the bad man.
Though it may appear to have done so incidentally, it never did
so finally ; and the stones will be faithful unto the last. There
shall come a day when men shall say to the rocks and to the
mountains, " Fall on us," and rock and mountain will stand without a sign. "Hide us from the wrath of the Lamb ! "—and the
rock and the mountain will stand upon their foundations without
a quiver or a spasm. " Acquaint now thyself with him, and
be at peace." This is science : we are invited into the astronomic movement. It is the call of gravitation, not of speculative theology. It is the music of the spheres, not some hymn
of despicable sentiment. What say you ? To be with Christ,
with God, is to be in the laws of gravitation. Have you any
objection to that ? It is to be marching step for step. Have you
any complaint to make against that appeal ? Why try to go the
other way when all the gates are locked and the keys are not
to be found ? Why not have on our side God, and all that God
implies and involves—the whole mystery of power and grace,

righteousness and wisdom? Then we shall know what it is to triumph. We shall hear a voice behind us and within us say, "It is God that justifieth, who is he that condemneth? It is Christ that died, yea, rather, that is risen again." Who shall lay anything to the charge of those who are in rhythm with God? The appeal seems to me so based on all that is true in science, in nature, in the reality and necessity of things, that but for the miracle which we indicated at the outset, it would seem impossible but that every man should rise and say, I will be on the Lord's side, I will live by the divine movement, I will find peace with God through our Lord Jesus Christ. That is what Jesus Christ came to do. He found we were opposing the law of spiritual gravitation; trying to create a universe of our own, and only making a hell; trying to silence music by discord, and being lost in the tumult which we made. He is our peace. In him we are safe evermore. When the hail pours down, it will be upon the enemy, not upon the friend; and when the lightning gleams and blazes and burns, it shall not come nigh the heart that rests in the Cross—in the infinite mystery of the infinite atonement. Bad man, you can go on a while if you like, but not for long: the hail is against you. You can make yourself so trusted as to be allowed to go and change the securities and rob the strong-box, but not for long: nature has her eye upon you, the constables of the universe are on your track. You can succeed for a while, you can do wonders for a while, but only for a while; you will be hanged, cut down, ruthlessly and contemptuously flung into a cave, and be forgotten. Do not imagine that your course is quite run yet: you may have twenty-four hours more; but the hand from which there is no release is already groping for you. There is no peace, saith my God, to the wicked. The ungodly are like the chaff which the wind driveth away. The triumphing of the wicked is short. Only righteousness is eternal; only honesty goes through the weather without getting wet; only the truth can put out to sea in any weather, plunging into the troughs, mounting up on the billows, swinging on the crest,—down again, up again, but all the time steering straight for the green summer shore. Oh, go not to sea in some paper boat of your own making! The vessel of God's righteousness and love is open to us all. Let us enter. It cannot be wrecked.

PRAYER.

ALMIGHTY GOD, we are alive this day to praise thee. Thou canst call upon living men to bear witness to thy rule and thy care. Thou art not the God of the dead, but the God of the living; thou dost not refer to the ancient time beyond our memory, thou dost appeal unto ourselves, thou dost ask us to read the record of our own life and to consider all the way along which thou hast conducted us. This we will gladly do. Herein is our joy, secret and public. We love to commune with our own hearts, and to take note of all the care thou hast shown unto us day by day from the first; and we love in the open sanctuary to make public mention of thy goodness, and to sing a loud song unto God, and to make a joyful noise unto the rock of our salvation. We have seen thy goodness, handled it, felt it, known it in the core of the heart; therefore we will not be silent, but will magnify thy name day by day, at the entering in of the city, in the place of public concourse, quietly at home, all but silently in the chamber of sickness: but we will not forget thy benefits, nor cease to remember the mercies of God. Thou hast led us by a way that we have not known. We have come upon strange names in the outworking of our history; unfamiliar places we have trodden; unfriendly tribes have accosted us and encountered us with stubborn resistance; we have looked round for water where there were no wells, and have gone out to pluck fruit where there were no trees; and, behold, thou hast not sent us back unrefreshed or empty-handed: thou hast created fountains in the wilderness, and trees thou hast planted on the rocks. Thou art a God of miracles, working wonders in light and in darkness. Thou dost send unto us messages in all the blowing winds, yea, in the cold and mighty tempest, and in the gentle summer breeze; and all the year long thou dost never forget us: we are graven upon the palms of thy hands. We will magnify thy name, and praise it. New mercies shall create new songs; new visions of truth shall touch the soul into nobler praise. Thus will we spend the few days of our life, a handful at the most, praying that the last may be brighter than the first, yea, that the last on earth may be the first in heaven. We pray that our own life may continue to be the object of thy care. We can only live in God. We can only live in God as we bear the fruit which is consistent with thy purpose in our creation. Every branch that beareth not fruit is cut down, and cast away, and burned in the fire. We would bear fruit unto thy glory: we would have living minds, clean hearts, responsive spirits, industrious hands, souls that live in prayer; the Lord grant unto us our heart's desire! For thy Book we daily bless thee: it is brighter than the morning; it is fuller of truth than the night is full of stars. Help us to read it patiently, sympathetically, devoutly; whilst we read, nay the Writer himself be present, the inspiring Holy Spirit, that so the inspired reader may peruse the inspired writing, and in thy light see light, and behold and wonder at the ever-expanding revelation of God. Be with us wherever we are in the twelve hours of the day and the twelve hours of the night. Make our bread pleasant to our eating; grant a blessing upon the water we drink from the streams which descend from heaven; give us the apt mind in business, the clear head, the eye that sees afar, the sensitiveness which men knowing not God cannot explain; be with us in all family darkness, trouble, bereavement: when sickness comes, or loss, or bare poverty, may we find room for them, because they may be angels in disguise. Direct us in all our path; give us the right word when a sudden answer is demanded; save us from mental perplexity when besieged by an unrighteous ability; the Lord give us steadfastness and love of truth in the soul, and the incorruptible sincerity which burns all evil and finds its way to God through storm and cloud, through rock and desert and difficulty. Send a plentiful rain upon thine inheritance; bless thy people with peace; crown their lives with forgiveness. Above all, make us like thy Son Jesus Christ, brightness of thy glory, express image of thy person; may we in our degree be beautiful as he: pure and noble and self-surrendering; may we know somewhat of the mystery of his Cross, the pathos of his suffering, the atonement which he wrought out in the mystery and passion of love. For his sake, hear us; for his sake, bless us; for his sake, withhold not any good thing from us. Amen.

Joshua x. 12-43.

FIVE MODERN KINGS.

WE are now travelling in the midst of wars and rumours of wars in our progress through these sacred pages. The reading is very exciting and distressing. Every page is a battle-field, and every sentence is like a stain of blood. Our distress can only be mitigated by taking in great breadths of time and viewing the course of Providence, not in detail, but in entirety, as a stupendous and well-composed unity. This is the law of just judgment in all life, so we are not creating a law for special application to exceptional circumstances. We do not fully know why this waste of human life was made. But why say " was " made, as if referring to an exhausted history? We need not speak in the past tense, but in the present, for this same waste of life is made, in some form or other, every day, and seems to be part of the very law of progress. We cannot understand it. We are not called upon to defend it. We must seriously stop and consider it. But there is the law: peace comes through battle, and life through death. Every garden is only a planted cemetery. Wherever you set your foot, you set it upon death. Who can understand the philosophy of destruction, the apparent wastefulness of God ? It is a mistake to suppose that destruction is unnecessary. Every day slays its countless thousands. War is not a term definable by one word, nor is it confined to one set of circumstances ; it is at the very heart of all imperfect and yet developing things. Life lives upon life. Blood is renewed by blood. A great mystery this and a tragedy that expresses infinite pain. But such is the devouring rapacity of life. It cannot live upon dead things. Life must live upon life, —cannibalism, not regulated, directed, and brought under some law of sanctification,—a great fact, a solemn and terrible thing ! What a hunger it is that gnaws our being ; it would soon develop itself into cruelty if civilisation did not limit it, and supply it with what it wants. No fire could deter it ; no force could restrain it ; it must be appeased from heaven. Which is to be uppermost? is the question of all life. What is to be uppermost ? is the question of Heaven, and God has declared for the righteous. So righteousness will win, and purity will sit upon the throne that is everlasting. We know all this, in part, without the Bible. There are many bibles upon this subject. Men have written revelations who never suspected what they were doing. They described their exercises by quite other and inferior terms, namely : they were observing, collating, laying down a basis of induction ; but do what they may, they all end in law, and the law would seem to be : destruction necessary to life, the out-crowding of some by others,—" the survival of the fittest." This is not the day of judgment upon which we can settle all these things, giving fully-matured opinions upon them and disposing of them decisively and finally. Thank God, we are permitted to speak as we think,—that is to say, God permits speech to relieve thinking ; so men publish immature books, speakers deliver immature speeches ; but their books and speeches are not to be regarded as final and unchangeable. Revelation is a growing quantity. Biblical interpretation is a progressive science. The observation of human life expands and clears and enlarges. Who, then, shall bind any man to his own punctuation, or search the foregone pages to charge him with inconsistency ? No man thinks two days alike. To-morrow is not responsible for this day, forasmuch as it will bring its own evil and its own good, its own light and its own darkness. It is needful to remember these things in reading the ancient books of Scripture, for they are full of terror and battle and cruelty and destruction and oppression and wrong, in many a detail, showing how easily the best men were tempted, how soon the noblest men fell into miserable humiliations, and how even women and children and innocent persons were borne down by a tremendous rush, as if the impulse were from heaven.

What use, then, can we make of these ancient instances? We can make great and profitable use of them if we be so minded. Before attempting to make some use of this incident, let us be thankful that the mystery of the sun standing still, and the moon being stayed until the people had avenged themselves upon their enemies, has been cleared up. What battles have been fought about these words! How astronomy has been subpœnaed as a witness, and all nature been forced into court! It was quite needless—as is much of the clamour and debate raging round strange things in the Bible. The writer himself asks, " Is not this written in the book of Jasher?—So the sun stood still in the midst of heaven, and hasted not to go down about a whole day." It was written in a poetical book as a grand instance of sublime imagining. It was as if it had been so. It appeared as if this battle must be fought out before eventide, and as if, strangely, men had so fought and so won that the great issue was completed before the setting of the sun. The instance is specially referred to even upon this page as a quotation from a poetical book; so there need not be any solemn summoning of astronomic science to contradict what has never been asserted.

Now we come to the slaying of the kings—the king of Jerusalem, the king of Hebron, the king of Jarmuth, the king of Lachish, and the king of Eglon. They were immured in a cave; they were kept for further uses: they were hanged upon a tree; they were burnt and condemned. Are there not five kings —yea, fifty, yea, countless hundreds—with whom we can do this very same thing—kill them, hang them, bury them? We have come to spiritual battlefields. The weapons of our warfare are not carnal; we wrestle not against flesh and blood, but against principalities and spiritual powers—invisible, but tremendous in strength, nor less tremendous in subtlety. We are not straining the instance by pausing to consider the meanings of the names of the places connected with the names of the king,—such as the king of Jerusalem, the king of Hebron, the king of Jarmuth, the king of Lachish, the king of Eglon. The names of the places may help us to consider the nature of their respective kings.

"The king of Jerusalem." That such a king should have been slain works violently in our memory and whole thought, for "Jerusalem" means peace—the city of peace, the restful city, the sabbatic metropolis, the home of rest. But is there not a false peace ? If we could not bring some good words into our use and qualify them by bad names, the case of the wicked man would be simply intolerable : the little truth he does tell, makes way for the much falsehood he wishes to propagate. Is there, then, not a false peace ? Do we not hear men crying, Peace, peace, where there is no peace ? Is it not possible to daub the wall with untempered mortar ? Do we not create a wilderness, and call it peace ? By banishing all anxieties, by stifling the voices within us that call to righteousness and truth and purity, by occupying the mind with other things, do we not suppose that we have entered into peace enough and realised all the rest we need ? Have we not shut out the light, and said, There is none ? Have we not given an opiate to conscience, and then said our life is going forward without rebuke ? Have we not declined to discuss certain things, and therefore imagined that the things are not open to discussion ? We have wronged our own souls in this matter. It is pitiful, yea, heart-rending, to mark how prone we are to close our eyes and consider that, because we have excluded the sense of danger, we have destroyed its presence. The king of false peace must be slain. He has ruled over some of us too long. He has lived upon us, plundered us with both hands, and all the while flattered us, until we have lost all power to criticise his baleful sovereignty. When men are not real with themselves, the case is hopeless. And who is real with himself ? Who can take out his very heart, as it were, and analyse it, sift its motives, cross-examine its purposes, and test its half-spoken words ? On all subjects of this kind we can but ask the piercing question ; it lies with every man to return the honest answer.

"Hebron" means conjunction, joining, alliance. Is not the king of false fellowship to be killed ? What concord hath Christ with Belial ? Why these ill-assorted marriages in life,—not marriages of a merely human and social kind, but all kinds of unions, fellowships, alliances, partnerships, that are founded upon rottenness, and are meant to mislead and deceive ? What fellowship hath light with darkness ? Yet we are beguiled into such associations, and we enter into them so gradually and in some cases so unsuspectingly that we hardly realise our relation to the false and the abominable until it is completed and sealed. God has always been against unholy alliances. Many a man he has, so to say, arrested with the words, Why this conjunction ? What right have you to be here, pledging your character to sustain a known dishonesty ? Why do you throw your respectability over this rottenness ? But who can be true to himself and to God in this matter ? Because we unite at certain parts or points of character, therefore we imagine that we do not include the whole line, and we decline responsibility in proportion to the number of points which our closure does not include. This is trifling with life ; this is making a fool of conscience ; this is giving to the moral power within us a dread narcotic : and we know it, and to pray after it is to crown our profanity with a lie. " Come out from among them, and be ye separate," saith the Lord. It is very difficult to be associated with some men merely for a temporary purpose, and then to leave them as if the association had never existed. Oftentimes that cannot be done. A certain contagion has operated, and although the formal association may be dissolved, the results of it may abide and express themselves in many insidious, but emphatic ways. Here, again, detail is out of the question. It is only possible to put the inquiry sharply, unflinchingly, and to leave every man to find out where he is, and why he is there. You may pay too much for high fellowships. A man may pay his soul as the price of being allowed to go into a saloon ; he may pay his manhood, he may pay his conscience. To spend a giddy half-hour in the gas-lighted saloon, he may be compelled to leave himself outside, that he may emptily and self-renouncingly play the fool in what he calls Society. That rule applies to all life, to all business, to all social fellowships, to all temporary associations. Have nothing to do with bad men, even though the purpose for which they seek your association is itself good. Do not believe any Scripture which the devil quotes to you. It ceases to be Scripture in his vile lips. He spoils all beauty, all loveliness, all honour. Take the same Scripture from the fountain, and carry it out; but do not say, He has quoted Scripture, and my relation to him is only that which ought to subsist between myself and a quoter of Scripture. We must have cleanness of conjunction, purity and reality of alliance, meeting on sympathetic ground. Even the Church of Christ, as constituted in some places, may be wrong in this particular.

And the king of Jarmuth. The word means high, that which is lifted up. And is not the king of false ambition to be slain and then hanged—to have contempt added to murder? Contempt is never so well expended as upon false ambition. This false ambition is killing many people. They do not see how foolish it is to be living under king Jarmuth. Why live a strained life—always trying to reach something that is just half an inch beyond your stretching power? If you were trying to seize the stars, men would simply smile upon you as imbeciles. It is the odd half-inch that deceives you, makes you think that, because it is only half an inch, surely you may reach it and use it. That is a false law of life. It means ruin. Whilst you are so stretching yourselves beyond your due proportion, men are robbing every pocket you have, and you do not know it; cutting the ground from under your feet, and you are not aware of it; and you yourselves are losing power to do the simple, real, needy business of life with both hands and undivided strength. The temptation to be just a little more than we are is the temptation we read of in the garden of Eden:—Eat, says the serpent, of that tree, "and ye shall be as gods,"—ye shall go into another kind of society, into a saloon higher up, larger, and better lighted; put forth your hands, eat freely, and become "as gods." See if the serpent is not still deceiving society by this very suggestion. Who can live simply and lovingly within the lines of his own conscious strength, and do the work which God has obviously designed him to do? It is when the wish to do something else and something better comes in, that many a man is thrown down and loses what strength he has, much or little, as the case may be.

Then the king of Lachish. The word means hard to be captured, almost out of reach, or so defended that it will be almost impossible to get at the king. Is not the king of fancied security to be slain and hanged? We say it is impossible to penetrate to our hiding-place and dislodge us from our ramparts, not knowing that our ramparts, which are supposed to be made of granite, are constituted but of ice, and the rising sun shall not smite them, but dissolve them, and they shall stream away from us and leave us exposed to every dart and every stroke of the assailant. What is our security? Not money, I hope: for riches take to themselves wings and fly away. Not physical strength, I hope: for even Samson has had his energy drawn out of him, and has been left a giant in carcase, but a cripple in power. Not ancestry, I hope: for who would live upon the dead and wear the respectabilities of an exhausted generation? There is only one security, and that is harmony with God, peace with Heaven, identification with righteousness, the absorption of the little imperfect will with the infinite will of God. You have seen the wicked in great power, spreading himself like a green bay-tree: yet he passed away, and, lo, he was not, yea, you sought him, and he could not be found. The mystery was that there was no violence; there was no record of the decadence in the newspaper of the day. It was a mystery. The man changed: his mental power deserted him: he put out his hands to take something when there was nothing to be seized; he spoke, as it were, upside down, in confusion that would have amused you if it had not too much distressed your sensibilities. He lost, he reeled, he groped at noonday, he went back to find his rampart, and, behold, it was gone! This we have seen in life in countless cases; but if we have *only* seen it, the sight will do us little good: such visions should be laid to heart.

King of Eglon. The word "Eglon" means pertaining to a calf, and may be taken as representing the whole system of false worship. A great mocking voice is heard in one of the minor prophets, saying, "Thy calf, O Samaria, hath cast thee off." It is the way of false gods: they betray their worshippers; they withdraw themselves when danger crowds the scene with innumerable hostilities; they will do in the sunshine—that is to say, they will do when there is nothing to be done; but they have no biding pith, no staying power, no quality divine. Such is the difference between men. Under some circumstances the men are, as it were, equal—equal in pleasantness, in cheerfulness, and willingness to assist; but some of them can bear no strain: so long as the whole business can be done by assurances that are without security, they are willing that the whole business should be completed. Men are known by their staying power. Many a man walks the first mile as if he were treading upon air. It is a kind of exercise in levitation, rather than in ponderous and literal walking. But there are ten miles to be walked. The second mile sees a difference; the third mile excites pity in the beholder : the man was never made for that task. So it is with false worship, with imperfect worship, with fancy worship. There are men who worship reason; but reason never worships them or trusts them : it does but coldly smile upon them and wonder at their philosophic insanity. And there are those who worship gold and fame and honour and ease; and these base deities cast them off at eventide. Be right in worship, if you would be right in character. Be right in religious conviction, if you would be right along the whole line of life and equally strong at every point.

Joshua, having slain these kings, goes upon his conquering way. Joshua said, in effect, There are not only five kings to be killed, but more and more, a line of kings, far as the eye can see. So, soldier-like, captain of God, he passed on from Makkedah to Libnah, from Libnah to Lachish, from Lachish to Eglon, from Eglon to Hebron; and there we lose sight of him for a moment. His sword is up, his eyes aflame, and he is the captain of the Lord towards all "devoted" things. And on, too, we must go—on from evil to evil, until the last bad king is slain: on from habit to habit till the whole character is purified : on until the whole life is cleansed; and this sweet old earth, so debased, so ill-used, shall become, in every land, in every clime, beautiful as a palace built for God.

PRAYER.

ALMIGHTY GOD, we pray with our hearts because thou hast taught us to pray, and we know that in heart-prayer the answer is found in the very petition itself. We are cleansed by this exercise; our mouth is purified and our lips are made clean. How can we speak the name of God, and then speak any other name that is not related to it by pureness or by love? How can we lift up our eyes unto heaven to behold the revelation of light, and then turn them downwards to look upon anything which that light has not created and approved? So thou dost make us better by our praying; we feel the stronger after we have spoken to God. Thou dost draw nigh unto those that address thee; thou dost put out thine hand towards them, and in thine hand is the sceptre of gold. We come by the way of the Cross. We have tried other ways, and they end in cloud and nothingness : but the way of the Cross is a way straight up to heaven; we meet angels upon the road and the spirits of the just made perfect,—a sweet and innumerable companionship of souls: all the dear friends we have lost, and the brave comrades, and the crowned ones of every name and quality whom we have known and with whom we have consorted; they have washed their robes and made them white in the blood of the Lamb. So we form one host : part of it in heaven, part of it on earth; still, we are one family in Christ, and we shall all be brought together into the larger house, and stand night and day in thy presence, whose look is heaven, whose breath is peace. For religious hopes we bless thee : they sing in the soul like angels from heaven; they make the night as the morning, and the morning they make as sevenfold noontide in the summer-time. We thank thee for them; they drive away dejection and fear and solitariness and all evil. We pray thee to multiply these hopes; increase not only their number, but their radiance, and in their light we shall work industriously and hopefully, and every hour shall create its own heaven. The days are few with many now before thee, because the pilgrims are hastening quickly to the end. The end may be to-morrow; the end may be to-night; the end cannot be far off, by reason of natural weakness and the increase of days. Some are young, and full of hope and high life and hot blood,—brave and chivalrous when good, but desperate and evil-minded when under the inspiration of the devil; the Lord send a message to such— a great gospel of love that shall seize the attention, attract the confidence, and save the soul. Help the young man in his struggle; it goes hardly with him sometimes. Now and again he is quite down, and but for thy touch he would remain there a dead man. Save him in the time of peril ! Kill the tempter that sits beside his ear to speak as he may be able to receive the bad communication. Some are engaged in good service : the Lord help them; their heaven is in Christian toil; their delight expresses itself in sacrificial labour. Give them courage and good cheer, and may they be able again to draw together their whole strength, in the name of Christ and for the sake of his Cross, and to go out and do valiantly for the Son of God. The Lord hear us when we pray, and be patient with us in our best endeavours. Pity our littlenesses and vanities and mean conceits. Pity us wherein we carry diseases, distresses of mind or body, brought upon us by no blame of ou' own; when the evil rises within us, consider our estate, we beseech thee, and remember whence we sprang and through what course we have come in all the ages gone. Take us into thine arms; give us rest awhile from storm and strife; quiet us with thy peace, thou tranquil one; and all this and more immeasurably do thou accomplish for us, because we pray in the name which must prevail. Amen.

Joshua xi.

TYPES OF CHRISTIAN WARFARE.

AGAIN there seems to be nothing for us in these historical records. Yet, properly understood, these records were only written yesterday, as if with ink of our own making, and by hands that are writing the story to-day. Surely we find here types of Christian warfare; and surely we find here lessons by which we may direct our energy, as well as our thought, in the great conflict which is going on as between light and darkness, right and wrong, Christ and Belial. Change the words only, and the spirit or thought may remain without modification. Nothing has gone out of this chapter but the mere terms, the proper names of men and of places. The law of warfare remains, because the fact of warfare abides; and the method of warfare is just the same to-day, substituting spiritual purposes for military thoughts and the usual armour of the battle-field. This might be substantiated incidentally by referring to the great forces which are set in array against the Christ of God. In the first five verses of the chapter we have a statement of the numbers that came out against Joshua :—

"And it came to pass, when Jabin king of Hazor had heard those things, that he sent to Jobab king of Madon, and to the king of Shimron, and to the king of Achshaph, and to the kings that were on the north of the mountains, and of the plains south of Chinneroth, and in the valley, and in the borders of Dor on the west, and to the Canaanite on the east and on the west, and to the Amorite, and the Hittite, and the Perizzite, and the Jebusite in the mountains, and to the Hivite under Hermon in the land of Mizpeh. And they went out, they and all their hosts with them, much people, even as the sand that is upon the sea shore in multitude, with horses and chariots very many. And when all these kings were met together, they came and pitched together at the waters of Merom, to fight against Israel."

That is a modern speech. The same kings, being spiritually understood, are meeting to-day in order to fight the Son of God. The kings have almost always been against him,—not the nominal kings only, as the kings of nations and of empires, but the kings of influence, the kings of society, the leaders of public sentiment, influential men—scribes, Pharisees, rulers, and the should-be guides of the people. The enemies of Christ are very many in number. We sometimes attempt to create Christian statistics. It is easier work upon that side than upon the other. Arithmetic is less distressed when called upon to state what good there is in the world, as represented by communities and activities, than when asked to give some dim hint of the evil that prevails. Who can give the statistics of the enemy? We have made some approach towards an enumeration of the persons and activities identified with the cause and kingdom of Jesus Christ, but where are the black books, the tables of figures that would represent the sin, the sorrow, the heartbreak, the baleful purpose, the selfish design, the cruel disposition, and all manner of evil known amongst men? We are told that there are ten thousand little girls upon the streets of London alone whose name is associated with sin. I do not blame them altogether. Judgment must not fall upon them solely. What do they represent? They must be taken in their symbolical character, as well as judged by their real conduct; and so taken, what is the meaning of it all? Who can trace the lines backward? Who can fix those lines in the proper centres and personalities, and identify those who are socially invisible with this infinite degradation? We are told that if all the drunkeries of Britain were set together, they would make a street six hundred miles long, and that street would be a double street, having a return line equal to the first, so that, if stretched out in one continuity, there would be twelve hundred miles representing the traffic which is doing more to destroy the earth than any other traffic which man can originate or invent. But what does this represent? The matter does not begin and end in thronged buildings, in flaming windows, in flowing poison; there is something behind, round about, and until we can get into the atmosphere of the case we shall not be able to state statistically how evil stands. As many as the sand upon the sea-shore in multitude are they who are busily engaged in propagating evil. The worst of all evil is the respectable evil, the well-dressed wickedness, the haughty, disdainful blasphemy against all good and truth and love. The worst of all evil is in our own hearts. We are prone to go out in quest of statistics that we may represent how other people are breaking the ten commandments and offending the sanctity of Heaven: " first cast out the beam out of thine own eye; and then shalt thou see clearly to cast out the mote out of thy brother's eye." Is there any irony more pitiable, is there any irony less excusable, than our figuring down upon paper, which we shock by the very violence of the figures, how other people are transgressing the law, and saying nothing about our own selfishness, vanity, jealousy, cruelty, and designs to which we dare not give audible expression? " All we like sheep have gone astray; we have turned every one to his own way." The Lord looked down from heaven to see if there were any that did righteously, and he said, " There is none righteous, no, not one." Nor do we add to our supposed morality by publishing statistics against other people. It is quite true that we ought not therefore to spare other vices which are more public and in a social sense more calamitous than the vices which characterise conventional respectability: it is perfectly true that there ought to be exposure and denunciation and judgment and penalty, and that hell is too good for those who work evil; but the two statements are perfectly compatible: whilst we are indignant, and justly and rightly so, with things that we see, we ought to be equally indignant with the things that are hidden in our own hearts. Purify the fountain, and the stream will be clean; make the tree good, and the fruit will be good. Thus there are two aspects, both of which may be zealously maintained, but no one of which ought to be maintained at the expense of the other. Blessed be every man who, having found evil, tears the mask from its face, and blessed be that man who is busy casting the beam out of his own eye whilst he is mourning the frailties, the follies, the wickedness and ineffable iniquity of others.

Not only are the enemies of Christ very numerous, but they are perfectly united. There is a common consent amongst them. They hate the good. They are unanimous, and their unanimity is power. Though they sin in different ways, so that the details seemingly have no relation to one another, yet there is an understood unanimity amongst bad men, there is a password of evil, there is a touch which is known throughout the infamous fraternity. Bad men support one another. Herein they set Christians an example. Christians are not united. There is no body of men so disunited as the Christian body. What are they doing? Setting one opinion against another, battling for *isms*, contradicting one another publicly and bluntly, assailing one another, creating indictments which involve petty heterodoxies or erratic thinkings amongst honest men ; whereas Christians ought to begin with this fact, namely : we are one brotherhood ; we are one in our worship of Christ, in our trust of the Cross, in our expectation from Calvary ; we are one in prayer. The moment we begin to pray, all hearts throb in one grand energy ; the moment we begin to speak to one another, contradiction sets in. Then let us leave everything of the nature of dispute contradiction, and variety of opinion, and show a common front to the common enemy. There is no occasion to say that we are undervaluing opinions, differences, and varieties of conviction and expression ; we are now speaking relatively, and I cannot but repeat that, in view of enemies many as the sand upon the sea-shore in multitude, with horses and chariots very many, the one grand question amongst Christians should be, How far are we one ? and not, How far can we divide and subdivide ourselves, and separate one from another as if in vital hostility ? All the world over the bad man supports the bad man. He may not do so openly, but there is an understanding between them : the one bad man knows that if his house falls, the other man's house is in danger ; or when the other man's house falls, his own dwelling is in peril. Whatever the differences in name and detail and circumstance, evil is one, and evil gathers itself together in tremendous concentration to fight against the Son of God.

The forces of evil are many, united, and desperate. They have made up their minds to work rack and ruin. We have covered over a great deal of enmity, but it is still there, as rank and virulent as ever. There are men within sound of the church-going bells who would tear down the bells, or use them to announce some other act and some other day than Christian service and resurrection morning. Within the sweep of our own observation there are men who would burn the Bible, dig up the very foundations of the sanctuary, destroy the memory of the Cross of Christ. We need not go to heathen lands or foreign countries, and talk about the opposition which is offered to the gospel of Christ. There is no such opposition in many of these places, for the simple reason that the name of Christ is not known. The rancorous and awful opposition to the Cross of Christ is in our own hearts, in our own life, and may be within the circuit of our own influence. Wicked men—let us repeat again and again—are desperate. Never undervalue the force that is against you. Nothing is to be gained by pouring contempt upon the numbers that are arrayed against the kingdom of Christ. There are those who would say, The enemy can be but few in number—why heed a dozen men? Why make any account of a hundred souls? What are they in relation to the great numbers which constitute the army of Christ? Pour contempt upon no one man. The kingdom of heaven itself is like a grain of mustard seed: it had a small beginning, and it has gone forward under the contempt and opposition of the world to its present position, whatever that may be, in beneficence and nobleness. One desperate man is an army. One really earnest man is a host, either on the one side or the other. There are so many ciphers; the number is very great, but the value is nothing; the value would be increased if even one unit could be set at their head: that one unit would shoot a value through every empty cipher and make it stand up the symbol of number and force and goodness. Woe betide the Church when, shutting her doors and closing her windows, she simply looks round upon her own congregation and supposes that congregation to be the world! At any given moment in Christian history the majority of men, taken by numbers, has been dead against the Messiahship of Christ.

What, then, is to be done ?   A dreary picture has been drawn ;
a very discouraging outlook has been taken in some respects and
in some directions : what is to be done ?   The answer is in
the sixth verse :—

" And the Lord said unto Joshua, Be not afraid because of them : for to
morrow about this time will I deliver them up all slain before Israel; thou
shalt hough their horses, and burn their chariots with fire."

It required the Lord's voice at that critical moment.   There are
times when, if God himself does not speak, the heart cannot live
any longer.   Hosts are gathering, the kings are coming down,
every man is a king, and every king has brought his army with
him, and his chariots ; the gathering-place is within sight, and in
one moment more the tremendous war will open,—" and the
Lord said—"   The Lord times his sayings.   He will allow
Joshua to look on until Joshua's heart becomes as water within
him, until his strength utterly declines ; and when Joshua is in
that condition, the Lord will say, " Be not afraid because of
them : for to morrow about this time will I deliver them up all
slain before Israel."   Who can tell what will happen within one
round of the clock ?   We must not be discouraged because at any
one moment the Christian cause seems to be overwhelmed.   The
Lord will suddenly come to his temple.   Many things are nearer
than we suppose, and in their bringing-in there will be no
violence or revolution.   The great spiritual victory may be won,
to our surprise, in the night-time, as though we had nothing to do
with it, but it were purely a conquest of heaven as against hell.
History is made in critical moments, and sometimes apparently
within measurable periods.   Yesterday the kings were in high
feather, yea, in great glee.   As king came in after king, the
shout of victory arose.   There was no terror-stricken man in all
their royal gathering.   The forces of the land had come together.
This was no deputation work ; it was original service : the kings
themselves were soldiers.   How long did it take to overcome
them all ?   What we should now term one round of the clock.
Surely there is a kind of latent contempt in the observation " for
to morrow about this time."   One day is as a thousand years,
and a thousand years as one day.   Great deeds are wrought in
a short time.   This is the hope of the Christian ; this is the

confidence of all noble workers in noble causes. We cannot tell how it is, but this miracle is promised—the last miracle— the miracle of suddenness, immediacy. Who can tell how the proud and the mighty shall be broken down "to morrow about this time"? Who can tell how short a period it will require God to work in to strike off the fetter from the foot of every slave, the manacles from the wrist of every bondman? Sometimes a grand emancipation or deliverance has appeared to be a thousand years off, and yet "to morrow about this time," even to morrow the whole blessed issue was wrought out and accomplished, and Right as against foul Might was crowned. This is the view we must take of our service. Our service appears in some respects to be even contemptible. We preach, but nobody hears, or they who hear do not believe; they laugh with their hearts, or put away Christ with silent disdain. He seems to be fighting a losing battle; he is no further on to-day than he was yesterday; even where his sentiments are acknowledged, and where the compli- ment of hypocrisy is paid to him, there is no sound progress of righteousness and verity and holiness. That is a false view, or it is a view which should be false by the testimony of all history. "To morrow about this time" there will not a king be found arrayed against the Son of God. "To morrow about this time" heaven will descend, earth will arise, and none will be able to tell the difference between the fair worlds; Christ shall have the heathen for an inheritance, and the uttermost parts of the earth for a possession. He seems to be now ten thousand ages away from that royalty, but "to morrow about this time" that astounded earth will throw down its arms, and say, in every language, "Galilean, thou hast conquered," or, "Son of God, reign over us; thine is the right to reign." Blessed is that servant who expects these things! He is inspired by the expectation: he comes up again to the fight, assured that "to morrow about this time" the victory will be won. Is it not possible for us to anticipate even the time which God has set, and, as it were, to surprise him by an early surrender? Is it not possible for some even now to say, I will not put it off until to-morrow; it shall be done now. Now I will part with all evil; I will dissolve alliance with all iniquity : I will, God helping me, be a new man, and serve the Lord in fulness of the heart's consent?

Joshua did his work thoroughly. In the twelfth verse we read, "he utterly destroyed them." We want thorough work. We have partially cut down many vices : we have shaved off the top of them, but the root is still there, and, as we have seen before, the vine is the root, not the flower, not the blossom. What would be said of the husbandman who simply took the top off the poisonous tree which was destroying the fertility of his land? We should describe him as thoughtless, foolish, unwise altogether, and exhort him to dig up the root and burn it with unquenchable fire. What would be said of the man who painted himself a healthy colour,—who, without taking note of the internal disease, simply concealed its symptoms under a coating of fine tint that should express to the casual observer real health? We should call him "fool;" we should describe him in the severest terms; we should designate him a madman. But what is that to what we ourselves may be doing,—washing the outside of the cup and platter, while the inside is full of rottenness and dead men's bones? The eyes of judgment will look upon the inside, and many an outside flaw or stain will be forgiven or excused because of the friction of life and the multitudinousness of our relations; but the inside, the interior, that will be judged, and that will be approved or condemned.

Sweet is the last word :—"the land rested from war" (v. 23). The tocsin sounded no more; the trumpet was not again heard. The whole earth is to be at peace with God, and therefore at peace with itself. The sword and the spear are to be turned into ploughshare and pruning-hook, and the shiel is to be hung up in the hall—a piece of ancient history, only preserved that it may stimulate to holier thanksgiving and profounder prayer. The land had rest from war. The fiend went abroad no more. Man came to man as brother to brother. Feuds and differences and separations were things of the past. Every man knew the Lord; every man prayed with his brother-man in happy consent. This is a great outlook from the Christian's specular tower : he sees the morning of peace, the day of light, the Sabbath of humanity; and he preaches in that tone—the great, glad, triumphant voice, like the voice of many waters; he says, Peace is coming; the battle-flag is furled; and the world is at last at peace! Towards that end we are moving. We are not ashamed of the issue; we are hoping for it, praying for it, working for it. Ask what the Christian Church is doing, and if in earnest, she is doing this one thing only—fighting for peace, praying against evil; and all she does tends in the direction of "the federation of the world."

SELECTED NOTES.

Jabin, king of Hazor.—(1) One of the most powerful of all the princes who reigned in Canaan when it was invaded by the Israelites. His dominion seems to have extended over all the north part of the country; and after the ruin of the league formed against the Hebrews in the south by Adoni-zedek, king of Jerusalem, he assembled his tributaries near the waters of Merom (the lake Huleh), and called all the people to arms. This coalition was destroyed, as the one in the south had been, and Jabin himself perished in the sack of Hazor, his capital, B.C. 1450. This prince was the last powerful enemy with whom Joshua combated, and his overthrow seems to have been regarded as the crowning act in the conquest of the Promised Land (Josh. xi. 1-14).

(2) A king of Hazor, and probably descended from the preceding. It appears that during one of the servitudes of the Israelites, probably when they lay under the yoke of Cushan or Eglon, the kingdom of Hazor was reconstructed. The narrative gives to this second Jabin even the title of "king of Canaan;" and this, with the possession of nine hundred iron-armed war-chariots, implies unusual power and extent of dominion. The iniquities of the Israelites having lost them the divine protection, Jabin gained the mastery over them; and stimulated by the remembrance of ancient wrongs, oppressed them heavily for twenty years. From this thraldom they were relieved by the great victory won by Barak in the plain of Esdraelon, over the hosts of Jabin, commanded by Sisera, one of the most renowned generals of those times, B.C. 1285. The well-compacted power of the king of Hazor was not yet, however, entirely broken. The war was still prolonged for a time, but ended in the entire ruin of Jabin, and the subjugation of his territories by the Israelites (Judg. iv.). This is the Jabin whose name occurs in Psalm lxxxiii. 10.

The question has been raised whether these two Jabins were not one and the same; and the affirmative has by some been assumed as an argument against the authenticity of the narrative in Joshua; while others think that the two narratives may be of events so nearly contemporaneous that they may have happened in the lifetime of the same person. This latter hypothesis, however, cannot possibly be retained; for even supposing that the ordinary chronology, which places the defeat of Sisera one hundred and fifty years after the time of Joshua, requires correction, no correction that can be legitimately made will render it possible to synchronise the two narratives, nor can we suppose that within the lifetime of one man Hazor could have been rebuilt, the shattered kingdom of its ruler restored, and that ruler enabled to tyrannise over his former conquerors for twenty years.

PRAYER.

ALMIGHTY GOD, we know that thou art love, but what love is, who can tell? Yet we feel after thee because of our need of One greater and better than ourselves. Our souls have often cried in the darkness, O that I knew where I might find him : I would come unto him, and order my speech before him. We know where thou art ; unto us who live in these latter days is the sanctuary of the Almighty well known. Thou art in Christ Jesus thy Son. Thou art in the Cross of redemption ; thou art always to be found there ; to that Cross, therefore, we now come, and our eyes are unto it with the eagerness of love and expectation. Thou wilt not disappoint the look of trust ; thou hast never denied the prayer of simple faith. Thou wilt not deny our prayer when we ask for pardon, saying, God be merciful unto us, sinners, and forgive us our iniquities, and cleanse us from all our sins. To this prayer thou hast but one reply. Whilst we are yet speaking, may we hear the answer, and stand up like men who have heard music from heaven. We rejoice in a pardoning God. We need pardon. We have done wrong ; but thou art merciful as well as righteous, and there are tears in the eyes of judgment. We come to thy compassion, not to thy righteousness ; we hasten to thy Cross, O Christ, and not to the throne of the judge. Who can stand when God inquireth for life ? What man may abide the look of justice ? But we come to Christ ; we stand at the Cross ; we hope in the mysterious blood, the wondrous sacrifice, not to be explained, but to be felt : an influence that touches the heart, a ministry that awakens the love. Send none unblessed from thy word ; let a portion of meat be given to each in due season ; and may we feel that in perusing thy Book we have been enjoying a spiritual feast, eating and drinking in the King's presence, and that we have been refreshed and satisfied and stimulated by the bounty of thy house. Amen.

Joshua xii., xiii.

A RECORDED LIFE.

THESE two chapters contain a good deal of hard reading. They are studded with unfamiliar and difficult words and names, so that reading them is like reading the writing upon gravestones in a foreign land. Still, there is much for our instruction here. For example, we are called to behold how good a thing it is to keep a detailed record of life. These chapters are in a certain sense diaries or journals. The men of the ancient time wrote down what they did—that is to say, they kept their story freshly before their memories : they lost nothing ; they wrote their accounts up to date ; and at any given moment they could peruse the record and derive from it the advantage of stimulus which such an exercise could not fail to supply. The twelfth chapter deals with the slaughter of many kings. Their names are given, or the names of their cities. Men were not slain, and forgotten. This was not a heedless fight, wherein the soldiers on the victorious side struck in the dark and knew not what men they slew or what progress they made. The whole matter is detailed, put down—simply, clearly, and definitely. Moses seems to figure but poorly in the record of slaughter. He killed but two kings ; and Joshua killed thirty-one kings. But who are the kings that Joshua killed, compared with the kings slain. by Moses ? The two which Moses slew have famous names ; they were great and mighty men. The thirty-one slain by Joshua did not add up to the two slain by Moses. Thus work is estimated by quality. We do not reckon by number in the sanctuary, but by quality and by relation, by just standards, and the weighing is done in scales of gold. The poor woman who gave all she had gave more than all the rich : for they gave out of the margin, out of the abundant and all but unreckonable profit, the surplus of their earnings or savings ; but she plucked out her whole heart and cast it into God's treasury, the only donation she could give ; said the Treasurer, It is more than they all. This shall be the law of judgment : according to what we have, according to the quality of our work. The fire shall try every man's work of what sort it is. He who has killed many kings, and he who has killed but two, shall be judged, not according to the number, but according to the difficulty, the dignity, the quality involved in the tremendous exercise. Do we keep a record of life ? How few men write their own story : in truth, there seems in many cases to be nothing to write. But this is quite a mistake. It is better to write the little nothing there is, than to omit the inscription altogether. A man may be shamed by the very nothingness of his entries to go out and do something worth putting down on paper and leaving as a record. We do not know what we do until we detail it. No man knows how much money he spends unless he puts down every coin. That is the difference between the wise man and the fool. The fool knows nothing as to what he is doing : he goes out in the dark, works in the dark, returns in the dark, and he cannot tell what he has made of the trust which was put into his hands. The wise man is his own judge, his own scribe and secretary ; and many a page he peruses which his hands wrote long ago with tears and penitence, with the difficulty of self-conviction. No man knows how much he gives in charity unless he puts it down. But who dare put that down ? Who can say how little paper would be required for the record in many cases ? Yet, on the other hand, who can say how much paper would be required by other men ? But there is a deadly sophism which relates, not only to the giving of money, but to the giving of service, which expresses itself in this form : I am always giving. If you think so, you are never giving. Have you put down what you have done, and added it up ? Now add up the other page on which the luxuries are written, the adornments of the house, the decorations of the person, the indulgences of appetite, the tribute paid to social ambition. Add up the figures : recite them if you dare ! Yet it is well to write down the story—the story of discipline and battle and sorrow : the story of spiritual kings that have been slain, of enemies that have been conquered by love, and of positions that have been seized by prayer.

Then, again, we see how time beats the strongest. This is set forth very pensively :—

"Now Joshua was old and stricken in years ; and the Lord said unto him, Thou art old and stricken in years, and there remaineth yet very much land to be possessed " (xiii. 1).

We have seen Moses go up to die with the fire of his eye unquenched. Joshua is said to be "old," but not in the sense of years ; he was "stricken in years," that is to say, the years had told heavily upon him. There was not much of him to begin with. He was fertile, keen, quick, flashing ; but he had not much stubborn stuff in him to stand the wear and the tear of a captain's life. He was only about a hundred and ten when he died, a sum counted as nothing in the ancient days.

But the word here used literally means, time has told upon thee ; this wear and tear has made havoc in thy strength, Joshua ; how old thou art !—not in days, but in anxiety, in care ; thou art whitened, blanched, withered ; and yet there is much work to be done, much land to be possessed. So God takes note of our failing strength. He says, concerning this man and that, Grey hairs are here and there upon him, and he knoweth it not. About some supposedly strong men, he says, They are wearing out ; they are old at forty ; at fifty they will be patriarchal, so far as the exhaustion of strength is concerned ; they will die young in years, but old in service. God's work does take much out of a man, if the man is faithful. A man may pray himself into a withered old age in one night : in one little day a man may add years to his labour. We can work off-handedly : the work need not take much out of us ; but if we think about it, ponder it, execute it with both hands,—if it is the one thought of the soul, who can tell how soon the strongest man may be run out, and the youngest become a white-haired patriarch ? But blessed is it to be worked out in this service. A quaint minister of the last century said, " It is better to rub out than to rust out." How many are content to " rust out " ! They know nothing about friction, sacrifice, self-slaughter, martyrdom. The work tells upon men in different ways. Moses was as young when he died as when he began. As for his spirit, his enthusiasm, he could have taken a thousand kings ; but it was time he was in heaven : God knew his life, God counted his pulses, God estimated his strength ; and God sends for a man when he wants him. Joshua came briskly forward, though at first we felt there was something wanting in the man somewhere. He needed so much encouragement. The opening of his story is full of " fear not ;" " be not dismayed ;" " only be of a good courage ;" hope in God ; keep your spirits up ; cheer yourself : now go forward. We wondered as to the meaning of this. We could not tell at first all it signified. Now it comes out. He is old already, stricken in years before he has begun to live ; and the land unconquered lies before him like a challenge, yet darkens upon him like a despair. No man completes the work. This is saddening, even to the point of agony. A man is permitted to build the wall of his tower half-way up, and then when he has got into the way of it, and could build blithely, because of added skill and experience, he is told to come down — and to die! Providence is thus a continual rebuke to human ambition. We cannot put on the topstone. How much we would like to do so! to see the last child thoroughly educated and comfortably settled in life; to see the last effort crowned with success! Then we should retire into the sylvan shade, and listen to the singing birds all day, and spend a quiet eventide, and glide into heaven, rather than die into its splendours! But the column is broken in the middle. A man is old whilst yet his friends are rallying him on the fewness of his years. And the uncompleted work testifies that God is the Builder and man but the labourer of a day. Seldom can a man complete his own work. There is always "much land to be possessed." The author has planned ten more volumes. Men, looking on, say, How active he is, and busy and prolific! He says, I have done nothing yet, I have not even begun; presently I will set to work and go through it like a man. It is not to be! The man who has lived well has a thousand schemes in his head when he dies. He says, I was just planning the noblest work of my life; I had just settled in my mind to begin what would have proved to be one of the most useful projections of the age; and now my right hand is withered, and the one strong arm falls by my side in impotence. "In the midst of life we are in death;" "boast not thyself of to morrow; for thou knowest not what a day may bring forth;" "work while it is called to-day, for the night cometh, when no man can work;" "whatsoever thy hand findeth to do, do it with thy might;" for the time of ceasing is at hand. Does God look at the worker only? No; he looks at the work as well:—"there remaineth yet very much land to be possessed." So he will have the land divided; he will have it allotted before the battle goes any further. What, is not this an allotment on paper? The battle has not yet begun in these other regions. We have seen the conquest of Jericho, and the burning of Ai, but as to these other portions of the land, the foot of Israel has not even been set upon them. God says, That does not concern you; take pen in hand, and write after my dictation. Then he maps out the land, fixes the boundaries, appoints the possessor, determines

the tribal relations, and creates a new geography. But suppose
that the fortunes of war should alter all these appointments?
What is God's answer to that? His answer is, There are
no fortunes of war, there are no accidents; life is not a speculation, human history is not a game of chance; all things are
ordered and appointed, and move by a massive and inevitable
law, the meaning of which in the long run is—righteousness,
beneficence, right. And the scribe wrote how the land was to
lie. This is the Christian's comfort! " The very hairs of your
head are all numbered." If we are doing anything on our own
account, in a kind of practically atheistic manner, God will allow
us to build a little more, but he will come down to see the tower
we have been building; he will put his finger upon it,—and in
the morning it will be found a ruin! Only they build wisely
who build under God's direction and by his daily inspiration.

Then, comes the alarming, yet comforting thought,—that *God*
keeps a record, if we do not. Read chapter xiii. 2-6, and see how
detailed is the knowledge and purpose of God :—" This is the land
that yet remaineth : all the borders of the Philistines, and all
Geshuri, from Sihor, which is before Egypt, even unto the borders
of Ekron northward, which is counted to the Canaanite: five lords
of the Philistines; the Gazathites, and the Ashdothites, the
Eshkalonites, the Gittites, and the Ekronites; also the Aviles :
from the south, all the land of the Canaanites, and Mearah
that is beside the Sidonians, unto Aphek, to the borders of the
Amorites : and the land of the Giblites, and all Lebanon,
toward the sunrising, from Baalgad under mount Hermon unto
the entering into Hamath. All the inhabitants of the hill
country from Lebanon unto Misrephoth-maim, and all the
Sidonians, them will I drive out from before the children of
Israel : only divide thou it by lot unto the Israelites for an
inheritance, as I have commanded thee." Yet we try to exclude
God from his own world. We think *we* make the fields to grow ;
whereas we have no power to make anything grow, except
we obey the unwritten and eternal law of nature. We can
do wonders in little patches of land; but who can strike a
light that will illuminate a landscape ? Who can kindle a fire
that will warm the earth ? We are such toy-makers ; we do all

our work on such a minute scale, that we deceive ourselves by
supposing that we are doing something : whereas, in reality, we
are only keeping the law.   We can break the moral law, but we
must keep the natural law.   Breaking the moral law, we call
ourselves free men ; keeping the natural law, we do not know what
we are.   But that is our position.   We work by the sun ; we take
our time from the meridian.   We are the slaves of nature: we
are the rebels of the sanctuary.   Blessed is the man who
meditates in the law of God day and night—the great law, the
whole law, natural, moral, spiritual : it is really one law, because
the Law-giver is one.   Why not be as obedient in morals as we
are in labour, in agriculture, in travel ?   Who counts it degradation to wait for the tide ?   Who calls himself a slave because
he waits for the seed-time, and cannot hasten it one hour ?   The
whole scheme of things is set in law, " the Lord reigneth."   All
we have to do is to study the law, understand it, obey it ; then
our peace will flow like a river, and our righteousness as the
waves of the sea.   God knows what has been done.   He says, in
effect, I have watched you, and I have marked down every step
you have taken : you are at this moment at this point; now from
this point the course is thus and so ; and all the land is to be
possessed.   God will have the land, even if we die.   Noble is the
thought that he has entered into covenant with his Son.   We
may smile at the old theological terms as we please, but noble
is the thought that there is a covenant pledging that Jesus Christ
shall have the heathen for an inheritance and the uttermost parts
of the earth for a possession.   Sometimes it seems as if this
could not be.   We say it never can be accomplished ; the so-called
Christian civilisation is going backward.   Only going backward
as we have seen the waves go backward, that they might come
in with a fuller force and throb against the appointed boundary.
We believe that all the land shall be possessed, because the
mouth of the Lord hath spoken it.

Then there is another consideration, and that relates to the
recurrence of bad names in the comings and goings of human
history.   We are startled on reading the twenty-second verse of
the thirteenth chapter :—

'Balaam also the son of Béor, the soothsayer, did the children of Israel
slay with the sword among them that were slain by them."

We thought we had done with Balaam. We made a study of him and closed the page. But who knows where his name may come up again? Who can tell in what relation he will stand to human history as the ages move on and circumstances vivify the memory of men? We think of names we will not mention to ourselves: they bring up nought but pain and shame and woe. We think of names we would speak all day long, for the mention of them is like a mention of summer flowers, and the record of the deeds in simple speech is like a gathering of such flowers, handful by handful, until the house is beauteous and fragrant as a garden. Our actions will come up in curious connections years after. People will say of one, He was a mean man, a selfish calculator and designer; he never did good to any living soul. Of another they will say, He was a brave creature, full of chivalry, quite lowly in heart, and so munificent that both hands were employed in helping the helpless and blessing those who needed comfort. A little incident will occur, and all memory will be lighted up, because the observer will remember how good some one was, and tender and sympathetic. The business man will help the young man because he will remember, when the case comes before him, that he himself was once young and needed a friend, and that a friend touched him as he lay in prison, and the chain fell off and he walked out a free man; and he will say, "In memory of that friend I do this deed." So the good does live after men, though the evil is not often interred with their bones. We will reverse the poet's moaning strain and say, Yes, the good does live, as well as the evil. Blessed are they who have laid up material for this kind of immortality. Even this, if the only immortality, is worth living for: in years after the name shall be a household word in many a family-circle, for it is associated with noble thought, generous impulse, self-sacrificing deed, and bravery to which the darkness was but as the light, and to which danger was a challenge rather than a dread. If we do not write our life, God is writing it. A man in his vision saw the great white throne, and the Judge was set, and the books were opened, and another book, which is the book of life. Wherever our name is written, may it be written in that book, and God will see that no fire can destroy the record.

PRAYER.

ALMIGHTY GOD, we pray for one another that, according to the necessity of each heart, thou mayest command a great blessing from heaven. Thou knowest what our life is— how full of pain and trouble and unrest, how much disabled, how weary oftentimes, yea, how dejected and even despairing. But thine eyes are upon us for good; the heavens are opened unto our prayer; the Cross of Christ is still the centre of our hope. We come to that Cross day by day, longing to understand more and more of its love, of its deep meaning in relation to our sin. We would be affected by that love; we would see what thou feelest and thinkest concerning men, and would exclaim, Herein is love! God is love; God is very pitiful and kind: his mercy endureth for ever. He is kind unto the unthankful and to the evil: while we were yet sinners, Christ died for us. May we be subdued by that love, chastened and elevated by its infinite spirit; and as thou dost love us, so may we love one another. We know that we have passed from death into life because we love the brethren. May this love grow within us, and find continual expression in our speech and conduct, so that others looking on may begin to wonder and inquire, saying, Behold how these Christians love one another in deed and in truth! We have come up to worship God. We would be bowed down before thee in penitence and humiliation, because of sin. God be merciful unto us, sinners! The blood of Jesus Christ cleanseth from all sin. There is a fountain opened in the house of David for sin and for uncleanness. We have no answer; we are without excuse or defence; all we like sheep have gone astray; we have turned every one to his own way. Have mercy upon us for the sake of thy Son Jesus Christ our Lord, who freely bore our griefs and carried our iniquities. Amen.

Joshua xiv.

CALEB'S CLAIM.

CALEB was a prince of the tribe of Judah, and before the allotment of the land was proceeded with he said, in effect, I have something to say about this; the allotment ought not to proceed until I have been heard: whether the word was written or not, Caleb said, in effect, I cannot tell, but it was surely written in my heart; I will tell thee what it was: A distinct promise was made to me some five-and-forty years ago,

and that promise was to this effect. Then Caleb quoted the
words or their substance, and set the case before Joshua, who, as
prince of the host, listened kindly and answered generously and
justly. How wonderfully the Past affects the Present! We
must not think that affairs are lying upon the surface and are open
to the handling of any'one; that the business of life is superficial,
easy, requiring no reference to the historical past, and no reference
to unwritten, but eternal law. There is nothing so simple as it
often seems to be. Sometimes simplicity is but the last result of
complexity. Beware, therefore, of all counsellors who treat life
in an off-hand, easy fashion, as if things could be set up, and pulled
down, and changed without much anxiety or without appealing to
the deepest affections and sometimes the tenderest memories of
the soul. Caleb referred to the past; Caleb said, A promise
was made to me in this matter, and I will tell you what that
promise was. Mark the wonderful consistency of Caleb's spirit.
He is the same at forty and at eighty-five. At forty he was a
man of chivalrous spirit: a tall man did not affright him; he
looked upon walled cities as upon paper castles. He returned
with Joshua, saying to Moses, The work can be done. All the
other princes or heads of houses had "melted" hearts; their
courage had gone out of them; they said, The people are very
tall, and the cities are very strong, and there is no more spirit in
us. But Caleb was a man of "another spirit." That spirit kept
him young to the last day of his life. King David was called
"very old" at seventy. We saw in our last reading that the
word "old" is not a time-word; it is a word that relates to
work, and to the effect of work upon the worker. The wear
and tear of work tells terrifically upon some natures; they are
so intensely devoted: there is nothing trifling to them; every
moment brings its own judgment, every day its own solemn
sense of destiny. David was old because his work had been heavy.
It is trouble that makes men old. Where is there a man that says
he has been overborne by mere work, mere labour? But a
thousand men could stand up if challenged to reply to the question
whether trouble does not wear down the spirit, take out the
very strength of the man, and make him old at five-and-
twenty, aged and venerable at half a century. So it was
with Joshua. He took hardly to the work; it was a great

study to him; he did nothing perfunctorily or within the limits
of the moment for the moment's sake; all he did, drew blood
—" virtue "—out of his interior nature. So it was with king
David —" very old " at seventy. Other men are younger as the
years pass on! They have a happy way of working; they are
blessed with the inestimable blessing of cheerfulness; they are
able to take everything, as it were, with a light hand and yet not
frivolously; they are so buoyant, so happy, so cheery altogether,
that, whatever comes, they approach it almost with friendliness,
and they pass through controversy as if it were but a variety
of life's pleasantness. The man who is now speaking in the
text is eighty-five years old, and he says he is as strong as
he was nearly half a century ago. May we not be so in our
degree? Why do we so soon give up the work? Why this
whining after rest, this desire to be let go, to be let alone,
and to be permitted to flee into the wilderness or "some
boundless contiguity of shade"? To touch such men as Caleb,
is to receive new life, new hope. The cheerful man comes into
history, bringing a warming influence with him, helping men to
carry their burdens more resolutely and more hopefully.

But perhaps Caleb was simply asserting this youthfulness
in order that he might claim the inheritance. Did he affect
juvenility? Was he for the moment buoyed up with a false
hope? The answer is very distinct, and there is no escape
from it. In the eleventh verse he says,—

" As yet I am as strong this day as I was in the day that Moses sent me:
as my strength was then, even so is my strength now " [what for?] " for
war, both to go out, and to come in."

It is a soldier's speech. It is not the utterance of a man who
simply wants his wages and then to be allowed to luxuriate amid
the uplands of Hebron. Caleb feels the old war-horse stirring
within him: I am eighty-five and as strong as ever for war, both
to go out and to come in,—to take the fortunes of the day, to be and
to do what the times would suggest and justify. So this boasted
youthfulness was neither an affectation nor a sentiment. What
did Caleb choose? By his choice we shall see somewhat into his
character. Did he choose a garden blown upon by the south-west
wind only—a very choice and well-screened portion in the new

land ? He chose Hebron! Those who have read the history know what that choice meant. Hebron was the metropolis of the Anakim, the country of the most warlike people in Southern Canaan. Hebron meant difficulty. For the moment, the Anakim had withdrawn, but they were still at a point of observation, and their intention was to return and take Hebron and its lands. Caleb, knowing all this, said, Send me where there is most danger. As for these people who went with me—or, at least, their descendants, for there is probably not a man of the original camp left— they would be affrighted by the tall Anakim : even to-day they would be as cowardly as ever. There is an heredity of cowardice, a descent of meanness. I have no patience with these people. Let me have Hebron, with its tall warriors and its defences and its positions fortified and all but invulnerable ; give me the hard lot. Now we know the meaning of his boast. We want some such men now. We must not dismiss old workers who are willing to continue the work. Have no faith in any Christian communion that wants to get rid of the old pastor who has borne the burden and heat of the day, who loved and strove and suffered long before many of his critics were born. And this doctrine would admit of application in all directions. Remember the men who cheered you in darkness, who were lights in the time of your despair, who brought you grapes from the land that was afar off, and brought you the true wine of heaven, in that they said, This work can be done : arise and do it. Such men ought not to be treated unkindly or discourteously. They were brave men in their day. Some of them are as young now as they were when they were forty. If they think they are young, do not discourage them ; if they suppose themselves to be as deeply interested in passing questions as they ever were, it is not ours to throw them into dejection ; it should rather be ours to encourage them and bless them, for, whatever they may be to-day, in the brave days of old they were our soldiers, and heads-men, and leaders. When they ask for hard work, they prove their mettle.

Who can estimate the indirect influence of such an example ? Indirect influence is a subject we do not perhaps sufficiently consider. There is a direct influence which is much spoken about and highly valued, and not improperly so ; but who can

tell all the mystery of radiation ?   Who knows in what direction
the warm rays shoot ?   Who can follow all the palpitation of
heat, and say it begins here and ends there ?   Who can tell the
indirect influence of Scripture well read, of a Gospel well
preached, of a life well lived ?   There are observers on the out-
skirts.   The prisoners were listening whilst the apostles were
singing.   Taking into account indirect influence as well as direct
service, many a life will in the judgment be surprised because
God attributes to it the outworking of so many and such gracious
results.   Who could refuse the better portions of Canaan when
Caleb said, "I will take the hard part.   Let the old man
grapple with the difficulty.   As for these young people, they will
get younger as they grow older perhaps ; they will become more
courageous as the years come and go.   Meanwhile, I will take
the land that is now peopled by the giants ; and in the strength of
God I will subdue the land and make it part of the inheritance of
heaven " ?   We want to hear such voices.   We are tired of the
moaning word, the despairing note, the sign of dejection, the
cowardice that betrays itself even in the voice.   Many persons
can follow a tune who cannot raise one.   We must have leaders,
captains, mighty men.   Who knows what influence Lebbæus had
in the first discipleship ?   He is a man of no historical account ;
he does not figure among the three mighties ; but "Lebbæus"
means "hearty, cheerful."   Who can tell what influence the man
had by virtue of his cheeriness ?   We are not all speakers ; we
do not all go to the front and lift up an ensign ; but many help
the good work who stay at home and make the house glad, make
every window face southward, wherever the builder has made
it turn, to catch all in the sunshine.   Who can estimate the
influence of home music, home love, home encouragement ?   When
we go home, carrying life's burden with us, and say we are
now exhausted and can return no more, who knows the effect of
a cheerful word, an encouraging expression ?   These things are
pointed out that many may be encouraged who suppose they are
doing nothing.   Apparently they are not engaged in much public
work of any consequence ; but they do so much good to us at
home or on the highway : we never met them in the dark night
but they brought all the stars out ; we never spoke to them in
the storm but within the tempest there was a great calm.   Let

every man discover what his gift is, and his vocation, what he can do, and let him do it in the name and fear, the sight and love of God.

Who could give up when the senior was willing to go forward? We are shamed into some good deeds. Who would give anything to a collection if the congregation was not present? Who would really give in the dark? Some people would: the darkness and the light are both alike to them; but is it any libel upon human nature to say that there are some other people who would not do it? We are moved by example. There is a subtle contagion in social unity and action. We thought we would not go out; but seeing Caleb arraying himself for the night and going out into the storm, we cannot for very shame stay at home. So we look to our leaders, our senior men, to be young, to speak the glowing word, and to show that what they say is not sentimental, but real, because they themselves are willing to keep the door, to watch the gate, to stand outside, or to accept the most difficult position. Are there not some secondary heroes in the Bible? Very little is said about Caleb. There are three men of the name of Caleb in the Bible, and if you put all the three Calebs together the space required for the record of their deeds would not be a large one. There are under-heroes, men who are not of the stature and volume and force of Elijah, who fills the whole space of the time he lived in: but there are Calebs, men who are less, and yet of the same quality; men who have accepted Heaven's vocation and are working it out with a rare courage and a sweet patience. May such a word as this touch many a man who is wondering what he is doing, and help many a woman to believe that in quietness and in peace in household privacy she may be touching with helpfulness some of the boldest and bravest lives of the time.

What was the secret of this continual cheerfulness? It was a religious secret. Caleb says,—

"Nevertheless, my brethren that went up with me made the heart of the people melt: but I wholly followed the Lord my God" (v. 8).

When does God allow a man to grow old in any sense that involves contempt or insignificance or worthlessness? No man grows old at the altar. The Church, properly understood in all

its relations and activities, is the ground where grows perennial
youthfulness. When did the aged preacher say he could find
nothing more in the Bible? The blessed difficulty is this : that
the older we grow, the larger the Bible becomes; the more we
read it, the less we seem to have perused it ; we want to begin
at the very beginning again and go through all the music, so
enchanting is it, so inspiring, yet so soothing. The religious
man ought to be young. The religious man is bound for the
heaven of God, for ‿mmortality ; he must not die into nothingness,
into extinction ; he must live upwards, so that when he dies he
ascends. Herein I would not hesitate to preach the religion of
Jesus Christ in what may be termed its spiritually sanitary
aspects. Christianity keeps the soul clean, pure, healthy. Christianity will not̓ abide in the heart with any enemy of Christ ;
there will be controversy, all-night fighting, but Dagon must go
down ; the Spirit of Christ will not abide peacefully by truce or
compromise in any heart in which is hidden iniquity. For
bright faces, for kindling eyes, for voices having in them soul
and expressiveness, to what can we look as we can look to the
Christianity of the New Testament—the moral precepts and
doctrines of the holy record? A beautiful image is this: "I
wholly followed the Lord my God." The Bible is a pictorial
book. Nearly all the words are pictures. Most of the proper
names certainly are pictorial or illustrative. Many of the
references belong to the same class. What is the image underlying the words of Caleb? "I wholly followed the Lord my
God," equal to, "I was like a ship in full sail and going straight
on." The figure was worthy of the man. He was not halting,
beating about the shore, wondering where he could find a night's
refuge, or how he could escape the voyage altogether. He said,
When I was forty years old my life might be described as a ship
in full sail, the wind blowing it on to the desired haven ; what
I was at forty, I am at eighty-five : not a sail taken in, not a
wandering thought, not a divided affection ; as I was then, so am
I now : so I claim the fulfilment of the promise spoken five-and-
forty years ago. Did Joshua say, "No ; many things have
happened since then"?—a politician's base excuse under some
circumstances for not carrying out his word, or doing what he
once promised to do. No. He said, "This is right, and because

it is right, it must be done." And it was not done with the right hand only, but with the left hand as well; and not with the right hand and the left hand only, but with the right hand, the left hand, and the whole heart.

So Caleb's cheerfulness was met by a buoyancy equal to itself, and Hebron was given to him with a blessing breathed from the sincere heart. Is not many a blessing kept from us because we have not been like a ship in full sail? Have not our iniquities kept good things from us? How can we claim the inheritance if we have never been ready for the battle? And why should we sit in contemptuous judgment upon the Calebs of any age, when we have not known the stress that was put upon them, or entered into their labour, which made their lives oftentimes a great burden? Understand that we have come into an inheritance of history. We enjoy a Hebron that has been made for us. The civilisation round about us to-day is none of our handiwork; at the best we have only put a kind of top upon it. To-day gathers up into its throbbing heart the energy of all the centuries that have gone. Blessed are they who live under the inspiration of this idea. They will be grateful to their forefathers; their forefathers will not be spoken of as dead men, but as men who are now living and historically ruling the sentiment of their age. One thing is certain: God will not forsake a man who has been "wholly" devoted to him. God knows the number of Caleb's years, and the promise shall be redeemed. O poor heart, wondering when the good time is to come, when Hebron is to fall in as part of the inheritance, thinking the time is long, long in coming, and there may not be many days left in which to enjoy the heritage, take courage! God knows every word he has spoken. He is not unfaithful or unrighteous to forget our works of faith and labours of love. When he does bring in the inheritance, he will surprise us by it. It will be no mere handful of mud, no little measurable Canaan, but all heaven's blessedness, all heaven's purity, all heaven's music. Cheer thee! He is faithful who hath promised; he is able to do exceeding abundantly above all that we ask or think.

PRAYER.

ALMIGHTY GOD, we are not discomfited because the lot is cast into the lap and the disposing thereof is of the Lord; instead of being disquieted, we are at rest: this is right, this is best; not our will, but thine, be done. We would desire to dwell on the sunny side of the hill, and to find out where the rivers flow all the year long, and where the soil is garden-land; but thou dost put some men in the wilderness, and some upon the mountain-top, and some in stony and rugged places. The earth is the Lord's and the fulness thereof. Every place is praying-ground, every stone is an altar, and everywhere there are paths straight up to heaven. We desire to see in our lot God's law, God's will. We are here,—we want to be there; but thou dost say, No, abide on thy lot unto the end of the day; be a good and faithful servant, and heaven shall find thee room. This is thy sweet word. It makes us glad and strong; it fills the night with great stars; it makes the winter a kind of summer. Once we did not understand all this, and we chafed as a bullock unaccustomed to the yoke; now our eyes are opened: we see that God is King, and Lord, and Father, Shepherd, Friend, Companion, that there is but one throne, and that it is established upon righteousness. Now, come weal, come woe, we are not far from God. The cup is sometimes bitter, but thou canst help us to drain it every drop; sometimes the cross is heavy, but thou dost send a friend to lift it for us, at least for a day or two; sometimes the road is all roses and song and joy, the very dust of the ground leaping up in praise, and then all is heavenliness;—whether it be thus or otherwise, guide us with thine eye, preserve us by thy grace, give us comfort in all sorrow, and chastening in highest ecstasy. Work within us all the good pleasure of thy will. Give us the joy that comes of rational obedience, and the higher joy that comes of loving faith. Give us some touch of heaven even upon the earth; surprise us by some little flower that cannot have grown under these cold skies, some leaf from paradise, rich with fragrance from above; then we shall be young again, and strong and mighty, and though the enemy have chariots of iron we shall drive him out, and God shall have the praise. Help every man to see life broadly, clearly, and hopefully; enable every one of us to lay hold of it with a strong man's hand; keep us from all fear, fainting, dejection; take not the spirit of hope from us: may it dwell within us, and sing to us, and make us glad. We can ask all this in the name of Jesus, who carried our sorrows, who bore our sins in his own body on the tree. He taught us to call thee Father, and to ask great things of thee, yea, even to ask the Holy Ghost—all gifts in one. Jesus is our Saviour; Jesus died for us. We know not all the meaning of this Cross of his, but in the night-time of tempest and sorrow and loneliness, there is nothing so grand, so good, so comforting. Amen.

Joshua xv.-xix.

DISTRIBUTION.

LOOKING at these chapters is like looking at infinite rocks. Most stony are these verses. The eye is affrighted by these Hebrew and other polysyllables. The land is being allotted and distributed. Why then dwell upon a picture whose chief feature seems to be its inhospitableness? Because the picture is full of suggestion, and full of abiding and useful truth. One tribe is ordered to the right hand, another to the left; one north, another south; one into the valley, another to the mountains; one to places where fountains spring, another is commanded to go to the wood country and cut down trees and clear a space for itself—make a civilisation. This is but an analogy of higher distributions. Is there not a great law of distribution in all human life? We have but to open our eyes and look upon it. We cannot alter it. We may here and there modify it a little, or pass laws concerning it, or make it a subject of scientific inquiry: but there is the law, and there is no lasting escape from its operation. Nor need there be in order to prove the goodness of God and the riches of his mercy. The whole globe is allotted. Every continent has its own people, every island its own socialism. Wherever man can be placed he is set down there by a law which he cannot control—a marvellous, but gracious predestination. We feel it to be so. Who does not know a foreigner the moment he sees him? We say within ourselves, if not in articulate speech, This man is a long way from home. Who said so? By what right do we determine his relation to the globe? We cannot tell, but we do it. Instantaneously we see that the man has come from over seas thousands of miles away; his colour, his dress, his aspect—something about him says, I do not belong to this part of the land, I am a foreigner here: have regard for me upon that ground; I speak your language imperfectly: do not impose upon me because of my ignorance, but guide me, protect me, and show me hospitality whilst I linger within your borders. Who made the difference? What is the meaning of the difference? Why are some men put in

tropical climates, and others are set among the eternal ice?
And why this spirit of contentment more or less evident in
every land? Because, whilst we would regard the man as a
foreigner, we must remember that, were we visiting his country,
he would regard us, even us—great and glorious and all but
infallible Englishmen—as foreign! It is sad to think of! It is
sometimes intolerable. But even an Englishman may happen to
know the mystery of the misfortune of being a foreigner in some
parts of the world—an idea almost impossible to drive into the
English mind, for an Englishman, whilst hating all boasting on the
part of other people, spends his time in boasting about himself.
But there is the law—the unwritten law—the imperious and unchangeable law. The bounds of our habitation are fixed. We
are tethered to certain localities; we have a fatherland, whether
it be here or there; we have an appointed place, where our
dead are buried, where our battles are fought, where our
progress is developed : hence the spirit of patriotism—that
marvellous spirit that burns within us when the country is the
question. We feel, therefore, in perusing silently these wondrous
chapters in Joshua that distribution is perfectly familiar to us :
we see it in every part of the globe; we see it in men, in
animals, in plants. There is no monotony in the divine allotment ; it burns with colour; and in so far as it accepts the law, it
throbs with music, with lofty, grateful song.

So it is with talent and faculty. The kingdom of heaven is as
a man who took his journey into a far country, and distributed
to his servants various talents—to one five, to another two, to
another one,—to every man according to his several ability.
There is the fact. Why enter into pedantic discussions about
the parable, and the allotment, and the outworking of the little
drama? Here in our own circle and within our own consciousness
we have the parable itself in every detail and syllable. We
may covet one another's allotment, but we cannot cross the hedge,
or steal the talent that we envy. Who would not play upon the
musician's harp? Who would not wear a poet's mantle? Who
would not dream great dreams, the very beauty of which creates
a language of its own, purifying all common terms and making
refined gold of them, and jewels precious as rubies? Who
would not be a great merchantman, knowing things, as it were,

without study ?   Where other men toil towards conclusions, the greater mind moves to them with natural ease and dignity, seizes them and applies them to wealth-producing purposes.   Who would not be the heroic soul that never goes out but when the wind blows from the north, and then in great gusts and thunder-blasts ?—the man who would not sail over a smooth sea, but wait till the wind seizes the infinite deep and torments it into agony ?   Who would not be so brave as to wait till the war is at the thickest, and then plunge into the very midst of it, and ask only for the privilege of fighting the strongest man ?   But we cannot interfere with the operation of the law.   Some men cannot sing : there is no poetry in their being ; they never dream ; they never see heaven opened and the Son of man standing at the right hand of God ; they never rise to that high ecstasy which treats miracles as trifles, as occurrences that trans-pired millions of miles beneath them.   Others are without courage, except the courage of subtle impertinence, which suggests that everything must be attempered to their timidity, and nothing must be done that can affright their souls.   Did they but know they were mean and small and worthless, they might be forgiven, but they do not, and therefore they keep society at prayer, for nothing but the profoundest prayer can enable us to tolerate their presence.   Why is not every man as able as his brother ?   Why is one man eloquent, and another speechless ? Why is one man gifted with the power of acquisitiveness in intel-lectual directions, and another unable to learn his first lesson ?   If we imagine that all these things can be rectified, in the sense of making all men equal, we shall toil at abortive reforms, and have nothing at the end but empty hands and disappointed hearts. The question is, What can be done ?   What is the divine will ? Or, if we shrink from theological or biblical terms, still we need not surrender our reason : we might stand back and make a philosophy of that of which we decline to make a theology : the conclusion is the same ; the fact abides.

The same law applies to distribution in heaven.   All the beings, white-robed, unstained, beautiful with purity, do not stand upon an equal plane in the celestial country.   There are angels and archangels ; cherubim and seraphim ; beings all fire, beings all vision, typical of wisdom all but immeasurable ; quick-flying angels speeding with messages from the throne, and brooding spirits hovering over our life, appointed to watch little children: in heaven their angels do always behold the face of Christ's Father. In heaven there is variety of mental stature, spiritual service,—a great distribution of faculty and force and ministry. And this is essential, from our point of view, to a complete and beautiful heaven. We must give up the idea of monotony. If we still think of heaven as a place of harps and harping and songs, we are quite right, the meaning being that all true life blossoms up into song : we could not complete any pillar of logic or of fact without putting upon the top of it the lilywork of music and gladness and victory. We have painted heavens the colour of which wears off, monotonous heavens that become burdensome, small heavens picked out for ourselves and our friends. We must burn these heavens, and let them pass away with a small noise, for such heavens could never make a great one. The true heaven is one of glorified earth, glorified facts as we know them ; heaven of variety and position, locality, service. We know now what it is. We do not need to die to be in heaven, or to know it and speak about it familiarly : the kingdom of heaven is within, in the deepest, truest, most living sense. There are father-spirits, and mother-angels, and little people—children playing. The child that does not play ought to be looked after, and the case should be inquired into with awful solemnity. Children must play everywhere—at church and in heaven. A glorious paradise that, by reason of its variety, personality, faculty, and colour, and engagement ! In it there is room for you, for me, for greatest, smallest, richest, poorest :—" in my Father's house are many mansions : if it were not so, I would have told you."

Remember that every man begins with gifts. This is the very law of these chapters of allotment. The people have something to begin with. No man made his first dowry ; it was in him, or handed to him ; he did nothing towards the first germ, the plasm of his fortune and his destiny. This is often forgotten in estimating human position and human progress. Every man has a faculty given to him—a first thing—a nest-egg—a wonderful beginning ! God gives us the light, the air, the land, the sea. We did not kindle the sun ; we do not loose the winds from their tabernacles; and no man ever made one inch of land, or added one pebble to the earth's surface. In this particular we are very limited and very small. Think! the man who built the greatest cathedral that ever domed itself out towards the skies never added an atom to the sum-total of the earth. He worked with stones that were laid up for him, banked for him in the treasure-house of the earth. So when the Lord goes into a far country he leaves with every man something which the man did not make—five talents, two talents, one talent, whatever it may be; that germ or starting-point or protoplasm was given. So we begin with grace, privilege. We are trustees to start with. With all this ability and wonderful inventiveness we have never invented a new pebble, in the sense of adding to the earth's stones something that was not in the earth and hidden there by its Maker. If we leave that central or primal thought, we get into detail that vexes us, then we begin to manipulate and rearrange and redistribute; but it all comes at last to this fact, that every man has something to start with,—a wealth that cannot be communicated, a property his alone; and that must be inquired into at the final audit.

Some possessions come as rewards :—

"And Caleb said, He that smiteth Kirjath-sepher, and taketh it, to him will I give Achsah my daughter to wife" (xv. 16).

There begins the test of talent and force and quality in men. The speech is, Come, now! the palm be to the brave, the crown to him who wins it. Up to a certain point all things seem to be appointed, settled, almost arbitrarily distributed; but then there are chances in life that seem to come afterwards, as it were, amongst ourselves, competitions of a personal and social kind. How early this competitive spirit was developed, and how wonderfully it has been preserved through all history! The spirit of Providence seems to say, in homeliest language, now and again, Here is a chance for you; you had something to begin with, to that you can add more, by pluck, bravery, force,—to the war! We need such voices; otherwise we would soon slumber off, and doze away our handful of years, and awake to find that the day had gone. So voices appeal to us continually, Here is reward for you : he who is up earliest in the morning shall have this; he who has most staying power shall have the prize which I now exhibit; he who can take the most strongly-fortified city shall have this crown—all gold, except where lit up with diamonds. We know that this offer is made; we are aware that these opportunities do exist. Now if they who obey such calls do it to obtain a corruptible crown, what shall they do who are called to the possession of an incorruptible? If before running a race, or engaging in a wrestle, men subject themselves to discipline, diet themselves, allow themselves to be directed, controlled, and overborne by another energy and wisdom, what should they do who say they are striving for heaven, fighting for a crown of life, aspiring for celestial citizenship?

Compromises are sometimes inevitable. This is made clear by the sixty-third verse of the fifteenth chapter :—

"As for the Jebusites the inhabitants of Jerusalem, the children of Judah could not drive them out: but the Jebusites dwell with the children of Judah at Jerusalem unto this day."

Here the mysterious alliances begin which mark our life. We do not know how it is, but there are some forces we cannot expel; we are obliged to make truce and compromise and workable arrangement. It is so. Why dispute it? We cannot have everything four-square, snow-white, absolute in heaven-liness or righteousness. The Jebusite will elbow the children of Judah. Good may come out of all this, in the sense of wonderful educational influence and social modifications and chastisements. How many men there are whom we almost want to die, and die they will not! We see fair creatures dying —sweet innocent things, flowers of heaven upon earth, wither away; and there are stubborn lives, perverted, conceived in a false key, operating upon mischievous lines,—and the night dew will not damp them, the fogs of winter will not choke them, they escape perils on land and perils on sea. Why do the wicked live? Why do men who are apparently useless and mischie-vous live? Why is poverty continued? There may be many answers to these questions, but all the answers seem to leave the mystery where we found it. Life now in this part of its educa-tional process is often a compromise. How then shall it be? Shall the Jebusite overpower Judah, or Judah overpower the

Jebusite, or shall they both grow together until the harvest ?
We must not carry on works of destruction.   Men are not to be
killed out of the way.   Even the worst men are not to be
despatched by poison.   There is a mystery which God will
solve ; but this we can do : we can so grow in the grace of God
and in the knowledge of our Lord Jesus Christ that we shall be
able to throw off all the baleful influence which otherwise would
fall fatally upon us by associations we are obliged to maintain.
"Why eateth your Master with publicans and sinners ? "   Why
does he not kill them off the face of the earth ?   Instead of doing
so, he goes to be guest with a man that is a sinner.   That is
true ; he can do it, because he is the Son of God : the sunlight is
not afraid to go anywhere ; the wind cannot blow out that candle
of the Lord.   Our little lights sway in the wind and die in the
cold, but the sunbeam looks upon carrion, and yet is pure ;
heaven's mid-day looks upon hell, but receives no taint.   By
Christly character, by Christly pureness, by Christly consecration
we can live even with the Jebusite : he cannot harm us, so long
as we are Christ-like ; we may do him good, for love is mighty : an
eloquent tongue hath love, charged with the power of persuasiveness ; and pureness has wonderful influence, operating day by
day as it does, with the most sacred and sacrificial constancy.
What if one day we should say concerning the Jebusite, " Behold,
he prayeth" ?   Sad will it be for us if the Jebusite should say,
" Behold, he hesitates in prayer ; we have mocked him so long
that he is now afraid of his own faith : we shall win at last."
Oh, tell it not in Gath, publish it not in the streets of Askelon ; lest
the daughters of Philistia rejoice, saying that the men of prayer
have been mocked into unbelief, and the men of high profession
and noble character have been brought down by arrows skilfully
shot by arms that are mighty.   We accept the lot : not our will,
but thine, be done.   Whether the talent is five in number, or
two, or one, give us the cheerful, grateful heart that goes to work
with a will, and that finds its heaven, not in the number of the
talents, but in their happy and beneficent use.

PRAYER.

ALMIGHTY GOD, in whom can we put our trust but in the Living One? Death is written upon all other securities. Thou remainest evermore the same, and in thy righteousness is no change. We hasten therefore unto thee as men hasten to the rock in which they can be protected against the tempest and the storm. Thou art indeed a refuge from the tempest. Thou dost hide thy people in thy pavilion from the strife of tongues; thou dost call them into the chamber in the rock until the storm be overpast. Enable us to take refuge in the Son of God, to find our home and our heaven in his protection; and thus shall our life be spent wisely, and our strength shall go out from us to return again abundantly enriched and honoured. We would live in thy fear, we would work in thy love, we would be comforted with thy consolations and none other. Heal our diseases; direct our steps; keep us in the time of strife, and give us solidity of confidence in the day of distress. We bless thee for all thy care, so patient, so tender, so minute, covering all things, and attending to each as if it were a solitary concern. This is thy greatness, thou Infinite One, that nothing is too little for thy notice. We put ourselves into thy hands. We would have no will of our own; we would listen for thy voice morning, noon, and night, and answer it with the readiness of love. We own our sins. We will not count them, for no number can set them forth; nor will we speak of them, for we cannot state them as they are in thy sight; but we will look towards the Cross of Christ; we will fix our attention upon the Son of God as he expires in agony. When sin torments us most, we will remember what Jesus, Son of man, Son of God, did in Gethsemane and on the Cross, and therein shall we find perpetual comfort. Enable thy servants to work better than they have ever done. Enable all to whom the ministry of suffering is entrusted to suffer patiently, unmurmuringly, and hopefully; yea, may they so suffer as to awaken the wonder of those who look on, because of gentleness, meekness, and patience. When we read thy Book, first read it to us, utter the music in our souls; then shall we see thy meaning, and answer it instantly and lovingly. Remain with us; yea, tarry with us, lingeringly, as if thou couldst not leave us: and in that lingering we shall see a pledge of eternal fellowship. Amen.

Joshua xv.-xix.

THE DISTRIBUTION OF THE LAND.

WE have taken our first survey of the distribution of the land, and noticed several particulars of some consequence to ourselves; other particulars are now to be noticed. The inquiry will be, How far the distribution and the particulars associated with it are true to human nature as we know it. In answering this inquiry we shall soon see whether the Bible is an old book, in the sense of being obsolete and pointless, so far as the conditions and requirements of this day are concerned. The case is a very simple one. The land is to be divided among a given number of people. How they took the distribution or accepted the circumstances is an important inquiry.

We soon come upon a line that might have been written yesterday. It was not enough to have a great general distribution, but there must be some particular and singular allotment, to one person at least. She had a petition to offer; she offered it, and the supplication was answered. She asked through another a request from her father. Her father had received his portion, even Hebron and the region round about, and his daughter Achsah would have a little gift all her own. She would say, "Give me a blessing." That is vague. Not only would she have a benediction, but a portion—quite a little one, but still a portion, belonging, as it were, to herself—a jewel for her own neck, a ring for her own finger. Who does not like to have something particularly his own? It is well to have some general stake in the country, but to have a little private piece of land—one little bubbling, singing, fountain; a corner quite one's own—is not that the very joy of proprietorship? No doubt there is a general sense of wealth, so general indeed as to be of little particular service under the occasional pressure of necessity : but when the child has six inches of garden-land all its own at the back-door, there is, after all, a landlordly feeling in the young heart that finds frequent expression. Caleb's daughter would have "a field :" "she lighted off her ass ; and Caleb said unto her, What wouldest thou ? " She answered, "Give me a blessing." That she could have in a moment, but said she, Give me more, "give me also springs of water in addition to the south land." "And he gave her the upper springs, and the nether springs " (vv. 18, 19). To whom did she pray ? To her father. Have we not a Father to whom we can pray for springs of water ? Yes, we have such a Father, and from him we can have the upper springs and the nether springs. The river of God is full of water. It cannot be drained

off. It sets a-going all the fountains of creation, and is more at
the end than at the beginning—the very fulness of God; a
contradiction in words, but a grand reality in experience. The
sun lights every lamp, and not a beam the less is his infinite
glory. We therefore may have a special portion, a little all
our own; yea, a double portion of the Spirit may be ours.
Do not let us be content with the general blessing of the Church.
That, indeed, is an infinite comfort. But that general blessing
is a pledge of particular donations on the part of the Father
of ligi ts. Here we can pray without covetousness; here we
can be ambitious without selfishness; here we can have great
desires, and be enlarged in our generosity by their very operation
in the heart. Let each say to the Father, Give me a field;
give me a faculty; give me some dear, sweet consciousness of
thy nearness and lovingness—something that nobody else can
have just as I have it; whisper one word to me that no one in
all the universe but myself can hear, and that whisper shall
be to me an inspiration, a comfort, a security, a pledge; not
that others may not enjoy the same in their own way, but I
want something mine own. To that prayer who can measure
the reply, if spoken in faith and love and noble unselfishness?

Now another voice is heard. Joshua was not going the right
way about the work, in the estimation of some people:—

"And the children of Joseph spake unto Joshua, saying, Why hast thou
given me but one lot and one portion to inherit, seeing I am a great people,
forasmuch as the Lord hath blessed me hitherto?" (xvii. 14).

These were the Ephraimites, the most arrogant and the most
cowardly of all the tribes. Arrogance and cowardice have been
bed-fellows all through time and all the world over. "The
children of Ephraim being armed, and carrying bows, turned
back in the day of battle." We expected no less. We were
sure from their vaunting boast at the time of the distribution of
the land that there was no quality in them. The bark of a
dog would be mistaken for the roar of a lion; the falling of a
leaf would be construed into the noise of advancing foes. Yet
not all the Ephraimites were of that quality. Joshua himself
belonged to that tribe. The contrast, therefore, is the more
beautiful, that they, the boasting leaders of Ephraim, should
come up to Joshua, the true leader, and talk to him in a tone

of arrogance and lofty demand.   They thought they would touch his pride, but his pride lay beyond their touch.   He was too great to be restless, too profoundly religious to be in a tumultuous state of mind, too much in heaven to care, from a selfish point of view, for all Palestine—a mere speck of mud upon the sea.   Yet they thought they had good standing before Joshua.   " We are a great people," said the Ephraimites, " and one lot is not enough."   Joshua answered them with infinite wit, with a fine touch of satire, as well as with high religious nobleness :—

" And Joshua answered them, If thou be a great people, then get thee up to the wood country, and cut down for thyself there in the land of the Perizzites and of the giants, if mount Ephraim be too narrow for thee " (xvii. 15).

The answer is the answer of statesmanship in all times, and the answer of wisdom to those who clamour for great spaces and for liberties worthy of their greatness.   Consider the answer well : If thou be a great people, go out and cut down the forests : create a space ; prove your greatness by your service ; great men cannot be kept back : if thou be a great people, go and fight the giant ; don't spend thy time in catching flies.   The Bible is not an old book in the sense of being outworn.   It is still the best business book in the world.   It is still the book that holds all things within its four corners ; no man can add to it, and none can take away from it.   That is the mystery of the Bible.   We have already seen that no man can add a single pebble to the universe.   With all man's greatness and ambition and fiery determination, and all his love of conquest, he cannot add one little pebble to the earth ; he labours with infinite toil within a very small circle.   With the book of God it is the same in the matter of addition and subtraction.   You cannot publish a supplement to the Bible.   You cannot really and vitally take anything from it ; you may do so feloniously and literally, but the Bible is the complete Book.   Call it a seed-house, and grow whole forests and beautiful gardens out of it ; but as to its vital substance, its eternal pith and music, you can neither add, nor subtract anything.

Joshua, continuing the high satiric strain, said :—

" Thou art a great people, and hast great power : thou shalt not have one lot only : but the mountain shall be thine ; for it is a wood, and thou shalt cut it down : and the outgoings of it shall be thine : for thou shalt drive out the Canaanites, though they have iron chariots, and though they be strong " (xvii. 17, 18).

This is how we should try all supposedly great men in the Church—put them down into barren positions, and tell them to make gardens. Send the very greatest professor to the most desolate missionary station, and tell him that it will be at his peril to write one word of discouragement; every post must bring news that gardens are growing, birds are singing, the desert is rejoicing and blossoming like the very garden of God. So should all great people be treated. They should not have merely hereditary blessings—the meanest of all wealth, the wealth that has no soul in it, no blessing with it—a great load set upon a sliding scale that goes on and on by its own impetus. If we think we have great faculty, go out and prove it by going into the mountain, and by battling with the Canaanites. If we suppose ourselves to have very superior talents, go to the most destitute parts of the city, to the east end of every city, and make it as the west should be in all hopefulness and in all spiritual purity and dignity.

We come now to another set of circumstances. It appears that when all was done up to this point, a good deal still remained to be accomplished. We read of this in chapter xviii. 2-7 :—

" And there remained among the children of Israel seven tribes, which had not yet received their inheritance " (xviii. 2).

Joshua said, Go and walk through the land and describe it, and come again to me, that I may here cast lots for you before the Lord at Shiloh. In other words, Go and see what can be done with the remainder; bring me a map of the country; state to me the possibilities of the situation, and I will make a religious question of it, as I have always done. That is how we must do now. There are more than seven tribes amongst us who have nothing. What have we to do ? We have to go out and look at the situation, in its length and breadth—measure it, grasp it, be master of its details; and come back and settle destiny by religious standards and considerations. To young men I would say, Do not stand there complaining to your fathers and your leaders; nothing is easier than to moan, and to complain, and to murmur; go out and look around and see what the reality of the circumstances is, and then address yourselves to that reality as you may be religiously directed.   What is the globe ? Let me understand something of the earth upon which I live. What is its size ?   Right through it, how far ?   Round about it, what distance in miles ?   How many people are there upon its surface ?   What is the history of its growth and trade ?   And as we map this globe out and understand something of its history, we see that the great thing to be done is to emigrate.   That is what young men of consciously great faculty and strength have to do.   You are playing the part of suppliants ; you are running after your fathers and mothers, asking for new garments when you ought to be away making them, weaving them, and making nature a bank yielding you what riches you require.   But the fathers and the mothers are somewhat to blame herein : the world is very great ; and to conquer it seems to break up the family circle, and to bring down grey hairs with sorrow to the grave. O foolish, mistaken love ! Nay, let us go further, and say that is not love at all.   There is space enough, land enough, and we can so act as to find liberty enough.   We may have to go into woody districts ; and says some dear, foolishly-mistaken father, "The idea of my boy going into a wood !" That is the right place for him ; he will be made a man of there.   The wood is necessary to complete the school, and the drawing-room, and the confectionery period, in which you have done your utmost to ruin your boy.   "But he is such a fine boy !" That is the very reason why he should go :—Thou art a great people ?—then go and cut down trees, and lay them out foursquare, and roof in the place as well as you can, and begin there.   To commence elsewhere is to begin to build a temple from the top of the steeple or the tower.   Or trade may take the place of emigration. How lies the globe of trade ?   What trades are too thickly thronged ?   Where is the congestion ?   Where is the difficulty ? Where is the point at which genius can operate in the construction of new relations and the creation of new possibilities ? What a field for the exercise of mind !   And what is true of young men who are complaining that they cannot get a living, is true of the Church of the living God—is true, in other words, of the great field of evangelisation.   A great Church staying at home, eating its own banquet, drinking its own wine, and talking over the number and excellence of its own luxuries—surely that is the way the end whereof is death. The larger the congregation, the more valorous should be the evangelistic assault upon the fortresses of darkness, ignorance, superstition, and heathenism. The hotter the centre, the further should radiate the beams that can touch with illumination and encourage with warmth those who are afar off. We must not take our greatness as a reason why we should do nothing, but as a reason why we should do more. Let those whose faculties are small and whose opportunities are limited remain at home and do the housework; but the children of the mighty—men who are conscious of strength—should be found, all the world over, heroes to fight; protectors to defend purity, innocence, and weakness; and leaders to inspire the faint-hearted.

And has Joshua nothing in all this—the great man himself, so quiet, so gentle? Caleb asked for his portion right boldly, but he asked—as a heroic man should ask—for difficulties. At eighty-five he wanted to prove that he was as young as he was at forty. Joshua might have taken that opportunity of saying, Caleb, I was with you in that matter of the espial of the land; if you want your portion now, I may as well have mine at the same time. Nothing of the kind. Joshua waited until the very last. So we read:—

"When they had made an end of dividing the land for inheritance by their coasts, the children of Israel gave an inheritance to Joshua the son of Nun among them : according to the word of the Lord they gave him the city which he asked, even Timnath-serah in mount Ephraim : and he built the city, and dwelt therein" (xix. 49, 50).

The greatest came last. Joshua could afford to wait. Sometimes the end is better than the beginning, even in this matter of distribution. But when he did get his portion, it was called "Timnath-serah"—in English, "an abundant portion"—afterwards called "Timnath-heres," "the portion of the sun." Herein he was the type of the coming Joshua : he shall have all nations for his tributaries, all kings for his servants; his dominion shall be as the circuit of the sun : "Timnath-heres" shall be the name of his empire, for the sun shall never set upon that wide dominion. Is it not also beautiful that Joshua *asked* to have the city Timnath-serah ? The city was given at his own request. What saith the Psalmist in the second Psalm ?—" Ask of me, and I shall give thee the heathen for thine inheritance, and the uttermost parts of the earth for thy possession." Ask thou ? The Joshua, the Jesus of the race, shall have Timnath-serah, Timnath-heres; and as the type was satisfied with his portion, so shall the Antitype be satisfied when he shall see of the travail of his soul.

A very tender word is found in regard to some of the tribes. "Gad, and Reuben, and half the tribe of Manasseh, have received their inheritance beyond Jordan." Sweet words !—" beyond Jordan." By a very legitimate accommodation these words may be applied to many a Christian. Some Christians have but little portion this side of the river ; their lot is a small one ; their riches could all be hidden in one hand ; yet how bright they are !—as radiant as a summer dawn, as songful as a wood in spring-time, when all the birds are swelling their feathery throats with song. Why ? Because the refrain of their hymn is " beyond Jordan." The crown is on the other side of the river ; the city lies beyond the stream ; the great inheritance is at the other end of the valley of the shadow of death : they are " begotten again unto a lively hope by the resurrection of Jesus Christ from the dead, to an inheritance incorruptible, and undefiled, and that fadeth not away." So their citizenship being in heaven, they have learned in whatsoever state they are, therewith to be content. Blessed are they who are rich in faith ; yea, blessed with sevenfold blessing they who can say that their souls are already in heaven, and the consciousness of the heavenly possession creates contempt for the vanities of time.

Looking at the whole matter practically, let us not forget that the land was given to be cultivated. This is not a mere matter of enjoyment. When Palestine was seized, it had to be brought under agricultural treatment, and men were to enjoy the fruit of their labour even in the Land of Promise. There was fighting to be done, there were trees to be cut down ; the centre of the country was a great forest, and the foresters must go into it and bring down the timber and root out the old roots, and make flowers ai d fruits grow in the old forests of

Palestine. Life is given to us to cultivate. We are not called upon to do merely the work—if so it may be termed—of appreciation and enjoyment; we are called to battle, to cultivation, to toil, to service, to disappointment, and to some fruition of our hope and love.

Nor must we forget that variety did not excite discontent. The lots were not all equal. Judah had twenty-nine cities and the villages thereof; Benjamin, fourteen cities with the villages; Joshua had Timnath-serah, in Mount Ephraim. So it is possible for us now to have variety of lot, and yet a sweet content of heart. The kingdom of heaven is as a man travelling into a far country, who called together his servants, and gave to one five talents, to another two, to another one—representing talent and opportunity and capacity. The Lord must distribute as he pleases. The great lesson for us to learn is, that it is possible for us to have little, and yet not to want more; to be called to a great opportunity, and yet not to boast over those whose limitation is so obvious. This sweet content, this hallowed peace, can only be enjoyed in proportion as we abide in Christ, like living branches in a living vine. This miracle is not a trick of the human hand; it is the miracle of the Holy Ghost.

SELECTED NOTE.

Eccentric Boundaries of the Tribes (Josh. xv.–xix.).—Thomson, in "The Land and the Book," writes: "The reason why the boundaries of the different tribes were so eccentric originally, and are now so difficult to follow, was that the 'lots' were not meted out according to geographical lines; but lands of certain cities lying more or less contiguous were assigned to each tribe. These cities were the capitals of small principalities or districts, just as Tibnin, and Hunin, and Bint-Jebail are now. The territory of one might extend far to the east of the city, that of the next to the west. It is now absolutely impossible to draw lines around the separate 'lots' with any degree of certainty. Their general positions with relation to each other, however, can be ascertained with sufficient exactness for all important purposes in the study of Biblical geography."

PRAYER.

O THOU who art the refuge of men, let us flee unto thee, assured that the door of thy mercy will not be closed against us. We have sung for a lifetime of Jesus as the refuge of the soul. We have found him to be a covert from the storm. We would abide in him, let come what may, strong in his strength, confident in the immutableness of his love. This is our daily thought and this our nightly rest: a very song in our mouth; a perpetual joy, like a singing angel hovering over the life. We turn and think of Christ, and behold our thought makes us glad. We muse about the Son of God in holy wonder, and as we muse the fire burns, and by its glow we know he is near who is the light of heaven. We would dwell upon the thought of his life; we would count his words as men count jewels; we would number them, and set them in order, and preserve them with all the eagerness of unutterable love, accounting each one necessary to the perfectness of the whole. Whilst we thus treasure thy Word, and find in it our true wealth, thou wilt not forsake us; thou wilt make us stronger, younger, happier, as we proceed in this faithful and delightful service. Reveal thy word to us day by day—a new light, a new beauty, a new possibility; may it be unto our eyes as the dawn of heaven, and unto our ears as the music of the skies. According to our necessity may thy word present itself to us—now a staff to lean upon, now a sword with which to fight, now a light that shall be as a lamp unto our feet, and now an unspeakable comfort, making even sorrow itself welcome, because sorrow brings the Saviour nearer. Thy word abideth for ever; thy word is patient like thyself, waiting for its opportunity, standing at the door of the attention and knocking and waiting until we be ready to hear what it has to say. It has waited for us many a year. When we hear it, we know it to be thy word, because there is an answering spirit in our own hearts which says, This is none other than God's word—a very speech from the heart of the universe. We thank thee for all thy mercies. Though thou hast set us in a time of depression, yet do we see that the stars are all in their places. It is indeed night-time with many, by reason of difficulty, poverty, distress, and hardship; yet not one star has gone out, and the heavens look brighter sometimes than they ever did. Thou hast not forsaken thy people, nor left in desolation those that trust in thee. This is their confidence and their song; yea, it has become their boast and their sure refuge in time of difficulty. Even now thy mercies are more than we can number: even when winter has set in and all the flowers have hidden themselves, thy mercies are full and thy compassion is near and thy kindness is loving-kindness. Even in the midnight of the year we can sing praises unto our God and shake down the prison of our distress.

Help us in all things to see thy hand, and to say, All is well. Enable us to prove our faith by the nobleness and clearness of our testimony. May we be enabled to say, Though he slay me, yet will I trust in him, and though the night be dark and dreary, it is but short at most, and the morning is already dawning on the higher hills. We commend one another to thy loving care; they are well kept whom thou dost keep; in their hearts shall be no unrest, but one continual radiant Sabbath-day; no lion shall be there, nor any ravenous beast go up thereon, it shall not be found there; all holy thoughts shall dwell there, and sorrow and sighing shall flee away, like birds of the night, afraid of the sunshine, terrified by the day. We are found again at the Cross. We wait at the altar of the atonement wrought by him who is thy Son, our Saviour. His blood is our prayer, his sacrifice our plea. Amen.

Joshua xx.-xxiv.

AFTER REST.

THE twentieth chapter deals with the Cities of Refuge. A very beautiful expression is that—" City of Refuge." Very suggestive, too. But there is a great black shadow in the middle of it: for why should men want refuge? The term is noble in itself, but what is it in its suggestion? Surely it means that there is a pursuing storm. We have heard travellers say that by making haste they will just be in time to escape the impending tempest; so they quicken their steps, and when they gain the threshold of the sanctuary they were aiming at, they breathe a sigh of relief and thankfulness. The sanctuary is doubly dear to them. Home is always sweet, or ought to be; but how sweeter than the honeycomb when it is reached under circumstances which try the spirit, exasperate the sensibilities, and weigh heavily on the soul! In this case there is a pursuing storm, but not of weather—a social storm. The man who is running has killed a man, and the one who is following him is " the avenger of blood." Who will be first in the city? God will help the first runner, if it be but by one step he will be in before the pursuer can lay hold of him. There is a wondrous ministry of helpfulness operating in the world. We are helped in a thousand ways, not always in the one way in which we want to be helped, but in some other way; yet the help always comes. Was the refuge then for the murderer? No; there was no refuge for the murderer. But is it not said that the man who is fleeing to the city of refuge has killed some person? Yes, it is so said ; but a definition is given which clears up all the moral side of the mystery :—

"The slayer that killeth any person unawares and unwittingly may flee thither" (xx. 3).

It was not murder, it was accident, an awful accident, and therefore not to be lightly dismissed ; still, not murder, and therefore not to be requited with blood. The suggestion of the arrangement is itself a gospel. Mark the discrimination of the great Governor of the universe. There is no confusion in his statute-book. There is no want of discernment in the eye of God ; that eye distinguishes between the intentional and the unintentional, the accident and that which was of malice prepense. All such distinctions give us confidence in the Book. God is not unrighteous. The spirit of moral criticism pervades the whole Book, so that none can escape by false plea or by special pleading, and none can be unjustly accused or over-weighted with impeachment ; God will hear the case, and judge it himself. So it will be in the summing-up of things. It will be found at last that many things were done "unawares and unwittingly," and were never meant to be done ; and who shall say what mercy will be revealed when that fact is made clear ? We may even now magnify it to the comfort of men. Life is not to be severely judged, but righteously examined and pronounced upon. Many a sin is committed unawares and unwittingly ; many a wrong word is spoken under the same qualification ; many a life plunges into disastrous relations without purposing so to do. Some lives get a wrong start. The young man is put where he ought never to have been placed ; his life began in a false key and with a false conception of things. From that point he has gone staggeringly onward : now tolerably steady ; now flat down in the dust, as though he had been smitten by an invisible, but mighty hand ; now crawling a little ; and now strong enough to run a few paces ; but altogether the life was wrongly started. Others, again, seem not to have any keen moral discernment : they blunder in making their distinctions ; in a moral sense they are colour-blind. God must be judge in all these matters, for he conceived the notion of the City of Refuge ; he has been trying to save men, to make the most and best of men, to give new chances to

men.   What wonder if at last he should set up the Cross, and
say, This is all that even God can do?   On the other hand,
whilst we magnify this thought for our comfort, we must not
pervert it to our soul's degradation and loss.   Let us not make too
free with the gentle utterances and gracious arrangements of
the inspired volume.   They were meant for encouragements
and the beginnings of hope ; they were not meant as excuses for
indolence, or malice, or selfishness.   Herein is the righteousness
of God revealed.   " Shall not the Judge of all the earth do
right ? "   He will not destroy the righteous with the wicked ; he
will rather make one righteous man balance a thousand bad men
than that a hair of a righteous man's head should perish.   So
then we take heart again.   All that we have done unawares and
unwittingly that was wrong is provided for ; but if we have done
wrong, aware of the error and wittingly, then " whoso sheddeth
man's blood, by man shall his blood be shed."   Murder cannot
be balanced by tears.   High treason against human life cannot be
blotted out by sighing.   Some one must die ; blood must answer
blood somewhere.   If God shall provide a Lamb, let him do it,
and let him be adored in the doing of it.   But sin means blood
somewhere—in the sinner himself or in God.   Herein is love,
that while we were yet sinners Christ died for us.   The law is
never altered.   Blood must pay for blood.   That is the eternal
law of the universe ; but by whom the blood shall be shed must
remain for the solution of God.   We believe that the precious
blood of Jesus Christ was shed for the sins committed by men ;
and it is our joy to hear a great voice, strong as thunder, musical
as love, saying in the midst of the ages, " Behold the Lamb of
God, which taketh away the sin of the world."

We read in chapter xx. 7-9 :—

" And they appointed Kedesh in Galilee in mount Naphtali, and Shechem
in mount Ephraim, and Kirjath-arba, which is Hebron, in the mountain of
Judah.   And on the other side Jordan by Jericho eastward, they assigned
Bezer in the wilderness upon the plain out of the tribe of Reuben, and
Ramoth in Gilead out of the tribe of Gad, and Golan in Bashan out of the
tribe of Manasseh.   These were the cities appointed for all the children of
Israel, and for the stranger that sojourneth among them, that whosoever
killeth any person at unawares might flee thither, and not die by the hand
of the avenger of blood, until he stood before the congregation."

That is the best fame.   Better be Kedesh and Shechem and

Kirjath-arba and Bezer and Ramoth and Golan than be cities
of infinitely more famous names.	These are mother-towns,
these are mother-cities.	We read of cities infinite in domination,
innumerable in population, marvellous in military resource and
prowess, but it is a smoking fame that goes up in clouds to
be blown away by the wind.	This refuge-reputation is the true
fame.	There would be no difficulty in learning these names.
When the names of great fighting cities have been forgotten, the
names of the refuge-cities would be repeated as men repeat
rhyme inspired with reason and made noble by love.	Such
fame we may have.	Are there not men who are in very deed
cities of refuge?	We can go to them by night or by day, and
there is always the genial welcome, the glad, Sit down and tell
me what it is; sob out all your sorrow, and keep back nothing of
your sin; let me know it through and through—the very worst
and blackest that can be told.	Are not these men as Kedesh
and Shechem and Kirjath-arba?	Are they not more beautiful to
us than Bezer and Ramoth and Golan?	There are other men
from whom you must expect nothing in the day of weakness and
distress.	They are critical men.	You can only go before them
with a clean white folio, and even then you will be coldly
received, for such men have no heaven to give; they are not
cities of refuge; in your poverty they will tell you that you ought
to have done very differently from what you have done, and they
will read you a lecture full of sternness, and punctuated with
stings and reproaches.	Who would go to them?	No one who
knows them; they will never be knocked up at midnight; they
will never be quoted in the hour of distress; they are not cities
of refuge; they are not sanctuaries of hope and love.	Let us,
however, dwell upon the thought that we may be cities of refuge
to men who need rest, defence, and comfort.	We may be blessed
with the enduring fame: "When the ear heard me, then it
blessed me . . . I was eyes to the blind, and feet was I to the lame."
We may share our last loaf with poverty; we may speak the
cheering word to despondency; our very smile may be as a fire
radiating hope and comfort in the house made bare and desolate.
To this fame we are called.	It is the fame of the Son of God:
"Come unto me, all ye that labour and are heavy laden, and I
will give you rest."

Now Joshua proceeds with his valedictory speech. Here and there he records a sentence which belongs to all time. The twenty-first chapter has little or nothing to say except to the people to whom it specially related; but in summing up the twenty-first chapter Joshua says,—

"There failed not ought of any good thing which the Lord had spoken unto the house of Israel" (v. 45).

The verse would end well there. But that is not a full-stop. After the word "Israel" in that part of the sentence there is but a semicolon. Four words remain, which contain all we want to know about God's promises and God's dispensations. These four words are all of one syllable. They might form a child's first lesson in reading—"all came to pass." What a testimony for the old man to bear! What more could be said? The note-of-hand had matured and been redeemed. The promised harvest had grown into golden abundance, and had been reaped and garnered. Can we bear this testimony to-day, or can we not? Christians ought to speak out upon these matters. There is a mischievous sophism, working endless disaster in society, which says that religious experiences lie between God and the soul, and are not to be talked about. There is a very little grain of truth in that assertion. The greater truth is :—"Come and hear, all ye that fear God, and I will declare what he hath done for my soul." This is the evidence that cannot be answered. It does not admit of criticism; it is personal experience; it is personal testimony. But for verses such as this the miracles would be incredible and the history of the Bible would sound like a romance. Now and again a great stone is put into the building, which seems to bind the whole structure together in unity and solidity, and this is one such stone :—"There failed not ought of any good thing which the Lord had spoken unto the house of Israel; all came to pass." Now after that we can do with matters local and transient. We seem to need some smaller stones after that great block of marble has been set in its place. Is not that same block put into the temple of to-day? What has failed of all Christ has spoken? Here we are thrown back upon a definition we have given before, that prophecy is not intellectual genius exercised upon an unknown future, but is simply a moral declaration— the declaration that right means upward and heavenward, and wrong means downward and perditionward. All men, therefore, may be prophets with regard to any city that now lives. Just as the old prophets spoke of Babylon and Tyre and Egypt, so men may speak of the capitals of the world and the countries greatest in history at this moment. Given selfishness, narrowness of policy, love of war, devotion to luxury, an obliteration of moral distinctions, heedlessness of moral responsibilities ; and the prophet gathering his mantle around him, and standing upon some eminence, may declare that the feasting shall be turned into mourning, lamentation, and woe : the satyrs and the owls shall hoot in the palaces of greatness, and all the renown of the bad men shall be turned into infamy. The colouring will partake of the nature of the imagination which depicts it : the colouring is not in the prophecy, but in the utterance of it ; the prophecy itself is moral : right—heaven; wrong—hell. Now let Ezekiel, Daniel, Jeremiah, Isaiah fill in the colouring ; the prophecy is not touched in its moral integrity and grandeur by the colour used by the prophet or the parabolist. We need no books upon the fulfilment of prophecy. Such books often stand in the way of the Bible. They turn prophecy into a narrow letter ; they want to insist upon coincidences which satisfy the merely literal mind. There is but one prophecy, with a thousand varieties of expression and illustration, and it is—" Say ye to the righteous, that it shall be well with him : Woe unto the wicked ! it shall be ill with him."

A noble testimony this, too, borne by the old man. It is not youth that anticipates, it is age that reviews. Old men never become infidels. We say sometimes that seldom is an old man converted to Christianity. How far that may be true we cannot tell ; but did ever an old pilgrim who had once seen heaven opened, turn round and say, in his wrinkled old age, that he was going to the city of Negation, or to the wilderness of Atheism ? Old men ought to be heard upon these subjects; they have lived a lifetime ; they have fought upon a thousand battle-fields ; they know all the darkness of the night, all the sharpness of winter, all the heat of summer, and they have a right to be heard upon his question; and their testimony on the side of the Bible is united, distinct, emphatic, and unanswerable.

Another point is found in chapter xxii. 5 :—

"But take diligent heed to do the commandment and the law, which Moses the servant of the Lord charged you, to love the Lord your God, and to walk in all his ways, and to keep his commandments, and to cleave unto him, and to serve him with all your heart and with all your soul."

The hurly-burly is done. What is to be the new turn of affairs ? After tumult—music, study, and worship. Our ears have been plagued with the uproar of war. Sometimes our faith has almost reeled under the historical tumult through which we have passed. Now and again we have come into a sanctuary, and there we have breathed a while ; and out of it we have come to join the rush and the roar of battle, and advance. Now the Lord has given rest unto Israel. What is to be done ? Now that the battle is fought and won, the old man speaks :—

"Return ye, and get you unto your tents, and unto the land of your possession. . . . But take diligent heed to do the commandment and the law" (xxii. 4, 5).

Thus is life balanced : great battle to-day, and great prayer to-morrow ; a period of solitude to-day, and a period of excitement and terrific assault upon evil fortresses to-morrow. Thus, let us say again and again, is life brought into equipoise. Life is not all sentiment, nor is it all action ; life is not all prayer, nor is it all war. The one must balance the other. Dark days and bright must contribute to one another, and make the common day between them. Let us not say that Providence has forsaken us because we are thrown into a day of war and misunderstanding, because one is taken and another left, and because there is a fire in the earth and a sword in society ; nor let us say that we have come into special favour of Heaven because there is nothing to do in our day but to dream ourselves off into imagined heavens. The times are many-coloured. Life is a great variety, but the thing that abides is the presence of the Son of God. Come who may, go who may, dig what graves we may, Jesus Christ is " the same yesterday, and to-day, and for ever." Activity should be balanced by knowledge. He who is not profoundly versed in the law cannot guide the battle. Hence, they who guide the State should be good men. They who are in charge of the nations of the earth should be men who take diligent heed to do the commandment and the law, and to walk in all God's ways, and to keep His com-

mandments and to cleave unto him, and to serve him with all
their heart and with all their soul. Piety should be in the
premiership; honour should be at the head of affairs. He who
speaks the guiding word should first have learned that word in
communion with God.

It would seem as if some interviews in life could not be
satisfactorily closed but with the language of benediction. An
ordinary word would be wholly out of place. There is a fitness
of things in human communication as in all other affairs and
concerns of life. It is fitting, too, that the benediction should
be spoken by the old man. Joshua was "old and stricken in
years," and he concluded the audience fitly by blessing the
children of Israel :—

"So Joshua blessed them, and sent them away; and they went unto their
tents" (xxii. 6).

Without that blessing, the interview might have been perverted
into a controversy; but the benediction ennobled all that had
gone before. Is it not often so, with the last word of even
ordinary human speech? Following the discourse, the mind
of the hearer wonders, interrogates, doubts: then coincides,
admires, believes: or, it may be thrown into a state of conflict,
weighing evidence and hardly knowing which scale is prepon-
derant; but as the speaker moves on to other strains, and
delivers himself in nobler tones, and gathers into one sublime
appeal all the religious considerations which can affect the issue
of his argument, it would seem as if by a grand Amen, all the
difficulties had been dispersed, and a great reconciliation and
sympathy had been established. Happy the interview that ends
in a benediction. All our interviews with God may so end. In the
benediction lies the very wealth and force of the argument. Who
can live upon contention, or be edified by wordy phrase? We
sigh for the blessing; we are unanimous in the benediction; we
are a church undivided, mute because so eloquent, when invoking
the seal of the divine love. But some blessings are full of subtle
suggestion. They mean what they do not fully say. Probably
the blessing of Joshua was one of those benedictions fraught with
suggestion—perhaps not always to the credit of the hearers and
receivers. It might mean, being broadly interpreted,—Begin
again : let the past be buried; now remember, and from this day

forth be your better selves; claim your inheritance divine; be at peace one with another; learn from all the past; now farewell: to your tents, and be blessed of God.   Have we not all been dismissed in this way now and again?   Has not the prodigal been sent to his chamber with a blessing which meant much of fear and much of suspicion, and yet was intended to act as an encouragement and an inspiration, a kind of divided blessing, a benediction with a rebuke in it, an effort lacking in stimulus, a hint which made the reproach the keener?   We should listen to the tone as well as to the words —the tone explains everything; the words explain nothing.   What poetry is not disabled and uncrowned by the very printing of it?   And Christianity has fought the battle and overcome the disadvantage of words. The Christianity spoken by Christ is one thing, and as spoken by those who do not understand it, another, wholly and pitiably.

Now the children of Israel go to their tents: They are to be at peace.   Ceasing war they are to be students of war. We shall hear no more of controversy; every man having received the blessing is a good man, and there is an end of a tumult which at one time threatened never to cease.   So we should imagine, but our imagining is wrong :—

"Now to the one half of the tribe of Manasseh Moses had given possession in Bashan: but unto the other half thereof gave Joshua among their brethren on this side Jordan westward.   And when Joshua sent them away also unto their tents, then he blessed them.   And he spake unto them, saying, Return with much riches unto your tents, and with very much cattle, with silver, and with gold, and with brass, and with iron, and with very much raiment: divide the spoil of your enemies with your brethren. And the children of Reuben and the children of Gad and the half tribe of Manasseh returned, and departed from the children of Israel out of Shiloh, which is in the land of Canaan, to go unto the country of Gilead, to the land of their possession, whereof they were possessed, according to the word of the Lord by the hand of Moses " (xxii. 7-9).

But in going they did something which excited the anger of Israel.   They built a great altar "by Jordan."   The altar is described in the tenth verse as "a great altar to see to," that is to say, it was very high, a piece of wonderful masonry, a thing that could not fail to attract attention; and the children of Israel said,—This is the beginning of a new idolatry; we are no sooner blessed by Joshua than we are cursed by the spirit of impiety, and misled and dishonoured by some seductive demon. See how the altar rises heaven-high! A great and influential deputation was despatched :—

"And the children of Israel sent unto the children of Reuben, and to the children of Gad, and to the half tribe of Manasseh, into the land of Gilead, Phinehas the son of Eleazar the priest, and with him ten princes, of each chief house a prince throughout all the tribes of Israel; and each one was an head of the house of their fathers among the thousands of Israel" (xxii. 13, 14).

They went up to war against the two tribes and a half. They would have no idolatry; they would put down superstition and false worship by the sword ; they were not going to have the sanctity of their history trifled with. How wonderfully consistent they were! The very people who had been building altars of their own and fashioning a god of their own were now warmed into right holy zeal, because the two tribes and the half tribe had built an altar! What was the issue of the interview? It turned out to be no altar at all. It was meant as an altar of witness and not of sacrifice. It was not for religious purposes, but for historical. They said :—

"Let us now prepare to build us an altar, not for burnt offering, nor for sacrifice : but that it may be a witness" (xxii. 26, 27).

So when the children of the one side and the children of the other say, What is the history of our people? they may point to this great altar as a mark of punctuation in all this noble and exciting story. So there was peace where war was threatened. But it is not safe to build altars if you do not mean to use them as such : the immediate and local circumstances may be forgotten, and the altar may remain a continual temptation to false thought and vicious desire, so that that which was at the beginning perfectly innocent and open to a rational and satisfactory explanation, may in the end be turned into a temptation and a curse. A great and lasting lesson arises here. We are not always present to explain how this or that was begun. Men will come upon our work without knowing its history, and they will turn it possibly to their own meanings, and to uses which would surprise and distress the original builders. Why create temptations for ourselves? Why adorn the walls with pictures which may suddenly become serpents, talking to us and making great promises, which can never be redeemed ? Why encourage practices which in themselves at their beginning and under certain local conditions are innocent enough, but which may become temptations to other persons, who coming upon them without the original explanation, use them as mere instruments by which to gratify desire or delight imagination ? We should search into reasons and follow with religious solicitude certain vital possibilities. We have to do with the impression we make, as well as with the actual work we accomplish. The two tribes and the half tribe had their own idea in building the altar, and that idea was perfectly defensible; its meaning was honest and good; but what impression did it make upon observers ? Abstain from the appearance of evil. To have a great argument is not enough. Sometimes we are bound to accommodate our argument to our listeners, and to save our contention from possible perversions and misuses. Have we not a right to do what we may ? Certainly not. If we have dug out a stone, may we not build it where we please, and as we please ? The answer is a solemn, No; you have no such right. No man liveth unto himself; no man dieth unto himself. The solemn question should be, What effect will this action have upon the young, the unsuspecting, the inexperienced ? Blessed is he with a right royal strength who can stoop down to the weakness of inferior men.

This being settled, a very tender scene occurs. Joshua gathers all the tribes of Israel to Shechem, calls for the children of Israel, and for their heads, and for their judges, and for their officers, and talks to them historically and grandly. He called the people themselves to witness what God had done for them :—

"And ye have seen all that the Lord your God hath done unto all these nations because of you " (xxiii. 3).

Not only so, but he uses a very searching expression :—

"And, behold, this day I am going the way of all the earth : and ye know in all your hearts and in all your souls, that not one thing hath failed of all the good things which the Lord your God spake concerning you; all are come to pass unto you, and not one thing hath failed thereof " (xxiii. 14).

Mark the precision of the appeal. The old man would not speak in vague generalities, nor will he have a vote as if by

majority; he must have a clear testimony as to the faithfulness
of God. To what does he appeal? To mere opinion? To
the common judgment of the people? No; his language is
more precise :—" Ye know in all your hearts and in all your
souls." These are the witnesses, and we can admit no other
We demand such testimony. Whatever it is, let us have it
from the heart and from the soul. A man can bear such
witness only now and then. No man has full command over
his heart and over his soul so as to summon the witness at
a moment's notice. A man may have to retire for awhile and
gather himself together, and prepare himself by daily meditation, before he is at liberty to speak a single word. Joshua
points to history, says in effect—Review it, put it together,
understand its meaning; then compare the history with the
promises you started with ; and let your souls speak and not your
vain intellect; let the heart make the avowal ; do not ask the
imagination to declaim. It is a solemn and grand appeal !
Would God men would speak from their hearts and from their
souls ! We should get rid of infinite lying, of every variety
of falsehood, of every misleading colour in the hue of social
intercourse; we should, too, have the right testimony about the
Bible and divine Providence and the whole quantity termed
divine revelation. We should also be driven back into realities,
and made to talk about real things. Who ever keeps to the
vital line? Who is not prone to run off into side-issues and
to dwell with meanness of mind upon merely incidental points
or accidental details? Is it not so in human intercourse?
Friendships of a life standing are broken up because one of the
parties being of mean mind—incurably mean mind—seizes upon
an incidental point and magnifies it unto absurd proportions.
Thus love is lost and life is turned into misery. What we have
to do is to review the whole day by day—the summer, the
winter, the seedtime, and the harvest—put altogether into one
complete quantity, and then say, from heart and soul, whether it
be not noble, massive, strong, beneficent. The judgment is not
to turn upon the detail of this day, or of that day, but upon
a review of the whole line of life. By this rule of judgment,
many men will be much better than they seem to be now
and then; by this rule of judgment, others will prove to be

worse than at one time they appeared to be, for whilst many
can do incidental acts of kindness, it takes something like
completeness of conviction to pursue a pure and useful life day
by day, year by year, until youth is supplanted by age, and
the cradle is exchanged for the tomb. An incidental kindness
does not make a beneficent life. An incidental mistake ought
not to destroy a lifelong friendship. Judgment must be upon
the whole ; and judgment must be spoken not by heated lips,
not in a feverish excitement, but deliberately, with the heart
and with the soul, with the innermost life, and under a sense
of the divine criticism.

Now Joshua changes his tone :—

> "Be ye therefore very courageous to keep and to do all that is written in
> the book of the law of Moses, that ye turn not aside therefrom to the right
> hand or to the left ; . . . But cleave unto the Lord your God, as ye have
> done unto this day" (xxiii. 6-8).

What is the call of these verses ? It is a call to moral courage.
The people were soldiers ; when they saw that an altar had been
reared to heaven which they did not like, and which they
misunderstood, instantly they sped from their tents and challenged
the builders to battle. That is the rudest courage; there is
nothing in it. Many men can fight who cannot suffer ; many are
brave in activity who are cowards in waiting. Joshua calls the
people now to thought, study, quiet and consistent and continuous
obedience—namely, " Cleave unto the Lord." Without this,
growth would be impossible. Men cannot grow in the midst of
continual or unbroken excitement. We grow when we are at
rest ; we grow not a little when we are in the shade ; we advance
when the burden is crushing us, and we are not uttering one
complaining word because of its fatal weight. When the history
of the land is written as it ought to be written, many a battle
which now fills pages and chapters will be dismissed with a
contemptuous sentence ; and sufferings at home, quiet endurances,
Christian manifestations of patience, will be magnified as indicative of the real dauntlessness, the heavenly bravery, the lasting
courage. Let every man examine himself herein. To say "No"
to a tempting offer is to win a battle : to receive a blow from an
enemy and not return it, is to reach the point of coronation in
Christ's great kingdom ; to hear a rough speech and make a

gentle reply is to evince what is meant by growing in grace. So the history rolls on, from battle to battle, from mistake to mistake, from point to point, until at last the moral displaces the material, questions of the soul put into their right place questions of rank ; and moral courage—simple, loving, unquestioning obedience —is set at the head of all the virtues ; and the quiet, meek, submissive, patient soul is crowned and throned, and stablished amid the hierarchy of heaven. We cannot dazzle the world by our greatness, but we can please God by our goodness ; we cannot harness the winds and make them bear our names far and wide, but we can so live, so suffer, so speak, as to constrain the enemy to say,—Verily, this man is a prophet ; verily, this man has been with Jesus and learned of him ; verily, there is in this supposed weakness a wonderful and enduring strength.

We cannot but be struck by the equality of the divine way as it is marked by the venerable leader. The fifteenth verse is very expressive upon this point :—

" Therefore it shall come to pass, that as all good things are come upon you, which the Lord your God promised you ; so shall the Lord bring upon you all evil things, until he have destroyed you from off this good land which the Lord your God hath given you " (xxiii. 15).

The way of the Lord is equal. We have already seen that there is no mere partisanship with God, or favouritism that is heedless of the position and needs of other people. The point which has been established beyond all dispute is that God's partiality is for character—that is to say, for truth, integrity, and holiness ; where these are found God's benediction rests ; and where these are not found no blessing of Heaven can descend or abide. We only hold what we have from God so long as we hold God himself. But had not Israel come into possession of the promised land ? Certainly ; and yet even the promised land itself was only to be held by the title of character. The sixteenth verse makes this clear :—

" When ye have transgressed the covenant of the Lord your God, which he commanded you, and have gone and served other gods, and bowed yourselves to them ; then shall the anger of the Lord be kindled against you, and ye shall perish quickly from off the good land which he hath given unto you " (xxiii. 16).

We cannot read such words without feeling that God is righteous and just in all his ways. We are not entitled to reason that because we are once in possession we are always in possession. We stand or fall by character. The kingdom of God is a kingdom of truth and goodness, and not of mere words and ceremonies, pretensions or technical rights. Even heaven itself cannot be held by sinful men. Were it possible for sin to enter into the celestial land, those who committed that sin would be cast out of heavenly places into deep and outer darkness, notwithstanding all that had gone before. What a sublime security is this for the peace and beauty of the universe! Might shall be without power, and royalty without a crown, and high descent without any value, except in the proportion in which character is maintained in unsullied purity. Only goodness is to be guaranteed in its possession.

Joshua having gathered all the tribes of Israel to Shechem, called for the elders of Israel, and for their heads, and for their judges, and for their officers, and delivered unto them his final speech. Again we are thrown upon the grand truth that men must bring all their history into one view at certain periods, that thereby they may renew their covenant and revive their best hope. The work of the Lord is not of yesterday; it goes back through all the generations; and he is the wise scribe, well instructed in holy things, who brings into one view all the course of the divine education of the world. This is what Joshua did in brief in the twenty-fourth chapter. Having given the historical outline, the old man began to exhort the people, saying :—

"Now, therefore, fear the Lord, and serve him in sincerity and in truth" (xxiv. 14).

Exhortation comes well after history. It is like flowers growing upon the top of the rock. In order to encourage the children of Israel to be faithful in their religious relations and responsibilities, Joshua solemnly announces his own determination :—

"—but as for me and my house, we will serve the Lord" (xxiv. 15).

This is the true spirit of leadership. The world will pay little heed to our exhortation if we do not follow it up by personal practice. Many can understand our religion who could never understand our theology. This is the secret, too, of all wide and

lasting evangelisation. The evangelist himself must be absolutely devoted to Christ's Cross and to Christ's truth. At the
centre there must be intense heat if there is to be any radiation
of warmth around the circumference. We cannot hear such
noble resolutions pronounced without ourselves being either
shamed into silence or encouraged into harmonious and equal
action. It is the earnest man who makes his impression upon
society. If preachers are doubting; if Christians are wavering;
if suppliants are halting in their prayers and endeavouring to
balance their sentences by remote considerations, or are troubled
by unexpressed fears, the Church can never make any deep
and lasting impression upon society. Resoluteness wins. Unanimity within the man himself is the secret of growth in grace.
If imagination is going one way and judgment another; if the
understanding and the will are in perpetual feud; if conscience
is disobeyed and appetite is gratified, the man is divided against
himself, and there can be no stability or duration in his character.
Joshua, in making this bold and noble resolution, has rebuked
the cowardice and the timidity of all inferior men, and has shown
them how they ought to deport themselves in the presence of
wavering and hesitation. We can kneel down the more gracefully and hopefully now that our venerable leader has declared
himself so emphatically and completely upon the side of God.
The people, indeed, answered Joshua with a good deal of
enthusiasm. They said :—

"God forbid that we should forsake the Lord, to serve other gods'
(xxiv. 16).

Then they review and repeat the solemn history and say that
all Joshua has said is true in fact. Then Joshua says unto the
people—"What you have now said amounts to little more than
mere words; you forget that God is a holy God and a jealous
God, and you are speaking from impulse rather than from settled
conviction." Then the people reply that Joshua himself is mistaken, and they have really made up their minds once for all to
serve the Lord. So be it, then, said Joshua—"Ye are witnesses
against yourselves that ye have chosen you the Lord, to serve
him." The people answered—That is even so; "We are
witnesses." Then said Joshua, There is one final word to be
spoken. If you have made up your minds to this course, you

must put away the strange gods which are among you; no taint
of idolatry must remain behind; not the very smallest image
must be taken with you one day longer or one inch further; the
expurgation must be immediate, complete, and final. The people
answered unanimously : "The Lord our God will we serve,
and his voice will we obey." It was indeed a solemn day; a day
of covenant, a day of memorial, a day which condensed into its
throbbing hours generations of history and strong and ardent
pulsings of devotion and prophetic service. A covenant was
made, and a statute and an ordinance were set in Shechem. To
make, if possible, the matter inviolably permanent, "Joshua
wrote these words in the book of the law of God, and took a
great stone, and set it up there under an oak, that was by the
sanctuary of the Lord " (xxiv. 26).

Then a very solemn scene occurs :

"And Joshua said unto all the people, Behold, this stone shall be a
witness unto us; for it hath heard all the words of the Lord which he spake
unto us: it shall be therefore a witness unto you, lest ye deny your
God" (xxiv. 27).

Then the assembly broke up. It broke up never to meet again
under the same wise and valiant leadership. All pathetic occasions should be treasured in the memory; the last interview,
the last sermon, the last prayer, the last fond lingering look; all
these things may be frivolously treated as sentimental, but he
who treats them so is a fool in his heart : whatever can subdue
the spirit, chasten the sensibilities, and enlarge the charity of
the soul should be encouraged as a ministry from God. Now
Joshua dies, at the age of one hundred and ten. He was buried
in the border of his inheritance in Timnath-serah, which is in
Mount Ephraim, on the north side of the hill of Gaash.

"And Israel served the Lord all the days of Joshua, and all the days of the
elders that overlived Joshua, and which had known all the works of the
Lord, that he had done for Israel" (xxiv. 31).

Now the history is done. The bones of Joseph, which the
children of Israel brought up out of Egypt, were buried in
Shechem, in a parcel of ground which Jacob bought of the sons
of Hamor the father of Shechem. Then men died quickly :

"And Eleazar the son of Aaron died; and they buried him in a hill that
pertained to Phinehas his son, which was given him in mount Ephraim"
(xxiv. 33).

Death, death, death ! The great man dies, and yet the work goes on. The minister ceases, but the ministry proceeds. The individual sermon closes, but the everlasting gospel never ceases its sweet and redeeming proclamations. Book after book is finished, but literature itself is hardly begun. Amidst all mutation there remains one everlasting quantity : "Thy throne, O God, is for ever and ever." All the new generations acknowledge it. They come up in great pride and strength, as if they themselves were to outlive God, and behold in a few years their pith is exhausted, their hope dies, and they know themselves to be no better than their fathers. When we are touched by the death of those whom we have known best, and wonder how light can ever shine again upon the circle in which we move, we should give the mind free scope to range over all the noble and marvellous history of the world, so shall we see that how great soever have been the men who have led us, the world could do without them ; God knew how to supply their places, and amidst all change and fear and dismay the purpose of Heaven went steadily forward in all the grandeur of its strength and all the tenderness of its beneficence.

In coming thus far in our Bible studies let us pause a moment to consider how many illustrious men with whom we have companied have passed away. Truly the dead are quickly becoming the majority. Adam died, but, though his years were many, how few are the deeds which are recorded of him ! He stands in history as the very Gate of Death. "By one man came death." We feel as if we might say—"But for thee, O Adam, all men would now have been alive; no grave would ever have been dug ; no farewell would ever have been breathed."—That is an overwhelming reflection. Consider the possibility of Adam himself now entertaining it, or following it out in all its infinite melancholy ! Think of him saying—"By my sin I ruined God's fair earth; to me ascribe all iniquity, all shame, all heart-break ; by my presumption and disobedience I did it all : I slew the Son of God ; but for me there would have been no Bethlehem, no Gethsemane, no Calvary, no Cross : lay the blame at the right door,—O ages of time, ye burdened and groaning centuries, curse my name in all your woe."—On such thoughts we may not dwell, for the mind reels in moral amazement, and the heart cannot quench the passion of scepticism. Enough is known to make us solemn. Count the graves until arithmetic gives up the reckoning in despair. Abel, Enoch, Abraham, Isaac, Jacob, Moses, all gone! Just as we had come to know them in the breaking of bread they vanished out of our sight. It was as if rocks had been uprooted, or as if planets had ceased to shine : nay more, for we have not only lost strength and majesty, we have lost guidance, stimulus, friendship, and the subtle ministry of eloquent example. Can history repeat such men? Does our story now lie all down-hill, from steep to steep until we reach the valley of commonplace or the plain of mediocrity? Jesus Christ has taught us how to regard great men, saying " Among them that are born of women there hath not risen a greater than John the Baptist : notwithstanding he that is least in the kingdom of heaven is greater than he." Here we have at once recognition of greatness and hope of greater history. What if we may know more than Adam, see farther than Enoch, embark in greater adventures than Abram, offer greater sacrifices than the priests, and see a deeper law than was ever revealed to Moses? In Christ are hidden all the treasures of wisdom, yea riches unsearchable, promises exceeding great and precious. My soul, bestir thyself, go out in the early morning, remain in the field until the stars come out, for every hour brings its own spoil, every moment its own vision. O my Lord, Father in heaven, Blessed One, made known to me in the Cross of salvation, inspire me, lift me up, and make me gladly accept thy yoke and do all thy bidding ; give me the aspiration that is untainted by vanity, and the consecration that is undefiled by selfishness, then shall I be willing to be baptised for the dead, and to stand steadfastly where princes and veterans have fallen by the hand of Time.

"HANDFULS OF PURPOSE,"

FOR ALL GLEANERS.

". . . *the Lord your God, he is God in heaven above, and in earth beneath.*"—JOSHUA ii. 11.

Everything depends upon a right conception of the personality and character of God.—The Hebrew conception was marked by great exaltation and comprehensiveness.—Again and again we have observed that a little conception of God means a little religion, and a little religion means a little morality.—We must in all our thinking strive after the largest conceptions, not simply for their own value as thoughts, but for their moral influence upon the whole circuit of thinking and action.—Joshua's description of God is absolutely inclusive: (1) he is "the Lord your God;" as if he were associated with the Israelites only, and with every Israelite in the whole community: thus he is made a personal, or social, or tribal God; but such a God can never be more than a mere idol; to save God from the rank of idols we must have a true conception of his greatness as well as of his moral qualities: (2) Then "he is God in heaven above;" there the thought receives wonderful and sublime enlargement: what "heaven above" is must be left to the imagination, and imagination itself reels in any attempt to comprehend the vastness and glory of the expression: though

the mind is thus bewildered, it is yet exalted and ennobled by the very endeavour to comprehend the incomprehensible: (3) Then he is God "in earth beneath;" thus all the dimensions are included; a beautiful method of education is this, for it enables the mind to begin at certain clear and ascertainable points and to move onward and upward to greater distances and to sublimer effects.—The Christian conception of God has never enlarged the thought of the Hebrew theology. Christianity has introduced tenderness into it by describing God by more familiar and endearing names, yet not at the expense of the sublimity, but rather in illustration of it, showing that true sublimity is not far from true condescension.—The Hebrew conception of God should have been followed by a grand conception of personal character. —To have a great God in the intellect, and no God in the life, is the most criminal atheism.—When a man with this conception of God does that which is unworthy of the conception, he not only drags himself downwards, but he drags also the conception of God along with him.—It is possible to have an intellectual conception without a moral realisation. This is the most painful irony that can occur in life.—When we speak of a great conception of God, it is not intended that the mind alone or the pure reason should be interested in that conception, but that it should fill the whole being, enlightening the mind, subduing the heart, chastening the disposition, and regulating the will. With such a conception immorality is simply impossible; because it is impossible that such light should be quenched by the darkness round about it.—The vital point to be ever remembered in these studies is that a great intellectual theology does not necessitate a grand moral purification. Theology must be made more than an intellectual science; it must supply the motive and the reward of sanctified impulse and action.

"*Come hither, and hear the words of the Lord your God.*"—JOSHUA iii. 9.

In the Old Testament, the question of place has never been regarded as inferior.—To us locality is a matter of little or no importance, but to the Hebrew locality was an element of true worship.—The Israelites were in this instance invited to a particular place, in order that they might hear the words of the Lord.—Christianity so far enlarges this idea as to find in the sanctuary the place in which God especially reveals himself to earnest and expectant worshippers.—Jesus Christ went into the synagogue on the Sabbath-days. Jesus Christ also withdrew from the crowd in order that he might alone commune with God in the silence of night and the solitude of the mountain.—There is no doubt an utter destruction of the idolatry of place in Christianity; but the destruction of idolatry is not equal to the deconsecration of given places of worship: the altar is still holy; the church is still recognised as praying-ground in an especial sense, namely, the sense of bringing together men of common sympathies and common aspirations, and giving them to feel the security of nearness and multitude.—Whilst it is possible to pray in the great throng, and even to commune upon deep subjects amid the noise of the world, yet Silence will ever be regarded as constituting a kind of sanctuary in which the soul more especially delights. Every Isaac will feel a pleasure in going into the fields at eventide to meditate.—There is a kind of thought which may be said to have its residence in the mountains, and a kind of praise which may be said to reach its noblest expression amid the waves of the great deep.—The mere act of "coming" is itself a religious exercise; it means withdrawment from usual avocation or entertainment, and specialty of thought and service: it breaks up the idea of commingling and intermixture, which too often tends towards earthliness rather than towards heavenliness, and constitutes in itself a severe trial of intellectual attention and moral expectation. Such coming means willingness to set apart time for Christian purposes, and to create opportunities for spiritual education.—Coming is thus, in some degree, a sacrifice, a token of the heart's willingness to obey God rather than yield to the clamour of earthly appeals.—All men are the better for coming together for religious service.—We get something in fellowship which we can never get in solitude. Men belong to one another in this sense, and are not complete in the absence of one another. —Even where physical association is impossible, the very act of yearning after the absent, and compelling them to be spiritually present, is in itself an expression of the noblest religious feeling.—Atmosphere will always have its effect upon moral education.—Here the great subject of environment shows its importance.—Whilst there may be some minds so strong and independent as to create their own atmosphere, yet looking at men in the generality, they require the help of locality and all the subtile suggestion of association and habitude in order to excite religious impulse and expectation to the highest point. —There is great plausibility in the sophism that men can hear the words of the Lord anywhere.—Jesus Christ did not mean to teach that doctrine when he told the woman at the well, "Neither in this place, nor at Jerusalem, shall men worship the Father;" he merely meant to destroy the idolatry of place, not its consecration; his idea was one of inclusiveness, not of exclusiveness; and his purpose was to show that men could everywhere pray, and that, when compelled to abstain from consecrated places, that compulsion would not interfere with the integrity or prevalence of prayer.— Men can *live* everywhere, but they can live best at home. Men can express their thoughts in any language, but there will always be about the mother-tongue a tenderness which cannot be communicated by any other. Men can see in other men brothers, but they can see in family likenesses and feel in family sympathies what cannot be found elsewhere.—It is so with religious life in relation to the Church.—The fact that some men are superstitious upon these points must not destroy rational veneration.—So long as the Church preserves the peculiarity of its function, and strenuously endeavours to meet the abiding demands of human instinct and reason, it can never lose its hold upon the confidence of the world.

"*God dried up the waters of Jordan from before you, until ye were passed over, as the Lord your God did to the Red sea.*"—JOSHUA iv. 23.

This presents God as doing the little and doing the great: in the one case he dried up a river; in the other case he dried up a sea.—The idea to be kept steadily before the mind is, that it is the same God that worketh all in all. —Omnipotence is as much required in the drying up of the Jordan as in the dividing of the Red Sea; and the Omnipotence that divided the Red Sea condescended to dry up the river.— Every action on the part of God must of necessity be a condescension.—When God made the universe he humbled himself.—When God made man he subjected the Deity to degradation.— This must not be looked upon in the light of experiment, but in the light of necessity. Terms which seem to indicate the contrary are merely terms of accommodation, and not terms which express the essence of things.—We are to reason from the greater to the less; thus, if God dried up the Red Sea, he will also dry up the Jordan; if God enabled us to kill a lion, he will enable us to slay a man; if God enabled us to climb a mountain, he will not forsake us when we have to pass over a molehill. —The text is an appeal to memory as well as an appeal to confidence.—That we may live well in the future we should live steadfastly in the past.—The witness of God's personality and presence in life must be found in a man's own experience; he can only assent to them with the intellect, but he can claim them as verities, and affirm them as the truest facts of life only in proportion to the richness of his personal experience in divine things. Thus growing life should be growing religiousness; old age should be itself an argument; memory should be a library of exposition and defence.—What is forgotten so soon as grace or favour even on the part of man to man? It is even so with God.— We forget that our whole life has been a miracle. We forget this in proportion as we draw a line beyond which our recollection is not permitted to go—

Recollection must be helped by association or analogy.—Thus we can go back to our own infancy by carefully regarding the infancy of others, marking its frailty and its continual exposure to fatal danger.—Life regarded thus from the beginning to its end becomes itself a piece of work which no human hands could have executed, a very miracle of mystery and beauty.—The Old Testament saints in particular were accustomed to reason from the past to the future. David did so in relation to Goliath. That is but a typical instance. Job did so when he contended that, as God had been with him in six troubles, he would not forsake him in seven ; or when God himself affirmed this to be the line of his treatment of mankind.— Our own hymn-writers have celebrated this truth in many a soothing and encouraging line,—" His love in time past forbids me to think," etc.

" *Up, sanctify the people, and say, Sanctify yourselves against to morrow.*"—JOSHUA vii. 13.

In this sense sanctification was equal to preparation.—There should be solemn days of scrutiny in every man's life.—We can complete the process of self-scrutiny even where social scrutiny is impossible.—The man who judges himself most severely has least to fear from the judgments of others : he can bear their criticism with composure when he knows it to be just ; he can treat it with disdain when he knows it to be malicious.—All these appointments lead up to the grand assize in which the whole world shall be judged. —To live without scrutiny is to live without the enjoyment of many a privilege.—Scrutiny is not all on the side of severity.—The Old Testament saints were sometimes enabled to plead their integrity under circumstances of persecution as a ground for divine protection.

They knew that the enemy had formed a wrong estimate of their character, and, being confident of this, they had also confidence in God.—Such scrutiny as is indicated in the text shows that there are circumstances in life which can only be met by severe moral inquest. Penetrating questions must be asked ; detailed examination must be conducted. A man must, so to say, retire within himself, and submit every part of himself to scrutiny, as if each part were a separate individuality. The sin may be found lurking in the imagination, the taste, the affections, the understanding, the selfishness or the ignorance of man.—The man must not look upon himself as a whole, and ask general questions regarding his conduct, but must regard himself as divided into many attributes and forces, and must seize each, and by severest cross-examination discover which is the Achan, the thief, the idolater, the miser, the blasphemer, the liar ; it is easy to talk about a general examination and to pronounce vague judgments ; we are called to analysis severe and exhaustive. —He does not love himself, but, on the contrary, bitterly hates himself, who is unfaithful in this matter of self-scrutiny.

" *He hath wrought folly in Israel.*"— JOSHUA vii. 15.

The charge seems to be a two-fold one. The first is that " He hath transgressed the covenant of the Lord ; " and the second is that " He hath wrought folly."—Look upon sin as being not only criminal but foolish.—The sinner is not only a criminal, but a fool. He plays with fire, and burns himself. He trifles with edged instruments, and maims himself. He tampers with eternal forces, and thus in every way disables and impoverishes himself.—It is pitiful to think that at the end the sinner will stand forth as a fool, and not as a hero. He mistakes the relations of things; the values of things; the consequences of actions.—A great French statesman was blamed because he pronounced a certain policy not only as a crime, but worse than a crime—a blunder.—Crime does not touch one side of the character alone, for then under some conditions it might claim somewhat of heroic importance, and be invested with a kind of transient grandeur.—According to the Christian conception the universe is a great moral constitution; not an infinite vastness of matter, but a symbol and expression of something within tenderly sensitive and ineffably pure: he, therefore, who operates in a manner contrary to its law and purpose undertakes to supersede Omniscience, and to re-create creation: at the end he stands forth in pitiable weakness: a man who is not only regarded as foolish, but who is constrained to call himself a fool.—Some men are more touched by the contempt which follows upon folly, than by the censure which follows upon crime; their pride is affected, their sense of dignity is lowered.—God thus attacks the sinner at every point; he shows that in the very act of playing the great man the sinner becomes a foolish man, and is obliged at last to confess that his conception of life has been a profound and pitiable mistake.— Folly has but a short day. The time of its revelation is always at hand.—No sinner has ever proved himself to have been both a genius and a criminal in the moral sense: genius there may have been in the conception of the crime as a merely mechanical or social act, but the folly of it has been demonstrated by its consequences.—It may be for this reason that God pities the sinner: he sees what a fool the sinner is; he sees to what fate of contempt and shame the sinner is hastening; he knows it is hard for the sinner to kick

against the pricks.—On every ground God hates the sin and pities the sinner.

" . . . _an altar of whole stones, over which no man hath lift up any iron._"—JOSHUA viii. 31.

This is a point in the spiritual education of man.—We must think ourselves back to the time when such mechanical exactitude was part of personal and national religion.—The uses of such studies may be to show how far we have advanced, and to inquire into the methods by which our progress has been realised.—We do not advance from those points unless we have really been at them ourselves, either literally or sympathetically.—It is not enough to know that the Israelites were at the point of literal detail, such as is indicated in the text; we must ourselves have been at that point in some clearly recognised sense; we do not descend upon great spiritual privileges, but we work up to them through processes of subservience; we are not born into this household of grace and liberty, but are brought into it by long processes of self-rebuke, self-chastisement, and self-denial; all men must begin at the alphabet, and pursue their way into the delights of literature.—It is the same with religion as it is with education.— We are born into a great literary estate, full of philosophy, poetry, history, and imagination; yet though we are born into this inheritance and have certain rights to it, we can only claim the inheritance by becoming patient inquirers and students: when the philosopher leaves his philosophy to the world, even his own children must begin at the alphabet, and toil up the ascent upon which the graet fortune stands.—Passages of this kind rebuke the idea that religion now is a merely off-handed exercise, a pleasure that can be taken up or laid down: a species of luxury which may be languidly enjoyed or languidly declined.—To build the altar is not to create the God.—To build the church is not to unfold the revelation.—There is a wonderful co-operation in the whole process of religion.—God will, so to say, be met half-way.—He will come to the top of the mountain, and meet us at the end of our opportunity.—A beautiful thought is this, that God sometimes will come no further down than to the top of the mountain; if he remained one league above it, we could not reach him; but it is in accord with his mercy that he begins where man ends; man toils to the top of the mountain, and cannot proceed one step further, and it is in this extremity that God creates his own opportunity.—Although altar-building may now have been done away, and much of mechanical process may have been abrogated, yet still there remains the great fact that man must always make some preparation to meet God and enter into the full enjoyment of religious privileges.—The preparation indicates the spirit of the worshipper.—When called upon to offer hospitality to a king, we prepare according to the dignity of the guest; when summoned to the presence of some great one, all our preparations are made with a view to the greatness of the man whom we have to meet.—We have only to apply these facts in a religious direction to discover what we ought to do when we are called upon to commune with Heaven.

"*. . . the Lord God of Israel fought for Israel.*"—JOSHUA x. 42.

Israel was an undivided name betokening a complete whole.—The Israelite, as an individual, had no existence from Israel, the whole number.—If one man wandered away from Israel, the whole body felt itself in a state of incompleteness, and was inspired by a spirit of solicitude and yearning after the absent one.—There is a nationality as well as a personality.—We miss a good deal by supposing that life is wholly a question of individualities.—In a very important sense it is so, but in another equally important sense it is not so.—England has a character as well as every Englishman.—We speak of the *health* of a country and say it is good, at the very moment when thousands of persons are lying without ability to walk or work : we speak of the *wealth* of a country, and call it exceedingly abundant, at the very moment that workhouses are crowded with inmates; we speak of the *intelligence* of a country, and may describe some countries as the most intelligent in the whole world, notwithstanding the fact that there are within them uncounted numbers of illiterate persons.—Thus there is another life beside the merely personal.—God is here represented as fighting for nations.—God never fights for any nation simply because it is a nation, but because as a nation it is on the right side of the controversy.—God has no partiality for any land, except in the degree in which that land is marked by righteousness of purpose and action.—Patriotism is folly unless it be based upon moral considerations as well as upon kindred and sentiment.—Throughout the whole Bible the Lord has always shown himself as ready to give up one nation as another when moral fidelity was impaired or perverted.—Men cannot be permitted to unite themselves with Israel on the ground that God always fights for that particular denomination. This would be selfishness, not piety.—God searches the heart, and judges absolutely by the motive.—No nation then must pride itself upon being a particular favourite of Heaven : God hath made of one blood all nations of men : God is the Father of the whole world : God is only on the side of the righteous man, be that man black or white, great in wealth or mean in poverty.

" He left nothing undone of all that the Lord commanded Moses."—JOSHUA xi. 15.

A 1 easy sentence, but a most difficult process.—First of all, here is an assumption that Joshua was a *student*. How did he know what the Lord had commanded Moses, except by diligent inquiry and study?—Not only was Joshua a student, he was a minute or critical student.—He did not take a merely general view of divine commandment, but went into particularity; " he left nothing undone of all that the Lord commanded Moses;" the word "all" is the critical point.—Here is a process of enumeration, weighing, balancing, and allotment : some things are to be done by day and some by night ; some things were essentially and others relatively important ; Joshua had to study the perspective of the moral outlook, and not to commit folly by the transposition of persons or events.—Not only was Joshua a student, and a critical student, he was a man of active obedience. His life was a process of doing. He found enough to do from the rising of the sun to the going down of the same.—God has left no vacant hours in all the day. God has made benevolent preparation for sleep or rest, but he has also made abundant arrangements for industry and service.—Not only was Joshua a student, a critical student, and a man of active obedience, but he was inspired by the thought that all he did was done under the direction and for the glory of God.—It is something to know that we are working, for what master we are acting, and in view of what reward.—The strength is often found in the motive.—Far behind all

outward instrumentality, we find our power in spiritual philosophy, thought, and confidence.—Herein is the supreme value of prayer : it shuts us up in close communion with God ; it leads us to the very fountain of power ; it clothes us with ineffable dignity.—A blessed thing it is to realise that our whole life-plan is laid down for us.—In the matter of moral purity and action we have nothing to invent; the commandments are all written, and will all be understood by the heart that really wishes to know their meaning.—It is a sign of a false life when a man hesitates on the ground that he really does not know what his duty is. Duty is perfectly and continually plain to the man whose motive is simple. "What doth the Lord thy God require of thee?" "What is written in the law?" "How readest thou?"—There can only be bewilderment in the matter of detail ; there can never be any confusion as to the distinction between right and wrong, noble and ignoble, upward and downward.

" There remaineth yet very much land to be possessed."—JOSHUA xiii. 1.

This is no threat. This is no sentence of discouragement. This indeed is inspiration.—It is true of every department of life. It is true, for example, of a man's own individuality : every man is not yet master of his entire self : some men have possessed themselves of their whole reason who have yet left their imagination unchastened and unsubdued.—Many men are chaste who are not generous. Many men are generous who are not just. Many men are impulsively good who are not rationally benevolent.—Such men may say to themselves, "There is yet very much land to be possessed."—It is true with all intellectual education.—He knows best how much land is yet to be conquered who has conquered the most.—The advanced student is the most modest.—The wisest man is most assured of his ignorance.—Sir Isaac Newton said that he was like a child on the seashore who gathered a few pebbles, while the great ocean of truth lay all undiscovered before him.—It is true with regard to the spread of the kingdom of Christ.—Take a map of the world, and show where Christianity has made progress, and where it is unknown ; and even the imagination will be appalled by the extent of land yet to be covered.—We need not rest because there is no more to be done.— We do not obliterate what is to be done by closing our eyes and resolutely refusing to look upon it. The infinite darkness is still round about us, and is not at all decreased by the closing of our eyes.—But instead of the text being a discouragement, it is an encouragement ; the land is there in order that it may be possessed ; it is not afar off and inaccessible, but is immediately in front of us, and is intended for our use ; we may have to obtain possession through battle and even through suffering, but the battle and the suffering do not destroy the possibility of possession.—What is worth holding that has not to be secured through suffering and loss of a temporary kind ? The kingdom of heaven itself lies at the end of a strait road ; but the very straitness of the road gives some hint of the value of the kingdom.—The Church must enter into a full realisation of the fact that the work yet to be done is greater than any work that has yet been accomplished : it is not an acre that awaits conquest, but a whole continent ; not a whole continent only, but a whole world.—The work to be done enlarges in proportion to the work that is done.—If the work were superficial only, it might be completed with comparative ease, but it is cubic, solid, through-and-through work, and, there-

fore, it is difficult, but its difficulty is an indication of its glory.

" The Lord God of Israel was their inheritance, as he said unto them."
—JOSHUA xiii. 33.

This was spoken of the tribe of Levi —in a peculiar sense the religious tribe of Israel.—The kingdom of God has an outward and an inward aspect : it has a land to be conquered, and it has a doctrine to be received and obeyed.— The idea of the text is that man may so live in God as to have no conscious need of outward things : and then the counterpart of the idea is that he who ascends to spiritual functions need have no fear with regard to the supply of physical necessities.—God is not the portion of religious men in the sense of feeding themselves only with thought and consolation and promise ; he is pledged so to act upon the impulses and consciences of other men as to see that every lawful necessity is abundantly supplied.—Whilst the Levites were asking for God, God was asking for them, in the very sense of finding them bread and home and security.—If we trusted God more we should receive more from God.—If we will always persist in undertaking our own business, what wonder if God should leave us to ourselves and give us the reward of disappointment ? " Seek ye first the kingdom of God, and his righteousness ; and all these things shall be added unto you."—Blessed is he who has God for a treasurer.—It is more than folly to say that all this is impossible.—We imagine that we must do so much ourselves, or God will do nothing for us ; and that statement is so far true as to give the sophism which lies at the heart of it some hold upon the confidence of the least earnest thinkers.—The text certainly suggests that God has appointed some men to be the spiritual teachers and guides of the world.—We cannot get rid of the idea of spiritual ministry.—It is right to disclaim all merely official dignity and importance, but infinitely beyond the merely official lies the grandly personal and real, which all men recognise with admiration, and many men honour with homage and generous support.—When spiritual thinkers and workers give themselves wholly to the function assigned them of God, they will realise more perfectly God's meaning when he says he has undertaken to be their inheritance; the meaning is not that they are to live upon fine thoughts and splendid conceptions, but that in addition to such thoughts and conceptions God himself will undertake to see that their house is watched and their table is supplied.—" He is able to do exceeding abundantly above all that we ask or think." " God is not unrighteous to forget your work and labour of love."—No man can work wholly and lovingly for God, and be neglected by him.—" Trust in the Lord, and do good ; so shalt thou dwell in the land, and verily thou shalt be fed."

" *Give me also.*"—JOSHUA XV. 19.

This was the petition of Achsah, the daughter of Caleb.—The father had given his daughter a portion already in the form of a south land, and now she asks him for something more, namely, " springs of water."—The emphasis of this text would seem to be on the word " also," if we accommodate it to the temper and desire of our own times.— Achsah was not content with the south land ; she wanted an addition.—Who ever is content with what he has? Does not one possession suggest another ? This suggestion may be base and selfish. It may indicate a spirit of greed or covetousness which can never be satis-

fied. We have a proverb which says " much wants more." Where such a spirit is manifested the possession already in hand is unworthily held.— Here is the secret of the amazing disparity between class and class, and the explanation of some of the grossest tyrannies of history.—Men should watch their desires in this direction.—All getting should be accompanied by corresponding giving.—Where there is no outlet there will soon be stagnation.— This desire, however, may be one of the noblest aspirations of the human mind.—There is a discontentment which is to be religiously encouraged. Say, for example, in the realm of knowledge : we go on from one advancement to another, earnestly desiring the completion of our study : say, for example, in the region of Christian donation ; Paul counted himself not to have apprehended, but he resolved his whole life into one action expressed by the attitude of pressing towards the mark for the prize of the high calling of God in Christ Jesus : he urged the Christians of Corinth to " covet earnestly the best gifts :" there is, then, a covetousness which is equivalent to prayer ; a desire for more which is a holy aspiration.— It is often difficult to distinguish between the legitimate and the illegitimate in human desire. As a broad rule it may be said that all desire for more material possession or personal gratification is wrong ; and all desire for more light, clearer insight into truth, and fuller realisation of duty, is right.— Every man must determine this for himself.—There must be no shrinking from the most penetrating inquiry.—When the soul is really anxious to know what its own desires are in the sight of God, there cannot be the slightest difficulty in obtaining the information.

" . . . . *the children of Israel gave
an inheritance to Joshua the son
of Nun among them.*"—JOSHUA
xix. 49.

Joshua had rights of his own, and
could have claimed such rights ; but
beyond rights which a man may claim
are still more precious rights which are
accorded to him by the conscience and
generosity of the community.—This is
the very law of divine providence.—
The fact that we are born into the world
is a fact which brings with it certain
natural rights, in the absence of which
we should hardly be men at all. But
this is not the limit of the divine bounty.
Beyond all that is merely legal and
necessary there is a region of grace, of
large and happy dowry, showing not
only the bare justice, but the sweet
mercy of the rule under which we live.—
In a social sense it is true that we might
get more if we claimed less.—Joshua
lived a noble life amongst his people,
and carried out his function of leadership with obvious justice and disin-
terestedness, and it is beautiful to
observe how the people seem to have
recognised this by their willing concession to him of an inheritance by their
coasts.—This should be true in all
family life. Obedience is due to parents
by an unwritten law, as well as by formal
decree ; but beyond obedience there
lies the whole region of voluntary testimony and service. Blessed is he who
gives his parent an inheritance in that
wide region !—The same thing should
be true in commercial relations : there
should be something more than a bond :
where the bond is carried out loyally on
both sides Duty will gracefully take upon
itself any crown which Gratitude may
be disposed to place upon its head.—
This should be also true ecclesiastically :
men who have laboured in season and out
of season for the good of others ought not
to be forgotten in the time of audit and
general winding up of life and service,
but should have accorded to them all
possible honour in view of a life unstained by sin, and crowded with acts of
beneficence and sacrifice.—The charm
of some possessions lies in the spirit
which dictated their ownership.—It is
a poor thing to have only those possessions which are bought and sold, and on
which merely commercial lines are inscribed ; such things, of course, every
man must have ; but the things which
are written all over with love and thankfulness are infinitely more precious, and
in an obvious sense are even more
enduring.—No man begrudged Joshua
his city in mount Ephraim : every one
felt that the city was due to the brave
captain and obedient saint.—It is well
when our honours are doubled by the
recognition of their desert by those who
know us best.—The Well-done of the
Master constitutes the best part of heaven.
—To go into heaven even as a mere act
of justice is to deprive the holy city of
its most fascinating charm. It is because
the city is given with the Well-done
of its King that residence in it becomes
the final and eternal joy of the soul.

" *Appoint out for you cities of refuge.*"—
JOSHUA xx. 2.

The law in Numbers xxxv. appointed
that the Levites should have six cities
of refuge and forty-two others.—The
law of the cities of refuge is given in
full in Numbers xxxv. and Deuteronomy
xix.—All cities should be cities of refuge.—How great the number of the
inhabitants, and how well-organised
the institutions ; how fitting, then,
that the young and the inexperienced
should find refuge in such highly-
civilised asylums.—The city is an ag-
gregation of homes, and should surely
bring the home feeling into wandering
and aching hearts.—Is not the city
crowded with churches ? And are there
not in them men of God appointed

to preach the great Gospel which was meant to heal the dying life of man ?—All these reflections suggest the gracious thought of refuge.—Where men are few it would appear as if the soul were more exposed to assault.—Solitude has dangers peculiar to itself.—When the young life is hidden amongst ten thousand times ten thousand others, surely it ought to feel a sense of security, because in such a number the spirit and genius of brotherhood should be developed and crowned.—Consider what libraries there are in the city ; how rich in literary treasure ; how impossible is solitude in the midst of such eloquent silence.—Is not a library itself a city of refuge ?—May not wandering thoughts be stayed amid all its treasures of learning and language ?—Who can be lonely in any sense of desolateness who has access to a library ?—Whilst all this is pictorially true, consider how different is the melancholy fact.—The city is full of trapdoors opening upon perdition.—Count the number of its inns, places of harmful amusement, people devoted to what has now become the fine art of knavery, sharp practice, and all manner of delusion.—Consider how the net is spread even in the sight of the bird, and the snare is laid on the open ground.— Compare a city as it might be with a city as it is, and see how steady and tremendous has been the process of degradation and corruption.—It has pleased God to represent his Church and kingdom under the image of a city.—We read in the Psalms of "the city of God."—Heaven is represented as a city whose walls are jasper and whose streets are gold.—This would seem to be a restoration of the ideal city.—It is a mistake to suppose that a city is bad simply because it is a city.—Association, companionship, interchange of opinion, the commingling of trusts and stewardships, ought all to combine to constitute an idea

of commonwealth, brotherhood, and home.—In proportion as the city is really bad, the Church should take care to provide refuges from all its malicious pursuers and an answer to all its seductive appeals.—Let there be a city within a city,—the city of God within the city of destruction.

———

" The avenger of blood."—JOSHUA xx. 5.

The text of course is limited by a local reference, but its suggestions spread themselves over the whole area of life and society.—Recognise the fact that there is in all civilisation an avenger of blood.—This indeed is necessary to the complete idea of civilisation.—If blood could be shed with impunity, civilisation itself would be a continual prey to passion.—God has set a high price upon blood ; its quality would seem to be kindred to his own ; it is full of fire, vitality ; it is the very alphabet of immortality.—Every human creature is of inexpressible consequence to God.—Given a globe consisting of twelve hundred millions of human beings, and who can assign the exact importance to any one of them ?—What is he but as a fleck of snow upon a landscape, a drop in the Atlantic, an insect hardly visible in the sunbeam in which it dances for a moment ?— Not such is the divine view ; the very hairs of your head are all numbered ; the providence of God is minute, personal, critical, exacting the uttermost farthing, and ruling all things with the severest economy.—Civilised society takes in its degree the same view of human life, for not a single child may be touched without society instantly arising as an avenger of blood.—Surely there can be no great offence in destroying an unconscious life, in putting an end to an infancy which has barely begun,—what can be the loss?—Yet even society itself instantly demands an answer to the accusation of child-murder : no excuse would be tolerated : no fine theory of limiting the population would be admitted for one moment : organised society instantly becomes as it were the parent of the child, and demands an account of its life and recompense for its loss.—This being so with regard to the body, are we not entitled to lift the argument to a higher level, and to contend that there should be an avenger of mind, thought, purpose, as well as an avenger of blood ?—They that kill the body can do but little ; they are indeed hardly to be feared in comparison with those who can sow the seed of wickedness in the opening heart, and suggest evil thoughts to the awakening mind.—If we slay him who slays the body, what should be done to him who takes away the life of the soul, who perverts the operation of motive and purpose, and who drags down the whole life to shame and infamy ?—All this anxiety about the body, its protection and its prerogatives, is but the beginning of an infinitely higher argument, if we are just to its logic.—He would be accounted a fool who cared for the child's clothing, but paid no attention to the child's health : how much greater a fool is he who pays attention to the child's health of body and utterly neglects the child's health of mind !—Consider how the avenger steadily proceeds in his task : men cannot sin with impunity : they are made to feel the result of their wicked-ness in their health, in their property, in their whole outlook of life ; their fellow men shrink from them ; they are distrusted, and handed over to repro-bation, if not always openly, and as it were by public demonstration, yet more or less secretly, silently, but surely : whatsoever a man soweth, that shall he also reap. There is an avenger of blood upon the track of every bad man ; as to when he shall be discovered and punished no man can tell the exact time, but God fixes it, and by the decree of Heaven, though hand join in hand, the wicked shall not be unpunished.

" *And they appointed Kedesh in Galilee in mount Naphtali, and Shechem in mount Ephraim, and Kirjath-arba, which is Hebron, in the mountain of Judah.*"—JOSHUA xx. 7.

The mountains of the Bible form an interesting subject of study as to their moral suggestiveness. — A beautiful thought is it that the cities of refuge should be upon the mountain-top, or should nestle in the sides of the moun-tain.—Two ideas of strength seem to combine here, the mountain itself being strong and the city built upon it in-violable.—Thus the works of God and the works of man unite in a holy effort to secure human life.—Are not all the works of God intended to save and edu-cate and complete manhood ?—When-ever the works of God fight against manhood we may be sure that sin is operating with deadly effect in some direction. — The whole world-house seems to have been built for the ac-commodation of the tenant ; for him the sun shines, the rivers flow, the earth grows her harvests, and the sea yields its population.—Man should add nothing to the works of God that is not in their own nature and according to the direction of their own purpose.— To build a home upon the fair land-scape is to add to its beauty ; to build a church on the noblest elevation on the surface of the earth is to lift the mountain to a higher altitude.—The earth is sanctified or desecrated by what is put upon it.—The schoolhouse ennobles the district in which it is placed.—Every benevolent institution is as a tree of the Lord's own planting, though it be set in the midst of a garden, or made the crowning point of a lofty summit. — On the other hand, how much has the earth been desecrated by the presence of buildings upon it devoted to evil purposes. — The public-house may be a blot upon the landscape ; the building in which evil arts are practised and evil professions are taught is as the presence of perdition in the very sanctuary of nature. — We should find more upon the mountains if we looked for more. — God has put cities of refuge upon every one of them. — The mountains themselves may be cities of refuge ; there the weary reap new strength ; there the over-driven and fevered brain cools itself and receives a tonic, enabling it to resume the battle of life and carry it on to conquest. — Not one thing in all nature has had its full meaning yet disclosed. — God burns in every bush ; his house is by the seashore ; his tabernacle is in the stars ; his temple is in the tiniest flower that blooms. — The day is coming when the whole earth shall be the mountain of God ; "no lion shall be there, nor any ravenous beast shall go up thereon, it shall not be found there ; but the redeemed shall walk there : . . . and sorrow and sighing shall flee away." — To bring about that day we are not called upon to be ideal, to dream away our time, to slumber in selfish contemplation ; we are rather summoned to activity, to discipline, to suffering ; every man should feel as if the dawning of that day depended upon his individual exertions.

" *Cities to dwell in.*" — JOSHUA xxi. 2.

This chapter deals with the distribution of the Levitical cities. — They were given to priests, to Kohathites, to Gershonites, and to Merarites. — We are told that in the camp of Israel there were two squares surrounding the tabernacle : an inner square of priests and Levites, an outer square of the tribes of Israel, three on each side. — Our point, however, is that every tribe had a city. — The distribution was so made as to involve each and all in some responsibility or trust. — The Kohathites carried the sacred vessels, the Gershonites the curtains and various fabrics of the tent and tabernacle, and the Merarites were entrusted with the bars and boards. — Wherever we find distribution in Scripture we find it so meted out that every man has his own particular vocation or trust. — The kingdom of heaven is like unto a man who took his journey into a far country, and distributed his goods to his servants, giving every one a portion to profit withal. — We have nothing to do with the amount of the distribution, but we have a distinct responsibility in relation to its fact. — Let every man ask himself, What have I, what am I expected to do, what burden have I to carry, and what is the strength wherewith I am endowed ? — No one man has all the talents : the greatest cannot do without the least. — Greatness is often misunderstood in this matter ; the probability is that there is nothing so dreary as the solitude of greatness when it is deprived of popular recognition and sympathy. — The mountains may be very great, but they are often very barren. — The valley can do better without the mountain than the mountain can do without the valley. — Though the talents be few in number they can be applied to great purposes. — The reward is not in the dowry but in the industry. — It is not humility to deny the possession of talents ; it may be simple dishonesty and unfaithfulness.

" *And the Lord gave unto Israel all the land . . . and the Lord gave them rest.*" — JOSHUA xxi. 43, 44.

The Lord is always giving. — He lives

to give.—"God so loved the world, that he gave . . . "—Trace the word "give" in connection with God throughout the whole of the Bible, and it will be found that the extent of his gifts is simply infinite.—The point to be observed here is in the contrast between the one gift and the other.—How much is implied in the word, "gave unto Israel all the land," when it is contrasted with the expression, "the Lord gave them rest !"—Was there no rest in obtaining the land? No, not so much as one day.—Although the land was given it must be fought for.—This is the great law concerning all the gifts of Heaven ; they are gifts only in a certain sense or in a limited degree, or are meant as provocatives to human energy or prizes for human patience.—The word "give" must thus be enlarged so as to represent its whole meaning : the Lord gives life, but man must train the life that is given : the Lord gives opportunity, but man must embrace the opportunity and fill it with all its significance : the Lord gives society, but society must enter upon a process of self-development and self-protection.—The thing that is given may be but the first seed, the germ, the protoplasm : all the rest may come of time, the succession of events, and the adaptations of educative influences and ministries.—In a larger sense the Lord gives rest.—He never gives rest until he has prepared men for it.—When men are not prepared for rest, they do not understand it as a blessing.—The six days' labour make the Sabbath what it is ; but for the six days' labour the Sabbath would be a mere institution, a religious ordinance, an arbitrary distribution of time ; but after the six days' toil it comes as a benediction—the very beginning and pledge of Heaven. —The true rest is the rest of the soul.—"Come unto me, all ye that labour and are heavy laden, and I will give you rest ;" "There remaineth therefore a rest to

the people of God ;" "Blessed are the dead which die in the Lord . . . that they may rest ;" "Let us therefore fear, lest, a promise being left us of entering into his rest, any of you should seem to come short of it."

" There failed not ought of any good thing which the Lord had spoken unto the house of Israel ; all came to pass."—JOSHUA xxi. 45.

Personal testimony is better than literary argument.—Of this testimony Biblical religion can always avail itself. Of this testimony Christianity can still more pointedly make account. It is no mean indication of the power of Christianity, that it constrains its disciples to bear witness to the power of Christ in the soul. The Bible writers are always particular to maintain that the word of the Lord never failed. Failure there would have been fatal to the whole idea of divine providence as disclosed in the Bible.—The ancient writers are, if possible, more particular to notice that the good things promised of God were assuredly given rather than that his threatenings were realised. There seems to be a subtle willingness to overlook the infliction of punishment in view of the daily and abundant manifestation of divine goodness.—We soon forget the darkness when the light shines. The day whose wind and rain gives us discomfort is speedily forgotten when the summer broods over the land and turns it into one garden of flowers. —A very marvellous thing it is, that in health we soon forget our sickness ; there may be in this some indication of that which will take place in higher states of being ; in heaven we shall forget every trouble of earth.—A text of this kind seems to challenge the reader to contradict it.—If it were a mere question of argument, one disputant might be outwitted by another ;

but where it is a question of direct personal witness, the character of the witness must be taken as equivalent to an argument.—The good things of God seem to grow in number and in magnitude in proportion as we look upon them from the point of advancing age. We do not see them in their true magnitude at first, or at the moment of their introduction ; we are then too near them to see exactly their bearing and colour ; a man at fifty knows more of the riches and blessedness of life than it was possible for him to know when but half that age.—The testimony in this case is most precise and inclusive. It is not a general commendation of the faithfulness of God, but a critical declaration that not one thing failed of all which God had spoken.—The argument of history is one of the most solid arguments in theology.—Doctrine is attested by providence.—We judge men by the manner in which they have kept their word to us, and where the word has been faithfully realised, honour is accorded and trust is increased. It should be so in our relations to the Creator and Ruler of life.

" What trespass is this that ye have committed against the God of Israel, to turn away this day from following the Lord, in that ye have builded you an altar, that ye might rebel this day against the Lord ? "—JOSHUA xxii. 16.

The children of Israel are here represented as coming unto the children of Reuben and to the children of Gad and to the half tribe of Manassch, and challenging them respecting a certain action.—Here is a great principle, the application of which is world-wide and time-wide : the principle is that men have a right to inquire into the trespasses committed by one another.—There is no right of trespass ; there is

no chartered sin.—Men are the keepers of one another, and ought to be severely critical as to the moral atmosphere which any man or number of men may create.—It is worse than a fallacy to suppose that a man has a right to do even with himself as he pleases.—There is a sense in which there is no mere " self" to be dealt with.—In a sense, every man is a part of some other man, or part of the body corporate.—There is no isolation in any sense that limits evil action.—Even an infamous example may be doing untold mischief in society, though the man himself may be taking no direct or energetic part in the propagation of evil.—Every householder has a right to inquire into the nuisances created by adjoining householders.—No man has a right to vitiate the common air ; it belongs to all the people, and they have a right to protect its purity, or to avenge any violation of its healthfulness.—This principle is not sufficiently recognised ; hence men are told to mind their own business and to let other people alone.—The merit of this speech consists entirely in its brevity, for it is wholly without wit, sense, charity, or beneficence.—The mother has a right to inquire into the nature of every road along which her child travels day by day.—The parent is called upon to inquire into the character of the school in which he may place his child.—He who detects any noisomeness in the air has a right to follow that noisomeness to its origin, if he possibly can, though in doing so he may have to trample down hedges and boundaries and landmarks.—The public health is of more consequence than the temporary integrity of mechanical boundaries.—If we had more challenging of one another in this matter of trespass, we should have a healthier state of society.—The time will come when men will not only be anxious about nuisances that vitiate the air or throw disquietness into the social life ; they will be still more anxious about thoughts that unbalance the mind, ambitions that fever the soul, and speculations that destroy the serenity and peace of the heart and mind.—It is in vain to preach a doctrine of brotherhood or commonwealth, and yet to desist from the exercise of those rights which belong to community and fellowship.—To preach that all the world is a brotherhood, and then to act as if every man had a right to do as he pleased, is simply to contradict preaching by practice.—When man asks, Am I my brother's keeper? the answer should be a grand and solemn affirmation.

" Choose you this day whom ye will serve."—JOSHUA xxiv. 15.

There is a point at which all religion becomes voluntary.—There is a sense in which natural religion is not voluntary, although there is a strained sense in which a contention may be set up for its voluntariness.—The whole value of spiritual religion consists in its expressing the supreme desire of the heart.—An appeal is thus made to reason, inasmuch as man is called upon to make a choice. To make a choice means, in other words, to examine, to attach values, weigh one thing against another, and to pronounce on rational grounds for the election of a certain course of conduct.—A beautiful union of words is here found, namely, " choose," and " serve." Here is a beautiful instance of voluntary slavery.—There is a service that is merely of the eye, regulated by selfish considerations and determined by self-indulgence : that service is of no account in the sanctuary : it is a vain oblation, and is rejected by God.—The apostles did not hesitate to describe themselves as "slaves of the Lord Jesus Christ ; " the word **slave** seems to mean more than servant,

and it was after that further and deeper meaning, that the apostles strained themselves when they described their service as slavery.—There is a slavery of love.—Love can never rise too early, or toil too severely, or give too lavishly ; it lives to give; it lives to gratify others ; its joy would be taken away if its service could be limited.—In such a case as is referred to in the text, "service" must not be taken as a merely intellectual or ceremonial relation,—it means downright hard work, genuine obedience, hearty devotion, complete, unsparing, and joyous consecration.—The profession of religion may be an aggravation of immorality.— To profess and not to do is to be guilty of the blackest falsehood.—Great mistakes about the service of God must be cleared away : it is a mistake, for example, to suppose that we may serve God by singing hymns, attending services, and patronising ministers, when in doing all this we only gratify our own desires without exposing ourselves to a single pang or loss. Exercises of this kind must be taken as merely part of the great consecration. The beauty is not the flower, nor is it the fragrance ; there must be root-life, hidden sources of nutriment, and direct connection with the sun.—We cannot serve God if we are not living in God, and God is not living in us. To serve God is to bring the spirit into activity at every possible point of life, thinking good, doing good, and. where necessary, suffering for good. —The greatness of this service may be seen in the fact that it is always associated in Christian teaching with concentration.—Jesus Christ said, Ye cannot serve God and mammon, as ye cannot be going east and west at the same time. Here, therefore, the meaning clearly is that divine service means undivided concentration, complete and absolute devotion to the will of God.— In view of this definition (a definition realised only by the Lord Jesus Christ) let every man say how far he is worthy to be called a servant of the living God.

" Behold, this stone shall be a witness unto us ; for it hath heard all the words of the Lord which he spake unto us."—JOSHUA xxiv. 27.

This is more than poetry ; this indeed is the greatest of realities.—We are accustomed to regard nature as a silent and unresponsive quantity, but it is never so regarded in holy Scripture.— We cannot tell the relation of nature to our own spiritual life. —There is nothing secret that shall not be revealed ; there is nothing spoken in whispers that shall not be repeated in thunders. Who cannot recall the places at which certain vows were spoken, or memorable prayers were poured out of the heart ? The world is full of trysting-places, altars of promise, mountains of aspiration, sanctuaries of vow and oath.— Every place at which we have kneeled will be a witness against us. Every time we have handled the Bible we have marked down a witness either in our favour or against us.—A recollection of these circumstances would hallow nature and give all life a new sensitiveness.—" God is able of these stones to raise up children unto Abraham." Had not the children praised Christ, the very stones would have cried out against them, and taken up a song of gladness in his honour.—There are places which we cannot pass without great memories leaping up from them, and making us live our years over again in sudden agony, now of pain, now of rapture.— The footprints we leave behind us may be seen by others, and may be encouragements to them. It is for us to say whether those encouragements shall be found on the upward road, crowned with heaven, or on the downward road, at the end of which there is a burning pit.—A very solemn thought it is that we are never really alone.—Time and space are God's witnesses, and the stones we accounted deaf may be alive to hear every oath and blessing uttered by our lives. It is a fearful thing to live !—What did you say at the child's grave ?—What at the wedding altar ?— What was the meaning of the gift of a mother's Bible ?—Recall the spot on which a great deliverance was wrought, and remember your many tears and vows.—How desolate the condition of a man against whom dumb nature exclaims !—The very stones cry out.— Every harvest rebukes spiritual indolence.—Every star puts to shame the life of darkness.—Every flower protests against moral hideousness.—O my soul, how many have been thy vows, and how few thy fulfilments ! Wilt thou always be a liar before God, and always dare the very faces of nature to put thee to shame ? I will arise and redeem my vows, and ask him who is merciful evermore to give me courage to own my cowardice, and strength to repair the waste places of my life.

EXCURSUS.

WE have now reached a point in our Biblical studies
from which we can look back to see the general
line of thought which the inspired writers have pursued.
As this is distinctively the *People's* Bible, we are entitled
to ask questions respecting what may be termed the
people's religion, by which is meant such a religion as
would be understood by the mind of the common people
who have not received specific or professional training
either in theology or philosophy. Given the Pentateuch
and the Book of Joshua in order to discover what impression the popular mind would receive from reading
them ; this is our problem, and at this point we are
prepared to make at least a tentative reply.

We must always distinguish between the people as
a whole and those specially gifted individuals who have
achieved great influence and renown as powerful thinkers.
We may judge either by the many or by the few ; and
in a case such as is now before us we are certainly
entitled to judge by the many, asking ourselves the
question, How will this or that doctrine or revelation
strike the average mind ? Unless we keep in view this
broad distinction as between the many and the few, we
shall do injustice to both. Judging by the many, we
might be inclined to view with contempt, certainly with
disesteem, the few who are supposed to plume themselves
on great gifts, and claim to be the leaders of the world.
Nothing would be easier than for the multitude to scorn

the little clique or sect or faction claiming to be all
but inspired, and asserting some kind of right to rule the
general thinking of mankind. The common people might
ask whether it is more probable that a thousand men
should be right than that one man should be right when
he differs from them. A good deal of supposed eminence
might also be traced to vanity, or set down to some
inferior motive. On the other hand, it is just as possible
to do injustice to the many by unduly magnifying
the gifts and rights of the few. Was the revelation of
God made to mankind, or was it made only to a man
here and there of superior intellectual capacity and force?
Is the Bible intended to be the Book of the People,
or is it meant that it should come to the people
only through the interpretation of priests, ministers, or
scholars? Is there not a spirit in man, and doth not
the inspiration of the Almighty give him understanding?
Did not the common people hear Jesus Christ "gladly"?
Are we not distinctly told again and again that many
sacred mysteries are hidden from the wise and prudent,
and revealed unto babes? Does not the whole tone of
the Bible sanction the thought that the revelation made
by God to man respecting the salvation of the race is
made to the humble, contrite, penitent, unassuming, and
is withheld from the princes of this world? It should be
remembered on all sides of an argument of this kind that
some men have what may be termed a theological faculty
or genius : they have insight, a kind of prevision, a
comprehensive glance as to power of grouping details
and setting facts and doctrines in their true perspective :
they may be emphatically termed theologians, and ought
to be duly respected as such ; but it is perfectly evident
that Christianity cannot come through merely scientific
theology, otherwise the great common world would never
receive the blessings of the Gospel, or if it did receive
them it would be with such a sense of obligation to
learned and gifted men as to constitute those men into
a kind of priesthood, and offer to them, more or less

consciously, a tribute scarcely distinguishable from idolatry. The theologian has a distinct function and position of his own ; keeping himself strictly to that function and position, he is to be consulted with the hope of spiritual advantage on the part of the inquirer ; but it must never be understood that the Gospel intended for the salvation of the whole world is entrusted solely to the custody of men of letters, men of metaphysical genius, or men of piercing insight, and can only be received through their mediation or instrumentality. Between the theologian and the Christian the widest possible contrast must be established : a man may be a profoundly scientific theologian, and yet know nothing about the Spirit of Christ ; on the other hand, a man may be imbued with the very Spirit of the Lord, and yet be totally unacquainted with the methods and results of distinctively scientific theology. We cannot be too careful in protesting against the erection of preaching into some kind of mere profession. It is in this way that priesthoods are formed, and that all kinds of spiritual tyranny are established. The people must never hold the idea that the Bible can only be understood by a certain kind of men to whom exceptional privileges have been granted. We must insist that the Bible is the people's book, that it can be understood by the people, that there is nothing in it necessary to salvation which people cannot find out for themselves, without the help of priest or preacher. This is true liberty of conscience, and this is the proper exercise of the right of private judgment. When questions of history, archæology, letters, ancient civilisations, or any species of criticism come up, then the assistance of learned and competent men is indispensable : but so long as the question relates to the method of reconciliation with God, and the building up of spiritual and beneficent character, the people must discuss and settle the whole matter without what may be termed, inoffensively, professional intervention. There is in human nature a **strong tendency towards priesthood, professionalism, or** official superiority. This tendency is to be resisted as if it were one of the most subtle and persistent temptations. The most eminent professor of Biblical learning would do well sometimes to sit at the feet of the humblest disciple. He would be all the better if he could hear some broken-hearted man read the Bible to him morning by morning. The great passages of the Bible are to be read through the tears of sorrow. Learning of a verbal kind can do only the very meanest sort of work in the house of God ; a needful work no doubt, a work by no means to be contemned when limited to its proper scope and uses, but the spirit of the Bible is in the heart of the people, and by that heart alone can that spirit be fully and influentially revealed.

Looking back upon the course we have traversed, what would be the people's idea respecting the God of the Bible ? The metaphysician might begin by some analysis of the elements or attributes of Godhead, but we are not now asking what the metaphysician would do, but rather what would be the impression of the people regarding the God of the Pentateuch ? There are two distinct ways of entering upon the question of the existence and sovereignty of God. The metaphysician has one way, and the non-metaphysician has a way quite different. We have now to do with the non-metaphysician—the plain, common, average mind of the world. Let that mind carefully go through the Pentateuch, and through such portion of history as is set forth in the Book of Joshua, and its impression must be that, according to the teaching of the Bible, God is great, good, mysterious in character, inscrutable in purpose, but always revealing himself in great acts of moral correction and beneficence. The ordinary reader might not be able to define with anything like exhaustiveness such terms as Omnipotence, Eternal, Jehovah, and yet the inability to give such definition would not prevent the mind entertaining the sublimest thoughts of God's nature, attributes, and government. We may have carried this matter of definition too far. In all religious thinking there is a point at which analysis must stop, and man must simply begin to pray and to wait patiently upon God. To this of course it will be replied that the people will insist upon saying, *What* have we to believe respecting God ? *Who* is God ? But this reply itself needs correction. The answer is both Yes and No. How are such matters settled in practical life ? You may as well say that before a man who is hungry can accept bread he is bound to ask certain difficult questions respecting bread,—as, for example, by what process did it grow, what chemical forces operated in the production of bread, what is the relation of the earth to the sun, of light to water, and what is the secret or mystery of germination ? Now whilst it might be most interesting to answer all these questions, the answer to them is not at all necessary to the appropriation of the bread which is offered. There is no violence in the suggestion that he who accepts bread without inquiring into all the chemical or other questions which relate to the mystery of germination or growth, acts upon faith rather than upon reason ; his reason is not at all satisfied simply because he knows nothing whatever regarding the processes which took place in the production of bread. Nor is the analogy to be thrown out simply because it does not cover the whole ground ; it covers ground enough for our immediate purpose, when it shows that in practical matters men are content to act in a practical way. We contend that there is no matter more practical than the moral settlement of the mind, the purification of motive, the acceptance of divine blessings, ending in reconciliation with God, a beneficent life, and sure hope of heaven. We must insist that these questions are themselves practical ; for, the moment we allow them to be taken out of practical relations, they become merely speculative, and can only be treated as so many high conjectures to which there is no definite answer. The people cannot read the

portion of Scripture through which we have come without
feeling that the existence of God is everywhere recognised ;
is, indeed, assumed as the one all-ruling fact of the
history ; is not brought up for discussion or consideration,
but is set down as the unit without which all processes
of calculation would be simply impossible. The mind,
therefore, might accept God as the Bible accepts him.
He is there assumed, taken for granted ; not a step is
taken except under the distinct conviction and happy
consciousness of the presence and rule of God in human
life. Because we begin at this point it does not follow
that we may end there. Experience itself will become
a means of education, and as we proceed in our spiritual
reading and Christian education we may be able to form
higher and clearer conceptions of the divine existence
and character, and so may be enabled to create a kind
of theology of our own. But the point to be observed
is that all this is after-growth, and is not at all necessary
to the formation of a really religious character. Because
metaphysical questions can be asked, it does not follow
that it is necessary to answer them. There is no mental
exercise that does not admit of severe metaphysical cross-
examination. If we did not act in common life until we
were able to answer all the metaphysical questions that
could be raised concerning it, we should never act at all.
What is will ? What is the origin of ideas ? What
is the scope of volition ? What is the final meaning of
responsibility ? What is the exact moral relation of one
man to another ? All these questions, and many more,
instantly present themselves when any undertaking is proposed, and if we were not to move until they were finally
settled, we should never move at all. The suggestion,
therefore, that men will ask certain questions respecting
God, and that we ought to be prepared to answer them,
falls to the ground, if there is any force in analogy. We
must ask men to be as reasonable in the higher things
of life as in the lower, and to adopt certain working
principles in order to find the way even to their prior

or ulterior intent and purpose. In adopting this course of inquiry and reasoning, the mind will be strongly supported by reflecting upon the kind of character which is thereby produced. Accepting God,—that is to say, the fact of his existence, the certainty of his government, and the reality of his judgment of human conduct,— what is the kind of character produced by this recognition ? We contend that the kind of character so produced is of the highest quality, ennobled by veneration, purified at the very fountain of its motive, and ruled by considerations which involve the claims, rights, and highest interests of other men. If a non-metaphysical acceptance of God ended in looseness or frivolity of character, such an ending would be a powerful answer to the argumentative contention ; but when facts all tend the other way— namely, to show that even where there is no metaphysical genius there may be thorough acceptance of the idea of the divine personality and rule, and profoundly religious character and feeling—the whole aspect of the argument is changed. Now up to this point in the Bible we have not had to deal with metaphysicians, philosophers, theologians, as these terms are now understood, but we have had to deal with many noble and righteous men, whose examples may be safely held up for imitation in all lands and all ages. They lived in God ; they moved and had their being in him ; some of them "walked with God," and some of them were hardly distinguishable from the very purest examples of piety which even Christian history affords. The people, then, may well come to the conclusion that in the portion of the Bible which we now close, there is certainly the revelation of a creating, sustaining, and directing God—mighty, merciful, good, and gracious ; having sympathy with men, pitying their infirmities, burning with anger against their sins, and yet in the very midst of his moral indignation seeking their redemption and restoration.

What would be the idea of the people with regard to

the Providence which is revealed in the Bible up to this point? We need not enter upon minute questions regarding government, relationships between the Governor and the governed, as involving nice questions of moral obligation; we have simply to ask, What would be the impression produced upon the ordinary mind by the perusal of so much of the Scriptures as we have now studied? Is there anything like shape or form in all the history that has passed before us? Is there anywhere a disclosure of a distinct purpose in divine rule? Have things but moved from one chaos to another, aggravating the tumult and confusion as they have passed from phase to phase? Has there been at all events the recognition of a Power which could raise up and put down; which could punish sin and reward righteousness; which could bind kings and princes and give authority to those who were previously without name? Is there anywhere in all this portion of Scripture a sense of centralisation, supremacy, authority? Is there at least the shadow of a throne, high and mighty, above all the affairs of men? I cannot but feel, in coming along all this open Biblical road, that everywhere we have been confronted by the gracious presence of an overruling Providence. The pages have been full of happy inspiration. True, we have had mystery upon mystery, one darkening upon the other like sevenfold night, but again and again we have had occasion to exclaim, Though "clouds and darkness are round about him, righteousness and judgment are the habitation of his throne." Curiously enough, we have seen deliverance come both unexpectedly and suddenly, but with a certainty which no human power could set aside. At the very point where we expected evil to triumph permanently, we have seen the light strike the evil one, and day displace all the horrors of night. We hold these to be simple matters of fact. They have ample correspondence and confirmation in our own consciousness and experience. We cannot account for these things; all things seem to be entangled one within the other, and hope of reconciliation or harmony there appears to be none ; the enemy is at the very door, and the hour of destruction has already come : yet in a moment deliverance has been wrought, and that which was dark and frowning has become bright, smiling, and hopeful. The common people can understand these things when they cannot enter into the mysteries of government, rulership, and moral relations of developing and sometimes apparently contending degrees. The thing to be kept in mind is what the people as such can understand, and never to tempt them away into fields of mere speculation and conjecture, where, because of want of adequate mental training, they would be sure to fall into deeper and deeper confusion. The people as such must be encouraged to stand upon solid ground, upon the facts which they themselves have known, seen, and handled ; and how tempting soever it may be to proceed from these solid rocks into the upper air of question-asking and speculation, the people must be exhorted to stand within the lines which they themselves have proved, for only within those limits have they adequate answer to the assaults of the enemy. Some men may pass beyond those lines. Here it is that we must always make room for the highly-qualified theologian or metaphysician. He is of unspeakable use, as we have again and again allowed, so long as he keeps within his proper sphere, but he must not sneer at the common people because they cannot philosophise, neither must the common people sneer at him because he sees higher heights than they themselves have yet beheld. The common man and the uncommon thinker belong to one another, are mutually complementary, and therefore they must hold one another in mutual honour.

Another interesting inquiry would relate to the conception of the common people as to the matter of Inspiration, so far as our studies have proceeded. Theories of inspiration have always been rife enough in the Church,

Our contention is that the people as such really cannot settle questions of inspiration, nor ought they to attempt their consideration. Not only are the people unable to settle the great question of inspiration, but even the most learned and gifted professors and teachers have not come to common ground on the question themselves. What the common people can do with regard to the matter of inspiration is to discover the moral tone and purpose of the Book which claims to be inspired. They can put to themselves the great question, What is the moral teaching of this book? What kind of character is this book designed to create and foster? What is the quality of the righteousness on which this book insists? Is this a book which is satisfied with expediency, training, compromise, or being right on the whole or in general? He would be an unwise teacher who denied that there are difficulties in the Pentateuch which even scholars cannot settle. Let us allow that there are discrepancies as to dates and events in the Pentateuch and in the historical books; let us admit that there are many questions on which no light can be thrown; it would be most unwise to rest the question of inspiration or non-inspiration upon such circumstances. The importance of these questions is not for a moment to be denied, but they are not to be regarded as taking rank with the highest moral inquiry and purpose on the part of the book. The heart can always tell what words are inspired when they address themselves to the moral nature. There is not a soul that would not revolt at the idea that a command to do wrong was inspired. Not a man would rise to uphold commandments contrary in spirit to the ten which constitute the law. Were a man to arise and say, The eighth commandment ought to be read, " Thou shalt steal," he would instantly be put down by the common voice of civilised humanity; it would be felt that such a doctrine aimed at the very constitution of life in all its social and dependent relations. Now whilst there are definite lines upon which the inspiration of the Bible can be tested, it may be quite

enough for the common people—that is, for the people as
a whole—to rest upon those lines, and not to trouble
themselves with the remoter questions which even the
most learned men cannot adjust.   No fault need be found
with the teachers who insist that the word of God is to be
found in the Bible, as against the theory that the Bible
is itself the word of God.   Considerable controversy has
arisen respecting this distinction.   Let us understand what
it is : one teacher says the Bible is the word of God ;
another teacher says the word of God is to be found in
the Bible.   In the first case the man undertakes to uphold
the doctrine of what is termed plenary or verbal inspiration : he will have it that every letter is inspired, that
every word is sacred ; in short, that there is nothing whatever, from the beginning of the Bible to the end, that is
not immediately and absolutely inspired and directed by
God.   The other teacher maintains that this is by no
means the case, and that it is not necessary that it should
be the case in order to prove that the Bible is a divine
revelation : he insists that the moral character of the Bible
is the best proof of its being inspired ; he looks upon
all matters of astronomy, geology, military history, local
movement, popular rumour, as being merely literary, and
as being strictly in accordance with the knowledge and
temper of the times ; in all these departments he is prepared to find literal discrepancy, or to be confronted with
considerable difficulty of many kinds ; but he contends
that, apart altogether from these incidents and details, there
is in the Bible an authoritative revelation of righteousness,
truth, and peace to the whole world.   The inspiration,
therefore, for which the second teacher would contend
may be termed moral as apart from literal inspiration : he
maintains that there is no difficulty whatever in ascer-
taining the real moral character of the book, and upon
that real moral character he establishes his claim that the
Bible is inspired and has become possible as a book only
because of direct divine intervention.   It is not in our
power to settle these contending claims.   But what is

there to find fault with in the claim of the man who insists that from beginning to end the God of the Bible requires of man that he walk justly, love mercy, and put his daily trust in God, looking to none other for direction, instruction, and judgment ? We continually insist that even in the parables of Christ the local incident or colouring is not to be regarded as part and parcel of the parable : in effect we contend that the truth is within the parable ; in other words, that the parable is within the parable, and that we must reach the kernel if we would understand the speaker's meaning. The teachers to whom reference is now made make the same contention with regard to the Bible : they say that the Bible is within the Bible : they say that the Bible contains incident, colouring, and detail of many kinds which really have no essential or vital bearing upon the supreme purpose of the book itself : they are thus enabled further to maintain that whatever may be said regarding the merely external circumstances associated with the development of the Bible, its central purpose remains inviolate and inviolable : from their point of view the Bible contains the very law of God, respecting which there can be no dispute, as to its sublime morality or profound and glorious character. Probably the common people would be prepared to adopt this view without saying anything at all respecting the other, simply because they are not qualified to discuss the other with adequate information and ability. A great point, however, is gained when any man is drawn to confess that the Bible contains and reveals the whole counsel of God regarding human character and human responsibility. It is of infinitely greater importance to establish this doctrine than to establish any other within the whole sphere covered by the term Inspiration. The one sphere does not indeed necessarily exclude the other, nor does the one sphere necessarily include the other. A man may be perfectly orthodox, and say that he is altogether unable to settle the contentions of doctors and critics regarding inspiration, but for himself he has come to the conclusion that, however much may be taken out of the Bible, its moral integrity is left unimpaired, it enshrines the very wisdom of God, and reveals the only conditions upon which man can walk acceptably with his Maker.

On these three questions of Godhead, Providence, and Inspiration, the people may up to this point be able to form distinct and profitable opinions for themselves. My exhortation must continually be, Prove all things ; never allow the priest to dispossess you of your right of private judgment ; read the book thoroughly from end to end, and believe that Almighty God never sent a message to the human race which could be understood only by a portion of that race—that whatever the great Father of us all has sent to the human family he has sent in language which cannot be misunderstood except by the perversity and selfishness of man. Wherever we come upon any mystery which is intended to interfere with the development of moral character, we may be sure that that mystery is an invention of priestcraft, and ought to be blown away with indignation and horror. Great and awful mysteries of another kind there must always be. Who can find out the Almighty unto perfection ? Who can lay a line upon Eternity and say, This is the measure thereof, and such and such number of days exhaust the meaning of eternal duration ? Again and again we must stand back in wonder and awe, not knowing where we are or what events are challenging our imagination. But apart from all these mysteries, speculations, conjectures, hypotheses, there are great solid rocks of history, fact, experience, upon which all men can stand, and where they can wait as in a sanctuary for the further revelation of God's kingdom. How foolish would that man be regarded in common life who would not build upon a rock because other men have attempted to build upon a quaking bog ! Look at your own life, its form, its progress, its gradual uplifting and purification, and say if within that boundary you have not encouragement enough to pray and hope and serve to the end. Religion without mystery would be incomplete religion, and would soon become the merest amusement of frivolous minds. All through the line we have traversed God has kept certain reasons to himself without the faintest hint of revelation. He did not explain to Adam why one tree was forbidden. He did not tell why one sacrifice was accepted and another rejected. In the wilderness he gave symbols which never fully conveyed the meaning of the thing signified. Even when he communed with man it was through the medium of a chosen servant, and not promiscuously to the multitude. But whilst there have been inscrutable mysteries, have there not also been countless mercies? To the mercies we must recur with thankful hearts when the mysteries dazzle and bewilder our helpless Reason. The beasts of the field shall teach us. The rocks shall be full of suggestion. The stars shall shed down their gospel of light. Our own home-life shall witness gratefully to the goodness of God. Thus, whilst the mysteries hide themselves in light unapproachable, the mercies shall sing to us by day and night, and be unto us as glad promises of still better things to come.

JUDGES.

THIS book abounds in human character, and thus differs very happily from the books of ritual through which we have just passed. Innumerable men come and go on this busy stage, each leaving a distinct impress on the memory, even the humblest having some touch of distinction which gives him importance. Think of Ehud the ambidexter, Shamgar the wielder of rough weapons, Deborah the mother in Israel, Barak woman-led, Gideon so majestic in self-control and patient simplicity, of Abimelech the hateful self-seeker, Jotham the father of fabulists, Jephthah despised yet crowned, Manoah domestic and melancholy, his wife quick at spiritual interpretation, Samson an elephant in strength a babe in weakness, Micah the priest, and Benjamin dissolute yet missed and lamented. Then there are innumerable little names, glittering like asteroids on that distant sky, as Othniel and Heber, Sisera and Jael, Tolah and Jair, the woman who stunned Abimelech with a millstone, and the old man who came out of the field at eventide and blessed the wayfarers. A book abounding in character truly! History, Romance, Song, War, Tumult, gather in this array, and it is our business to observe and ponder, consider and learn what we can. The study of this book has been most profitable to my own mind, as a study of human nature under conditions which severely test it at every point, and also a study of that spiritual and mysterious action which we justly name Providence. Though the tumult is great the central line never changes. An unseen but mighty Hand guides the tremendous storm, and is never more evident as to omnipotence than when the history is most confused and bewildering. How many are the servants of Jehovah, and how various in faculty, disposition, and capacity! Who could hold them together in one happy service but the Lord God omnipotent? This consideration opens up the whole subject of the Providence which governs and unites the infinite mass which we call Society. Think of it as a Society that has been kept together thousands upon thousands of years and yet has always seemed to be upon the point of dissolution! Always about to be dissolved yet never dissolving. The dispute never ceases; collision and contention occur every moment; yet in the midst of continual contention there is continual progress. Society has come again and again to the point of ruin, yet it has always escaped the last peril ; again and again Might has seemed to have Right utterly in its power, yet the Right has thriven in adversity, and clothed itself with new beauty even in the fire ; in a word, human history is a constant crisis, yet it never reaches the point of extinction. Society is marked by the widest contrasts, such as master and servant, rich and poor, learned and ignorant, refined and vulgar ; and the moral distinctions are endless,—you have every variety of temper, purpose, desire, sensibility, and service ; you have the brave and the timid, the generous and the mean, the unsuspecting and the distrustful, the man who faces the world with high courage, and the coward who shrinks in darkness ; you have the earnest soul who prays for his race like an intercessor, and near him (or born of the same mother) one to whom the light gives pain. The nursery is full of infant life, and the hillside alive with childish movement and glee, and on the other side of the same hill you have the dying child, the good man sighing for home, and the bad man ending a wild day in a wilder night. Look abroad still. Yonder are the blind, who know only of morning by hearsay ; the dumb, the imbecile, the mad, and on and on the exciting panorama stretches and palpitates, until the eye is tired by the endless spectacle. Realise, as far as you can, all distances, differences, contrasts, and antagonisms, and then ask, How can all this be accounted for ?

I hold that this is as purely a matter of scientific interest as the formation of rocks or the distribution of plants. I am interested in social man as much as the naturalist is interested in physical man.

This in passing. Now look at your own individual life, and thus bring the mystery nearer home. You had no control over your birth. You had no control over your constitution. You come into a world and assume responsibilities of the most appalling magnitude. You come in a helpless infant, you go out either to heaven or to hell. You learn, you work, you suffer ; you fight, and lose the battle ; you run, and lose the race ; you are just going to drink the cup of joy, and behold it is thrown out of your hand ; the child that is to be your mainstay and comfort dies first ; the man who never prays succeeds in this world better than you, though you pray seven times a day. You cannot get a footing anywhere. The rock melts into water the moment you touch it, and the water becomes a rock again when some other man puts his foot upon it. You are confounded, bewildered, lost.

Now account for all this. Suppose we say that it is all a matter of chance, would that satisfy any thinking, reasonable man ? Look how the suggestion degrades us ! It contradicts the very instincts that make us human. Have we not power to protect ourselves against chance ? We protect ourselves against infection, and against fire and water ; we build bridges, lay telegraphs, and do all manner of wonderful things : how is it that we cannot overcome so contemptible an agent as chance? Why do we not assemble in solemn congress and get the upper hand of a power that makes everything else so uncertain? If we could bring chance under our control nine-tenths of our troubles would be at an end.

Suppose we say that it is the operation of the law of averages, we have only used a long word for a short one, for after all it comes back to chance put down in figures. Is any sensible man really satisfied with that explanation? Is it enough for me, looking at my disappointments and losses, my trials and griefs, my heart-breaks and temptations, to say that they all fall under the law of averages? We feel that the answer is insufficient. It does not go to the root of the matter. It is a reply that would be put down in politics as a fool's answer, and that would be regarded in business as the road to bankruptcy. How, then, to account for the facts? Suppose that it should be suggested that above all and around all there is an Almighty Providence, that all things are naked and opened unto the eyes of him with whom we have to do? Does not the heart leap at that suggestion and say it is true?

I accept the doctrine of Providence not because I am told to do so without any reason being given, but because the facts of my own daily life make such a doctrine essential; they demand it; they fall to pieces without it; they are lifted up into coherence and meaning and expectation by it.

Observe how this method of reasoning operates. If you start from the point which says, There is a Providence, go and find it; you will meet with many things in the course of your study which will appear to contradict and destroy the theory, and because you have started to prove a theory the difficulties will be all the greater. But if you begin at the point which says, There is human history with all its ups and downs, its ambitions and limitations, its ebbings and flowings, go and account for it, you will be compelled to attribute it to chance or to Providence, and I leave it to any sensible man to say which is the more probable, not to say the more satisfactory, solution.

If we say chance, the answer not only insults our intellectual dignity, it positively contradicts and stultifies itself, for the chance which is so regular, so consistent, so uniform, that in many departments of life it can be made the basis of arithmetical calculation, proves that it is no chance at all. Chance is capricious. Chance is unmanageable. Chance is treacherous. If chance has become law, law is no chance, and it has to be shown how chance chanced to become law, and how having become law it has lost the chance of becoming chance again. No, no. The theory of chance is absurd and untenable. But if we make Providence our answer we still have to face the many difficulties of human history; children die; good men suffer; bad men prosper; the scroll in the hand of pensive Time is written all over with mourning, lamentation, and woe. Let us now note the action.

Judges 1. 7.

"As I have done, so God hath requited me."

ADONI-BEZEK.

THESE words were uttered by Adoni-bezek (king ot ʋezek). He had conquered seven of the little kingdoms in and around Palestine, and he showed their kings the rough hospitality of cutting off their thumbs and their great toes, and of allowing them to gather their meat under his table. In due time, however, Judah, who succeeded Joshua in the leadership, went up to do the Lord's work and took with him Simeon that they might fight against the Canaanites. In Bezek they slew ten thousand men. There they found the king, and they fought against him, and when he fled they pursued after him and caught him and cut oft his thumbs and his great toes. "And Adoni-bezek said, Three-score and ten kings, having their thumbs and their great toes cut off, gathered their meat under my table : as I have done, so God hath requited me." This fact is an illustration of a severe yet most holy law. "The Lord God of recompenses shall surely requite." Nor was this an ancient law only ; it was repeated by Jesus Christ himself : "With what measure ye mete, it shall be measured to you again." The same doctrine was laid down by the Apostles : "He shall have judgment without mercy, that hath shewed no mercy." Adoni-bezek shows his wisdom in making this comment upon his own suffering. Though he was a tyrant yet he was not a fool. The difficulty of the spiritual teacher is with heedless men ; all other difficulties may be subdued or even turned to advantage, but heedlessness, inattentiveness, careless-ness, who can overcome ?

Set it down as a central and abiding truth that wrong-doers cannot escape divine judgment. "Be not deceived ; God is not mocked : for whatsoever a man soweth, that shall he also reap." A man may deny this ; he may theoretically disregard it ; but all history shows that he cannot escape it. At the heart of things is the spirit of judgment. Life appears to be confused, but before the Almighty it has shape and plan and purpose. God overtakes a man at the last, and comes before him with such vividness of action as to constrain the man himself to admit that the punishment is divine and not human. There is an answering voice in the human heart. When a man is suffering from any amputation whatsoever, either physical or social, either ecclesiastical or commercial, let him profoundly reflect upon the whole case and scourge his memory so that nothing may be omitted from the review, and he will find that there is a marvellous law in life whose watchword is : "Breach for breach, eye for eye, tooth for tooth" ! "As thy sword hath made women childless, so shall thy mother be childless among women." Only the fool can be satisfied by tracing his punishments to ill-luck.

Seeing that there is this law of punishment or requital in constant operation, no man should take the law into his own hands. That is the most pitiful form of the attempted readjustment of things. When the reformation is worked out it must come from a greater distance and operate by an infinitely greater sweep. "Thou shalt not avenge, nor bear any grudge against the children of thy people." "Say not, I will do so to him as he hath done to me." "Dearly beloved, avenge not yourselves, but rather give place unto wrath : for it is written, Vengeance is mine; I will repay, saith the Lord." Adoni-bezek acknowledged his punishment as a divine visitation. He did not look upon it as a petty resentment on the part of his enemies ; he took a high moral view of his condition. Why have we suffered loss in business ? May it not be that we have oppressed the poor and needy ? Why are our schemes delayed and thwarted ? Is it not because we have been obstinate and unfriendly towards the schemes of others ? Why are we held in disesteem or neglect ? Is it not because of the contempt with which we have treated our brethren ? Let us look at the moral working of things, and see in the results which are forced upon us, not the petty anger of men—something that might have been avoided—but the inevitable judgment of God against which all resistance is vain.

This law does not operate in one direction only. The God who punishes also rewards. "God is not unrighteous to forget your work and labour of love." "The liberal soul shall be made fat." "Give, and it shall be given unto you; good measure, pressed down, and shaken together, and running over, shall men give into your bosom." This is the other side of a law which is full of awful suggestion. The way of the Lord is thus equal. Nothing that we do for him or for his cause goes without reward. Whosoever shall give a cup of cold water only, in the name of a disciple, shall be surprised by the approbation of Heaven, and amazed at the degree in which every simple deed of duty or love is magnified by the Judge of the whole earth. But we must not work merely for the sake of a reward, for then all the process would end only in disappointment. It is possible to do good deeds with a selfish hand. If a man shall set himself to convert the whole world, simply in order that he may secure heaven at last, all his efforts will be thrown away and he himself will be cast into outer darkness. The reason is plain. There is no similarity between the motive and the action; they are not only not co-ordinate, they do not belong to the same universe; they can only be regarded as abortive and pitiful attempts to serve God and mammon. Where the motive is right the good deed is always its own reward. We realise heaven in the doing of it. No man ever yet relieved the necessities of poverty without himself being abundantly fed and satisfied by the very act of benevolence. A very curious law is this, yet that it is a law is proved by innumerable instances, and not a single instance to the contrary can be quoted in modification, much less in disproof. It would appear as if eyes were watching us from heaven, noting all the way that we take and all the deeds that we do, and that instantly some communication was set in motion by which our hearts were encouraged and refreshed immediately upon the accomplishment of every good deed. Hence come our holiest raptures, our sublimest ecstasies, the enthusiasms which lift us into the gladness of heaven: hence, too, comes that sweet content which never fails to crown the day's labour done by the hands of the good man. If we would know how happy human life can be, how like God's own life, peaceful with the very quiet of heaven, let us go about doing good, and thus imitate the Son of God.

Then coming back to the other side of the great truth, there

stands before us the solemn fact that though justice be long
delayed yet it will be eventually vindicated. Adoni-bezek had
run a long course of wickedness : seventy kings had suffered
under his cruel knife. It seemed as if all power had been
given into his hands. As king after king entered within the
shadow of his dominion all courage must have sunk and died
Yet even Adoni-bezek came within the grip of the law and
learned that the time of punishment is with the Lord and not
with man. We are apt to suppose that after a certain time we
have outwitted the law of retribution. When half a lifetime has
been lived we say, Surely there can be no revival of the forgotten offence. We pass an act of oblivion regarding our own
moral misdeeds. God's hour is coming ; a stormy and terrible
hour. Adoni-bezek acknowledged his punishment to be just ;
he saw it to be God's act ; so at last every wicked man will own
that hell is his proper place. Could there be any comfort in
perdition, it would arise from the fact that the punishment there
inflicted is just. Surely some such reflection as this alone
can enable the criminal to bear the tremendous penalty of life-
long servitude. Innocence might enable him to bear it, because
of the sureness of an ultimate vindication and reward ; and
consciousness that the punishment is deserved might mitigate
the severity of the penalty, because the conscience would be saying all the while, " As I have done unto others, so hath the Lord
requited me." Let us then be solemnised and yet comforted.
Life is not a haphazard movement as in some aspects it occasionally appears to be. Above it all is seated the ever-watching and
incorruptible Judge. Let us give ourselves no uneasiness about
the punishment of offenders ; let us do our work honestly and
straightforwardly whoever may oppose, and in the long run we
shall see that there is a rod for the wicked, and a crown for
those who do well. An awful message the pulpit must ever
have to deliver to the wicked man : " Though hand join in
hand, the wicked shall not be unpunished ; " " Be sure your
sin will find you out." The judgment of the last day may
therefore be the briefest of all exercises, forasmuch as every man
will be a witness either for or against himself, and will answer
the look of the Judge in a way which will signify beyond all
misinterpretation either heaven or hell.

PRAYER

ALMIGHTY GOD, we bless thee for the wonderful words of our Saviour. We often cannot understand what he saith; yet from what we do understand, we know that the very mystery of his speech is itself a blessing. The noontide of revelation will come, the full light will shine upon all his words; then shall we see how beautiful they are, as flowers of summer, and how rich they are, as sheaves of harvest. Who can find out the Son of God unto perfection? Who can say, This is his meaning, and there is none other? Sooner can we lay a line upon the whole heaven, and measure the height thereof, than we can understand unto perfectness the wisdom of the Son of God. Never man spake like this Man. Verily he is no man only : there is a reach in his arm which is not found in human arms : he raises it to the stars, he lays his hand upon the throne of God, he searches all heaven. His words are full of love, full of mystery, full of grace. We wonder at the gracious words which proceed out of his mouth—the words themselves so gracious and made doubly gracious by the tenderness and majesty of his tone. Give us at all times when Christ is the speaker, the hearing ear, the understanding heart, and the obedient will; then shall our hearing be a means of grace, and the sight of Christ by the vision of the soul shall be a ministry of transfiguration : then shall we be like him when we see him as he is. To gather round thy book is our chief delight; this is the very jubilee of time, the hour of joy and growth and liberty. May no man miss the sacredness of the opportunity: may every moment be begrudged that is not spent in eager attention, and may the one desire of every listener be to know what God the Lord hath spoken—the invisible God in heaven, or the visible and human Christ on earth. Thou knowest all the burdens we carry, and with what little strength we bear them. Every perplexity of our life is known unto thee. We are baffled, disappointed, turned back, surprised by the proportion of our foes, and amazed by their uncalculated number; but God is with us, and when the Omnipotent One shall make bare his arm, behold all enemies shall be dispersed and all difficulties overcome. Help any men who are being crushed by their burdens. They dare not tell all the tale of distress; they hide it in their hearts, and grow old by the very concealment of the misery. The Lord look upon all men, read the secret of life, send salvation from the Cross, and help from the sanctuary. Amen

Judges i. 27-36.

27. Neither did Manasseh drive out the inhabitants of Beth-shean and her towns, nor Taanach and her towns, nor the inhabitants of Dor and her

towns, nor the inhabitants of Ibleam and her towns, nor the inhabitants of Megiddo and her towns : but the Canaanites would dwell in that land.

28. And it came to pass, when Israel was strong, that they put the Canaanites to tribute, and did not utterly drive them out.

29. Neither did Ephraim drive out the Canaanites that dwelt in Gezer : but the Canaanites dwelt in Gezer among them.

30. Neither did Zebulun drive out the inhabitants of Kitron, nor the inhabitants of Nahalol ; but the Canaanites dwelt among them, and became tributaries.

31. Neither did Asher drive out the inhabitants of Accho, nor the inhabitants of Zidon, nor of Ahlab, nor of Achzib, nor of Helbah, nor of Aphik, nor of Rehob :

32. But the Asherites dwelt among the Caananites, the inhabitants of the land : for they did not drive them out.

33. Neither did Naphtali drive out the inhabitants of Beth-shemesh, nor the inhabitants of Beth-anath ; but he dwelt among the Canaanites, the inhabitants of the land : nevertheless, the inhabitants of Beth-shemesh and of Beth-anath became tributaries unto them.

34. And the Amorites forced the children of Dan into the mountain: for they would not suffer them to come down to the valley :

35. But the Amorites would dwell in mount Heres in Aijalon, and in Shaalbim : yet the hand of the house of Joseph prevailed, so that they became tributaries.

36. And the coast of the Amorites was from the going up to Akrabbim, from the rock, and upward.

TRIBUTARIES.

THE only profitable use we can make of this section is to consider its spiritual applications. We are always engaged in battle or in progress, and, do what we may, we are not always able to carry everything our own way. The signature of defeat is somewhere upon our proudest achievements; again and again shadows appear, which can only be accounted for by the presence of the enemy. The body remains, and social contact and sensuous appeal ; in a word, the very spirit of evil is continually appearing and reappearing even in the best moods of our life. We want to drive away the enemy, and we but partially succeed. Sometimes we think we have wholly banished him, and behold, he suddenly returns from concealment, and is more malignant and furious than ever. Our life is thus a continual series of surprises, and the surprises are often very stinging disappointments. Again and again we say to our souls, Take your ease, and even venture to be mirthful, for the horse and his rider are thrown into the sea, and the whole land is cleansed of the pollution of the presence of the enemy ; and whilst the song of triumph and thankfulness is in our mouth, the sea gives up its dead, and the land becomes as foul as ever.   When we would do good evil is present with us; our prayers are punctuated with overtures to the enemy ; even in our supplications we half promise the devil to return, and serve him as eagerly as ever.   All this is full of mystery and full of pain.   What, then, is to be done ? There remains the sweet and comforting doctrine that even where extinction is impossible tribute may be charged and enforced ; not only so, sometimes tribute is better than extinction.   What if in the end it should appear that it is better that we should be conscious of the presence of the enemy than that we should feel too secure in our spiritual position ?   What if it should be proved that the enemy himself is to be made tributary to our spiritual greatness and influence ?   Even this is within the possibility of the grace and sovereignty of God.

The *world* itself is to be laid under tribute, and must be so laid if the full Christian life is to be lived.   The Christian is not removed out of the world, but is set in a totally new relation to everything which the world contains and represents.   The world becomes one of two things : it becomes either a limit, or a symbol ; whether we take it in the one sense or in the other will depend upon our spiritual state.   To the worldly man the world is enough ; he wants nothing that cannot be found in its gardens, or drawn from its fountains, or descried upon its horizon ; its summer is heaven, its night is Sabbath, its wealth is honour.   The worldly man in so reasoning is perfectly consistent with his fundamental conception.   Whatever he may do theoretically, he practically accepts but one world, and, accepting that one world, he is bound to make the most of it ; it becomes large to his vision, and valuable to his sense of importance : whatever other worlds there may or may not be is to him a matter of no consequence ; he has found space enough for the exercise of his energy and the satisfaction of his desires.   On the other hand, the Christian man cannot be content with this view.   However great the world may be in miles and leagues, it becomes smaller and smaller to the Christian as he grows in spiritual relationships.   What before was vast dwindles into insignificance; what before was important becomes trivial; and what before had about it the traces of durability becomes transient and uncertain. To the spiritual mind the world is a symbol, and in this view it is of infinite consequence as supplying countless starting-points upon which the sanctified imagination can operate : all light, all force, all beauty, all fruitfulness—yea, and even all darkness, and judgment, and fear, can be turned into texts upon which the Christian imagination dilates, with ever-growing power, and profit to itself. In this sense the Christian man makes the world his tributary. He does not destroy the world, but says to it in effect, You shall give me everything you can supply to stimulate my imagination, to encourage my aspirations, to disclose to me new possibilities, and to hint to me sublime destinies ; the very stones of the field shall be sermons to me, and the running brooks shall be books, and in everything I will find good. The Christian man is thus placed in a right relation to all material nature : it no longer overpowers him by its vastness and brightness; it has become to him a comparatively little thing in itself, yet most useful as a pedestal, on which he can stand, and from which he can view ultimate issues and the welcoming hospitalities of still wider spaces, even of the heavenly citizenship itself. This was the meaning of Christ's prayer when he said that he did not desire that his disciples should be taken out of the world, but that they should be kept from the evil in it. This was the meaning of Paul's desire that certain things should be used and not abused. This also is the full interpretation of the policy that men should marry as if they married not, buy and sell as if they bought and sold not, plough and sow as if they ploughed and sowed not : all this constitutes an experience which must be lived in order to be understood ; when set forth in words it is simple contradiction and impossibility, but when advanced upon from the point of actual personal realisation, it becomes a massive and instructive harmony. Every man has to answer whether he will treat the world from a bodily or a spiritual point of view. Let it be fully known that he is at perfect liberty to treat it from either point ; but whichever point he may choose he must accept the responsibility of the election. It cannot be too emphatically declared that spiritual goodness is not forced upon us—in fact, if the operation admitted of the presence of force, the goodness itself would be destroyed in that proportion. Man has the liberty to choose the wrong, but not the right to choose it. It should be considered an immorality to take any view either of mankind or time or space which is belittling, or which partakes of the nature of reduction to contempt; where the value goes down in things material it should only be because the value of things spiritual has risen in the thought and imagination, in the judgment and reason. Here, then, is comfort for the rich and the mighty. If they account their wealth enough, the world is no longer their tributary, but their master : if they accept their position in the spirit of stewardship and discharge its responsibilities with spiritual fidelity, then the world is made to contribute to their strength and usefulness, and is in very deed held in tribute to their spiritual suzerainty.

Coming into closer quarters, and making the question still more personal, it will be found that it is possible for every man to constitute his own nature into a series of tributaries to his spiritual wealth and force. For example, every passion which agitates the human spirit should be made tributary to moral excellence. Take, for example, the passion of Ambition. Men wish to become more and more, greater and greater, richer and richer, and to exercise an ever-growing influence, and to live in the midst of ever-increasing applause. This desire may be mean or great, according to the use which is made of it; nothing is more contemptible when limited to selfish ends, and nothing more desirable when applied in disinterested directions. There is a holy ambition; there is a fever for power and influence which may burn to the glory of God. Such an ambition is never satisfied with little conquests or small delights; it contemplates the possession of the uttermost parts of the earth in the name of the King, and would hand over to him the whole heathen world as his lot and inheritance. Ambition thus becomes spiritual enthusiasm; the fire of it flames towards heaven with infinite energy. It is not the little ambition which dwindles into meanness and pitiable calculation as to means and ends; it is the heroic ambition which claims all creation as the theatre of i's action, and all nature as its assistant in working out the conquest of peoples and nations, kindreds and tongues for Christ. Take again, for example, the passion of Resentment; that, indeed, is dangerous fire to play with. Some men seem to be naturally and almost incurably resentful; they love to avenge themselves; they are positively delighted when they see how judgment overtakes their personal enemies, and how their foes are dragged in the dust; they do not scruple to call this action providential, or to trace it to divine causes, which seem to recognise with just partiality their own peculiar virtues. Is it possible for resentment to be made tributary to goodness? Yes; even this miracle can be wrought by the Lord Jesus Christ. The resentment itself may not be destroyed, but it may be turned against the sin rather than against the sinner; by this use it is made tributary to the highest purposes. This is the kind of resentment which attests real spiritual growth. At first we burn against the evil-doer. Our animosity may be said to be concrete or personal, and we suppose that resentment is gratified by the punishment of the individual offender; it is enough to satisfy our pride or to satiate our vengeance to see the bad man crushed or even destroyed. Christianity entirely corrects this view of penalty and this use of resentment. Instead of allowing us to fix upon the sinner, as if he in his person comprehended the whole problem and difficulty, it binds us to look at the sin, the boundless quantity, the infinite hugeness, that raises its black form into the heavens and casts a shadow upon the sky. Then resentment is divested of its pettiness, its selfish animosity, its evil humour, and is turned into a divine engine and an expression of the very heart of God against sin, which is the abominable thing which God hates. The man who has so treated his resentfulness has, by the Spirit of the living God, turned that resentfulness into a tributary to all that is best and strongest in his spiritual nature.

Looking at this question from the directly opposite point of view, we shall find that all the higher faculties which distinguish man must be made to pay tribute to the spiritual dignity which makes him immortal. Our higher faculties may either be debased or exalted; that is to say, they may be made to impoverish us or to contribute towards the enlargement and strengthening of our character. Take, for example, the faculty of *imagination*. How easily we may become its victims! A life of utter falseness may be created or stimulated by the action of fancy. The whole world of deceit lies within the compass of imagination. By the perversion of imagination we tell lies to ourselves, we blot out all moral distinctions, we fail to discriminate between the right and the left, the upward and the downward; and imagination delights to show its genius by the multiplication of its falsehoods. On the other hand, imagination is absolutely essential to the interpretation of nature and revelation. Imagination sees possibilities, reconciles discrepancies, makes the rough places plain, and the high places low, and prepares the way of the Lord in every wilderness. Imagination delivers the soul from the narrowness and deceitfulness of the letter, and leads it into the gracious liberty of the spirit. Imagination is the flying faculty of the mind. Reason walks, halts, pauses to take its breath, looks round in wonder, half-religious, half-misbelieving, and puts down its conclusions haltingly and self-distrustfully; Reason stands by the side of the precipice and shudders at the contemplation of its depth; Reason looks out upon the unmeasured ocean, and wonders how any mariner dare tempt the deceitful waters: Imagination, on the other hand, flies across the abyss, spreads its infinite pinions and hovers over the sea as over a drop of dew; Imagination sees in the darkness as clearly as in the light, and is even more at home amid the multitude of the starry lights than in the companionship of the solitary sun. Men must, therefore, determine what use they will make of their imagination, being assured that it will either tend towards their destruction or towards the enlargement and beauty of their soul's life. Take, again, the high faculty of Wit or Humour, near to which is the kindred faculty, if it may be so called, of Pathos—the wondrous gift of tears. Wit may be turned into a tributary as certainly as may the power of prayer. Christ has room for wit in his great household; but wit must be a servant, not a master: it must teach by laughter what cannot be easily taught by philosophy: it must do by a flash what never could be done by a tedious process. Wit, irony, raillery, humour, pathos, all these may be so used as to loosen the solidity of character, or so employed as to increase its massiveness. Christianity never designed to drive away these faculties from the possession of man ; on the contrary, it meant man to realise their presence, and turn that presence to the highest use.   To lay down the contrary doctrine is to teach that Christianity can only live by the cutting away of one half of our human nature.   In this sense, as in all others, Christ is to have the heathen for his inheritance and the uttermost parts of the earth for his possession. Things which seem to lie farthest away from his Cross, his awful sacrifice, his infinite solemnity, are to be brought into service and laid under tribute ; this also cometh forth from the Lord of hosts, who is excellent in counsel and wonderful in working.   What is said of imagination and wit, of humour and pathos, may be said also of Eloquence and Music.   These latter may be made into seductions that shall lead the soul away from the altar and the Cross : or they may be made into servants of the living God, unfolding his kingdom with all the splendours of expression and all the fascinations of melody.   Christ must have these as well as every other faculty of the soul.   Eloquence must wait upon him to receive the message, and then must turn that message into persuasive appeal.   Music must stand by his side to learn his will, and then make it a life-long study to turn the expression of that will into an unanswerable persuasive brought to bear upon the judgment and the will of the world.

There is still another point of view from which this question of tribute may be regarded.   Let us lay it down without misgiving, that all the *practical conditions* of life must be made tributary to Jesus Christ.   Our social advantages will either overweight us or enable us to stand upon them as upon a pedestal whence we can view further distances and greater possibilities.   It is sad to see manhood crushed by the very respectability of its environment.   Are there not men who are overpowered by their own respectability ?—such men, I mean, as have to consider the bearing of any spiritual action or attitude upon their social consequence : they wonder how such and such a course will be regarded in society.   Such men are not masters but slaves ; they live for others in the base sense of being ruled by the whims and policies of others, and not in the holy sense of service and sacrifice.   What good the rich man might do!   What a contribution of influence the man of honour might make to every Christian cause ! and the contribution would be the greater in proportion as that cause was shadowed and depressed by the haughtiness of other men. Then there is the condition of *leisure.* Surely leisure ought to be made tributary to the cause of the Saviour. To how many men may not the question be addressed : Why stand ye idle all the day ? What a comfort they might be to their churches, to the sick, to the poor, to the ignorant ! Even leisure shall be reckoned as an element in the judgment of our life. There are men so toil-bound and toil-driven that they have actually no time to render services of benevolence to their fellow-creatures; from early morning until late at night they are grinding at the wheel, and God knows how their energy is strained and their resources are exhausted, and he will be gentle in his judgment of men so hard driven. But there are others who have no need to toil in this servile fashion, who ought to consider whether they cannot withdraw from certain engagements and devote the time thus saved to more distinctively Christian purposes. There are others who have positively retired, in the general acceptation of the word, from the business of the world, upon whom leisure seems to rest as a burden, who might, were they rightly disposed, be eyes to the blind and feet to the lame, centres of strength and security to every good cause, pillars and supports of the very Church of God. The poorest of all poor things it is to have nothing to do. But I deny that any man has a right to the use of these words. When a man says he has nothing to do he simply blinds himself to the reality of his circumstances, or denies the reality of his responsibility. Such a man must be condemned because he uses false language or because he deceives himself by sophisms of the most selfish description. When all our men of wealth and men of leisure bind themselves in a holy bond to consecrate their time to the service of Christ, the poor, and the ignorant, the Church will be marked by an intenser and holier activity. God speed the coming of that time ! The Church is cursed by indolence. Christians are doing nothing until they are doing everything. It is not enough for them to criticise, to pass opinions, to offer judgments, and thus indirectly to magnify their own importance ; to work, always to work, every one to work, should be the motto of the Church which is blood-redeemed.

Then there is another and final point which is not wanting, indeed, in surprise. Let it never be forgotten that even *suffering* itself may be made tributary to Christian character. We cannot escape suffering; but we can determine the use to which suffering shall be put. It may either be a dark presence to affright us, or a veiled angel to cheer us on our way. But this experience can only come out of real life. "No chastening for the present seemeth to be joyous, but grievous: nevertheless afterward it yieldeth the peaceable fruit of righteousness unto them which are exercised thereby." Jesus Christ endured the Cross, despising the shame; and when we inquire into the reason of this sublime contempt, we learn that he was animated by the joy that was set before him. The Apostle Paul rises into one of his noblest raptures as he crushes suffering under his feet and makes it contribute to his Christian steadfastness and joy. He says, "We glory in tribulations also: knowing that tribulation worketh patience; and patience, experience; and experience, hope: and hope maketh not ashamed; because the love of God is shed abroad in our hearts by the Holy Ghost which is given unto us." The Apostle James continues in the same strain, saying, "My brethren, count it all joy when you fall into divers temptations; knowing this, that the trying of your faith worketh patience. But let patience have her perfect work, that ye may be perfect and entire, wanting nothing." Nor is the voice of the Apostle Peter wanting in this grand testimony as to the tributary position of suffering in the Christian life. His words are: "Rejoice, inasmuch as ye are partakers of Christ's sufferings; that, when his glory shall be revealed, ye may be glad also with exceeding joy." And, again, he says, "If any man suffer as a Christian, let him not be ashamed; but let him glorify God on this behalf." Here, then, we have a great tributary system established at the very centre of the Christian life. Nothing is destroyed but sin. Everything else is turned to a holy purpose. We use the world as not abusing it. In the coming and going of its lights and shadows we see a high spiritual symbolism; in the uncertainty of its joys we see how foolish it is for the immortal to attempt to find its satisfactions in the temporary; in all its beauty and fruitfulness we see the beginning of heaven: the morning is a benign encouragement; the night is a gracious rest; the summer is a hint of paradise, and death itself is a door opening upon heaven. Thus we come into a right relation to all things round about us. Until we knew Christ we stood in a false relation to everything; but now living in Christ and breathing his Spirit, we know exactly what the world is and what it can do, and whilst in some moods we despise its littleness, in others we are enabled to accept every one of its intimations as an assistant to our faith and an increase to the brightness of our hope.

SELECTED NOTE.

"But the Amorites would dwell in Mount Heres in Aijalon, and in Shaalbim: yet the hand of the house of Joseph prevailed, so that they became tributaries" (Judg. i. 35). We find the Amorites first mentioned in Gen. xiv. 7—"The Amorites that dwelt in Hazezon-tamar," *the cutting of the palm-tree*, afterwards called Engedi, *fountain of the kid*, a city in the wilderness of Judæa not far from the Dead Sea. In the promise to Abraham (Gen. xv. 21) the Amorites are specified as one of the nations whose country would be given to his posterity. But at that time three confederates of the patriarch belonged to this tribe: Mamre, Aner, and Eshcol (Gen. xiv. 13, 24). When the Israelites were about to enter the promised land, the Amorites occupied a tract on both sides of the Jordan. That part of their territories which lay to the east of the Jordan was allotted to the tribes of Reuben, Gad, and the half tribe of Manasseh. They were under two kings—Sihon, king of Heshbon (frequently called king of the Amorites), and Og, king of Bashan, who "dwelt at Ashtaroth [and] in [at] Edrei" (Deut. i. 4, compared with Josh. xii. 4, xiii. 12). Before hostilities commenced messengers were sent to Sihon, requesting permission to pass through his land; but Sihon refused, and came to Jahaz and fought with Israel; and Israel smote him with the edge of the sword, and possessed his land from Arnon (Modjeb) unto Jabbok (Zerka) (Num. xxi. 24). Og also gave battle to the Israelites at Edrei, and was totally defeated. After the capture of Ai, five kings of the Amorites, whose dominions lay within the allotment of the tribe of Judah, leagued together to wreak vengeance on the Gibeonites for having made a separate peace with the invaders. Joshua, on being apprised of their design, marched to Gibeon and defeated them with great slaughter (Josh. x. 10). Another confederacy was shortly after formed on a still larger scale; the associated forces are described as "much people, even as the sand upon the sea-shore in multitude, with horses and chariots very many" (Josh. xi. 4). Josephus says that they consisted of 300,000 armed foot-soldiers, 10,000 cavalry, and 20,000 chariots (*Antiq.* v. 1, 18). Joshua came suddenly upon them by the waters of Merom, and Israel smote them until they left none remaining (Josh. xi. 7, 8). Still, after their severe defeats, the Amorites, by means of their war-chariots and cavalry, confined the Danites to the hills, and would not suffer them to settle in the plains: they even succeeded in retaining possession of some of the mountainous parts. "The Amorites would dwell in Mount Heres in Aijalon, and in Shaalbim: yet the hand of the house of Joseph prevailed, so that they became tributaries. And the coast of the Amorites was from *the going up to Akrabbim* (*the steep of scorpions*) from the rock and upwards" (Judg. i. 34-36). It is mentioned as an extraordinary circumstance that in the days of Samuel there was peace between Israel and the Amorites (1 Sam. vii. 14). In Solomon's reign a tribute of bond-service was levied on the remnant of the Amorites and other Canaanitish nations (1 Kings ix. 21; 2 Chron. viii. 8).

PRAYER.

ALMIGHTY GOD, let thy goodness appear unto us as a new light shining from heaven. We know it is as venerable as thyself; still, may it be new to us as the dawning of another day; may we have a new sense of thy goodness, a new feeling of its largeness, and may we answer its appeal with the service and sacrifice of a whole life. Thou dost send the years upon us one by one, that we may work in them, and study thy will, and do what we can to realise thy purpose: enable us to see thy meaning, to trace thy hand, to obey thy will; condescend to fill us continually with the Holy Spirit. We bless thee that we have a religious idea of time: no longer are the hours silent to us; they cry unto us to arise, and work, and suffer, and pray, and hope; we would answer their appeal; we would rise early and toil late, if haply by thy grace we may do thy holy will. For all the helps thou dost give us by the way we bless thee; for the day of rest we especially thank thee: for a moment thou dost drive back the great flood, and still the noises of the world, and give us rest in thy house within the shadow of the altar; whilst we are there may we hear thy voice, and see the image of thy love, and be filled with thy Spirit: then shall the coming week answer our hand; we shall be able to guide its affairs with discretion, with enlarged wisdom which is never baffled, and with Christian hopefulness which gives songs in the night time. Thus would we begin the year in God's strength and in God's fear, hoping continually in God, living in the Son of God, Christ Jesus the Saviour, eating his flesh, drinking his blood, partaking of his Spirit, and entering into the mystery of his love. May no vow that is good be broken; may no purpose that is noble be frustrated; may our will be set steadily in the direction of heaven, and may thine angels come around us as ministering spirits, giving us assistance, light, stimulus, according to the need of the day. Thy mercies towards us have been beyond all number. As for thy compassions, there is no figure by which we can make them known: they are tender beyond all tenderness, they yearn over us with infinite solicitude,—because thy compassions fail not, therefore we are not consumed. We would live upon thy love; we would find everything within that gracious mystery—all aid to read the Bible, all comfort in sorrow, all light in darkness; we would see it become the resurrection and the life in the presence of our dearest dead. According to the days wherein thou hast afflicted us, be gracious unto all thy people; give them double in exchange for all thou hast laid upon them, that by multiplied joy they may be enabled to see the meaning of discipline, and by added comfort they may know what thou dost mean by the rod of humiliation. Let our homes be precious in thy sight, our little dwelling-places, where the fire means hospitality, where the door means security, where the window means an outlook upon heaven's light; the Lord grant unto us in our houses security, protection, comfort, and make our table as a banqueting-table of God, whereat we eat what is good for the soul and drink of the wine of the Saviour's blood. Be with us in our businesses; they are many, trying, fluctuating,—now so hard, now too easy; now a great temptation, and now a violent distress; the Lord help us to get rid of these by working at them patiently and lovingly, in the spirit of heavenly citizenship, and encountering all earthly trials, losses, difficulties, with contempt, because we look for an inheritance incorruptible, which cannot fade away. Regard the children with a father's love. We are all children in thy sight. Thou hast nought but little ones in all the nursery of the universe. But thou knowest to whom we refer as the children. Give them strength of body, brightness of mind, hopefulness of spirit, and open their way in the world, that they may see that all affairs are under God's hand and all issues are with the Lord. Heal the sick, if healing be good for them; and if thou dost not heal the body with health that must again decline, heal the spirit with immortality. Grant a blessing to every heart; specially to those hearts made sore and twice tender by chastisement, loss, bereavement, new visions of the littleness of life, and new glimpses of the possible eternity. In all good things and wise ways and holy resolves strengthen, stablish, settle us; and as for our sins, having first seen them, may we next see the Cross, and in that higher sight we shall lose the memory and the sting of guilt. Amen.

Judges ii.

DIVINE AND HUMAN INFLUENCE.

DO not trouble yourselves about the personality or name of this angel that "came up from Gilgal to Bochim." He is always "coming up." Why do we miss great meanings by fastening upon little pedantic points? The angel charged the people with having broken God's conditions, upon which he promised to be with them and keep his covenant with their houses. That angel still lives. Now we call him Memory, or Conscience. What is there in the change of name? He is an angel still. He is the wonderful Presence in life which takes note of all our goings, thoughts, and doings,—an invisible, unslumbering Spirit that, so to say, keeps the covenant in one hand, and our life in the other, and looks to see how the harmony is sustained. If now and then the Spirit should turn from the covenant and say to the life, Think! you are wrong; you are out of course; you have lost step and touch with Heaven—surely we should say the voice is the voice of an angel; it is no common rough tone of accusation, but an appeal spoken sweetly to the innermost heart and thought of the man, and should be answered according to its own quality. Thus we get great meanings in the ancient records. But if we stand here and ask questions about angels, their history, their figure, the law of their movements—inquiries to which there can be no possible answers—we shall feel ourselves no longer in a flowering garden, golden with the richness of summer, but in a burning and waste wilderness. Give the angel good hearing. Never arrest unduly or impatiently the voice of reproach and accusation, but answer it rationally, fearlessly: if there is nothing in the accusation, the answer will be short and easy; but, contrariwise, if the accusation is really sound and true, consider it, be not afraid of it, and with reverent familiarity interrogate it, apply it, and escape from its honest charges by better behaviour.

The people having heard the accusation, "lifted up their voice and wept. And they called the name of that place Bochim"—a place of weeping, a place of many tears. So they were not lost. This is the value of emotion : its presence indicates that the heart is not utterly dead to all solemn appeal and heavenly judgment. However fickle the life—and the best life is fickle—let us thank God if we can feel the tone of accusation, the language of reproach, and answer it even with the feeble answer of tears. Oftentimes tears are the best words. Were we to answer the accusation of the angel with words, we should get into controversy, and controversy lies at an infinite distance from repentance. When we lose speech we may gain power. It is better to bow down the head in silent, tearful sorrow, when the accusation is poured down upon us, than to attempt to answer it by petty excuses, or by inventing replies which are as feeble as they are dishonest.

So the people cry, and begin again. They were human. In this respect we ourselves are of the same race. Our days represent but a series of evil actions and late repentances. A singular mixture is life:—prayer, and blasphemy; high-handed rebellion, and meek humiliation; great vows, majestic in their moral nobleness, and lies of which lost spirits might be ashamed.

In the seventh verse we come to a more human aspect of the exciting history :—

"And the people served the Lord all the days of Joshua, and all the days of the elders that outlived Joshua, who had seen all the great works of the Lord, that he did for Israel."

Here is a great principle—the principle that those who have seen God's works,—that is to say, who have had real experience of them—never go wrong; not only do they never go wrong themselves, but they keep other people right.   Joshua and the leaders who were his contemporaries and survivors "had seen all the great works of the Lord, that he did for Israel "—not only seen them with the bodily eye, for many had so seen them and denied them, but seen them with the inner eye, the eye of faith and love and thankfulness.   The moment you get into a generation that has not seen religious verities, you get into an age of scepticism or religious feebleness.   We cannot live upon tradition; we cannot be courageous because of something which happened to other people : there must be personal contact with divine realities, an individual touch, a present and indestructible consciousness of God's nearness and of the reality of things ; then there will be courage and testimony, and service and sacrifice. The men who have been in slavery know the value of freedom. To those who have only heard of slavery " by the hearing of the ear," freedom is a theme for poets,—weave it into song, beat it into music, turn it into picture, for the men have only heard of slavery as men might hear of a storm that gathered and burst a thousand years ago.   It is so with religious persecution.   The men who have made the nations great are the men who have actually seen trouble and felt it.   Other men are not competent to speak about them, and it is impertinence for such men even to offer an opinion upon them.   The men who felt the pressure of the steel, who paid blood as the price of every hymn they sang and every prayer they prayed, were not likely to be taken up with new-fangled notions, or to be seduced by cheap temptations : they "had seen all the great works of the Lord, that he did for Israel ; " they did not, as in romantic poetry, pay the blood of some other man for their liberties, they paid their own. Yet the children of such men will arise and ask insane and pointless questions, and join the posterity of the very people who slew their fathers, and dug their graves.   Nor is this to be wondered at.   We cannot live on the experience of other people for long.   Whilst the exciting anecdote is ringing in our ears we may make some answer superficially heroic : only as we suffer can we profess ; only as we have seen can we speak ;

only as prayer has been answered can we vindicate its authority and utility. Marvellous it is to watch how people deport themselves in all these relations. There is no hereditary piety ; there is no hereditary heroism : we need to see for ourselves before we can speak with authoritative tone to others. That is the secret of authority. When the heart speaks, when the sufferer testifies, when the victim makes oath and says,—I saw it, felt it, knew it,—that is the true authority ; not an announcement made in cold blood and on the sunny side of a successful controversy, but an announcement made with the pathos of personal suffering and with the emphasis of personal loss. It is distressing and discouraging that people should lose their own history ; that sons and daughters of heroes should sink into drivelling commonplace ; that heroic fires should die into white ashes. Every generation must have its own experience, must keep steadily along the line of its own facts : the moment the life fritters into words, controversies, theories, and schemes, the all-sustained and all-sanctifying energy is lost.

What a noble influence may be exerted by one consecrated life ! "The people served the Lord all the days of Joshua." We have had similar experience. We say : Since the leader died the followers have gone sadly astray. Or we say : Had the leader lived, it would not have been thus ; he would have kept us together ; his gracious domination would have ruled us aright ; our reverence for him amounted to a species of religion. Or we say : Since the just critic died things have become demoralised ; he was a just judge ; he was generous withal ; he saw the best side of every man, and took the kindliest view of every subject : but he was so strong, so true, so honest ; his voice was a judgment, his look was an approbation or a disfavour ; everything about him was of a noble, healthy, beautiful kind ; since he died there is no judge in the land. So we may come by an examination of our own experience to understand many of these old biblical incidents.

What a compliment is this to Joshua ! How little, perhaps, did Joshua know what he was doing ! If you ask for a eulogium upon Joshua, where will you find it ? Is it set forth in any special form ? Can we turn to a given page and say, Behold the

eulogy spoken by the most eloquent lips of the time; see how
paragraph follows paragraph, how climax heightens above climax,
till the noble panegyric makes one feel how good a thing it was
to live in the days of old? There is no such page, there is no
such eulogy; but read this seventh verse and say whether it is
not praise enough for any son of man :—" And the people served
the Lord all the days of Joshua." That is the only eulogium
worth having: a great social influence, a sublime, beneficent
action, operating all the time and upon everybody, and yet the
man himself saying little and seldom seen. There are many
eulogies : some in noble words that can only be credited by the
imagination ; some in out-of-the-way actions and silent deeds and
subtle influences which can only be fully comprehended by a
kindred spirit—yea, even by God himself. Let us thank God
for our leader. The father is a Joshua in the family. So long
as he lives there will be no controversy amongst the children :
they all love him, so that one word of his will be final ; were
there tumult in the house he could by one sentence settle it,—
not by arbitrary authority, but because of something in his quality
not to be defined or measured, something that begets a magnificent moral reverence and trust. So it is in business, so in the
State, so in the Church, so everywhere. The one true life may be
keeping a thousand other lives in the right direction.

A beautiful picture is given in the eighth verse :—

"And Joshua the son of Nun, the servant of the Lord, died, being an
hundred and ten years old."

Was he two men then? Yes: he was "the son of Nun"—our
little earthly relations must not be ignored—he was also "the
servant of the Lord"—our great religious relations must be regarded with thankfulness. A medal this with two sides : on the
one side "Joshua the son of Nun"—some plain good soul unknown to fame, but with a sweet heart, a good honest mind, plain
enough as to his position and manners, but great in his greater
son ; on the other side of the medal, "Joshua the servant of the
Lord." Realise all the relations of life. The higher our service
for the Lord the readier are we to think of the old folks at
home—the people that thought of us, and nursed us, and sat up
long nights with us, and were strength to our weakness and

eyes to our blindness, and that went near to telling many lies
in describing our imaginary excellences and virtues; people who
died for us by living for us; the people that saw themselves in
us magnified and glorified. They must not be dropped out of
the reckoning. The greater you are the more are you indebted
to those who went before you. Then comes the second and
greater and eternal title—" the servant of the Lord," the slave of
God, the bondman of Christ. Live the complete life; not only
the natural, physical, social life, but that other and higher life
which is indicated by the words " the servant of the Lord." How
few *serve* the Lord of heaven! How many profess to do so! To
serve God is not to assent to propositions, to attend a certain
place of worship, to pass through a given routine of ceremony;
it is to live in him, to him, for him; to live, move, and have our
being in God, to have nothing that is not his, and to do nothing
that he bids us not. It is easy to describe ourselves as servants
of God; it is difficult to realise the sublime position.

Joshua gone. All that generation gathered to their fathers:—
" There arose another generation after them, which knew not the
Lord, nor yet the works which he had done for Israel "—a blind
generation, utterly poor, historically penniless; men without anything that was more than one day old. These are the weights
which time has to carry; these are the burdens of the ages;
these are the men who let history die. What men should we
be if we realised our history! Could we see the past as it
ought to be seen, it would be like a cloud of spirits, a great army
of angels, a sky shaded rather than darkened by heroic spirits,
master souls that ruled their time. The other generation is
always coming—the poor, penniless generation, the non-related
generation; the generation that thinks every man a separate atom,
or individual without any relation to the sum-total of things,—
this is the generation that loses religion. Why? Because
religion is historical. Religion binds man fast to the past.
Religion does not incline itself towards the future in some
selfishly expectant attitude; it lies back upon the past, and by
the past seizes the future. We should be ashamed of some
people—the people that talk mincingly, vain-gloriously, with
affectation, with superficiality, who look upon life as a thing

begun yesterday, and to be enjoyed to-day, and left to-morrow; they make us sore of heart; we feel poor in their presence; they have not seen "the great works of the Lord;" they have not bowed down to some worthy leadership and accepted its discipline and chastisement; they have influence only for a moment because they speak of things that endure but for a moment. Let us pray for the preservation of heroic memories. Let us remember that we never could have had a Bible to read if some men had not printed it as with their blood and bound it with their martyrdom. Let us think that we could not meet in many a Protestant church if there had not been men who counted not their lives dear unto them that they might stand up for liberty and defy the whole brood of hell. Now we ask little questions about things that our fathers died for! We now use the liberty they bought to praise the very tyranny which killed them.

So the generations come and go :—

"And the children of Israel did evil in the sight of the Lord, and served Baalim : And they forsook the Lord God of their fathers, which brought them out of the land of Egypt, and followed other gods, of the gods of the people that were round about them, and bowed themselves unto them, and provoked the Lord to anger. And they forsook the Lord, and served Baal and Ashtaroth" (vv. 11–13).

These are the incredible incidents of history; these are the fables we should laugh at if we did not know them to be true in our own experience! The people "followed other gods," "the gods of the people that were round about them"—the fashionable gods, the popular deities, the little divinities that ruled the little time. Beware of all visible gods. Beware of any god that can be known. We accept the reproach of God's unknowableness, because to know God would be to be God.

How did the Lord answer them? He could not answer them in words. There are times when words are useless. The answer is in the fourteenth verse :—

"And the anger of the Lord was hot against Israel, and he delivered them into the hands of spoilers that spoiled them, and he sold them into the hands of their enemies round about, so that they could not any longer stand before their enemies."

He took the pith out of them ; he watered down their muscle until it became flabby ; he confused their minds until they reeled at noonday and stumbled like drunken men ; he set all heaven on fire against them ; the horizon burned them, scorched them, and they withered away : they who might have been the foremost princes crouched behind, they who might have worn white robes were lying crushed in the dust. God's anger was hot against them, and it will be hot against any corresponding generation in the w l. Forsake God, take up with idols, follow the fashions, yield to the spirit of the times, forsake prayer, and regard the Bible as only some ancient document, and your business will leave you, your fields will not yield half their increase, the enemy will laugh at you. They who forsake the altar shall be forsaken of God. It is a covenant that binds us, and a covenant with two sides : to trifle with it on the human side is to have judgment poured down through it from the divine side. O lands of the earth, O peoples of the day and of every clime, if you would have plentiful harvest-fields, thriving businesses, happy homes, joyous times, forget not the living God. " Let the people praise thee, O God ; let all the people praise thee. Then shall the earth yield her increase "—a bountiful harvest shall follow in the wake of a praying, active, sacrificing Church.

SELECTED NOTE.

" *And they called the name of that place Bochim* " (Judg. ii. 5).—Bochim (*the weepings*) was the name given to a place (probably near Shiloh, where the tabernacle then was) where an " angel of the Lord " reproved the assembled Israelites for their disobedience in making leagues with the inhabitants of the land, and for their remissness in taking possession of their heritage. This caused the bitter weeping among the people for which the place took its name.

PRAYER.

ALMIGHTY GOD, thou hast heard the prayers of thy saints, and answered them with great love. We ourselves know this, and our hope in God is as a strong trust. We know when we have prayed unto thee, because the answer is in our hearts whilst we are yet speaking. We know the heavenly Presence; we can tell when we have reached thy throne: behold, thou dost come to us and turn our prayers into sweet replies in the very act of offering our supplications at thy throne. We are thankful as we look back upon the years that are gone. We will think of thy mercy, and not of our sin; we will dwell upon the lovingkindness of God, and not upon the rebellion of our own hearts. The years have been full of thy mercies; thy compassions glitter in them like jewels: thou truly hast been good unto Israel, even to them that are of a clean heart; and thou hast also been kind unto the unthankful and to the evil: whilst thy rain and thy sunshine have fallen upon the good, they have not been withheld from the unjust. We look onward with hope. Thou wilt not forsake us in the seventh trouble; thou wilt redeem thy covenant to its utmost letter, yea, thou wilt add to it and exceedingly multiply thy grace towards us. Keep us in the holy way; show us the sanctuary that is on high, and may our hearts desire to be in it night and day; may we measure all things by its weights and balances and standards: then shall we know when we are right and when God is pleased. Give us to see more and more of the grace that is in Christ Jesus, Son of man, Son of God. He was the express image of his Father, the very brightness of his glory. May we study his words profitably, lovingly, seeking out their meaning with earnest hearts and receiving the same in all its fulness. We commend one another to thy tender care. Thou knowest what we need most—in ourselves, in our houses, in our businesses. Thou knowest the serpent that is pleading with us, telling us the lies we like to hear. Thou knowest the weak point in the character, where the assault tells most immediately and most disastrously. Thou knowest every trap set for our feet, and gin and snare, cunningly laid, that we may be taken and overthrown. We know nothing about it ourselves. We look on, and see nothing but a great cloud. We will therefore trust in the living God, putting our hand into his and asking to be led and directed and sustained by the eternal Spirit. Whether our days be many or few, may they be bright with thy presence, and wealthy with honest and good service. Where there is a difference between man and man, oh heal the controversy and restore the love; where there is difficulty at home, dissolve the perplexity; where there is sorrow because of the family—wandering, unfilial, broken— speak some new parable that shall bring the wanderers all back again, or the old parable, but with the sweetness of a new tone. Be with those who are in trouble on the sea—that great, weary, unfriendly, threatening sea. Be with those who are in deeper trouble—the trouble of mind and heart, who are suffering from the sting of accusation and remorse, and the bitterness of·just reproach ;—yea, according to our varied necessity do thou come to us, and love us, and heal us, and do us good.

We pray every prayer at the Cross, and we feel it not to be a prayer until we have spoken the crowning name of Jesus—Jesus Christ—Immanuel—God with us. Amen.

Judges iii. 9-11.

9. And when the children of Israel cried unto the Lord, the Lord raised up a deliverer to the children of Israel, who delivered them, even Othniel the son of Kenaz, Caleb's younger brother.

10. And the Spirit of the Lord came upon him, and he judged Israel, and went out to war : and the Lord delivered Chushan-rishathaim king of Mesopotamia into his hand ; and his hand prevailed against Chushan-rishathaim.

11. And the land had rest forty years. And Othniel the son of Kenaz died.

OTHNIEL.

A GREAT prayer marks a historical point in the life of any man or any people. We know when we have prayed. The people who ask questions in a controversial tone about prayer never prayed themselves, and so long as they are in that spirit they cannot pray. This exercise is not to be explained to outsiders ; this is an inner mystery. The publican knew that he had prayed when he said, "God be merciful to me a sinner." He needed not to ask any man whether a prayer had been offered, for he himself, the contrite suppliant, had the answer in his heart before the last word escaped his lips. We are dull indeed if we do not know when we have struck a full chord. Something in us says, That is right. We have uttered many words, and at the end we have said, That is not prayer ; the words are devout, the phrases are devotional, they would read well in print, some good spirits might turn them into prayer, but we who uttered them did not pray. Why then debate about this matter, or talk about it as if it were subject for analysis and definition and formal treatment of any kind ? We know when we have touched the hem of Christ's garment by the healing that instantly takes place in the spirit. Answers in detail may require long time to work out, but the great answer is in the healed heart, the comforted soul, the quieted and resigned spirit. Other replies there may or may not be,—all these must be left : the great answer to prayer is an answer to the soul which the soul only can hear and apply.

"When the children of Israel cried unto the Lord"—an energetic term is that—" cried." It was a piercing shout of the heart. The words did not come out of the mouth only ; they were hardly in the mouth at all ; they shot from the heart within—the burning, lowly, broken heart. We know a cry when we hear it or when we utter it ; there is fire in it, a touch of immortality, a strange ghostliness. Truly in such case the voice is the man, the tone is the prayer. There are calls to which we pay no heed. We say they are calls expressive of merriment or folly, or intended to play upon our credulity; we know them to be hollow and meaningless ; but there are cries we must answer, or get somebody else to answer: they come so suddenly, they strike the very soul so truly, there is so much of real earnestness in them, that if we ourselves are frightened by their energy we tell the next person we meet where the trouble is, where sorrow cries for help, where weakness pleads for assistance. You cannot talk about prayer in cold blood. This is not a subject to be discussed in current conversation, passing along the thoroughfare, or upon some quiet occasion : you have dragged the subject to a base level ; you are speaking about it as if you were masters of the situation : you can only speak about prayer whilst you are praying, and then you will never speak about it controversially but sympathetically and confirmingly ; and when the heart has really cried—that sharp cry which cuts the clouds—you will know that the heart in its agony has touched God's love. Turn away, then, from those who would make prayer a matter ot controversy and inquiry and analysis and vivisection ; it is not to be so treated ; it is a secret masonry with a password all its own between the soul and the soul's God.

The prayer was answered :—"The Lord raised up a deliverer." The answer came in a human form. That is a remarkable circumstance. The answer might have come otherwise ; but God delights in incarnations. He aims at something in all these human leaderships ; he is conducting a process of evolution. Many a man bearing the title of Leader has come before us, and each has, so far as he has been faithful to his vocation, been an incarnation of God's thought and purpose and will. The matter cannot end here. All these are temporary incarnations, but charged with infinite suggestiveness, and always leading the mind to higher expectation—subtler, deeper yearnings for some broader and brighter disclosure of the divine personality. But we must not anticipate. The Bible is given to us in pages, and every page must be read, and there must be no vain haste. This is still God's method, to answer by incarnation. A friend is sent who has the key of the gate which you cannot open ; a brother is met who speaks the word your poor heart most needed to hear ; an occasion is created suddenly or unconsciously, and it shapes itself into a temple, becomes a holy sanctuary, a sphere of radiant revelation. This is what we mean by providence. Why has not every man an equal influence over us ? Because every man is not sent to our life with a special message. There are men who can sing, there are men who can preach, there are men who can read the Bible and read it as it were into inspiration as to its influence upon the hearer,—these Othniels are God's creations ; in a sense,—God's presence, divine incarnations.

"The Spirit of the Lord came upon him." There is no mistaking that Spirit. It was not an awakening of anything that was in the man himself, but a descent from heaven of the Supreme Influence. Othniel, a common man yesterday to all observation, is to-day an inspired man, "a little lower than God." As a consequence the man was not vainglorious. No inspired man can be conceited. He does not know that he is great. He knows that he is the instrument of God. The most inspired of men have said, "We have this treasure in earthen vessels, that the excellency of the power may be of God, and not of us." Inspiration means modesty ; genius means retirement, self-obliviousness, disregard of circumstance or applause. The inspired life is the unconscious life. To us who look on, the inspired man is great, wonderful,—we cannot understand the miracle ; to himself he is but a child in God's house, quite a little one, hardly able to walk, asking questions by his looks of wonder, praying himself into ever-deepening lowliness. The poet does not know that he is a poet in the sense which is applauded by those who understand not his spirit ; he breathes his poetry. Paul breathed his Christianity; to him to live was Christ, to breathe was to pray, to look was to rejoice. We shall know when the Church is inspired by its lowliness. Find men who are fretful, peevish, always susceptible to offence, complaining men, "ill-used" men; and you will find men who know nothing about the Spirit of Christ : their money perish with them; their patronage would be a great shadow laid upon the Church. The Church must be healthy in her goodness, mighty in her inspiration. Othniel could not communicate his power. Inspiration is not an article of barter. Nor could Othniel keep his inspiration without conditions. Everything we have we hold upon certain understandings of an eternal kind : they need not be expressed; they are unwritten, but indelible; they cannot be seen with the eyes, nor can they be blotted out by the hand : they belong to the necessity of things, the fitness and harmony of the universe. Whatever we hold we hold upon our good behaviour. We are tenants at will. The greatest Othniel in the Church would be cast out of heaven if he allowed his purity to be spotted, his honour to be stained, his stewardship to be tampered with. Not one of us is essential to God. The first archangel holds his mighty wings on his good behaviour : let him lie, or touch the forbidden tree, and his great wings would fall powerless, his eye would be smitten with death. "Once inspired always inspired" is no doctrine of the Scriptures. We stand or fall by our spiritual relation to the divine. "Let him that thinketh he standeth take heed lest he fall;" and let the chief of the apostles keep himself in constant check lest when his mightiest discourse is ended he himself become a castaway. We live in character. Our immortality—blissful, heavenly—is in our relation to Christ. We have no independence, no charter entitling us to invent a morality of our own; we are measured by eternal standards, we are judged in the court of the Infinite Righteousness.

Othniel had a special work to do : he was raised up to deliver Israel, to destroy the power of the king of Mesopotamia ; and having done that work he died. When shall we come to know that every man is called to one work, particularly if not exclusively?

Herein do we not judge one another harshly and unjustly?

The work of Othniel was not a manifold work; he was not a multitudinous genius, able to see behind and before, on the right and on the left, and to be equally strong by day and by night; he was not so much a statesman as a deliverer; he was mighty in war, he might be but second in counsel. Each man, therefore, must find out his own faculty, and be just to it; if he fail in discovering it, then he will be unjust to his true self. If you are aiming to be some other self, you will fail and be unfaithful to God's purpose. One man is sent to do business, to show how business ought to be done, to make commerce a religion. Another man is sent to sing, to make us glad, to show us by tones that there must be some other world—to touch our highest sensibilities and move our noblest impulses, and comfort us in our distresses and make new stars for the darkness of the night; let him keep his singing robes on, rising high up in the sky so that everybody may hear him and answer him with electric joy: he has a great vocation, has that singing man; he helps even the commerce of the world. Another man is sent to pray. He must live upon his knees. He knows how to speak human want in human words. He never says one word too much, never one word too little; he knows the measure of the sorrow, he knows where the burden presses most heavily, he knows where the heart's sore is most painful; and his is surely a holy vocation. Let him keep at the altar; never let him rise from his posture of prayer. He will do us good, and not evil. He, too, though seemingly so far away from the world's real strife, is helping the world in its most prosaic servitude. When the Church acknowledges this doctrine, the Church will receive more from her leaders, teachers, and supporters. We must not live a divided life: "This one thing I do" must be the motto of every man. Nor must there be judgment of one another, saying, You should do this, or do that. Let alone! Touch not the prerogative of God!

We, too, needed a deliverer. We had given up the idea of self-emancipation. Once we thought we could break our own manacles and fetters, and set ourselves free, and sing the songs of liberty. We tried, we tried often, we all tried,—we failed, we all failed. When there was no eye to pity and no arm to save, God's eye pitied and God's arm wrought salvation. "Who is this that cometh from Edom, with dyed garments from Bozrah ? this that is glorious in his apparel, travelling in the greatness of his strength ? I that speak in righteousness, mighty to save." It is the joy of the Christian Church to believe that there is only one Redeemer, one Lord, one Christ, one Advocate, one Paraclete. This is the gospel. This is the good news itself. When we preach it, we shatter all idols of a selfish kind ; we say to Invention, to Genius, You are of no use here : you cannot break a link, you cannot shed a light upon this infinite gloom. Preaching Christ, we denounce all other helpers and deliverers, except in some secondary and related capacity. There is one Son of God; there is one Cross ; there is one atonement; there is but one hope. We read history, and recognise deliverers, and are thankful when they appear, and we doubt not the reality of their deliverances : why should we in the presence of Jesus Christ forget to adore and forget to trust ? They who have known most about Christ have most to say in his favour. Those who have not known Christ are not asked for their opinion about him. We do not ask the blind to pronounce upon colours, or seek from the deaf a criticism upon music: Christians alone can testify in this court, and their evidence is conclusive because it is sustained by character and can be tested and appreciated. Who is looking for a deliverer ? let him turn his eyes to the Son of God. Who is saying in the bitterness of his soul, "O, that I might be saved from this horrible distress and delivered from this unfathomable abyss " ? let him turn his eyes to the Son of God. Who is mourning sin, having felt its bitterness and seen its abominableness ? let him turn his eyes to the Son of God. He came to deliver, to emancipate, to save : "this Man receiveth sinners." He is able to save them to the uttermost that come unto God by him. Let us feel this, believe this, and commit our souls unto Christ as unto a faithful Creator.

Judges iii. 15.

"But when the children of Israel cried unto the Lord, the Lord raised them up a deliverer, Ehud the son of Gera, a Benjamite, a man lefthanded : and by him the children of Israel sent a present unto Eglon the king of Moab."

EHUD.

A DELIVERER with a lefthand seems to be a contradiction in terms or a piece of practical irony. The Divine Being, in sending Ehud in reply to the cry of the children of Israel, seems to mock the very prayer which he answers. Such a reply is full of subtle suggestion, to the effect that the Israelites really need not have made such a cry about their circumstances, because even in their forlorn condition a lefthanded man would show himself to be equal to the occasion. When we pray to God for help it is with some idea that an angel will be sent, and that all Heaven's artillery will be placed at our disposal that we may resist or destroy the foe. Instead of an angel there comes a man with a lefthand, or as he is elsewhere called an "ambidexter"—that is, a man who can use both hands with equal ease. Has not God continually disappointed the expectation of people in the matter of leadership ? Again and again it appears in sacred history as if the leader were altogether unlikely to accomplish his task either by reason of bodily infirmity or mental incapacity. What was Moses but a stammering shepherd ? And was not Christ himself regarded with disdain because of the lowliness of his origin ? Between these two great captaincies a number of others will be found illustrative of the same principle.

On the matter of lefthandedness we are reminded of the boast of Hector: "Many a Greek hath bled by me, and I can shift my shield from right to left." In another part of the book of Judges we read respecting the children of Benjamin : "Among all this people there were seven hundred chosen men lefthanded ; every one could sling stones at an hair breadth, and not miss." Plato recommended all his soldiers to acquire equal facility in the use of both hands, but these very references show that lefthandedness is quite a peculiarity. We do not remark upon a man that he has the use of his right hand, that he writes with it, points with it, or performs the usual duties of life with it ; but when a man is left-handed the incident instantly strikes us as a peculiarity. All these peculiarities are noticed in the Bible. We have already seen that men were known in many instances by little circum-stances or trifling peculiarities. All such identifications lead us to the great consolatory doctrine that the very hairs of our head are all numbered. All kinds of men are made use of in the Bible. There is no peculiarity, however strange, that may not be used as an instrument for the promotion of truth and goodness, or the defence of right and weakness. No man should be discouraged because of his peculiarities, for in truth though in some re-spects his weakness, they may in other respects be his strength. It has been noticed by close observers of human affairs that almost every cripple is endowed with some speciality of power which gives him pre-eminence among his fellows. What he wants in dignity he may make up in skill. The very infirmity which drives him into solitude may be the occasion of his acquiring richer learning, or training his insight to profounder and clearer views of providence and humanity. Men ought not therefore to be discouraged because of peculiarities.however striking.

Does not the text throw us back upon the oft-recurring doctrine that the many may be dependent upon the one ? All the ciphers are turned into value by the single unit that is placed at their head. Without that unit they would be simply nothing, but with that unit they become millions strong. The children of Israel were many, even a great host, numerous enough to turn their desires into a great noise which they dignified by the name of prayer. Why then did they not work out their own deliverance ? Have we not been wrong on this subject of majorities ? Is there not a quality as well as a quantity to be considered in estimating human influence ? Eglon, king of Moab, had oppressed Israel, yet as soon as Ehud was raised up their liberation vas effected, and the sorrows and burdens of

eighteen years were forgotten when the deliverer appeared upon
the scene. Theie is unquestionably a philosophy of monopoly
in the matter of human influence. One man keeps the key of
secrets. Another man speaks the word which inspires the
courage of dejected hearts. Another man is blessed with farsightedness and can see the very spectre of deliverance when it
first appears upon the distant horizon. Another man has such
richness of character as to be a tower of strength in the day of
shaking and desolation. One man may be in a better position
than a great number of men can possibly be. The individual
moves rapidly from place to place; he can move noiselessly; he
can take his own time for the making of certain observations;
above all things, he can keep his own counsel; for who does not
know that whispering is the ruin of confidence and the very annihilation of strength? The Ehuds of society find that their power
lies in their individuality. They know the difference between
leading the crowd and consulting it. In all great leaderships consultation must be a kind of compliment and in no wise a necessity.
At a critical point in important affairs it is the one man who must
decide the course of the journey or the policy of the battle. Is it
then altogether well with the great man? Probably not. We
see his greatness and admire his elevation and wonder about his
gifts, but we forget that all high qualities bring with them severe
taxation, and that power is the measure of responsibility. It may
be that to obey is easier than to direct. Certainly the responsibility is of a higher grade. Beyond all question he who cannot
obey cannot rule. The men pray for a deliverer, and a deliverer
is given in answer to prayer; their business should be to receive
the deliverer, hold him in honour, obey his commandments,
and do all that within them lies to consolidate his power. All
this is true in merely political directions. The great statesman
keeps his party together. The great professor unites and glorifies
the university. The brilliant commander makes his army as
the heart of one man. But these are exceptional cases and can
hardly be quoted for daily purposes. There is, however, a truth
in connection with this doctrine that is constantly available in all
the practical conditions of life, and that truth is that the good
man who is also wise may command a deep and gracious
influence in social affairs. Goodness is always influential; not

necessarily in the sense of continuousness, without break or interruption, for there are times when goodness itself is silenced, but
always in the sense of appearing at critical times and under
circumstances which give its word infinite weight and consequence. In illustration of this, read the account in the Acts of the
Apostles of a shipwreck, in which Paul took command of all things
and was more than captain. "By the blessing of the upright the
city is exalted : but it is overthrown by the mouth of the wicked."
Covet earnestly the best gifts.

We are very dainty about our instruments. In this matter we
have committed the most mischievous errors in the administration of Church affairs and the appointment of spiritual ministries.
Who ever prayed God to send a lefthanded man to save the
country ? Who has not been disappointed when a lefthanded
man actually came and said he had been sent to do the work ?
The prayers which the Church sends to heaven for ministers are
prayers in many instances which the Divine Being can only
reject with contempt. Our prayer asks that God would send into
the Christian ministry men of great intellectual capacity, men of
burning eloquence, men capable of receiving the highest educational culture, men able to address the most gifted classes of
society ; what is all this but dictating to God or making our own
conception of the situation the measure of God's bounty ? All
such prayers are impertinences. The consolation is that God
pays no heed to them but sends the kind of men who can do the
work after his own will and in defiance of many preconceptions
on the part of men. Let us pray God to make his own choice,
to send whom he will—king or peasant, man of stammering
tongue or eloquent speech ; he must choose the labourers, and
thrust them forth into his own harvest. It must not be supposed
that a man is necessarily an Ehud simply because he is lefthanded. In this direction our thoughts need to be continually
guarded. We may see the lefthandedness and generalise too
broadly concerning it. The peculiarity must have something
behind it, for in itself it is nothing. We must not reason that
because Ehud was lefthanded every lefthanded man is an Ehud.
Bunyan was a tinker, but it does not follow that every tinker is a
Bunyan. There is a danger of mistaking an eccentricity for a

law and setting up false or inadequate standards of judgment.
Moses stammered or was of slow speech. It does not follow that
every stutterer is a Moses. Do not magnify the peculiarity, and
certainly do not disdain it. We say about some men that appearances are not in their favour. Were appearances in favour of
this lefthanded man ? We imagine that we show our sagacity
by discovering in a candidate for favour some littleness or infirmity or awkwardness which disentitles him to confidence.
" Look not on the height of his stature."—" Man looketh on the
outward appearance, but the Lord looketh on the heart." Paul
was aware that his bodily presence was weak and his speech
contemptible, at least in the estimation of those who looked upon
him with evil eyes. The great instance is of course always to be
found in the Son of God himself. He had no form nor comeliness, and there was no beauty that men should desire him. He
was as a root out of a dry ground. He took upon him the form
of a servant and was made in the likeness of man. Like the
psalmist he was "a reproach of men, and despised of the people."
Thus we are brought again to the great doctrine which he
himself laid down : " Judge not according to the appearance, but
judge righteous judgment."

SELECTED NOTE.

Ehud, of the tribe of Benjamin, was one of the "judges" of Israel, or
rather of that part of Israel which he delivered from the dominion of the
Moabites by the assassination of their king Eglon. These were the tribes
beyond the Jordan, and the southern tribes on this side the river. Ehud
obtained access to Eglon as the bearer of tribute from the subjugated tribes,
and being lefthanded, or rather ambidextrous, he was enabled to use with
a sure and fatal aim a dagger concealed under a part of his dress, where it
was unsuspected, because it would there have been useless to a person
employing his right hand. The Israelites continued to enjoy for eighty
years the independence obtained through this deed of Ehud (Judg. iii.
15-30).

"And after him was Shamgar the son of Anath, which slew of the Philistines six hundred men with an ox goad : and he also delivered Israel."

SHAMGAR.

SHAMGAR was the third judge in Israel. He was at the beginning a labouring man, a tiller of the ground, and it is thought that on account of the exploit recorded of him in the text he was raised to dignity. According to the Song of Deborah (Judges v. 6) life was very insecure at that time :—" In the days of Shamgar the son of Anath, in the days of Jael, the highways were unoccupied, and the travellers walked through byways." What is termed an " ox goad " in the text is literally " a thing to teach oxen." Ox goads have always been regarded as formidable instruments some eight feet long and pointed with a strong, sharp iron head. The Thracian king Lycurgus is said to have chased the Bacchanals with an ox goad. According to Ellicott's Bible— " The Athenians in their painting of Marathon represent the gigantic rustic Echetlus, who was supposed to have slain so many Persians with his ploughshare." A traveller who had seen Eastern ploughing thus writes : " It was observable that in ploughing they used goads of an extraordinary size ; upon measuring several I found them about eight feet long, and at the bigger end six inches in circumference. They were armed at the lesser end with a sharp prickle for driving the oxen, and at the other end with a small spade or paddle of iron, strong and massy, for cleansing the plough from the clay which encumbers it in working." Shamgar was working in the field with one of those goads when six hundred Philistines made their appearance but so vigorously did he wield it that not a man of the whole crowd escaped with his life. According to the authority already quoted, " it has been most needlessly assumed that he slew them single-handed, and not, as is probable, at the head of a band of peasants armed with the same rude weapons as himself . . . . But the question here is merely one of interpretation, and nothing is more common in Scripture, as in all literature, than to say that a leader personally did what was done under his leadership."

One of the most obvious lessons deducible from this incident is that we should not complain of our tools when we have hard work to do. When the work is done badly we are apt to blame the tools. Shamgar used an ox goad ; Samson wielded the jaw-bone of an ass ; David had but a sling and stone. Sometimes we think what wonders we should do if we had better instruments. The bad writer blames his pen. The unskilful carver grumbles at his knife. The unsuccessful preacher says that he could do better if his church were in a better locality, or if some rearrange-ment of woodwork could be made. Who ever blames himself for failure ? Or even if blaming himself, who does not suggest that he could have done much better if the tools had been more distinctly adapted to the service he had to accomplish ? Our success in the great battles of life depends more upon spirit, intelligence, devotedness, and enthusiasm, than upon merely mechanical arrangements. What is a feeble instrument in the hands of one man is a mighty instrument in the hands of another, simply because the spirit of that other burns with holy determi-nation to accomplish the work that has to be done. There is one thing which ought to be noticed with special care, the proper noticing of which will greatly enlarge the charitableness of our social judgments ; namely, men should work with those instru-ments which they can handle most skilfully. Shamgar knew how to use the ox goad, and David knew how to use the sling and stone. Other instruments may be far heavier, keener, and likelier altogether, but if we are not accustomed to them why should we run the risk of a failure ? Men are strong in propor-tion as they keep within the circle of their own tried ability and experience. The instrument may be the grandest in the world, but if we do not know how to handle it we can accomplish infinitely bett r results with instruments which expose them-selves to the contempt of advanced civilisation. There are preachers who ould do incalculable good if they would confine

themselves to the subjects which they understand and to language
which is spoken by the people whom they address. The moment
such preachers begin to talk finely they lose all their ease and
power, and stumble like men who are endeavouring to speak in a
foreign tongue. How foolish it would be to ridicule the instrument when the results are so obviously good ! Look at the six
hundred dead men ; look at the slain giant ; look at the prostrate
walls of Jericho. The rule applies to every department of life.
Why set up some arbitrary standard of judgment when the
results are open to scrutiny and estimate ? This rule should be
applied to preaching. Why say that the sermons are not skilfully proportioned or expressed according to the usages of the
schools, and therefore are not valuable sermons, when sinners
are being converted and believers are being edified through their
instrumentality? Let the result determine everything. Whilst
military critics might be unfavourably criticising the ox goad,
Shamgar was standing rejoicingly over six hundred defeated
foes. This is the best answer of the Church to unfriendly
criticism. When souls are converted, when households are
reconstructed, when lives are inspired and encouraged, when
clouds of distress and fear are driven away, the Church may well
point to such results and be stirred to multiplied efforts rather than
be deterred by the criticism of men who pay more attention to
instruments than to results. God hath chosen the weak things of
this world to throw down the things that are mighty. We are
not called upon to defend this divine method ; it is enough
for us to know that it is God's way, and to accept it and obey it
with loving thankfulness. "Not by might, nor by power, but
by my Spirit, saith the Lord of hosts." " All this assembly shall
know that the Lord saveth not with sword and spear : for
the battle is the Lord's." He who fights for the right has God
upon his side. If God be for us, who can be against us ? The
army on the other side is but a multitude of shadows ; one ray
of light from the rising sun shall disperse the host of emptiness.
What meaner instrument can there be than the Cross of Christ ?
Hath it not pleased God, by the foolishness of the thing that is
preached, to save them that believe? Were not Peter and
John accounted unlearned and ignorant men? Are not the
highest things hidden from the wise and prudent, and revealed

unto babes ? Such is the way of God, that no flesh should
glory in his presence. All these thoughts are necessary to
comfort the earnest worker against the pitiful criticism which
is directed against Christian service. There are men so skilled
in the use of bitter words that they might even discourage
Shamgar himself by dwelling upon the ugliness and the un-
wieldiness of the weapon which he used. They might laugh
him into a kind of shame. The thing to be done is to point
men to the results which they have been enabled to secure,
and to ask them to trust the instruments which have served
them in good stead in the day of opposition and conflict.
David said concerning the sword of Goliath—"Give me that ;
there is none like it." Do not easily give up tried methods,
proved instruments, machineries and utilities which have been
of service in the time of war. The same rule applies to
trusty comradeships. We fight better in the society of some
men than we could do in the society of others : we know their
voices in the dark : we know their touch even when they do
not say a word to us: we can depend upon them when the
strain is greatest. New methods should be well studied in
secret before they are tried in public, or they may bring their
patrons to disappointment and chagrin. The Cross of Christ
will stand when all things fail. Let us be determined to know
nothing among men but Jesus Christ and him crucified. God
forbid that I should glory, save in the Cross of our Lord Jesus
Christ. Our speech and our preaching should not be with
enticing words of man's wisdom but with demonstration of the
Spirit and with power. The instrument indeed is mean enough.
To the Jews it is a stumbling-block, and to the Greeks foolishness ; nevertheless it works its daily miracles and finds in
renewed hearts and brightened lives the only needful proof of its
divinity and sanction.

PRAYER.

ALMIGHTY GOD, thy word is full of love. It draws us towards thee with a sweet compulsion. It is a word of grace, of light, of pity, and tenderness. Thy word knows us; it is familiar with our nature, and all the mystery thereof, and it speaks to us in music, in thunder, in judgment, in sharp exhortation, and in tender consolation; it is in very deed a wondrous word, coming all the way from heaven, and yet touching our hearts as the light touches the flower. We bless thee for thy word, for thy house, and for everything that is specially thine. We know that all things are thine : but some things seem to be twice thine, specially and wholly thine—the Lord's Day, the Lord's Book, the Lord's Portion, the Lord's own Spirit. Take not thy Holy Spirit from us ! May it abide with us—a sun that never sets, a gracious presence that never tires, a gift that grows by giving. We bless thee for all the love we have seen in all the way of life. The way of life has been made beautiful by thy love; even the uphill parts have been rendered quite easy because of thy sustaining grace ; and the winding ways and the dark valleys have not been so fearsome when we have come to them, because thou didst go before us and prepare a path. Thy comforts have been our strength ; thy grace has been our sun and our shield, and we have good hope of heaven. We pray thee to regard us as sinners, and have pity upon us, yea, mercy—saving pity and redeeming mercy, such as we have seen in Christ Jesus thy Son, bleeding, dying, rising, praying for us. If thou hast freely delivered him up for us all, thou wilt with him also freely give us all things; so we shall have no necessity ; we shall carry no burden, because, though the weight be great, the strength shall be more than equal to it. Let the whole year be a new year—new in thought, new in resolve, and new in sacrifice : thus shall the years not take away from our strength, but add to it, and make us younger as they fly, because bringing us nearer to the land where there is no sin, no death. Be this our good hope in Christ Jesus ; in this hope may we stand together as Christian students and worshippers, growing in grace and in the knowledge of our Lord Jesus Christ. Let our prayer prevail in heaven; let us have the answer hidden in our heart, a secret treasure, a great, yea, an infinite prize. Amen.

Judges iv., v.

DEBORAH AND HER SONG.

THE fourth and fifth chapters bring into view quite a host of secondary characters, such as Jabin and his chief captain, Sisera ; Deborah and Barak ; Heber, and Jael his wife ;

and in the great song of triumph and judgment names come and
go with flashes of colour full of history and criticism. Sometimes we are told of a song that the words are nothing—the tune
is everything. That may be a happy circumstance as regards
some songs, but that criticism has no place in reference to the
Song of Deborah; it is all words, all thoughts, all spiritual music.
This song has in it something more than tune. If we do not
know the words we shall never understand the music. Poor is
the singing in which you cannot hear every word; it is then but
a performance, it is but a vocal trick; we must hear every word,
every syllable, every sentiment, and judge whether the music
is worthy of the great intellectual conception. It is so with the
Song of Deborah. We shall find in it words as well as tune.
Jabin, king of Canaan, had held Israel in oppression twenty
years. Jabin had resources which astounded people who lived
in the hill country. Among the mountains chariots were no use;
the bow and arrow were everything, but the chariot could not
be driven over a craggy steep or unfathomable abyss. Jabin
had nine hundred chariots of iron, and he made the plain of
Esdraelon tremble as they rolled along. People who peeped
down out of the crags, and saw the nine hundred chariots rolling
in the plain of Jezreel, thought Jabin a mighty king, and obeyed
his behest with meekest submission. Do not blame Jabin for
oppressing the children of Israel twenty years. Jabin did not
begin the oppression. Do not let us ruin ourselves by looking
at second causes, and pouring out our denunciations upon the
king of Hazor in Canaan. He, like many other poor kings, had
nothing to do with it except instrumentally. There is but one
King. It pleases us to call men kings and rulers, but there is
only one sovereignty; the Lord reigneth, and there is room for
none other; his throne fills the universe, and his kingdom
ruleth over all. Jabin was an unconscious minister of God.
Many men occupy that relation to Heaven who are not aware of
it. The Lord has many servants at his threshold : he maketh
the wrath of man to praise him; he finds music in strange places,
and brings all kinds of instruments into the band that plays the
music of his purpose. No doubt, Jabin thought himself a great
man over Israel—lord and ruler and oppressor. Probably he
counted Israel among his riches ; in adding up his little store he

put Israel down at a plain price, and said, " Israel is mine, and is worth so much in the coming and going of things." He did not know what he was talking about. The reason why Jabin had anything to do with Israel was that Israel had done "evil in the sight of the Lord" (iv. 1). It is putting the case too lightly to say that Israel "did evil in the sight of the Lord." That might have been a first offence, and twenty years' penal servitude under a king without a harp, was a heavy sentence for a first violation. But we have missed the explanatory word. How often we do this in reading the Scriptures! How prone we are to leave out the key-word, and thus create confusion for ourselves! The text literally reads, "And the children of Israel again did evil in the sight of the Lord." How great the emphasis which ought to be laid upon the word " again "! It may not mean a second time or a third time ; it may be the thousandth time for aught the word "again" says to the contrary. Israel did evil upon evil, as if building a black temple with black stones, and purposing to consecrate it to the service of the devil. Twenty years' servitude was a small penalty. God did not plead against Israel with his great power when he sentenced Israel to this period of oppression and sorrow. How readily we look at the oppression and forget the sin ! This is characteristic of human nature. We pity the sorrow ; we would even count the tears of human distress, and make a great number of them, and turn that number into a plea for Heaven's mercy. We are wrong. We have started the argument from the wrong end ; the point of view is false ; the perspective is out of line : the whole vision suffers from wrong drawing and colouring. We have nothing to do with the oppression. We must look at causes. We must say,—How did this come to pass ? and in answering that inquiry we shall vindicate Eternal Providence, and justify the ways of God to men. We are moved more by the oppression than by the sin. That is a test of our own spiritual quality. Men are more frequently annoyed than they are wronged. Many men suffer more from an assault made upon their self-conceit than an assault made upon the proofs of eternal righteousness. Hence men resent what are termed personalities, whilst they look benignantly, if not approvingly, upon sin in the abstract—violated law that hurts the vanity of no man.   All this is indicative of character.   Here we see what Sin really is.   It binds the sinner to his outrages against God; it endeavours to modify its own force and gravity, and it seeks to turn attention to outside matters, accidents, passing phases, and temporary troubles.   Were we of God's mind and of Christ's heart we should dwell upon the evil, the evil twice done and twice repeated, and continued until it has become a custom—a custom so established that the repetition of it brings with it no new sensation.   But we will look at accidents and circumstances, rather than probe into real causes, profound and true origins.

A new period dawned in Israel.   Deborah the wife of Lapidoth was judge.   Great questions are settled by events.   There was no inquiry as to whether it was meet that a woman should be a judge.   Israel needed a mother, and Deborah was a mother in Israel.   If we make questions of these subjects, we shall entertain one another with wordy controversies : but when the true Deborah comes, she comes of right, and sits a queen, without a word.   There is a fitness of things—a subtle and unchangeable harmony—and when its conditions are satisfied, the satisfaction is attested by a great content of soul.   As Deborah sat under her palm-tree in Mount Ephraim, no man said : Why are we judged by a woman ?   The answer was in her eyes : she looked divine; the vindication was in her judgment: when she spake, the spirit of wisdom seemed to approve every tone of her voice.   There is a spirit in man : he knows when the right judge is upon the bench ; the poorest listener can tell when he is in the presence of Justice ; the unsophisticated heart knows when attempts are being made to quibble and wriggle and misrepresent, and to substitute the jingle of words for the music of righteousness.   The people came up to the famous old palm-tree, and told their tale to Deborah day by day, until the motherly heart began to ache, and her trouble was very great.   She saw, as motherly eyes only can see, how the wrinkles were deepening, how the faces were not so plump as they used to be, how strong men were bending under invisible burdens.   She said : By the help of Heaven we will see more clearly into this.   A hundred miles away in the north there lived a man, Barak by name—"Barak," which is, by interpretation, "the lightning"—and on Barak

Deborah fixed her heart as on the hope of Israel. She sent for him; but he said No. She said in effect, You must come. But he said in reply, You do not know the case as a soldier knows it; Jabin has nine hundred chariots of iron, and the plain of Jezreel seems to have been made into a way on purpose for them to roll in; if it were Jabin only, I might attempt the task, but think of nine hundred chariots of iron! Deborah said, You must come, for the time has arrived; Heaven's hour of deliverance has struck; and I look to you to espouse the cause of Israel. Barak said, No, I cannot, except on one condition. Deborah said, Name your terms; what are they? Then replied Barak, My terms are that you go along with me. Instantly she said, I am ready to go. And Deborah, a mother in Israel, became the soldier of Israel, and Barak was her humble servant. The news soon spread. Sisera was on the alert. This was the very thing he had been longing for. When a man has nine hundred chariots of iron he wants something for them to do. Kings who have standing armies are bound to create occasions of war; hence the injustice, the turpitude, the hellishness of battle. Sisera was the chief captain, and the nine hundred chariots of iron were under his direction, and he said, Now Esdraelon shall tremble under this weight of iron, and Israel shall be crushed as a fly upon a wheel. "Why do the heathen rage, and the people imagine a vain thing? The kings of the earth set themselves, and the rulers take counsel together, against the Lord, and against his anointed, saying, Let us break their bands asunder, and cast away their cords from us. He that sitteth in the heavens shall laugh" at them, and laugh again at their chariots, though they be iron in quality and nine hundred in number. The chariots of the Lord are twenty thousand, yea, thousand of thousands. The battle is the Lord's, not ours. But the Lord will not loose his chariots upon Jabin and his nine hundred curricles. There is a river on the field of battle, Kishon by name, quite a little silver threadlet in summer, but soon swollen by tributaries from the hills; and a river once getting charge of a plain makes swift work in its progress. The rains had fallen, all the hills seemed to pour out their treasures of water, the stream expanded, the water burst and flowed over the plain, and the nine hundred could not move. They were overcome by water! Kishon was more than all Jabin's iron host. Then came awful doings—men slaying one another. As for Sisera, the captain of all the iron chariots, he fled—ran away like a hound that had seen a tiger, and pantingly he came to a woman's tent, and said to Jael, the wife of Heber the Canaanite, Can you give me shelter? What are nine hundred chariots when the Lord is against them? What are all the chariots of the earth as against the sea? They could be sunk in the Atlantic, and the great ocean not know that they had descended to its depths. Jael said, Come in. And Sisera went in to come out no more. "The mother of Sisera looked out at a window, and cried through the lattice, Why is my son's chariot so long in coming? why tarry the wheels of his chariots?" At that moment Sisera was lying in the tent of Jael with an iron nail through his head. Sisera had chariots of iron—Jael had but one nail, but the hammer must have been God's. There is no defence of Jael's conduct. Viewed in the light of our morality, it was base in and out—bad, corrupt, horrible. As she walks softly, the softlier, the deadlier, and takes the nail and the hammer, she is the picture of incarnate depravity. This we say, unless there be some law which takes up all our laws and moves them into greater meanings through infinite orbits. There are greater laws that take up all our local movements and relations, and set them in new attitudes and invest them with new values; but of these laws we know nothing, and it is right that we should speak frankly about the ancient morality as represented in the action of Jael, and that Christian teachers should condemn it within the limits which are known to them. A woman began the war and a woman ended it, judging by the literal history. The inspiration of deliverance was a divine inspiration. Wherever there is a movement towards freedom, that movement began in heaven. Wherever any oppressed man, conscious of his sin and penitent for it, lifts himself up in an attitude of independence and looks his oppressor in the face with a calm determination to be free, there is a distinctively divine act. God is the God of liberty. He permits slavery or uses it, and may sanctify the use to higher issues and advantages; but beneath the oppression, below all the trouble, there is that spirit which is akin to his own, which asserts itself and says:—I cannot always live under this cloud, or carry this weary load; I will be free. When such a word is spoken reverently, solemnly, honestly, it is neither more nor less than the living voice of the living God.

Now Deborah sings. She seems almost to excel Moses in song. There is hardly such a piece of composition in all known literature. It has everything in it. This is a manifold song. Some persons have points of power, individual faculties of notable strength ; but this woman seems to have all human faculties, and all human faculties in their largest proportions. She praises the people for their willing offering of themselves (v. 2). She recognised the spontaneous action of the people ; they wanted to be free. She also regards kings as occupying a subordinate position :—" Hear, O ye kings ; give ear, O ye princes " (v. 3). They had to receive the news, not to create the event ; they had to hear of it next day, not to plan it the day before. Who can tell the ways of Providence ? God setteth up the poor amongst princes, he plungeth the princes down into meanest places ; the first shall be last, and the last shall be first. God shall have the record and the register written, and rewritten and redistributed, so there shall be no vanity in Israel, no conceit in the hosts of Christ. There is, too, a tone of judgment in the song. Deborah could not forget who had forsaken her on the day of trial. She said : Reuben was not there—" For the divisions of Reuben there were great thoughts of heart." Reuben abode among the sheepfolds, and listened to the bleating of the flocks, and let the woman go out alone to fight the chariots of Jabin. " For the divisions of Reuben there were great searchings of heart." Gilead was not with me ; he " abode beyond Jordan " : Dan was not with me ; he " remained in ships " : Asher got behind the creeks and the crags, and peeped out, and then withdrew : " Zebulun and Naphtali were a people that jeoparded their lives unto the death in the high places of the field." So Deborah makes mention of severe troubles even in the roll of her triumphal song. She did not confuse things. She was not so lost in enthusiasm and transport, as to forget whether Reuben was present, and Gilead and Dan ; nor did she neglect Zebulun and Naphtali. This woman's song is reason set to music, judgment in rapture —yea, say in rhapsody, but judgment still, awarding to the good that which is good, to the evil that which they deserve, and thus setting forth in song a picture of the ultimate and final judgment.

Meroz was cursed even in song. Why? Meroz was in the heart of the country; Meroz might have struck the first blow, and Meroz did nothing:—" Curse ye Meroz, said the angel of the Lord, curse ye bitterly the inhabitants thereof; because they came not to the help of the Lord, to the help of the Lord against the mighty." The Lord might have been torn to pieces for aught that Meroz did. The winding up of all things shall be a great song, a triumphant burst of music; but moral distinctions will not be forgotten in those jubilant strains. Then it will be known who did his duty, who remained at home, who was content with criticism, and who hazarded his life that his Christ might be made more widely known.

SELECTED NOTE.

The song of triumph which was composed in consequence of the great victory over Sisera, is said to have been " sung by Deborah and Barak." It is usually regarded as the composition of Deborah, and was probably indited by her to be sung on the return of Barak and his warriors from the pursuit.

Deborah, the prophetess, was wife of Lapidoth. She dwelt, probably, in a tent, under a well-known palm-tree, between Ramah and Bethel, where she judged Israel (Judg. iv. 4, 5). This probably means that she was the organ of communication between God and his people, and probably on account of the influence and authority of her character, was accounted in some sort as the head of the nation, to whom questions of doubt and diffi- culty were referred for decision. In her triumphal song she says:—

"In the days of Shamgar, son of Anath,
In the days of Jael the ways lay desert,
And high-way travellers went in winding by-paths.
Leaders failed in Israel, they failed,
Until that I Deborah arose,
That I arose, a mother in Israel."

PREACHING
THROUGH THE
BIBLE

BY
JOSEPH PARKER

VOL. 6

JUDGES VI—I SAMUEL XVIII

Originally printed
under the title,
The People's Bible

CONTENTS.

ANNOTATED CHAPTERS.

(Giving the result of the best available criticism.)

THE BOOK OF JUDGES

(Continued).

PRAYER.

ALMIGHTY GOD, we would rest in thee. Thou hast welcomed us to thy rest, and made us, in promise, sharers of thy feast. The Lord will bless his people with peace, yea, with peace that passeth understanding. Thou dost cause men to possess their souls in peace and confidence when they look unto the Lord and set their expectation eagerly upon him. We have said unto our souls, Look unto the hills whence cometh your help: your help cometh from the Lord which made heaven and earth. Thus the heaven and the earth have become images to us of thy greatness, wisdom, goodness, and continual superintendence; and thus through heaven and earth we have found the living God who made them both. All things tell of thy power, and all things sing of thy love. Why should man be silent? His should be the loudest, sweetest voice of all. Let the people praise thee, O God; yea, let all the people praise thee; let the time of silence now past more than suffice, and let the time of singing, and rejoicing, and testifying, come in upon us like a new year. Truly thy mercies deserve our songs. We will sing of mercy, and of judgment: for is not thy judgment a mercy? and is not thy mercy a judgment? art thou not continually looking upon us through the cloud, and blessing us every day with sunlight? We would join the innumerable company of angels in praising God. We would think of the great host in heavenly places joining the hymn of adoration and thankfulness; we would unite in the great and solemn praise, and be as glad as earth will permit its children to be amid its night and winter and cold. We praise thee for a day that is all thine own: the four-and-twenty hours are four-and-twenty jewels; we bless thee for a house that is all thine own, built upon a sure foundation, rearing itself towards heaven, excluding all profanity, offering hospitality to all necessity; and we bless thee for a book that is all thine own, written as it were with thine own finger, having in it gospels from heaven infinite as the love of God and grand as his glory: may we have the seeing eye, the understanding heart, that, beholding the writing we may comprehend the meaning, and then proceed to live it over again in useful and happy life. We desire that our religious aspirations may grow in number, in intensity, in loftiness; may our whole character be lifted up by their energy, so that our citizenship may be no longer upon earth,

I

but already in heaven. Thy care of us, who can doubt? The very hairs of our head are all numbered. If for a moment we distrust thee, it is that we may pray some nobler prayer, because of contrition and the heart-break of penitent sorrow; if we have turned from the Lord, we will come back again, renewed, stronger than ever in faith, tenderer than ever in love. Oh heal our backslidings, and love us freely. Thou knowest our life, for thou didst make it. We do not know what it is. We suffer it, and are afraid of it; for a moment we enjoy it, as we might enjoy an angel's presence, but all our joy is troubled by a distant and speechless fear, and we say, This is none other than the house of God, and this is the gate of heaven; and our pulse is as the beat of God's eternity within us. Help us through our life to know somewhat of thine; enable us to know through our hearts somewhat of God's love: then shall our life be profitable, and shall help itself to higher uses because to higher devotion. We pray for one another. The Lord's blessing be upon us every one. Thou hast a portion of meat for each in thy house; thou wilt not send any empty away; if our hunger is great, thy resources are greater still. Blessed are they that hunger: behold, our very necessity is turned into a blessing; our capacity to receive is the measure of our capacity to enjoy. O that we might praise the Lord every day—that we might know that all our time may become sabbatic, restful—a period of peace, an anticipation of everlasting tranquillity! Help us to live out the few more days that remain: they come and go so quickly we can hardly number them; between the sunrise and the sunset there is so brief a time, hardly an opportunity to breathe. May we know the measure of our days, and knowing that, may we redeem the time, buying up every opportunity eagerly, and using it as a trust from heaven. Guide all who need special guidance. Show men where the lock is they cannot find, and when they have found it and cannot open it, put the key into their hands. Send light upon those whose way is wrapped in darkness. Speak a word in season to him that is weary; show the weeper that his tears are but for a time and may be the precursors of joy. Help those who are called to carry the burdens of others, who think about them until they are weary—until their wonder becomes a distress, and their solicitude an intolerable pain. We pray for those in trouble on the sea. We pray for those in trouble because of bodily weakness. We pray that in houses where Sorrow has long been the one guest he may this day flee away. As for our sin, we bring it to the cross: the blood of Jesus Christ is the answer of God to the sin of man. Help us to believe in Jesus, to trust in the Son of God, to give up all hope in ourselves, and to find all satisfaction in Christ. Amen.

Judges vi.–viii.

GIDEON.

AT the close of the song of Deborah "the land had rest forty years." The sixth chapter begins with the usual black line:—"And the children of Israel did evil in the sight of the Lord." These comings and goings of evil in human history seem

to be fated. Men never get so clear away from evil as never to
come back again to it; at any moment the course of life may be
reversed, and the altar, the vow, the song, and the prayer may
be forgotten like vanished summers. This makes the reading of
human history a weary toil. We have only to turn over a leaf,
and the saints who have been singing are as active as ever in
evil. It would be difficult to believe this if we did not know
it to be true. This Bible-history is indeed our own history
written before the time. Our life seems to be spent upon a
short ladder, in going up, in coming down : in going up to pray,
in coming down to sin, and drying the tears of penitence ; and
climbing again, and then coming down; miles short of heaven.
The weariness is not in the literature—it is in the fact. We
are many men : when we would do good, evil is present with us ;
when we would do evil, the angel looks at us and reproaches
our purpose. The history of Israel is the history of the world.
Israel was given over to the hand of the Midianites seven years.
This was not, as in the former case, an oppression ; it was an
attack. In our last study we saw Israel oppressed ; here we see
a foreign invasion, crowding upon the land inhabited by Israel.
Whether in this way or in that, God will not let the battle end
until he has punished evil and destroyed it. He is continuing
the same policy now. Seated in the heavens, he is watching
the earth as if it were the only world he had,—blessing the
good, punishing the evil, threatening everything that is of
another nature than his own, and keeping perdition for those
only who must inevitably be lost. In the olden times there
were oppressions, invasions, assaults, and the like; to-day Providence seems to be operating by subtler methods, but always
operating to the same end : to punish the evil, and bless the
good. A very vivid picture is given of the state of Israel in
chapter vi. 2. Israel was dwelling in "the dens which are in
the mountains, and caves, and strong holds." The proud and
princely Israel was burrowing in the torrent gullies, instead
of building cities that should have lifted their towers and spires
like ascending psalms to the approving heavens. Think of it
well! It is the same to-day. Men who might have been in
the thoroughfare are hidden away in some distressing obscurity.
Men who ought to have been foremost are left so far behind

they can hardly be seen,—dim spectres in the far-away distance. The Midianites were coming up like locusts. No sooner did the Israelites sow their seed than the Midianites had their eye upon it; and it was only by strategy, cunning almost surpassingly human, that Israel could save a handful of corn for itself. Israel was "impoverished." A very remarkable word is that. It means that they were like a door swinging on broken hinges. Israel, the redeemed people, Israel without whom there might have been no history, Israel had so sinned as to be at last like a door swinging on hinges that were broken : the door could not be shut, the door was no security, the door was a perpetual irony, yea, a daily reproach and taunt. There is a poverty that is the result of what we call misfortune ; that is to be pitied and to be assisted : there is a poverty that is only the social and punitive side of sin ; that is to be recognised as such—a black blot on the snow of God's holiness, a sad brand on the righteousness of things. Or the figure may be changed, for it is a double one. Israel was like a sear leaf, just hanging by one frail thread to the branch, all the juice gone, all the beautiful green dead for ever, all possibility of fruitfulness exhausted ; and there hung great Israel, a leaf—sear, yellow, dead, just hanging to drop ! We must realise this condition of things before we can understand the arduousness of the mission of Gideon. If we do not understand the situation we cannot understand Gideon's distress, hesitation, hopelessness. The times were out of joint. All things beautiful were dead. The whole time was given over to idolatry. There was but one man who kept to the true faith, and he seemed to worship in secret ; he alone was not swallowed up in the great idolatrous passion ; his father had gone religiously astray, but he himself still thought of old histories, and had in him flickering, but, oh, quite dyingly, some hope of returning faith.

Then came the inevitable " cry " :—" The children of Israel cried unto the Lord " (vi. 6). It was a mean prayer. Some cries must not be answered ; they are unworthy screams or utterances of selfish desire. The Lord will not be too critical about these " cries," for who then could stand before him and hope for any thing from his hand ? What prayer is there worth being heard, not to say worth being answered ? Search it, probe it, and what is it but religious selfishness—a plea for self? But men must pray as best they can. We cannot expect perfect prayers from imperfect men. In the cry there may be something which God can hear to which he will make response. But prayers are not answered, because they are not prayers; they are self-excuses, self-pleadings, desires inspired by selfishness: so they are narrow, shortsighted, out of the rhythm of the music of the universe, notes that cannot be smoothed into the general utterance of the divine purpose; they may do the suppliant good by heightening his veneration or exciting within him some inexpressible desires, but as words they fall back again like birds whose wings have been broken.

Israel cried unto the Lord. What was the divine answer to that cry? It was a prophet. Jewish legend says it was Phinehas, son of Eleazar. The prayer was answered by a man:— "The Lord sent a prophet unto the children of Israel" (vi. 8). A "prophet" is a teacher, a man who sees the largest relations of things, one who lives above the cloud and can see what is going on underneath it; a seer, a man of penetrating vision, a man whose eyes are within, and from whom God has hidden nothing of wisdom, grace, purpose, and issue. The age must be prepared for its prophets. When the age is haughty, self-contented, self-idolatrous, prophets go for nothing; they are the object of sneering remark; they may be caricatured, they may be turned into food for merriment; but when the age becomes like a door swinging on broken hinges, or like a sear and yellow leaf when all hope has died out of it, then men ask if there be not a prophet, or one who can pray—a seer who can penetrate beyond appearances and discover germs of life or hints of hope? It was so now. The prophet came, and delivered a judicial speech :—

"Thus saith the Lord God of Israel, I brought you up from Egypt, and brought you forth out of the house of bondage; and I delivered you out of the hand of the Egyptians, and out of the hand of all that oppressed you, and drave them out from before you, and gave you their land; and I said unto you, I am the Lord your God; fear not the gods of the Amorites [the Amorites were the highlanders of Palestine, and as they were the strongest of all the Canaanitish tribes they are often spoken of as representing or including the whole of them], in whose land ye dwell: but ye have not obeyed my voice" (vi. 8-10).

Here you find a reminder,—that is to say, a reference to history.

Memory was awakened and turned upon the days that had gone. God works through recollection. Marvellous are the miracles which God works by the power of memory : memory goes back, and brings to mind things forgotten, uses them in the light of to-day, observes their action upon the circumstances which make up the immediate present ; and oftentimes a man needs no hotter hell than an awakened and stimulated memory. The recollection was followed by a reproof:—"But ye have not obeyed my voice," saying in effect: I have not changed; I was continuing the line; my purpose was one of deliverance and success and honour for Israel, but ye failed in obedience : first you became reluctant, hesitant, then weary, then you complained of monotony, then you said the yoke galled your shoulders, then you fell clean away, then you built Asherah and worshipped Baal ; this is the reason of all that has come upon you; blame yourselves : for men who fall away from the road of obedience fail of the heaven of blessedness.

All this is intelligible. We have been accustomed to these reminding and accusing voices ourselves, and we do not hear in them anything that startles our reason or taxes our faith. Now the prophet is succeeded by an angel. A most mysterious instance occurs, challenging our faith in its loftiest moods. Gideon was threshing wheat by the winepress, to hide it from the Midianites. He was in a little sheltered corner, not daring to use a flail, perhaps, lest the beat of it should attract the attention of some listening Midianite ; Gideon was almost rubbing the wheat between his hands. He was in a little cave rather than in a winepress, which is hardly the literal translation. He was in a corner by himself, rubbing out the wheat which he had industriously sown, painfully watched, and honestly gathered. It was weary work for Gideon. He felt that he was a prisoner, almost stealing his own bread. This is not unknown to ourselves. Men sometimes have to hide their food from their own relations. Some men dare not even seem to be prosperous, because they know what havoc would be wrought by those who have been watching their honourable and successful labours. Men sometimes have to hide themselves from their own flesh, and to rub out their little handful of wheat behind some sheltering crag. Some men are bound to look poor, because they know they would

be fleeced and robbed. Is that not strictly according to our own
personal experience ?   This is the picture presented by the
position and action of Gideon [hewer]: a hidden man, doing
an honest work in the quietest possible way, only thankful
if he can get his wheat turned into bread to satisfy his
hunger.   Watch Gideon, the one religious man of the place
and time.   If any one were to come from heaven now, he
would come to Gideon.   Like descends upon like.   " And there
came an angel of the Lord, and sat under an oak which was
in Ophrah [in Western Manasseh], that pertaineth unto Joash
the Abi-ezrite."   For a time the angel was silent.   How will he
speak to a weary man ?   He will say to him : Poor laden one, this
is sad work for Israel ; poor weary Gideon, I am sorry for thee
in my heart ; Gideon, thou shouldst have been out in the open
air swinging thy flail and separating the chaff from the wheat
right cheerfully and hopefully—poor Gideon ! Such sympathy
would have overborne the man ; it would have been the one
drop that would have made the cup of his sorrow overflow.   No,
there must be sharp reaction ; a note must be struck that will
awaken the man wholly : he must not continue his dream-trouble,
he must have his sleep driven away.   What said the angel ?
" The Lord is with thee, thou mighty man of valour."   The
speech seemed to be ironical.   Gideon had about him the look
as to weariness of a man who was exhausted.   But he was a
king, and he had a kingly presence, a face that only needed to be
awakened to answer the angel's own in the likeness of kinship.
There was no fairer man than Gideon in all the land ; the make
of him was a miracle of God.   When he stretched himself right
out to his full compass and looked his best self, one could understand how it was that he had " faithful among the faithless been,"
and had kept Jehovah's altar even amid the riot of the Baal-
worshippers.   Who shall say there is no kinship between
angels and men ?   Who has wisdom enough to declare that
there is no connection between the spiritual life or lives of the
universe ?   It is not only a higher faith but a nobler reason
which would say : All we, men, women, children, angels, spirits
of the blessed, are one, warmed with one fire, radiant with one
glory, expectant of one destiny.   We cannot settle anything about
this angel that is definite and final.   What do we know that is

at all of the nature of counterpart? We know something about unexpected meetings, strangers speaking to us, and yet so speaking that we know them,—speaking to us in our mother tongue, speaking to us words which we have wanted to hear but dare scarcely speak to ourselves; people making beginnings which have had happy endings;—that we know right well. We know something of unforeseen opportunities: the cloud has suddenly opened, and we have seen where we were. Clouds often do open quite suddenly. We have seen the mariner watching for the sun for days: the mariner is ready, his glass is in his hand; if there be but one little rift in that great cloud, he will avail himself of the opportunity to know where the sun is that he may know where his ship is. A rift has come, a sudden chance; it was but a moment, a glimpse, but in that moment there was communication between earth and heaven. So far we are upon familiar ground. We know something of unaccountable impressions also; and sometimes we utter prayers that angels might have inspired, for the prayers have surprised ourselves and made sudden Sabbath in the midst of the tumultuous week. If then we know something of unexpected meetings, unforeseen opportunities, and unaccountable impressions, we seem to be not far from the angel vision, the angel touch.

When Gideon heard the angel's message, he said, in a tone we cannot reproduce, a tone made credulous by incredulity, yet with some resonance of strength in its very halting and shaking, —a tone representing a strange struggle between hopelessness and faith, experience and possibility,—" Oh, sir "—for the term Gideon used in the first instance was but a term of courtesy and not a title of religious veneration—" Oh, sir, if the Lord be with us "—but the angel did not say so; the angel said " thee." Who can listen critically? Who can distinguish between person and number in the grammar of an angel?—

"Oh, sir, if the Lord be with us, why then is all this befallen us? [*see* Deut. xxi. 17] and where be all his miracles which our fathers told us of, saying, Did not the Lord bring us up from Egypt? but now the Lord hath forsaken us, and delivered us into the hands of the Midianites" (vi. 13).

It was a right answer so far. It was better that Gideon should know the exact circumstances. " To know ourselves diseased is half the cure." Gideon must not have any false hopes. He must not be taking up any broken splinters of wood and saying : These splinters will be swords which we shall thrust through the bows of the enemy. It is well that he is driven into obscurity, that he is made to do his work with the utmost quietness, that he is compelled to act almost as a thief on the threshold of his own house. To be down so far is to be in that darkness which oft precedes the dawn.

What did the angel do? The angel did two things. (1) He " looked." Who can interpret that word ? Some biblical words must remain without interpretation. Sometimes in translating books from foreign languages into our own we are obliged to quote certain words and let them remain untranslated ; we hover over them, point to them, give clumsy paraphrases of their possible meaning, but think it better after all to set down the word itself, for it has no equivalent in our own language. It must be so with this word " look." That look begat attention, inspired confidence, elevated thought, stimulated veneration, and *looked* Gideon into a new man. There are looks which do so. There is one look which is yet to do this in all the fulness of its meaning : the day is to come when we shall be like Christ, for we shall see him as he is. These are spiritual looks that we read of in the Old Testament, and that we have experience of in the current of our own lives. (2) The angel, however, not only looked but "said"—changed his tone, used human speech, addressed the man in his mother tongue. He said, " Go in this thy might, and thou shalt save Israel from the hand of the Midianites : have not I sent thee ? " (vi. 14). But Gideon was astounded, and said in effect : Impossible—

"Oh, my Lord, wherewith shall I save Israel? behold, my family [my thousand] is poor [the meanest] in Manasseh, and I am the least in my father's house" (vi. 15).

This is quite in the line of biblical history. Sarah " laughed " when the angel said that she should be the mother of one who should be supreme in history ; Moses was shocked when he was told that he, a wandering, stammering shepherd, should face the Pharaohs of Egypt and demand justice to Israel; Paul was amazed that he should be chosen for great missions of deliverance.

Speaking of Gideon, the quaint commentator Trapp says: "He was well-descended, but had mean thoughts of himself. True worth is modest. Moses had distributed the people into thousands as Alfred did the English into shires, hundreds, and tenths, or tithings, whereof the ancientest were called the tithing men." Such was Gideon's view of himself and his chiliad, or thousand. But there is the accusing and stimulating question: "Have not I sent thee?" accusing men of unfaith in a tone that stimulates them to seize their grandest opportunities. Are there not new births? Are there not vivid realisations? Are there not new selves? Behold, the angel must confirm his own message and vindicate his own revelation.

What is the application of all this to ourselves in addition to what has already been said? Are we not often hopeless? We say Jesus Christ is in a minority. Put down the great leaders of the world's religions, and Jesus Christ must statistically take his place near the bottom of the list. That is the arithmetical condition of affairs to-day. Even if every man in the church be a sound man, yet, reckoning up the sum-total, the figures often sink into insignificance. But are there not these two great lessons lying upon the very face of the history, namely, that we grow in social power as we grow in spiritual consciousness? Just as Gideon saw the angel and was conscious of a divine presence did he grow in social power. He was warmed into a larger self. It is when we see God most clearly that all difficulties vanish from our sight. See God, and you need behold no other sight to make the soul majestic and clothe the life with social beneficence. Fear God, and have no other fear. Be sure that the heavens are with you, then be confident that the harvests of the earth will he gathered even to the last grain of wheat, and the enemy shall not prevail in any degree. Then there is a second lesson lying upon the same line, namely, that we need not be socially great to be spiritually useful. Gideon said, "Behold, my family is poor in Manasseh, and I am the least in my father's house." "Blessed are the poor in spirit; for theirs is the kingdom of heaven;" and anything but blessed are they who say, "We are rich, and increased with goods, and have need of nothing,"— knowing not that they are poor, and blind, and miserable, and naked. It is like God to choose the poorest tribe and the poorest man in the tribe. When did God change that plan ? When did he vary that mysterious policy ? Is it not that no flesh may glory in his presence ? Not many wise, great, m ghty, noble are called, but God has chosen the weak things to trouble the strong, —yea, things which are not—things which seem to have no existence—to bring to nought things that are : ghostly ministries operating upon material fortresses, spiritual agencies crumbling down temples in the night-time, mysterious influences rending the mighty and bringing down that which is high.

SELECTED NOTE.

Palestine, which is only about the size of Wales, and was still largely held by the former inhabitants, was subdivided by the Hebrews into many tribal governments, as England in the Saxon period was broken up into Essex, Wessex, Mercia, Kent, Sussex, and several other kingdoms; and was, hence, in constant danger of inroad and subjugation. To the nomadic tribes of the desert, which stretched to the borders of the land on the east and south, the valleys of Gilead and Bashan, and the fertile plains of Central Canaan, were an irresistible temptation, stretching out as they did like paradises of green, before eyes wearied with the yellow sand or dry barren-ness of the wilderness. Israel itself, when only so many wandering tribes, had forced a way into these oases, and had held them, and there seemed no reason why other races should not, like them, exchange the desert for a home so fair, at least during the summer and harvest of each year, by overpowering Israel in turn.

The forty years' rest after Deborah's triumph was rudely broken by inroads excited in this hope. A great confederation of the Arab tribes, like that which, at an earlier day, had given the Shepherd Kings to Egypt, poured into Palestine. Midianites, Amalekites, and all "the children of the east," far and near, in countless numbers, with immense trains of camels, and of cattle, and flocks, streamed up the steep wadys from the fords of Jordan, and swept all resistance before them, from Esdraelon, on the north, to Gaza, on the extreme south. No sooner had the fields been sown each year, than these wild hordes reappeared, covering the hill pastures and the fertile valleys, in turn, with their tents; driving off every sheep, or goat, or ox, or ass, they could find, and seizing all hoards of grain they could discover, saved from the few fields that had escaped destruction by their endless flocks and herds. No visitation could be more terrible, for there was neither food nor live stock left in the land. Fire and sword spread terror on every side ; desperate resistance by isolated bands of Hebrews only led to the massacre of these brave defenders of their homes, and at last safety and even existence seemed possible only by the population taking refuge in the numerous caves of the hills, and in strongholds on hill tops.—*Geikie.*

PRAYER.

ALMIGHTY GOD, come to us as thou wilt—a great fire, or a great wind, or a still small voice. We shall know thee when thou comest, for we are akin to thee; thou didst make us and put thy name upon us. We are fearfully and wonderfully made; we are a continual surprise unto ourselves: sometimes we are self-afraid; sometimes we are tempted to be as gods. Now we know ourselves to be but men, and we sigh about our frailty, and say we are as a withering leaf, as a speck of dust blown about by the wind, a vapour that cometh for a little time and then vanisheth away; then in some other mood, created by thyself, we lay our hands upon all heaven and claim it as an inheritance in Christ Jesus, saying, This is the meaning of his blood, this is the true interpretation of his Cross,—glory, honour, immortality; service without weariness, worship accompanied by growing knowledge, trust in God untroubled by a doubt. Whether we are in this mood, or that, low down or high up, moaning about our littleness or rejoicing in our spiritual sonship, take not thy Holy Spirit from us: Holy Spirit, dwell with us! As for these varying tempers and conditions of ours, are we not still prisoners of time, bondmen of the flesh? Are we not oppressed by circumstances we cannot control? But of all these we shall presently be rid, and then we shall claim thy great creation for the development of our powers, for the continuance and consummation of our worship. For all high religious feeling we bless thee; for all sweet Christian hope we thank thee: whilst the angel of hope shines within us and sings its sweet song of heaven, we know nothing of death or of restraint or of littleness; we are already in the celestial world mingling companionlike with the angels. Read thy book to us thyself, with thine own voice, in thine own tone, and the tone shall be explanation: we shall know what thou meanest when we hear thine own voice. Above all things give to us the seeing eye, the hearing ear, and the understanding heart, when we come into the sanctuary of revelation, lest we exalt ourselves and say our own right-hand hath gotten us what spiritual prey we have: rather would we say, This is the Lord's doing, and it is marvellous in our eyes,—is not his love a continual wonder? Is not his grace a perpetual revelation? Hold us, Mighty One, to-day and to-morrow, and on the third day perfect us. Amen.

Judges vi.-viii.

GIDEON.—(*Continued.*

WHEN the angel "looked" at Gideon the good man's heart was troubled, and yet his hope was revived. His faith went so far that he would submit to receive some test and proof that the angel was in very deed the messenger of God. It is something to have got so far along the road of the better land; anything in this direction is better than deafness, blindness, and utter indifference. Gideon said, " If now I have found grace in thy sight, then show me a sign that thou talkest with me " (vi. 17). According to the laws of Oriental hospitality, Gideon withdrew to prepare refreshment for his wondrous visitor :—" Depart not hence, I pray thee, until I come unto thee, and bring forth my present, and set it before thee." And the angel said, " I will tarry until thou come again." " Gideon went in, and made ready a kid, and unleavened cakes of an ephah of flour : "— unleavened bread being more easily-prepared than any other— " the flesh he put in a basket, and he put the broth in a pot, and brought it out unto him under the oak, and presented it." The angel said, " Take the flesh and the unleavened cakes, and lay them upon this rock, and pour out the broth." And Gideon did so.

" Then the angel of the Lord put forth the end of the staff that was in his hand, and touched the flesh and the unleavened cakes ; and there rose up fire out of the rock, and consumed the flesh and the unleavened cakes. Then the angel of the Lord departed out of his sight " (vi. 21).

It was enough. It was the beginning of lasting and all-sufficient comfort.

Now there came a practical test to be applied to Gideon. Sooner or later that test comes to every man. If we put God to the test, what if God should in his turn put us also upon our trial ? The test to which Gideon was about to be put was a practical one. As the foreign invasion of Midian was traceable to Israel's evil-doing, so the beginning of the divine deliverance must be moral, spiritual, and religious. That same night the Lord said to Gideon : Take thy father's young bullock, even the second bullock of seven years old, attach it to the altar of Baal by rope or iron, and drag it down. That was a negative beginning. We must get down the old altar before we put up the new one. " And "—when thou hast done this—

" build an altar unto the Lord thy God upon the top of this rock, in the ordered place [build an altar with the wood laid in order] ; and take the second bullock, and offer a burnt sacrifice with the wood of the grove which thou shalt cut down " (vi. 26).

The grove or Asherah was an image of nature-worship, a huge piece of clumsily-carved wood set up beside the altar : so the altar and the Asherah, or grove, must be cleansed out. Nothing could be done until the religious distemper had been healed.

Gideon made one reservation. We do not wonder that he should have done so. He said, in effect : I cannot do this in the daytime; I will do it by night.—Who can blame him? Who will call him coward? It was a natural device. Men cannot be courageous all at once. Some men need to be trained and nursed into courage ; be gentle with them, patient and hopeful,— who can spring into lionhood all in one sudden moment? "Gideon took ten men of his own," rather than "ten men of his servants," and pulled down Baal's altar by night. When night gives up her history, it may be found that many a man has attempted to begin a better life under the cover of darkness. We should not taunt men for want of boldness in spiritual things ; sometimes they are bolder than we have imagined them to be : they may even have attempted to pray aloud when no one was present. That is a trial of a man's spiritual sincerity. It is not every man who can listen to his own voice in prayer and continue the supplication with any composure. A man's first audible prayer might smite himself down as by a great thunder-stroke : the voice seems so loud, the exercise so audacious ; it is as if the universe had halted to hear the new appeal. Who shall say that men who are dumb in church have not tried in darkness and in loneliness to sing some little hymn of praise when they were quite unheard? Who knows what papers have been written, what plans of battle have been drawn up, at night-time, wherein men said they would certainly begin at this point, or at that point, to renounce a companionship, to change a custom, to release themselves from the tyranny of a habit : next time they would say No to the invitation which sought to seduce them to evil-doing. Who is not courageous when he is alone? Who is not most eloquent when there is none to hear him? We must not, therefore, fall foul upon the memory of Gideon and charge him with want of courage.

But the morning came. What the city then saw! The cathedral, so to say, was pulled down ! When the men of the city

arose early in the morning they missed the altar and the Asherah,
"and they said to one another, Who hath done this thing?"
And inquiry resulted in the information that Gideon the son of
Joash had done it.

"Then the men of the city said unto Joash, Bring out thy son, that he
may die: because he hath cast down the altar of Baal, and because he hath
cut down the grove that was by it " (vi. 30).

Joash was not a born Baal-worshipper; the foreign religion sat
uneasily upon him. He had inwardly no great respect for Baal;
outwardly he was addicted to his worship, but really he had
serious misgivings about Baal's godhead. What if all idolators
be afflicted with the same scepticism? Scepticism does not
grow in the Church with relation to the true God alone; unbelievers in the true religion have scepticism often with regard
to their own: they cannot tell what to make of their dumb gods;
they have great philosophies about them, but no direct consequence comes of it all; so when an assault is made upon them
the resistance is but reluctant or careless. Joash was a wise
man; he said: Men of the city, hear me: my son has torn down
the altar of Baal; if Baal be a god in very deed let him avenge
the wrong himself; do not you interfere as to Baal's sovereignty
and godhead: in so far as Baal is a true god he will see to it that
the man who insulted his altar shall be punished for his sacrilege and audacity. The men thought this was a good answer,
and they accepted it. This is the challenge of the God of the
Bible. God is always challenging the false gods to come forward
and show what they can do. God mocks them, taunts them, tells
them they are nothing,—says they are things made out of iron
and stone and wood, and not a single thought is in their carved
heads. This is the challenge of Elijah; said he, " The God that
answereth by fire, let him be God," whatever his name be;
this is not a test of names, forms, ceremonies, dogmas: if Baal be
God, let us all worship him, and if the Lord be God, let us bow
down in adoration before him :—"the God that answereth by
fire, let him be God." The position taken up by Joash is the
position we should all take up with regard to religious things.
Let God defend himself. The Christian religion is never so
humiliated as when men attempt to defend it. God needeth not
to be ministered unto by men's hands; nor does he require the

patronage of trained intellect and swift and eager mind. God is
continually vindicating himself in his providence. God's appeal
is : Look at the world ; look at it in great breadths of time; not in
a handful of days, or in a nameable measure of months, but look
at it in the light of centuries; give yourselves field of vision
enough ; look at the distribution of men, and the distribution
of all natural products ; consider the occasion well : see what
boundaries are set, see what issues are inevitable, observe how
ambition is cut in two at a certain point, and must begin again
to raise its shattered head ; watch all the ebb and flow of civilisation; observe keenly as well as widely ; and if providence be not
its own vindication, it is useless for any man, however swift of
thought or copious in expression, to attempt to vindicate what the
facts themselves do not support. Christian teaching will be strong
in proportion as it takes this ground. We are not engaged in
matters that can be settled by words. We look abroad and see a
law operating—a law of restraint, a law of culture, a law of rewards and punishments ; we try to check it, modify it, avert it, but
it comes on with quiet irresistibleness—an infinite force : who can
ascend beyond a certain height ? or who can descend without
being suffocated ? Who can stretch himself out so as to touch the
horizon ? and who has not chafed as Job chafed when he said,
"Am I a sea, or a whale, that thou settest a watch over me ? "
If a man would take this wide vision, and bring into focus all
these infinite relations, let him look carefully at his own life ;
let him, as it were, write his own story in his own language, and
see how the chapters fall into happy sequence. See what training
the man has had, what narrow escapes, what afflictions, what
deliverances,—how disappointments have been turned into the
roots of prosperity, and how the grim discouraging negative has
been the beginning of boldest and most successful endeavour ;
and when the reviewer has concluded his retrospect, let him say
if he can, "All this was of chance, and luck, and incalculable
fortune."

Gideon, however, was punished by the people in some degree.
The people must interfere a little, even in the case of avenging
insults offered to Baal. So they called Gideon by a new name,—
they called him "Jerubbaal." The least one can do is to give a
reformer a nickname. If we may not smite him, we may at

least throw some appellation at him which we hope the enemy will take up and use as a sting or a thong. So Gideon was called Jerubbaal—literally, " Baal's antagonist ": let Baal strive, let Baal take up his own cause; Gideon is the man who has defied the gods. That was not a severe punishment for the beginning of a revolution. The name itself was taken up afterwards and sanctified. There is nothing the enemy can do that God cannot turn into happy issues.

Now came the open conflict :—

"Then all the Midianites and the Amalekites and the children of the east were gathered together, and went over, and pitched in the valley of Jezreel " (vi. 33).

They were there first. They said, They will be well off who are soonest in the field. What had Gideon to present in reply to this tremendous muster ? The story reads well at this point : " But the Spirit of the Lord came upon Gideon," and he was a thousand men in himself. Inspired, he knew no fear ; the tabernacle of the living God, he trembled not before the wind and the tempest. We need inspired men, mad men, enthusiasts, men who know not whether they are fasting or feasting, men who use the world as not abusing it, who hold every thing lightly but their trust from the living God. Gideon " blew a trumpet ; and Abi-ezer "—his little flock—" was gathered after him. And he sent messengers throughout all Manasseh "—the people of the tribe— " who also was gathered after him : and he sent messengers unto Asher "—who once proved faithless—" and unto Zebulun, and unto Naphtali "—who had won immortal fame in the battle last fought by Israel—" and they came up to meet them " (vi. 34, 35). Spiritual endowment is power. It is of no consequence how many swords the Church has if it has not the living God : " Put up again thy sword into his place : for all they that take the sword, shall perish with the sword." Christ's kingdom is not of this world : it is a kingdom of thought, feeling, love, sacrifice ; be true to that spirit, and none can stand before you.

Now Gideon became afraid again, and must therefore be encouraged by another sign from heaven. We must not blame him. He is not the less earnest that he wants to be assured that he is right. Gideon invented a little test for God :—

" Behold, I will put a fleece of wool in the floor; and if the dew be on the fleece only, and it be dry upon all the earth beside, then shall I know that thou wilt save Israel by mine hand, as thou hast said " (vi. 37).

Did God reply ?　God accommodated himself to human weakness as he has always done.　Gideon arose early in the morning, " and thrust the fleece together, and wringed the dew out of the fleece, a bowl full of water" (vi. 38).　["Wool, as a good radiator of heat, would, under ordinary conditions, receive a plentiful deposit of dew, but so would the surrounding grass and soil.　The second miracle was still more remarkable, inferior radiators receiving dew, when a better radiator, wool, remained dry."]　Gideon was half persuaded: Now, said he, if the reverse process can be completed, I shall be strong in faith, giving glory to God :—

" Let not thine anger be hot against me, and I will speak but this once : let me prove, I pray thee, but this once with the fleece; let it now be dry only upon the fleece and upon all the ground let there be dew. And God did so that night : for it was dry upon the fleece only, and there was dew on all the ground " (vi. 39, 40).

[" The double sign in connection with the fleece, which Gideon asked of God, is an illustration of a tendency in him to ask for signs : and nothing could be more ingenious, nothing more satisfactory, than the alternate wetting by dew of the fleece and of the whole ground.　Possibly he was led to use such boldness in repeated pleadings with God, by the example of Abraham's repeated requests when interceding for Sodom (Gen. xviii. 23–33).　And he may have asked for the dew first to concentrate on the fleece, then to spread out over the ground, as he saw how the grace bestowed first upon himself, was spreading out over Israel." —*Douglas.*]

We may not set these fancy tests.　They were proper enough at the time when Gideon applied them.　The day was not then so far advanced ; it was quite early morning, grey twilight, and men did not see clearly, so they asked for much assistance to their vision ; and God graciously answered them.　Even in apostolic days the freak of the lottery was tried, and we hear but little of the happy consequences which flowed from the adventure. We have nothing to do with putting tests for God now.　Why ? It would seem a natural and beautiful thing to say, as Gideon

said, If the fleece be wet, or if all the earth be wet, and the fleece
be dry, then God is with me, and the right way is open before
mine eyes. Why may we not submit God to these tests?
because the day is far advanced. This is the age of the Spirit,
the age of true spiritual or religious faith. We have now to be
guided by those inward and spiritual convictions which often
have no words for their adequate and precise expression. We
are to be students of providence. Providence itself is a succession of trials, tests, proofs. We are to see how things go,
to watch their origin, sequence, consummation. We are to get
rid of the superstition that life is a series of isolated incidents.
Instead of being right in this particular case, or that, we ourselves
are to be right, and all these things shall be regulated for us.
The man who is anxious to know merely detailed right has not
entered into the Spirit of Christ. He is a man who would keep
a book regarding himself, and separate or distribute his life into
independent lines and items. That is the Baal we must cast
down,—the Baal of being right in instances, in mere details, and
writing a little maxim-bible of our own. What, then, is the
great aim of Providence to-day? To make right *men*, to create
new and clean hearts and spirits, to make the *soul* right. Is that
represented to us in any formal, quotable words? Surely:—
" Seek ye first the kingdom of God, and his righteousness; and all
these things shall be added unto you." Expand that thought,
and what happens but this great philosophy of life, namely: Be
right in your soul, be right in your purpose, have a single eye,
do not be playing a double game; " do justly, and love mercy,
and walk humbly with thy God;" and as for the details of this
opening life, they will fall into great laws of divine Providence,
and will be ministers of grace to the trusting soul. What an
insidious sophism lurks in this thinking, namely, that if we could
have lotteries by which to test individual actions we could not go
wrong. So long as you are meddling with individual actions,
and trying to be guided by a kind of travelling time-bill, you
cannot be right. Here is the distinctive glory of Christ's religion.
"If any man be in Christ, he is a new creature: old things are
passed away; behold, all things are become new." The man
does not say, What shall I eat; what shall I drink; wherewithal
shall I be clothed; what shall I do to-morrow; and on the

second day how shall I be occupied ; and in what spirit shall I encounter such and such a possible occasion ? That is to live a little life,—to split up, and separate, and individualise, and to act cleverly, not religiously.   Life is not to be a system of scheming, managing, arranging, balancing, outwitting those who are half-blind, outrunning those who are cripples or unable to run; life is a religion, a consecration, a spiritual sacrifice, a continual living in the sight and fear and love of God ; that being granted, all the rest comes in musical sequence, everything else comes and goes by a rhythm divine in its swing and throb.   Foolish are the men who want to be right in particular instances, who desire above all things not to be outwitted on set occasions.   There was a time in human history when such desires were natural and wholly seasonable, but that time is not now ; for Christ is amongst us, and says to us : Children, be the children of your Father in heaven ; be ye holy, as your Father in heaven is holy ; be ye perfect, as your Father in heaven is perfect ; trust your Father, little flock ; be not disheartened ; live in your Father's good pleasure : seek first the kingdom of God and his righteousness, and all details will settle themselves.   Why, who would kindle a little fire in his own field to dissolve the snow, and say he will have at least a little garden there ?   Is the great snow to be broken up into patches in that way, and are we to have little summers and little forces of nature, and little clever attempts to grow something under the most discouraging circumstances ? Do not interfere with God's law in that way.   God will send a south wind and a warm sun, and the snow will flee away. There must be a great astronomic movement—a high, mighty far-reaching movement, a change of atmosphere : and that will drive back the winter, and in due time "throw a primrose on the bank in pledge of victory."   So must it be with the winter-bound heart of man.   It is not by lighting little fires here and there so as to warm great feeling, or create a momentary benevolence, or rise into a temporary ecstasy ; the Spirit of the living God must descend upon the whole man, must take possession of the heart ; and, reigning there, ruling there, working out the mystery of inspiration there, all the life shall bud and blossom, and be gracious and hospitable as summer.   This is the better plan ; **this is the grander philosophy of life.**   We do not **pronounce** judgment upon Gideon in any adverse terms; he did what he could. God smiled upon his infantile endeavours; the great day of spiritual inspiration had not then fully come. Gideon's purpose was to know whether God was with him. The purpose is eternal—the method of discovery was temporary. Let us also know whether God is with us, not in this particular case, or in that particular case, but whether God is with us in very deed within, ruling the mind, and heart, and will, and judgment of the whole soul; and then if we go downhill, it will be downhill on the highlands: even the valleys are lifted up in these great heights; and if we do stumble, we shall rise again—yea, though we fall seven times, the eighth endeavour shall bring us home. He who lives upon any other principle lives a sharper's life,— often very clever, often very skilful, a good deal may be said in defence of it as to particular instances and individual successes, but he is a charlatan, an empiric, an adventurer; he is setting traps for God, and fancy devices wherein to entangle the Eternal. The great life—the grand, true, simple life—is to be in Christ, in God, as to thought, feeling, purpose: then let the days bring with them what they may, all their bringing will be overruled and sanctified, and even our very faults shall help us in our higher education.

SELECTED NOTE.

"*Cast down the altar of Baal*" (vi. 30).—The word *ba'al*, as it signifies *lord, master*, is a generic term for *god* in many of the Syro-Arabian languages. As the idolatrous nations of that race had several gods, this word, by means of some accessory distinction, became applicable as a name to many different deities. Baal is appropriated to the chief male divinity of the Phœnicians, the principal seat of whose worship was at Tyre. The idolatrous Israelites adopted the worship of this god (almost always in conjunction with that of Ashtoreth) in the period of the Judges (ii. 13); they continued it in the reigns of Ahaz and Manasseh, kings of Judah (2 Chron. xxviii. 2; 2 Kings xxi. 3); and among the kings of Israel, especially in the reign of Ahab, who, partly through the influence of his wife, the daughter of the Sidonian king Ethbaal, appears to have made a systematic attempt to suppress the worship of God altogether, and to substitute that of Baal in its stead (1 Kings xvi 31); and in that of Hoshea (2 Kings xvii. 16), although Jehu and Jehoida once severally destroyed the temples and priesthood of the idol (2 Kings x. 18, *sq.*; xi. 18).

PRAYER.

ALMIGHTY GOD, thou hast made the sanctuary a place of explanation: within thy house we understand all that is needful for us to know. Outside of it we cannot tell what things really are; we are in the midst of tumult and strife and anger; wrath and malice and bitterness exclude thy presence, but when we come into the house of God we see in the true light, we know somewhat of thy meaning, we are privileged to behold the outworking of thy purposes, and as we look we wonder, and as we wonder we pray, and our prayer speedily becomes a song of praise, because we see that the Lord reigneth and that the end of things is in his hands. Enable us often to come to the sanctuary. Blessed be thy grace for establishing it, so that now we may say, the tabernacle of God is with men upon the earth; God's house is in the midst of our dwellings. When we come into the sanctuary may we find the spirit of the house there,—the spirit of reverence and love, the spirit that loves the truth and follows after it and will eventually establish it; and being in the spirit in thy house, may thy book appear to us in all its breadth and lustre: wide as the great heaven, brighter than the sun when he shines in his strength; and may our hearts be comforted by the messages which they most need; and if first we must be humbled and chastened, stripped and impoverished, that we may know our right condition, thou wilt not end the process there, but having shown us our blindness and nakedness and wretchedness thou wilt give us fine gold, and ointment wherewith to anoint ourselves, and truth upon truth, until the soul is filled with the riches of Christ. So let it be now and evermore. May the sanctuary be a place of elevation whence we can see afar, and a place of revelation where we can see sights let down from heaven and hear voices meant for our instruction and comfort. To the sanctuary we bring our sin. Here we leave it, because the Cross is here; we may not—need not —take it back with us; for the blood of Jesus Christ thy Son cleanseth from all sin. Here let our sin be crucified; here let our sin be pardoned.

This prayer we pray at the Cross; and we tarry at the Cross until the answer come. Amen.

Judges vi.-viii.

GIDEON.—(*Continued.*)

THERE are critical words in every life, and critical moments. Everything seems to happen all at once,—a curious sense of suddenness affecting the whole life. The word "then," with which the first verse of the seventh chapter opens, marks a critical point of time. How easily the word is written; and how easily said; but all Gideon's life seemed crowded into that ardent moment. So it is with our own lives. We crush the whole life into one day. Or we seem to see for what our whole life has been preparing by the light which shines upon one special moment. The time of battle had come; but the time of battle came in the case of Jerubbaal, as we have seen, after long and singular preparation. All that is happening should be regarded as of the nature of preparation. We should ask ourselves now and again, even amid the monotony of life, What is the meaning of this rest? What is the point of this delay? God always has a purpose, and we ought to find it. Why all this schooling, this long and weary study, this knocking night and day at Wisdom's door? These intellectual inquiries touch the very region of prayer. What is the meaning of all these providences? In all these undulating lines of life read the philosophy and purpose of heaven regarding human service and destiny. Why these sharp trials, these rains of sorrow, these rivers of grief? Why these bereavements, losses, deprivations, disappointments, surprises? Has the tale no end? Is there no point of fire, no final climax? Is it all tumult, change, gain, loss, pleasure, pain,—on and on, and the last pain the greatest,—the pain of saying farewell before dropping into eternal silence? This cannot be. The question, then, should come to every man when he is seeing visions, hearing voices he never heard before, receiving unexpected and startling visits, What is the meaning of it all? This means action: presently the story will open upon the battle chapter. Surely some of us have had preparation enough. Long since we ought to have been in the thick of the fight. Why all this book-reading? Is there room in the crowded memory for one more volume? Surely we may say to some students, Why continue the bent head, the midnight lamp, the vigil out of season? What is the meaning of all this? The battle waits, or the battle might now begin: the world might turn round and ask, Are you not ready now to speak some gospel word, or at least look some look of hope, lifting upon our weariness eyes that might be as revelations and encouragements. It is weary work to watch how long some men are in putting on their armour. It tires the soul to see how long some men

are in whetting the sickle, whilst the white harvest almost
withers because of their unaccountable, if not criminal, delay.
The critical morning dawned upon the life of Gideon. He took
up his new name, having no objection to it. When his fellow-
citizens called him Jerubbaal, he said, in effect : So be it :
that name expresses my relation to the false god exactly,—
namely : " Let Baal strive ; " or " Let me be Baal's antagonist : "
I yoke a bullock to the god, and drag him down ; now let my
father's advice be accepted, and let Baal defend his own case. It
is wonderful to notice how many of these Old Testament people
take their new name with fine grace, as if with deep sense of
the fitness of the larger appellation. We, too, are called upon to
pass into new names, or new categories : have we done so ?
Have we been called Christians ? Or are we hiding the new
faith under the old name, so that the people know not that a
change has taken place in our title ? " Beloved, now are we the
sons of God." Yet some of us have hardly dared to claim and
wear the name. If to some there belongs a name of controversy,
battle, antagonism, take it up : it suits the times ; the world
wants warriors. Take the name which God gives you, or which
is brought to bear upon you by the order of his providence.
When does God give a less name than the old one ? He adds a
syllable, and thereby adds a destiny : he changes one letter, first
or last, and therein changes the course of a lifetime. " Jerubbaal,
who is Gideon," took his place at the head of his people, " rose
up early." When did the great worker ever rise up late ?
Early-rising is a necessity of divine vocation. There need be
no mechanical arrangement about it. The work is terrific, and
the worker is straitened until it be accomplished. There is an
impatience that is inspired. Gideon and his people " pitched
beside the well of Harod,"—that is, beside the well of " trembling," beside the well of " fear." It is well to begin at that
point. Many a man who has begun his work nervously has
turned out at the end to be quite a giant. Take heart ; you
are indeed now at the well of Harod,—at the waters of fear and
trembling,—but if you are there on God's business, have no vital
fear ; you may shake off all fear and pray in the church as a child
might pray at home, and fight in the field as consciously called
of God to do the work of battle. We must not pour contempt

upon men who are nervous, timid, hesitant in their first
speech, afraid to pray their first audible prayer. History
ought to have taught us a good deal upon such matters. Men
who have begun thus have ended in great renown. Everything
depends upon our spirit, upon our reliance upon the living God,
upon our knowing that the work is not ours but the Lord's.

This would seem to have been the course of the divine
thought, for " the Lord said unto Gideon, The people that are with
thee are too many." They are but thirty-two thousand in all ;
yet they are too many. But how can they be too many, for the
Midianites are a hundred and thirty-five thousand strong ? That,
said God, is making a human calculation. We get wrong by
applying human arithmetic to divine decrees ; or we get wrong
by trying to measure God's eternity by the tape of our time. He
was an inspired man who invented the phrase " for ever and
ever." That is the point at which time gives up the race, falls
down dead, and lets eternity stand in its nameless mystery. But
to-day we will play the arithmetician, and deal in figures and
tables and returns audited and well avouched. When will we,
can we, learn that all numbering is with the Lord, and that
because the battle is his he will fight it as it pleases him ? Israel
would make a wrong use of numbers, as most men do. Israel
would say, " Mine own hand hath saved me : I was thirty-two
thousand strong on that memorable day, and that was force
enough to slay the Midianitish power." God will stain the pride
of all glory. God will not allow any flesh to glory in his presence.
If we are gospel preachers, " we have this treasure in earthen
vessels, that the excellency of the power may be of God, and not
of us." Human ambition must be restrained.

The so-called law of cause and effect, which has victimised so
many men in the spiritual universe, must be upset and contemned. When the Church comes into this temper we shall hear
news of victory : God will surprise his trustful Church with
tidings of great joy. Two-and-twenty thousand men returned
unto their houses because they were fearful and afraid. Do not
contemn this cowardice, for it is the very colour and temper of
our own time. Many men are bold the day after the battle;

many have *nearly* said the word of courage, the word of just reproof. Are not the greatest numbers most cowardly ? In a sense this is true. If they could fight as a crowd they would be partially courageous : but real fight comes to man by man, assault and answer. So two-and-twenty thousand men said, We had better continue in oppression, in slavery, in loss, than challenge these unequal odds. But the Lord said, " The people are yet too many ; " and the number was reduced to three hundred men by a very curious and interesting test, namely, the different methods in which water was taken. Are there no such tests now ? We suppose that this test has passed away and settled in venerable history, to be occasionally exhumed and wondered about : the particular instance itself may no longer be literally repeated, but the principle that is in it is the principle which is operating in the very men who deny the accuracy of the literal incident itself. Men are chosen now by curious signs. We do not know how we are chosen to any particular work ; but it may be found incidentally that some little unexpected circumstance, of which we took no note or heed, determined our being where we are. Men who want servants, lieutenants, allies, co-operative assistants, are looking round ; the people upon whom they are looking may be unaware of the critical inspection, but it is proceeding nevertheless. Those who are looking on say, He walks lazily, his gait is lacking in energy ; he will never do for my particular work. Or : See how he walks ; what fire there is in him ; every action is half a battle ; he needs but to be put in the right circumstances, and he will turn out a satisfactory man ; or : He talks too much ; his speech is without pith or regard to the number of its words ; he patters and gossips and is cursed with a detestable fluency : listen ; he never ceases, he never pauses, he evidently loves to hear himself chatter,—he will never do. Or : He is an excellent listener ; he does not commit himself : observe, he never plunges into anything that he cannot fully grasp and comprehend ; he looks more than he speaks ; not a word escapes that listener : when he does speak there is marrow in his speech ; he is young, but he will get over that disadvantage ; he shapes well already. This process is going on through all society. Men are noting one another ; seeing whether they lie down upon the ground and devour the water, or whether, being men in wise haste and under self-control, they lap it, and pass on. The little local incident has changed, but the principle of curious and even eccentric election is operating in all life, and the men who deny the Bible live over again its most curious instances.

Gideon was one of those men who require continual encouragement. It was not enough to say to him once for all, " I will be with thee ; " he did not doubt the divine presence : but see how Israel had been weakened, impoverished, crushed, these last seven years by the invasion of the Midianites ; see how they dare not thresh their corn in the open field or accessible winepress, but had to beat it out in the concealment of the crags and rocks ; observe how Israel had to listen and look to assure himself that no Midianite was looking on before he rubbed out his handful of corn and got it ready for the baking ;—then say if a man could instantly become a great religious and courageous character ; and then see how loving it was of God to deal with him according to his weakness, to encourage him, little by little to lead him on. Why, this is the Christly spirit : he will not break the bruised reed, nor quench the smoking flax ; he has the tongue of the learned, and can speak a word in season to him that is weary ; he will not urge his omnipotence against our nothingness, but will accommodate his approach, and breathe upon us quietly, and send to our sinking spirits a still small voice. So Gideon needed to be encouraged again. The Lord said to him : I have made a man down in the Midianitish camp dream a curious dream ; I will so operate upon him that he will begin to talk as it were in a half-sleep : go down and listen. Gideon looked afraid ; the Lord noticed the blanched face and said: If thou fear to go down alone, go thou with Phurah thy servant ; two may be better than one. This is an anticipation of the time when the Lord sent out his servants " by two and two." Gideon took heart when he was allowed to take a servant with him.

"Then went he down with Phurah his servant unto the outside of the armed [the same word is rendered *harnessed* in Exodus xiii. 18. The probable meaning is *arrayed in divisions*] men that were in the host. And the Midianites and the Amalekites and all the children of the east lay along in the valley like grasshoppers [locusts. Compare Numbers xxii. 4, 5] for multitude; and their camels were without number, as the sand by the sea side for multitude " (vii. 11-12).

When Gideon came near a man told a dream to his neighbour; he said, " Behold, I dreamed a dream, and, lo, a cake of barley bread "—such bread as Israel has been reduced to, the bread of poverty—" tumbled into the host of Midian, and came unto a tent, and smote it that it fell, and overturned it, that the tent lay along." It is an extraordinary dream; what is the meaning of it ? The other man had the faculty of interpretation; he said, " This is nothing else save the sword of Gideon the son of Joash, a man of Israel." Once let the enemy have within him the fear that the opposing host will succeed, and the battle is won. Battles are lost and won in the soul. The Church has feared, and the Church has lost.

The battle opened. Israel, represented by three hundred men, did according to the instructions of Gideon :—" When I blow with a trumpet, I and all that are with me, then blow ye the trumpets also on every side of all the camp, and say, The sword of the Lord, and of Gideon,"—and that will correspond in instructive harmony with the dream which I have overheard; the name of Gideon has entered into the speech of the Midianites; associate that name with this great battle, and say, " The sword of the Lord, and of Gideon." So the battle opened. " And the three companies blew the trumpets, and brake the pitchers, and held the lamps in their left hands, and the trumpets in their right hands to blow withal : and they cried, The sword of the Lord, and of Gideon ; " and as the torches were shaken in the air, for they were torches rather than what we understand as lamps, and as the sound came from every quarter at once, Midian was afraid, and Midian was destroyed. Make the most of yourselves. You are but three hundred, but symbolically you are all heaven. This manner of assaulting the enemy is no dramatic manner, no pretence or affectation ; this is a battle which is being fought on divine principles : therefore, if three hundred men seem to be three millions, they *are* such, multiplied by themselves and multiplied by infinity in their symbolical and representative capacity.

Gideon took princes that day, even " Oreb and Zeeb," the

Raven and the Wolf. The heads of the raven and the wolf were
brought to Gideon on the other side Jordan,—see him with the
one in one hand and the other in the other. It was an old and
barbarous plan to bring the head of the enemy to the hand of
the conqueror. It is not a thing to be reproduced or counten-
anced by Christanised civilisation ; but it was the ancient mode
of warfare, and must be judged by the morality of the age.
This is typical. "Who is this that cometh from Edom, with
dyed garments from Bozrah ? this that is glorious in his apparel,
travelling in the greatness of his strength ? " He has trodden
the winepress alone. He is mighty to save ; he is mighty also
to destroy. " His enemies will I clothe with shame : but upon
himself shall his crown flourish." In this faith all Christians
live and work, serve and suffer, and, blessed be God, the inspiration is in us also. Men call themselves by symbolical names, as
Midian was called " the Raven," but God's hand is in the heavens,
and the air shall be cleansed of his enemies :—" the Wolf," but
God's eyes are in the forest and the jungle and the wilderness,
and he will destroy the ravenous beast. Men have called
themselves by ideal and typical names, as the " Gracchi "—the
jackdaws. We respect them under the name of the Gracchi,
because we do not know what it means, but when it is understood that the interpretation thereof is " jackdaws " we feel that
we ourselves might encounter them in battle. The Aquilini
—the eagles. So our great warriors have called themselves
bull, and wolf, and lion. All these names have histories behind
them ; but we can never fight with names only : they must
represent realities, spiritual inspirations, moral convictions,
gospels we have died for, heavens we have seized with crucified
hands ; then the battle will go the right way. Enter the fight
and always turn your eyes to the blood-stained banner on which
is written, as with pen of lightning, The battle is not yours, but
God's. Fighting under that banner and in its spirit, the fight can
have but one end—grand, complete, eternal victory.

PRAYER.

ALMIGHTY GOD, evermore be with us; evermore give us the bread of life: evermore keep us within the hollow of thy hand. We have learned to distrust ourselves. We have hewn out to ourselves cisterns, but have found them to be broken cisterns that could hold no water. We have thought to plant gardens and sow fields of our own, and behold thou hast withheld thy sun, and all our efforts have perished in darkness. So now, if thou wilt not disdain so mean an offering, we would, under the drawing of a power not our own turn to thy grace, and offer ourselves in sacrifice unto thee: do thou now accept the oblation and give us answers from heaven. We thought our life would never end, and behold we have come to know that it is but a breath in our nostrils. We said of our strength, It is enduring, and cannot fail; and behold, whilst the boast was upon our lips our juice was dried up and there was no sap in all the life. We all do fade as a leaf. We are but as the wind, blowing for a little time: or a vapour dying upon the breeze. We cannot tell what we are, for there is no language that can set forth our poverty, and feebleness, and littleness; yet, when we come to know thy Son Jesus Christ our Saviour, and by living faith in him enter into the mystery of his being, then are we the sons of God, and it doth not yet appear what we shall be, but our hope is that we shall be like our Saviour, for we shall see him as he is. So we are little, and great; worthless, yet all-worthy; children of time, yet sons of immortality. Help us to understand somewhat of this mystery, to accept it, to walk in its spirit, to pray mightily unto God that we may grow in all purity, nobleness, and holy power. Thy hand has been outstretched to us in all goodness; no good thing hast thou withheld from us. If we judge by thy rain we cannot tell the just from the unjust; if we judge by thy sunshine we know not the difference between the good and the evil: for thou art kind unto all, and thy tender mercies are over all thy works; the mercy of the Lord endureth for ever, and to his love there is no measure. Bless the Lord, O my soul, and all that is within me, bless his holy name. We confess our sins, and mourn them with bitterest lamentation, and seek thy pardon at the cross. God forbid that we should glory, save in the cross of our Lord Jesus Christ: it is the hope of the sinner; it is the way to heaven; it is the very glory of the divine love. Help us to handle our life with great sagacity, understanding the mystery of it as revealed in thy holy book; may we see its littleness, yet its infinite possibilities; may we judge between that which is for a moment and that which is for ever; as wise builders, may we build upon the rock and not upon the sand; may it be found at last that through apparent folly we have been practising the most solid wisdom, and though

men have imagined that we had forgotten that which is temporal, yet by
seeking first the kingdom of God and his righteousness, all the lower worlds
and their meaner concerns have been put under our dominion. We give
one another to thee. We would be wedded unto the Christ of God; we
would serve him with all faithfulness, love, sincerity, and hopefulness : may
he accept our offering. We bless thee for all good men, whose word is
their bond, whose signature is never forsworn, who know what is righteous
and do it at the cost of life itself. We thank thee for all patience, as shown
in the house, in the business, in the church, in every sphere of life—divine
patience, motherly, womanly, Godlike. We ask thee to be with us in all our
special troubles and turn them into special joys : may our losses be the
beginning of our gains, and through our failing health may we see the
meaning of immortality. Guide the blind; save the helpless; give speech
unto the silent; and be the friend of the friendless. Thus may we live in
thy fear, in thy Spirit, in thy love, triumphing over life, time, space, death,
already knowing that our citizenship is in heaven. Amen.

Judges vi.-viii.

GIDEON.—(*Continued.*)

I N the eighth chapter we have quite a gallery of portraits. We
may call these allusions to character, aspects, rather than full
delineations. Unless we look very vigilantly we shall miss a
good deal of the colour and meaning of this panorama, for the
action is extremely rapid. You find a character in a line; a
history in a sentence ; the whole man almost in one trembling
or urgent tone. Everything in this chapter is of the nature of
condensation. More matter could not be put into this space.
Hardly a word could be omitted without interfering with the
solid integrity of the composition. He who built this chapter
was a master-builder. What fire there is in it ; what anger ;
yea, what zeal ; what delay inspired by impatience ! thus constituting an almost contradiction in terms. Here is a man too
impatient to do what he wants to do at the moment, but he says,
I will do it by-and-by ; when the greater purpose is accomplished
the smaller design shall be fulfilled. But we anticipate. Let
us travel the road step by step.

Take Gideon's answer to Ephraim as showing that not only
was Gideon a great soldier but a great man. That is the secret
of all official greatness—namely, greatness of manhood. There
can be no great officer in any sense except as expressive of a

reserve of strength, a great manhood. **There can** be no great soldier, great statesman, great preacher, great business man, without there being behind all that is official and visible a great wealth of nature, a great fulness of life. The men of Ephraim did chide sharply with Gideon, saying, "Why hast thou served us thus, that thou calledst us not, when thou wentest to fight with the Midianites?" We shall see presently that Ephraim was both a bully and a coward. He is proud of having descended from Joseph, and proud of being connected with the illustrious Joshua; but in himself there was more foam than ocean, there was more splutter than divine energy. Ephraim was always finding that he had been left out in the cold. In a page or two we shall see that he met with the man who had the right answer to that foolish self-idolatry. Gideon will reply softly and gently, but Ephraim shall not always have it thus; he will ask this very question again of another man, and we shall see how that sterner man will answer him. Ephraim represents the kind of man who comes in after the battle has been turned to victory and says what he would have done if he had been invited. Ephraim represents the man who is always a day after the fair, a day after the battle,—he who comes in when the sun of prosperity is shining and says that if only he had had an invitation he would have been the first subscriber to the fund, the most liberal supporter of the movement, the most energetic member of the faith. Presently he will tell Jephthah that, and Jephthah will answer him otherwise than Gideon replied. It was well that Gideon,—whose name means "Hewer," —should show that he was as gifted in the quality of self-control as were his three hundred followers. His answer is intellectually energetic, and in it—far away in it—is just a little suggestion of irony and the kind of flattery which has a sting in it. It was a wonderful answer. Haughty, proud Ephraim apparently could have crushed the Hewer and his three hundred men; so Gideon said: What have I now done in comparison with you? think how little I am! Why, you mis-spend your anger in being at all annoyed by anything that was in my power to do. Is not the gleaning of the grapes of Ephraim better than all the vintage of the house to which I belong? the few odd grapes you leave on the vine, are they not of more value than all the grapes that ever

cluster on the vines of Abi-ezer? It was well to put the inquiry
so. There is a skilful use of interrogation. The form of
question has been adapted to strange uses. Gideon reminded
Ephraim of what had been done, though even that was only
done incidentally. Then he asks the other question: And what
was I able to do in comparison with you? You are such a
great people; if I had asked you to join in a war you might
have contemned so insignificant a creature; look how tall you
are, and how scarcely visible I am! "Then their anger was
abated," showing that it was a bully's anger, and not a hero's.
Their anger was abated when they were flattered. Yet this is
the soft answer that turneth away wrath. The question well-
planted, quite a thorn of a question, yea, a sharp sting; yet
Ephraim, being of the mean quality he was, accepted the flattery
and felt not the reproach. We almost long for Ephraim to come
into contact with the other kind of man. Ephraim finding how
this movement ended will try it again. Ephraim looked so well.
What he would have done if he had only been invited! We wait
for the man who can see through his falsehood and answer it
with slaughter.

Was Gideon, then, soft and foolish? Has he lost the pith of
his character? Take his treatment of the men of Succoth.
Gideon asked that they would give loaves of bread unto the
people that followed him, "For," said he, "they be faint." He
seemed to ask for the people and not for himself: I am pursuing after kings—give the people loaves of bread that they may
be able to keep up with me in this fierce haste. The princes of
Succoth took advantage of weary men. There are cruel hearts
that can take advantage of the hunger of other men—hearts that
can say, Now is our opportunity; whilst they lack bread and are
suffering from hunger, now we can vaunt it over them, now we
can tread upon them. The princes of Succoth said, Your victory
is not yet complete; you have to fight Zebah and Zalmunna
before you can say the battle is ended; when Zebah and Zalmunna are in thy hands, then come, and we will give you bread
enough; but do not suppose that you have found those whom
you are only pursuing. Gideon was instantly fed with a nutriment that made him strong; forgetting his weariness, he said,

"When the Lord hath delivered Zebah and Zalmunna into mine hand, then I will tear your flesh with the thorns of the wilderness and with briers." And he made the same answer to the men of Penuel : "When I come again in peace, I will break down this tower." So we must not argue that because a man gives a civil answer to a violent assault, therefore he is of mean quality, and is craven in spirit, and afraid of that which is high and mighty. The quiet answer is an illustration of self-control ; the soft reply, the gracious retort, shows that the heart is trusting in the living God, and not in any accidental strength : they who dwell in the tower of heaven can speak quietly from the window to those who are looking up and who are expressing dislike far down at the base. In quietness possess your souls, and in sweet patience. Never answer fury with fury. The princes of Succoth and the men of Penuel were cold in their cruelty, mocking in their hostility ; they were not in red-hot anger, but they were taking advantage of temporary weakness. Such persons were answered with fire red-hot. Gideon was thus a manifold character : a quiet man, few in words, threshing out his corn behind the rock that no Midianite might see him, quietly proceeding about his domestic affairs ; suddenly taking fire when the touch from heaven came upon him, and a voice other than human told him he was a "man of valour," right mighty in battle, but most suave and gentle and gracious in the presence of unreasonable men, who did chide with him sharply for what they supposed to be an omission of duty or a breach of courtesy ; then flaming up again into the very divinest anger because men refused weak soldiers bread, and mocked pursuers because they appeared to be unable to complete the journey. "I will tear your flesh ; " literally, I will thresh your flesh, as he had been found by the prophet and the angel threshing his corn ; "I will break down this tower," and those who are in it must take the consequences of its overthrow.

Was Gideon selfishly ambitious ? To this inquiry there is a sublime reply. When the men of Israel saw the prowess of Gideon they said, "Rule thou over us, both thou, and thy son, and thy son's son also : for thou hast delivered us from the hand of Midian" (viii. 22). That was his opportunity. All great

prophets and soldiers have had such chances; John the Baptist
had when he was asked if he was "that prophet." Then, everything depended upon his answer; and he answered, "I am not."
The people would have taken Jesus and made him a king "by
force," but he stood back from the mob and disdained their
crown. "And Gideon said unto them, I will not rule over you,
neither shall my son rule over you: the Lord shall rule over
you" (viii. 23). There is the real quality of the man. Probe
him where you will, you find his motive to be inspired by a
consciousness of God's sovereignty and control. Gideon might
have been a king, but was not; and, because he was not, he
really was. There are many kingships, some crowned, some
uncrowned; some material, imperial; some spiritual, intellectual, moral: the crown is *in* the man rather than upon him;
if only upon him, the wind may blow it off, or some fool's hand
may suddenly dash it to the ground. Gideon believed in what
is known as the Theocracy,—that is, the reign of God,—God's
kingship of Israel, God's headship of the Church, God's defence
of all faith, truth, righteousness. It is not every man who can
start a victorious war so nobly. Gideon lost nothing in the fight,
but gained all things. So may we. Life is a battle. Every day
has its controversy, its sharp tug, its fierce wrestling, its great
conflict—a conflict within or without; a temptation addressed to
the soul, or a fury assailing the estate. How are we to come out
of the great combat; to bring out of the onslaught a clear character,
a clean heart, a right spirit, a motive undamaged, and a probity
unstained?—that we may so come out of the clash of arms and
the spiritual assault should be our continual prayer. "Take
unto you the whole armour of God, that ye may be able to
withstand in the evil day, and having done all to stand." Stand
therefore, panoplied from head to foot, the left hand as the right,
and the eyes fixed now on God, now on the foe.

Was Gideon, then, perfect? Is he by all these just encomiums
removed from competition and enshrined in altitudes absolutely
inaccessible? Is he an historical figure to be almost worshipped?
Is he bone of our bone, flesh of our flesh, snared by the same
gins and traps, and falling now and again under the same
blandishments? The perfect man, whom we feel to be so per-

fect as to lose touch with our humanity, really would do us more harm than good. Gideon was no perfect man. He had a vulnerable heel ; there was a bruise upon him which showed him to be mortal. Having had the offer of the crown and the throne and the rulership that was to be hereditary, Gideon said, No, but " I would desire a request of you." What is that ? said Israel cheerfully. I would request " that ye would give me every man the earrings of his prey " (for they had golden earrings, because they were Ishmaelites). Gideon could make some use of these little crescent-shaped ornaments. " And they answered, We will willingly give them. And they spread a garment "—perhaps the very overcoat that Gideon himself wore—" and did cast therein every man the earrings of his prey. And the weight of the golden earrings that he requested was a thousand and seven hundred shekels of gold ; " and, being in the giving mood, they said, Give him " ornaments, and collars, and purple raiment that was on the kings of Midian," and add to the store " the chains that were about their camels' necks." We do not blame them. They were royal-hearted in their liberality ; therefore they gave with both hands. Gideon had but to make his mind known, and the people who followed him instantly responded with abounding, yea, with redundant generosity. Wherein, then, was the littleness of Gideon or his imperfectness ? It was in the use which he made of the golden store : " Gideon made an ephod thereof, and put it in his city, even in Ophrah : and all Israel went thither and whoring after it "—lusting after it, desiring to make an idol of it and worship it—" which thing became a snare unto Gideon, and to his house " (viii. 27). We did not expect this. Yet we might have expected it had we studied human nature closely. The very man who pulls down one idol sets up another. Gideon had an eye for colour. He liked the sleeveless coat of the priest. He noted its beautiful structure, its marvellous adornment, its oracular gems ; and he was minded to make an ephod of all the gifts the people had given. This ephod became an idol, a charm, an amulet. It was looked at as if the very spirit of Gideon was in it. He who disestablished the national idol set up an ephod of his own ! Alas for human inconsistency ! The same Gideon, the man who took one of the bullocks and yoked it to Baal and dragged down the helpless god manufactures a little idol of his own! It was a shame; and yet it seems to be partly well, for now we can join Gideon at the point of his imperfection; perhaps we can get further into his character, and pray with as intense an energy, and grasp the eternal with as strong a faith. Take the man in the entirety of his character, in the sum-total of his being, and not in points and phases. Is it not so with all great reformers? The men who can finance the affairs of Europe can very seldom pay their own private accounts! The great and mighty reformers who could reconstruct the universe sometimes omit to wash their own hands! Are we not all human? Is it not perfectly possible to be both great and small—to have dragged down a god and to have set up an ephod?

Now surely Israel will be good. Israel has had schooling enough, and the time has now come when Israel will take up the policy of good behaviour, and be honest and true evermore. "Gideon the son of Joash died in a good old age, and was buried in the sepulchre of Joash his father, in Ophrah of the Abi-ezrites" (viii. 32). Now Israel will remember the old man's grave, and never be insincere or faithless any more. The thirty-fourth verse will disillusion us: "And the children of Israel remembered not the Lord their God, who had delivered them out of the hands of all their enemies on every side." Well, they may have gone down theologically, but still they are men. Agnostics claim to be men, and honourable men. History has never been very much on the side of those persons who imagine that theology can be given up and yet morality retained. We are bound to accept the evidence of the ages. What was the case of the children of Israel? They "remembered not the Lord their God," but they remembered Gideon. They will be kind to his children. They will say, We may have changed our theological views, but we are still men; we may have left the church, but we are still honourable citizens. The thirty-fifth verse will disenchant us: "Neither shewed they kindness to the house of Jerubbaal, namely, Gideon, according to all the goodness which he had shewed unto Israel." The retirement from the soundly religious point of view is accompanied by lapses of another kind. A man cannot close the Bible and say,

Though I have abandoned that book, yet I am as honourable and true and pure and good as I ever was. If so, then history has been inverted ; the facts of the centuries have been proved to be false. A man cannot give up prayer, and give his attention in any profound and enduring sense to the culture of a noble life. A man cannot love his neighbour until he has loved his God. There is logic in the sequence of the commandments : the first, "Thou shalt love the Lord thy God ;" the second, "and thy neighbour as thyself." It is a very dangerous thing for any of us to attempt to-day, in the face of so vast a body of historical evidence, to say that we will give up the Church, the sanctuary, the altar, the Bible, and be as good as we ever were. It is like the train saying, We will give up the engine, and travel just as easily and swiftly as we ever did. It is like the spring flower saying, I will give up the sun, and be as beautiful, delicate, and fragrant as before. It is like the body saying, I will stop the pendulum of the heart, and be as vigorous, strong, and energetic as I ever was. Do not attempt the risk ; do not rush upon the mad adventure. The stream can only run in proportion as the fountain is filled and flowing ; the earth is nothing of itself, but, being attached to the sun, being a little tiny servant in the great astronomic household, it swings on usefully, and yields us enough for the body. Said Christ, "I am the vine, ye are the branches." "As the branch cannot bear fruit of itself, except it abide in the vine ; no more can ye, except ye abide in me." "Abide in me, and I in you." "He that abideth in me, and I in him, the same bringeth forth much fruit : for without me ye can do nothing."

Judges vi.-viii.

GIDEON.

(*A Varied Treatment.*)

"And the children of Israel did evil in the sight of the Lord: and the Lord delivered them into the hand of Midian seven years" (vi. 1).

GOD punishes indirectly as well as directly. He has agents —strange, rude servants of his, who unconsciously do his will. He can turn the wrath of man as it doth please him. According to the text it hath pleased God sometimes to punish man by man. Instead of calling Israel up into a mountain apart, and there with some great scourge chastising Israel for iniquity, he chooses to hand over his people to the rod of the tyrant; he allows Midian for seven years to torment Israel. We can punish one another. We do not know always what we are doing; sometimes in our apparent lawlessness and riotousness we are actually carrying out some divine decree, and God has chosen us, in the very intensity of our madness, to do some terrible thing for him, that some side or other of his holy government may be fully vindicated.

"And the hand of Midian prevailed against Israel: and because of the Midianites the children of Israel made them the dens which are in the mountains, and caves, and strong holds" (vi. 2).

If we had looked at the dens, and caves, and strongholds, we should have said: "Some wild beasts have made these; we see the marks of their great paws; see how they have torn the mountains and made themselves beds and chambers in the strongholds." So rudely and mistakenly do we interpret some things. The rough homes, these poor hiding places, that the wind could get at so fiercely, and the storm could rage in, were made by men. They who ought to have made the Most High their refuge, who ought to have made God himself their sanctuary, dug in the earth for a home and sought shelter among the rocks, when they might have rested in the secret places of heaven. We are doing every day—in so far as we are doing wrong—very much of the same thing. We are seeking to ourselves hiding places, we are planning for our own security, we have taken the defence of our life into our own hands, and we have said to money, "Thou shalt be my sanctuary;" to the poor power of our own arm, "Thou shalt be my defence," and we have said with pagan Ajax to his sword, "Thou art my God." Alas! poor man, thou hast been burrowing in the dust, scratching in the mud, hollowing out the rocks for a resting place, when God has asked thee to find security in his own power, quietude in his own peace, amplitude and beautifulness of home in his own infinite love. Think of a man tearing the mountains to pieces that he might get security from an enemy; think of a man tearing the rocks out of their places that he might hide himself from some storm of human fury! To such straits men are driven. Oh, that in being so driven they might catch some notion of the great moral purpose which is being worked out even by their torment and homelessness!

"And Israel was greatly impoverished because of the Midianites" (vi. 6).

Thus God gets at men through various means. The Midianites came out and spoiled the fields of the Israelites. The camels of the Midianites were without number; they entered the land to destroy it. Wheresoever they laid their hand they crushed the hope of Israel. Has God a way into our life, then, through corn and grass? Has he a way to chastise us through the medium of our business? Can he turn a client away and send a customer in another direction, and blind a man whilst he is counting his money? And can he so arrange things that prosperity shall crumble into adversity, and a dense darkness shall settle upon the brightness of prosperity? This is God's way of working. He gets at men through their skin; he smites them with leprosy that they may learn to pray; he curses their bread that they may cry out for the better life; he drops poison into their water that they may learn that they have committed two evils—they have forsaken him, the fountain of living water, and have hewn out unto themselves cisterns, broken cisterns, that can hold no water. These things should bring us to study, to reflection, to inquiry. Why has this adversity come upon me? Why do men actually pine and die? Is there not a cause? Israel cried unto the Lord, and the

Lord sent a man amongst them, to tell them exactly how the whole thing had happened. How did the man proceed? He proceeded to recall history. God always challenges his doings to mankind in the past. God reads the book of history, and says, "See what I did for you, where I found you, how I delivered you, how I interposed for you in the hour of extremity; see how, by a mighty hand and outstretched arm, I wrought out this whole salvation for you, and no sooner did I recover you to life and to hope, than you turned your backs upon me, and stopped your ears with your fingers, and your hearts went astray from my throne." There is, then, a moral explanation of this whole thing that we call difficulty, or pain, or discipline, disappointment, sorrow, and death. "Ye obeyed not my voice." That is the explanation of it all. The explanation of death, pain, poverty, homelessness, friendlessness, sorrow of every degree, is to be found in the fact, that we have disobeyed the voice of God. There has been the moral lapse, the great spiritual slip; the heart has not retained its integrity, and we have got wrong at the centre, and having become disorganised there, all the outwardness of life has gone off into confusion and riot and darkness, and God has justly vindicated himself by a multitude of pains and penalties, keen distresses and intolerable agonies, all of which are the servants of his righteous and gracious will. How long can God set himself against the cries of the heart of his people? Not long. Israel cried unto the Lord! Did the Lord remove himself ten thousand miles further into the depth of the great solitude that is above? No. He is full of compassion, he is tender in mercy, he is gentle in spirit. When Israel cried God came. Though he might have said, "No," yet he came—for God is love. He knoweth our frame, he remembereth that we are dust. "As I live, saith the Lord, I have no pleasure in the death of the wicked." "Turn ye, turn ye, why will ye die?" is the utterance of his expostulating hope and love. So when Israel cried unto the Lord, the Lord inclined his ear, and heard the cry of pain and the prayer of want.

Then comes a most beautiful arrangement: Gideon was threshing wheat, and as he was pursuing his business the angel of the Lord appeared unto him and said, "The Lord is with thee, thou mighty man of valour." God answers the prayers of the many by touching the life of one. As God had tormented man by man, so God will redeem man by man. This is a great mystery; but it is a mystery of love, it is a secret of the divine education of the world. As God did not take Israel apart into the wilderness, or to the top of a mountain and there scourge him with his own hand, so when he comes to deliver, he will make arrangements which show that in all his government of mankind he proceeds upon the principle of mediation; he saves us by making us to one another instruments of salvation. He blesses man by man, he redeems man by man,—the Son of man is come to seek and to save that which was lost. What was Gideon doing? Threshing wheat. It seems a long way to us—because we will look at things only in their outward relationship—from threshing wheat to the command of a delivering army. It is a long way, if we measure the thing superficially and externally. But to God it is all one, whether you are blacking a shoe or studying a star; whether you are threshing your father's wheat when he had many servants and might have sent one of them to thresh it, or whether you are wearing the crown of God's empire. He says to a man, "A thousand men can plough that furrow, but one only here and there can do the work which I have for thee to do. Come away from the sycamore tree; come away from the receipt of custom." God calls men by his great and wondrous word from one duty to another. All duties, humble and lofty, obscure and imposing, stand equal before God, if so be we have a servant's spirit and a son's love. My friend, there is a call comes to you through your business every day. When you are threshing your wheat, God speaks to you; when you are counting your money, an angel finds you. When God wants a man he knows exactly where to find him. So let me rest content in my sphere. Why should I be chafing myself? Why should I be complaining of the iron bars that cage me in? If God wants me to do some greater work, he knows where I am, and what I can do, and what I am capable of attempting, and at his own time and in his own way he will come for me and promote me to rulership and empire. If I seize that principle, I am strong; I have repose, I have quietude; but if I let go that, I find I am the victim of everything that may happen; the Bible is a chapter of accidents, and verily it is the Bible of a fool!

So Gideon, startled at his work by the presence of an angel, said he did not see how God could be with Israel.

"If the Lord be with us, why then is all this befallen us? and where be all his miracles which our fathers told us of, saying, Did not the Lord bring us up from Egypt? but now the Lord hath forsaken us, and delivered us into the hands of the Midianites" (vi. 13).

Gideon approached the proposition of the angel very cautiously. He said, "If thou art an angel of the Lord, give me some proof of thine identity as such." He put God to the test. He was so startled by the revelation of God, that he was to be the deliverer of Israel, that he proposed test after test. He was a cautious man. Let us beware lest our caution be mere pedantry, and lest it degenerate into sophism. It is right to be cautious. Make sure, in the first instance, and then, having made your ground secure, proceed, and the gates of hell shall not prevail against you. But Gideon, having put the angel to the test, was in his turn put to the test. The angel told Gideon that he was to do a work at home. The idol had been worshipped by Israel, and now the idol was to be torn down. The angel said unto him, "Take thy father's young bullock, even the second bullock, of seven years old, and throw down the altar of Baal that thy father hath, and cut down the grove that is by it : and build an altar unto the Lord thy God upon the top of this rock, in the ordered place, and take the second bullock, and offer a burnt sacrifice with the wood of the grove that is by it" (vi. 25, 26). What was the meaning of all this? "Gideon, you must be tested." He who would make great revolutions must begin at home ; he who would go out and strike a foreign enemy must begin reformation within his own circle. If you are going to fight the Midianites successfully you must reform at home. Take down the idol that thy father hath set up ; tear down the idol from the elevated place ; begin at home. He who begins there will fight well abroad. But if a man shall leave the idolatry in his own house, and go to fight some enemy that is on the outside, behold his victory shall perish, his renown shall be but the flash of a moment, and he shall have no real and abiding success. So must it be with us ; we must go into our own hearts and do the great work of demolition there, so far as the empire of the devil is concerned, before we go out to revolutionise, to correct and to educate the public. How is it with our home life? How is it with the condition of our hearts? Are we preaching against idolatry in others and yet falling down before Baal ourselves? Are we filled with righteous indignation because of the evil doing of persons who are far away, whilst we ourselves have temples in our hearts set up to the idol gods? These inquiries search the very secrets of our lives; these questions are like the candle of the Lord held over the depths of our own being. Gideon will have a powerless arm when he challenges the Midianites if he go not forth and begin this moral revolution at home.

How did Gideon proceed? He was cautious here again. We shall find that caution was a characteristic trait in Gideon. He did not like to do this in the daytime because he feared his father's household and the men of the city. So what was he to do? The angel had appeared unto him, and a new light had shed itself over his life; a great destiny was proposed to him; he himself had suggested a test of the credentials of the angel, and had been satisfied with that test; in his own turn he himself was to be tested. Now what did he do? He said, "If I go out in the daytime the men of the city will seize me. What am I in their hands? Yea, my own father's household will fall upon me, and I shall be crushed by their cruel power. What shall I do?" And because he could not do it by day he did it by night. Earnest men can find opportunities if they want to do so. He is making a frivolous and impious excuse who says, "I do not like to do it; I am afraid to attempt it; I shrink from going forward; I prefer a modest retirement;" and so lets the work and the call of God slip out of his fingers. If you cannot do it in the morning brightness, you may do it in the evening twilight; if you cannot do it in the noontide glory, you may do it in the midnight darkness. Earnestness always finds opportunities; earnestness always finds the sycamore tree up which it can climb and see Christ. There is always a course open to tact, to reality, to sincerity, to determination. If any man is saying that he cannot make his way through all the difficulties that beset his life so as to get near to God, in the name of all history that is true, in the name of all history that is holy, in the name of all history that is worth preserving, I charge him with a mistake or a lie.

There was sad excitement on the morning of the next day. People finding that Baal had been overthrown were all astonished, and inquiry proceeded. How had this thing been done so suddenly? Done in the night-time? When it was discovered who had done it, they went to the father of Gideon and said, "Now shall thy son be slain for this. Bring out thy son that he may die, because he hath cast down the altar of Baal, and because he hath cut down the grove that was by it." And Joash was changed in a moment: you can touch a man through his child. You can touch his keenest sympathies. When they proceeded to lay a bloody hand upon the head of Gideon, he said, "If Baal be a god let him plead for himself." A grand tone, a right tone! If Baal be a god let him plead his own cause. What is a god worth if he cannot gather himself up again when somebody has thrown him down? The grandest things have been said by men when they have been cut to the quick, when their child's life has trembled in the balance. Joash was a new man from that moment. He made the grandest proposition that ever was made in the whole kingdom of idolatry. He saw Baal on his face. He said, "If Baal be a god let him get up again!" This is exactly what we say to all the gods of England. Have you been trusting to money, to power, to health, to friends, to luck, to chance? Let them help you in the hour of extremity, but, beware, there was once a scornful laugh among the nations, a scornful laugh ringing along the courses of the whirlwind: It was this, "Thy calf, O Samaria, hath cast thee off!" Samaria had worshipped the calf; God had risen in judgment to vindicate his government, to vindicate his claim to human attention, and when Samaria went to the calf it turned Samaria off. He is but a poor god who cannot save us in extremity—who cannot speak for himself—in whose arm there is no power of self-defence.

Gideon, having been satisfied that he was called of God to do this great work, betook himself to it. But there was one difficulty in the way,—a strange difficulty, too, and peculiarly worthy of note. The Lord said, "Gideon, the people that are with thee are too many." When did God ever complain of having too few people to work with? Tell me. I have heard him say, "Where two or three are gathered together in my name, there am I." I have heard him say, "One shall chase a thousand, and two shall put ten thousand to flight." But I never heard him say, "You must get more men, or I cannot do this work; you must increase the human forces, or the divine energy will not be equal to the occasion." I hear him say, in the case before us, "Gideon, the people are too many by some thousands. If I were to fight the Midianites with so great a host, the people would say, after the victory had been won, 'Mine own hand hath saved me.'" Now the Lord proposed that a proclamation should be made unto the people, saying, "Whosoever is fearful and afraid, let him return and depart early from Mount Gilead." How many of the people think you returned? Twenty-two thousand went off at once. You cannot do much with a crowd. The crowd never did anything for the world or for itself. Twenty-two thousand went away, ten thousand remained. Now the Lord will say ten thousand is just enough. No. He said, "Gideon, the people are yet too many; they will still boast of their numbers, and they will take all the credit to themselves, if I delivered Israel from the Midianites by their instrumentality; we must have fewer still." So they were taken down to the water, and every one that lapped of the water with his tongue as a dog lappeth he was set by himself, and he alone was taken; and out of the thirty-two thousand Israelites, but three hundred men were called upon to do the great work. Most people are afraid. It is only a man here and there can set himself up with true courage; there are only about three hundred out of every thirty-two thousand that are worth anything for real fighting, for real endurance, for real enterprise. The work of the world has always been done by the few; inspiration was held by a few; wealth is held by a few; poetry is put into the custody of but a few; wisdom is guarded in her great temple but by a few; the few saved the world; ten men would have saved the cities of the plain; Potiphar's house is blessed because of Joseph; and that ship tossed and torn upon the billows of the Adriatic shall be saved because there is an apostle of God on board. Little child, you may be saving all your house—your father, your mother, your brothers, and your sisters. Young man in the city warehouse, a blessing may be coming upon the whole establishment because of your prayer and sobriety, truthfulness, honour, and religious faith. We cannot tell how these things work. There is a secret behind all appearances, and we know not the meaning that underlies all the unrest, and storm, and confusion of life. Still, we may be of some use in other ways. If we cannot go forward to the fight, we can go back to the fields and plough. If I am not one of the three hundred men that can go and take Midian captive, I may be a quiet, homely man, who can repair a fence, or set a gate in order, or plough a furrow, or continue and complete the work which was interrupted by the calling away of the three hundred men. We can all do something. Cyphers are inexpressive and worthless by themselves, but when a unit is put at their head, they are gifted with articulation and value. So let the three hundred mighty ones lead the world; and those who can fight, and think, and scheme, and govern a state, and make law, and write books, go on, and God bless them! But let us who are of a humbler mould and poorer nature know that still there remains some kind of really useful good work for us to do. "Blessed is that servant, whom his Lord when he cometh shall find so doing!"

What does this teach us? What is the application of this to the men of to-day? It is this: that human history is under divine control. God's eye, though in heaven, is looking upon the children of men. Afflictions do not spring out of the dust. If the rod be laid heavily upon our backs, it is because God would take out of us some desire that is evil, punish us for some way that is corrupt, seeking thus to recover us from the error we have committed. This history further teaches that the Lord himself finds a deliverer. Israel did not call upon Gideon, Israel did not call a council of war, and by some lucky stroke of genius deliver themselves. The Midianites were to be overthrown. This was a divine proposition, this was the arrangement of God. Salvation is from on high; deliverance is from the Lord of hosts. When there was no eye to pity, when there was no arm to save, his own eye pitied, and his own arm brought salvation. What is true in this little local case is true in the great and universal condition of humanity. The Redeemer is from heaven; the Deliverer is not a creation of earth. He who delivers mankind comes from the depths of eternity, having the ancientness of unbeginning time upon him, and the power of omnipotence in his arm. We cannot be delivered by ourselves. "O Israel, thou hast destroyed thyself; but in me is thine help." God hath laid help upon one that is mighty, and the name of that one is Jesus Christ, God the Son, who came into the world to save sinners, and redeem from a worse than Midianitish bondage.

Then God by all this teaches us that no flesh shall glory in his presence. Man shall not arise, and say, "We have devised a scheme of salvation; we have bought ourselves with gold of our own coining; we have found a file, by the use of which we can cut in twain the iron chains that bound us." God does the work. Our salvation is of his own mercy, of his own grace and power. It hath pleased God by the foolishness of preaching to save them that believe. He hath chosen the foolish things of the world to confound the wise; and base things of the world, and things which are despised, hath God chosen, yea and things which are not, to bring to nought things that are. It hath pleased God to withhold the battle from the strong and the race from the swift, and give honour to whom he will, that no flesh shall glory in his presence!

See, yonder a man glorying in God's presence. He lifts up his hands, he lifts up his eyes, he lifts up his voice and says, he is "not as other men." He tells God how clean his hands are, how often he washes them, and to what perfection he has brought his character. There is also another man with downcast eyes, who has smitten his bosom, and who can only say with a sob, "God, be merciful to me a sinner." He is the man who takes heaven back with him to his home. But where there is a spirit of self-trust and self-glorying, there can be no true honour, there can be no true salvation. It is when I am nothing, when I renounce myself, when I cast my whole life upon the Son of God, that I know what it is to be gathered into the love of God, and to be hidden in the sanctuary of his power. The day of salvation is come, the Deliverer is amongst us. This is a faithful saying, and worthy of all acceptation, that Christ Jesus is come into the world to save sinners. There was a man in the ancient time, who, having been called to a charge, allowed his charge to slip from him, and when he was asked the reason, he said, "As thy servant was busy here and there, he was gone!" Let us be busy here and there, and yet mind the great business. Let us be threshing our wheat, and still be willing to show hospitality to the angels of God. Let us be doing the duty of the passing day, and yet let our doors be ajar that God may come in whenever it doth please him to visit us in our low estate !

SELECTED NOTES.

Though he resisted the offer of a throne, Gideon fell into the error of meddling with the priestly office; a snare into which he may have been betrayed by the command, which he received and obeyed, to build an altar in his city of Ophrah, and offer on it a sacrifice to Jehovah. This isolated act, connected with his rescuing the people from the worship of Baal, and, with the manifestation of the Angel of Jehovah to him (compare and contrast 1 Chron. xxi. 28, xxii. 1), was perhaps made the beginning of a system of sacrifices there; at all events, he prepared an ephod, the well-known high-priestly garment used in consulting God (Exod. xxviii. 6-30; 1 Sam. xxiii. 6, 9). Whether he meant no more than to have a memorial of the divinely-appointed ephod, and the way of approaching God by it, as the eastern tribes had built an altar merely for a memorial (Josh. xxii. 26-29), it is impossible to tell; even so, there was a serious risk that he might go farther than he intended. But it is an old opinion that the high priests at Shiloh had early lost the confidence of the people, and had sunk into insignificance; certainly they are never mentioned or referred to in the Book of Judges, after Aaron's grandson the illustrious Phinehas (xx. 28); and long before Gideon's time there had been a schismatical and even idolatrous priestly system set up by the tribe of Dan in the town to which they gave their patriarch's name, and this, too, arose out of an unlawful family sanctuary and its ephod (xvii. 5, xviii. 30, 31). There is no warrant whatever for imputing the same sin to Gideon; yet he did something which looked in that direction, possibly bringing the high priest from Shiloh to use his ephod at Ophrah, possibly using it himself. Even if he himself escaped the more serious consequences, yet (ver. 27), all Israel went a-whoring after it there, and it became a snare to himself and his house, with evil lurking in it, and ere long bursting forth with lamentable results. The high priest's ephod, with all its attendant ornaments in the breastplate, and with its precious stones, must have been very costly; we need feel no surprise that Gideon laid out upon his ephod 1,700 shekels of gold, or about 53 lb. avoirdupois; nor that so much gold was obtained from this vast multitude of the enemy, since the Arabs to this day manifest an extraordinary love for golden ornaments. Perhaps Gideon thought himself like Moses, when he received the contributions for the tabernacle (Exod. xxxv. 20-23), many of those also being the spoils taken from their oppressors; while the men of war who willingly responded to his request may have felt like their ancestors when they made a similar free-will offering after an earlier Midianite war (Num. xxxi. 48-50). *There were other dangers in Gideon's position, of which his polygamy is an evidence.* Even had he been king, the law of God against multiplying wives was explicit (Deut. xvii. 17): yet though he refused to be ruler, in those forty years of rest and prosperity, he must have assumed something of royal state in its worst oriental form, with a harem. And there is enough in the language of the original (comp. Neh. ix. 7; Dan. v. 12) to lead to the conjecture that the name Abimelech, "A king's father," was one which he gave to his concubine's son in addition to the name given to him originally, one of those epithets or descriptive names which were common among the Jews: if so, the lad was one of those spoilt children like Adonijah (1 Kings i. 6), who brought misery and shame upon their families. Gideon himself died "in a good old age," an expression used elsewhere only of his father Abraham (Gen. xv. 15, xxv. 8), and of David (1 Chron. xxix. 28); but his death was the signal for the renewed outbreak of all evil. It seems to have taken the form of open apostasy, substituting "Baal of the Covenant" as their covenant God instead of Jehovah; though possibly there was an attempt to combine the worship of the two. And when the people did not remember Jehovah their deliverer no surprise need be felt at their thankless forgetfulness of his earthly instrument and representative, whose two names seem united into one at ver. 35, as if to recall and combine all that he had procured for Israel both of temporal and of spiritual blessings.—*Rev. Principal Douglas, D.D.*

"*And Israel was greatly impoverished because of the Midianites*" (vi. 6).— The Midianites had oppressed Israel so grievously that the people were forced to flee from the open country, and to seek an asylum in mountain fastnesses, in caves, and in fortified cities (vi. 1, 2). Midian was now at the head of a great confederacy, comprising the Amalekites and the leading tribes of Arabia, called by the sacred historian *Beni Kedem* ("children of the East," [v. 3]). In early spring the confederates assembled their vast flocks and herds, descended through the defiles of Gilead, crossed the Jordan, and overran the rich plains of central Palestine, plundering and destroying all before them (vi. 5). In their distress the Israelites cried unto the Lord, and he sent a deliverer in the person of Gideon (8-13). The invaders were concentrated on Esdraelon—their flocks covering the whole of that splendid plain, and their encampment lying along the base of "the hill of Moreh," now called little Hermon (vi. 33; vii. 1, 12). Gideon assembled his band of warriors at the well of Harod, or fountain of Jezreel, situated at the foot of Gilboa, and famed in after days as the scene of Saul's defeat and death (vii. 1). Gideon having collected the forces of Israel, followed the fugitives across the Jordan, up the hills of Gilead, and away over the plain into the heart of their own country. There he completely overthrew the whole host (viii. 12). The power of Midian was completely broken. In a single campaign they lost their princes, the flower of their warriors, and their vast wealth. "Thus was Midian subdued before the children of Israel, so they lifted up their heads no more" (viii. 28). Their name as a nation appears no more in history.

PRAYER.

ALMIGHTY GOD, is not all our life a parable, full of instruction, full of rebuke, yet full of comfort? Thou art always coming to us in figures and incidents, and in things we cannot explain, mysteries that darken upon us, and lights above the brightness of the sun. Thou dost whisper to us in the night-season, when the darkness is round about us like prison walls; then thou dost call us out into the warm morning, into the liberty which is beyond, large and glorious liberty. Thou dost teach us by our disappointments and sorrows: our losses thou dost make eloquent with instruction; and, behold, night and day thy purpose is to make us wise unto salvation. O that we had the hearing ear, the understanding mind, the attentive heart; then thy gospels would not be lost upon us, but would be to us as light from heaven. Make thy word live as we read it. May we know it to be true because of the answering voice within. May our judgment witness, and our conscience testify, that this is none other than the voice of the living God. So shall our life be strengthened, beautified, and introduced into great freedom. We come before thee evermore to seek thy pardon, for our sins are as numerous as our days: we spoil every hour by some touch of rudeness, some act of violence, some aversion of soul from light and truth. But that we know this sinfulness is itself a blessing: if we confess our sin, we know that whilst we are confessing it at the cross of Jesus Christ thy Son, our Saviour, thou dost look upon him rather than upon us, and for the sake of his work thou dost pardon the iniquity which we repent. This is our joy, this is the good news from heaven: we accept it, and answer it, and are glad because of thy forgiveness. Direct us all our days. Their number dwindles; their light is uncertain; their messages are more urgent. Help us to seize the passing time, and inscribe it with love and service and sacrifice. Dry the tears of our sorrow. Lift the burden from us when it is more than we can carry. Attemper the wind to the shorn lamb. Undertake for us in all perplexities and embarrassments and difficulties, and give us the joy of those whose perfect trust is in the God and Father of our Lord Jesus Christ. Amen.

Judges ix.

ABIMELECH—THE BRAMBLE KING.

IS Abimelech dead? Has he reappeared in our own days? Or after the devil made Abimelech did he throw the mould away? These questions are not difficult. We can easily determine them, either in the positive or in the negative. It would be something worth doing to be able to establish as a fact the absolute certainty of the death of Abimelech and all his progeny. But we must take the evidence as we find it, and abide by the issue to which it points, whatever that issue may be. This is the only just way of reading human history, and we must not suspend it, or pervert it, simply to confirm our own prejudices or inclinations. The broad lines of the career of Abimelech are written in this chapter, and are easy of comprehension. Abimelech was the son of Gideon. So far that may be put down to his credit. But his mother was only a concubine, or a wife of the second rank. So Abimelech stands somewhat on one side in history. It is often awkward to have incidental relations in life : they surprise the parties interested at unexpected times ; they flash out light in the darkness ; they make a noise when deep sleep falleth upon man. Still, Abimelech had advantages arising from the concubinage of Gideon. He was related to the Ephraimites on the one hand and to the Canaanites on the other. It has been pointed out in the case of our own Henry II. that he boasted that he was the first Norman son of a Saxon mother. Abimelech may make use of this peculiarity in his history, and may work along that line of policy and adventure. Still, we must not blame Abimelech where no blame is due. We are not asked how we will be born into the world, or where ; otherwise some of us would never have been born at all. Do not throw a man's disadvantages in his face. There are misfortunes as well as crimes, and a just criticism of character and of history will ever distinguish between the one and the other. Abimelech must speak for himself. When he begins to talk we shall understand somewhat of the quality of his mind, but even there we must make critical and perhaps generous allowance. We do not now begin the human race. Even now we are tainted or blessed by our past. Only God, therefore, can judge the world. We see but the individual man, the narrow and open circumstances of life ; and the basis of inference is too narrow to justify us in supposing that it is in our power to form a comprehensive and final judgment. " Judge not, that ye be not judged. For with what judgment ye judge, ye shall be judged : and with what measure ye mete, it shall be measured to you again." Abimelech himself may illustrate these fundamental principles.

Abimelech was ambitious. By so much he lives to-day. He would be king; who would not? There is a taking of the lowest seat at the feast which is the veriest pride. When Diogenes trampled upon the robe of Plato he said, "Thus I tread on Plato's pride;" Plato answered, "With greater pride of your own." So if we find Abimelech wanting to be king, the air is full of Abimelechs. There are various kingdoms and thrones and primacies for which men are striving night and day. Who has not his own little ambition? It looks innocent enough in some cases: it is but to add a letter or two to the name; or to live in a larger house; or to be able to give hospitality that will create a reputation for itself; or to be named by some distinguished writer; it does not lie at all along the high line which is supposed to be terminated by a throne: but, as a mere matter of analysis the action or purpose underlying it is as full of ambition as if the man, actuated by that motive, had fixed his eyes upon the supreme throne of the world. Abimelech was adroit. He put a question. Are interrogators dead? He put a question that was noble and unselfish in its letters, namely, "Whether is better for you?" as if to say, It is no matter of mine; your interests are supreme: I open my business on the public highway for the good of the public; it is of no consequence to me whether you buy my goods or not; I lay them before you and give you the golden opportunity, and you must say what you will do in the matter. Is that man dead? Why, he is a thousand strong in nearly every great thoroughfare! Time cannot kill him; he can be found at a moment's notice. But Abimelech was unjust in his benevolence. The question he put had no right to be put, because it involved others, namely, "Whether is better for you, either that all the sons of Jerubbaal, which are threescore and ten persons, reign over you, or that one reign over you?" (v. 2). Would you like to have seventy kings, or one king? Now the spirit of Abimelech was false, because the seventy men had never said anything about wishing to be kings. Why do we first credit men with bad motives, and **then charge those bad motives upon them as accusations, as if** they had originated in the spirit of the men themselves? We must not put one another into false positions. If the seventy sons of Jerubbaal had said, "We would all like to be kings," the case would have been put precisely in the terms which Abimelech used. But Gideon had refused the kingship. Long ago, when the Israelites said, Rule thou over us, and thy house, he said, No, I will not rule over you, nor my house : the Lord is your king. How subtle is the temptation to misconstrue a man's purposes, and then to treat him as if he had actually originated those purposes! We transfer ourselves to the man, and having invested him with an enforced personality we judge him by that investiture. The spirit of injustice is a cruel spirit.

The action which Abimelech took was to kill the sons of Gideon. That was the rude method of the times. Seventy men were in the way, and the answer to the embarrassment was— Murder! So the sons of Gideon, seventy in number, were murdered "upon one stone"—probably flung from one rock and dashed to pieces. How will Abimelech die? We must wait to see. But one son escaped, namely, the youngest, Jotham by name. How is it that one always does escape? Account for the one little Fleance always getting out of the way and coming back at unexpected times, and facing society like a living judgment. It is in so-called little things that the providence of God is vividly shown. Not the oldest, strongest son, but little Jotham, we may call him, for he certainly was the youngest. He came upon a given day, and spake a parable upon the top of Mount Gerizim. He "lifted up his voice, and cried, and said"—and then comes the parable, or fable, of the trees. It is rather a fable than what we now understand by a parable. It is more after, as we should say, the lines of Æsop than the lines of Christ. But a fable may be the larger truth. How is it that the men living at the time cannot write the history of what they see? We say, This statesman, or that reformer, must be left for critical judgment to the historian. Or we say, The event is too near us to be correctly judged. That is to say, a man who is not yet born will arise and tell the world the exact meaning of what we are now doing! Why, then, this wonderful objection to Biblical prophets and Biblical judgments? It is the very principle upon which we ourselves operate day by day. There can be nothing much more startling to what we call common-sense than that a man who is not yet born shall arise and give a true version of the men's motives, purposes, and histories who lived a thousand years before he himself was born. So fable takes up the real meaning of things,—that marvellous composition we call fiction, dramatic interpretation, the lifting of things up from low levels, into right line and colour,—that most wondrous of all God's gifts to man, the gift of Imagination. Jotham displayed amazing intellectual sagacity, and expressed himself with exquisite verbal beauty. It required an attentive mind to follow him. The man speaks about trees; the trees going forth to anoint a king over them; the trees asking the olive, and the olive declining; then asking the fig-tree, and the fig-tree saying No; then asking the vine, and the vine refusing the throne; last of all, the bramble—lean, prickly, sharp—asking in a taunting tone if they were willing to put their trust in his shadow; if so, he, the bramble, would reign over the cedars of Lebanon. Pride at first says, Who shall we have to reign over us? At last Pride says, Who can we *get* to be our king? God humbles pride. The first inquiry made by a Church may be, Who shall we have for our minister? and the last may be, Who can we get? who will come? It is right: all really good people are pre-engaged. The olive-tree says, "Should I leave my fatness, wherewith by me they honour God and man, and go to be promoted over the trees?" The fig-tree says, "Should I forsake my sweetness, and my good fruit, and go to be promoted over the trees?" The vine says, "Should I leave my wine, which cheereth God and man, and go to be promoted over the trees?" All the good trees are pre-occupied. All the men worth having to reign over us are already enthroned. Kings are not falling about the streets to be picked up by any passer-by. Last of all, the trees becoming a little disappointed, actually renounced their courtesy, and said to the bramble, somewhat brusquely, "Come thou, and reign over us." No question was asked; no opportunity of declining was given; but, with a kind of satiric brutality, the trees said, We must have a king—here, come, and take the throne. The parable is spoken. It is sprinkled, so to say, on the air, and is apparently lost. No;

the air is full of sermons yet to be applied. They will take fire some day, and come back upon us with startling, if not destructive, energy No wise word is lost; no fable charged with sacred meaning has vanished with the smoke of the day in which it was spoken. Cheer thy heart, godly teacher; the sermons appear to be all lost. They are listened to, but not answered. The appeal, warm with thy very blood, accentuated by the fire of life, may apparently be lost. But there is a time of resurrection in these things, and swift application, a day of judgment before the judgment day, and then it will be known what every man has done in endeavouring to serve his age. Again and again in the life of Christ we read such words as these, "Then remembered they,"—that is to say, circumstances had gathered themselves into such proportions, and had addressed themselves with such vigour to the mind and the memory, that something within was awakened, the old word was sounded in the ear, and it came with its full and noble meaning. The man who can make a beautiful parable can make a beautiful sermon also. Jotham made a magnificent appeal :—

"Now therefore, if ye have done truly and sincerely [a bitterly ironical supposition], in that ye have made Abimelech king, and if ye have dealt well with Jerubbaal and his house, and have done unto him according to the deserving of his hands ; (for my father fought for you, and adventured [*cast,*—"he hath poured out his soul unto death,"] his life far, and delivered you out of the hand of Midian : and ye are risen up against my father's house this day, and have slain his sons, threescore and ten persons [Jotham himself is counted in this number], upon one stone, and have made Abimelech, the son of his maidservant [intentionally contemptuous], king over the men of Shechem, because he is your brother ;) if ye then have dealt truly and sincerely with Jerubbaal and with his house this day, then rejoice ye in Abimelech, and let him also rejoice in you : but if not, let fire come out from Abimelech, and devour the men of Shechem, and the house of Millo; and let fire come out [exactly fulfils vv. 45-49] from the men of Shechem, and from the house of Millo, and devour Abimelech " (vv. 16-20).

The *epimuthion*, or application of the fable, was magnificent in moral tone. Jotham comprehended the great philosophy that water cannot rise above its level : men cannot rise above the honour that is in them. Little men cannot be great ; ungrateful men cannot be just ; mean souls can never be majestic. Jotham said in effect : If this is your idea of honour, so be it, take the consequences; if this is your reading of history, and this your tribute to the illustrious dead, let it be so. Men must act according to their own quality. Men do not gather grapes of thorns, nor figs of thistles. The criticism with which your life is followed will be according to the quality of the critics: tainted men will see putridity in you; men of ungenerous mind will never write or speak one glowing word about your action. They are hardly to be blamed; they cannot help it: every tree grows after its own kind, so does every man. The appeal of Jotham is the appeal which men may address to the ages, though they run away as Jotham did, and flee into darkness; but the appeal will abide when the speaker has gone. Children, if this is your idea of what is due to your father and your mother who lived for you, suffered for you, had but one thought, and that a thought for your comfort and progress, if this is your idea of gratitude and justice to their memory, carry out your programme, and let the times that are coming judge you. Nations, if this is the way in which you treat your statesmen, your patriots, your reformers, so be it: nations cannot rise above their level: by your treatment of your leaders and patriots we shall know your own quality. Nations write themselves in the deeds which they do to those who have led and instructed them. Congregations, if this be your idea of what is due to your ministers and teachers, so be it; if after the men have prayed themselves into agony for you, studied your distresses that they might heal your wounds, lived for you, thought for you, sacrificed themselves on the altar of your welfare, if you care to forget the past, to throw out the old men and let them die where they may, so be it: congregations cannot rise above their level. Congregations must carry out their own idea of honour. They find it convenient to forget, to obliterate, the noblest service which man can render to man. Be it so. Do not reason with them. It is an inevitable meanness. Then the other side is true: there are grateful children; there are nations loyal to their chiefs; there are congregations greater than the ministers. So be it. On both sides we can but say with Jotham, So be it; rejoice, and rejoice in one another.

After three years peace was broken. Abimelech conquered until he came to Thebez, where there was a strong tower; and full of his father's intrepidity and daring courage, he went straight up to the tower and said he would destroy it, or over-throw it, or burn it. The people went to the top of the tower, and a woman among them looked out, and saw this man fighting against its very walls, and she dropped a stone, and it crushed the head of Abimelech. He killed the sons of Gideon with a stone : God also can throw stones. Let us take care : "With what measure ye mete, it shall be measured to you again." When Adoni-bezek had his thumbs and great toes cut off he said, "As I have done, so God hath requited me." The treacherous idolaters had their temple burned by the treachery of their enemies. "It is a fearful thing to fall into the hands of the living God."

"Thus,"—we read :

"God rendered the wickedness of Abimelech, which he did unto his father, in slaying his seventy brethren : and all the evil of the men of Shechem did God render upon their heads : and upon them came the curse of Jotham the son of Jerubbaal" (vv. 56, 57).

To some curses we must say Amen. They vindicate themselves. We cannot do other than concur in some judgments. We may revolt from them, turn aside with great feeling of sorrow : yet there have been cases in which parents have been obliged to concur in the sentence which doomed their son to death. This is the view we shall be made to take in the great summing-up of things. None shall be "lost, but the son of perdition." Christ is mighty to save, and none shall be taken out of his hand but the son of waste—the man of whom nothing can be made, the man who is in very deed a suicide, not killing the body, but slay-ing the self, the soul, the thing that made him a man. Let us so read history as to take warning from its bad men, and encourage-ment from its good men ; and let us learn that there is but one place of safety, Jesus—the Rock eternal !

SELECTED NOTES.

Cast a piece of millstone.—So that ambitious King Pyrrhus was at last slain with a tile-stone thrown upon his head by a woman. And the like deadly blow by a like hand, upon the head of Hermanius, Earl of Lucelberg, whom Pope Hildebrand had set up in opposition to Henry the Emperor, whom he had excommunicated. Simeon De' Monteforti also, another of the Pope's champions, fighting against those ancient Protestants, the Waldenses, was brained with a stone at the siege of Toulouse. That scholar that took his death by the falling of a letter of stone from the Earl of Northampton's house at the funeral of Queen Anne, was to be pitied. But commentators observe it for a just hand of God upon Abimelech, that upon one stone he had slain his seventy brethren, and now a stone slayeth him : his head had stolen the crown of Israel, and now his head is smitten.

The vengeance which he had wreaked upon Shechem, he intended also for Thebez, a town placed by the Onomasticon thirteen Roman miles from Neapolis (Shechem) on the road to Beth-Shean, or Beisân ; which is therefore the modern Tûbâs, twelve miles E.N.E. of Shechem. One might infer from this that the son considered himself the lawful successor of his father in the government of Israel, and meant to punish these two cities as Succoth and Penuel had been punished for their rebellion. But his utter failure, his death by the hand of a woman (like Sisera, iv. 9), and his miserable effort to escape by suicide from this disgrace, to a bold warrior, were the tokens in providence that he wanted the moral and spiritual qualities of Gideon. And his personal ruin, together with the immediately resulting collapse of the government which he had established over Israel, marked the fulfilment of Jotham's curse. It is mere ignorance of old English which in many copies of the Bible changed "alto brake," that is, "altogether brake," into "all to break " in ver. 53.

In the providence of God a spirit of rebellion and hatred was allowed to work its influence upon the Shechemites. Gaal, probably a Canaanite, came to the city, and excited the inhabitants at the time of the vintage festival, urging that Abimelech was half an Israelite, and that it behoved them to establish a pure native rule. Abimelech was privately informed of the conspiracy by Zebul, one of his followers, whom he had made ruler of Shechem ; and with an energy and promptitude that recall the military abilities of his father, at once proceeded to quell the revolt. He defeated Gaal, who attempted to exclude him from Shechem, and on the following day took the city with much slaughter of his former subjects. The temple-citadel in which the rest took refuge he burned to the ground, and then besieged Thebez, which had borne a part in the insurrection. The people fled to the citadel, and Abimelech proceeded to lay fire at the gate. Here, however, his reign and his life came suddenly to an end. A piece of a mill-stone, flung by a woman from the battlements, fractured his skull, and, at his own request, his armour-bearer thrust him through with a sword. Thus ended the dark, dishonourable career of "the Bramble King," after a tyranny of three years, and thus closed one of the most degrading chapters in the history of Israel.

PRAYER.

ALMIGHTY GOD, we are part of thy purpose in the creation of the world. We know not why we are here. We are here by no will of our own : the times are hard, the temptations are a million in number, the chances are that we may be lost. We cannot tell what all this means. Thou didst not ask us to be here. We are often full of pain and sore distress, hardly knowing the right hand from the left; mocked in our prayers; disappointed, not only in our ambitions, but in our rational hopes; borne down by a great weight, threatened by an immeasurable cloud, full of blackness, charged with thunder. What we love we lose : we grow flowers only to see them wither, and rear children that they may break our hearts, and pet the household lamb that it may be stolen. This is a great mystery. We knew not any of its meaning in ourselves. We bless thee for a book which interprets the riddle. We hear in that Gospel-book music from heaven, voices from beyond, assurances that the darkness is but for a moment, and that a great light has already started from the eternal throne and will be here presently. We have read the story of thy Son, and we know it to be true : this Man receiveth sinners; this Man talks to the broken heart, and holds up pictures of the kingdom long enough for us to see them through our tears. He loved us : he preached in our towns and villages ; he gave us bread when we were hungry ; he cured the sick man whom the physicians had abanuoned; he allowed us to approach him by night when we dared not go by day : he saved others,—himself he did not save ; he forgave his enemies dying, and he sent gospels to them living; and now he is exalted, a King, a Prince, a Saviour, to give repentance unto Israel and remission of sins; and he carries the little earth in his heart like a thing loved with all heaven's love. We know Jesus Christ. We love him. His name is wrought into the very texture of our life : to take it away is to take away our breath. He was our visitor when none else would come near the house; he lighted the lamp when the chamber was all darkness ; he came out into the wilderness to seek and to save that which was lost. We cannot forget his cross : if we forget that cross, may our right hand forget its cunning; if we cease to remember that death, may our tongue cleave to the roof of our mouth. Lead us to see that all other deliverances point to the one redemption. As we move along the line of Biblical story, may we feel that One greater is yet to come than any deliverer who has appeared. May we find our way through providence to redemption, through history to revelation, and through the altars built by men to the cross set up from before the foundation of the world ; thus will our reading be profitable, full of spiritual nutriment, and our souls shall grow in the school of God, and around them shall be wrought the mystery of grace, as we spend our nights and days with Jesus. We put our hands into thine. The way is too long for us, and too rough; who made the road we cannot tell, but our feet are weary, and our eyes are distressed by the vast monotony. But in thy society there is no weariness; in thine inspiration, O Holy Spirit of the living God, heaven begins. Feed us; lead us; keep us;—may no wanderer be lost! Amen.

Judges x.

AFTER ABIMELECH.

WE have had much excitement in many of the pages through which we have inquiringly passed. We now come to a period of extreme quietness. For five and forty years nothing occurred in Israel worth naming in detail. Tola and Jair, though judges in Israel, lived and died in the utmost quietness. They occupy about four lines each in the history of their people. Quietness has no history. Events are recorded; stories, anecdotes, incidents,—these claim the attention of the historical pen; but peace, quietness, industry, patience, inoffensiveness, these have no historian: a line or two will do for them,—the war must have chapter after chapter. The popular proverb is, " Blessed are the people who have no annals." Within a narrow sense that is true; the sense is very narrow.

Read verses 1, 2 :—

" And after Abimelech [who is not counted among the judges] there arose to defend [or save, equal to deliver] Israel Tola the son of Puah, the son of Dodo, a man of Issachar [probably the only judge furnished by this indolent tribe]; and he dwelt in Shamir in mount Ephraim. And he judged Israel twenty and three years, and died, and was buried in Shamir."

Is that dull reading? Of what tribe was the man? "Issachar." Has Issachar any fame? Let us bethink ourselves: who can remember anything said in the Bible about Issachar? The solution of the mystery may be in that direction. The individual man may have no great repute, but he may belong to a tribe quite renowned for some virtue. Mark these words: "The children of Issachar, which were men that had understanding of the times, to know what Israel ought to do." Then Tola the son of Puah, the son of Dodo, belonged to a tribe of statesmen. It was nothing to them to propound great schemes, work out great reforms, propose wholesome ameliorations: great things came naturally in their way. If a little tribe had attempted any one of the reforms proposed and executed by Issachar he would have become famous. A very short pedestal would make a giant of a dwarf. But the men of Issachar were accustomed to statesmanship; they were famed for their sagacity; they had the piercing eyes that could see through all surfaces, veilings, sophisms,—that could read the necessity of the age, the temper and desire of the heart of Israel. So we must not pass by these negative characters as if they were really nothing. A touch of their hand might be equal to the stroke of a powerful instrument. One word spoken by a man of the tribe of Issachar might have in it a volume of wisdom. We must not measure men by the lines which the historian spends upon them. There is family history, household training, sagacity that makes no noise, farsightedness that disappoints the immediate ambition, but that prepares for the discipline and schooling and perfecting of a lifetime. Let those who spend their lives in the shadow think of these things : they may have a fame distinctively their own, not noisy, tempestuous, tumultuous, but profound, healthful, lasting,—blessed are they who have the renown of wisdom, the fame of understanding : that will endure when many a vaporous reputation has been exhaled, forgotten. The men of Issachar were wise men,—men of solid head, clear brain, comprehensive vision ; men who put things together, and deduced from them inferences which amounted to philosophies ; they had understanding of the times : they were not fretted and chafed by the incidents of the passing day ; they saw the meaning that underlaid the event, and they knew what Israel ought to do. Bless God for good leadership—in the state, in business, in the family, everywhere ; the greater it is the more silent it may sometimes be.

"And after him arose Jair, a Gileadite, and judged Israel twenty and two years. And he had thirty sons [representing an ostentatious polygamy] that rode on thirty ass colts [implying the great wealth of the household], and they had thirty cities which are called Havoth-jair [Havoth, meaning villages] unto this day, which are in the land of Gilead. And Jair died, and was buried in Camon" (vv. 3-5).

That is the great danger of times of quietness. When there is little to excite attention and develop energy the tendency is that men may notice little things and make much of them. There

was not much to do in Israel when it could be noted how many
sons any man had, and whether they rode on ass colts or otherwise. That danger besets all life. In the absence of great
questions, thrilling problems of an imperial or social kind, men
betake themselves to little pedantries, frivolous amusements,
trifling inquiries : the greater nature sleeps, and little, active,
nimble fancy presides over the life, and fritters it away. We
want every now and then some great heroic occasion that shall
swallow up all our little fancies, whims, and oddities, and make
men of us. We need visitations of a providential kind to shake
us out of our littleness and frivolity, and make us mighty in
prayer, almost sublime in thought, certainly heroic in self-control
and patience. Thus God has educated the world. Mark how
the marvellous history has gone; in what measured undulation :
sometimes the mountains have been very high, and have been
untouched except by the feet of the eagle, unploughed except by
the lightning of God,—far away, lost in the cloud ; sometimes
the heights have been quite accessible, so green, so velvetlike in
their sward, and so rich in new and surprising flora ; then we
have come further down into great gardens, quiet villages, places
sacred to slumber, and whilst we were revelling in the luxury of
quietness a great clang tore the air and a trumpet summoned us
to sudden war. So the Bible story has proceeded, and as the
sun has set upon the day quiet, or the day of strife, we have felt
a sense of incompleteness, which has often become quite religious,
and has said to itself, This is not all ; the punctuation is intermediate, not final ; surely all these occurrences mean a greater incarnation than we have ever yet beheld. We need great excitements
or solemn occasions in the family, or we should drivel away into
the most frivolous existence. Given sound health, abundant
prosperity, everything the heart could desire,—what is the issue
of it all ? Satiety ; great difficulty in being pleased ; an outworn
appetite or desire ; taking up with trivial things ; a sensitiveness
that is easily offended ; a pride that would be contemptible if it
were not so transparent. How they talk who have much goods
laid up for many years ! How difficult to please with their
books, which they never read, and their pictures which they only
buy because others have recommended them ! How difficult to
please with their friends, their feasts, their entertainments ! How

sensitive to cold! How extremely sensitive to draughts! How altogether peculiar! The Lord could not allow this to be going on, or the people would decay, fall away from manhood, and disappoint the very purpose and decree of heaven. So affliction must come, and loss, and the whole house must rock under the wind; then the people will become themselves again; they will think, pray, ask serious questions, and look at the reality and gravity of life. So must it be with the Church and with the nation. We must not have too much quietness. Our quiet periods must be alternated by periods of great stress and difficulty. Watch how God has trained the world. We do not see the method in any one verse or incident. Herein is the peculiarity of the Bible, that it must be read consecutively, page after page in sequence, until we begin to feel we are perusing a great architectural design, or a marvellous plan of war, or a sublime philosophy of education. Men may read the Bible in fragments, and know nothing about it. The Bible must be read continuously and cumulatively, until it prove its inspiration by its unity, and arrest human confidence by manifest proofs of divine dictation. Therefore we cannot stop in the historical books. We are thankful for them: so full of life, colour, action; many chapters have been written with the sword, others with rough pens, and others are but living hints of things that cannot be expressed; yet on we must go to the end, until the time when the whole book satisfies itself and satisfies its readers by a grand Amen.

"And the children of Israel did evil again [added to do evil] in the sight of the Lord, and served Baalim, and Ashtaroth, and the gods of Syria [see Gen. xxxv. 2, 4,], and the gods of Zidon [1 Kings xi. 5], and the gods of Moab [1 Kings xi. 7], and the gods of the children of Ammon [Lev. xviii. 21], and the gods of the Philistines [observe how the seven idols correspond with the seven retributive oppressions], and forsook the Lord, and served not him" (v. 6).

We are sometimes afraid of *religious* excitement, but who ever is afraid of *irreligious* enthusiasm? It is supposed that all the exaggeration and sensationalism must be on one side; hence Christians are often foolishly and unjustly charged with religious fanaticism. There are revivals of godlessness; there are revivals of worldliness. What think ye of that? This sixth verse burns with unholy enthusiasm. Hear the list:—Having taken to idolatry, Israel took to it earnestly, with both hands—" and served Baalim, and Ashtaroth, and the gods of Syria, and the gods of Zidon, and the gods of Moab, and the gods of the children of Ammon, and the gods of the Philistines,"—any number of gods. Yet if Christian people are at all warm in their subject, they become " fanatics," and are blamed for sensationalism, by men who work seven days in the week to increase their balance at the bank ! Let us keep the matter steadily in view. Which is better, a great excitement in the Church in the direction of bringing men to Jesus Christ, saving souls from death, converting the world ; or a devotion to Mammon, in which the name of God is never mentioned, in which the Church is forgotten, in which every religious impulse is annihilated ? One or the other of the enthusiasms we must have—an enthusiasm of life (and it is hardly a contradiction in terms so to say) or an enthusiasm in death. Christians must not allow themselves to be too easily rebuked : they must rather say with the Apostle, " Whether we be beside ourselves, it is to God : or whether we be sober, it is for your cause." Israel could hardly have gods enough. There is a marvellous licence in irreligion. Even Cicero said it was not sufficient for the majesty of Rome to have but one god ; Rome must have a multitude of gods, said he, for reasons of State. There is then enthusiasm in idolatry; a keeping up of idolatry to its very highest pitch. These revivals are published, too. The idolaters were not ashamed to say to how many gods they had bowed down. Is all courage to be on the side of the opposition ? and are Christians to sit down in the quietness of death, because they are afraid of the criticism of the world ?

"And the anger of the Lord [compare 1 Sam. xii. 9] was hot against Israel, and he sold them [or, gave them up] into the hands of the Philistines, and into the hands of the children of Ammon. And that year [imperfect, as no year is specified] they vexed and oppressed the children of Israel: eighteen years, all the children of Israel that were on the other side Jordan in the land of the Amorites [the kingdoms of Og and Sihon], which is in Gilead. Moreover the children of Ammon passed over Jordan to fight also against Judah, and against Benjamin, and against the house of Ephraim; so that Israel was sore distressed " (vv. 7-9).

Desperate diseases require desperate remedies. The Lord said in effect : If you will have the gods of the Philistines, you may take the Philistines also; if you will have the gods of heathen, you may have the whole yoke of heathendom to carry : you must not pick and choose, taking out the gods and leaving the customs, following the idolatry and escaping the tyranny. This is the reason why the Lord sends upon us all manner of evil,—because we have forsaken him. We may not have forsaken him nominally, but there is a forsaking that is worse than a merely nominal and formal renunciation. A man may not be forsaken in any public or mechanical manner by his family, but if they neglect him, if they allow him to mourn in his loneliness, and to cry in the bitterness of an unrelieved solitude,—if they hear his complaints without replying to them, he is indeed forsaken. It is impossible, therefore, to have a church, and an altar, and a merely nominal God, and a creed full of points innumerable, and yet never to turn the living, loving heart to the Father in heaven. Providence is full of chastisement in relation to evil-doers. The Lord is very pitiful and kind, but pity may be exhausted, and kindness may come to an end. So health is broken ; the strong man is bowed down ; those who were proud of their vigour have now to sigh their wants because they cannot express them in words. And the business is all broken up. Nobody can account for it. All the arrangements have been as usual ; every appointment has been kept ; attention has been paid to the whole circle ; but there is no response : everything goes wrong ; every figure is turned into a cipher, old books become practically blank. And bereavement is sent,—the choice one is taken away, the best one dies, and the bird with the brightest wing takes flight ; the sweetest singer becomes dumb. And the way is shut up ; yet no man can see where the bars are : there is no gate of wood or brass or iron that can be touched, for then it might be broken through or opened ; but the air is full of bars, and we cannot make any progress. We earn wages, and put them into bags with holes in them. Is God always going to allow himself to be mocked ? The point of sovereignty must be found somewhere : shall it be found in the riotous mob, God-forgetting, God-insulting ; or in the eternal unchangeable throne of righteousness ? Blessed be God for broken health, depressed trade, graves without number, ways that are barred up with invisible iron, if our use of these things should lead us to thought, repentance, and better life. Israel was " sore distressed." There is a moral in agony. It is not every pain that will make a man pray. Some pain may be treated lightly, referred to as a momentary inconvenience ; but the pain becomes sharper, the agony more burning, the fire more intolerable, and men who thought they could not pray are made to "cry," for they are "sore distressed." Do not let us suppose that we can outrun or outwit the living God. He will overtake us, and trip us, and scourge us, and it shall be found that among the multitude of the deities there has been in reality but one God.

"And the children of Israel cried unto the Lord ["cried they had before, as very brutes will do when they are hurt, but not with their whole heart; their cries were the fruits of the flesh for ease, not of faith for God's favour"] saying, We have sinned against thee, both because we have forsaken our God, and also served Baalim" (v. 10).

That is a true conception of the case. Both the points are put effectively. Not only was there a forsaking of God, but there was a taking up with Baalim. Men cannot throw off their church robe without putting on some other garment. It is impossible simply to "leave the church." Yet there are men who deceive themselves with the idea that they have simply given up attendance upon religious duties and observance—have merely withdrawn from church appointment and action : nothing else has occurred. That is a profound mistake. No man leaves the true Church, wherever and whatever it may be,—no man abandons its ceremonies and observances and duties without exposing himself to a thousand assaults and temptations : he is more easily trifled with ; he listens more eagerly to temptations which appeal to his ambition or his cupidity. He who goes down in veneration goes down in every faculty of his nature that pointed towards heaven or aspired after nobler life. Israel proved this. Having forsaken God, Israel took up with Baalim, with all the gods of the heathen ; with many gods—yea, countless in number—absolutely forgetting the true God. There are losses which never can be made up. Loss of character is never made up by gain of wealth : there is no correspondence between the two quantities. Loss of the true God cannot be amended by the multiplication of false gods. The many do not total into the one.

Now comes a sad word. The Lord said in the course of his reply,—

"Go and cry unto the gods which ye have chosen; let them deliver you in the time of your tribulation" (v. 14). [Compare very carefully Deut. xxxii. 37, 38; 2 Kings iii. 13; Jer. ii. 28.]

We do not wonder at the " cry." The wonder is in heaven, not in man : the wonder is that we have anything, not that we are left with a solitary staff; the surprise is that we have a coal in the grate, or a loaf in the cupboard, not that we die of cold and perish with hunger. The taunting word we must all approve, if it comes to a question of bare justice, fair and honourable revenge. But when God laughs the universe grieves. "I also will laugh at your calamity." Who can bear it ? There is a laughter which we can return with disdain equal to its own contempt. But there is another laughter, the laughter of mocked love, the laughter of avenging affection, the laughter of dishonoured holiness : who can abide its scorn ? "I also will laugh at your calamity," I will refer you to the gods you have served ; I will say, " Cry aloud : for he is a god ; either he is talking, or he is pursuing, or he is in a journey, or peradventure he sleepeth, and must be awakened." Cry aloud ! " Acquaint now thyself with him, and be at peace." The day of " sore distress " overtakes every life. Is the Lord Jesus Christ only to be sought after when everything gets darkened, and when the pathways round about the house are so treated as to prevent any noise reaching the dying life ? Is he never to be invited to the wedding, where he would make the water wine ? Is he never to come to the evening feast, where all the children would grow in his presence like flowers opening in the sun ? Is he never to go out with us into the fields, golden with vernal and summer flowers ? Is he never to be invited into the best rooms of the house, but always to be kept outside until he is asked into the chamber darkened because light means pain, and only to be spoken to when we need something from him ? The question is a solemn one, and the answer is with ourselves. The voice of warning we have heard ; the voice of redemption we have also listened to. "Choose you this day whom ye will serve." Keep to your god ! If Baalim be god, keep to him, serve him ; if the Lord be God, cleave unto him with full purpose of heart. That the Lord is God we know—we know in our heart, in our best feeling, in our least-perverted instincts; that there is a throne in the universe we know by the history of humanity upon the face of the earth, —a living Bible, a moving apocalypse, and obvious inspiration. Many deliverers have arisen, many redeemers have appeared in time of stress and sorrow, but each of them has said in mysterious language, " I am not he : there cometh one after me." We pass through a whole array of deliverers, emancipators, soldiers, ardent in patriotism,—the meaning of them all being that there is one coming whose name is Jesus Christ. He must reign till he hath put all enemies under his feet. In heavenly vision I see him, and on his vesture and on his thigh is written, " KING OF KINGS, LORD OF LORDS." On his head are many crowns, and all heaven is filled with the thunder of his praise. Be Christ our captain. Be the Son of God our infinite deliverer.

SELECTED NOTE.

" *The children of Ammon passed over Jordan* " (v. 9). These were the descendants of the younger son of Lot (Gen. xix. 38). They originally occupied a tract of country east of the Amorites, and separated from the Moabites by the river Arnon. It was previously in the possession of a gigantic race called Zamzummims (Deut. ii. 20), " but the Lord destroyed them before the Ammonites, and they succeeded them and dwelt in their stead." The first mention of their active hostility against Israel occurs in Judges iii. 13 : " The king of Moab gathered unto him the children of Ammon and Amalek, and went and smote Israel." About one hundred and forty years later we are informed that the children of Israel forsook Jehovah and served the gods of various nations, including those of the children of Ammon, " and the anger of Jehovah was hot against them, and he sold them into the hands of the Philistines and of the children of Ammon " (x. 7). The Ammonites crossed over the Jordan, and fought with Judah, Benjamin, and Ephraim, so that " Israel was sore distressed." In answer to Jephthah's messengers (xi. 12), the king of Ammon charged the Israelites with having taken away that part of his territories which lay between the rivers Arnon and Jabbok, which, in Joshua xxiii. 25, is called " half the land of the children of Ammon," but was in the possession of the Amorites when the Israelites invaded it ; and this fact was urged by Jephthah in order to prove that the charge was ill-founded. Jephthah " smote them from Aroer to Minnith, even twenty cities, with a very great slaughter " (xi. 33). In the writings of the prophets terrible denunciations are uttered against the Ammonites on account of their rancorous hostility to the people of Israel ; and the destruction of their metropolis, Rabbah, is distinctly foretold (Zeph. ii. 8; Jer. xlix. 1-6 ; Ezek. xxv. 1-5, 10 ; Amos i. 13-15).

PRAYER.

ALMIGHTY GOD, it is our joy to know that thou art on the throne, and that thy judgment is true and righteous altogether. We trust our all to thee, for thou didst give us all. The mystery of our being we cannot understand; but when it is most painful, we see how truly great is thy meaning towards us. Surely thou didst not make man in vain; thou didst purpose concerning him great glory and honour, because great service, in the spheres which thou thyself wilt appoint. Some come into the world under infinite disadvantages; still, they are thy children; thou knowest their whole story; thou wilt not leave them without a friend; the burden is very heavy, the cloud is very threatening, but the Lord reigneth, and his name is Love. They wonder why they are here; they dare not escape from the little prison; they would galdly do so, but thou hast wrought within them the mystery of patience, which most sweetly says, Not my will, but thine, be done. And others are crowned with advantages which they cannot use: they are filled with pride and haughtiness, and the self-trust which they boast is only idolatry; they cannot tell the meaning of all the riches with which thou hast crowded their life: behold, their wealth is multitudinous, and they listen not to the cry of the poor, nor understand the pain of necessity. Others thou hast gifted until their gifts become temptations and snares, and seem to lie close to the dread region of madness; thou dost give them dreams they cannot realise, and flash upon their eyes visions which dazzle them; they seem to be able to pluck what they want, and yet they just fall short of the tempting fruit. So life is very hard to some men, most difficult, full of pleasure, full of pain—a great distress; the joy seems to be occasional, the sorrow permanent; the delight is but for a moment, and then the bright heavens close again in great thunder-clouds. Yet still thou hast so made us that we cling to life. Herein is a great mystery. We cannot give it up. We still hope that to-morrow will redeem to-day, and that in the coming gladness we shall forget the sorrow that is gone. So we stand in a great mystery. Come to us with the light of Christianity, the glory of the Cross, the revelation of thy love in Christ Jesus thy Son. May he bring life and immortality to light, and show us that in the by-and-bye, which we hope for under the name of Heaven, we shall see thy purpose, and glorify thy goodness, and say thou hast done all things well. Amen.

Judges xi.

["The history of Jephthah appears to be an independent history inserted bodily by the compiler of the Book of Judges. For it is obvious that vv. 4, 5, introduce the Ammonitish war without any apparent reference to chap. x. 17, 18, though in perfect agreement with what is there related."—*The Speaker's Commentary.*]

Annotated Text.

(Giving the results of the best available criticism.)

1. Now Jephthah the Gileadite was a mighty man of valour, and he was the son of an harlot: and Gilead begat [may mean, was the ancestor of] Jephthah.

2. And Gilead's wife bare him sons; and his wife's sons grew up, and they thrust out Jephthah [in perfect accordance with the law, see Deut. xxiii. 2, 3], and said unto him, Thou shalt not inherit in our father's house; for thou art the son of a strange woman.

3. Then Jephthah fled from his brethren, and dwelt in the land of Tob [a Syrian district on the north-east of Peræa]; and there were gathered vain ["These are exactly analogous to the *doruphoroi*,—a body guard of spear-bearers, which an ambitious Greek always hired as the first step to setting up a tyranny. We find David (1 Sam. xxii. 2), and Absalom (2 Sam. xv. 1), and Rezon (1 Kings xi. 24), and Adonijah (1 Kings i. 5), and Jeroboam (2 Chron. xiii. 7), all doing the same thing."] men to Jephthah, and went out with him [as fellow freebooters].

4. And it came to pass in process of time [after days], that the children of Ammon made war against Israel [this has been fully related in chap. x].

5. And it was so, that when the children of Ammon made war against Israel [at the close of eighteen years of oppression, chap. x. 9], the elders of Gilead went to fetch Jephthah out of the land of Tob:

6. And they said unto Jephthah, Come, and be our captain [our leader in time of war], that we may fight with the children of Ammon.

7. And Jephthah said unto the elders of Gilead, Did not ye hate me, and expel me out of my father's house? and why are ye come unto me now when ye are in distress?

8. And the elders of Gilead said unto Jephthah, Therefore we turn again to thee now, that thou mayest go with us, and fight against the children of Ammon, and be our head over all the inhabitants of Gilead.

9. And Jephthah said unto the elders of Gilead, If ye bring me home again to fight against the children of Ammon, and the Lord deliver them before me, shall I be your head? [more than merely leader in times of war.]

10. And the elders of Gilead said unto Jephthah, The Lord be witness [be hearing] between us, if we do not so according to thy words.

11. Then Jephthah went with the elders of Gilead, and the people made him head and captain [civil as well as military leader] over them: and Jephthah uttered all his words before the Lord in Mizpeh [by some solemn religious ceremony].

12. And Jephthah sent messengers unto the king of the children of Ammon, saying, What hast thou to do with me, that thou art come against me to fight in my land? [He speaks officially in the name of all Israel.]

13. And the king of the children of Ammon answered unto the messengers of Jephthah, Because Israel took away my land [plausible, but not factual], when they came up out of Egypt, from Arnon even unto Jabbok [the space

occupied by Gad and Reuben], and unto Jordan: now, therefore, restore those lands again peaceably.

14. And Jephthah sent messengers again [because he disputed the king's facts] unto the king of the children of Ammon:

15. And said unto him, Thus saith Jephthah, Israel took not away the land of Moab, nor the land of the children of Ammon : ["What they took was the territory of Sihon which they had never been forbidden to take, and had, indeed, been forced to take by Sihon's attack upon them."]

16. But when Israel came up from Egypt [compare Numb. xx, xxi.], and walked through the wilderness [in the second year of the wanderings] unto the Red sea, and came to Kadesh;

17. Then Israel sent messengers unto the king of Edom [as narrated in Numb. xx. 14, etc.], saying, Let me, I pray thee, pass through thy land : but the king of Edom would not hearken thereto. And in like manner they sent unto the king of Moab : but he would not consent: and Israel abode in Kadesh [where they may have encamped for a great part of forty years].

18. Then they went along through the wilderness, and compassed the land of Edom, and the land of Moab, and came by the east side of the land of Moab, and pitched on the other side of Arnon, but came not within the border of Moab: for Arnon was the border of Moab.

19. And Israel sent messengers unto Sihon king of the Amorites, the king of Heshbon [king of the Amorites by birth, king of Heshbon by conquest] ; and Israel said unto him, Let us pass, we pray thee, through thy land into my place.

20. But Sihon trusted not Israel to pass through his coast : but Sihon gathered all his people together, and pitched in Jahaz, and fought against Israel.

21. And the Lord God of Israel delivered Sihon and all his people into the hand of Israel, and they smote them: so Israel possessed all the land of the Amorites, the inhabitants of that country.

22. And they possessed all the coasts of the Amorites, from Arnon even unto Jabbok,.and from the wilderness even unto Jordan.

23. So now the Lord God of Israel hath dispossessed the Amorites from before his people Israel, and shouldest thou possess it ? [a theological as well as a military view.]

24. Wilt not thou possess that which Chemosh thy god ["The expression shows the close connection between Ammon and Moab. Chemosh was distinctively the god of Moab, and Molech of Ammon : but the two nations were of kindred blood and allied institutions."] giveth thee to possess ? So whomsoever the Lord our God shall drive out from before us, them will we possess.

25. And now art thou any thing better than Balak [are you the good, good in comparison with ?]·the son of Zippor, the king of Moab ? did he ever strive against Israel [except with pure hatred], or did he ever fight against them,

26. While Israel dwelt in Heshbon and her towns, and in Aroer and her towns, and in all the cities that be along by the coasts of Arnon, three hundred years ? [An argument drawn from undisputed possession. The

time mentioned may be a marginal gloss which has crept into the text] why therefore did ye not recover them within that time [at that crisis] ?

27. Wherefore I have not sinned against thee, but thou doest me wrong to war against me : the Lord the Judge be judge this day between the children of Israel and the children of Ammon. [A familiar appeal. See Gen. xvi. 5, xxxi. 53, xviii. 25 ; 1 Sam. xxiv. 15.]

28. Howbeit the king of the children of Ammon hearkened not unto the words of Jephthah which he sent him.

29. Then the Spirit of the Lord came upon Jephthah [endowing him with courage and wisdom], and he passed over ["he swept through the land from end to end to kindle the torch of war, and raise the population"] Gilead, and Manasseh, and passed over Mizpeh of Gilead, and from Mipzeh of Gilead he passed over unto the children of Ammon [went to attack them].

30. And Jephthah vowed a vow ["A practice among all ancient nations, but especially among the Jews : Gen. xxviii. 20-22 ; 1 Sam. i. 11 ; 2 Sam. xv. 8 ; Ps. lxvi. 13."] unto the Lord, and said, If thou shalt without fail deliver the children of Ammon into mine hands,

31. Then it shall be, that whatsoever cometh forth ["Jephthah ignorant as he was,—being a man of semi-heathen parentage, and long familiarised with heathen surroundings—contemplated a human sacrifice." St. Augustine ridicules the idea that there is any reference to a mere animal.] of the doors of my house to meet me, when I return in peace from the children of Ammon, shall surely be the Lord's, and I will offer it up for a burnt-offering.

32. So [And] Jephthah passed over unto the children of Ammon to fight against them ; and the Lord delivered them into his hands.

33. And he smote them from Aroer, even till thou come to Minnith [Maanith, four miles from Heshbon], even twenty cities, and unto the plain of the vineyards, with a very great slaughter. Thus the children of Ammon were subdued before the children of Israel.

34. And Jephthah came to Mizpeh unto his house, and behold, his daughter came out to meet him with timbrels and with dances: [As Miriam went to meet Moses (Exod. xv. 20) ; and the women to meet Saul and David (1 Sam. xviii. 6, 7)] and she was his only child ; beside her he had neither son nor daughter.

35. And it came to pass, when he saw her, that he rent his clothes ["Every Jew on approaching Jerusalem for the first time has to submit to the *Krie, i.e.,* to a cut made in his sleeve, as a sort of symbol of rending his clothes."], and said, Alas, my daughter ! thou hast brought me very low [crushing, thou hast crushed me], and thou art one of them that trouble me : for I have opened my mouth unto the Lord [a vow to be binding, must have been actually expressed in words], and I cannot go back [no room was left for mental reservations : Lev. xxvii. 28, 29].

36. And she said unto him, My father, if [omit if] thou hast opened thy mouth unto the Lord, do to me according to that which hath proceeded out of thy mouth ; forasmuch as the Lord hath taken vengeance for thee of thine enemies, even of the children of Ammon.

37. And she said unto her father, Let this thing be done for me : Let me alone two months, that I may go up and down upon the mountains, and bewail my virginity, [The thought most intolerable to a Hebrew maiden was

to die unwedded and childless. In this case there was additional bitterness because she was an only child, and in her early death prophecy would seem to come to nought.] I and my fellows.

38. And he said, Go. And he sent her away for two months: and she went with her companions, and bewailed her virginity upon the mountains.

39. And it came to pass at the end of two months, that she returned unto her father, who did with her according to his vow which he had vowed [offered her up for a burnt offering] : and she knew no man. And it was a custom in Israel [the Targum of Jonathan adds—"in order that no one should make his son or his daughter a burnt offering as Jephthah did, and did not consult Phinehas the priest," who would have redeemed her with money],

40. That the daughters of Israel went yearly to lament [to praise or celebrate] the daughter of Jephthah the Gileadite four days in a year.

JEPHTHAH.

JEPHTHAH was an illegitimate son. His brethren were cruel to him : they thrust him out, and said unto him, "Thou shalt not inherit in our father's house; for thou art the son of a strange woman." (v. 2). So the man was driven away. That is the first picture. The man was unfortunate, not criminal. He was the victim of circumstances. Why should society be so cruel? Is a man to be blamed because he was born blind? Who does not thrust the cripple away when there is a great feast, or a grand show, or some occasion of family pride and delight? Who does not hide the thing that is unpleasant? This is the mystery of society—that we should fix responsibility where there is none, and be very light in our thought concerning responsibility where it is evident and incommunicable—that is to say, where it is fastened upon the individual and cannot be transferred to any other person. There is something wrong here in social thought. Who does not gather himself up in a kind of conscious or unconscious disdain and look severely and repudiatingly upon a man who has come into the world under infinite disadvantages? We should show a better quality if we were more kindly disposed towards such, saying to them in effect : Poor souls! you had a bad beginning; the time will go heavy with you ; you have somehow come into a world that is lacking in compassion and magnanimity ; but, in God's name, some of us will stand by you, and help you, and make the world as glad for you as we can. That would be noble chivalry; that would be

the very Spirit of Christ. So Jephthah is doomed to everlasting
obscurity : is he ? The Lord is very pitiful and kind. Jephthah
was disreputable in birth, but he was illustrious in faith. That
is your opportunity! However you came into the world you
may go out of it a gentleman, a hero, a saint. Says the Apostle :
" What shall I more say ? for the time will fail me to tell of
Gideon, and of Barak, and of Samson, and of Jephthah." So
when his mocking brothers or alien kin are all forgotten, the
bastard Jephthah stands out elect, precious—a mighty man in
faith as in valour. Cheer ye! you may yet have a time of
gladness. There is no difficulty that is not conquerable. Many
a time your disadvantages will be thrown in your face. When
you are advancing with terrific pace upon the foremost men and
threatening to overrun them, they will not forget your birth and
your disadvantages. Every one of them will be turned into a
stone, which will be thrown at you, but not one of the stones
will strike you. Never mind what is thrown—have your purpose right and good, and God will defend you.

So " Jephthah fled from his brethren, and dwelt in the land of
Tob " (v. 3)—perhaps in the land of his maternal ancestors.
There is room enough in the world. Do not crowd one another
so. If there is a family difference, a disagreement of a painful
kind, you will find that Space may be turned into a kind of
reconciliation. Divide, separate : there is wonderful healing in
fresh air, and in new sunshine, and in new scenery and surroundings. If you are thrust out, it may be the making of you.
Some men would have been better to-day if they had been
driven from home. They have grown not one visible inch
during the last quarter of a century. A little hardship would
have been the making of them ; it would have awakened them all
through and through, so that most of them would not have been
asleep, but every faculty would have become a burning point, a
centre of new vitality. Jephthah went, and he left the shame
with his brothers. That must be the law of life, if we would
follow Christ. Behave you like a gentleman, however much
others may mock you and persecute you. Let the shame be
theirs! Wear them out by the very patience of goodness ; be so
constant in all nobleness, truth, honour, and genuine goodness,
that at last they will give up, saying, Truly this man is a son of

God ! Marvellous are the healings of time and space, mountains and seas.

Was there, then, no compensation ? Was there nothing but disadvantage in the life of Jephthah ? The question turns us back again to the first verse :—" Now Jephthah . . . was a mighty man of valour." Even his mother might not be without great qualities. Surely the mother lives again in the son. She was a giantess of a mother, fit to be the mother of kings. Do not scatter your contempt about too freehandedly. You cannot tell whom you are undervaluing, and whom you are attempting to deride. Your virtue may consist of some one point of respectability, and the person you contemn may be a person whose shoe's latchet you are not worthy to unloose. God knows what is in every man, woman, and child. He does not fix his eye upon little points or great, but takes in the whole man, the entire life, in its whole bulk and weight and force. Jephthah has a fortune in himself. The young man who went out from his father's house with the portion of goods that fell to him, had a fortune in his hand, not in his head—not in his heart ; and whatever is in the hand only may be spent, for there is nothing so easy as spending : any fool can learn the art without a premium. Jephthah's fortune was internal, spiritual; within him, in his mind, not yet awakened : for that gigantic body habited a mind worthy of itself. Study the law of compensations. If a dozen boys are playing at a game, and there is a cripple amongst them, the cripple is the winning man ; nothing can stand before the cripple ; all the handsome boys will be behind. You may have seen this again and again. It seems to be a kind of law of nature. Where a man is unable to speak much, you should see one of his letters—every sentence meaning something, and there is more in one page of his letters than in all the epistles some of the most fluent speakers ever wrote. See a man who is very timid under some circumstances, and that same man may be as bold as a lion under others : in the first instance the circumstances were not equal to the man—they did not awake him ; the latter appealed to his best quality. So it is all through and through life. The unsuccessful man may have a happy temperament, which is worth a very great amount as to quietness and happiness and music. God hath not left any of his creatures without some token of blessing, some point of

light, some gift all his own. Search for that particular gift, and
make it the beginning of heaven. You may be driven out, but
how strong you are! You may be derided by others, but how
wonderfully you can take care of yourself! Look at the bright
side, and though you be driven into far-away lands, yet, with a
soul touching God's great economies, and drawing out of them all
nutriment and inspiration, every land is home.

Now came a period of trial. The brethren got into trouble :
"The children of Ammon made war against Israel" (v. 5).
But a bastard might not reign in Israel ; so it was written in the
law. Jephthah, therefore, must keep out of the way ; the
captaincy is forbidden to him. There were social reasons for
this, strong enough for their time, adapted to the civilisation
which they ruled. What, then, was to be done ? A provision
was made for overgetting the difficulty. Such a man must be
called to the captaincy by the elders. Hence we find "the
elders of Gilead," including the brethren, in a formal and official
manner "went to fetch Jephthah out of the land of Tob " (v. 5).
Now we see a turn in the wheel of Providence which is not
unusual. The elders said unto Jephthah, "Come, and be our
captain, that we may fight with the children of Ammon " (v. 6).
Jephthah was but a man ; who can be more, unless he be
crucified with Christ—unless the life he now live in the flesh be
a life of faith of the Son of God ? "And Jephthah said unto the
elders of Gilead, Did not ye hate me, and expel me out of my
father's house ? and why are ye come unto me now when ye are
in distress ?" (v. 7). Your opportunity will come, and you
will feel that question though you may not ask it. When men
are in distress they seem almost inspired to be able to find out
one's address. We think we are well concealed, and it will be
impossible for any person whom we wish to avoid to find out
where we are ; but there is a kind of invisible directory they get
hold of, and as soon as the wolf is upon them they are upon us.
Who could keep back the question, "Why are ye come unto me
now when ye are in distress ?"—remember the old times when
you were hard with me, and thrust me away, hardly giving me
a garment with which to cover my shoulders, sending me away
from my father's house without a blessing or a cheer, without

one word of prayer or benediction, without a single " God bless
you " to shorten the road and brighten the end; why are ye
come to me now ?   If we push the question too much, we shall
show that we are unworthy of the honour which is sought to be
conferred upon us.   Joseph showed a right spirit when he said
to his brethren, "Now, therefore, be not grieved, nor angry with
yourselves. . . . It was not you . . . but God." Jephthah was
not so well instructed.   Presently we shall find that he did not
know the law of Israel, for if he had known it he would have
saved himself infinite pain.   How could Jephthah know the law ?
We thrust men out of their houses, drive them away into far
lands, and then blame them for not being as civilised as we are,
as highly educated, as fully trained.   This is the evil way of the
human spirit when it is not subdued and sanctified.   We give
men no chances, we turn them out into the bare desert, we treat
them as if they were of inferior quality : and then if they make
a slip or mistake, or commit offence, we charge them with
ignorance of the law.   We first make the heathen, then we
deride him, and at last we feebly attempt to convert him !   Have
we not driven away many ?   What this land has to answer for,
and many other lands, in the way of exiling men from their
natural positions and opportunities !   Surely the day must come
when our Christian preachers will not be afraid to read and
preach the *whole* Bible.   When that day comes there will be a
sword in the country, there will be a fire in the earth !   Now we
read the comforting promises, the tender exhortations, we apply
all the needful solaces, and call such reading and preaching
honouring the Bible !   There is no fire so hot as the fire that
burns in God's Book, in relation to all sin, injustice, irrational and
oppressive inequality.   The wrath of the Lamb is such wrath as
cannot burn in evil breasts.   Jephthah said, " If ye bring me
home again "—we cannot get rid of that word " home"; it
follows us into the land of Tob, and into every land, and makes
a song for itself—"to fight against the children of Ammon, and
the Lord deliver them before me, shall I be your head ?   And
the elders of Gilead said unto Jephthah, The Lord be witness
between us, if we do not so according to thy words " (vv. 9-10.)
It is really a pitiful moment when one gets the better of the
enemy.   There is something so crouching in the humiliation of

the foe that we almost wish the conquest had never been effected. The elders of Israel would do anything, give anything, promise anything, if this great Samson in anticipation would only come and deliver them from the children of Ammon.

Then came the battle and the victory. Jephthah stated his case in a statesmanlike manner (vv. 12-27, *ante*, p. 71).

There is nothing furious in the claim ; history is stated, victories are avouched, and a claim is made. Jephthah wishes to be strong in justice. If a man is not morally strong even an arm of iron may be broken and sinews of brass may be melted. Have right on your side. That is the coat-of-mail. There is no crevice in it. Let the arrows come with the thickness of rain ; they will fall harmlessly at your feet. Jephthah was a superstitious man, not well trained in the law. How could he be ? He was full of a wild kind of superstition. " Then the Spirit of the Lord came upon Jephthah, and he passed over Gilead, and Manasseh, and passed over Mizpeh of Gilead, and from Mizpeh of Gilead he passed over unto the children of Ammon " (v. 29)— passed like a mighty tempest ! Who can arrest a man who is made mad by the divine presence ? He was not inspired in the prophetic or apostolic sense of the term, but he was " possessed " ; he was no more himself, but a tabernacle of the living God. He had a purpose to realise, and God was in him that that purpose might be consummated.

Jephthah made a vow. He said that whoever came out of his house when he returned should be offered in sacrifice (vv. 30-31). " And Jephthah came to Mizpeh unto his house, and, behold, his daughter came out to meet him with timbrels and with dances : and she was his only child ; beside her he had neither son nor daughter " (v. 34). Here he was just as steadfast as at the earlier points of his history. There is a wonderful consistency about the man. When he saw the child, " he rent his clothes, and said, Alas, my daughter ! thou hast brought me very low, and thou art one of them that trouble me ; for I have opened my mouth unto the Lord, and I cannot go back " (v. 35). So he was a great man even in his heathenism. But he did not know the law, we have said. If he had been allowed to remain at home, and to study the law and **acquaint** himself with the ordinances of Israel, he might have known that provision was made for this very crisis. Oh, had one been at hand that day to whisper in his ear, "And if it be a female, then thy estimation shall be thirty shekels" (Levit. xxvii. 4)! Jephthah did not know that in the law there was mercy hidden. Jephthah was not aware that all the great necessities of life have been anticipated by providential economies, and that heaven's great, sweet law provides against the rashness and the madness into which we are plunged by our sin. For "thirty shekels" he could have redeemed his vow, and his only child might have been spared! Search the Bible for the way out of your difficulty. Everything is in the Book of God. Whatever your sorrow or strait, sit down to the inspired volume and read it until you find the gate that opens upon liberty; it is unquestionably in the Bible. All the deepest questions man has ever asked were answered before they were propounded. Who can be before the Lord, or prevent the Eternal?

Into the mystery of what then happened we cannot enter. The daughter was worthy of the father. She said, "If thou hast opened thy mouth unto the Lord, do to me according to that which hath proceeded out of thy mouth" (v. 36). We sometimes understand fathers best by studying the children. Jephthah's child had in her the making of a great woman. So the compensations of Providence are a million in number. They come upon a man at unexpected points, and they cheer him in the most critical distresses. Jephthah might have felt himself filled with a pride pleasing to heaven, as he heard his child utter this sublime reply. Men are sacrificing their daughters to-day in quite as heathenish a manner as Jephthah ever sacrificed his only child. There is less hope of them. They have passed through Moses and the prophets, the evangelists and the apostles, in so far as their moral teaching is concerned; and the men in question have come out of the process more obdurate and worldly than ever. Are there not men to-day who are saying, If I can marry my child to a rich man I shall be satisfied; no matter what his belief, no matter what his conduct, wealth is the one condition? Such men are cruel; they are not fit to live. They may not put **the case** to themselves quite so boldly; **they may throw a good** deal of social decoration around their proposals; but if at the heart of those proposals there is this idea of wealth, then truly their condemnation is just.   There is only one thing perhaps worse than this, and that is that a daughter should vow herself away on this mean altar.   But are there not people who are saying, If there is wealth, no matter what else there is or is not? What can come of an association of that kind, but disappointment, bitterness, death?   Are there not some also who are saying: I dedicate my children to enjoyment; they must have a good opportunity in the world, for life is brief and chances are few, and they must not be brought up to slave as I have slaved: they must be saved from hard work, and drudgery, and humiliation; they shall run with the footmen and outstrip the horsemen in the race of time?   Poor fools! they, too, are cruel.   There is no kindness like the kindness of bringing up a child to work.   He ought to be punished by society who leaves his child without a trade or a means of obtaining an honest living.   These are the vices to frown down.   These are the injustices that ought to be put down. The children will arise to condemn the memory that ought to have been for ever kept clean.   Dedicate your children to honesty, industry, self-reliance, sobriety, honour.   Tell them there is a poverty which is wealth, and a wealth which is poverty: a repute which is infamous, and a repudiation of a social kind which amounts to a real crowning and enthronement.   If we cannot look for these things from Christian people, from whom can we expect them?   This is the Spirit of Christ.   In all things he was our example—in making his living, in giving an equivalent for everything he received, in giving himself for the life of the world.   "If ye know these things, happy are ye if ye do them." "To him that knoweth to do good and doeth it not, to him it is sin."   I know of no cruelty so great as to substitute a momentary kindness for a lifelong discipline.   Let us learn that every direction suited to the education and development of human life is to be found in the Book of God.   He who walks by this book will walk straight into heaven; he will make no permanent mistakes; he may sometimes have a rod in his hand; sometimes his face may be darkened by a frown; sometimes his voice may tremble with menace; but, pursuing the course of education marked down in God's Book, at the last his children shall bless him, and they will speak with their father's enemies in the gate, if he should ever need to be vindicated or his honour to be upheld.   Let us stand by the Bible—preach, read, study, proclaim the Bible. Human life has no necessity that has not been anticipated by the living Book of the living God.

SELECTED NOTE.

Volumes have been written on the subject of " Jephthah's rash vow ; " the question being whether, in doing to his daughter "according to his vow," he really did offer her in sacrifice or not.   The negative has been stoutly maintained by many able pens, from a natural anxiety to clear the character of one of the heroes in Israel from so dark a stain.   But the more the plain rules of common sense have been exercised in our view of Biblical transactions, and the better we have succeeded in realizing a distinct idea of the times in which Jephthah lived and of the position which he occupied, the less reluctance there has been to admit the interpretation which the first view of the passage suggests to· every reader, which is, that he really did offer her in sacrifice.   The explanation which denies this maintains that she was rather doomed to perpetual celibacy, and this, as it appears to us, on the strength of phrases which to one who really understands the character of the Hebrew people and their language suggest nothing more than that it was considered a lamentable thing for any daughter of Israel to die childless. To *live* unmarried was required by no law, custom, or devotement among the Jews ; no one had a right to impose so odious a condition on another, nor is any such condition implied or expressed in the vow which Jephthah uttered.   To get rid of a difficulty which has no place in the text, but arises from our reluctance to receive that text in its obvious meaning, we invent a new thing in Israel, a thing never heard of among the Hebrews in ancient or modern times, and more entirely opposed to their peculiar notions than anything which the wit of man ever devised, such as that a damsel should be consecrated to perpetual virginity in consequence of a vow of her father, which vow itself says nothing of the kind.   If people allow themselves to be influenced in their interpretations of Scripture by dislike to take the words in their obvious meaning, we might at least expect that the explanations they would have us receive should be in accordance with the notions of the Hebrew people, instead of being entirely and obviously opposed to them. The Jewish commentators themselves generally admit that Jephthah really sacrificed his daughter ; and even go so far as to allege that the change in the pontifical dynasty from the house of Eleazar to that of Ithamar was caused by the high-priest of the time having suffered this transaction to take place.

Professor Bush maintains with us that a human sacrifice was all along contemplated.   But he suggests that during the two months, Jephthah might have obtained better information respecting the nature of vows, by which he would have learned that his daughter could not be legally offered, but might be redeemed at a valuation (Lev. xxvii. 2-12).   This is possible, and is much more likely than the popular alternative of perpetual celibacy ; but we have serious doubts whether even this meets the conclusion that "he did with her according to his vow."   Besides, in this case, where was the ground for the annual "lamentations" of the daughters of Israel, or even for the "celebrations" which some understand the word to mean ?—*Kitto.*

Judges xii.

1. **And the men of** Ephraim gathered themselves together [literally, were called together; the same phrase in chap. vii. 23, 24], and went northward [in order to cross the Jordan fords. Mizpeh in Gilead lay to the north-east of the tribe of Ephraim], and said unto Jephthah, Wherefore passedst thou over to fight against the children of Ammon, and didst not call us ["the tribe of Ephraim throughout the book of Judges is represented in a most unenviable light." Compare the similar complaint of the Ephraimites to Gideon, chap. viii. 1; see also Josh. xvii. 14-18] to go with thee? We will burn thine house upon thee with fire [that is, we will burn thee alive in thy house; a threat which shows somewhat the wildness of the times. See a similar threat in chap. xiv. 15, and an execution of it in chap. xv. 6. Burning was a mode of capital punishment; see Gen. xxxviii. 24; Josh. vii. 25].

2. And Jephthah said unto them, I and my people were at great strife with the children of Ammon [literally, I was a man of strife, I and my people, and the children of Ammon exceedingly. For a similar phrase, see Jer. xv. 10]; and when I called you, ye delivered me not out of their hands. [The Ephraimites held themselves selfishly aloof. When Jephthah says, "I called you," he speaks in the person of Gilead or of the Gileadites].

3. And when I saw that ye delivered me not, I put my life in my hands [in the hollow of my hand], and passed over against the children of Ammon, and the Lord delivered them into my hand [Jephthah makes his appeal to Jehovah]: wherefore then are ye come up unto me this day [for the phrase "come up," see chap. i. 1-16], to fight against me?

4. Then Jephthah gathered together all the men of Gilead [under great provocation. By "the men of Gilead," understand the eastern tribes generally], and fought with Ephraim: and the men of Gilead smote Ephraim, because they said [here the translation and meaning are regarded by eminent critics as highly uncertain: one says that it seems to be "implied that in spite of Jephthah's perfectly reasonable answer the Ephraimites advanced to attack Gilead, and goaded the Gileadites to fury by intolerable taunts, which prevented the Gileadites from giving any quarter when they had won the victory"], Ye Gileadites are fugitives of Ephraim [an extremely obscure passage. *The Speaker's Commentary* gives the following as the most grammatically correct and natural rendering of this and the two following verses: "The men of Gilead smote Ephraim, for they, the Gileadites, said, Ye are fugitives to Ephraim (Gilead lies between Ephraim and Manasseh); and Gilead took the fords of Jordan before Ephraim, and it came to pass,

when the fugitives of Ephraim said, Let me pass over, and the Gileadites asked him, Art thou an Ephraimite? and he answered, No; then said the Gileadites to him, Say Shibboleth, etc., so they, the Gileadites, slew them at the ford of Jordan], among the Ephraimites, and among the Manassites.

5. And the Gileadites took the passages of Jordan [because only through them could the Ephraimites escape to their own tribe] before the Ephraimites [literally, to Ephraim]: and it was so, that when those Ephraimites which were escaped [fugitives to Ephraim. It has been suggested that a bitter retribution may be implied in these words. "The Ephraimites had taunted the eastern Manassites with being fugitives to Ephraim, and in the next verse they themselves appear to be in another but fatal sense fugitives to Ephraim] said, Let me go over; that the men of Gilead said unto him, Art thou an Ephraimite? If he said, Nay;

6. Then said they unto him, Say now Shibboleth [a ford; depth of waters; water-flood; channel]; and he said Sibboleth [according to *The Speaker's Commentary,* this is a curious instance of dialectic difference of pronunciation between the east and west Jordanic tribes. . . . The *sh* may have been as impossible for an Ephraimite to pronounce as *th* is to a Frenchman]: for he could not frame to pronounce it right. ["Archdeacon Farrar says, 'On May 25th, 1802, all the French were detected by their inability to pronounce the words,' *scilt, end, friend.*"] Then they took him, and slew him at the passages of Jordan [the Arabic version says, they led him across, but the word means rather massacred, butchered]: and there fell at that time of the Ephraimites forty and two thousand [not necessarily that they were all butchered, but only that that was the number of the invading army; it may include the slain in battle and those killed at the fords; see chap. iv. 16].

7. And Jephthah judged Israel [his authority embracing all Israel after the subjugation of the Ephraimites] six years. Then died Jephthah the Gileadite, and was buried in one of the cities of Gilead [literally, in cities of Gilead; according to the LXX. in his city, Gilead,—that is, Ramoth-Gilead, or Mizpeh of Gilead].

8. And after him Ibzan [about whom nothing further is known than is found in these three verses; some have supposed him the same as Boaz] of Bethlehem [Josephus assumes that Bethlehem-Judah is here meant] judged Israel.

9. And he had thirty sons, and thirty daughters [implying polygamy, wealth, and great state. Compare 2 Kings x. 1 and Judg. viii. 30], whom he sent abroad [whom he gave in marriage out of his house], and took in thirty daughters from abroad for his sons. And he judged Israel seven years.

10. Then died Ibzan, and was buried at Bethlehem.

11. And after him Elon [the name means a Terebinth: it is customary for Orientals even now to name their children from trees. Archdeacon Farrar says that one of his muleteers in Palestine was named "Father of Olives"], a Zebulonite, judged Israel; and he judged Israel ten years.

12. And Elon the Zebulonite died, and was buried in Aijalon [a place in the tribe of Zebulun, not elsewhere mentioned: where the vowel-points are omitted, the names Elon and Aiialon are identical in Hebrew] in the country of Zebulun.

13. And after him Abdon [*servant*] the son of Hillel [praising. The Rabbi called Hillel is regarded as by far the greatest and best of the Rabbis], a Pirathonite [and therefore of the tribe of Ephraim], judged Israel.

14. And he had forty sons and thirty nephews [the Hebrew has, *sons of sons:* the word "nephews" in our version always means *grandsons,* "nieces" is a word which means *granddaughters* in Wyclif's Bible], that rode on threescore and ten ass colts [implying wealth and distinction] : and he judged Israel eight years.

15. And Abdon the son of Hillel the Pirathonite died, and was buried in Pirathon [now called Feratah, six miles west of Shechem] in the land of Ephraim, in the mount of the Amalekites [pointing to an early settlement of Amalekites in Central Palestine. "The twenty-five years, apparently consecutive ones, occupied by the judgeship of Ibzan, Elon, and Abdon, seem to have been very uneventful and prosperous, since the only record of them preserved in the annals of their country relates to the flourishing families and peaceful magnificence of two of their number. . . . Jephthah's victory over the enemies of Israel was followed by twenty-five years of peace under three judges. . . . All the three belong to the western tribes. The first from Bethlehem, the second from Zebulun, and the third from Ephraim.]

[The venerable John Trapp, remarking on verse 6, says, "They were discerned by their lisping, their dialect betrayed them. How many have we that can hardly lisp out a syllable of good language, and if they attempt it, falter fearfully." On verse 14 he quaintly remarks, "In Persia the peasant never rideth; the gentleman never goeth on foot, but fighteth, tradeth, conferreth, doeth, all on horseback."]

SHIBBOLETH.

WE have just inquired, Is Abimelech dead ? and to that inquiry we received a very decisive reply. Are the Ephraimites dead ? Are they clean gone for ever ? To this inquiry what reply can we discover in the history which is now before us ? Why concern ourselves about an extinct tribe ? Principally because we deny that the tribe is extinct. There are no extinct tribes where great moral characteristics and inspirations are concerned. Men die, but Man lives. The individual type seems to modify, and to pass away by development or by extinction, but a certain ground-line runs through all human history ; there is a purpose in it, there is a grand central idea which abides. This we shall see if we study the history of Ephraim, as revealed in this incident connected with the war of Jephthah upon the children of Ammon.

Are the Ephraimites dead ? Are they dead who are hard upon a man when he is in circumstances of extremity ? Are they dead who do not fear to strike the last blow upon a man who is supposed to be staggering and to be unable to resist ? Jephthah was exhausted. The war had been a triumphant one, but even triumph is succeeded by exhaustion. Prosperity takes out of a man the very energy which he was required to show in securing the honour. Great efforts are followed by great weaknesses. Added to this, there was a vow claiming execution. The only child was away upon the mountains on a two months' respite, and in this time of extremity and agony, proud and arrogant Ephraim came to ask a question and deliver a threatening. Are the Ephraimites, then, dead ? Have they no successors ? Are we now quite patient, after the manner of Christ, with men who are tired, for the moment outworn, and to whose physical exhaustion great mental prostration is added ? If so—if there are no such men ; if there are no such cruel proposals and demands ; if there are no such untimely and aggravating threats, then the Ephraimites are dead, and shame be to the preacher who would exhume such men even that he might rebuke their forgotten wickedness.

Are the Ephraimites quite dead ? Are there not men who cannot bear that anything should be done but by themselves— men who will deny the victory rather than award the merit ? Are there not men who would not allow even the world to be converted but under their inspiration, and guidance, and co-operation ? Are there Christian communions which deny to one another that they are accomplishing real and solid good in society ? Is there a spirit of criticism which says, " The work may be only in appearance—a kind of superficial work is no doubt being done, but time will test and time will tell," a spirit which hampers and frets great Christian aggressions by narrow-minded and impious criticism ? Ephraim could not bear that the battle should be won in which Ephraim had taken no part. We measure successes by the part which we ourselves have in them. If we were not in the fray, leading it, and causing it to issue in victory, how can we suppose that the fray was other than a tumult in which there was neither reason nor righteousness ?

Are the Ephraimites quite dead? Are there not people who profess to be offended because they were not invited? Ephraim said, "Wherefore passedst thou over to fight against the children of Ammon, and didst not call us to go with thee?" (v. 1). We stand much upon the etiquette of invitation. We are so self-restrained, and so conscious of intolerable modesty, that unless we are properly invited to pray we will not worship God, and unless we are besought almost by deputation to take an interest in Christian service we will stand back in unchristian resentment. There are people who must be invited every day. What they suppose themselves to be it is almost impossible to tell. But they must be invited, entreated; the impression must be produced upon them that the universe would go out like a dying spark if they did not come to its patronage and sustenance. They have to be courted by the Church, waited upon, sedulously attended to. If a card should be sent to other people and not to them they would have no part or lot in the matter. Their dignity perish with them! They have no right to be in the Church. They are spots in the feast of charity. Who issues the invitations? The Lord. Whose battle is it? The battle is not yours, but God's. For whom do we work when we open the door, light the lamp, throw in the coin of charity? Is it for the minister—for some man? Then why this sensitiveness? Why this retirement to bed, and covering oneself up with all the clothes, and sweltering in an undeserved and unrecognised obscurity? Who called us to the service? Our call is from eternity. We respond to a divine decree and purpose, and as we were not born of men into this service we do not own their rulership: we are the sons of God, and we will work, whoever sends for us, or ignores us, or praises us. That is the spirit of consecration, and any other spirit in any man, in the pulpit or out of it, is not of God. Reason would be shocked were we to go into detail upon this matter. The childishness, the pettishness, the resentment, which we see in some poor souls, would discourage the strongest heart, were not our trust put in the living God. When such Ephraimites retire, are they any loss? Yes, they **are**: when they have gone we have lost folly, pride, petulance, **arrogance and a great burden which we carried with a sense of intolerable pain.**

Are the Ephraimites quite dead? Are they dead who have curiously forgotten their own faithlessness in the past? Jephthah said, " When I called you, ye delivered me not out of their hands. And when I saw that ye delivered me not, I put my life in my hands, and passed over against the children of Ammon, and the Lord delivered them into my hand " (vv. 2-3). Men curiously forget the invitations that they have actually received. They put them aside, because they were not willing to obey them ; and having put them out of sight, they have put them out of memory ; and having put them out of memory, they impiously deny their existence. The heart is deceitful above all things, and desperately wicked. Were the Ephraimites, then, so brave and bold and constant in all faithfulness that they should criticise the action of Jephthah? People should be very careful how they criticise. The popular proverb is a wise one which says, " They who live in glass houses should not throw stones." Jephthah remembered the case. He had not forgotten sending for the Ephraimites at a critical time in his history, and the Ephraimites paid no heed to his cry. We cannot always be sending for the men who are supposed to be neglected. There is a point at which common reason says, No ; we will send no more for you. There is a point indeed at which decency can proceed no further. The people who have always to be sought, and always to be sent for, and always to be implored to come, will break the patience they have misunderstood, and will come to the ruin which they deserve.

Are the Ephraimites quite dead? Are they dead in whom envy culminates in revenge? " We will burn thine house upon thee with fire " (v. 1). They had better have reckoned with the enemy first. Some houses are not easily lighted. The spirit of men, however, is here clearly revealed. They envied Jephthah his honours, and envy has but a short distance to go to reach revenge. What will not envy do? Of what is it compounded? Of what hateful juices is that devil's cup made up,— envy, the spirit that has no generous word even for a friend, much less an antagonist ; envy, that reduces everything that is done to the lowest possible point ; envy, so critical in vision, so unjust in criticism ; envy, that, serpent-like, entwines itself around the

heart, and transforms what ought to be a fountain of benevolence
into a fountain of deadly bitterness ?   Envy cannot rest in mere
criticism.   Envy must do mischief : not only is there a con-
demnatory word, but there is a word of menace : the inward fire
expresses itself in outward conflagration.   Beware of the very
first symptom of envy, jealousy !   Cultivate the noble spirit,—
the spirit of appreciation and recognition, and if in this respect
you water others, you shall be divinely watered yourselves ;
your heart shall be as an abundant harvest field, laden with the
very gold of heaven.

Are they dead who are insolent, who descend to the use of
contemptuous taunts ?   If not, then the Ephraimites are not
dead.   The Ephraimites said to Jephthah and his tribe, "Ye
Gileadites are fugitives of Ephraim among the Ephraimites, and
among the Manassites" (v. 4).   You belong to neither one
tribe nor another ; ye upstarts, ye off-scouring, how dare you
fight without asking us to lead you ?   That tribe can come to no
good.   Watch its history, and see whether such vaunting can
end in honour.   Are insolent men dead ? the men who stealthily
pick up stones and carry them until a suitable opportunity arises
for throwing them at those who have outrun them and outfought
them in the war ?   Are you ever reminded of your lowly parentage ?   Is it ever whispered that you were not born in royal
circles ?   Does any adversary ever give the hint, quite in a
Christian spirit, and in a fine and beautiful hypocrisy, that you
were not born as highly and famously as he was, albeit the place
of his birth has not to this day been discovered, though it might
possibly have been found out if the lowest creature on earth had
thought it worth while to put the vain and useless inquiry ?
Jephthah was stunned by this taunt.   Many a man can bear a
threat to have his house burned who cannot endure too much
impertinence.   Some noble natures have chafed under insolence
who could have gone with some steadfastness even to martyrdom.
Jephthah was roused.   He now came to a kind of war he would
have avoided if he could.   So long as it was a heathenish war
a battle with the enemy, he was equal to the occasion ; but when
the battle became internecine, of the nature of a family feud,
partaking somewhat of the quality of civil war, his soul revolted.

So long as it was Ammon, the outward heathen enemy, he was
not unprepared to go forward even alone to fight the foe. But
who would enter into a family feud, a tribal dispute? Who
would not rather half apologise, and explain as far as possible,
and swallow somewhat, rather than play the foul game of Cain
and Abel? Jephthah was quiet, almost as quiet as Gideon at
the first when the same Ephraimites assailed him. Jephthah
said : I did send for you ; I wanted you to come ; I did not forget
your high position; but when ye did not come I put my life in
my hand ; I had my life on my palm, like a loose bird that might
at any moment fly away, and in that condition I went out to fight
Ammon, and I take no merit or undue praise to myself: "The
Lord delivered them into my hand : wherefore then are ye come
up unto me this day, to fight against me?" He reasons well!
There is a touch of condescension in his reasoning which
detracts nothing from its dignity and cogency. Presently they
will go too far with him. Ephraim said, "Ye are but the fugitives of the tribes, ill-born, ill-bred ; Ephraim will not have you ;
Manasseh will not have you ; you are playing between the two,
being outcast of both,—away with you!" It was enough! We
shall see who was overthrown. The Gileadites took the fords of
the Jordan, and said in effect, "Every man who passes here will
have to give a good reason for his doing so." When any man said,
"Let me go over," the men of Gilead said unto him, "Art thou
an Ephraimite?" Now we have come to real conflict. Apologies
are no excuse at this point, nor explanations. Every man now
holds his life who can hold it. If the man said, No, I am not an
Ephraimite, they tested him : they said unto him, "Say now
Shibboleth : and he said Sibboleth : for he could not frame to
pronounce it right. Then they took him, and slew him at the
passages of Jordan : and there fell at that time of the Ephraimites
forty and two thousand." Do not interfere with divinely-
qualified soldiers. They may expose themselves to your
criticism now and again, but in so far as they are divinely
qualified they will conquer at the last. There will be a period
of apology and self-exculpation, there will be moments given up
to explanatory statements ; but let them alone, they cannot be
slain. If you apply fire to their houses, the very houses will not
burn. They must win, because they are sent of God.

Sometimes we misapply the use of this word Shibboleth—as, indeed, what do we not misapply when we come into the spiritual interpretation of the Bible? Now the phrase is used in this sense,—namely: if we cannot pronounce the Shibboleth of a sect we are regarded as heterodox. It has become quite a proverb amongst us, has this use of the word Shibboleth. Men defend themselves by saying one to another, Although we cannot pronounce your Shibboleth, we claim to be independent and accurate thinkers. The term Shibboleth has no relation whatever to that kind of remark. The test was put, not as a test of orthodoxy, but as a test of character, and is it not true that character is tested by little things? Regarding a Christian country, the men are comparatively few in number who are guilty of great crimes or aggravated transgressions against the state, or against one another. How many men could arise and indignantly repel great impeachments: but the question relates to little matters: and what can test character more than little experiments, minute utterances and observances? We may not have sinned against God, or against one another, in a manner that could be called romantic or tragical, but what about the little offences, the minor immoralities, the white lies, the leaving out the words of letters which give them their real meaning? What about mispronunciation, false accent, calculated emphasis so laid on as to give false colour to the thought that is being uttered? What about attitudes, postures, hints? What about unuttered defamations? What about "hesitated dislike"? It is along that line you know whether men can say Shibboleth or Sibboleth. The leaving out of a syllable changes the whole message; the introduction of false emphasis is destructive of integrity. Let us, therefore, examine ourselves in so-called little things and minute ceremonies and utterances: then what hand has not done the wrong deed? What tongue has not spoken in the wrong tone, if not in the wrong language? Who, then, can claim to be white-robed? Who can say of himself that his purity is like the snow, untrodden, and unstained? We must not recede from the application of such passages by limiting them to sectarian differences, or metaphysical contrasts; but follow out the exact line of the thought, and then we shall come to a test of *sincerity*, a test of truthfulness, a test of character,—we shall know whether a man is trying to save his life at the expense of truth. The Ephraimite said in effect : " I will tell any number of lies, if you will only let me escape." But the Ephraimites have mocked the Gileadites—let them mock them *now!* So it shall be at the great upwinding of things. Sceptics, assailants, enemies of Christ and his cross, have yet to meet that same Christ in an official examination. The war does not end just now. All things are to be brought up for arbitrament and final decision, and we read of those who shall pray the rocks and the hills to fall upon them and hide them from the face—the wrath, the burning countenance —of the Lamb. We must be prepared for these test interviews and final examinations ; then it will be seen that all pride, and arrogance, and insolence, and flippancy will have no reply in that day. Be wise ere the sun go down. Kiss the Son, while his anger is kindled but a little. If we have spoken haughtily even against the Son of God it may be forgiven us, if we repent with our hearts. He himself has said so. He never shut the door upon contrition, repentance, or attempts at restitution. Wherein we have been unjust to the Bible, unjust to the Church, unjust to Christ,—wherein we have been excusing ourselves from joining the war on petty grounds of not having been invited, let us repent this very day, call ourselves not only sinners, but fools in the sight of God for such a mean exculpation ; and with one heart and mind and soul, let us say or sob, " God be merciful to me a sinner ! "

PRAYER.

ALMIGHTY GOD, do thou bless us according to our need, and have mercy upon us according unto the multitude of our sins. Thy loving-kindnesses cannot be reckoned up: behold, they are more than the sands upon the sea-shore, and they exceed the stars in multitude. We live upon them: without them we could not live. We are fed by the mercy of the Lord; we are led by the light of his glory; we stand on the rocks which he has laid as foundations, and our whole life is rooted in his eternity. We look up unto heaven expectantly and gratefully. We love thee for all thou hast given, and we must continue to live upon thy regard for us. Thou hast redeemed us at a great cost: thou hast called us to the cross of the Saviour; thou hast made known unto us thy purpose to save our souls. We are therefore full of gladness, and a new song is in our mouth, and our expectation is from on high. We commit one another to thy tender care, for they are well kept whom thou dost keep. Lead us by still waters and in green pastures, and show us where thou dost make thy flock couch at noon; and may we always be in thine arm, or guided by thine eye, or sustained by thine hand. Let thy wisdom be within us a continual light, and thy grace an abiding hope. Make our way straight before our feet: bring down all high places; make all rough places smooth; lift up the valleys; and thus do thou, preparing a way for us, delight us with the city which is at the end. We bless thee for the hope of heaven— the all-completing world, the place all light, all purity, all love. We have heard of it with the hearing of the ear, and thou art daily satisfying us that it is more than eye hath seen or ear heard or heart conceived—the sublimest of thy wonders, a city worthy of thyself. Meanwhile help us to work more, to dig deeply, to do our present duty with both hands earnestly. May our eyes be in our head, may our hearts be true and loyal to God's doctrine, and in all the way of life may we know that to do is to learn, that to obey is to be instructed, and if we do the will we shall know the doctrine, and the mystery shall not appal us, but draw us on by a marvellous fascination. This life we want to live; this discipline we are prepared by thy Spirit to undergo. The Lord work in us all the good pleasure of his will, and the work of faith with power, and then call us into upper places to behold sights we cannot now see, and enter upon work which at present is too much for our poor strength. Amen.

Judges xiii.

1. And the children of Israel did evil again [see chap. iii. 7, iv. 1, vi. 1-11, x. 6] in the sight of the Lord; and the Lord delivered them into the hand of the Philistines [who from this point to the reign of David play a most

important part. By Philistines we are not to understand Canaanites, but foreign conquerors ; the name means *camps*] forty years [terminating with the battle of Ebenezer, 1 Sam. vii. 13].

2. And there was a certain man of Zorah [*place of hornets*], of the family of the Danites [the words "family" and "tribe" are often used interchangeably. The tribe of Dan is said to have consisted of the single family of Shuham, Numb. xxvi. 42], whose name was Manoah [*rest*]; and his wife was barren, and bare not.

3. And the angel of the Lord appeared unto the woman, and said unto her, Behold now, thou art barren, and bearest not : but thou shalt conceive, and bear a son.

4. Now therefore beware, I pray thee, and drink not wine nor strong drink [intoxicating liquor not made from grapes], and eat not any unclean thing [a law which applied to all Israelites] :

5. For, lo, thou shalt conceive, and bear a son ; and no razor shall come on his head [see the law of the Nazarite in Num. vi.] : for the child shall be a Nazarite unto God from the womb ; and he shall begin to deliver Israel out of the hand of the Philistines ["begin," but not complete : many men are permitted to begin good works, but they die without their full accomplishment].

6 Then the woman came and told her husband, saying, A man of God came unto me [angels always appear in human form], and his countenance was like the countenance of an angel of God, very terrible [see Matt. xxviii. 3, 4] : but I asked him not whence he was, neither told he me his name :

7. But he said unto me, Behold, thou shalt conceive, 'and bear a son ; and now drink no wine nor strong drink, neither eat any unclean thing : for the child shall be a Nazarite [Samuel was also a Nazarite, so was John the Baptist, so was James the Lord's brother] to God from the womb to the day of his death.

8. Then Manoah intreated the Lord, and said, O my Lord, let the man of God which thou didst send come again unto us, and teach us [we should ask for second and completing inspirations] what we shall do unto the child that shall be born.

9. And God hearkened to the voice of Manoah ; and the angel of God came again unto the woman as she sat in the field : but Manoah her husband was not with her.

10. And the woman made haste, and ran, and shewed her husband, and said unto him, Behold, the man hath appeared unto me, that came unto me the other day.

11. And Manoah arose, and went after his wife, and came to the man, and said unto him, Art thou the man that spakest unto the woman ? And he said, I am.

12. And Manoah said, Now let thy words come to pass. How shall we order the child [what shall be the order of the child and his work?] and how shall we do unto him ? [Not a step would they take without divine direction.]

13. And the angel of the Lord said unto Manoah, Of all that I said unto the woman let her beware.

14. She may not eat of any thing that cometh of the vine [see Numb. vi. 3-5], neither let her drink wine or strong drink, nor eat any unclean thing : all that I commanded her let her observe. [The wine is described as the

vine of wine—the grape-bearing vine; thus distinguishing it from the wild cucumber vine ; see 2 Kings iv. 39].

15. And Manoah said unto the angel of the Lord, I pray thee, let us detain thee, until we shall have made ready a kid for thee [literally, before thy face. Compare with this the narrative of Gideon. A kid was a special delicacy; see Gen. xxvii. 9 ; 1 Sam. xvi. 20].

16. And the angel of the Lord said unto Manoah, Though thou detain me, I will not eat of thy bread : and if thou wilt offer a burnt offering, thou must offer it unto the Lord [literally, a burnt offering unto the Lord thou mayest offer it. Compare chap. vi. 20. The worship of angels is nowhere encouraged by angels themselves; they invariably point worshippers to God himself. The angel did not understand Manoah as preparing a simple meal, but as really making preparations for sacrifice. Cautions given by angels should be studied with care—Rev. xix. 10, xxii. 8, 9; and see Acts x. 25, 26]. For Manoah knew not that he was an angel of the Lord.

17. And Manoah said unto the angel of the Lord, What is thy name [compare Gen. xxxii. 29; Exod. iii. 13; Prov. xxx. 4], that when thy sayings come to pass we may do thee honour [the word implying that some gift would be presented to the angel] ?

18. And the angel of the Lord said unto him, Why askest thou thus after my name, seeing it is secret? [In Isa. ix. 5, this word is rendered "wonderful": the word must be taken as an adjective. The only angel who names himself in scripture is Gabriel].

19. So Manoah took a kid with a meat offering, and offered it upon a rock unto the Lord : and the angel of the Lord did wondrously [as in some sense verifying his name]; and Manoah and his wife looked on [all they could do].

20. For it came to pass, when the flame went up toward heaven from off the altar [that which was a rock at first now became an altar], that the angel of the Lord ascended in the flame of the altar. And Manoah and his wife looked on it, and fell on their faces to the ground.

21. But the angel of the Lord did no more appear to Manoah and to his wife. Then Manoah knew that he was an angel of the Lord.

22. And Manoah said unto his wife, We shall surely die, because we have seen God ["as seeing him who is invisible"; Exod. xxxiii. 20; see also Gen. xxxii. 20 and Deut. v. 24].

23. But his wife said unto him, If the Lord were pleased to kill us, he would not have received a burnt offering and a meat offering at our hands ; neither would he have shewed us all these things, nor would, as at this time, have told us such things as these.

24. And the woman bare a son, and called his name Samson [*to minister*, a name denoting Nazaritic consecration]: and the child grew [see Luke i. 80, and ii. 40], and the Lord blessed him ["with a heroic spirit and extraordinary strength of body, far above that which the poets feign of their Hercules with his twelve incredible labours "].

25. And the Spirit of the Lord began to move him at times [literally, to agitate or thrust him—"to move him hither and thither, as the bells which hung in the skirts of Aaron's garments ; these bells have their name from a word which signifies that they were shaken to and fro "] in the camp of Dan between Zorah and Eshtaol.

Judges xiii. 23.

"But his wife said unto him, If the Lord were pleased to kill us, he would
not have received a burnt offering and a meat offering at our hands; neither
would he have shewed us all these things, nor would, as at this time, have
told us such things as these."

MANOAH'S WIFE.

THIS is part of a family scene. It is quoted from a conversation which took place between husband and wife. Let
us treat the incident as showing some aspects of family life,
some methods of reading divine Providence, and some sources of
consolation amid the distractions and mysteries of the present
world.

Look at it as showing some aspects of family life. Here is the
head of the house in gloom. Is he not always more or less in
gloom, this same head of the house all the world over? Who
ever knew a head of the house that was not more or less low-
spirited, worried by a hundred anxieties, tormented by sudden
fear? Perhaps naturally so: after all he *is* the head of the
house; and probably the lightning conductor, being higher than
any other part of the building, may have experience of thunder-
storms and lightning discharges that lower parts of the structure
know nothing about. As the head of the house you are in the
market-place, you see things in their roughest aspects, you have
to bear many a thing that you cannot explain to strangers, and
there is an under-current in your consciousness which perhaps your
truest friend has never seen, or seeing, appreciated; and therefore when we hear the head of the house complaining in tones that
have no music in them, how know we but that the poor man has
been undergoing vexations and distresses that he does not feel at
liberty to explain? At any rate Manoah took this view of the
angel's visit: "We have seen God: no man can see God and live
—we shall surely die." Here we have a wife comforting her
husband. Like a true woman, she let Manoah have his groan out.
There is a beautiful cunning in love. It does not break in upon
a sentence at a semicolon. It lets the groan get right out, and
then it offers its gentle consolation. If we had heard Manoah
alone, we should have said, A terrible thunder-storm has burst

upon this house, and God has come down upon it with awful vengeance ; and not until we heard his wife's statement of the case should we have any clear idea of the reality of the circumstances. You complain of this word " *but* " when a statement is made to you and it proceeds fluently and satisfactorily ; the speaker says *but*, and you say, " Aye, there it is again." We carelessly abuse this *but;* it sometimes, however, introduces all the light and all the music, and is found to be the key, long lost, of the gate which had impeded our progress. " But his wife said unto him "—" *but* a certain Samaritan came that way." Therefore remember that help sometimes comes after words that seem only to promise some greater distress. Be the complement of each other. The husband does not know all the case. Perhaps the wife would read it a little too hopefully. You must hear both the statements, put them both together, and draw your conclusions from the twofold statement. People are the complement of each other. Woe to that man who thinks he combines all populations and all personalities in himself. He must be a miserable man who thinks that he is the only man in the world. You would get more help from other people if you expected more, if you invited more, if you put yourself in circumstances that would justify the offering of more. There is not a poor creature in the world who cannot fill up the drop that is wanting to complete the fulness of some other creature's joy. You would not be half the man that you are except for your wife, and yet you never say " Thank you " with any degree of heartiness or sincerity. You listen to her suggestions with a half contempt, as if she did not know what she was talking about, and then you go and work out her idea and get the profit of it, and say what a clever man of business you are. That is not honest, it is not just —" Thou shalt not steal."

Here we have a husband and wife talking over a difficult case. Is not that a rare thing in these days of rush and tumult and noise, when a man never sees his little children, his very little ones, except in bed ? He leaves home so early in the morning, and gets back so late at night, that he never sees his little ones but in slumber. Is it not now a rare thing for a husband and wife to sit down and talk a difficulty over in all its bearings ?

Have we not known in our own experience many a wife wronged because of the husband failing to show proper confidence? The man has been in difficulties, wherever he has gone he has been pursued by a haunting dread, and he has suffered all this alone; whereas if he had but stated the case with all frankness and loving candour, who knows but that his wife might have said some word which might have been as a key to the lock, and as a solution of the hard and vexatious problem? You will always find it an inexpressible comfort to take your husband or wife, as the case may be, into your confidence, and talk any difficulty right through, keeping back no part of the case. "It soothes poor misery hearkening to her tale." If we lived in more domestic confidence, our houses would be homes, our homes would be churches, and those churches would be in the very vicinage of heaven.

Let us now look at the incident as showing some methods of reading divine Providence. There we have the timid and distrustful method. Manoah looks at the case, reads it, spells where he cannot read plainly, and then, looking up from his book, he says to his wife, "There is bad news for you: God is about to destroy us." There are these same timid and doubtful readers of Providence in society to-day. There are some men who never see the sky in its mid-day beauty, who never see summer in July at all, who really have never one day's true elevation of soul. I do not blame such people altogether. We are fearfully and wonderfully made. We cannot all read with equal facility, and see with equal distinctness. There are causes or sub-causes, intermediate, secondary influences arising from physical constitution and other circumstances over which we have no control, which trouble our vision even of God himself. Let us, therefore, put in a word wherever we can for those who are not constituted hopefully, who have not been gifted with a sanguine temperament. There are men amongst us whose life is a continual pain. It is possible so to read God's ways among men as to bring upon ourselves great distress. Is a man, therefore, to exclaim, "This is a punishment sent from heaven for some inscrutable reason, and I must endure it as well as I can; I shall never see the sky when not a cloud bedims its dome"? No, you are to struggle against this, you are to believe other people; that is to say, you are to live in other people's lives, to get out of other people the piece that is wanting in your own life. You are not to put ashes upon your head and say, "There is nothing in the universe that I do not see." You are to call little children and to say, "What do you see?" and young men and say, "How does life look from your point of view?" and you are to live in other people. We are to walk by faith and not by sight; we are debtors both to the Jew and to the Greek; and we must get from one another a complete statement of the reality of God's way among the children of men. This is the inductive and hopeful method of reading divine Providence. Some cynical people who have no licence, and therefore ought to be arrested as metaphysical felons, say that women have no logic. And that sentence sounds as if really it ought to be true. It is so pat. It is one of those little weapons that a man can pick up and use as if he had always had it. I think that Manoah's wife was in very deed learned in what we call the inductive method of reasoning, for she stated her case with wonderful simplicity and clearness. "If the Lord were pleased to kill us, he would not have received a burnt offering and a meat offering at our hands; neither would he have shewed us all these things, nor would, as at this time, have told us such things as these." That is logic! That is the inductive method!—the method, namely, of putting things together and drawing a conclusion from the aggregate. Thank God if you have a wife who can talk like that. Why, if they had both been gloomy parties, what a house it would have been! They need never have taken the shutters down, and summer might have ignored their existence. But Manoah's wife was of a hopeful turn of mind. She had the eye which sees flecks of blue in the darkest skies. She had the ear which hears the softest goings of the Eternal. She was an interpreter of the divine thought. Oh, to have such an interpreter in every house, to have such an interpreter in every pulpit in England, to have such a companion on the highway of venture and enterprise! This is the eye that sees farther than the dull eye of criticism can ever see, that sees God's heart, that reads meanings that seem to be written afar. Have we this method of reading divine Providence? I call it the appreciative and thankful method. Why, some of us can take up our loaf and say, "Only this!" and say

it in a tone that means practical blasphemy; others can take up
a crust and say, "Praise God from whom all blessings flow!
This is God's gift. He cannot mean me to die, or he would not
have put this into my hand." A litany in one sentence, worthy
to find its place amid the hallelujahs and blessings of the better
world. Who was it that said, "When I look at those who are
higher than I am, I am tempted towards discontent, but when I
go out amongst the poor and compare their condition with my
own, my heart overflows with loving thankfulness"? How dare
we complain, the worst, the poorest among us! Taking the
average—and a low average—what man, what woman is there
that ought not to join in heartfelt praise to Almighty God
for mercies innumerable as the moments, delicate as the light,
present as the living air round about one's poor life! Manoah
droops, pines, dies; his wife goes out, gathers the flowers in the
Lord's garden, brings them back to him and says, "Manoah, be
a man: would God have given us these things if he meant to
kill us?" And poor Manoah lifts up his drooping face to the
light. Put together your mercies, look at them as a whole and
say, Can this mean death, or does it mean life? and I know what
the glad answer will be.

There are some sources of consolation amid the distractions
and mysteries of the present world. Every life has some blessings. I charge it upon you when the year closes to reckon up
your blessings. Men eagerly count up their misfortunes and
trials, but how few remember their mercies! One man says, I
have no wealth. No, but look what a pair of shoulders you
have! Another man says, I have but feeble health. True, but
look what investments you have! Another voice says, I am disposed to be fearful and dispirited. But look what a wife you
have! Every life has some blessing, and we must find what that
blessing or those blessings are. We must put them together,
and reason from the goodness towards the glory of God. Amid
these blessings religious privileges are sure signs of the divine
favour. We have religious privileges: we can go into the
sanctuary: we can take counsel together; we can kneel side by
side in prayer; we can go to the very best sources for religious
instruction and religious comfort. Does God mean to kill when he

has given us such proofs of favour as these? Does he mean to kill us when he has sent the minister of the covenant to tell us glad tidings of great joy? Let us find in religious blessings proof that God means no evil to us. We will persist in looking at a distress till it seems to be the only thing in our life. We need to put two and two together. Do not be losing yourselves in the midst of details that have apparently no connection. Gather up your life until it becomes shaped into meaning, and then when you have seen things in their proper relationships pronounce calmly upon the ways of God towards you. Let us put away religious melancholy. Many people are saying, "I fear I have committed the unpardonable sin; I seem to have offended God for ever, and put him far away from me, so that I can never see his face again." Wouldst thou have any anxiety about the thing if he were clean gone for ever, and had drawn the skirts of his garments after him so as to leave thee but the blackness of darkness? By the very fact of thy concern, understand that God has not purposed to kill thee. Cry mightily for him; say, "Oh that I knew where I might find him!" "Why standest thou afar off, O God?" And if thou criest so, he will surely come again, saying, "For a small moment have I forsaken thee; but with great mercies will I gather thee."

Let us learn from this family scene that great joys often succeed great fears. Manoah said, The Lord intends to kill us; his wife said, Not so, or he would not have received a burnt offering at our hands. And behold Samson was born, a judge of Israel, an avenger of mighty wrongs. Is it ever so dark as just before the dawn? Are you not witnesses that a great darkness always precedes a great light—that some peculiar misery comes to prepare the way for some unusual joy? If we could only lay hold of life in this way, and read it, not with unreasonable expectation of deliverance and joy, but with hopefulness, we should never become old, desiccated, or tuneless—to the last we should wear like old silver, to the very last there would be in us a light above the brightness of the sun. Let us read the goodness of God in others. Many a time we have been recovered from practical atheism by reading other people's experience. When things seem to have been going wrong with us, we have looked over into a neighbour's garden and seen his flowers, and our hearts have been cheered by the vision.

Oh, woman, talk of your mission! Here is your mission described and exemplified in the case of the wife of Manoah. What do you want with your School Board and platform experiences, and those mysterious abstractions which you call your *rights?* Here is your field of operation. Cheer those who are dispirited ; read the word of God in its spirit to those who can only read its cold meagre letter, and the strongest of us will bless you for your gentle ministry. Did not Paul write to the Church at Rome saying, "Greet Priscilla and Aquila," putting the wife's name first, and that in no mere spirit of courtesy, but probably in recognition of her supreme influence in spiritual direction and consolation ? Who was it in the days of Scottish persecution ? Was it not Helen Stirk—a braver Helen than the fiend Macgregor —who said to her husband as they were both carried forth to be executed, "Husband, rejoice, for we have lived together many joyful days ; but this day wherein we die together ought to be most joyful to us both, because we must have joy for ever ; therefore I will not bid you good-night, for we shall suddenly meet within the kingdom of heaven "? Who was it when Whitefield was mobbed and threatened, and when even he was about to give way,—who was it but his wife who took hold of his robe and said, "George, play the man for your God"? Oh, woman, talk of your rights, and your sphere, and your having nothing to do ! We should die without you. The man is fit for murders, stratagems, and spoils who is not a worshipper of woman—a worshipper of his mother, of his sister, of his wife, of the ideal woman. Have a sphere of labour at home, go into sick-chambers and speak as only a woman can speak. Counsel your sons as if you were not dictating to them. Read Providence to your husband in an incidental manner, as if you were not reproaching him for his dulness, but simply hinting that you had seen unexpected light. Women have always said the finest things that have ever been said in the Bible. She was a woman that—we speak it with reverence—outwitted the Lord himself. He said "No" to her request. And he was not accustomed to say that word ; it fell awkwardly from those dear lips. "I am not sent but unto the lost sheep of the house of Israel. It is not meet to take the children's bread and cast it unto dogs." But the woman outwitted him. Scribes and Pharisees would have been silenced, but the woman said : "Truth, Lord ; yet the dogs eat of the crumbs that fall from their masters' table." Christ yielded himself a willing prisoner of love. Trust the heart of love to outstrip the brain of genius !

SELECTED NOTE.

Samson was the son of Manoah, of the tribe of Dan, and born A.M. 2848, of a mother whose name is nowhere given in the Scriptures. His destination to great achievements began to evince itself at a very early age by the illapses of superhuman strength which came from time to time upon him. Falling in love with a woman of Sorek, named Delilah, he became so infatuated by his passion, that nothing but his bodily strength could equal his mental weakness. Betrayed by her, and forsaken of Heaven, the Philistines having deprived him of sight, at first immured him in a prison, and made him grind at the mill like a slave. As this was an employment which in the East usually devolves on women, to assign it to such a man as Samson was virtually to reduce him to the lowest state of degradation and shame. In process of time, while remaining in this confinement, his hair recovered its growth, and with it such a profound repentance seems to have wrought in his heart as virtually reinvested him with the character and the powers he had so culpably lost. Of this fact his enemies were not aware. They kept him like a wild beast for mockery and insult. On the occasion of a feast in honour of their god Dagon, Samson was ordered to be brought out to be made a laughing-stock to his enemies. He secretly determined to use his recovered strength to tremendous effect, and persuaded a boy to conduct him to the two pillars upon which the roof of the building rested. Here, after pausing for a short time, while he prefers a brief prayer to Heaven, he grasps the massy pillars, and bowing with resistless force, the whole building rocks and totters, and the roof, encumbered with the weight of the spectators, rushes down, and the whole assembly, including Samson himself, are crushed to pieces in the ruin. Thus terminated the career of one of the most remarkable personages of all history, whether sacred or profane. The enrolment of his name by an apostolic pen (Heb. xi. 32) in the list of the ancient worthies "who had by faith obtained an excellent repute" warrants us undoubtedly in a favourable estimate of his character on the whole, while at the same time the fertility of the inspired narrative has perpetuated the record of infirmities which must for ever mar the lustre of his noble deeds.

PRAYER.

ALMIGHTY GOD, thou openest thine hand, and satisfiest the desire of every living thing. Thou knowest when to open thine hand and when to close it, and it is ours but to watch the opening and the shutting. Thou art King : we are the subjects of thy crown. The Lord reigneth. That is the highest note in our song, the gladdest tone of our rhapsody. We abide under the shadow of the Almighty, and take nothing into our own hands, for they are not only unclean, but weak because unclean. We come to the God and Father of our Lord Jesus Christ, the Unknown One, and the for-ever Unknowable, yet still always coming to our heart's best feeling, a new light, a new warmth, a new gladness. We know thee by our love. Our hearts grope for thee, assured that thou art hidden in the darkness, and concealed in the light, and everywhere present to bless and heal and redeem. Now we know thee in Christ Jesus—the heart of God, the will of God, the whole meaning of eternity in relation to man. This is wonderful in our eyes. Sometimes we touch him, so near we are, and so reverently familiar ; yet we feel that it is like touching a cloud hiding mysteries ; and sometimes we stand afar off, because we do not know his language, we cannot follow his words : we know them as terms, but we cannot see all the meaning with which he charges them. Nevertheless, he is with us to-day, to-morrow, and on the third day ; then he rises again, and we see him no more after the flesh : but we know that he lives ; he left his promise with us : we claim it, we rejoice in it, our heaven begins in its music, and our eternity of bliss is assured by a living faith in the living Christ. Thou hast done all things well. Sometimes we have thought otherwise, and at those times of ignorance thou hast graciously turned away thine eyes from us, that thou mightest not see our folly ; but we have come to repent ; we have seen the larger work, the fuller meaning, somewhat of the ultimate intention —then our mouth has been filled with singing, and our heart with joy, and our eyes with tears of gladness. Henceforth we will trouble thee no more. Be the rain heavy and the storm bitter, or the sky burning with gracious summer, it shall not be ours to murmur at the reigning, living, loving Father. Thou doest all things as thou wilt ; the time is kept in the upper sanctuary, and the law is with the Lord and not with man. This is the gift of Christ—this glowing, triumphant faith ; this is the miracle of the cross ; this is the meaning of the resurrection as to our own spiritual victory. Now we glory in tribulations also. They were the last to come into the song ; they stood back, far off, frowning and hesitant, unwilling to be made use of for Christian sacrifice ; but now by faith we have brought them in one by one : and we glory in tribulations also—yea, we are exceedingly filled with gladness, and we forget our sorrow as the sea might forget in its fulness the stone which lies in its depths. We bless thee for all these high emotions, these noble impulses, these upward outgoings of the soul : they do us good; they cleanse the heart; they give elevation to the whole scale of life—they are the very miracles of heaven. We put our whole being into thine hand, saying, Do as thou wilt : thy will, not mine, be done; what thou choosest is best, what thou doest is right. This we have learned in Jesus Christ; this is the lesson we have received in our crucifixion with the Son of God. Thou dost administer thy discipline to us in various ways. Sometimes thou dost bring us down from great heights; sometimes thou dost chasten us with heavy sorrows, so that men pity us, so that human creatures who are strangers cannot look on without sympathetic tears. Yet the sufferer is the most rejoicing, because where pain abounds grace doth much more abound; where the background is blackest every touch of thy light shines with a new and dazzling meaning. Thou hast brought us together again after separation—some for one week, some for a few days, some for a longer period. For all renewal of fellowship, and trust, and love, we bless thee. We need all these intermediate helps, that we may be continued in our faith and patience in reference to the eternal communion. Some are in great sorrow; some cannot see for tears; many have no helpers, and a few have none to speak to : a few words of uttered misery would be a help in the wilderness, but there is nothing present but the great glaring light or the heedless wind. Say to such that thou art near, and that everything may be told to thee, even things that may not be told to sweetest mother, or most trusting and loving friend. Help us during the few days that remain. How they fly ! Presently they will all be gone, and we, who were going to enjoy ourselves some day, will find that our proposals are lost in the wind, and that the opportunity is gone. Help us, then, to begin now, to enter into the joy of the Lord now, to know that now is the accepted time and now the day of salvation. Amen.

Judges xiv.

1. And Samson went down to Timnath [a portion], and saw a woman in Timnath of the daughters of the Philistines [such intercourse was forbidden, Exod. xxxiv. 16; Deut. vii. 3, 4].

2. And he came up, and told his father and his mother, and said, I have seen a woman in Timnath of the daughters of the Philistines : now therefore get her for me to wife.

3. Then his father and his mother said unto him, Is there never a woman among the daughters of thy brethren, or among all my people, that thou goest to take a wife of the uncircumcised Philistines ? [a term of the intensest hatred]. And Samson said unto his father, Get her for me; for she pleaseth me well [she is right in my eyes].

4. But his father and his mother knew not that it was of the Lord [that there was more in it than at first sight appeared], that he sought an occasion [a quarrel] against the Philistines : for at that time the Philistines had dominion over Israel.

5. Then went Samson down, and his father and his mother, to Timnath, and came to the vineyards of Timnath : and behold, a young lion [a lion of lions] roared against him.

6. And the Spirit of the Lord came mightily upon him [pervaded him], and he rent [throttled] him as he would have rent a kid, and he had nothing in his hand : but he told not his father or his mother what he had done [absence of vanity].

7. And he went down, and talked with the woman [the requisite betrothal arrangements having been made], and she pleased Samson well.

8. And after a time [an absolutely indefinite period] he returned to take her, and he turned aside to see the carcase of the lion : and, behold, there was a swarm of bees and honey in the carcase [rather, skeleton. The burning sun of the East soon dried the body] of the lion.

9. And he took thereof in his hands [a skeleton not being treated as a dead body], and went on eating, and came to his father and mother, and he gave them, and they did eat : but he told not them that he had taken the honey out of the carcase of the lion [he had not told of the slaying of the lion].

10. So his father went down unto the woman : and Samson made there a feast ; for so used the young men to do [in all ages, Gen. xxix. 22 ; Rev. xix. 9].

11. And it came to pass, when they saw him [perhaps saw him in some new aspect], that they brought thirty companions [paranymphs, children of the bridechamber], to be with him.

12. And Samson said unto them, I will now put forth a riddle [from a word which means "to knot"] unto you : if ye can certainly declare it me within the seven days of the feast, and find it out, then I will give you thirty sheets [shirts] and thirty change of garments :

13. But if ye cannot declare it me, then shall ye give me thirty sheets and thirty change of garments. And they said unto him, Put forth thy riddle, that we may hear it.*

14. And he said unto them, Out of the eater came forth meat, and out of the strong came forth sweetness. And they could not in three days expound the riddle.

15. And it came to pass on the seventh day [being in despair], that they said unto Samson's wife, Entice thy husband, that he may declare unto us the riddle, lest we burn thee and thy father's house with fire : have ye called us to take that we have [to spoil us] ? is it not so ?

---

* "Cassel quotes a curious parallel from the annals of North Germany. The judges offer a woman her husband's life if she can make a riddle which they cannot guess. On her way to the court she had found the carcase of a horse, in which a bird had built its nest and hatched six young ones, which she took away. Her riddle was (I venture rudely to translate the rude old lines) :—

> 'As hitherwards on my way I sped,
> I took the living out of the dead,
> Six were thus of the seventh made quit :—
> To rede my riddle, my lords, 'tis fit.'

The judges failed, and the husband was spared."—*Archdeacon Farrar.*

16. And Samson's wife wept before him [marriage wine made sour] and said, Thou dost but hate me and lovest me not : thou hast put forth a riddle unto the children of my people, and hast not told it me.   And he said unto her, Behold, I have not told it my father nor my mother, and shall I tell it thee ?

17. And she wept before him the seven days, while their feast lasted : and it came to pass on the seventh day, that he told her, because she lay sore upon him : and she told the riddle to the children of her people.

18. And the men of the city said unto him on the seventh day before the sun went down, What is sweeter than honey ? and what is stronger than a lion ?   And he said unto them, If ye had not plowed with my heifer, ye had not found out my riddle.

19. And the Spirit of the Lord came upon him, and he went down to Ashkelon, and slew thirty men of them, and took their spoil [armour or suits of armour], and gave change of garments unto them which expounded the riddle [paid them out of their own purse].   And his anger was kindled, and he went up to his father's house.

20. But Samson's wife was given to his companion [the chief of the paranymphs : the bride-conductor], whom he had used as his friend [to the companion whose friend she was].

SAMSON.

THE whole story of Samson is romantic, yet many of its lessons are most practical and useful.   No such prodigy is known in our days, and indeed, such a man would, in many respects, be out of keeping with our civilisation.   We have no room for him ; we have no need of him.   There are some respects in which history could not repeat itself with advantage in our civilisation.   But the temptation is that we should look upon our progress as the measure of human history.   We want a wider outlook.   We must take in more field, if we would see things in their right perspective and proportion.   We certainly did need this very type of man to complete the divine conception of humanity.   If Samson had been left out, we might have said, there is one type which God never allowed to come upon the stage of human history.   We have had the sanguinary man, Cain ; the believing man, Abraham ; the cunning man, Jacob ; the meek and much-enduring man, yet a man full of enterprise and soldiery daring, Moses ; we have had wise men and valiant men, not a few, but a man entrusted with all-abounding strength —the man of iron muscle—the elephantine man, we have never had in perfection. God leaves out nothing. God will finish the picture if we will not interrupt him with our provoking impatience. We needed just this man—huge, overwhelming, mountainous, and in very deed terrible ; we needed to see what sheer strength could do, mere bone and muscle and bulk—what part they could play in the shifting and urgent drama of human history. We have never met the like of this man before. He does not know himself. There is so much of him that he cannot really take in the whole prospect and meaning. A kind of Adam over again ; so new a thing, and such a baby. What will he do ? How will he compare with his forerunners ?

Physical power is the most rudimentary and imperfect form of strength. Yet it has its uses. It is full of high suggestion, if spiritually interpreted. There is a sense in which God glories in the very make of a man. Sometimes he becomes quite an angel. " Thou hast made him a little lower than God." God can have no delight in mere weakness for its own sake. He will not make the halt, the cripple, the deformed, the insane, merely as such ; he will make use of them in his great economy, and he will sometimes turn disadvantages into advantages. But almightiness can take no pleasure in mere weakness, simply as such. But what is the strongest man known to us ? Is there a tiger in the forest or jungle that could not tear him to pieces ? What is *mere* strength—sheer physical energy ? A man boasts that he has climbed some astounding height ; and, behold, when he looked up, the wild goat was fifty feet higher, looking down upon him with a kind of superb and unconscious contempt ! The fleetest man is outstripped by the tiniest bird that ever fluttered a wing. Who, therefore, would worship *mere* strength ? Yet without health what is the world to any man ? and strength is nothing if it be not expressive of health. Health is a compound term. It means equality, harmony, the fine, happy working of all faculties, so much so that we do not know they are working at all. Who knows that the earth is moving ? and why is there no knowledge of the motion ? Because the motion is so great, so regular. So it is with health. Whilst, therefore, we pour contempt upon mere strength, taking it singly and alone, we cannot but rejoice in that balance of faculty and motion expressing itself in the sweet, clean word, health—a state of being in which every happy influence is felt, responded to, acknowledged as a religious visitation, and turned to religious uses. The reason we dwell upon this matter of strength is that under some form or other, outward and measurable, it exercises a disastrous influence upon the imagination of many men : they judge by bulk, vastness, strength, all of which are as nothing compared with the infinite and the eternal, yet every one of them may be made of use in helping the mind to a larger and truer realisation of that which is infinite and everlasting.

Pitiable is a strong body and a weak spiritual nature. Samson was all force, his strength he played with. How infantile was his mind ! It is beautiful to watch this huge elephant-man as he moves clumsily about. He is so pleased with little things. He delights in the very things that are weak. He feels that he is a stupendous contrast to everything that is within reach of his vision. How he was delighted with a riddle ! how he shook with internal laughter as he thought he would propound a riddle to his wife and her friends ! and when the idea of giving prizes for answers to riddles occurred to him, he was as pleased as a modern journalist. He said to the people about him : I have a riddle, and if you can give me the answer I will give you clothing, and almost anything you like to ask for; and he turned aside to hide the smile of triumph with which he regarded the imbecility of his contemporaries in the matter of answering riddles. Then what fancies he took ! dreaming new dreams, and pleased with them as a child blowing blue bubbles from a clay pipe. Oh, how charmed he was with all things little, weak, fanciful ! How we do eke out ourselves by taking in all that is contrastive and dissimilar ! The man of slow, hesitating speech, whose words all counted do not number more than three hundred, is amazed at the volubility of a man who can speak a long time without stopping. He delights in that man ; calls him a phenomenon ; regards him as a prodigy. That is exactly what Samson did in relation to the little things and the little people who were round about him : he liked to have them there ; they seemed to make up something that was wanting in his own vastness. Now, the other contrast is possible to every one of us.

We may have a great spiritual nature, however weak and deformed may be our physical condition. The spirit can be born
again. The interior man can be turned, like one of old, "into
another man," so that his friends shall not know him, but shall
wonder at his chastened, sweet, loving disposition, and speak of
him as men might speak of a heavenly miracle. Wonderful is
the providence of God in this direction! We cannot all be great,
but we can all be good. All men may not have an abundance of
this world's wealth, but every man may be rich in faith, and
otherwise rich towards God and society. Who may not store his
mind with thoughts of the great and bright minds of the days
that have gone? With what poetry he may enrich his imagination! With what gems of thinking he may stud his memory!
The door of the temple of Knowledge stands wide open, and the
poorest man may go in and find himself at home under that
lofty and hospitable roof. The body a man may not be able to
carry up to Samson's strength, but the mind every man can
cultivate with diligent industry, and patience, and faith, until he
find in his own intelligence bread to eat that the world knoweth
not of, a comfortable sustenance which hands can never steal.
Grow in grace, and in the knowledge of our Lord Jesus Christ, so
that whatever may be the outward man—poor, dishonoured, mean
—the inward man may be full of intelligence, and goodness, and
truth. There was One of whom it was said, "There is no
beauty that we should desire him;" and of that same One it was
said, through his miracles, his graciousness of speech, his
wisdom, his love, his Cross, his blood, he should become
"the desire of all nations." The time will come when the
nations will not look on bulk, strength, guns, swords, standing
armies, and glittering diadems; but upon libraries, good actions,
noble beneficences, and in that day all outward strength and
pomp shall be considered vanity; for the soul alone shall be
valiant for its attainments in the highest lore.

Samson's strength was quite unregulated. There was no
soldierly discipline about the elephant. When he rose he seemed
to wonder that he ever sat down; when he sat down he was
larger every way than any other man he had ever seen. Who
can be trusted with great strength that is ill-regulated? Hardly

a man, and not a nation. Only give a nation guns enough, and
that nation must quarrel, must fight. Samson, looking round
and remembering his huge strength, thought he would tie the
tails of about three hundred foxes all together—just by way of
showing what he could do—and light them as a weak man might
strike a match, and send them into the growing fields (xv. 4, 5).
It was an unregulated strength. Only the one man could do that
deed, and where that power is not balanced by another which
checks it, chastens it, subdues it, nothing can happen but wanton-
ness, destruction, ruin. Then Samson would praise himself; he
said, " I will go out as at other times before, and shake myself"—
(xvi. 20)—all that I want to put on my very best power is to
shake myself, as a lion might shake the dew from his mane and
hold his great jaw aloft proudly in the air. That is the tendency
of all great endowment if it be not held back by spiritual
ministry. That is the tendency of all strength unless it has
learned the lesson that in the sight of God's almightiness there is
no strength. We must be conquered by omnipotence. There
is a great danger in one-sided strength. The great aim of life
should be to cultivate an all-round—that is, a happily-balanced
and harmonious—strength ; otherwise we shall have eccentricity,
erratic experiment, tremendous dash, and pitiable failure. This
lesson should be applied to spiritual education. There is a
danger of being too strong in this direction, or that, at the expense
of equal culture along other lines. What is the consequence ?
Bigotry, stubbornness that is stupid, and self-opinionatedness—
that is, self-idolatry. No one man knows everything ; no one
church is *the* Church. When all Churches are brought together,
with their strength, weakness, and every possible variety of
thought, attainment, and purpose, you begin to see the Church,
complete as the rainbow which is round about the Throne.
Until that time come, we are parts of the Church—little parts,
awaiting the upcoming of our stronger brethren and our weaker
brethren, that we may be all one in Christ. The danger is,
too, that men boast of ill-regulated strength. They say, in
dubious terms, Whatever I may be in this or that direction, I
am, at all events, strong at this point. That may be an impious
boast. The boasting, if any, should take effect in a different
direction—namely : being comparatively strong at this point,

thank God, I must go on to be equally strong through the whole series.   Then the triumph divinely ascribed may be the beginning of a complete and lustrous manhood.

We cannot read the life of Samson without being struck with the perishableness of all outward strength.   " Tell me, I pray thee, wherein thy great strength lieth ? "   Herein Samson plays the gigantic baby.   He tantalises the people, and then smiles at them.   But he is lured, and persuaded, and conquered.   He has won in two or three instances.   When they bound him with green withs that were never dried—which he himself proposed as an experiment—" he brake the withs, as a thread of tow is broken when it toucheth the fire" (xvi. 9).   Then he smiled at the lords of the Philistines.   Then another experiment he would try :—" If they bind me fast with new ropes that never were occupied, then shall I be weak, and be as another man.   Delilah therefore took new ropes, and bound him therewith, and said unto him, The Philistines be upon thee, Samson.   And there were liers in wait abiding in the chamber.   And he brake them from off his arms like a thread" (xvi. 11, 12).   Then he told about his hair :—" If thou weavest the seven locks of my head with the web.   And she fastened it with the pin, and said unto him, The Philistines be upon thee, Samson.   And he awaked out of his sleep, and went away with the pin of the beam, and with the web" (xvi. 13, 14).   And then he told her about the vow.   He came to the religious mystery—the mystery that holds everything in a great cloud.   "He told her all his heart, and said unto her, There hath not come a razor upon mine head ; for I have been a Nazarite unto God from my mother's womb : if I be shaven, then my strength will go from me, and I shall become weak, and be like any other man" (xvi. 17).   And it was so.   " He awoke out of his sleep, and said, I will go out as at other times before, and shake myself" (xvi. 20).   He went out, and he shook himself ; but having lost his religion, he had lost his power.   When a man loses his character, all the life-house that he has been building falls, and great is the fall thereof !   He may conduct a few experiments, and thereby may mock the malice of many who have watched him with envy and despair : so long as his character remains he is a mighty man ; but when he breaks his vow, the other breaking is a matter which an infant can accomplish. When a man tears down the altar, his house follows in the tremendous collapse.

How much strength there is that is only outward! We say of Samson that his strength lay in his hair, and therein we do not represent the whole truth : but is there not much strength that is only external—beauty, which is said to be but skin-deep at the best; money, which may take to itself wings and flee away ; great bodily strength, which time can suck out of a man, so insidiously and imperceptibly, that he will not know until he is a tottering pilgrim within a step of the tomb ? But the point which is often overlooked in connection with Samson is, that his strength was not in the hair, but in that which the hair represented—namely, constancy to a vow, faithfulness to a period of consecration. The hair was nothing : there was no strength in that ; but it was symbolical of a grand religious process which had been accomplished in Samson, and, having been faithful to God, God was faithful to him. "Them that honour me I will honour, and they that despise me shall be lightly esteemed." Let a man take care how he treats his vows. "When thou vowest a vow unto God, defer not to pay it ; for he hath no pleasure in fools." Who has not entered into a vow ? Who has not in some time of loneliness said, If God deliver me, I will be his slave in love and service evermore ? Who has not said, If the Lord deliver me out of affliction, my life shall be a daily consecration ? Who has not said, when men pressed heavily against him, and the best friend of all human friends deserted him, If God will give me another chance in life to make an honest livelihood, I will give him a tenth of all that I possess ? Every man must remember his own vows, bring them into full view, apply to them searching and godly criticism, and know exactly what position he occupies. When we talk about times that are depressed, business that is paralysed, circumstances that are but so many impediments and obstructions in the way of progress, we are talking about effects and not about causes. Until we find the fount and origin of the evils which we mourn, the evils will but multiply under our lamentation. If we heal our hurt slightly; if we daub the wall with untempered mortar ; If we cry "Peace,

peace," where there is no peace, God will not deliver us out of the consequences of our mad infatuation.

Where, then, shall strength be found—the true, abiding, generous, beneficent strength ? One man answers the question : he says, " Though our outward man perish, yet the inward man is renewed day by day." The same man says, " If our earthly house of this tabernacle were dissolved, we have a building of God, an house not made with hands, eternal in the heavens." Another man, writing to a dear friend, says, " Beloved, I wish above all things that thou mayest prosper and be in health, even as thy soul prospereth,"—not that the soul may be as the body, but that the body may be as healthy as the soul. But in these expressions we lack definiteness. The expressions themselves are grand, no doubt copious in meaning, certainly very musical in utterance, but there is something wanting to centralise and define them. Then let the same man who spake the first two sentences speak again :—" I can do all things through Christ which strengtheneth me." That is what we wanted—the Name, the living Name, the redeeming Name. There will be periods when our strength goes down. Christ himself was weak in Gethsemane. There appeared an angel unto him, " strengthening him," fortifying him, holding him up, lest he dash his foot against a stone. Do not be afraid, then, if times of weakness beset our own Christian life—times when the devil seems to play with us, and have it all his own way with us—when he mocks us, taunts us, runs around us in laughter filled with contempt, and challenges us to repel or subdue him ; such are times of darkness, times of weakness, times of fear—the very power and agony of hell. In that hour, oh that Paul would speak to us ! His word would be as a resurrection voice. Let us remember this word in our wilderness temptations and Gethsemane agonies —" I can do all things through Christ which strengtheneth me." " Mighty Saviour, dwell with me ! "

PRAYER.

ALMIGHTY GOD, we know thee by thy sweet name of Love. Surely it is a fearful thing to fall into the hands of the living God. But we know thee in Christ Jesus, forbearing, patient, continually seeking us that we may be saved and made like unto thyself. We remember thy word concerning the terrible things in righteousness which thou didst to those who lived long ago. Surely then thou didst shake the heavens and the earth, and thine anger burned like a fire; it was then a fearful thing to behold thy face, for thy jealousy and thine anger burned there against the sins of men. But now thou art coming to us day by day by the way of the cross. Thou dost on beholding the city weep over it; thou dost send gospels of grace to those even who are furthest away; thou dost keep the door open that the prodigal may re-enter and establish himself in his Father's house. Thou art a gracious God, a loving Father. Behold, thine hand is stretched out towards us, not in wrath, but in welcome, and we would answer thy appeal as thou mayest inspire our hearts. We bless thee for the great words thou hast taught us, for they lift up all other speech, and sanctify all other intercourse. We find them nowhere but in thy Book, and finding them there we run unto them as unto a strong tower; they are part of thy very self; therein we read of thee as the eternal, the everlasting, the gracious Lord, the pardoning and forgiving God, the Lord of mercy and of might, the God of love. We feel that we in very deed are now on strong ground, building our life upon a rock, and that all we are and do is under thy control. So now we leave all that is below and mean and unworthy of us, and we ascend unto the hill of the Lord, standing upon the high and lofty places, overhearing the music of heaven, and catching early intimation of thy will. This is the Lord's doing, and it is marvellous in our eyes. Help us to live in the spirit of these gracious truths, that we ourselves may be gracious, having large-hearted feeling towards all the children of men, and even those who have strayed the most and are the most obdurate. Fill us with the spirit of redeeming pity. May we long to save the souls of men; may this be our burning concern, our daily zeal, growing in intensity and compelling us to many an act of sacrifice. Again and again we plead for one another—that necessity may be relieved, that the pressure of heavy burdens may be mitigated, that those who are weary and ill at ease may be lifted by thy gracious hands, and enabled to prosecute their journey with renewed strength and hope. We pray for all who have great plans before them, daring schemes, new enterprises, which touch the imagination, and sometimes stun the ear, though, alas! sometimes ignoring the conscience. The Lord look upon such: give them wisdom in the day of sudden temptation; enable them to consult the heavens before committing themselves to the exactions of earth. The Lord be with all those who cannot be in the open sanctuary; make a little chamber for them at home, a secret altar, a place of wordless communion, where tears will be speech and sighs will be eloquence; the Lord grant this favour: then shall all thy people rejoice with a great gladness, and there shall be Sabbath day all the world round. Amen.

Judges xiv.-xvi.

SAMSON.—LIGHT AND SHADOW.

IT would be unjust to consider this as a finished picture of the man of strength. In all that we have said we have endeavoured to establish by good reasoning and clear reference. But it would be unjust to pronounce upon any life after merely looking at a few incidental points in its course. That is a danger to which all criticism is exposed. We are prone to look upon vivid incidents, and to omit all the great breadths and spaces of the daily life, and to found our judgment of one another upon peculiarities, eccentricities, and very vivid displays of strength, or very pitiful exhibitions of weakness. This is wrong; this is unjust. Samson has indeed done many things that have startled us. We have been inclined to say now and again in the course of our study, This is the man—the whole man; in this point, or in that, we have the key of his character. Now the reality is that Samson is a greater man than the mere outline of the romantic part of his history would suggest. There was another man than that which we have just seen pass before us—the great giant, the man who played with things that were burdens to other men, the man who was infantile in mental weakness on many occasions; there is another man within that outer man, and until we understand somewhat of that interior personality we cannot grasp the whole character of Samson. We must judge men by the *mass* of their character. Who would not resent the idea of being tested by the incidents of a few months, rather than being judged by the level and the general tone and the average of a lifetime? Man does not reveal himself in little points, except incidentally and illustratively: hence we must live with the man, and so far as history will allow us to do so we must become identified with him: when we get to understand his motives we shall begin to comprehend his conduct, and when we put together the night and the day, the summer and the winter, the fair youth and the white old age, then we may be in some degree prepared to say what the man in reality was. When this rule of judgment obtains we shall get rid of all pettishness of criticism, all vain remark upon one another : before pronouncing the final judgment, and especially a harsh verdict, we shall say : We do not know enough about him ; we have only seen a few points in the man ; he seems to be a greater and fuller man than he disclosed himself to be on the occasions when we saw him ; had we seen more of him, and known more of him, we should have come probably to a more generous conclusion. That is the rule of Christian charity, and whoso violates it is no friend of Christ. He may show a certain kind of critical ability, and the very malice of hell in the power of sneering, but he knows nothing about the agony and the love of the Cross.

Is the life of Samson, then, comprehended within these few incidents which have just passed before us ? The incidents upon which we have remarked might all have occurred within a few months. What was the exact position of Samson in Israel ? He judged Israel twenty years. How often is that fact over‾looked ! we speak of the great strong man, the elephantine child, the huge monstrosity, but who thinks of twenty years' service—the consideration of all the necessities of the people, the frown which made the enemy afraid, the smile which encouraged struggling virtue, the recognition which came very near to being an inspiration ? Who knows what headache and heartache the man had in prosecuting and completing the judgeship ? Who can be twenty full years at any one service without amassing in that time features, actions, exhibitions of strength and weakness, sagacity, folly,—all of which ought to be taken into account before pronouncing final judgment ? Thus may it be with us, or it will go hard with us in the day of partial and prejudiced criticism. Who will condemn you for one little month in your life ? Then you were in very deed a fool ; you know it ; you own it : you broke through the sacred law ; you did things you dare not name ; you reeled and stumbled and fell, but were up again in a moment. Shall he be judge of your life who saw the reeling and the falling? or shall he be judge who knows that for ten years, twenty, or more, you walked right steadily, a brave soul, charged with generous thoughts, and often doing good with both hands? So it must be with all men. But we are prone to break that rule. How small we are, and unjust, herein; we will turn off a friend who has served us twenty years because of one petulant word which he spoke! Who has the justice, not to say generosity, to take in a whole lifetime, and let little incidents or great incidents fall into their proper perspective? Until we do this we cannot ply the craft of criticism : we are ill judges, and we shall do one another grievous injury.

Some physical constitutions are to be pitied. Samson's was particularly such a constitution. He seemed to be all body. He appeared to have run altogether into bone and muscle. He was obviously only a giant. How seldom we see more than one aspect of a man! call up any great name in Biblical history, and you will find how often one little, or great, characteristic is supposed to sum up and express the man. We call up the name of Moses, and think of nothing but his meekness : whereas, there was no man in all the ancient gallery of portraits that could burn with a fiercer anger; he brake stones upon stones, and shattered the very tablets written by the finger of God. We say, Characterise Jeremiah, and instantly we think of his tears, and call him the weeping prophet : whereas who concealed an eloquence equal to his?—a marvellous, many-coloured eloquence, now so strong, and now so pathetic : now all lightning, and now all tears. We must beware of the sophism that a life can be summed up in one little characteristic. Herein God will be Judge. Some men cannot be radiant. They may think they are, but they are only making sport for the Philistines when they are trying the trick of cheerfulness which they cannot learn. Other men cannot be wise. If they have conceived some plan of so-called wisdom, and submit it to you, and take it back again, they set it upside down, and forget exactly where it began and where it ended. They are to be pitied. Weakness is written right across the main line of the face ; weakness characterises every tone of the voice. They are not to be judged harshly. Blessed be God, the judgment is with himself, and what if the first be last, and the last be first?

Is there hope of renewal for overthrown men? One would hope so :—"Howbeit the hair of his head began to grow again after he was shaven"—(xvi. 22). Is this real renewal or only apparent? It was not the hair that was in fault, but the soul. We have seen that the strength lay not in the hair, but in the vow which that hair represented and confirmed. If the matter had been one purely of person adornment, the hair might have grown again on the strong and noble head, and covered it as luxuriantly as before; but it was the soul that was shorn of its honour; it was the spirit that parted with its oath. How difficult to renew a broken character! Thank God, it is not impossible. It cannot be done mechanically,—that is to say from the outside, by skilful manipulation, by obedience to tabulated rules and orders,—"Ye must be born again : " it is not enough to renew the profession, to rehabilitate the reputation, to seem to be just as you were before,—"Ye must be born again." Samson's hair comes, the locks are as raven-like as ever, but has the soul been renewed ; has the strong man cried mightily unto God for the restoration of his character? That is the vital point, and to trifle with it, pass over it hurriedly, is to lose the wisdom and the music of the occasion. Looking at men outwardly, we say, They seem to be as before; all the outer semblances are excellent, but who are we that we should judge what has taken place within? Outwardly the circumstances may be as before, but the man himself should take care as to what has happened within his soul. He should hold himself in severe and close monologue upon this matter, saying, These people form a good opinion of me ; they think now I am a sober, upright, reliable man ; I am regular in my church attendances, I keep up with the foremost in the public race, and the general impression seems to be that I have recovered myself,—but have I done so ? I will not look at the outer man, but at the heart. Is that stead-fast toward God—constant in holy love, burning with pure zeal for righteousness and truth? Man must not judge me in these matters—I must therefore judge myself the more austerely and exhaustively. Blessed are we if we can apply such criticism to ourselves; and blessed if outward appearances dimly typify a spiritual life, an unseen and undying probity of mind.

Samson died a curious death. He prayed in his blindness that he might yet show himself a strong man. The Philistines would have sport: Samson would that the occasion of sport might be turned into an occasion of what appeared to him to be just vengeance. Said he: Let me touch the pillars of the house; lay my poor hands on the pillars of this unholy place. And the giant's hands were lifted and put upon the pillars, and Samson cried mightily towards the heavens and shook the pillars, and the house fell, and he himself died with innumerable others. It was a poor way out of the world. But judge nothing by the death scene. In many instances the death scene amounts to nothing. Many a man has gone to heaven straight from the act of suicide. Many a man has died into heaven about whom we are prudently silent, because of some little or great incident which has disturbed our judgment of his character. It is not enough to leave the last transaction to be completed in a few moments of words without sacrifice, of profession without possible realisation. And some may have died and gone to heaven about whom we have our secret fears. Let us entertain no such apprehensions about any man whose twenty years of life lies open for public judgment. Nothing was said at the last; nay, more, the poor man got wrong within the last year of his life: he slipped, he fell, he was laid up a long time; what happened then between him and his Lord we cannot tell; but we have before us an instance or two of such secret and unreported interviews. The man who saw his Lord and plunged into the water, and came to him, had a talk with Christ all alone, and after that he became the most fervent of the apostles. The man is not to be judged by what he did in the last week of his life. It is the *life* that God will judge—the tone, the purpose, the main idea of the life. What is life indeed but a main idea—a grand central thought and aspiration? We shall delude ourselves and do injustice to others by thinking of collateral circumstances, things on the surface, things that come and go. Many a man has stolen who is no thief. Many a man has been overcome by strong drink who is no drunkard. Many a man has been guilty of innumerable weaknesses who is a strong man in the soul and heart of him. That these generous constructions may be perverted is perfectly possible; but I would rather that wicked men should pervert them than that the men who need such encouragement should go away in despair. We cannot tell what the dogs will do, but the children must nevertheless be fed. If any man should leave this study of Samson saying that licence has been given to do this or that which is wrong, he but aggravates his profanity by a final falsehood. On the other hand, many a man must be cheered, or he will be overwhelmed in despair, and we shall never hear of him any more. What is the central purpose of your life? what is the main idea? Answer that in the right way, and God will be merciful to you.

We have still to notice the most important point of all, which, in the mere matter of literal sequence, ought to have come earlier. Samson said he would go out and shake himself as at other times—"and he wist not that the Lord was departed from him" (xvi. 20). All the outer man was there, but it was a temple without a God. The giant was as grand to look at as ever, but his soul was as a banqueting-hall deserted. And Samson knew it not! that is the painful point—the unknown losses of life, the unconscious losses of life: power gone, and the man not aware of it,—is there any irony so humbling, so awful to contemplate? We may be walking skeletons: we may be men without manliness; we may be houses untenanted: yet the eyes are where they always were, and just as bright, the voice is as vibrant as in olden time; and yet the divinity is dead. And for a man not to know it! We have had experience of this in other than merely religious directions. The writer that used to charm thinks he writes as well as ever, and only the readers are conscious that the genius is extinct: the right hand has forgotten its cunning; the writer does not know it; having filled his page, he says, That is as bright as ever: I never wrote with greater facility: in my old age I have become young again;—he wist not that the spirit of genius had departed from him. So with the preacher. He supposes he preaches as energetically and as happily and usefully as ever; he says he longs for his work more than he ever did; and only the hearers are conscious that the man has been outworn by all-claiming, all-dominating time. The statesman, too, has lost his wizardry : he cannot see afar off ; yet he supposes himself to be as great as in his most lustrous prime. All these are common incidents, and are referred to simply to show that they point towards the most disastrous effect of all—that a man may have lost the Spirit of God, and not be aware of his loss. Others look on, and pity him. The prayer has lost its pleading tone ; the tears which stream from his eyes are but common water ; the upward look sees nothing but cloud ; the universe has become a great blank space : the stars glitter, but say nothing ; the summer comes, but creates no garden in his soul ; and the man does not know it. Who dare tell him ? This points towards a possible ghastly condition of affairs. The Church is as large as ever, but Ichabod is written upon its door. The old words are all said, one by one with formal pomp and accuracy, but they are only words—no longer bushes that burn and are not consumed. Again and again remember that the point is that the man did not know it. Had he known it, he would have been a better man ; had he really felt that the Lord had gone out from him, he might have begun to cry at last like a child, if he could not pray like a priest. How is it with us ? Put the question right into the very centre of the soul. We may have more words, more dogmas, more points of controversy, more little orthodox idols ; but what are we in the heart, the spirit, the purpose of the mind ? Seeing that this great danger is before us, there is one sweet prayer which every day should carry to heaven from our pleading soul. A child can pray it ; an angel cannot add to it. That deep, high, grand, all-inclusive prayer is—" Take not thy Holy Spirit from me,"—take health, take friends, take happiness, take all the world values as good and necessary, but take not thy Holy Spirit from me ! "Holy Spirit, dwell with me."

PRAYER.

ALMIGHTY GOD, our hope is in thy Son; other hope in very deed we have none. We have hewn out unto ourselves cisterns, but we have found them to be cisterns that could hold no water. So by this experience, so sad and deep, we have come to know that there is no help for man but in the living God, the Saviour of all, who will have all men to be saved. We lay down our arms of rebellion, we renounce our various inventions, and we now come to thee, empty-handed, full of sin in the heart, conscious of great and aggravated wickedness, and casting ourselves upon the work of the Lord Jesus Christ, we say each for himself, God be merciful to me a sinner! We know thine answer; it is a reply of love: where sin abounds, grace shall much more abound; wherein we have grieved thee, we shall be mightily brought back again to thy side, to take part in thy praise, and to be active in thy service. May the time that is past more than suffice; may our inquiry be about the few days that remain; with earnestness, simplicity, fidelity, may we gird ourselves to the work that lies before us, and with all-burning zeal, most constant love, may we do thy will gladly, hoping only for a reward in thine own heaven. Help us in all our life. Its necessities are as numerous as its moments. Our life is one crying want. Let our life be turned into a sacred prayer, by being lifted upwards towards the all-hospitable heavens, and no longer left to grope in the earth for that which can never be found there. As for our burdens, we shall forget them if thou dost increase our strength; our sins shall be cast behind thee, our duty shall be our delight, and our whole life a glowing and acceptable sacrifice. Guide men who are in perplexity; soothe the hearts that are overborne by daily distress; save from despair those who think they have tried every gate and beaten upon every door without success or reply: save such from the agony and blackness of despair; at the very last do thou appear, a shining light, a delivering day, wherein men can see what lies about them, and address themselves to their tasks with the help of the sun. Be round about us in business; save us amid a thousand temptations; direct us along a road that is sown with traps, and gins, and snares; take hold of our hand every step of the journey, and in thine own good time bring us to rest, to death—to life. Amen.

Judges xvii.

["A wholly disconnected narrative here follows, without any mark of time by which to indicate whether the events preceded or followed those narrated in the preceding chapter. The only point of contact with the preceding history of Samson is that we are still concerned with the tribe of Dan.—*The Speaker's Commentary.*]

1. And there was [before the days of Samson] a man of mount Ephraim, whose name was Micah [a contraction of Micayehû = who is like Jehovah].

2. And he said unto his mother, The eleven hundred shekels of silver [£136] that were taken from thee, about which thou cursedst [thou didst adjure ; see Matt. xxvi. 63], and spakest of also in mine ears, behold, the silver is with me ; I took it. [See Prov. xxviii. 24.] And his mother said, Blessed be thou of the Lord, my son.

3. And when he had restored the eleven hundred shekels of silver to his mother, his mother said, I had wholly dedicated [consecrating, I consecrated] the silver unto the Lord from my hand for my son, to make a graven image and a molten image : now therefore I will restore it unto thee.

4. Yet [And] he restored the money unto his mother ; and his mother took two hundred shekels of silver, and gave them to the founder [see Isaiah's opinion of founders, xlvi. 6-10], who made thereof a graven image and a molten image : and they were in the house of Micah.

5. And the man Micah had an house of gods, and made an ephod, and teraphim, and consecrated [installed] one of his sons, who became his priest.

6. In those days there was no king in Israel, but every man did that which was right in his own eyes. [See this forbidden in Deut. xii. 8.]

7. And there was a young man out of Beth-lehem-judah of the family [tribe] of Judah, who was a Levite, and he sojourned there. [See Gen. xlix. 7.]

8. And the man departed out of the city from Beth-lehem-judah to sojourn where he could find a place : and he came to mount Ephraim to the house of Micah [probably having heard of Micah's chapel], as he journeyed.

9. And Micah said unto him, Whence comest thou ? And he said unto him, I am a Levite of Beth-lehem-judah, and I go to sojourn where I may find a place.

10. And Micah said unto him, Dwell with me, and be unto me a father and a priest, and I will give thee ten shekels [the shekel weighed about half an ounce] of silver by the year, and a suit of apparel, and thy victuals. So the Levite went in.

11. And the Levite was content to dwell with the man ; and the young man was unto him as one of his sons.

12. And Micah consecrated the Levite [which none might lawfully do but the high-priest] ; and the young man became his priest, and was in the house of Micah.

13. Then said Micah, Now know I that the Lord will do me good, seeing I have a Levite to my priest [see next chapter for the answer].

A SERIES OF SURPRISES.

THE book of Judges properly closes with the sixteenth chapter. What follows after the sixteenth chapter has been described as an appendix—two appendices, indeed, dealing with the case of two Levites. From the seventeenth chapter onward the matter was probably written long before other portions of the book, in the days of Joshua and the greater judges. Certainly, this part of the book was written when there was no king in Israel, and when every man was left to do that which was right in his own eyes. The history of the two Levites is full of romantic interest. The first history is to be read aloud and preached about quite freely; the second is to be read in secret—hardly read at all, and yet fully comprehended, because of the following chapter in which vengeance, just and tremendous, is dealt out to men who inflicted upon Israel a scandal that was never forgotten. Let us publicly and openly read the case of the first Levite, and then read in shame and secrecy what follows ; then come into the light once more, and close the book of Judges amid a blaze of glory.

Is not this a fair picture of life ? What undulation ! What incessant variety ! what visions of beauty ! what disclosures of shame ! how bright is the fair, great heaven ; and yet how near the deep and awful hell ! Micah dwelt in mount Ephraim, and stole silver from his mother : Micah afterwards became a maker of gods. What rapid transitions in character ! what wonder if the rapidity of the transitions sometimes excites suspicion as to the reality of the conversion ? But is not history condensed ? The verses read in flowing sequence, as if no time had elapsed between one line and another : hence the shock with which we come upon the fact that the man who was but yesterday a concealed criminal is to-day a manufacturer of gods and churches. Is there not a punctuation in life which is inserted by the hand of God ? Are not the observers to blame for a good deal of what is called unnatural and too swift transition in character ? Who knows what may happen in one hour when God is the minister and a repentant soul is the subject ? Sometimes life is wrought out very swiftly, so far as public observation can detect ; yet it is being lived very slowly in the consciousness of the man : he is so fired with pain because of conscious sin that he would have himself transported in unnamable swiftness of time into a new consciousness and a blessed individuality. At the same time, a sober lesson does reveal itself at this very point. Whilst conversion may scarcely be too sudden, the manufacture of gods and churches ought not to take place with indecent haste, if at all. It is difficult to believe that a man can spring at one bound from being a concealed felon into being a patron of the universe—a builder of gates that open heaven, a creator of altars and priests. There should be some time spent in solitude, in secrecy, in earnest wrestling prayer : the whole night should be thus spent, and the morning light will shine upon a new personality, bearing a new and larger name. At the same time, recognising the sobriety and gravity of the lesson, let no man be discouraged should he really feel what by its purity must be a divine impulse to move instantly and to act like a man who, having wasted many days, seeks to redeem the time, and to make one day as long as two, by diligent industry, by the passion of consecrated love.

This chapter is full of surprises. What can be more surprising than that a layman should consecrate a priest? This is what Micah did. Micah began where he could. Everything was to be done at once. So Micah consecrated one of his sons, who became his priest. Men do things in high passion which would be unnatural and almost irrational if done in cold blood. We must always calculate the influence of spiritual temperature upon human action. Some things we must have heard, and not read ; the whole meaning was in the way of saying them. The Bible only tells us that certain persons "cried unto the Lord,"—verily a poor report, utterly inadequate, yet all that was possible : for who can write down a "cry"? who can paint, even in letters, an agony? So some allowance must be made for the new spiritual passion of Micah. A man can do great things when he is really on fire. No man knows himself, as to the full volume and bulk of his being, until he is possessed—no longer a little measurable self, but part of an infinite immeasurable totality. We speak of men being "mighty in prayer." They cannot account for it. Yet they know that sometimes they have hold of God, and that omnipotence graciously yields to the gracious violence. Indeed, man must at certain historical periods make priests. Whether we are in such a historical period now, is not the immediate question, but following the unfolding of history along the biblical line we see how now and again man must be almost almighty. Despair finds new energies. Religious despair, religious helplessness, finds God, or makes an image supposed to be like him. Do not let us mock at idolatry of a really heathen kind too flippantly ; there may be an aspect of idolatry that touches our sense of the ludicrous, but there is also an aspect of it which touches our tears. To be an idolater in a Christian land is not only an anachronism, it is a blasphemy : but follow the whole history of idolatry and study its pathetic side, and see if it be not true that in man's attempts to make gods, and altars, and priests, there is something infinitely touching. To that mystery in our being a divine revelation may one day be made. It may be at that very point God will begin the miracle of self-revelation—of incarnation. Man must have a priest. There are necessities which cannot be denied—urgencies of soul which must be appeased, soothed, if not gratified. Are not all men looking round—some hopelessly and indistinctly—for helpers, spiritual assistants, for brother-men larger than they and altogether mightier in the nobler life, to lift them up, to eke out their poor expressions, to find prayers which their poor lips may utter as if their own ? Is there not something in the heart that cries— "Master, Lord, teach us how to pray" ? The fault does not lie in the impulse, but in its perversion ; nay, rather, there is an unmistakable touch and signature of divinity in the impulse. Blessed are they who have received the ministry of sanctification and have responded to the divine provision made for great human passions, and great spiritual necessities. Yet no man can make a priest. Priests are the miracles of manhood—men who have the gift of prayer, men who by looking on human sorrow are moved heavenward to intercede on man's behalf. A strange gift, signalised by fire, is that of being able to pray in every tongue, so that every man may hear in the tongue in which he was born an interpretation of his soul's poverty and need. Such intercessors are not made by man : these are the gifts of God to every age. "The effectual fervent prayer of a righteous man availeth much." Yet this is confining the idea of priesthood to intercession. If it be so confined, what possible objection can be lodged against it ? To make a priest anything more than one who is mighty in prayer, mighty in sympathy, keen in moral insight, patient more than woman, is not the work of man.

A surprising thing it is that a converted thief should elaborate a religious system : "And the man Micah had an house of gods and made an ephod "—a gorgeous priestly robe—" and

teraphim "—little Syrian images. This is a condensed statement. Who can go into the detail of these two lines ? "An
house of gods "—a consecrated place—a gods' house : what
patience in the elaboration of the deities ; what painstaking in
the fabrication of the ephod ; what detailed and critical, if not
artistic, care, in the shaping of the teraphim ; we are apt to overlook the detail of all worship. Look upon the poorest little
church, on the bleakest hillside, and what does it look like but a
handful of stones rudely put together,—a sight that might be
remarked upon at the moment, and passed by and forgotten ?
yet who can tell the history of these few stones ? who knows
with what hands they were carried and shaped and put in place ?
who knows how the labourers toiled when the day's work was
done that they might put up the simple structure, to have a home
in which to worship God ? Who knows at what sacrifice the
Bible was bought by these poor peasant worshippers, how small
Sums were laid by from week to week, and how as the little pile
neared maturity the thrifty one almost had the Bible by the
anticipation of love, how the Bible was preserved, loved, almost
worshipped ? Do not let us pass by all these things carelessly as
if they meant nothing ; they are full of tears, full of pathos, full
of that finest quality of manhood which is the real wealth of any
nation.

Yet Micah was ill at ease. Who can make one of his own sons
into his superior ? The son was but a makeshift after all. How
superstition tyrannises over men ! To have a son for a priest as
Micah had was like a kind of illicit marriage. A sense of un-
naturalness marred the service. The son was quite right in
many respects, worthy of confidence and honour and love ; but
in his official capacity he was still a son. Who does not like his
minister to come down out of the clouds ? Who likes to see a
minister grow up before his very eyes—to know the child at
home, to follow the boy at school, to see him pass through various
processes, and at length appear as a recognised minister of
Christian truth ? Who does not feel slightly uneasy if he knows
the minister's mother and brothers and sisters ? Who does not
say, "Are they not all with us ? Is not this the carpenter's son " ?
To some people, if a man is once a carpenter's son, he never can

be anything else by all the miracles of Heaven. Why? Because they themselves could never be anything else: they measure themselves in measuring him. Who does not like a species of ghostliness to be round about a minister? Who likes to think that his minister eats and drinks and sleeps? In very deed, some quite hide that aspect of the ministry and graciously pay no attention to it. Micah was but a man. It would be a beautiful thing if ministers could come down from the clouds and go back to the clouds, and we could have nothing to do with them but enjoy a momentary revelation. This has many applications. The man who felt somewhat uneasy or dissatisfied as to his son being priest, represents a great many men. Who could be so grand a minister as the brother sitting at our side, who, suddenly inflamed by the divine presence, rises and speaks to human need in human speech? If we were not so little, so superstitious, so denuded of the higher and sublimer reason, we should find in man—known man—our truest representative. It is because we have misunderstood humanity that we have undervalued the true ministry.

But fortune seemed to be upon Micah's side. We are now in times of wandering and adventure and bold enterprise, and in those times a young man was travelling out of Beth-lehem-judah of the family of Judah, and he happened to be a real Levite; and when he came to mount Ephraim, to the house of Micah, Micah elicited his story, and instantly said to him, "Dwell with me, and be unto me a father and a priest." The Levites in those days were driven about. It was mourned in one of the prophetic books that the portion of the Levites was withheld from them. They were under Heaven's frown:—"I will divide them in Jacob, and scatter them in Israel." So this young man was wandering, more or less in a spirit of enterprise and curiosity; and he came, as we now say, by chance to the house of Micah. There was something interesting about him. He certainly was not a money-seeker; the terms were these:—"And I will give thee ten shekels of silver by the year, and a suit of apparel, and thy victuals" (v. 10)—twenty-five shillings a year was not much for a priest, even including one suit of clothes and victuals. A man who had spent hundreds of shekels upon his gods thought he

was liberal in spending five-and-twenty shillings a year on his
priests ! There are persons who think more of the church as a
building than of the minister as a servant of the soul. Who
was this Levite ? Was he a man of any name ? Not much in
himself, but he was the grandson of Moses. To what adversities
may we come in life, and to what " base uses " ! The grandson
of Moses, the caretaker of Syrian images, and the priest of an
idolater ! Who can say to what we may be driven ? Once let
the centre go ; once depart from the vital point ; take one step in
a wrong direction, and who can calculate the issue ? Be steadfast ; hold on to the ascertained—to that which is proved to be
beneficent, pure, noble ; or you may come into a servility which
not only disennobles you but throws unjustly a slur on the most
famous memory. No man liveth unto himself. We have to
take care of the past, if we would really take care of the future.
Now Micah was comparatively happy. Micah consecrated the
Levite. The Levite was not a priest, but he seemed to have an
odour of sanctity about him, and, for the rest, Micah, having once
got his hand into priest-making, made no account of it. The
young man became his priest, and was in the house of Micah ;
then Micah was at rest.

The greatest surprise of all remains. Here is an idolater
appealing to the true God ! " Then said Micah, Now know I
that the Lord will do me good, seeing I have a Levite to my
priest" (v. 13). Here is a false worshipper unconsciously
throwing off his own idols ! He keeps the idols as men keep
cabinets of curiosities. He has a house, a little museum, a small
miniature pantheon ; but in his finer moods he appeals to the true
and living God. So literal are we, we like to have something to
lay the hand upon. Men like a substantial and visible religion.
Yet Micah felt that God would do him good, seeing he had a
Levite for his priest. The son did not quite fill up the space,
but now with a real living Levite on the premises, the Lord—the
eternal God, the Father of every living thing—will do this man of
mount Ephraim good. How we degrade God,—that is to say,
how we misconceive him and misrepresent him to ourselves !
The Lord will do us good if our heart is right towards him. The
Lord will make up for the absence of all priests, ministers

churches, books, and ordinances, if we are unable to avail ourselves of such help: God will allow us to eat the shewbread, if
there be no other food with which to appease our hunger.   The
true Church is where the right heart is.   God himself is a Spirit.
There is no image of him that can be made by human hands.
There is one Priest—Jesus Christ, the true Melchizedek.   He
alone can sacrifice and has sacrificed and is sacrificed for us.
There is one altar—the cross—the cross of Jesus Christ: God
forbid that we should even know any other altar than the cross
of our redeeming, atoning, glorious Saviour.   For what are we
looking?   We cannot appease our deepest needs, silence our
most poignant cries, by any manufactures possible to our
ingenuity and skill: the Son of God is the Saviour of the world;
he is able to save unto the utmost all that come unto God by
him, seeing that he ever liveth to make intercession for us.   If
any man should now say that he himself is needful to our communion with Heaven, he is more than wrong in opinion, the case
is infinitely more serious than that which can be measured by
mere mistakenness of judgment: he usurps the place of Christ,
he dethrones the Son of God, he at least divides the prerogative
of the one Advocate.   This, then, is our Christian position: Man
needs a priest—that Priest is Jesus Christ; man needs communion with Heaven—that communion is spiritual; man needs
an answer to the agony of his own accusation—that answer is in
the cross of Christ.   These are great mysteries, but the soul
may become reverently familiar with them, after great suffering,
prolonged prayer, and simple trust in the living God.

PRAYER.

ALMIGHTY GOD, thou hast recorded thy name in thy house, and there thou wilt meet them that seek thee. The heart seeketh God in all its pain and need; the spirit crieth out for the living God, as a land that is thirsty cries out for the great rain. We bless thee for this hunger and for this thirst; a blessing follows this desire, for this desire is none other than the gift of God. Now we know the meaning of the blessing pronounced upon those who hunger and thirst after righteousness. Hereby know we that we are not of the earth earthy, but that we have in us the fire of God, the spark of deity, the mysterious power which makes us thy children. We cannot be satisfied with what we see, or hear, or touch; beyond all this we have needs they cannot satisfy. Our satisfaction is in the living God; our rest is in heaven; we are at peace only when we are reconciled unto God by our Lord Jesus Christ; therefore, being justified by faith, we have peace with God, and now we rejoice as those who have entered into harmony with the spirit of heaven, and to whom is reserved an inheritance incorruptible, undefiled, and that fadeth not away. Our joy is pure; our peace is unspeakable; our heaven has begun below. We bless thee for all that is meant by the name Jesus Christ; in it is all eternity, and in it is all time; it is the music of creation; it is the Gospel addressed to human hearts; it is a refuge in time of need. When we need refuge, Jesus Christ is more to us than at any other time; when we feel our own littleness, then we see Christ's majesty. We come to the throne by the way of the cross. We bring with us no virtue of our own, but crying necessity, burning pain, consciousness of a great void; and yet we bring with us also a great hope; we feel that we shall not be disappointed whilst we linger at the cross, and pray where Jesus died. Our heart is full of thankfulness because of thy great mercy and care. Every day witnesses to thy tender loving-kindness. Thou dost live for thy creation; thou dost live in it, and through it all thou dost send currents of life, utterances of music, gospels of grace. So would we live that we may enter into thy purpose, and embody it, and realise it to those who look on. This being our desire, it shall surely be answered; for thou canst not deny thine own inspirations: these longings are part of the yearning of thine own solicitude. Thou wilt reply to us graciously, even when thou dost contradict and repel us in the mere letter. Why should we importune thee in the letter, when thou hast taught us to pray in the spirit and to fall into happy harmony with all thy will, first crucifying ourselves with Christ, and then having known the fellowship of his sufferings, knowing also the power of his resurrection? We will cast ourselves into thine hands, not daring to utter one petition lest we should offend thy purpose, but comprehending all our prayer in the one complete desire that thy will may be done on earth as it is done in heaven. We bless thee for all the hints of a better life, which we obtain from the existence through which we are now passing : we are walking in the night-time ; we have nothing but the stars to read ; but they are thy lights ; thou hast set them in appointed places ; thou hast taught them to glitter according to thy will, and to speak to the observant eye in significant light : and are not the breezes, too, full of hints of a better land ? are they not tinctured with a fragrance not of earth ? do they not come to us bringing health and revival and sweetness—all hints of a greater state ? And the earth is for man : it is full of symbol and suggestion and strange writing, to be made out by the scholars of Christ. We will walk on—now up the steep places, wishing they were not so high ; now down into the valleys, wishing they were not so long : but thou wilt not allow these selfish wishes to mar the perfectness of our resignation when we say with the spirit, Thy will be done on earth as it is done in heaven. All our ways are in thine hands. Keep us wherever we are ; keep us near the altar, near the cross, and thus near thine own heaven. We commend one another always to thy gracious keeping : we can only be kept as we are held in the hollow of thine hand : outside that hand there is no security ; within it is the security of almightiness. Help us in all good purposes ; give us steadfastness therein—that sacred determination, that faithful constancy, which comes of conviction akin to inspiration. Be with all who are on the sea—that great, wide, troubled sea. Be with all our friends who are far away—in the colonies, in other lands, speaking other languages, seeking to establish friendly relations with other peoples, struggling for bread, promoting the interests of civilisation, living a hard life that they may make the lives of others easier. Forget not our sick-chambers—the churches in our homes, the abodes of pain, chambers set apart for whispering, and thought, and patience, and prayer. Be with all persons in difficulty, extremity, intolerable anxiety, and grant unto such answers to their pain from heaven ; then shall they sing in the night-time and glory exceedingly even in tribulation, knowing the dominion of God in human life, and answering with glad belief the gospel that thou doest all things well. Let thy word flame like a sun, or descend like the dew, or breathe into our hearts like the still small voice. Let it come as thou wilt, under what symbol thou dost ordain, only let it come—a word of emancipation, a word of benediction, a word of comfort, gracious as the speech of Christ, and sacred as his blood. Amen.

Judges xviii.

1. In those days there was no king in Israel : and in those days the tribe [may mean a tribe, or the division of a tribe] of the Danites sought them an inheritance to dwell in ; for unto that day all their inheritance [a description of their inheritance is given in Josh. xix. 40-46] had not fallen unto them among the tribes of Israel.

2. And the children of Dan sent of their family five men from their coast [their lords], men of valour [sons of force], from Zorah, and from Eshtaol, to spy out the land, and to search it ; and they said unto them, Go, search the land : and when they came to mount Ephraim, to the house of Micah, they

lodged there [Pythias was rich enough to entertain the whole army of Xerxes, a million men, yet he died a beggar].

3. When they were by the house of Micah, they knew the voice [perhaps by its dialect. He had lived in Bethlehem] of the young man the Levite: and they turned in thither [into the room where he was officiating], and said unto him, Who brought thee hither? and what makest thou in this place? and what hast thou here?

4. And he said unto them, Thus and thus [according to this and according to that] dealeth Micah with me, and hath hired me, and I am his priest [because of the dearth of priests, Jeroboam made priests of the lowest of the people].

5. And they said unto him [having seen glittering ephods], Ask counsel, we pray thee, of God [for censure upon such inquiry, see Isa. xxx. 4; Hosea iv. 12], that we may know whether our way which we go shal¹ be prosperous.

6. And the priest said unto them, Go in peace: before the Lord is your way wherein you go [carefully ambiguous].

7. Then the five men departed, and came to Laish [the mound of the judge], and saw the people that were therein, how they dwelt careless, after the manner of the Zidonians [they were supposed to be a colony from Zidon], quiet and secure; and there was no magistrate in the land, that might put them to shame in any thing; and they were far from the Zidonians, and had no business with any man [some read—they had no business with Syria].

8. And they came unto their brethren to Zorah and Eshtaol: and their brethren said unto them, What say ye?

9. And they said, Arise, that we may go up against them: for we have seen the land, and, behold, it is very good [Num. xiv. 7; Josh. ii. 23, 24]: and are ye still? be not slothful to go, and to enter to possess the land.

10. When ye go, ye shall come unto a people secure, and to a large land [wide on both hands]: for God hath given it into your hands; a place where there is no want of any thing that is in the earth.

11. And there went from thence of the family of the Danites, out of Zorah and out of Eshtaol, six hundred men appointed [girded] with weapons of war.

12. And they went up, and pitched in Kirjath-jearim [city of forests: nine miles from Jerusalem] in Judah: wherefore they called that place Mahaneh-dan [camp of Dan] unto this day: behold, it is behind [to the west of] Kirjath-jearim.

13. And they passed thence unto mount Ephraim, and came into the house of Micah [or precincts of the god-house].

14. Then answered the five men that went to spy out the country of Laish, and said unto their brethren, Do ye know that there is in these houses an ephod, and teraphim, and a graven image, and a molten image? now therefore consider what ye have to do [whether, and how, you would possess yourself of them].

15. And they turned thitherward, and came to the house of the young man [Jonathan] the Levite, even unto the house of Micah, and saluted him [" won with an apple, lost with a nut "].

16. And the six hundred men appointed with their weapons of war, which were of the children of Dan, stood by the entering of the gate.

17. And the five men that went to spy out the land went up, and came in thither, and took the graven image, and the ephod, and the teraphim, and the molten image : and the priest stood in the entering of the gate [having been inveigled thither to talk to the six hundred men] with the six hundred men that were appointed with weapons of war.

18. And these went into Micah's house, and fetched the carved image, the ephod, and the teraphim, and the molten image [not to destroy but to worship]. Then said the priest unto them, What do ye?

19. And they said unto him, Hold thy peace, lay thine hand upon thy mouth [finger on the lip, is the attitude of the Egyptian god of silence], and go with us, and be to us a father and a priest : is it better for thee to be a priest unto the house of one man, or that thou be a priest unto a tribe and a family in Israel [the papists offered Luther the cardinalate to be quiet]?

20. And the priest's heart was glad [and this was a grandson of Moses], and he took the ephod, and the teraphim, and the graven image, and went in the midst of the people [where he was well guarded].

21. So they turned and departed, and put the little ones [so it was a regular migration] and the cattle and the carriage [the baggage] before them [expecting to be pursued].

22. And when they were a good way from the house of Micah, the men that were in the houses near to Micah's house were gathered together, and overtook the children of Dan.

23. And they cried unto the children of Dan. And they turned their faces, and said unto Micah, What aileth thee, that thou comest with such a company [the grim humour of a tribe like a serpent on the way, an adder in the path, Gen. xlix. 17]?

24. And he said, Ye have taken away my gods [remember Laban, Gen. xxx. 31] which I made, and the priest, and ye are gone away : and what have I more? and what is this that ye say unto me, What aileth thee?

25. And the children of Dan said unto him, Let not thy voice be heard among us, lest angry fellows [men bitter of soul] run upon thee, and thou lose thy life, with the lives of thy household.

26. And the children of Dan went their way : and when Micah saw that they were too strong for him, he turned and went back unto his house.

27. And they took the things which Micah had made, and the priest which he had, and came unto Laish, unto a people that were at quiet and secure : and they smote them with the edge of the sword, and burnt the city with fire ["Dan was no gainer. His name disappears from the records of 1 Chron. iv. 1, and he is not mentioned among the elected tribes in Rev. vii."].

28. And there was no deliverer, because it was far from Zidon, and they had no business with any man; and it was in the valley that lieth by Beth-rehob [at the foot of the lowest range of Lebanon]. And they built a city, and dwelt therein.

29. And they called the name of the city Dan, after the name of Dan their father, who was born unto Israel; howbeit the name of the city was Laish at the first.

30. And the children of Dan set up the graven image [some say it was in

the form of a calf]; and Jonathan [the name has been withheld until this moment], the son of Gershom, the son of Manasseh, he and his sons were priests to the tribe of Dan until the day of the captivity of the land [probably the Philistine captivity].

31. And they set them up Micah's graven image, which he made, all the time that the house of God was in Shiloh.

MICAH'S SORROW.

WE now reach a very disturbed state of the history of Israel. All is anarchy. We have thus an opportunity of seeing what men will do when they are left to themselves without government, discipline, sense of social or natural responsibility. We shall see what the bridge is when the keystone has dropped out of it. We are told again and again in these latter chapters that "there was no king in Israel," so "every man did that which was right in his own eyes." What is the meaning of this? The meaning goes further back than the mere letter; there was no king in Israel, because in Israel there was no God. The Lord is King. You cannot have a king if you have not a God. There was no nominal renunciation of God, no public and blatant atheism, no boastful impiety; there was a deadlier heresy—namely, keeping God as a sign but paying no tribute to him as a King, worshipping him possibly in outward form but knowing nothing of the subduing and directing power of godliness. That is more to be dreaded than any intellectual difficulty of a theological kind. Intellectual heresies can do but little to impede the progress of the kingdom of truth; but dead consciences, prayerless prayers, mechanical formalities—these are the impediments which overturn for a time the chariot of Progress. This was the case in Israel. Where God is the king is. Not in any limited and measurable sense, as a man with a crown on, constituted of so much gold and so many precious stones; but a king in the sense of kingliness, sovereignty, authority, rule—the spirit of obligation and responsibility. You may have a king under any form of government. Republicanism itself is monarchical. You find the monarch everywhere—the right monarch where you find the right God. Herein is the utility of spreading far and wide right conceptions of the divine Being, as Sovereign, Father, Shepherd, Judge; let such conceptions be received into the mind; let them constitute part of the very substance of life, and you need not exhort men to keep correct weights and measures, and to pay the wages of the hireling; where the sovereign idea is right, and the supreme and dominating conviction is pure and noble, every finger of the hands serves the living God, and the whole breath is a continual sacrifice upon the altar of Righteousness. So, without going into narrow definitions of terms, we rest on the broad philosophy and reason that a right conception of God means a right conception of Man; a true, deep, complete love of God means an equal love of one's neighbour; a true theology, properly understood, is the uppermost side of a true morality.

Every man was king in the anarchical days of Israel. What does anarchy do for society? Anarchy and society are irreconcilable terms. Where *Self* is king there can be no society; the ghastly image of it must be symbolical of injustice. The illustration and proof are found in this very chapter. Dan went out to see what could be had:—

"The children of Dan sent of their family five men from their coasts, men of valour, from Zorah, and from Eshtaol, to spy out the land, and to search it; and they said unto them, Go, search the land" (v. 2).

In other words: Let us see what can be done. They followed the good old rule, the simple plan,—Let those take who have the power; Let those keep who can. This is the history of anarchy in a couplet: the strongest is the wisest, might is right, usurpation is justice. Things are turned upside down in their moral relations and applications when the great central thought is destroyed. Here a curious incident occurred. Dan, searching out the land and seeing what could be done, "knew the voice of the young man the Levite" in the house of Micah; "and they turned in thither, and said unto him, Who brought thee hither? and what makest thou in this place? and what hast thou here?"—(v. 3). Such are the coincidences of life—the little points at which so-called providences are created by selfishness and injustice. Singular chances arise, and we construe these into visitations of Heaven, made directly on our behalf. The young man explained his circumstances; and the children of Dan said unto him: "Ask counsel, we pray thee, of God, that we may know whether our way which

we go shall be prosperous " ₍v. 5₎. Here you have social
injustice connected with the holiest names. It is sad to see
how religion has been abused. It is mysterious, beyond all
other mystery, to note how men, given up to injustice, usurpation, and plunder, must now and again be religious. Thieves
go to church as well as honest men. Again and again it strikes
the roughest mind and the most ill-treated conscience that another
attempt at prayer may be an excellent investment. For irony,
look to the history of the human conscience ; read the history of
the Christian Church. Men have thought they could build their
way half up to heaven with stones taken by unjust hands out of
the quarries of earth. Men " have stolen the livery of the court
of heaven to serve the devil in." Men, who would not for a
moment deny God in words, have denied and rejected him in
action. We should analyse our prayers, and cross-examine ourselves at the altar, and keep a strict watch upon ourselves at the
holy board,—even there the whole nature should undergo a
species of vivisection, that out of its agony we may extort the
truth.

The seventh verse presents a picture of the dangers of solitariness and self-security :—

" Then the five men departed, and came to Laish, and saw the people
that were therein, how they dwelt careless, after the manner of the Zidonians,
quiet and secure ; and there was no magistrate in the land, that might put
them to shame in any thing ; and they were far from the Zidonians, and
had no business with any man."

These circumstances have a wide application. They must not
be limited by geographical lines, for they apply to the history of
civilisation and to the position of every man in human society.
There is a solitariness which means weakness ; there is a " care
lessness " which amounts to a temptation to those who behold it.
Is this not so with regard to *mind ?* Are there not persons who
have intellectually no commerce with the world ?—they read no
books, they hear no discourses, they listen not to the voice of
education or of progress ; they live retrospectively ; they live
upon themselves, and are in a sense suicides. This intellectual
solitariness is often but another name for weakness. We should
know all men, all nations, all languages ; all civilisations should
be familiar to us. Without such large commerce with the world

we shall become little and less and less, day by day, falling swiftly backward to the vanishing point. We should travel more ; otherwise we shall think that one country is the world, and be amused with a fool's merriment when we hear of what is being done, in some distant kind of way, by nations which we are conceited enough to pronounce " foreign." There should be no " foreign " nations now. Modern civilisation should have rendered that an impossibility. Every language should be a man's mother-tongue—in the ideal of it, in the innermost meaning of it; not that it is possible literally and mechanically, but perfectly possible sympathetically and philanthropically. It is sad to see people dwelling within their own little sect, wondering how other persons can have the "audacity " to differ from them —forgetting that they themselves have the " audacity " to differ from other people. Why this fear of man ? We should be familiar with the history of barbarism, so far as it may be said to have a history ; or we should construct a history out of what we know concerning it, and out of the history extract a philosophy. This is the way to rebuke our own mind, to humble our own ambition, and to have our asperities struck off or smoothed down, by a large and continuous friction. So it should be in Christian culture. All Christian communions should intermingle. They would do one another good. They can never be constituted into one mechanical society, because of temperament, but they can realise a common brotherhood, because they may be stronger at the point of agreement than they are at the point of difference. What havoc the enemy makes upon solitary Christians ! Sympathy is strength. Little trust is little support. No one Church can be the whole Church of the living God. But who does not like to live "quietly," and " carelessly "—that is, without care, not indifference—at home, sitting, as we say, under his own vine and fig-tree ? If there is a pitiable sight on the whole earth to-day, it is to see a man sitting under his own vine and fig-tree, when the rest of the world is in poverty, weakness, or necessity. Times there will be, sabbatic and sacred, when there will be sense of home, sense of security, sense of the blessedness of having a vine and fig-tree ; but that should never be the dominating feeling in the Christian breast ; the dominating feeling should rather be one of large-heartedness, spreading a table for every man, asking a blessing in every language, and preaching a gospel to every creature. This was Christ's life ; this was Christ's philosophy ; this was Christ's practice. Let us be followers together of Christ, of God, " as dear children."

The history having advanced so far, and the men of Dan having reported that they had found in certain houses " an ephod, and teraphim, and a graven image, and a molten image," a singular transaction took place :—

" And the five men that went to spy out the land went up, and came in thither, and took the graven image, and the ephod, and the teraphim, and the molten image : and the priest stood in the entering of the gate with the six hundred men that were appointed with weapons of war " (v. 17).

This was a capture of shrines and images. Rather than not have a god they thought it better to steal one ; and having stolen the gods, of course they stole the priest. They put a case to him, saying : " Hold thy peace, lay thine hand upon thy mouth, and go with us, and be to us a father and a priest : is it better for thee to be a priest unto the house of one man, or that thou be a priest unto a tribe and a family in Israel ? "—(v. 19). It was an appeal to ambition. That was offering the man a " larger sphere of usefulness." We have seen what his salary was in the house of Micah—namely, twenty-five shillings a year, a suit of clothes, and his victuals. Now comes a " call of Providence." Woe be unto us when we receive intimations of Providence through the lips of thieves ! Distrust the devil even when he preaches a good doctrine ; repel him even when he quotes Scripture by chapter and verse. What was the answer of the grandson of Moses ? " And the priest's heart was glad, and he took the ephod, and the teraphim, and the graven image, and went in the midst of the people "—(v. 20). To trust a thievish priest one would say would be impossible. But such contradictions are repeated in human history. The children of Dan knew that all had been stolen, including the priest himself, and yet they had some kind of grim trust in all this wild arrangement. Truly, there was no king in Israel ; truly, there was no God in Israel ! We should simplify our relations to great central truths. We have managed, by some process not to be explained in words, to turn religion into a great complication, so that, not understanding it, we often pervert it. To what humiliation may the human intellect and conscience be reduced! To think that stolen images could do any good! On the other hand, to suppose that the gods stolen should consent to be the protecting divinities of thieves! Yet this is the danger of every day's religious experience—namely, the danger of a perverted conscience, an unbalanced judgment, a blurred confusion as to moral relations and obligations, so that having brought ourselves into intellectual and spiritual tumult, we justify our bad conduct by our bad metaphysics! Men may steal a god, but they cannot steal a character. They may take away a whole house of gods—as Micah's building was called—and yet have no living temple, no inner sanctuary, in which to worship and to love.

Micah's part in the matter is singularly illustrative of much that is taking place to-day. Micah having discovered the theft,

" overtook the children of Dan. And they cried unto the children of Dan. And they turned their faces, and said unto Micah, What aileth thee, that thou comest with such a company? And he said, Ye have taken away my gods which I made, and the priest, and ye are gone away : and what have I more? and what is this that ye say unto me, What aileth thee?" (vv. 22–24).

Micah had gods that could be taken away—have we any better divinities? Have we even a Bible that can be taken away? If so, we have no Bible at all. It is possible to make a mere idol of the Bible—possible to be most careful that no injury should be done to the book, and yet never to peruse its spiritual meaning and apply its spiritual doctrine. The Bible should not be outside of us—something that a thief can take away ; it should be in us, part of us, so that a man stealing our Bible must first steal ourselves ; for it is the very inspiration of memory, the very treasure of recollection, the very wealth of the soul. But where are the men to whom the Bible is thus much? The danger of Christ losing the battle—were such danger possible—would be in Christ's people neglecting Christ's Book. There is no volume held in such contempt as the Bible, even by some who profess to honour it. You cannot honour the Bible by binding it, gilding it, protecting it from dust and injury, walking round it, looking at it ; you can only honour the Bible in one way, and that is by reading it, taking it into the soul, reproducing it in living literature, in epistles "known and read of all men." A beautiful thing it seems to be to teach a child that even a king would not allow the Bible to be stood upon. The king was right, but he was only right in a limited sense. The true honouring of the Bible, let us say again and again, is having it dwelling in us richly, and reproducing continual fruitfulness in good.

The process of deprivation went on quickly. Having stolen a god, the thieves next stole a city; having corrupted a priest, they debased a memory; and they called the name of the stolen city Dan, "after the name of Dan their father." So swiftly may men run on the smooth road to hell! Once get the hand well into wickedness, and the rest comes by daily custom and practice. We sanctify our bad deeds by attaching to some of them the names of illustrious ancestors. How deceitful is the heart and desperately wicked! What a mixture is life! what lines of various hue are shot through and through this fabric of being! Here are men stealing gods, and asking counsel of Heaven; stealing a priest and all the shrines they could lay hold of, and then justifying themselves thereby in taking a city; seizing a city occupied by inoffensive people, burning it, building another upon its ashes, and calling it by the name of a dead man. Who can analyse human life? Who can really take to pieces the mystery of human action? The whole history is not bad; certainly the whole history is not good. This, indeed, is the summary of life. Where is there a man—speaking only now of the individual— who is all bad? Surely there is not one; surely the drunkard sometimes pauses in his madness to think some good thought of the days of long ago when he tried to pray; surely even the thief does not take everything, and partly excuses himself for having taken something by saying that he has left something untaken; surely the liar sometimes strikes some note of truth; surely the unjust man has a sudden impulse upon him which leads him to do not only justly but generously. And where is the man who is all good, without stain or taint or flaw or draw- back? Where? So, on the one hand, we have some reason for hope; on the other, much reason for humility and continual self-examination. But the time of judgment is not yet. God will judge us all, and he will find out the supreme motive of life, and by that he will determine everything. This is a gospel, and yet it is a judgment terrible to hear. Blessed be God, we stand in this conviction—namely, " God is a Spirit : and they that worship him must worship him in spirit and in truth." God dwelleth in the humble heart and contrite spirit. God cannot be stolen, though his image and symbol may. Blessed are they who have passed beyond the letter into the meaning of the spirit of things, knowing somewhat of God's own heart and entering sympathetically into God's own purpose ; then though the literal Bible be burned, revelation remains untouched ; though the church built with hands—" the sacrifice in stone "—is demolished, the temple indestructible is in the heart ; though forms and ceremonies are unremembered things, the soul goes up in continual aspiration, seeking the living God and desiring only to be found in the living Christ.

SELECTED NOTE.

The worship in Micah's house, in its object and intention, was the worship of Jehovah. Both mother and son did what they did " to the Lord." Their " gods," as they are called—their " images," "teraphim"—were set up for the purpose of a service which was meant to honour "the God of Abraham, Isaac, and Jacob." . . . They were significant emblems, something having a sacred meaning, which embodied religious ideas, and were to be used as a help in approaching God. They were visible types of spiritual things ; material representations of what was unseen ; vehicles, so to speak, by which the mind could be aided in rising upwards towards heaven, and through which divine virtue could flow down to man upon earth. It was the same with Aaron's golden calf and the calves set up by Jeroboam. In each case the professed object of the service was Jehovah. The visible things were not to be worshipped ; God was to be worshipped through them. " But the thing that was done displeased the Lord." All such unauthorised attempts to aid devotion through "the likeness of anything in the heaven above or in the earth beneath " were rejected and stigmatised as sinful. Whenever employed, they " became a snare," and " caused Israel to sin."

Micah was, in his way, very religious. He was not pre-eminently honest ; he had but a slight sense of relative duty, and cannot be supposed to have known much of personal moral culture. It is possible, indeed, that he stole his mother's property with the pious intention of making it into images for " the honour of God." His religion consisted in a blind and superstitious veneration for the outward and visible in divine worship, and in depending for spiritual grace (if ever he thought of that) on ceremony and ritual. Hence his anxiety to have " a father and a priest," that the priest should be consecrated, that he should minister in the proper sacerdotal robe, and especially that he should be of the sacred tribe, and belong to the legitimate Levitical succession. His highest expectations were founded on this ; not on *character*, either in the Levite or himself ; not on intelligence and capacity to edify and instruct ; simply on the fact that " he had a Levite for his priest."—*Thomas Binney.*

JUDGES xix., xx. (ANNOTATED).

Judges xix.

1. And it came to pass in those days [not long after Joshua's death, and before Othniel was judge], when there was no king in Israel, that there was a certain Levite sojourning on the side of mount Ephraim, who took to him a concubine [such relations were not legally forbidden] out of Beth-lehem-judah.

2. And his concubine [wife or concubine,—a wife with inferior rights] played the whore against him, and went away from him [Prov. xxx. 21], unto her father's house to Beth-lehem-judah, and was there four whole months [literally, days four months ; or, one year and four months].

3. And her husband arose, and went after her, to speak friendly [to speak to her heart] unto her, and to bring her again, having his servant with him and a couple of asses [one was meant to convey his wife] : and she brought him into her father's house : and when the father of the damsel saw him, he rejoiced to meet him.

4. And his father-in-law [so the relationship was recognised], the damsel's father, retained him [with hospitable and affectionate intentions] ; and he abode with him three days : so they did eat and drink, and lodged there [" in token of hearty reconciliation "].

5. And it came to pass on the fourth day, when they arose early in the morning [to avoid the burning heat], that he rose up to depart [" It is good hearing when the Levite maketh haste home. An honest man's heart is where his calling is "]. And the damsel's father said unto his son-in-law, Comfort thine heart [literally, prop up thine heart] with a morsel of bread, and afterward go your way.

6. And they sat down, and did eat and drink both of them together : for the damsel's father had said unto the man, Be content, I pray thee, and tarry all night, and let thine heart be merry.

7. And when the man rose up to depart, his father-in-law urged him [to test his good intentions towards a faithless woman] : therefore he lodged there again.

8. And he arose early in the morning on the fifth day to depart : and the damsel's father said, Comfort thine heart, I pray thee. And they tarried [lingered] until afternoon, and they did eat both of them.

9. And when the man rose up to depart, he, and his concubine, and his servant, his father-in-law, the damsel's father, said unto him, Behold, now the day draweth toward evening [literally, is weak or has slackened to evening], I pray you tarry all night : behold, the day groweth to an end [literally, it is the bending or declining of the day], lodge here, that thine heart may be merry ; and to-morrow get you early on your way, that thou mayst go home [to thy tent].

10. But the man would not tarry that night, but he rose up and departed, and came over against Jebus [so called in the days of David], which is Jerusalem ; and there were with him two asses saddled ; his concubine also was with him.

11. And when they were by Jebus, the day was far spent [he had been detained too long by hospitality] ; and the servant said unto his master, Come, I pray thee, and let us turn in into this city of the Jebusites [which they would reach about five o'clock], and lodge in it.

12. And his master said unto him, We will not turn aside hither into the city of a stranger [think of Jerusalem being so described !], that is not of the children of Israel : we will pass over to Gibeah [the Gibeah of Saul,—the birthplace of the first king of Israel].

13. And he said unto his servant, Come, and let us draw near to one of these places to lodge all night, in Gibeah, or in Ramah [two miles beyond Gibeah].

14. And they passed on and went their way ; and the sun went down upon them when they were by Gibeah [which determined them to stay], which belongeth to Benjamin [there were many other Gibeahs in Palestine].

15. And they turned aside thither, to go in and to lodge in Gibeah [Poneropolis, or city of the Evil One] ; and when he went in [through the city gate], he sat him down in a street [open place, or square] of the city : for there was no man that took them into his house to lodging [Deut. x. 9] [They would have gone on to Ramah, two miles farther north, had the daylight held out. Sunset in that latitude is almost immediately followed by darkness].

16. And, behold, there came an old man from his work out of the field at even [an old man ; an old man working ; an old man working out of doors], which was also of mount Ephraim [a fellow countryman of the Levite] ; and he sojourned in Gibeah : but the men of the place were Benjamites.

17. And when he had lifted up his eyes, he saw a wayfaring man in the street of the city : and the old man said, Whither goest thou ? and whence comest thou ?

18. And he said unto him, We are passing from Beth-lehem-judah toward the side of mount Ephraim [the depths of the hill country of mount Ephraim] ;

from thence am I : and I went to Beth-lehem-judah, but I am now going to the house of the Lord [or, I am a Levite engaged in the service of the Tabernacle at Shiloh] ; and there is no man that receiveth me to house [Hesiod reckons this as supreme wickedness].

19. Yet there is both straw and provender [any grain fit for food of cattle] for our asses ; and there is bread and wine also for me and for thy handmaid, and for the young man which is with thy servants : there is no want of any thing.

20. And the old man said, Peace be with thee [not merely a greeting, but an assurance of help] ; howsoever let all thy wants lie upon me ; only lodge not in the street [Gen. xix. 2].

21. So he brought him into his house, and gave provender unto the asses [it was the custom of the East to attend first to the wants of the animals] : and they washed their feet, and did eat and drink.

22. Now as they were making their hearts merry, behold, the men of the city, certain sons of Belial [sons of worthlessness], beset the house round about, and beat at the door, and spake to the master of the house, the old man, saying, Bring forth the man that came into thine house, that we may know him [Hosea ix. 9].

23. And the man, the master of the house, went out unto them, and said unto them, Nay, my brethren, nay, I pray you, do not so wickedly ; seeing that this man is come into mine house [an appeal to the sacred rights of hospitality], do not this folly.

24. Behold, here is my daughter, a maiden [see from what depths the world has risen], and his concubine ; them I will bring out now, and humble ye them, and do with them what seemeth good unto you : but unto this man do not so vile a thing.

25. But the men would not hearken to him : so the man took his concubine, and brought her forth unto them ; and they knew her, and abused her all the night until the morning : and when the day began to spring, they let her go.

26. Then came the woman in the dawning of the day, and fell down at the door of the man's house where her lord was, till it was light.

27. And her lord rose up in the morning, and opened the doors of the house, and went out to go his way : and, behold, the woman his concubine was fallen down at the door of the house, and her hands were upon the threshold [as if in one last appeal of agony and despair].

28. And he said unto her, Up, and let us be going. But none answered. Then the man took her up upon an ass, and the man rose up, and gat him unto his place.

29. And when he was come into his house, he took a knife, and laid hold on his concubine, and divided her, together with her bones, into twelve pieces, and sent her into all the coast of Israel [that he might rouse a spirit of vengeance].

30. And it was so, that all that saw it said, There was no such deed done nor seen from the day that the children of Israel came up out of the land of Egypt unto this day [and so soon after the death of Joshua] : consider of it, take advice, and speak your minds.

[The nineteenth chapter would be intolerable but for the twentieth ; the two must be read together. When men remark upon the awful depravity of the one they should remember the awful vengeance of the other.]

Judges xx.

1. Then all the children of Israel went out, and the congregation [the whole community of Israel] was gathered together as one man [a phrase which disappears after the days of Solomon], from Dan even to Beer-sheba [from one extremity to another,—a proverbial expression for all Israel], with the land of Gilead [the transjordanic tribes], unto the Lord in Mizpeh [not the one mentioned in xi. 11].

2. And the chief [literally, the corner-stones] of all the people, even of all the tribes of Israel, presented themselves in the assembly of the people of God, four hundred thousand [so the number had been diminished by one third] footmen that drew sword [the Israelites were forbidden to use either chariot or cavalry].

3. (Now the children of Benjamin heard that the children of Israel were gone up to Mizpeh.) Then said the children of Israel, Tell us, how was this wickedness ?

4. And the Levite, the husband of the woman that was slain, answered and said, I came into Gibeah, that belongeth to Benjamin, I and my concubine, to lodge.

5. And the men [lords or masters] of Gibeah rose against me ["The Levite colours the story in a way most favourable to himself"], and beset the hou e round about upon me by night, and thought to have slain me : and my concubine have they forced, that she is dead.

6. And I took my concubine, and cut her in pieces, and sent her throughout all the country of the inheritance of Israel : for they have committed lewdness and folly in Israel.

7. Behold, ye are all children of Israel : give here your advice and counsel.

8. And all the people rose as one man [1 Sam. xi. 7], saying, We will not any of us go to his tent [the transjordanic tribes were principally graziers], neither will we any of us turn into his house.

9. But now this shall be the thing which we will do to Gibeah ; we will go up by lot against it ["The shape of the ground probably made it impossible for the whole force to operate at once"] :

10. And we will take ten men of an hundred throughout all the tribes of Israel, and an hundred of a thousand, and a thousand out of ten thousand, to

fetch victual for the people, that they may do, when they come to Gibeah of Benjamin, according to all the folly that they have wrought in Israel.

11. So all the men of Israel were gathered against the city, knit together as one man [fellows of one college or club].

12. And the tribes of Israel sent men through all the tribe of Benjamin, saying, What wickedness is this that is done among you [even Benjamin had a chance of self-defence]?

13. Now therefore deliver us the men, the children of Belial, which are in Gibeah, that we may put them to death, and put away evil from Israel. [The verb implies extermination, such as the burning out of diseased flesh.] But the children of Benjamin would not hearken to the voice of their brethren the children of Israel [an evil solidarity] :

14. But [and] the children of Benjamin gathered themselves together out of the cities unto Gibeah, to go out to battle against the children of Israel :

15. And the children of Benjamin were numbered at that time out of the cities twenty and six thousand men [diminished by about a third since the census] that drew sword, beside the inhabitants of Gibeah, which numbered seven hundred chosen men.

16. Among all this people there were seven hundred chosen men [these words are omitted by the LXX. and the Vulgate] left-handed [not an accidental defect, but an acquired art] ; every one could sling stones at an hair breadth, and not miss [Cyrus valued his four hundred slingers].

17. And the men of Israel, beside Benjamin, were numbered four hundred thousand men that drew sword : all these were men of war.

18. And the children of Israel arose, and went up to the house of God [Bethel], and asked counsel of God [by the Urim and Thummim], and said, Which of us shall go up first to the battle against the children of Benjamin? And the Lord said, Judah shall go up first.

19. And the children of Israel rose up in the morning, and encamped against Gibeah.

20. And the men of Israel went out to battle against Benjamin ; and the men of Israel put themselves in array to fight against them at Gibeah.

21. And the children of Benjamin came forth out of Gibeah [the whole tribe adopted the bad deed,—an evil *esprit de corps*], and destroyed down to the ground of the Israelites that day twenty and two thousand men.

22. And the people, the men of Israel, encouraged themselves, and set their battle again in array in the place where they put themselves in array the first day.

23. (And the children of Israel went up and wept before the Lord until even, and asked counsel of the Lord, saying, Shall I go up again to battle against the children of Benjamin my brother ? [" showing a sort of compunction "] and the Lord said, Go up against him.)

24. And the children of Israel came near against the children of Benjamin the second day.

25. And Benjamin went forth against them out of Gibeah the second day, and destroyed down to the ground of the children of Israel again eighteen thousand men ; all these drew the sword.

26. Then all the children of Israel, and all the people, went up, and came unto the house of God, and wept ["The two battles must have caused an almost universal bereavement "], and sat there before the Lord, and fasted that day until even, and offered burnt-offerings and peace-offerings before the Lord.

27. And the children of Israel enquired of the Lord, (for the ark of the covenant of God was there in those days ;

28. And Phinehas [the noble and heroic grandson of Aaron], the son of Eleazar, the son of Aaron, stood before it in those days,) saying, Shall I yet again go out to battle against the children of Benjamin my brother, or shall I cease ? And the Lord said, Go up ; for to-morrow [the first promise of success] I will deliver them into thine hand.

29. And Israel set liers in wait round about Gibeah ["acting with more humility, caution, and wisdom "].

30. And the children of Israel went up against the children of Benjamin on the third day, and put themselves in array against Gibeah, as at other times.

31. And the children of Benjamin went out against the people, and were drawn away from the city ; and they began to smite of the people, and kill [the wounded or beaten of the people], as at other times, in the highways, of which one goeth up to the house of God [Bethel], and the other to Gibeah in the field [probably Geba, Josh. xxi. 17], about thirty men of Israel.

32. And the children of Benjamin said, They are smitten down before us, as at the first. But the children of Israel said, Let us flee, and draw them from the city unto the highways.

33. And all the men of Israel rose up out of their place, and put themselves in array at Baal-tamar [Lord of the palm] : and the liers in wait of Israel came forth out of their places, even out of the meadows [a word which occurs nowhere else] of Gibeah.

34. And there came against Gibeah ten thousand chosen men out of all Israel, and the battle was sore [Benjamin was attacked both in front and rear] : but [and] they knew not that evil was near them [that the hour of ruin had come],

35. And the Lord smote Benjamin before Israel : and the children of Israel destroyed of the Benjamites that day twenty and five thousand and an hundred men : all these drew the sword.

36. So the children of Benjamin saw that they [the Israelites] were smitten : for the men of Israel gave place to the Benjamites, because they trusted unto the liers in wait which they had set beside Gibeah.

37. And the liers in wait hasted, and rushed [set upon ; see ix. 33] upon Gibeah ; and the liers in wait drew themselves along, and smote all the city with the edge of the sword [an expression which denotes extermination].

38. Now there was an appointed sign between the men of Israel and the liers in wait, that they should make a great flame with smoke rise up out of the city

39. And when the men of Israel retired in the battle, Benjamin began to smite and kill of the men of Israel about thirty persons : for they said, Surely they are smitten down before us, as in the first battle.

40. But when the flame began to arise up out of the city with a pillar of smoke, the Benjamites looked behind them, and, behold, the flame of the city ascended up to heaven.

41. And when the men of Israel turned again, the men of Benjamin were amazed : for they saw that evil was come upon them.

42. Therefore they turned their backs before the men of Israel unto the way of the wilderness ; but the battle overtook them ; and them which came out of the cities [Benjamites] they destroyed in the midst of them [that is, in their own cities].

43. Thus they inclosed the Benjamites round about, and chased them, and trode them down with ease over against Gibeah toward the sunrising. ["The language and construction of this verse is poetical ; it seems to be an extract from a song, and to describe, in the language of poetry, the same event which the preceding verse described in that of prose."]

44. And there fell of Benjamin eighteen thousand men ; all these were men of valour.

45. And they turned and fled toward the wilderness unto the rock of Rimmon [the rock of the pomegranate]; and they gleaned of them in the highways five thousand men ; and pursued hard after them unto Gidom [mentioned nowhere else], and slew two thousand men of them.

46. So that all which fell that day of Benjamin were twenty and five thousand men that drew the sword ; all these were men of valour.

47. But six hundred men [compare 1 Sam. xiv. 2] turned and fled to the wilderness unto the rock Rimmon, and abode in the rock Rimmon four months.

48. And the men of Israel turned again upon the children of Benjamin, and smote them with the edge of the sword, as well the men of every city, as the beast, and all that came to hand : also they set on fire all the cities that they came to.

" Having utterly destroyed the Benjamite army, except the six hundred men who were shut up in Rimmon, the Israelites returned through the Benjamite country and put to death all the remaining inhabitants, destroyed the cattle and burnt the cities " (*The Speaker's Commentary*). Keeping the whole tragedy vividly in mind, we shall the more profitably enter upon the study of the following subject.

Judges xxi. 3.

"O Lord God of Israel, why is this come to pass in Israel, that there should be to day one tribe lacking in Israel?"

ONE TRIBE LACKING.

THE spirit of this inquiry is the spirit of the whole Bible. It is, indeed, not so much an inquiry as a wail, a burst of sorrow, a very agony of kinship and disunion. The three-fold repetition of "Israel" indicates supreme distress. Israel was meant to be a unity—a constitution not only complete but inviolable—foursquare, without break or flaw, vital at every point —a noble integrity! And now Benjamin is threatened with extinction : Benjamin is not in the house of God. From the beginning, Benjamin was but a little tribe, the least of all in Israel, numbering at first from thirty to forty thousand fighting men. Over an extremely difficult and delicate question Benjamin came into conflict with the rest of Israel, and after an almost superhuman resistance was overborne, all but extirpated indeed, only some six hundred men being left, and they hiding themselves in the rock Rimmon—the impregnable Rock of the Pomegranate—some four months, thinking of the eighteen thousand men of valour who had been " trodden down with ease over against Gibeah toward the sunrising." But there was a time of heart-breaking in Israel. In the battlefield men thought only of victory, but they went up unto what is called in the text "the house of God." That is the right point of observation. Until you have looked at your fellow creatures from the house of God, from the altar, from the cross, you have never looked at them. Israel was now in the house of God, and began to reckon, to say, Who is here? Who is not here? Then they sighed, and shed tears, as only strong men can shed them, and in their tears they said, "O Lord God of Israel, why is this come to pass in Israel, that there should be to day one tribe lacking in Israel?" Thus men come to their better selves; heat dies away, vengeance halts in its desperate pursuit, all deepest and truest instincts come to the support of reason, natural affection stands by the side of justice, and great questions are quieted by great answers.

Does not the text exhibit the human aspect of the solicitude of God's own heart? In this respect, as well as in other ways, is not man made a little lower than God? In all such emotion there are suggestions infinite in scope and tenderness—suggestions of unity, family completeness, absolute unselfishness, redemption, forgiveness, reconstruction, everlasting joy! There is of course a sentiment which is without value, but this must not blind us to the fact that there is also an emotion without which we cannot sound the depths of God's own love. When we feel most truly, we often see most clearly. "Where art thou?" was the inquiry of God when Adam did not come towards him in the fearless joy of innocence. "Where is thy brother?" was the divine inquiry when Cain was found in criminal loneliness. Rather than Israel should be lost Moses would be blotted out of God's book. Christ came to seek and to save the lost. And Paul—that marvellous compound of Moses and Christ—honouring the majesty of the law, yet feeling its weakness in the presence of sin—did he not tremble under the same emotion? The answer will be found in the most doctrinal and logical, yet the most profoundly emotional of all his Epistles. In the Epistle to the Romans not only is one tribe threatened with extinction, but all Israel seems to be lost. The writer cannot rest, therefore. He has "great heaviness and continual sorrow in his heart." It is not enough for him that the forces of the Gentiles are moving towards the Cross, that from Midian, and Ephah, and Sheba men are arising to show forth the praises of the Lord; nor is it enough that the flocks of Kedar and the rams of Nebaioth shall be acceptable sacrifices: all this is good, beautiful, and an exceeding delight, but—but Israel is, not in the number of those who rejoice, Israel is hard of heart, and remembering this Paul says, "I could wish that myself were anathema from Christ for my brethren, my kinsmen according to the flesh." "My heart's desire and prayer to God for Israel is, that they might be saved." It was a sublime emotion. But who is the speaker? Take his own account of himself— "Of the stock of Israel, of the tribe of Benjamin"—the very tribe which in the text is lacking! Thus history rolls round in amplified and ennobled repetition. In the Book of Judges all Israel mourned that Benjamin was lacking, and in the Epistle to the Romans, Benjamin, in the person of its most illustrious descendant, laments that all Israel is away—far off in the wilderness of unbelief—he an alien who ought to have been a prince in the house of God.

Nor does the evidence of the presence of this emotion in the Bible end here.   In the Apocalypse there is One—" faithful and true Witness, the beginning of the creation of God," and he says, " Behold, I stand at the door, and knock : if any man hear my voice, and open the door, I will come in ; " the same who said, " O Jerusalem, Jerusalem, which killest the prophets, and stonest them that are sent unto thee, how often would I have gathered thy children together, as a hen doth gather her brood under her wings, and ye would not ! " the same who went after the lost sheep of the house of Israel ; the same who said, " Preach the Gospel to every creature," for good news must evermore do good.

There is, then, what may be called a distinct unity of emotion, call it pity, solicitude, compassion, or by any equal term, through-out the whole Bible.   The Bible varies a good deal in historical and even in moral colour, but it never varies in pity, and love, and mercy.   From the *first*, God loved man, even with atoning and redeeming love.   Marvellous, truly and instructively, is the development of Biblical history.   It changes page by page— now barbarous, now gentle, here an altar, there a commandment, yonder a ritual, and afar off an experience full of confusion, and riot, and tragedy : but in all the infinite tumult God looks after the wanderer with longing love, pursues him, pleads with him, says "Turn ye, turn ye, why will ye die ? " importunes him : " Cries,—How shall I give thee up ? Lets the lifted thunder drop."   Even divine righteousness varies its aspects without vary-ing its nature ; in some sense it measures its demands by human weakness : now it is an order for a place or a time ; then it is a series of initial and suggestive commandments ; then it is an accommodation to hardness of heart,—never losing a ray of its eternal glory, it yet creates an atmosphere suited to the vision of the beholder ;—but love, pity, mercy, care for the absent, wonder about the one lacking tribe,—this begins the book, ends the book stirs the book like the throb of an infinite heart.

The love of God, the mercy, the pity, the compassion of God
is not a revelation of the New Testament only, it is the revelation
of the whole Bible.   In Eden there was a Promised Seed ; in
the wilderness there was a mercy-seat ; in Genesis there is a
covenant ; in Malachi there is a book of remembrance ; in
Exodus the Lord keeps mercy for thousands, and forgives
iniquity, and transgression, and sin ; in Numbers " the Lord is
longsuffering and of great mercy, forgiving iniquity and transgression ;" in Judges " the Lord was grieved for the misery of
Israel ;" in Samuel he recalled the avenging angel ; in Chronicles
(a book of annals) he says, if his people will seek his face and
turn from their wicked ways, he will hear them from heaven,
and will forgive their sin, and heal their land ; the Psalms are
songs of forgiveness ; Isaiah, Jeremiah, and Ezekiel are books
glowing with the love of God ; and Daniel says, " To the Lord
our God belong mercies and forgiveness, though we have rebelled
against him ;" in Hosea, God heals the backsliding of his
people, and loves them freely ; even Joel—that burning furnace
—says that God is gracious and merciful ; Jonah, in solemn
anger, says he knew that God was " a gracious God and merciful,
slow to anger, and of great kindness ;" and all the minor prophets
praise the tenderness of God.   So we find that this pity, compassion, mercy—by whatever name we call the emotion—is
present from the beginning to the end of the Old Testament.
Paul was the most Old Testament writer in all the New Testament.   When he speaks of God being rich in mercy, good,
forbearing, longsuffering, Paul is in very deed a Hebrew of the
Hebrews, of the tribe of Benjamin.   When the Jews at Jerusalem heard that Paul spake unto them in the Hebrew tongue
they kept the more silence.   We ought to do the same ; for we
have understood that Paul was the Apostle of the Gentiles, that
his place was far off among the heathen, that special grace was
given unto him that he should preach among the Gentiles the
unsearchable riches of Christ, and at the very time he was
preaching in Syria and Cilicia he was unknown by face unto the
Churches of Judea which were in Christ.   Yet this man, consecrated to preach in Gentile tongues, spake in the Hebrew
tongue.   Why ?   He missed his own people.   He thought that
the mother-tongue might fetch some of them.   His heart was

ill at ease. But was not the Hebrew tongue doubly dear to Paul ?
Surely. For when he, as Saul, was fallen to the earth as he
went to Damascus, he heard a voice speaking to him " in the
Hebrew tongue, saying, . . . I am Jesus." So it was the mother-
tongue of his Christian life. It suited the great gospel better than
any other language : what other could speak with such unction
of "blood"? Any other tongue would make it vulgar—a
measurable thing : but in the Hebrew it was lifted up into
symbolism and grandeur. " Sacrifice," " redemption," " pro-
pitiation," " pardon,"—why, how could he speak in any other
than the Hebrew tongue ? Thus the Apostle of the Gentiles
is also the Apostle of the Jews : the foreign missionary is the
home missionary, and the home missionary is the foreign
missionary, for it was the whole world that God thought of when
he freely delivered up his Son for us all. Paul knew nothing of
an Israel reduced to eleven tribes ; speaking to Agrippa, he said,
with a wonderfully suppressed pathos, " Our twelve tribes ";
Paul knew nothing of a broken household, he knew only of the
whole family in heaven and on earth : Paul knew nothing of
an exclusive gospel ; when he witnessed he witnessed " both
to small and great." And James—a mind without poetry, a
church without a spire—wrote his letter to the full number of
the tribes, " The twelve tribes," said he—still twelve, though
" scattered abroad."

Is it possible for a tribe to be " lacking " for ever ? To become extinct ? To lose its election and be damned ? Where,
for example, is the tribe of Dan ? It disappears from the record
in 1 Chronicles, and it is not counted in the Apocalypse. Were
its few faithful members amalgamated with some other tribe,
say this very tribe of Benjamin ? Yet even in the Apocalypse,
the number of the tribes is twelve. God's promise shall stand
sure and steadfast, and his supper chamber shall be filled with
guests ! We may be unfaithful, and may lose our place, but
the Blessed One who died for us shall see of the travail of
his soul and be satisfied !

From another point of view we shall see that this yearning
over the lacking tribe was no mere sentiment. This high feeling had also a disciplinary aspect, and was, therefore, a whole

feeling—a complete and ardent loyalty. When Deborah sang her triumphal song she disclosed the second and sterner aspect of this emotion. She knew who was lacking from the war against Jabin King of Hazor, and did not scruple to mention by name the guilty absentees. Why should there have been, said that mother heart, one tribe lacking on that day of war ? Reuben remained among the sheepfolds, and listened to the bleatings of the flocks, when he ought to have answered the call of the battle horn and repulsed the chariots of Sisera ; and Deborah named him : "For the divisions of Reuben there were great thoughts of heart ; for the divisions of Reuben there were great searchings of heart." Why was he lacking that day ? He sent promises, but remained at home. He was busy amongst the flocks when he ought to have been suffering with the army ! Oh, these prior engagements ! these other occupations ! these domestic excuses ! They went for nothing in the tempest of Deborah's enthusiasm, and they ought to stand for nothing in our consuming zeal for the honour of our Lord and the dominion of his cross. Nor was Reuben the only absentee. Gilead abode beyond Jordan, Dan was concealed in ships, and Asher—are we not ashamed to say it ?—peeped in cowardly curiosity from behind the creeks, and wondered how the war was going on. Yet the battle was won. No credit to the absentees. Where men failed women succeeded : whilst "Zebulun and Naphtali jeoparded their lives unto the death in the high places of the field," Deborah and Jael made their names great in Israel. You may keep away from the war, but the battle will end in victory.

There is another variety of the principle of the text which cannot be wisely overlooked. There is a lacking or absence which affects great indignation because it has not been observed. Men stand back for a space that they may see whether they will be missed. Others come in after the victory and demand to know why they were not allowed to share in the fight ! Let history be our proof. We stand or fall by facts in an argument like this. When Gideon overthrew the Midianites, and held in one hand the head of Prince Oreb, and in the other the head of Prince Zeeb, the Ephraimites chided him sharply because they had not been sent for. This was a trick of Ephraim—a trick he dearly paid for when he tried it upon Jephthah. "Wherefore," said Ephraim to Jephthah, "passedst thou over to fight against the children of Ammon, and didst not call us to go with thee?" Jephthah told them why. He reminded them that once he did send for them and they did not come, and now that they began to chide him the Spirit of the Lord and of true judgment burned in him, and that day he choked the passages of the Jordan with forty-two thousand Ephraimites. Ephraim was a coward. Ephraim is a branded name. For ever will it be said of him, "Ephraim being armed and carrying bows turned back in the day of battle." Ephraim was famous for archery. Ephraim might have done wonders with bow and arrow, but he turned back, and then blamed others because he was not sent for! Is it so with any who may smile at Ephraim's cowardice? Are there not those who would have done wonderful things if they had known of the opportunity? They knew not when Christ was an hungered, or athirst, or naked, or sick, or in prison, or they would have given unto him: they say so, but—"These shall go away into everlasting punishment."

So the text taken in all its aspects is no mere sentiment. In presence of some gaps in the line of Israel the tears of the text become sparks of fire, because of the treachery of some and the cowardice of others. We have forgotten that Christianity is a battle as well as a gospel. Is the whole fighting strength of the Church under discipline? Are any skulking at home? Are any enjoying the delights of civilisation who ought to be in the wilderness of heathenism; nay, come closer still; are any sitting in luxury and idleness who ought to be in some department of Christian service—say in the Sunday-school, in the diaconate, in districts inhabited by poverty and ignorance? Why should there be this day one tribe lacking in Christian Israel? There is a tremendous foe. We are all needed. There is room for all— for wealth, for genius, for learning, for love, for age, for youth. Come! Surrender yourselves to Christ! Be soldiers of the Cross!

> "Sound, sound the clarion, shrill the fife;
> To all the sensual world proclaim,
> One crowded hour of glorious life
> Is worth an age without a name."

But here a word of consolation may be fitly given. Some are no longer in the hot battle, yet they must not be thought of as absent or lacking from the household of God. Even the mighty David " waxed faint." He was but seventy when he died. Yet when we say " but seventy " do we not speak carelessly ? What a seventy ! what years they were ! When he tottered under his weakness, in one of the closing battles, he nearly fell. A Philistine, Ishbibenob by name, had a new sword, and he was heavy upon the king, for the king was no longer what he used to be. The Philistine pressed hard upon him— upon him who slew the lion and the bear and the giant of Gath— upon him who made Jerusalem rich with the golden shields of Hadadezer. But he was getting old ; he was but poor at last in the stroke of the sword ; then came his loyal captains and said, so sweetly, with heart-breaking pathos, " Thou shalt go no more out with us to battle, that thou quench not the light of Israel." David had fought enough ; the shades of eventide were gathering around him ; he had been a great warrior, but it was time he retired from the field. May not this also be the experience of many ? After a long fight they stand aside, but, blessed be God, they are not " lacking." They have retired from the pastorate, from the public office, from the battlefield generally, but we do not mourn over them as Deborah mourned over Reuben and Gilead and Dan and Asher. They are not willingly absent. The old feeling again stirs in them. They sometimes think they could go back and fight just as well and as successfully as ever, and could preach just as richly and effectively and reverently as they ever did. They are not in the battlefield, but they are not lacking from the hosts of God ; the light of their example abides, and their remembered service is a perpetual and gracious inspiration.

The text is full of tender feeling, showing itself in anxiety about the absent, though the absent one was both insignificant and ill-behaved. This anxiety is, we know, the very spirit of the whole Bible. It is the Spirit of Christ. It is the explanation of the cross. Remembering all this, we venture to say that this feeling—this feeling of profound and anxious emotion— *alone* can sustain constantly and worthily all Christian and missionary service. When we lose this sacred feeling we lose our inspiration. When we cease to care for others, to long for the absent, to yearn over the poor and the out-of-the-way, our Christianity can live no longer. All Christian funds will languish when Christian feeling dies. Let us speak to ourselves plainly upon this matter. Many professing Christians are learned, controversial, orthodox in words, and idolaters of propriety: but where is the feeling which cannot rest until the lacking tribe is brought back? The preacher may do more by his tears than by mere dry reasoning. Only love, like God's, like Christ's, can persist in unselfish service—observe, *persist*, keep on, press forward, forgive injuries, forget neglects, begin again, stand at the door and knock, never give up, keep the door ajar for the prodigal, set a candle in the window for the wanderer,— only love can do these miracles: the mother can watch longer than the doctor: the shepherd will endure better than the hireling: pity will spare where law will destroy. What is it that is troubled on every side yet not distressed, perplexed yet not in despair, persecuted but not forsaken, cast down but not destroyed? What is it? It is the faith that works by love! Why continue in the ministry and prove it in much patience, in afflictions, in distress, in stripes, in imprisonments, in tumults, in labours, in fastings—why? "The love of Christ constraineth us." *That* is the eternal motive, or the motive which alone can endure to eternity. Macaulay has well reminded us of Lord Bacon's just observation that mere negation, mere epicurean infidelity, has never disturbed the peace of the world. "It furnishes," says he, "no motive for action. It has no missionaries, no crusaders, no martyrs." When Christian institutions lose their feeling they become but useless and costly machines.

But, it may be urged, the feeling of the text was a feeling expressive of kinship, a family feeling, an *esprit de corps*. What argument can be built upon a domestic or tribal instinct? The question is out of place. Happily the answer is ready. The Christian conception of human nature is that it is *one*. "God hath made of one blood all nations of men to dwell on the face of the earth." The question of Malachi, "Have we not all one Father? hath not God created us?" we answer in the words of

Christ—" Our Father which art in heaven." **There are** supreme
moments in human experience; they **cannot be** long-continued,
but what a memory they leave behind!—moments when we
realise the unity of the human race, saying, "There is no
difference between the Jew and the ˙Greek : for the same Lord
over all is rich unto all that call upon him." Man is one : for
God is one. A traveller in his book on tropical South Africa tells
us of a tribe called the Damaras, who have no knowledge of
arithmetic, enumeration, or numbers, as we understand them.
He gives many amusing instances illustrative of this lack of what
may be called numerical knowledge. But amidst all he says,
" how does the herdsman know when an ox is missing, when he
looks upon the herd under the shadows of evening ? He knows
not because the number is less, but because of a face which he
misses." Oh, that shepherdly look ! The man says, "There is
one lacking." Then the face is painted before the eye of his
imagination. We are not numbers in an hostelry ; we are not
figures in an arithmetical series ; we are faces, lives, souls,
spirits, sons of God. What wonder if sometimes even in heaven
the question should be asked, Why is there one face missing ?
Why is David's place empty ?

We now reach the final and most pathetic point, namely, that
there may be some who are saying in their hearts, not being
able to say it aloud because of grief, Why is my child lacking
from the Church ? Why is my son not by my side at holy
Sacrament ? Why has my firstborn left his old father's faith
and gone away ? Oh, why ? Be encouraged. He may return.
He may come back to-day or to-morrow. Never give up your
prayer. It is very hard to pray again after praying for years,
and to mention a name that never seems to get into heaven ; and
the poor old heart gives way and says, " I cannot pray any
longer about this : I am killed by the prodigal's very name : I
will cease." Never! Hold on! After the next prayer there
may be a sign in heaven—very small, but still a sign and a
beginning. Sorrow may bring back the wanderer. God's veiled
angel called Affliction may some night knock at the door and say,
" I have brought back that which was lost." Great commercial
distress may do it ; an utter annihilation of the young man's

foolish ambitions may do it. God hath many ministers. His chariots are twenty thousand, and who shall say in which he will go forth, in the morning, at midday, or in the evening? Hope on then. One more prayer—the greatest, the best, the fullest of heart—almost an atonement, going nigh to the shedding of sacrificial blood. Do not despair. It may be that even yet you shall have the joy of completeness :—

> "When, soon or late, you reach that coast,
>   O'er life's rough ocean driven,
> You may rejoice, no wanderer lost,
>   A family in heaven."

"HANDFULS OF PURPOSE,"

FOR ALL GLEANERS.

" The children of Israel asked the Lord."
—JUDG. i. 1.

Notice the simplicity of this.—The conscious nearness of God.—The very easiest form of worship.—No enlargement of this form has been given even in Christianity, whose exhortation is, " Ask, and it shall be given you."—Speaking to God elevates the soul.—Communion with God compels the spirit to search out acceptable words.—Such asking is really part of spiritual education.—The soul is called upon to recount its needs, and to set them in order before God.—The impossibility of imposing upon the Omniscient.—The suppliant must not do more than ask ; that is to say, he must not make the answer a condition of his piety, or a standard by which he will judge the reality of the divine existence, and the goodness of the divine government.—All we can do is to put our case before God, and to plead it, and then the answer must be absolutely left with him.—We are to ask about everything.—We shall undervalue the sacredness of life if we suppose that some things are not worth asking about.—The life is equally sacred at all points when it is hidden in God. Nothing unimportant can ever arise in human life.—Spiritual wisdom is shown in making every point of consequence and needing the direct intervention and blessing of God.—The word "children," as descriptive of Israel, comes suggestively before this act of asking.—Are we not all the children of the living God ? What have children to do but to ask ? —not to dictate or demand, but simply to state in terms of supplication.—All such asking is to be done in the name of him who taught us how to pray.—God is still approached through priesthood, only now the priesthood is not human, but divine.—We should so cultivate communion with God that our prayer will be reduced to the simplicity of "asking." The question is put as if from child to parent, or from friend to friend, or from scholar to teacher ; all traces of formality, ceremony, servility are absent, and the communion is marked by frankness, directness, and childlike simplicity.—This is the true genius of prayer.

" And when the Lord raised them up judges, then the Lord was with the judge."—JUDG. ii. 18.

A picture of society when divinely constructed.—The economy of mediation is here, as everywhere, observed.—The great principle of election is here also affirmed.—The judges were raised up by the Lord.—Men did not make themselves judges, nor did the people arbitrarily appoint and dismiss the judges. — The appointment was divine. — So it ought to be considered in all magistracy, judgeship, and government. — Society is a piece of mosaic wrought out by the loving hands of God. — God will only speak through the judges whom he himself has created and appointed. — The judge should recognise this himself, and be modest and self-restrained in proportion. — The true leader is always himself a follower of the divine guidance. — Elevation to office does not mean release from responsibility, but rather a responsibility that is enlarged and sanctified. — In times of national crisis men should pray that God would send the right leaders into the land, and clothe those leaders with appropriate influence. — It is in vain to have an orthodox Church and an atheistic State — that is to say, that the Church may be guided by God, but that the State may attempt to govern itself. — The Church should continually pray for the State, and thus acknowledge that God is the God of nations as well as the God of churches. — It is marvellous to observe how throughout the whole Scripture, all great appointments are acknowledged to be in the hands of God. — The children of Israel cried unto the Lord, and Moses was sent ; again they cried, and judges were raised up ; and so throughout the whole historical line, until Jesus Christ says, " Pray ye therefore the Lord of the harvest, that he will send forth labourers into his harvest." — This is a lesson quite as much to those who suppose themselves to be appointed to high authority, as for the peoples whom they rule or attempt to direct. — The true judge, minister, leader, statesman, will recognise that he is divinely appointed, and therefore accountable to God. — This will give moderation to his counsels, and invest all his thoughts and purposes with supreme solemnity, and will subdue the pomp of office by the consciousness of personal obligation to God.

" And they were to prove Israel by them, to know whether they would hearken unto the commandments of the Lord, which he commanded their fathers by the hand of Moses." —JUDG. iii. 4.

This may show us the part which our enemies have to play in the education and development of our lives. — The Lord left so many nations, as the Canaanites, the Zidonians, and the Hivites, that they might subject Israel to continual testing to prove their quality. — It is so that hardships are permitted to continue in the life. — When we ask why we should be surrounded by limitations so exact, and even by opponents so hostile, we should remember that this was the plan which God pursued in the training of his ancient people. — This is the divine purpose of all human affliction. — God must be left to determine what tests are best for our quality. — Men are not to choose their own tests and standards, but are to accept the chastening of the Lord, and to go into the furnace which the Almighty has specifically appointed. — Different men are tried in different ways, but the object of the trial is the same. — Your business perplexities are sent to prove your honesty ; your bodily afflictions are imposed to test your courage and trust ; your family difficulties are allowed to continue that the life of the household may be strengthened and refined ; your bitterest rival is permitted to run his course side by side with you that your temper may be sweetened, your charity enlarged, and your whole tone of mind elevated. — Thus we are brought to consider the religious uses of opposition and hardships, and to identify their very presence with the distinct purpose of God. —

When we can take this view of them we shall use them rather than fear them, and in due time shall come to account them as in some sort friends and teachers.—" My son, despise not the chastening of the Lord.'

" A mother in Israel."—JUDG. v. 7.

We need the womanly element in the Church.—The mother is the soul of the family.—We cannot live upon hard law and severe discipline ; there must always be a tender element in our education, for we are weak, and need the ministry of compassion and love.—We speak much about the fathers of the Church, and the fathers of the nation, and are apt to forget that the "mothers in Israel" have often been more heroic than the fathers, and that their very gentleness has become their strength in time of danger.—Whilst discouraging some aspects of what are termed sisterhoods, and whilst deprecating what is known as the worship of the Virgin Mother, we should seek for the truth which underlies all this womanly ministry.—Many could serve the Church by miracles of love, patience, compassion, and encouragement, whose voice could never be heard on public questions.—Every woman can at least be "a mother in Israel" within the limits of her own family.—She is not called upon to be a theologian, a scholar, a pedant, a source of alarm to the ignorant and the incompetent, but she is called upon to be compassionate, sympathetic, and encouraging.—It is a mistake to suppose that the Church is either a drill-ground or a school alone. —It is a house, a home, a nursery ; it is a place of healing, education, and comfort ; many a strong man would be the better if to all his strength he added a touch of tenderness.—Beautiful is the service of mothers in the Church of Christ.—They can speak with an in-fluence all their own, absolutely indisputable, even by the most learned and eloquent men.—They know how to whisper to sorrow, how to touch weakness without burdening it, how to speak a word in season to him that is weary.—All womanly influence in the Church and in the family should be abundantly and gratefully encouraged.

" There were great searchings of heart."
—JUDG. v. 16.

These searchings are always wanted. —We gain in solidity by such scrutiny. —It is impossible to live long and satisfactorily upon mere appearances, or upon vain hopes that all will turn out right at the last.—There is a great lack of heart-work in the Church and in the individual. — We are to search into causes of absence from the field of danger, of abatement of zeal and enthusiasm, and of every form of unbelief. —The great court of inquiry is the heart rather than the intellect.—We can never get at foundations and realities until we have pierced the region of motive, the region of secret and unconfessed purpose.—We should judge others less than we judge ourselves. —Let every man put to himself the penetrating question, What have I done, or what have I left undone ; and why is the case so, either on the one side or the other ?—Let there be no fault-finding with other people ; let there be no self-sparing.— Force the question to its uttermost extent, and be severer with yourself than with other men.—All this may mean bitterness, pain, disappointment, and shame, but in the long run it will mean healing, inspiration, strength, and renewed encouragement. " If we confess our sins, God is faithful and just to forgive us our sins."—If we say we have no sin, we are liars.—Our sins are transgressions of the heart, and until the heart itself is cleansed the hands never can be pure.—Let every man examine himself.—Let every man hold the candle of the Lord over the secrets of his heart.

" Faint, yet pursuing."—JUDG. viii. 4.

A description of many a Christian heart.—We shall be judged, not by the faintness, but by the pursuit.—Not what the heart does, but what the heart would do, will be God's question.— Sometimes we are so faint that we can only look in the right direction, but the direction being right, the look shall be regarded as equal to pursuit.—There is a moral meaning in attitudes.—Endeavours are often construed into actions.— He who would give a cup of cold water to a disciple if he could, will be accounted as having done it.—Men will be judged by what has been in their hearts ; then the first will be last, and the last will be first.—Allowance is made for faintness, for there is only One that fainteth not, neither is weary.—God knoweth our frame ; he remembereth that we are dust.—Men must not be too deeply discouraged because of their faintness, but must often look upon it as part of their very mortality.—Even the apostle said the flesh was weak when the spirit was willing ; but he knew that God would judge by the spirit, and not by the flesh. —At the same time we must be severe in our judgment upon ourselves, lest we suppose that a pleasant dream, which imposes no sacrifice, should be enough as proof of our Christian fidelity.—We must not assume faintness by easily giving way to discouragement.—Against some faintness we can bravely struggle, and our very struggling may overcome it.—Indolence must not be mistaken for this faintness.—Selfish calculation must not be allowed to take its place.— We must be true to ourselves in all these matters, or we cannot realise the blessing that is promised.—When a man

tells lies to himself about his faintness, he will soon relinquish his pursuit.—We can whisper where we cannot speak aloud.—We may be able to hold out a hand when we cannot utter a tone.— We can put large meaning into looks and postures.—There is no mistaking an earnest man. Even his feebleness may be so used as to become an element of spiritual strength.

" But the youth drew not his sword : for he feared, because he was yet a youth."—JUDG. viii. 20.

Too much must not be expected from youth.—It was a hard thing that Jether was here asked to do.—We may discourage youth by expecting too much from it at once.—It is well for that youth who understands the limits of his strength, and keeps well within them.— There is an audacity which it is hard to distinguish from impiety.—By imposing too heavy responsibilities upon youth, we may either inflame its vanity or discourage its modesty.—Every man is to consider what he can do, with propriety, and not to force himself to the front, unless others have proved unworthy of the occasion.—Under other circumstances youth is called upon to do the very hardest work. When that is the case, the revelation of duty will be made clear.—It was David who was called upon to slay Goliath.—David said, "Is there not a cause ? " He was the subject of an inspiration unknown to others ; he was obeying a voice which others could not hear.—It is easy to rebuke youth for not doing certain things from which young modesty shrinks ; it is better to recognise the modesty than to magnify the fear.— Young people do not become accustomed to the sword all at once. For a time they must be kept at home, watching the "few sheep in the wilderness," or planting a few flowers in the domestic garden ; by-and-by they may grow up to be soldiers and valiant men.—In the meantime, let us not condemn the Jethers of the age when they hesitate to shed blood.

" Thou seest the shadow of the mountains as if they were men."—JUDG. ix. 36.

This text may be used as showing how possible it is to be magnifying dangers, or creating illusory enemies. —Whilst this is historically true, it is spiritually indisputable.—There is a tendency in the spiritual life to magnify all difficulties, and so to discourage the soul.—Who has not been frightened by shadows? Who has not shrunk from the conclusions of his own just reasoning?—The hill always looks to be highest when viewed from a distance. —When approached it subsides and becomes really easy of ascent.—We may turn some men into enemies by looking upon them from a great distance, or seeing them under unfavourable circumstances.—We must come near them, and estimate them at their proper strength.—Approach is sometimes the best solution of difficulties.— Boldness often dissolves the mystery which it has feared.—The Christian should set it down as an article of his faith that they can be only shadows which are arrayed against the Lord and against his anointed.—Even Pharaoh, king of Egypt, was "but a noise."— The mightiest men who set themselves against Christ are not so much men as shadows.—All this has been proved again and again in history, and the proof should be taken as an inspiration and an encouragement by the age now living and by all the ages to come.— All clever arguments, all elaborated scepticisms, all new heterodoxies are but so many shadows, and are on no account to be feared by the soldiers of Christ.—Remember that shadows are

not to be destroyed by swords and guns, or by violence of any kind ; the shadows can only be chased away by light : "Ye are the light of the world." —If we were more radiant we should see fewer shadows, or the shadows would flee away before the approaching glory.—Pray for an increase of luminousness, that the whole character may be as a sun, shining in his strength, and dissolving and dispersing every shadow.

" What ye have seen me do, make haste, and do as I have done."—JUDG. ix. 48.

This exhortation may be adopted by Christian believers.—What ye have seen me do in difficult business circumstances.—What ye have seen me do in the presence of great temptations.— What ye have seen me do in the way of self-sacrifice.—What ye have seen me do in great afflictions.—This may be adopted also by Christian teachers.— The Apostle Paul said, "Be ye followers of me, even as I also am of Christ."— What ye have seen me do in the way of energy, in the way of faith, in the way of self-expenditure, in the way of forgiveness, make haste, and do as I have done.—Is the Christian believer prepared to make himself an example to others? What Christian man would be willing to say, You need not at present look any further than to myself, for I am guide and standard enough to the Church?—This exhortation may also be adopted by parents when addressing their children : each father or mother should be able to say, What ye have seen me do in the thick of domestic difficulties, in the night of pain, in the assured oncoming of poverty, in the very cloud and overshadowing of despair.—If we were to accustom ourselves to the thought that we have to show forth our own conduct as a standard, it would make us more careful to see that that standard is noble and right.—Even if we do not call attention to our actions ourselves, yet men are looking on, and may well claim that they have a right to copy us.—We may affect humility, and say, Do not look at us, but look at our Master; but after all the men of the world have a right to say, No : Christ is too high for us : we will look at his followers, and judge his Christianity by their spirit and their action.—A point, too, might be made of the words "make haste," because that which is an example to-day may be no example to-morrow in relation to certain practical matters; the circumstances altering, the adaptation to them must alter also. Beside, if we do not copy the example of to-day we may not be living to copy it to-morrow. —There are circumstances under which everything depends upon a prompt use of time.—The train goes at a certain moment, so does the post; the bank closes at a given hour : opportunities of all kinds are limited.—Hence the great importance which ought to be attached to the words "make haste."

___

" *His soul was grieved for the misery of Israel.*"—JUDG. x. 16.

We must first have sympathy, then action.—Action based on sympathy is likely to be permanent and pure.—If we do not see the miseries of mankind we shall not be moved to preach the gospel of salvation or to do the necessary work of mercy.—He who denies the existence of poverty will not be likely to become liberal in his donations.—He who does not pity the wounded traveller will not be likely to dismount and attend to his wounds.—We have learning, genius, eloquence ; but what about our grief for the miseries of the world?—Men who are moved by sympathy may have to listen to many a bitter tale, and may often have to be shut up in face-to-face

communion with scenes that shock and pain the heart.—Some men can only see the misery, and then relate it to others, and thus move them with their larger resources to go forth to its relief, or empower agents to represent them in the ministry of help.—The first thing we have to do is to consider the length and breadth of the case—the case of poverty, oppression, helplessness—and then our hearts having become affected by the presence and action of indisputable facts, we are to ask what can be done by way of remedy or redress.— " If thou forbear to deliver them that are drawn unto death, and those that are ready to be slain ; if thou sayest, Behold, we knew it not ; doth not he that pondereth the heart consider it ? and he that keepeth thy soul, doth not he know it ? and shall not he render to every man according to his works ? "— We do not destroy the miseries of the world by shutting our eyes to them.— No man can be truly grieved for the miseries of the world without instantly attempting to mitigate them. He may fail in his attempt, but he will make it resolutely and self-sacrificingly.—If we are merely attempting to satisfy the fancies of the world, or gratify the whims of the world, we shall often fail in our service, and continually be disappointed with its results ; but if we are fellow-workers with Christ in attempting to relieve the miseries of the world we shall find that the work is its own inspiration and its own reward.

___

" *Why are ye come unto me now when ye are in distress?* "—JUDG. xi. 7.

A proper inquiry to address to all applicants.—A rebuke is implied in the terms of the question.—The men had not come before. Up to this time they had disowned Jephthah ; now in distress they wished to make use of him.

—Circumstances test friendships and the reality and unselfishness of appeals. —God is always exposed to this kind of prayer.—Why thus ill-treat and dishonour God in the very act, as we suppose, of recognising his existence and goodness?—God does not ask us why we have come to him, but why we have come to him in distress; the coming itself is right, but the time—namely, the time of distress—may give peculiar significance to our approach.—This is a great hold which God has upon the human race.—The time of distress comes in every life, and in that hour men ask the greatest questions, and are, as it were, forced into the exercise of prayer. —When pain seizes the body, or when difficulty perplexes the circumstances, when severe family affliction clouds the house, when death has sent its forecast into the heart of the family, then men may begin to cry out for the living God. —God interrogates us, as Jephthah interrogated the elders of Gilead.—Our answer must often be one of pitiful humiliation.—God does not intend to disown us or repel us by asking the question; his purpose is to make us acquainted with ourselves, and to show us how complex is the structure and action of human motives.—Selfishness cannot pray.—Selfishness can beg, implore, intreat, whine, and make tragical appeals; but selfishness cannot get near enough to God to commune with him, or in the true sense to ask a favour at his hands.—The prayers of the wicked are an abomination unto the Lord.—If the prayer of our selfishness is answered, it is not because it is a selfish prayer, but because of God's infinite graciousness.

" *How shall we order the child, and how shall we do unto him?* "—JUDG. xiii. 12.

The supreme question which parents should ask.—A question which God permits to be put to himself.—God alone can know the true way of training a human life.—It is in vain to ask God's guidance after the foundations of the life have been laid and its policy has been determined upon. The child is to be trained up from its earliest moment.— There is a sense in which there is no time of unconsciousness to the child: we are making impressions even when those impressions are not accompanied by acts of intelligence.—Surely blessed is that child who has never seen anything in father or mother that is not true, beautiful, and good.—It would seem the easiest thing in the world to train a child; in reality it is the most difficult. —Every child has its own peculiar psychology.—Every child has its own peculiar motive, impulse, vision of things, and purpose.—The very wisdom of God is required in the right training of children.—But the child cannot be trained aright until the parent has a correct conception of life itself.—If life is a question of this world, of immediate health, wealth, and enjoyment, then the policy of child-training is easy and simple enough; but if life here is but the beginning of real life, if the present state of existence is but a gate opening upon true destinies and illimitable spheres of action, then light from above is needed, and guidance and comfort from the Father of all men.—Let parents be encouraged to consult God about child-training.—Let every child be the subject of special prayer.—Let the parent be able to say, should occasion arise, to each child, "I have prayed for thee," as Christ said to Simon Peter.

" *Why askest thou thus after my name, seeing it is secret?* "—JUDG. xiii. 18.

Men are continually driven back from secret altars, and forbidden to indulge their curiosity in sacred places.—We may receive anonymous blessings.—It is difficult to distinguish sometimes between curiosity and reverent inquiry.— Sometimes we are more interested in the secret things than in the things revealed. When we are conscious of such interest we may know that we are animated by curiosity, and not by the spirit of reverential inquiry.—In coming to the Bible we must come for ripe fruit, for practical blessings ready to be handled, for the things which we can immediately understand and apply; and we must not be deterred from our use and enjoyment of these because a secret seems to be hidden within them all, and a ghostly presence seems to be moving in shadow across the pages as we peruse them.—There is a point at which the knowable ends: at that point we may either become fools or wise men—fools because we say there is nothing worth knowing, or wise men by saying the temporal must be conducted in the light of the eternal, the finite must be ennobled by a consciousness of the infinite, the human must be lifted up to its noblest significance by the assured presence and judgment of the divine.

" *And he wist not that the Lord was departed from him.*"—JUDG. xvi. 20.

This is the saddest of all mental experience.—It has its counterpart even in business and in professional life.— There are men of business who suppose they are as competent and energetic as ever, whilst those who are looking on observe how great is the decay, and how lamentable the weakness.—Men suppose themselves as capable as ever of giving advice in perplexity, yet when they come to counsel the bewildered mind they lose the centre of thought, and miss altogether the purpose which the counsel was intended to serve.—We go away from such men filled with a sense of pity.—Let us apply the same truth to the religious nature.—Note the ghastliness of having a form of godliness without the power thereof.—No irony so distressing.—A man may use the very words of prayer, and yet may not enter into the spirit of fellowship with God.—The picture is that of a man on whose outward appearance no change has been wrought which he himself accounts of any consequence, but within the house of the soul has been stripped of all that was valuable, and is left in emptiness and desolation. —A terrible thing it is to bow down in prayer after God himself has forsaken the altar. —But is it possible for a man to have lost fellowship with God, and yet to be unaware of the loss? All history says that it is possible.—Familiarity with certain places and modes and actions may delude the mind into believing that whilst the usage is repeated the spirit is retained.—We grow into a species of self-idolatry sometimes without intention, and often without knowledge.—How are we to know that the Lord is still with us? Always by the simple test of obedience.—But is not obedience itself sometimes a delusive action? Possibly, and therefore we should esteem most highly that obedience which imposes upon us the pain and loss of sacrifice.—How does the Lord depart from a man?—The intellect is apparently as acute as ever, external offices are fulfilled as punctiliously as before, no blemish is found upon the public reputation,—how, then, can God have departed from the man? —The mystery lies in the fact of our composite nature : we are body and soul, flesh and spirit, in us there is both time and eternity, dust of the earth and fire from heaven ; and, our life being so complex, we do not instantly know when the very centre of life and thought has been changed—that is, we go on for a little while by a momentum originally received, but which has no power of self-replenishment, and therefore must die when the original inspiration is withdrawn.—Let us not make any religious experiments as Samson did.—He got into a mood of speculation and adventure, saying, If you do this or that, I shall be as other men.—He did not mean at first to tell his secret, but little by little we are led to the giving up of that which is the very mystery and glory of life.—It is infinitely dangerous to tamper with temptation.—There may be a kind of pleasure in taunting the Philistines, misleading them, mocking them, and laughing at them in their disasters, but he should be stronger than ever Samson was who ventures to play with the enemy, and to practise tricks and puzzles for the sake of bewildering and annoying them.—It is impossible to say when the last temptation may come, or how we ourselves may be tempted to try if in reality our strength lay where we supposed it to lie.—The lesson comes back again and again from all quarters, and with a thousand voices—" Watch and pray, lest ye enter into temptation."

" When Micah saw that they were too strong for him, he turned."—JUDG. xviii. 26.

Different estimates of strength.—Men are tested by circumstances.—If the pursuers had been fewer, Micah would have summoned up courage and acted differently.—He gave way, as men are now doing, to the force of numbers.—" Follow not a multitude to do evil."—The lesson is repeated in the experience of many ; as, for example, in the experience of the young man who explains his conduct by saying that all his companions are pressing in one direction, and that it would be folly for him to

attempt to resist them.—It applies also to the custom or fashion of the day.—Men say, As well be out of the world as be out of the fashion. When they see that the customs of society are too strong for them, they themselves turn, sophistically and foolishly arguing that it is in vain for one man to suppose that he can turn back the tide of public opinion or the flood of universally-established custom.—All history proves that solitary men have often been stronger than multitudes.—The only counting which we should permit ourselves to adopt is a reckoning as to the presence of God with us in our enterprises ; assured that he goes forth with us, we have nothing to do with any other arithmetic.—Though an host should encamp against us, God will be our confidence, and will bring in our judgment and triumph.—Always ask on which side is God, on which side is Jesus Christ, on which side is conscience ; and, having ascertained that side, there need be no further enumeration of forces.—The good man always says, and in saying it redoubles his courage, They that be for me are more than those that be against me.

" Tell us how was this wickedness ? "— JUDG. xx. 3.

We should not shrink from scrutinising evil, and asking it piercing questions as to its origin and cause.—We cannot deal with wickedness until we have got at its roots.—Evil is not an accident which is found upon the surface, varying with the climate and the light ; it is a disease of the heart, and only a heart-cure can utterly extirpate the evil and restore health to the whole man.—Men who cannot conduct a great philosophical inquiry as to the origin of evil may conduct a very searching scrutiny into their own questionable or wicked actions.—" How was this wickedness ? "

Was it because of a desire to fulfil a selfish ambition?—Was it done in order to quench a fiery appetite?—Was it done suddenly, in a moment of madness, or after long consideration and ample preparation?—Was it one of the sudden blasts which seize the soul without notice?—Or did we roll the iniquity under our tongue as a sweet morsel and enjoy the wickedness long in advance?—Sometimes it will do the soul good to tell the tale of its wickedness to friendly inquirers.—There is a sense in which confession even by man to man may do the soul great good.—The confession must not be made in any sacerdotal sense, as if man had power to forgive sin, but it must be told to force the soul itself into contrition, shame, self-renunciation, and to constitute a kind of judgment outside itself which it may continually fear.—It is possible by this kind of confession to create a species of criticism on the part of others which may hold us in restraint in days to come.—The great thought is that we are not to cover up wickedness, or lessen it, or decorate it, or excuse it; we are to tell the plain and shameful tale straight out from end to end, that we may know how the disease is to be treated.—"If we confess our sins, God is faithful and just to forgive us our sins." "Let the wicked forsake his way, and the unrighteous man his thoughts." The Gospel tells us that there is a Man who receiveth sinners. His name is Jesus Christ. No man ever came to him with broken-hearted desire to repent of his sin and abandon it who was turned away with one word or look of discouragement.

THE BOOK OF RUTH.

RUTH and Esther no Bible reader could well spare from the sacred volume, nor could we do without the Song of Solomon, which also supplies a feminine element which softens and chastens a volume so full of judgment and thunder, sovereignty and grandeur. A great famine broke out in the days "when the Judges judged." So father, mother, and two sons migrated from Bethlehem to the land of Moab, where the two sons, Mahlon and Chilion, took two Moabitesses, Ruth and Orpah, to wife. After ten years' sojourn, Naomi, the mother, returned to Judah, leaving behind her Elimelech her husband and her two sons, all of whom had died in the strange land. The rest of the story is told in the brief book. A few useful notes may be cited from a mass of criticism, which will help the general reader better to understand the tale. Ruth was the great-grandmother of David, and probably lived one hundred years before him. In the genealogy given by Matthew, the father of Boaz is called Salmon, who was the husband of Rahab. Boaz is supposed to have been born not many years after the taking of Jericho. As to the authorship of the book, the Talmud says Samuel wrote as one book the Judges and Ruth. A most painstaking German critic supposes the book to have been written during the Babylonian captivity. It has been suggested that the Book of Ruth is given in the Bible on account of David, of whose lineage no mention is made in the books of Samuel. This may be so, but I cannot consider it enough. Criticism may easily err in assigning reasons for the composition of the Bible. Certainly we need such little stories to help us in our human life and to show us how true it is that the Bible is a human Book, dealing with things that we can see and test ourselves, and not only with transcendent speculations which lie beyond the line of reverent reason. The Bible might easily have been too grand. Even Isaiah, in whose radiant pages prophecy seems to attain its supreme sublimity, must now and again come down from infinite heights to sing some sweet song adapted to human ears. The Book of Ruth shows that the Bible is the Book of the people, a family Book, a record of human life in all its moods, circumstances, passions, and volitions. Many can follow Ruth who cannot understand Ezekiel ; as many can understand the parable of the Prodigal Son who cannot enter into the mystery of the Apocalypse. If we were to ask what right has a story like Ruth's to be in the Bible, we might properly reply, By the right of human nature, by the right of kinship to the universal human heart. We may make even our personal religion far too grand. We are surprised by the little things that are in the Bible, wondering why they should come to fill up so much space in a book which we think ought to have been filled with nothing but stupendous events. This is not the way of God in the ordering and direction of human life. All things are little to God, and all things are equally great to him. It is our ignorance that calls this little, and that great, this trivial, and that important. If not a sparrow falls to the ground without our Father, we may be sure that he regards all such little stories as that of Ruth and Esther as of great consequence to the completion of the whole tale of human history. This attempt at monotonous grandeur springs from a spirit of vanity. The men who would have written nothing but what is great and dazzling in the Bible are very likely to be men who think they are doing nothing in life unless they are working upon a heroic and stupendous scale. In quite another spirit does Jesus Christ lay down his doctrine and law. We are to attend to so-called little things, to the details of life, to gathering up the fragments, to make the most of our moments, and to turn every day into a school

for the accomplishment of some task that shall bear
upon the final culture of manhood. We cannot always
be doing great deeds. Nor can we always be living in
a spirit of ecstasy. We must make room in the
Christian life for quietness, patience, silent suffering,
humble service. No one man is required to represent the
whole Bible in his own experience. Some may be as
the Book of Ruth or of Esther, others as the Song
of Solomon ; some may be as glowing and brilliant
as Isaiah and Ezekiel, while others must be content
with being classified with the minor prophets : the great
matter to be considered is that we all constitute God's
volume of revelation, that every man has something to
say to his age which no other man can say for him ; in
this way we realise our unity, and express the purpose of
God. The man who asks why should so little a book as
Ruth be in the Bible may also ask why obscure lives are
found in human history. Why should there be any
simple annals of the poor ? Why should children be
anything accounted of ? Why should other than great
soldiers, leaders, statesmen, and patriots have a place in
the human record ? God takes up little children and
blesses them ; God gives women a special status in
society ; God sets up and puts down according to his
own sovereignty, and he looks upon the human family as
one,—not as a series of units only, but as constituting
one great idea of unity and development. It is true
that there is one point of grandeur in Ruth ; so there
may be in every human life. In attempting to account
for the presence of Ruth in the Bible, this point of
grandeur has, as we have said, been fixed upon. Let
every man look for the point of supremacy in his own
life. Even in the lowliest and weakest there are points
of immeasurable importance. It is because we are men
that we are permitted to live in a spirit of hope and
faith. It is because we bear the image and likeness of
God that we are sought by the Divine Shepherd, and
that we are implored to return. To be a man is to be

great. To be human is to be almost divine. We are not to look for explanations of God's action in regard to us in any accidental greatness or importance, but in the fundamental and unchangeable quality of human nature itself. Some lives are mirror-like ; that is to say, they reflect the image of the reader. Few can read the whole story of Ruth without feeling that here and there her experience is common with the lot of humanity. No one reader may have lived the whole life of Ruth ; yet all may be able to join her at some particular point, in sorrow, in need, in the restoration of hope, and in the culmination of purest aspiration and desire. God avails himself of the dramatic mode of interpretation in order to reveal his inmost purpose. We can only understand some truths in proportion as they come to us in parable or figure, or imagined drama. For other interpretations we must look to human life itself in its most naked and repulsive realities. God cannot be understood by the monastic thinker who deals only with introspection and metaphysic : God is the God of history, of nations, of progress, and he is continually writing his Bible in the elaboration and culmination of events. We should pray for the eyes that see the signs of the times, and for the heart that understands the things that are being done on the right hand and on the left. Political history is a section of God's Bible. All art, science, and philosophy contribute pages to the revelation of God. Every little child's life, properly read and comprehended, will show some new aspect of the tender providence of Heaven. Blessed are they who have eyes to see, ears to hear, and hearts to understand, for the going forth of the Lord is from the rising of the sun to the setting of the same : in the winter he speaks in severity, in summer he addresses us in gentleness : in our filled barns he discourses to us of the Bread of Heaven ; and in all the way of life he has messages to deliver to us which enlarge the vision and comfort the heart. Under these convictions let us now proceed to read the sweet story of Ruth.

RUTH. (ANNOTATED.)

Chapter i.

1. Now [And,—an intro-copula which connects it with some other book] it came to pass in the days [a very early period in the days] when the judges ruled [judged], that there was a famine in the land. And a certain man of Beth-lehem-judah [Judah is added to distinguish it from the Bethlehem in the tribe of Zebulun] went to sojourn [to tarry as a stranger] in the country of Moab [exceptionally rich and fertile: see Isaiah xvi. and Jeremiah xxxviii., and often an asylum for the Israelites], he, and his wife, and his two sons.

2. And the name of the man was Elimelech ["my God is king";—probably, according to some Jewish doctors, a noble and powerful man], and the name of his wife Naomi ["to be pleasant," some say it means "ornament"], and the name of his two sons Mahlon ["sickness"] and Chilion ["wasting"], Ephrathites [Ephrah was the old name of Bethlehem] of Beth-lehem-judah. And they came into the country of Moab, and continued there [before and after this the Moabites had been conspicuously hard-hearted towards Israel].

3. And Elimelech, Naomi's husband, died; and she was left, and her two sons.

4. And they took [always used in this connection in a bad sense] them wives [after the father's death] of the women of Moab; the name of the one was Orpah ["kind"], and the name of the other Ruth ["comeliness"]: and they dwelled there about ten years.

5. And Mahlon and Chilion died [as young men] also both of them; and the woman was left of her two sons and her husband.

6. Then she arose with her daughters in law, that she might return from the country of Moab: for she had heard [Prov. xxv. 25] in the country of Moab how that the Lord had visited his people in giving them bread.

7. Wherefore she went forth out of the place where she was, and her two daughters in law with her; and they went on the way to return unto the land of Judah.

8. And Naomi said unto her two daughters in law, Go, return each to her mother's house [a picture of unselfish love]: the Lord deal kindly with you, as ye have dealt with the dead, and with me.

9. The Lord grant you that ye may find rest, each of you in the house of her

husband [residence in a heathen land had not heathenised Naomi]. Then she kissed them ; and they lifted up their voice, and wept.

10. And they said unto her, Surely we will return with thee unto thy people.

11. And Naomi said, Turn again, my daughters : why will ye go with me ? Are there yet any more sons in my womb, that they may be your husbands ?

12. Turn again, my daughters, go your way ; for I am too old to have an husband. If I should say, I have hope, if I should have an husband also to night, and should also bear sons ;

13. Would ye tarry for them till they were grown ? [" Every Jew at this day is bound to marry before he is twenty years old, else he is looked upon as one that liveth in sin."] Would ye stay for them from having husbands ? nay, my daughters ; for it grieveth me much for your sakes [it is far more bitter for me than for you], that the hand of the Lord is gone out against me.

14. And they lifted up their voice, and wept again : and Orpah kissed her mother in law ; but Ruth [the Rabbins say that Ruth was the daughter Eglon king of Moab] clave [" was glued," would give the more literal meaning] unto her.

15. And she said, Behold, thy sister in law is gone back unto her people, and unto her gods [local gods] : return thou after thy sister in law.

16. And Ruth said, Intreat me not to leave thee, or to return from following after thee : for whither thou goest, I will go ; and where thou lodgest, I will lodge : thy people shall be my people, and thy God my God :

17. Where thou diest, will I die, and there will I be buried : the Lord do so to me, and more also, if ought but death part thee and me.

18. When she saw that she was stedfastly minded to go with her, then she left speaking unto her.

19. ¶ So they two [types of the Jewish and Gentile Churches] went [the distance cannot have been less than fifty miles] until they came to Beth-lehem. And it came to pass, when they were come to Beth-lehem, that all the city was moved [rang with the news] about them, and they [the women : the verb is feminine] said, Is this Naomi ?

20. And she said unto them, Call me not Naomi, call me Mara [" bitter "] : for the Almighty [a name almost peculiar to the Pentateuch and the Book of Job] hath dealt very bitterly with me.

21. I went out full, and the Lord hath brought me home again empty : why then call ye me Naomi, seeing the Lord hath testified against me [hath humbled me], and the Almighty hath afflicted me ?

22. So Naomi returned, and Ruth the Moabitess, her daughter in law, with her [" so Jews and Gentiles walk to heaven together "] which returned out of the country of Moab : and they came to Beth-lehem in the beginning of barley harvest [ordinarily falling about the end of April].

Chapter ii.

1. And Naomi had a kinsman of her husband's, a mighty man of wealth ["yet religious ; a rare bird "], of the family of Elimelech ; and his name was Boaz [fleetness—alacrity, or strength : a contrast to the name of her former husband].

2. And Ruth the Moabitess said unto Naomi, Let me now go to the field, and glean ears of corn after him in whose sight I shall find grace [not afraid of hard work]. And she said unto her, Go, my daughter.

3. And she went, and came, and gleaned in the field after the reapers : and her hap [literally, her hap happened] was to light on a part of the field belonging unto Boaz, who was of the kindred of Elimelech.

4. And, behold, Boaz came from Beth-lehem, and said unto the reapers, The Lord be with you. And they answered him, The Lord bless thee [a beautiful picture of relations between the master and his servants].

5. Then said Boaz unto his servant that was set over the reapers, Whose damsel is this ?

6. And the servant that was set over the reapers answered and said, It is the [a] Moabitish damsel that came back with Naomi out of the country of Moab [as a stranger Ruth had a special claim to the gleaning: see Levit. xix. 9, 10] :

7. And she said, I pray you, let me glean and gather after the reapers among the sheaves ["handfuls"] : so she came, and hath continued even from the morning until now, that she tarried a little in the house.

8. Then said Boaz unto Ruth, Hearest thou not, my daughter ? [hinting at the seniority of Boaz] Go not to glean in another field, neither go from hence, but abide here fast ["cleave to "] by my maidens :

9. Let thine eyes be on the field that they do reap, and go thou after them : have I not charged the young men that they shall not touch thee ? and when thou art athirst, go unto the vessels, and drink of that which the young men have drawn [shall draw from time to time].

10. Then she fell on her face, and bowed herself to the ground, and said unto him, Why have I found grace in thine eyes, that thou shouldest take knowledge of me, seeing I am a stranger ? [The Moabite language differed little from the Hebrew].

11. And Boaz answered and said unto her, It hath fully been shewed me, all that thou hast done unto thy mother in law since the death of thine husband ; and how thou hast left thy father and thy mother, and the land of thy nativity, and art come unto a people which thou knewest not heretofore [literally, yesterday and the day before].

12. The Lord recompense thy work, and a full reward be given thee of the Lord God of Israel, under whose wings thou art come to trust.

13. Then she said, Let me find favour in thy sight, my lord : for that thou

hast comforted me, and for that thou hast spoken friendly [comfortably] unto thine handmaid, though I be not like unto one of thine handmaidens.

14. And Boaz said unto her, At mealtime come thou hither, and eat of the bread, and dip thy morsel in the vinegar [wine which had become sour]. And she sat beside the reapers : and he reached her parched corn, and she did eat, and was sufficed, and left.

15. And when she was risen up to glean, Boaz commanded his young men, saying, Let her glean even among the sheaves, and reproach her not :

16. And let fall also some of the handfuls of purpose for her, and leave them, that she may glean them, and rebuke her not.

17. So she gleaned in the field until even, and beat out that she had gleaned : and it was about an ephah [four pecks] of barley.

18. And she took it up, and went into the city : and her mother in law saw what she had gleaned : and she brought forth, and gave to her that she had reserved after she was sufficed.

19. And her mother in law said unto her, Where hast thou gleaned to day ? and where wroughtest thou ? blessed be he that did take knowledge of thee. And she shewed her mother in law with whom she had wrought, and said, The man's name with whom I wrought to day is Boaz.

20. And Naomi said unto her daughter in law, Blessed be he of the Lord, who hath not left off his kindness to the living and to the dead. And Naomi said unto her, The man is near of kin unto us, one of our next kinsmen [one of those who must redeem].

21. And Ruth the Moabitess said, He said unto me also, Thou shalt keep fast by my young men, until they have ended all my harvest.

22. And Naomi said unto Ruth her daughter in law, It is good, my daughter, that thou go out with his maidens, that they meet thee not in any other field.

23. And so she kept fast by the maidens of Boaz to glean unto the end of barley harvest and of wheat harvest ; and dwelt with her mother in law.

Chapter iii.

1. Then Naomi her mother in law said unto her, My daughter, shall I not seek rest for thee, that it may be well with thee ?

2. And now is not Boaz of our kindred, with whose maidens thou wast ? Behold, he winnoweth barley [though a mighty man of wealth, still a workman] to night [for the sake of the breeze] in the threshingfloor.

3. Wash thyself therefore, and anoint thee, and put thy raiment upon thee, and get thee down to the floor ; but make not thyself known unto the man, until he shall have done eating and drinking.

4. And it shall be, when he lieth down, that thou shalt mark the place

where he shall lie, and thou shalt go in, and uncover his feet, and lay thee down; and he will tell thee what thou shalt do.

5. And she said unto her, All that thou sayest unto me I will do.

6. And she went down unto the floor, and did according to all that her mother in law bade her.

7. And when Boaz had eaten and drunk, and his heart was merry [not necessarily implying any excess: see Judges xix. 6, 9], he went to lie down at the end of the heap of corn: and she came softly, and uncovered his feet, and laid her down.

8. And it came to pass at midnight, that the man was afraid [Gen. xxvii. 33], and turned himself [bent himself] : and, behold, a woman lay at his feet.

9. And he said, Who art thou? And she answered, I am Ruth thine handmaid : spread therefore thy skirt ["wing "] over thine handmaid; for thou art a near kinsman.

10. And he said, Blessed be thou of the Lord, my daughter [Origen compares Ruth to the Gentile church, the engrafted olive tree] : for thou hast shewed more kindness in the latter end than at the beginning, inasmuch as thou followest not young men, whether poor or rich.

11. And now, my daughter, fear not; I will do to thee all that thou requirest : for all the city of my people doth know that thou art a virtuous woman.

12. And now it is true that I am thy near kinsman ["Goel"] : howbeit there is a kinsman [Goel] nearer than I.

13. Tarry this night, and it shall be in the morning, that if he will perform unto thee the part of a kinsman, well; let him do the kinsman's part : but if he will not do the part of a kinsman to thee, then will I do the part of a kinsman to thee, as the Lord liveth : lie down until the morning.

14. And she lay at his feet until the morning : and she rose up before one could know another. And he said, Let it not be known that a woman came into the floor [this is the narrator's paraphrase].

15. Also he said, Bring the vail [" mantle : " Isaiah iii. 22] that thou hast upon thee, and hold it. And when she held it, he measured six measures of barley [twice as much as she gleaned], and laid it on her : and she went into the city.

16. And when she came to her mother in law, she said, Who art thou, my daughter? [Rather, How hast thou fared?] And she told her all that the man had done to her.

17. And she said, These six measures of barley gave he me; for he said to me, Go not empty unto thy mother in law.

18. Then said she, Sit still, my daughter, until thou know how the matter will fall : for the man will not be in rest [will not keep quiet], until he have finished the thing this day.

Chapter iv.

1. Then went Boaz up [the town stood on a hill] to the gate, and sat him down there : and, behold, the kinsman [the Goel] of whom Boaz spake came by ; unto whom he said, Ho, such-a-one ! [the name of the kinsman was either unknown or purposely concealed] turn aside, sit down here. And he turned aside, and sat down.

2. And he took ten men of the elders of the city [every city was governed by elders], and said, Sit ye down here. And they sat down.

3. And he said unto the kinsman, Naomi, that is come again out of the country of Moab, selleth a parcel of land, which was our brother Elimelech's :

4. And I thought [literally, I said I will uncover thy ear] to advertise thee, saying, Buy it before the inhabitants, and before the elders of my people. If thou wilt redeem it, redeem it : but if thou wilt not redeem it, then tell me, that I may know : for there is none to redeem it beside thee ; and I am after thee. And he said, I will redeem it [not knowing the whole case].

5. Then said Boaz, What day thou buyest the field of the hand of Naomi, thou must buy it also of Ruth the Moabitess, the wife of the dead, to raise up the name of the dead upon his inheritance.

6. ¶ And the kinsman said, I cannot redeem it for myself, lest I mar mine own inheritance : redeem thou my right to thyself [literally, redeem my redemption] ; for I cannot redeem it.

7. Now this was the manner in former time in Israel [showing that the custom was now obsolete] concerning redeeming, and concerning changing, for to confirm all things ; A man plucked off his shoe, and gave it to his neighbour : and this was a testimony in Israel :

8. Therefore the kinsman said unto Boaz, Buy it for thee. So he drew off his shoe [and so resigned the right of walking on the land as master].

9. ¶ And Boaz said unto the elders, and unto all the people, Ye are witnesses this day, that I have bought all that was Elimelech's, and all that was Chilion's and Mahlon's, of the hand of Naomi.

10. Moreover Ruth the Moabitess, the wife of Mahlon, have I purchased to be my wife, to raise up the name of the dead upon his inheritance, that the name of the dead be not cut off from among his brethren, and from the gate of his place : ye are witnesses this day.

11. And all the people that were in the gate, and the elders, said, We are witnesses. The Lord make the woman that is come into thine house like Rachel [her death and burial associated her with Beth-lehem] and like Leah, which two did build [from the Hebrew word *to build*, are derived the words for *son* and *daughter*] the house of Israel : and do thou worthily in Ephratah, and be famous in Beth-lehem :

12. And let thy house be like the house of Pharez [see Gen. xxxviii.], whom

Tamar bare unto Judah, of the seed which the Lord shall give thee of this young woman.

13. ¶ So Boaz took Ruth, and she was his wife : and when he went in unto her, the Lord gave her conception, and she bare a son.

14. And the women said unto Naomi, Blessed be the Lord, which hath not left thee this day without a kinsman [a Goel], that his name may be famous in Israel.

15. And he shall be unto thee a restorer of thy life, and a nourisher of thine old age : for thy daughter in law, which loveth thee, which is better to thee than seven sons, hath born him.

16. And Naomi took the child, and laid it in her bosom, and became nurse unto it.

17. And the women her neighbours gave it a name, saying, There is a son born to Naomi ; and they called his name Obed ["serving"]: he is the father of Jesse, the father of David [the first mention of David in Scripture].

18. ¶ Now these are the generations of Pharez : Pharez begat Hezron,

19. And Hezron begat Ram, and Ram begat Amminadab,

20. And Amminadab begat Nahshon, and Nahshon begat Salmon,

21. And Salmon begat Boaz [in Matthew it is said that the mother of Boaz was Rahab], and Boaz begat Obed,

22. And Obed begat Jesse, and Jesse begat David. ["Some links of the chain have been dropped, and if so, then doubtless in the period before Boaz . . . We have here the distinguished names, others of less note being passed over."]

PRAYER.

ALMIGHTY GOD, the heavens and the earth are thine: they are the work of thine hand; they are the witnesses of thy power; they are unto us as a great wonder by day and by night. Behold, who can measure thy strength, or understand thy wisdom? Thou settest creation fast upon the pillars of thy strength, and none can overturn them. We rest in the security of almightiness. Our hope is in the living God. We have no fear: perfect love casteth out fear; and in so far as thou hast wrought that love in our hearts we are delivered from the slavery of fear. We rejoice in all the work of thy hand. All thy work is ever new: every morning is a creation, every night a benediction, and all the time thou art doing us good because of thy tender mercy and thy lovingkindness. We would love thee in Christ Jesus more and more. In him thou hast outdone all thy greatest works: he is the brightness of thy glory; he is the express image of thy person; he is the fairest among ten thousand, and altogether lovely; he is the bright and morning star; he is our sun and shield; he is our all in all. We bless thee, therefore, most of all for the revelation of thyself in thy Son Christ Jesus. How gracious his word! how gentle his speech! how tender his Spirit! how full of love altogether! He died, the just for the unjust, that he might bring us to God. Surely he hath borne our griefs and carried our iniquities. This is our last and greatest joy: than this there is surely no greater gladness in heaven. Is not a Lamb, slain from the foundation of the world, seated upon heaven's own throne? and is not the anthem of heaven devoted to the praises of the Lamb? Bring us all nearer to Christ. May we feel more and more our need of him. May we answer his love by our faith; and, being sprinkled by his blood—yea, cleansed by it from every stain of sin—may we walk as those who are clothed in white, and keep our garments unspotted from the world. Thou hast set us in a strange place; thou hast caused us to pass under varied discipline: but thy rod is a rod of love, and it is in the hand of mercy. Help us to receive our daily task thankfully, resignedly, and to do it well in thy strength and love, knowing that God will judge us all, therefore may we not judge one another. We bless thee for all our hope, for all our secret gladness, for all the glory we have by faith seen beyond death and beyond the grave, so much so that we have mocked the monster and taunted him to his face, saying,—O death, where is thy sting? O grave, where is thy victory? Behold, we have triumphed in Christ, and because of his omnipotence we are delivered and are set in a great security. Help us to be wise men, truly knowing the times in which we live, fearlessly doing our duty, patiently awaiting God's verdict and the whole issue of providence. May there be in us no sign of terror, no sign of evil apprehension, but with stout hearts, and constant faith, and diligent industry may we do thy will on earth. Comfort those who are distressed ; dry the tears of anxious sorrow, intense and intolerable pain, and, above all, that secret and wordless misery which eats itself and which cannot draw upon the sympathy of those who observe it. The Lord direct us, protect us, be round about us— be our shield and safety, be our buckler and our defence ; then the battle shall be gladness, hard work shall be rest, and the eventide shall be a hint of that Sabbath all morning—the glad, glad day of heaven. Amen.

Ruth i. 1-18.

RUTH.

"She was a phantom of delight
When first she gleamed upon my sight ;
A lovely apparition, sent
To be a moment's ornament.
＊　　　＊　　　＊　　　＊
I saw her upon nearer view,
A spirit, yet a woman too ;
Her household motions light and free,
And steps of virgin liberty ;
A countenance in which did meet
Sweet records, promises as sweet;
A creature not too bright or good
For human nature's daily food."—*Wordsworth.*

"Think not the good,
The gentle deeds of mercy thou hast done,
Shall die forgotten all : the poor, the pris'ner,
The fatherless, the friendless, and the widow,
Who daily own the bounty of thine hand,
Shall cry to Heaven, and pull a blessing on thee."

The Preacher's Homiletical Commentary thus describes the scene of action :— At first Bethlehem, then Moab, then Bethlehem and the regions around once again. Bethlehem, two short hours' journey south of Jerusalem. The most attractive and significant of all the world's birthplaces (Schubert). Under ordinary circumstances a fruitful land. Remarkably well watered in comparison with other parts of Palestine (Benjamin of Tudela). Even in the present state of Palestine, deserves its old name. Ritter says, "Notwithstanding poor cultivation, the soil is fruitful in olives, pomegranates, almonds, figs, and grapes." Hepworth Dixon thus describes its present appearance :—

"A string of gardens, a few steep fields, much crossing of white roads— so many that the point of junction may be called the Place of Paths—a glen which drops by leaps and steps to the great Cedron valley, makes the landscape. Yet the slope which is thus bound in by higher tops and more barren crests, has a winning beauty of its own, a joyous promise of bread and fruit, which puts it first among the chosen places of Judea. The old word Ephrath meant Place of Fruit, the newer word Bethlehem meant House of Bread; one following the other, as barley and maize come after grapes and figs, and the sower of grain succeeds to the breeder of goats and kine. The little bit of plain through which Ruth gleaned after the young men, together with a level of stony ground here and there in the glen toward Mar Saba, are the only corn lands occurring in the hill country of Judea for many a league. . . . The lovely green ridge of Bethlehem is the scene of some of our most tender and gracious poems: the idylls of Rachel, of Ruth, of Saul, of David, of Chimham, of Jeremiah, of the Virgin-mother; the subjects of these poems being the foremost passages in Israel's religious life."—*Dixon's Holy Land.*

Moab, on the other side, and S.E. of the Dead Sea, from Bethlehem. A district about forty miles long by twenty in width. In parts a luxuriant land when cultivated. The uplands are very fertile and productive (Professor Palmer). Now but scantily populated, but presenting evidences of former plenty and fertility.

RUTH'S ELECTION.

"THERE was a famine in the land" (v. 1). Necessity drives men forth, and is therefore to be regarded as a blessing rather than a curse. It is prosperity that may be looked upon, in some senses and under obvious limitations, as a danger, if not a malediction. "Necessity is the mother of invention." We owe nearly all we have to necessity: we owe next to nothing to prosperity. Why do men hasten to the city every morning, pouring in great living floods out of every railway terminus, and hastening away, scarcely speaking to one another, scarcely knowing one another? What is the explanation of this rush and tumult and speechless haste? Necessity—necessity of some kind, necessity real and proper, or something that is a mistaken necessity; still, *need* is the word of explanation and solution. Why are all those ships upon the sea, full of men, women, and little children? What is the meaning of this leaving of father-land, this cutting asunder of tender and vital associations? Necessity. Men are going out to make lands, to create civilisa-tions, to establish themselves in free, independent, secure, and happy life. Prosperity does not drive men out; prosperity keeps them at home. Hardship is the real blessing of life, when properly measured and properly received. All children should have "a hard time of it," under proper regulation. The children of this day are being ruined. They are being confectioned and

coddled to death. By the time they are fifteen years of age they
have seen everything; there is nothing more to be seen: they
have travelled over the picture-galleries of Europe; they have
heard all the great speakers, musicians, and others; they have
seen all the great sights;—they are over-powered with weariness.
This should not be so: but it must continue to be so until
parents see the reality of the case. Five years in the workhouse,
the expenses being discharged by the parents, from five years
of age to ten, would make men of the children. How they would
then enjoy daisies, buttercups, little birds, half a day's rollicking
freedom in the green meadow! How pleased they would be
with any occasional dainty found upon the table! how doubly
valuable the sweet kiss! But we will not have it so. Hence,
the children are brought up to be pests to themselves, and
nuisances to the public. God however takes this matter into his
own hands, and he graciously sends famine and need and
difficulty, sickness and death, and a thousand black teachers
down into his great public school, to show men the real charm of
life, and to bring to bear upon them the most sacred and ennobling
impulse which can inspire and sanctify their industry.

"There was a famine in the land." There is always a famine.
Not always a famine of bread and a thirst for water: that is
the poorest of all famine; the real famine is a famine of the
heart—a famine of love, trust, sympathy, longing for help and
not finding it, hoping and praying for sympathy and care, and
the hope dying without an answer. Even that is not the worst
famine of all :—"Behold, the days come, saith the Lord God, that
I will send a famine in the land, not a famine of bread, nor a
thirst for water, but of hearing the words of the Lord;" there
shall be no voice from heaven : the communication between the
worlds shall be cut off, and men who would try to pray will
have their prayers sent back as the only possible reply; bu
even these days, properly received, may be turned to high
advantage. Religion has now become a satiety. We can go to
church so much that we hardly care to go at all. The gospel is
preached to us in so many ways that we have become quite
critical about them, and have "opinions" concerning them,—
what hungry man asks metaphysical questions about the bread

that is set before him in the pangs of his necessity ? Were there
more conscious need there would be less criticism and infinitely
greater enjoyment.

So the little story moves on. "And a certain man of Beth-
lehem-judah went to sojourn in the country of Moab, he, and
his wife, and his two sons" (v. 1). And the husband died,
and the two sons also departed this life. How is it the men
die first ? Surely, this is cruelty, from our point of view, that
the men should thus have the best of it—that the men should be
rid of the burden whilst they are quite young, and the women
left to weep and wonder, and slave and suffer unspeakably,
displaying a patience that might reverently be called divine.
Why should not they have the best of life and go into heaven
first, and be there to meet those who need more discipline—meet
those to whom longer exposure in the bleak air would do good ?
But it is well.

> " God keeps a niche
> In heaven to hold our idols; and, albeit
> He brake them to our faces and denied
> That our close kisses should impair their white,
> I know we shall behold them raised complete,
> The dust swept from their beauty—glorified,
> New Memnons singing in the great God-light."

Women can stand out better. There is more divinity in them.
What could men do left alone upon the earth—clever men, able,
skilful, inventive men ? Why, they dare not turn round because
of the great emptiness which bereavement has occasioned in
their lives ; their hearts go stark out, and their strength is like
flowing water, and there is no constancy in their fortitude. A
man left with four little children—say, is there a more helpless
creature in all the world, a picture of drearier desolation, and
a more ghastly spectacle of industrious thriftlessness ? These
things are all ordered in heaven : but surely it does seem cruel
now and then that the men should die first and get away to
the daylight, and the wealth of heaven's harvest-time, and all the
gladness of eternal day, and leave their companions struggling
far down in the world.

The two sons of the woman married, and they, as we have
seen, also died, after dwelling in Moab about ten years ; and this

was her position—a position of widowhood—three souls in heaven, three new stars in the crown of night, three openings into the better land, where even she had an inheritance in the God of Israel. Then good news came to her :—" She had heard in the country of Moab how that the Lord had visited his people in giving them bread " (v. 6). To live in this Hebrew faith would be life indeed; " the Lord " was always so near to the pious Hebrew ; it was " the Lord " that sent rain ; it was " the Lord " that sent the delivering angel ; it was " the Lord " that spread the field with abundant harvests ; it was " the Lord " who turned on the fountains of water and made them gush and sparkle in the sunshine. Account for it as we may, there is a warmth in the thought, which now and again touches us according to the pressure of our necessity and the stinging of some mortal pain. We have not gained much by striking out " the Lord " from our vocabulary, and putting in " the laws of nature," and " the courses of creation, " and " the natural evolution of material ; " —the gain is on the other side. Blessed are they who have faith to stand by the living words, and to run unto them as men who are pursued run into a strong tower. The time will come again when " the Lord " shall be a name used with reverent familiarity : men shall own the Lord in the breaking of bread, in the lying down to slumber, in the resurrection from sleep, in every pulse of the living day. Even so, Lord Jesus, come quickly.

Here we have a beautiful little picture :—

" And Naomi said unto her two daughters in law, Go, return each to her mother's house : the Lord deal kindly with you, as ye have dealt with the dead, and with me " (v. 8).

What a speech !—to be worthy of such a testimony ; to have so lived at home as to elicit this benediction. What a glimpse into home-life ! What a quiet sabbatic house—a house sacred as an altar, secure against evil as a fortress ! Is there aught so lovely, so attractive, so invaluable as a real, sunny, happy, gladsome home, where the opening of every door is an enlargement of hospitality, where the windows are all too small to receive heaven's benison of light, where every life considers every other life, and the whole household economy is as a concerted piece of

music ? In this direction all men, women, and children should
move. Home should be the sweetest, happiest place on earth.
On closing the household gate, the one who enters in should be
able to sigh relief—release from pursuing anxieties; and the
whole house should be beautiful and sacred as a church dedicated
to God. In words such as we find in the eighth verse we have
family life embodied in a sentence :—" The Lord deal kindly
with you, as ye have dealt with the dead, and with me." Her
throat swelled with a great sob as she referred to the dead. Oh,
to have no cruel reflections concerning the dead—to know that
whilst they were living we did the best we could for them : we
spared no trouble to lighten their burdens ; we never said we
were tired ; we seemed rather to invite the labour than to evade
it, if we could make their pillow easier and could add to their
day's outlook one brighter beam of light ;—then the very death
sanctifies the memory, and throws a singular charm upon all the
future—akin to a happy expectancy, akin to the possibility of a
sudden surprise by reappearance and re-junction. Do not mourn
the dead, for you can do nothing to repair the injury which was
inflicted upon them in their lifetime ; they are beyond the reach
of reparation. The only thing possible now is to do good twice
over to those who are living with you, to set up—not stones,
but—living tablets, sacred to the memory of the misunderstood
and the ill-used, the neglected and the distressed.

" Then she kissed them ; and they lifted up their voice, and
wept " (v. 9). Not a word was said. There are times when
words are simply useless ; there are sacred hours when the
best-chosen words fall upon our ear with a sense of irritation.
" They lifted up their voice, and wept ; " they kissed to one
another all their meaning. A lifetime was in that pressure,
memories not to be spoken in detailed expressions consecrated
that kiss of love. Who can without tears cut the associations of
memory and of happy and sacred life ? The heart that can do so
is a heart no more ; it is but a piece of stone. Look upon Naomi
and her daughters-in-law, see them kissing one another, and hear
their weeping, and say, This is dying ! What we call death is
hardly so to be named at all ; it is translation, liberation, sanctification, coronation ; but this parting, sundering, tearing of human

hearts, this division of the life-currents—this is death! The reflection should be laid to heart in all directions. The old man at home died when his prodigal son left him. The house became a cemetery when the evil deed was done. This is the kind of death men should think about. The other death—expiration, throwing off the " mortal coil "—call not this death in any sense that is distressful! The death is in parting, the giving up the dear associations of life, in sacrificing the whole store of blessed memory.

Now we approach the issue. After further speech, reasoning on the one side and on the other, we come to this conclusion:—

"And they lifted up their voice, and wept again : and Orpah kissed her mother in law; but Ruth clave unto her " (v. 14).

Precisely how people are characterised and distinguished to-day. We do not blame Orpah ; she was loving, but Ruth was more loving. That is the patent, and yet in some senses subtle, distinction. It is hard to fix upon the point where one man's quality exceeds another. For a long time they seem to be equal, but a critical juncture occurs, and at that point the quality of the man is determined. Still, let us not forget that the distinction is between loving and loving more,—not between hatred and love, not between aversion and attachment, but between love and love. Orpah loved Naomi, and indeed wanted to go with her, with a constancy, however, that was open to reasoning ; Ruth loved her and shut out all reasoning, because of the passion of her affection.

> "I am constant as the northern star,
> Of whose true, fixed, and resting quality
> There is no fellow in the firmament."

We shall be judged according to our capacity : all people cannot love alike ; all people do not hear with equal quickness; all people could not be trained to an equal state of refinement : but God will judge us all. God knoweth our frame ; he remembereth that we are dust. The Lord knows that sometimes we are in circumstances which do admit of being stated in two ways, and he sees us at the point of perplexity—now looking on the reasons for going, and now looking at the reasons for not going. He is not harsh with us. He knows our nature; he made us, and not we ourselves. It is hard to determine in some cases what is the right thing and the best thing to be done. How, then, will the judgment proceed? According to motive and purpose: where the conscience is clean, where the motive is right, the issue will be judged accordingly; the action may be a mistake, all the consequences arising out of the action may be disastrous, but in the judgment it will be the motive that will be determined :—"Create in me a clean heart, O God; and renew a right spirit within me,"—in other words: let my heart be clean, let my spirit be right, let my motive be pure, let my purpose be good and honest, and then, come weal, come woe, at the last thou wilt not forsake thine erring servant. Are there not people who do precisely what Orpah did, and what Ruth did? There are certainly persons who will go with you part of the road, but they always secretly reserve the right of abandoning you: they will see how events turn out; they will draw up a kind of balance sheet of *pro* and *con*; they hold themselves at liberty to take an independent course. Ruth did nothing of the sort—she plunged into this great stream and said she would go wherever the river went. Orpah could not have done so; it was not in her nature; she is not, therefore, to be condemned, blamed, and spoken of in contemptuous terms; even she did what she could: Ruth was Orpah *plus*.

> "So from the heights of will
> Life's parting stream descends,
> And, as a moment turns its slender rill,
> Each widening torrent bends.
> From the same cradle side,
> From the same mother's knee,
> One to long darkness and the frozen tide,
> One to the peaceful sea."

Who can read the next two verses without punctuating them with tears?—

"And Ruth said, Intreat me not to leave thee, or to return from following after thee: for whither thou goest, I will go; and where thou lodgest, I will lodge: thy people shall be my people, and thy God my God: where thou diest, will I die, and there will I be buried: the Lord do so to me, and more also, if ought but death part thee and me" (vv. 16, 17).

That speech was never made by an artist; that eloquence was

never elaborated by a cunning hand in which the heart took no part. We recognise the spontaneousness of the speech. This is untaught and unteachable eloquence—the uprising and outgoing of a grand human heart. This is the human heart at its best. If any would say what is the human heart in its finest mood, he cannot do better than point to the speech made by Ruth to Naomi. What a heart it is when it is at its best, even this fallen, corrupt, deceitful human heart! How even yet it can love, suffer, enter joyously into the mystery of sacrifice, and be glad of the opportunity of giving itself away to another! Never neglect that view of the heart. Other views of the heart are sound and good, profoundly scriptural, and sorrowfully actual; they are not to be denied, mitigated, or put into false perspective; at the same time, what a heart it is! How forbearing! how loving! how forgiving! how it dreams itself into new opportunities of sacrifice! how it keeps the door ajar that the prodigal may easily come into the old homestead! how it invents surprises for those whom it loves! how it can still the footstep into a kind of whisper as the ministrant comes into the sick chamber to do good to the sufferer who is in the last extremity! What a heart it is! Surely God must have taken that view of the heart when he purposed to redeem the world! It was no cruel heart, or heart of perishable beast, but a heart like his own, touched with the mystery of the same love and quality, that Jesus came to save. We may take both views. But one is not complete without the other, and we cannot understand the mystery of redemption until we understand, in some measure, the mystery of the human heart. What a speech is Ruth's! She says in effect: Further entreaty would give me intolerable pain: do not continue the importunate suggestion that I should leave thee. To leave thee!—in what direction should I go? If I turn my face from thine, I am as one who turns from the light into a great darkness: if I leave following thee, I am as one who abandons a garden that he may walk in a wilderness; nay, we are one; we have been one these many years; we are one more than ever now that the link has broken, —we must live and die together! What is the Christian application of this absorption? No words are needed to explain it. It means that this should be the relation of the heart to Jesus Christ. Sometimes Jesus Christ seems to propose our leaving, at least he

suggests the possibility of our going away. He said to his
disciples, "Will ye also go away?" Peter made the speech
nearest akin to the quality of Ruth's ever made by mortal lips—
"Lord, to whom shall we go? Thou hast the words of eternal
life." Is this characteristic of our personal Christianity? Is it a
passion of love? The question is not, Do we esteem Christ? do
we venerate him? have we a word of gracious recognition to
accord to his name? The question is, Do we love him—love
being pronounced with the heart, having nothing taken out of it
that is essential to the completeness of its emphasis and the completeness of its sacrifice? "Simon, son of Jonas, lovest thou
me?" Can we answer—"Lord, thou knowest all things—my
sin amongst them, my inconstancy, my blasphemy—thou knowest
that I love thee"? What we need in human life is not so much
more information, higher intelligence, more refined culture: about
these things not a word is to be said that is derogatory; but the
great demand is for passionate love, clinging love, constant love,
self-sacrificing love,—love always the same, never changing,
never faltering, never hesitating. Who has such love? Without
it we have no Christianity that is worth having. We may have
all its trappings, ceremonies, mechanical pass-words, ecclesiastical
privileges and honours, but we have not the love which is akin
to Christ's own affection. When did love ever turn back from
the living Christ? The intellect has sometimes gone away,
being imperfectly trained, being marred by voluntary or in-
voluntary ignorance, or being irritated by irrational impatience.
Worldliness has gone away: "Demas hath forsaken me, having
loved this present world;" respectability sometimes turns away,
afraid that the next stoop of condescension may be too lowly for
its dignity: but when did love go away—real love, burning,
passionate, sacrificial love? when was love offended? Love
suffereth long, and is kind; love outliveth all things; love never
complains of the dark night, the cold wind, the heavy burden,
the undesirable task, the steep hill, the stony pathway through
the desert; love asks one question—Is it the Lord who is gone
before? Am I walking in his footprints? Enough! Then labour
is rest, and pain is sweet; disappointment is the inspiration of a
larger prayer, and mortified fleshly desires are turned into nutriment ministering to the broadest, grandest, spiritual strength

Let this gospel be sounded far and wide—sounded musically, tenderly, importunately,—namely, to our information, intelligence, education, culture, critical power, genius, add burning, inexpressible love ; then discord will die, and the Church will live a life of holy emulation, each member desiring and aiming to surpass the other in deeds of charity, in acts of nobleness.

SELECTED NOTE.

" There was a famine in the land" (v. 1).—The first mention of a famine which occurs in Scripture is in Gen. xii. 10, where we read that so early as the days of the patriarch Abraham " there was a famine in the land," which is described as so grievous as to compel the father of the faithful to quit Canaan. The country to which he resorted was, as we might expect, the land of Egypt, the early and lasting fertility of which is a well-known historical fact. In Gen. xxvi. 1, this famine is designated as "the first," that is, the first known, or of which there was any record. The same passage informs us of another famine which afflicted " the land " in the days of Isaac, who seems to have contemplated a descent into Egypt, but who, being instructed of God, removed to a part of Arabia Petræa (Gen. xxvi. 17) named Gerar, a city of the Philistines, whose monarch's name was Abimelech.

Even Egypt, however, was not exempt from the desolations of famine (Gen. xli. 30). The ordinary cause of dearth in Egypt is connected with the annual overflow of the Nile. . . . This famine was made by Joseph the occasion of one of the greatest social revolutions which history records. The details may be found in the book of Genesis ; and it is enough to say here that, as the special administrator of the affairs of the country, Joseph got into his hands all the property of the kingdom, including the land (excepting that which belonged to the priests), and gave the same back to the people as tenants-at-will, on condition of their paying to the king " the fifth " probably of the annual produce.

From these statements it appears that three successive generations were in these early days visited by famine. The Scriptural narrative shows that in after-ages famines were, in ancient times, more frequent than they are now ; and this justifies the use which is made of so terrible a scourge by the sacred writers, and especially the prophets and our Lord himself, in the highly figurative language which they employ in their righteous endeavours to turn wicked men and wicked nations from the evil of their ways (Ezek. vi. 11 ; Matt. xxiv. 7). In Amos viii. 11 *sq.*, a heavier woe than even the want of bread is appropriately spoken of under the appellation of a famine : " Behold, the days come, saith the Lord God, that I will send a famine in the land ; not a famine of bread nor a thirst for water, but of hearing the words of the Lord ; and they shall wander from sea to sea, and from the north even to the east ; they shall run to and fro to seek the word of the Lord, and shall not find it : in that day shall the fair virgins and young men faint for thirst." The ensuing verse shows that idolatry was the moving cause of this heavy punishment.

PRAYER.

O THOU that hearest prayer to answer it in great love, we come to thee in Christ thy Son, the Priest of the whole creation. He only knoweth how to pray. Lord, teach us also how to pray; inspire us with reverence; elevate us with a sense of awe; subdue and chasten us by all the sweet influences of the altar. May we look far on high, no cloud coming between us and the Father whose face our soul seeks. We would talk with God; it hath so pleased him that we may talk in our own way, out of our broken heart, telling all the tale of our sin and shame, our trespass and misery, and receiving in reply the eternal gospel that Christ Jesus came into the world to save sinners. Thou knowest all our life—every stain upon it, every flaw, every shortcoming; every honest purpose, every resolute endeavour to be right and to do thy will. What, then, can we tell thee? Yet thou art pleased to hear our speech, for the very utterance of our words thou hast made a means of grace. We speak to thee of thy goodness first, for it is first, midst, last; it is like the sky: we cannot tell where it begins, where it ends; we have measured the earth, and weighed it, and written our signature all over its face, but we know nothing about thy sky; it is an image of thyself—in vastness, in grandeur, in majesty. As the heaven is high above the earth, so are thy thoughts above our thoughts and thy ways above our ways. We therefore speak of thy mercy as ever-abiding: it is the light of the morning; it is the rest of night; it is the song of all time. Because thy compassions fail not, therefore are we not consumed. We live upon pity; we owe our existence to thy tears; if thou didst hate us surely thou wouldst crush us with some great bolt of thunder. Yet thou dost spare us, and visit us, and care for us: herein is a love beyond all words. By thy providence thou dost draw us to thy grace. Thine is a gradual process, so that having looked upon the great letter of thy goodness in life we ask for further instruction, and are led, step by step, into the inner and upper sanctuary where is the eternal truth. We first see the great cross of wood—we are amazed, we are struck with horror, our soul dies within us in very disgust; then we look at the Sufferer, and he transfigures the cross and makes it like a living tree, the leaves whereof are for the healing of the nations; we still look on, and out of his death there comes new life, new hope, new grace; we then say, Truly this Man was the Son of God; then we cast ourselves upon him, having no other refuge, no other hope—our sin our only plea, our penitence our only hope. Thus the cross of Christ becomes heaven's brightest treasure, the very centre of all glory, the very majesty of the throne. We come to that cross night and day. Thou hast not yet taken it down; thou wilt continue it until thy purpose is all served: then cometh the end, when Christ shall have delivered up the kingdom unto God and the Father, and the Lord shall be all in all. Meanwhile, we would be saved by the cross, elevated and ennobled by the cross; we would be crucified upon it, that knowing the mystery of its pain, we may also know the power of the resurrection of Christ. We speak of thy goodness, but we know not what we say until we see the cross. Our first acknowledgments are full of selfishness. Thou hast given unto us loaves and fishes in the wilderness, and found a couch for us in the night-time and fountains of water in unexpected places, and we feel glad: but the gladness is stained through and through by self-regard. It is nothing to be glad for these things: these are appeals to our inferior nature; but when we are glad for Christ, for the spirit of grace, for the revelation of truth, for the opportunity of suffering for Christ, and for the occasion of serving him, for all the hopes which point to a destiny of deeper consecration, then we begin to touch the very magnanimity of thy Son. Our life we would live in thy sight. It is a poor little thing, cooled by the cold, affrighted by that which is high, troubled by that which is unknown; yet, nursed by thy grace, inspired and inflamed by thy Spirit, it becomes invested with somewhat of thine own almightiness—a grand life, a gift of God, not less than any donation of his hand; a mystery full of hope and full of dignity. Do with us what thou wilt. We like to be on the mountain-top first lighted by the sun, on which the eventide lingers; we like to have our own way; we like to turn our wishes into realities; we like to be strong, rich, full of friends, and having everything according to our own desire. Herein is our fault. It is this self-enlargement and self-idolatry that shames us when we really understand it. We thought it faultless once; it seemed to be quite right; it is now all wrong. This we have been taught in the school of Christ—a hard lesson, the last lesson that is taught there. So now we know what is meant by self-denial, self-obliteration. Yet we hardly know it. When we think we are dead behold we rise up again—the old pride, the ineradicable vanity, starting up in self-defence. Lord, slay us! Lord, kill us, that we may enter into our nobler selves. Take away the old man and his deeds; slay him; put him where he never can rise again; yea, banish him from our memory, and set up within us the kingdom of the new man, Christ Jesus, self-denying, self-obliterating, the great man, who lives for others, in others, and in their gladness becomes his true self. Rule all things; we know thou wilt. We are startled by the little foam, and run away as if it could do us harm. The floods lift up their voice, but they cry themselves to rest. The Lord reigneth. We put ourselves within the sanctuary, and from its open windows we behold the method of God in the world—so wise, so good, so unknowable in all its mystery, yet so gracious in its accessible points. Feed us evermore with the bread of life. Lord, evermore give us this bread! make us slaves of Christ that thus we may become freemen. Amen.

Ruth i.

THE CHARACTER OF NAOMI.

" We leave
Our home in youth—no matter to what end—
Study, or strife, or pleasure, or what not;
And coming back in few short years, we find
All as we left it outside : . . .
But lift that latchet,—all is changed as doom."

" IS this Naomi ? " (i. 19)—literally, is this *the* Naomi ?—the reference being to a person well known, and well known because of quality and station. The name was known to every one as the name of a lady of notable degree who had been obliged to give way to circumstances that were irresistible, and who had therefore become poor, dispossessed even of bread, and sent away in great distress to undergo what would seem to be the chief punishment which Heaven could inflict. Naomi said : Do not call me by my old name ; it is a name associated with joy, laughter, gladness, merry-heartedness ; literally you are right : my name is Naomi, but it ought now to be Mara, associated with bitterness, real grief of soul.—Let us look carefully into the characteristics of this brave woman, and learn what we can from her name and history.

Naomi had preserved her piety in a heathen country. Some have blamed Elimelech for leaving the land of Israel and going where the god Chemosh was the ruling deity. Some people have a genius for blaming others. There have not been wanting critics who have found in the punishment inflicted upon Naomi proofs of God's disfavour in the matter of the family having run away when the famine was sore in Israel. But who are these hard-hearted critics, who are so gifted in the detection of divine punishments, and who can seat themselves upon a throne of iron and declare who is right and who is wrong in all the inter-mingled story of human affairs ? Providence does not so come within our measurement. We had better attend to our prayers than to our criticisms. It is indeed a severer punishment still than any that fell upon the house of Elimelech to be cursed with the spirit of criticism. When an accident occurs, there are those who can tell exactly why the accident took place, and can trace it to a direct judgment of God upon certain evil-doers. Unfortunately, the facts are against the criticism : for there were neither evil-doers nor evil-doings in many cases: the men were known to be good, the object they had in view was unquestionably right, and yet in the midst of it the collision occurred, the bridge gave way, the fire leapt upon them and left them hot ashes. We cannot tell what God is doing. We must await the issue, and when the circle is quite sphered off, then say whether it could have been drawn by any compasses made by the hands of men. Undoubtedly, however, Elimelech was in the land of Chemosh—in the land of other gods—idols, and vain images. Yet, in the midst of an atmosphere that was poisoned through and through, Elimelech was able to pray, and Naomi to refer to the God of Israel. Let us not take undue encouragement from this, and say that in any company we are safe, and in any land we can maintain our piety, and under any circumstances our prayer cannot be violated or even shortened. Men ought not to try to play with fire. There is no bravery in courting danger. Even the boldest man has need to utter the sweet prayer of modesty that he may be kept night and day within the grasp of God. It is beautiful, though, to see the widow returning from the far country, with her piety intact, never referring to the heathen idols, or confessing their sovereignty or deity : as she went out she returned, deeply thinking about God—not a great thinker, but having in her that spirit of wonder which sometimes becomes almost genius, and that strange awe of heart which enables the listening ear to detect the going of the eternal. She is home now.

Naomi suffered from the worst form of trouble. She explained her sorrow in these pathetic words :—" Why then call ye me Naomi, seeing the Lord hath testified against me, and the Almighty hath afflicted me ? " (i. 21). What is the worst form of trouble ? The conscious absence of God, religious melancholy ; a sense of spiritual desertion, or a smarting under supposed divine judgments ? No trouble can compare with that sorrow in the very blackness of darkness. It does not admit of comfort ; it looks at the comforter as an intruder—yea, as an audacious and most dangerous person. To the soul that is loaded with darkness as with a burden, there is no Bible; there is a book large enough, but all the leaves are blank; if there are black letters upon it, they run into one another, and mean nothing in their mocking confusion. Who can speak to a soul that is religiously bruised? Who knows the tongue of that soul? Who can drop his voice into the still small whisper that can touch such a life without further wounding it? To this deep trouble we have not come, for the Bible is open before us and God's words still give us spiritual interest and satisfaction. Short of that trouble, all other distress is manageable. The presence of God sanctifies all other good, makes the dead live twice over, throngs all heaven with images of love and welcome. Let us pray, saying, "Take not thy Holy Spirit from me!" We should take care not to fall into this great agony. There is a possibility of giving way to certain influences and suggestions of a destructive character. Feeling them coming on as an armed host, we should seek immediate relief amid the healing mountains, the great mysterious waters, and all the genial influences of wise society. Who has not heard of poor creatures who have known when insanity was near at hand? Who has not read the heart-breaking story of Mary Lamb, who begged her brother to take certain measures when she felt the darkness fast deepening? That would seem to be the worst insanity—namely, the conscious approach of madness. Is there not a reason why we should take care in time with regard to this religious melancholy? May we not waste our lives away, allow our spiritual energy to ooze out of us, so that in some fell moment the devil may spring upon us, and capture us like a lawful prey? Let us watch, and be sober. While the light lingers about us in all its sacred laughter and joy, let us add to our spiritual strength, so that when the thief cometh to steal our soul's treasure we may handle him like strong men.

Naomi brought others to the true God by the might of personal character. We are not told that she preached to Ruth in any formal manner, yet Ruth said to Naomi these words,—"Thy people shall be my people, and thy God my God" (i. 16). That is our opportunity of showing which is the true divinity. People watch us, see how we act in famine, in bereavement, in

mortal distress; and in proportion as they see our integrity
untouched, our prayer enlarged rather than diminished, our confidence established upon everlasting rocks, they may begin
through our character to understand our theology. Herein every
man may become a preacher,—that is to say, he may become a
mystery of endurance, patience, hopefulness, trust in God. What!
—the enemy may say—is he not shaken off yet? Does he still
cling to God? Has he not had enough of Heaven's displeasure?
His house blown down, his children killed, his flocks stolen—
does he still trust God? There comes a time when even a
shattered life becomes an instrument of power. All men are
awed by great character, by sublime endurance, by heroic
patience, by tears that enlarge the eyes but never blind them.
What an opportunity is this! Hardly a word spoken, no
eloquence of the tongue needed, no charming imagination, no
fascinating words, no wizardry of speech; yet great conversions
going on night and day; persons first despising, then wondering,
then admiring, and finally ascribing the mystery of sanctified
endurance to the very grace of God. Although we may not be
able to work great wonders in this direction, we can forbear
working great destruction in the other. It will soon be discovered what our piety is worth. If the Christian man is just as
afraid in a shipwreck as any other man, what is his Christianity
worth? If a Christian soul is just as much troubled in times of
commercial depression as the souls that resent the idea of
religious faith, what is the value of his Christian sentiment?
If his face is all marked over with anxiety, fear, apprehension,
mourning, what has the peace of God done for him? Though we
may not work mightily as heroes, we may still do a most useful
work in society by quiet, silent, patient endurance. If the
question be asked, as it sometimes is, To what do you trace your
conversion? how often the reply is, To what I saw of Christianity at home; without understanding the books and the
preachers, without being able to follow them in their arguments,
I saw what Christianity could do in a house of poverty, affliction,
and great sorrow many-hued, and from what I saw of it there I
wish to embrace it, understand somewhat of it, love it, and ex-
emplify it: the Christianity that made my home what it was is
the religion I want. Who could give a finer reply? and blessed

be God, the reply is just. Christianity has worked these home-miracles; Christianity has furnished a house as with blessings and treasures from heaven, and having done this, he who would embrace that religion is justified by reason and fact.

Shall it always be thus with Naomi ? Shall she die in sorrow ? We find the answer in chapter iv. :—

"And the women said unto Naomi, Blessed be the Lord, which hath not left thee this day without a kinsman, that his name may be famous in Israel. And he shall be unto thee a restorer of thy life, and a nourisher of thine old age : for thy daughter-in-law, which loveth thee, which is better to thee than seven sons, hath borne him " (vv. 14, 15).

Naomi saw the light again. So it shall be with us in all our sorrows if we cling to the altar, and hope steadfastly in the cross. When times are dark and our bread is moistened with our tears, when every door seems to be shut, and everything we touch fades and perishes, let us hope in God. Though weeping may endure for a night, yet joy cometh in the morn-ing. Let us sing the old songs that made our fathers glad in the ancient days; they will be none the worse sung in Heaven's ear if stopped with sobs and tears and quite broken as to time and tune : it is the meaning that is accepted in heaven; no mechanical music is needed; the correctness is in the earnest-ness, the acceptableness is in the sincerity. Are we to sing in the night-time ? The answer is, Most certainly. The meanest birds can sing in the day-time, what little singing they can do· What bird is it that charms the night ? Even upon us light shall arise, the morning shall break, and we shall have hope in God, and our song at mid-day shall lose nothing of loudness and sweetness because of our song at midnight. Christians are called to hope. The Lord will surely appear unto his people, and turn their sorrow into joy; and there is no joy like that which comes out of sanctified distress. They are poor joys that come without preliminary sorrows : they are mere bubbles on the water, rising, sparkling, for a moment, breaking, and passing away into forgetfulness. Great joys that abide steadfastly through all heaven's eternity are the joys that are associated with a crucified Christ, who knew the darkness of religious desolation and felt the bitterness of spiritual orphanhood, saying, "My God, my God, why hast thou forsaken me ? "

PRAYER.

ALMIGHTY GOD, we bless thee for all the children of Abraham, for all the inheritors of his faith. May our faith be as his was. May our trust in God be simple, deep, unchanging. Take charge of our whole life; keep our life in thine own eternity; touch the springs of our being, that the streams of our life may be pure. May all our springs be in God, in the living God, the Creator of the ends of the earth, the Redeemer of the family of man. May we have no charge over ourselves, no care concerning our own life; may our present and our future be entirely under the control of our Sovereign Father, as revealed unto us in the person and mediation of Jesus Christ thy Son. We thank thee for every man who, in a loud, clear, sweet tone, has declared his faith in God before all men : for every one who has been simple in his testimony, who has convinced the world by the argument of a sober and solid life of faith in the Living One,—who has in thy strength done all things wisely and well. Let this hour be holy to us ! May every heart feel that it has alighted upon a flower in which there is much honey. May weary travellers know that there is a springing well here, —the well of the Lord's revelation which is never dry. May hungry hearts eat of the bread of life and be satisfied; may bruised reeds be protected; may no smoking flax be quenched; may the feeblest aspiration after the living God be answered by wondrous revelations of love to the waiting and eager heart. Give us release from the importunities of the world ! Help our recollection to remember thy goodness. Save our love from the distraction of many rivals. Draw all our faculties and powers, every desire of our soul, towards thyself in profitable concentration, that in this holy hour of worship we may become strengthened for all the engagements of life. May the strong man give thee his strength. May the wise man know that thou didst light the lamp of his understanding. Save the weak man from regarding his weakness as a temptation. Turn every eye to thyself, thou Eternal Light, and bind around thy heart all the affections of our own. God be gracious unto us ! Show us a love deeper than our mother's— tenderer than we have ever seen. Gather us unto thy great heart, and the storm shall never reach us there ! Amen.

Ruth ii.

BOAZ A TYPE OF CHRIST.

"The fragrant sheaves of the wheat
Made the air above them sweet;
Sweeter and more divine
Was the scent of the scattered grain,
That the reaper's hand let fall
To be gathered again
By the hand of the gleaner:
Sweetest, divinest of all,
Was the humble deed of thine,
And the meekness of thy demeanour."

BOAZ was not only a forerunner but a type of Christ. As compared with some of the greater luminaries of the Bible, Boaz was but a secondary star; yet, in two aspects, he is amongst the brightest lights in the Biblical constellation. Even socially, Boaz is a man worth knowing—quite a healthy soul, the winds of heaven getting well around him, and the sunshine falling amply into every fold and crevice of his gracious life. Boaz had fields, and lived much in the open air. A man of cheerful voice and well-controlled hilarity; a model agriculturist, quite a man to be copied and lived over again, age after age: so hospitable, so blithe, so strong, so bright-eyed altogether. When he came into the harvest fields he said to his reapers, "The Lord be with you;" and the reapers answered, "The Lord bless thee." That was farm-life in the olden times. There is nothing humiliating in that scene, nothing merely sentimental; there is the pledge of happy fellowship, sacred and prosperous co-operation. Who will not say, when looking upon scenes of this kind, that the former times were better than these? Have we improved so very much? Is our boasted advancement a reality in very deed? Without pronouncing any opinion upon this, let us consider the inquiry and lay it solemnly to heart. Say, is there a sweeter picture in all domestic history than this? Look at it: a barley field, the blue heaven like a song in colour, the blithe birds, the sharp whisk of the keen sickles amid the falling barley, the reapers turning labour into music, the master saying, "The Lord be with you," the reapers answering, "The Lord bless thee" (ii. 4).

What a welcome Boaz gave to Ruth : "Hearest thou not, my daughter? Go not to glean in another field, neither go from hence, but abide here fast by my maidens" (ii. 8). Ruth was astounded. How did Boaz know anything about her? "Then she fell on her face, and bowed herself to the ground, and said unto him, Why have I found grace in thine eyes, that thou shouldest take knowledge of me, seeing I am a stranger?" (ii. 10). Some people never can be strangers. We may never have seen them before, but to see them once is to own a kinship ; we know their touch, we know their voice, we have seen them before in some dream of love or some vision of sacred fancy; they are strangers only in a very limited sense,—profoundly and truly they are of our own kith and kin, of the same quality of soul and heirs of the same expectation. "Boaz answered and said unto her, It hath fully been shewed me, all that thou hast done unto thy mother in law since the death of thine husband : and how thou hast left thy father and thy mother, and the land of thy nativity, and art come unto a people which thou knewest not heretofore. The Lord recompense thy work, and a full reward be given thee of the Lord God of Israel, under whose wings thou art come to trust" (ii. 11, 12). That is the way to welcome a heathen traveller. Make the pagan feel at once that all the past is forgotten, forgiven, and a new glad morning has dawned upon the enfranchised soul. Said Ruth, Why this welcome? Boaz answered, I know all about thee; I have heard the little dramatic tale; it is full of sweetness and music—God bless thee, my daughter. Yes, our deeds live after us, and go before us, and make a way for us, and come up again and again in many a fashion, and touch society with the spirit of judgment or with the spirit of friendliness. We do not shake off our yesterdays, and sustain no further relation to them; they follow us, they constitute our life, and they give accent and force and meaning to our present deeds.

But Boaz was more than all this. He was a gentleman in every feature, and he was also an unconscious prophet. Who knows all the meaning of his own word? Who can explain all the issue and ultimate relationship of the simplest things which he does, in the Church, or in the harvest-field, or in any sphere of life ? We know not what part we are taking in the building-up of God's fabric. Sometimes when we little suppose we are doing anything at all towards building the temple of God, we are working most industriously and definitely in that direction. Boaz was but a farmer, a valiant man and wealthy, beloved by his servants, prosperous in his day ; but beyond all that he was permitted, by the grace of God, to fore-cast the future. He was more than himself, or his whole self he had failed to recognise. This is the view we must take of life if we would live largely and usefully in the broadest sense of that term. Sometimes the work appears to come back to us without profit or gracious answer ; but we know that it shall not always be so : the preaching of the word is seed cast into the ground, and the seed does not grow in one night. Sometimes life's monotony wearies us ; we say, As it was yesterday, so it is to-day, and to-morrow will see no change ; and we are overborne by this sad dreariness. Let us look back into history in order that our cheerfulness may be revived. Men do not know what they are doing, even in prosecuting their ordinary avocations. The barley harvest may be as a sacrament, the open field an unroofed church, the gracious words spoken to strangers may come back again in prophecy and its sublimest fulfilment.

Boaz was a type of Christ. Boaz was the Goel of his family. Boaz was the next-of-kin—in other words, he was the Goel. What part did the Goel play in the Hebrew family ? The Goel was the redeemer in the first place, and the Goel was the avenger in the second place. In both these respects Boaz was a type of Christ. Let us understand something in detail which ought to be interesting to the youngest readers respecting the functions of the Goel. If a Hebrew was so poor, reduced to such extremity of distress, that he had to mortgage—to use a modern expression—his land, to encumber it, to bring it under obligation to a stranger, it was the business of the Goel of that particular family to redeem that land, and restore it to its rightful owner. When the silver trumpets of Jubilee sounded, all the land was free ; but even in the years between one Jubilee and another, if the Hebrew tiller was so reduced as to be obliged to borrow upon his land, the Goel was bound to redeem it. The land itself never could be ceded. The Hebrew had no land to sell; he had only current rights, temporary interests, immediate advantages to dispose of: the land itself belonged to Israel, and in the year of Jubilee that doctrine was broadly asserted and minutely realised: but, as we have said, in the meantime men might be reduced to poverty, or be glad to avail themselves of the kindness of those who were round about them, or even to ask the stranger and alien to lend them something upon their lease. Then came up the next-of-kin—literally, the Goel—and redeemed the land, and restored the citizen to his place in the commonwealth of Israel. Is not Jesus Christ our Goel in this respect? Are we not all poor, dispossessed of everything, mean, self-helpless? That was our condition before God; that was the condition upon which Christ looked when he took up his position as our Goel, or Redeemer. But we have said the Goel was next-of-kin—was Christ akin to man? That was his peculiar glory in his official or redeeming capacity: "Forasmuch then as the children are partakers of flesh and blood, he also himself likewise took part of the same . . . he took not on him the nature of angels"—then he would not have been akin to us—" but he took on him the seed of Abraham," and thus became our Kinsman; thus he was not ashamed to call us brethren. As our elder Brother, he is our Goel. He has come to redeem humanity, to enrich it with infinite and eternal wealth.

Take another view of the Goel's function in Hebrew history. If a Hebrew sold himself into the service of another Hebrew he lost none of his rights; his citizenship was still recognised, and his prospects were honoured and fulfilled; but if the Hebrew sold himself into servitude to an alien or heathen, it was the place of his Goel or next-of-kin to come forth and emancipate him; there could be no slaves of that kind in Israel: the next-of-kin was bound to espouse the cause of the bondman, to redeem him, to break his chain, to buy him off, and to invest him with liberty. Here, again, at the time when the trumpets of Jubilee sounded, liberty was proclaimed to all; but in the meantime the Goel took up his function and discharged his gracious responsibility: he redeemed the slave. Herein it is easy to see how Boaz was a type of Christ. We were all bondmen, sold under sin, heavy

laden with the chains of bondage; and when there was no eye
to pity, no arm to save, our Goel pitied, and his right arm
wrought deliverance.   He is our Emancipator, our Redeemer.
Job said, "I know that my Goel liveth."   That noble verse
loses nothing of its best meaning by the use of the Hebrew
word.   In the English Bible the reading is, "I know that my
Redeemer liveth;" but the verse is still invested with ineffable
meaning and suggestiveness when it is read: I know that my
Goel—my next-of-kin—liveth, and that he will appear to redeem
and bless.

There was another function—namely, the function of the
Avenger.   If an Israelite had been wronged, injured, or slain,
who was to see to the rectification of the case?   who was to
demand and execute justice?   The Goel.   This he was bound to
do.   It was not left to his choice whether he would do so or
not; it was the prerogative and place of the Goel to avenge
wrong, injustice, murder.   And is there not an avenging element
in the priesthood and sovereignty of the Lord Jesus Christ in his
Church?   Do we take a complete view of the Saviour when we
think of him only as meek, lowly, gentle, loving, forbearing—a
Man all tears?   He can be described by such compassionate and
gracious terms; not a word can be too endearing to apply to the
Son of God in his office in relation to sin-destroyed humanity;
but we read also of "the wrath of the Lamb;" he rules sometimes
"with a rod of iron:" in some cases he "dashes" the enemy
"in pieces like a potter's vessel;" and men are exhorted to "kiss
the Son lest he be angry," to make peace with him "whilst his
wrath is kindled but a little;" into that mystery of wrath we
may not enter; who would force his way into that thunder-
cloud?   Enough it is to recognise its blackness and its terribleness, and to remember that "it is a fearful thing to fall into the
hands of the living God."   Whatever hell may be, it is something
indescribably awful.   There all thinkers may agree.   Whilst
controversy may rage about definitions and the right application
of terms, about etymologies and figures of speech, there remains
the tremendous and unchangeable reality, that whatever the fate
of the impenitent sinner may be, it is inconceivably and indescribably appalling.   (My soul, come not thou into that secret!)

Boaz, as we have said, was described as the next-of-kin—literally, the Goel—and to their own Goel all the distressed families of Israel had a right to look. Blessed be God, we have been invested in that right by Jesus Christ. He desires to be looked to; he invites our appeal; he says in effect : Tell me how your land is situated, what burdens rest upon it ; tell me what are your domestic conditions : is the father dead ? Is the house full of widowhood and orphanhood, and all forms of distress ? Relate all the circumstances to me ; I am your next-of-kin, and I will deliver and redeem, avenge and bless. Into his ever-listening ear pour all the tale of human want and woe, as speaking to One who is akin—next-of-kin—the Goel of humanity. We need the assurance that there is some such Goel. At times all things seem to be against us, and no voice is lifted up in our defence and for our comfort : all men seem to forsake us and flee. In that hour we need some such inspiration as comes from the assurance that our next-of-kin—our Goel—will never leave us nor forsake us. When we need him most he is nearest to us.

Not only was Boaz a Goel, he was a Menuchah, or rest, in whose protection Ruth found security. Menuchah means an asylum of rest, a protection of honour, a security that cannot be violated; and then in its last signification it means the very omnipotence and pavilion of God. In this respect Boaz was the type of Christ. In chapter iii. 1, we read, " Then Naomi her mother in law said unto her, My daughter, shall I not seek rest for thee—shall I not seek a Menuchah for thee—that it may be well with thee ? " The house of her husband was called the Menuchah of the wife—that is to say, the asylum of rest and protection. The orphanage is the Menuchah of the orphan. All homes, Christian institutions, asylums founded in the spirit of Christ and for the use of Christ, might be appropriately termed Menuchahs—places of rest, asylums of security, pavilions defended by the almightiness of God. There was a certain land promised to Israel. In the hope of attaining that land Israel lived and toiled for many a year. What would Israel call that promised land ? The Menuchah. To reach that Menuchah was the hope of Israel ; to stand upon the soil of that promised Canaan was to be sure of the nearness and protection of the God of Abraham, of Isaac, and of Jacob. Then, in its highest religious meaning, the Menuchah signifies the peace, favour, rest and protection of God. Jesus Christ said, " Come unto me, all ye that labour and are heavy laden, and I will be your Menuchah —I will give you rest "—sabbatic rest, complete peace, infinite reconciliation, the harmony in which there is no discord, the rest unbroken by a dream, undisturbed by any fear in the night-watches. All this is made the more vividly clear if we look at the case of Boaz and Ruth. Boaz was a near kinsman. There was one nearer still, but he declined to take up the functions of the family Goel ; then what we might call the Goelship fell to the lot of Boaz, and he assumed the responsibility and prosecuted the task. Then Boaz was, moreover, a rest—the man who afforded a sense of security to the poor wandering Moabitess. He was the Menuchah, the grand living asylum, in whose love Ruth found peace and security.

> " She stood breast-high amid the corn,
>   Clasped by the golden light of morn,
>   Like the sweetheart of the sun,
>   Who many a glowing kiss had won.
>   On her cheeks an autumn flush
>   Deeply ripened—such a blush
>   In the midst of brown was born,
>   Like red poppies grown with corn.
>   Round dark eyes her tresses fell,
>   Which were blackest none could tell,
>   But long lashes veiled a light
>   That had else been all too bright.
>   And her hat, with shady brim,
>   Made her tressy forehead dim ;
>   Thus she stood amid the stocks,
>   Praising God with sweetest looks.
>   ' Sure,' I said, ' Heaven did not mean
>   Where I reap thou should'st but glean ;
>   Lay thy sheaf adown and come,
>   Share my harvest and my home.' "

Transfer all these images to the Lord Jesus Christ, and see how beautifully they apply in every instance to the Messiah. He is our Goel ; he will mightily redeem us : he will take back from the hands of the enemy all the prey which the enemy has seized ; the foe will have to deliver up whatever he has possessed himself of that belongs to God and humanity.   The Goel will see us put into a secure position ; a position of righteousness, of solid defence, of truth and probity.   Then is he not the soul's Menuchah—the soul's resting-place, the soul's eternal asylum ? Have we not sought peace everywhere and failed in the pursuit ? Have we not hewn out to ourselves cisterns, and found them to be broken cisterns that could hold no water ?   Have we not made a bed for ourselves in the wilderness, and found that we were pillowing our heads upon the sharp thorns ?   Amid all life's tumult and the maddening pain of the soul, there has come this sweet voice : Come unto me, all ye that labour and are heavy laden, and I will be your Goel, your Menuchah ; I will mightily deliver you and lead you into the rest of God.   This is what we teach about Jesus Christ.   These are the sublime truths we associate with his name.   In all history men have needed a Goel or a deliverer, a Menuchah or a rest ; and all the anxiety, strife, pain of the world's history, seemed to point in the direction of One who himself would combine the strength of the Goel and the grace of the Menuchah.

Thus a great historical gate is opened.   Boaz was the father of Obed, Obed was the father of Jesse, and Jesse was the father of David—the darling of Israel and the man after God's own heart.   How little we know what we are doing !   Who can tell what the next link in the chain will be ?   Let us persevere in our work as God may give us opportunity and grace.   Sometimes it is very heavy ; sometimes quite dreary ; sometimes the sun is practically blotted out, and all the sky is in mourning. But if we rest on eternal principles, if we believe in the omnipotence of God, we shall live to see the return of the sun, and in the brightness of morning we shall forget the blackness and the sadness of night.

Looking at the Book of Ruth as a whole, we are struck with the marvellous working of providence.   The book had a sad opening.   It opened like a cloudy day.   It began with famine and misery, and went onward into widowhood twice told ; and the first chapter is like a rain of tears.   We could not understand why it should be so—why there should be a famine in Israel. The famine might have been otherwhere : why not afflict the heathen with famine, and let Israel, and Christian peoples, as we now term them, enjoy bountiful harvests, pulling down their barns to build greater ? Why does the lightning strike the very steeple of the church ? On the story goes, and God is working in it all. In the darkness his hand seems to be groping after something that he may loop on to something that had gone before. The movement of God is a movement of very subtle and intricate connections. Sometimes we wonder how the next link can be found, and often it is found in the night-time when we cannot see either the finder or the link he has found. Look at such portion of society as is open to our survey, and see how wonderful are the associations which have been made in life—the unexpected relationships, the strange coincidences, the marvellous creations of help, deliverance, and friendship culminating in the most practical affection. How are these people brought to-gether ? There was no plan in it on the human side ; there was nothing on the human side but surprise ; yet how the movement has proceeded, and how out of mysteries has happiness been consolidated ! You heard a discourse, and it became the turning-point in your life; you listened to a prayer, and whilst it was arising to heaven you made solemn oath and vow that you would be better, and that vow has been redeemed : you went into a public assembly, and saw a face, the seeing of which has changed the whole course of your life. The providence of God is not an Old Testament story ; it is the action of the day, the movement now circling around us,—the rustling of the leaves, the ploughing up of the land, the singing of the birds, the occurrences at home and abroad. Behold the hand of the living God, and in that hand put your trust. The most mysterious action of this providence was the bringing-in of the Gentiles. A new thing has been wrought in Israel : a Moabitess is numbered among the chosen children. Now that we read the story backwards we see the meaning of it all. Reading it as the facts occurred, the reading was often rough and most difficult. How true it is that we must wait to the end to see the real meaning of the beginning ! When God's way is finished, God's way will be clear. We ought to take an interest in the introduction of Ruth into the sacred lineage, because she was the first-fruits of the people to whom we belong. She was a heathen woman, an outsider, a

Gentile, and we belonged once to that outlawed class. Mean it is of us to say we do not take any interest in the conversion ot distant nations, when we ourselves were once a distant nation, and have been converted to the faith and crown of Christ. We are not true to our own history, or grateful for our own deliverance, in the degree in which we are indifferent to the conversion of those who are afar off. Ruth was our first-fruits; Ruth was our kinswoman in the larger sense. Blessed be God for the introduction of our sister into Israel. She was in the direct line of the Son of God. The Gentile woman became a progenitor ot God's own Christ. A strange genealogy! Having perused it line by line we know what it is :—the great king, the unknown man, the harlot, the Gentile Ruth,—they all stand there, a symbolic humanity, so that when the Son of God comes, he comes not in one direction alone, not as born of the Jew only, but of a line of kings ; in him all men are gathered up—the mightiest, the weakest, the wanderer, the homeless. Verily this Man was the Son of God—the Incarnate Deity !

NOTE.

IF the PEOPLE'S BIBLE has to be limited to twenty-five volumes, and certainly I do not think it would be wise seriously to increase the number, it is evident that the point has been reached when condensation must begin. In my judgment compression will be least felt in the books which come between Ruth and Job, not only because they are almost wholly historical, but principally because they are marked by much repetition of detail. This explanation would seem to be necessary in view of considerable change of method within the indicated limits: when we come to the Book of Job we shall need all the space which can be allowed, for in that immortal drama the battles of the world are fought. Were I to mark down what might be called my chronological experience as a Bible reader, I should not hesitate to say that, up to this moment, my careful perusal of the Bible has increasingly confirmed my faith in its divine inspiration and authority. Without proceeding one page beyond the Book of Ruth, I know of a surety that the preceding portions of the Bible are not the work of inventors, dreamers, or impostors. The composition is too artless for a schemer, the history is too vivid for a dreamer, and the morality is too exacting for a libertine. My knowledge of the Bible increases my reverence for it in every aspect.

THE FIRST BOOK OF SAMUEL.

PRAYER.

ALMIGHTY GOD, thou comfortest those that be bowed down. Thou liftest up those whose souls cleave unto the dust. The Lord is very pitiful and kind, and truly his mercy endureth for ever. It comes to us before the light of the morning, it remains with us when the sun has gone down, it is our guardian by night, it doth beset us behind and before and defend us from all evil. We desire, therefore, humbly to recognise thy mercy in the whole course of our life; we would see it everywhere giving strength and beauty, and meaning and pathos, to all the affairs of our daily history. Help us evermore to know that our power is in thy mercy; that we have no strength but in thy strength; that out of thy fulness alone can we receive grace upon grace. May we be released from all worldly memories, from all tormenting anxieties. May our souls be led away into the light! May our spirits be blessed with unspeakable peace! Ever teach us how to pray. May the desires of our heart be pure; may our purposes before God be simple, and may our whole supplication rise from the Saviour's cross, that even in our prayers we may know the mystery of self-sacrifice. What we pray, we pray in the Mediator's name; there is one God and one Mediator between God and man, the Man Christ Jesus, through whom, the Child of Bethlehem, the Man of sorrows, the mighty and only Redeemer of our souls, we offer every desire of our hearts. Forgive our sins. Cleanse our thoughts by the inspiration of the Holy Ghost. Establish thy counsels in our hearts that they may be repronounced in our daily life; and may our whole course be elevated and sanctified by the ministry of the Holy Spirit. Now what wait we for, but for the opening of heaven, that we may receive the blessing we have no room to contain, that we may be satisfied with the peace which passeth understanding! Unto the Father and the Son and the Holy Ghost, whom we adore as Three Persons in one God, be the kingdom and the power and the glory, world without end. Amen.

1 Samuel 1.

1. Now there was a certain man [literally, one man] of Ramathaim-zophim [abbreviated to la-Ramah. The village of Ramah was built on two hills], of mount Ephraim [the hill country of Ephraim], and his name was Elkanah, the son of Jeroham, the son of Elihu, the son of Tohu, the son of Zuph, an

Ephrathite [this tracing through four generations agrees with the family registers in 1 Chron. vi. The epithet belongs to Elkanah, not to Zuph]:

2. And he had two wives [Lamech was the first to violate the law of one wife only]; the name of the one was Hannah [grace or favour], and the name of the other Peninnah [modern: Margaret, coral or pearl]; and Peninnah had children, but Hannah had no children.

3. And this man went up out of his city yearly [to the feast of unleavened bread] to worship, and to sacrifice unto the Lord of hosts [the first time in the Old Testament that the name Jehovah Sabaoth occurs,—it occurs two hundred and sixty times in the Old Testament. It is used sixty times by Isaiah, and about eighty times by Jeremiah] in Shiloh [rest: a sacred city in Ephraim]. And the two sons of Eli, Hophni and Phinehas, the priests of the Lord, were there [Eli himself is not mentioned. He was still high priest, but too old to take part in the offering of sacrifice].

4. ¶ And when the time was that Elkanah offered, he gave to Peninnah his wife, and to all her sons and her daughters, portions:

5. But unto Hannah he gave a worthy portion [one portion for two persons: a double portion]; for he loved Hannah: but the Lord had shut up her womb.

6. And her adversary [her rival] also provoked her sore, for to make her fret [so much for polygamy !], because the Lord had shut up her womb.

7. And as he did so year by year, when she went up to the house of the Lord, so she provoked her; therefore she wept, and did not eat [of her portion].

8. Then said Elkanah her husband to her, Hannah, why weepest thou? and why eatest thou not? and why is thy heart grieved? am not I better to thee than ten sons [a round number to signify many]?

9. ¶ So Hannah rose up after they had eaten in Shiloh [after the sacrificial meal was over; literally, after she had eaten in Shiloh, and after she had drunk], and after they had drunk. Now Eli the priest sat upon a seat [a chair, or throne of state] by a post of the temple [palace] of the Lord.

10. And she was in bitterness of soul [literally, bitter of soul], and prayed unto the Lord, and wept sore ["Prayers and tears are the saints' great guns and scaling-ladders."—*Luther*].

11. And she vowed a vow, and said, O Lord of hosts, if thou wilt indeed look on the affliction of thine handmaid, and remember me, and not forget thine handmaid, but wilt give unto thine handmaid a man child, then I will give him unto the Lord all the days of his life, and there shall no razor come upon his head [a perpetual Nazarite].

12. And it came to pass, as she continued praying [as she multiplied to pray] before the Lord, that Eli marked her mouth.

13. Now Hannah, she spake in [to] her heart; only her lips moved, but her voice was not heard: therefore Eli thought she had been drunken [made possible by the moral degradation of the time].

14. And Eli said unto her, How long wilt thou be drunken [knowing that she had newly risen from a feast]? put away thy wine from thee.

15. And Hannah answered and said, No, my lord, I am a woman of a sorrowful spirit : I have drunk neither wine nor strong drink, but have poured out my soul before the Lord.

16. Count not thine handmaid for a daughter of Belial [the devil] : for out of the abundance of my complaint and grief have I spoken hitherto.

17. Then Eli answered and said, Go in peace : and the God of Israel grant thee thy petition that thou hast asked of him.

18. And she said, Let thine handmaid find grace in thy sight. So [having cast her burden on the Lord] the woman went her way, and did eat, and her countenance was no more sad.

19. ¶ And they rose up in the morning early, and worshipped before the Lord, and returned, and came to their house to Ramah : and Elkanah knew Hannah his wife ; and the Lord remembered her.

20. Wherefore [and] it came to pass, when the time was come about [literally, at the revolution of the days] after Hannah had conceived, that she bare a son, and called his name Samuel [heard of God], saying, Because I have asked him of the Lord.

21. And the man Elkanah, and all his house, went up to offer unto the Lord the yearly sacrifice, and his vow [vows were characteristic of this particular age of the Judges].

22. But Hannah went not up ; for she said unto her husband, I will not go up until the child be weaned [weaning took place very late among the. Hebrews—usually for two years, sometimes for three], and then I will bring him, that he may appear before the Lord, and there abide for ever.

23. And Elkanah her husband said unto her, Do what seemeth thee good ; tarry until thou have weaned him ; only the Lord establish his word [may the Lord fulfil his designs]. So the woman abode, and gave her son suck until she weaned him.

24. ¶ And when she had weaned him, she took him up with her, with three bullocks [one for a burnt offering, the two were yearly], and one ephah of flour, and a bottle of wine, and brought him unto the house of the Lord in Shiloh : and the child was young.

25. And they slew a bullock, and brought the child to Eli.

26. And she said, Oh my lord, as thy soul liveth [an oath peculiar to the Books of Samuel and to the Books of Kings], my lord, I am the woman that stood by thee here, praying unto the Lord.

27. For this child I prayed ; and the Lord hath given me my petition which I asked of him.

28. Therefore also I have lent him to the Lord ; as long as he liveth he shall be lent to the Lord. And he ["Neither Elkanah nor Samuel have been mentioned, and cannot therefore be meant. Hannah must be the subject, and the masculine of the verb is used, as in v. 7, though the subject is feminine."—*The Speaker's Commentary*] worshipped the Lord there.

1 Samuel i. 20.

"Samuel . . . because I have asked him of the Lord."

THE BIRTH OF SAMUEL.

HANNAH, the wife of Elkanah, besought the Lord for a man child. This draws our attention to the scope of human prayer. Men cannot pray by rule. We do but mock men when we say, You must pray for this and not for that. Such an exhortation may do for a man when his heart is not inflamed by the passion of godly desire ; it may do for him in his coldest and most indifferent mental states. But when he is in his most vehement and determined moods, he cannot be fettered and limited by such exhortations. We need something more for our guidance than mere maxims. A maxim is too narrow for life. We need principles which can shrink into maxims and can expand into revelations as the exigencies of life may require. Sometimes we are cold and dull,—then a maxim will do : sometimes our strength rises to full flood,—then we need inspiration. You cannot conduct life in its highest phases and its intensest desires by any set of maxims. You can only control and elevate life by having principles which can shrink and expand,—adapt themselves when man's moral temperature rises, when his strength rises, and suit themselves to all the varying phases and wants of his life. Tell Hannah that she ought not to pray for what God has not seen fit to give her, and she scorns your formal piety and your tabulated counsels. Why ? She is not in a mood to receive that kind of instruction ; there is a hunger in her heart ; through her own love she sees far into the love of God ; and by the eagerness of her desire she goes far away, with bleeding weary feet, from beaten paths and accepted roads, that she may bind God by the very importunateness of her love. That is not the kind of woman into whose ear you can drop a little formal maxim with any effect. Your religion will be to her profanity, if you cannot address her in a higher tone—meet her just where her soul is. She is borne away by the passion of her desire ; there is one dominating force in her nature that transfigures everything, that defies difficulties, that surmounts obstacles, and that waits with trembling nervous patience till

God come. What is love if it be not fiery? What is prayer if it be not the heart on a blaze? Prayer is not mere articulation; prayer is not mere words. Prayers are battles; prayers are the thunders which call for God when he seems to be far away!

Yonder is a wild goat, living on stony hills and desert places. He has wandered a long way from pasture, from food of any kind. In the madness of his hunger he sees on farther edge, five hundred fathoms above the level, just one little tuft of grass—the only green thing within a circuit of miles. It is a dangerous place, but then he is in a dangerous condition. He climbs to it,—the rock almost trembles under him. A moment more, and, hundreds of fathoms below, he lies a bleeding mass. But impelled by hunger, he does what only the fierce courage of despair dare do. So it is with that keener hunger of human souls. We do sometimes pray for things that lie away from the line of ordinary devotion; we would not pray for them but for that over-mastering, irresistible, spiritual force that holds us in its mighty hand. If we were in coolness and sobriety of spirit and temper, we should be able to reason about it and to put things together and to draw inferences. Man is not fully man when he stands upon his feet; he touches the highest point of his manhood when he lifts the pinions of faith and hope, and goes off into the Unknown if haply he may find God! If you do not know what the hunger is you do not know what the prayer is. You cannot feel as Hannah did without you have been in great straits, and when for the time you have been the willing victim of a glowing and grand desire. But is there not a limit? Yes, there is a limit, and it is sometimes well not to look at it in the light of a limit. It is true that we are shut up like the sea and watched like the whale, but that is no reason why we should shrivel into a pool or dwindle into a minnow. What is the limit of our prayer? This: "Not my will, but thine, be done!" Is that a limit?—it is glorious liberty! Not my will, but thine,—not a little will, but a great will,—not my thought, but thine,—not my love, but thine! Is that a limit? It is the lark rising from its field-nest into the boundless liberty of the firmament! Truly we do not limit ourselves when we exchange the creature for the Creator. When we take up our little thought

and say, "Lord, this is what we want,—but not our will but
thine be done," do we then throw away the greater for the
less? It is a contrast, and only such a contrast as you find in
the earth and heaven, in the blazing sun and the misty night.

Need we say that there are some things which are not fit
subjects for prayer? that there are some things which do not
lie directly in the devotional line? For example, no man is at
liberty to pray for wealth, merely as such. "Lord, give me
riches," would not be prayer; it would be profanity, it would
be covetousness carried to the point of blasphemy. Wealth, as
such, does not lie in the line of devotion, but far away from it,
and can only be made incidental to it by certain moral considerations which the possessor of wealth may possibly know nothing
at all about. Looked at in itself, Hannah's prayer was selfish
and poor in its spiritual tone; but the woman did not know
what she was praying for altogether. It is so with us in our
highest devotions. God inspires the prayer, and then answers
it; dictates the language, and then satisfies the petition. So
that persons who are asking for what may be called a little
ordinary daily blessing, may, in reality, be asking for a gift the
influence of which shall reach through ages, shall palpitate
through eternity. Hannah says, Give me a man child! She
knows not the destinies that are involved in that prayer. And
that prayer is not her own. Her petition is but the echo of a
higher voice. Herein is the mystery of prayer. There be cold,
formal, rudimentary prayers; there be labial prayers—prayers
that come from the lips only; and there be words which are
revelations of Christ—subdued sighings of the soul, which God
prompts and regulates, and which are sent for the trial of our
patience and strength, that God may bring in upon our little
petition a greater answer than our fancy ever dreamed, than our
love ever dared expect!

We shall see in what an extraordinary mental and spiritual
state Hannah was, as we read from the twelfth to the sixteenth
verses :—

"And it came to pass, as she continued praying before the Lord, that Eli
marked her mouth. Now Hannah, she spake in her heart; only her lips
moved, but her voice was not heard : therefore Eli thought she had been

drunken. And Eli said unto her, How long wilt thou be drunken? put away thy wine from thee. And Hannah answered and said, No, my lord, I am a woman of a sorrowful spirit: I have drunk neither wine nor strong drink, but have poured out my soul before the Lord. Count not thine handmaid for a daughter of Belial: for out of the abundance of my complaint and grief have I spoken hitherto."

A beautiful speech of the heart! Alas, men may be drunk, but not with wine! There is grief that has upon us all the effect of poison in the blood. There are anxieties that make us stagger to and fro like drunken men. There are paroxysms, hungers, and straits in life which take away from us our balance and equipoise, and which make us look almost insane in the eyes of men who are calm and cool, and who are limited by the ordinary conditions of life. The ordinary cannot judge the extraordinary. A man when he has all his senses about him, and would therefore feel himself in his most judicious mood, cannot reach certain cases—they lie mile on mile beyond him. Only grief can understand grief; only poetry can understand poetry; only love can interpret love; and only a woman in Hannah's mood can understand the trembling of Hannah's lips. We should be careful how we judge one another. Here is Eli, a priest of the living God, calling a woman drunken,—when she is insane in worship, when she is mad in the ecstasy of waiting upon God. There is a madness that is not lunacy; there is an insanity that is the sublimest serenity. Priests do not always understand people. Official persons seldom do understand extra officials. Eli had been accustomed to look upon persons, and to see them behave themselves under certain limits; he had observed them displaying certain decorums when they came into the neighbourhood of the holy place. But here is something he never saw before; and the priest of the living God, ordained and consecrated —who ought to have had a word of charity for the lowliest creature beneath his feet—instantly, with that little remnant of devil that is in the best men, says, "Thou art drunken!" Oh, when will priests be charitable! When shall we put the better and not the worse construction on extraordinary signs and tokens! When shall we speak hopefully! "Men would be better if we better deemed them."

There are three remarkable things in this case. First: Here is a religious household disquieted by one unhappy element. Hannah's life was lived under the harrow of Peninnah's reproach. The household was a religious one. Elkanah went out of the city to worship and to sacrifice unto the Lord of hosts in Shiloh. Hannah was a praying woman. We have every reason to suppose that, speaking in general terms, the household was markedly religious; yet there was shot through it one unhappy, disquieting, poisoning element. Let us get away from all that is merely local in the incident, and dwell upon the principle that one sinner destroyeth much good. The head of the house is a worshipping man, reverent, strong in faith, punctilious in religious observances; those that are round about him have religious convictions and religious strength. Yet there is something in the household—just one little microscopic thing—that spoils the heaven. You cannot exhort people to get out of that. The element is little and insignificant in itself; but still it requires a vital remedy. The disquieting cause is different in different houses. In almost every house there is some little spiteful spirit; in almost every family there is somebody that has the power of sneering at other people; in most households undoubtedly there are members who can drop just one scalding drop into a sore place and make it sorer. It can be done so that you cannot print it and publish it; it can be done so that you cannot report it; it can be done so that you can only feel it. These are the miseries that spoil many lives. Who are we—happily situated, having little or nothing to interrupt our domestic joy—that we should in an off-handed manner exhort people to be more patient, and to be this and that and the other, when we ourselves could not be so if we were under the same circumstances? Understand, it is these little, insignificant things that destroy the happiness of a human home. Not great fights, not periodical revolutions in the domestic state; but hasty little words, untimely shruggings of the shoulder, and sneers that are no sooner on the lip than away. What is the cure for all that kind of disease? There is only one cure, and that is, Crucifixion with Jesus Christ. Observe, not mere crucifixion. You may nail a man's hand—both hands, both feet—and crush thorns into his temple till he is bathed in blood; but you may not touch the devil that is in him. He must be crucified; but he must be crucified with Christ in his spirit, thoughts, and purposes. Sympathy with the cross of Christ takes out of human nature the last drop, the final dreg and sediment of evil, hatred, and bitterness ; and nothing but that will touch the disease. We may compromise ; we may bear and forbear ; we may make our life a game at setting up little pieces of wood, and piling up little cards in a certain shape, keeping every breath of wind away lest the little structure should be overturned. That is not life. The only true life is based on right, love, nobleness, law, charity, kindness. All this we find only in that manly, womanly, godly Heart that burst on Calvary.

The second remarkable thing is : A religious use of a daily provocation. Peninnah persecuted Hannah daily ; laughed at her, mocked her, jeered her, provoked her sore to make her fret ; provoked her to tears, to fasting, to grief of heart. Hannah was in bitterness of soul and wept sore. What use did she make of this daily torment ? Do not let us fix upon the one particular thing that she had in view, or the one special difficulty that annoyed and perplexed her ; but get into the principle of the case. What was the use which she made of this daily torment ? It was a religious use. She prayed unto the Lord ; she rose up and went forward that she might pray mightily before God ; she spake in her heart and she poured out her soul before God. That was conquest,—that was victory ! There is a possibility of having a daily annoyance, and yet turning that daily annoyance into an occasion of nearer and nearer approach to God. Let us then endeavour to turn all our household griefs, family torments into occasions of profound worship and loving homage to God. It was in human nature to avenge the insult; to cry out angrily against the woman who delighted in sneering and in provoking. But there is something higher than human nature, something better. And is it not our business, is it not better, indeed, that we should try, at all events, to get away from the human nature, which we are too prone to worship in its generalisation, and seek the divine nature, which has in it the interpretation of every difficulty and the remedy for every affliction ? It could not be easy to bear the daily annoyance. A footfall heard in the house might mean a coming sorrow ; a sound heard in the distance might awaken painful **memories; a turn of a** sentence, though it might be unintentional and unconscious on the part of the guilty individual, might afflict the soul. The worst suffering is subtle and unspeakable, and hardly to be told or to be hinted at,—made up of ten thousand little things, any one of which is not worthy of a moment's consideration. Yet here is a woman who was able to triumph over all these things, and to bring them in as helps to her continual prayer.

The third thing that is remarkable is,—the religious recognition of family mercies. When the son was born—the son for whom Hannah had been praying many a day—she called his name Samuel, "heard of God." Let us dwell carefully on this point, because everybody is embraced in the application of this truth. We have prayed for a long time for a given object; that object has at length been yielded to us. What then?

"And Hannah prayed, and said, My heart rejoiceth in the Lord, mine horn is exalted in the Lord: because I rejoice in thy salvation. There is none holy as the Lord; for there is none beside thee: neither is there any rock like our God. . . . The Lord maketh poor, and maketh rich: he bringeth low, and lifteth up. He raiseth up the poor out of the dust, and lifteth up the beggar from the dunghill, to set them among princes, and to make them inherit the throne of glory: for the pillars of the earth are the Lord's, and he hath set the world upon them. He will keep the feet of his saints, and the wicked shall be silent in darkness; for by strength shall no man prevail" (ii. 1, 2, 7, 8, 9).

So sang the rejoicing woman whose prayer had been answered. Praise should always follow answered prayer.

It was thus with one man. He was very ill; a great strong man in his day; yet disease touched him, shrivelled him up, laid him upon a lowly bed, made him pray to the humblest creature in his house for favours hour after hour. As he lay there, in his lowliness and weakness, he said, "If God would raise me up I would be a new man, I would be a devout worshipper in the sanctuary, I would live to his glory." And God lifted him up again; did not break the bruised reed, did not quench the smoking flax, but permitted the man to regain his faculties. And he was not well one month before he became as worldly as he was before his affliction. He prayed as if his heart loved God; and when he got his health back again he was a practical atheist—he was virtually the basest of blasphemers.

It was thus with another man. He had nothing when he started in life. He used to run errands; to sweep doorsteps, and burnish bells in order that he might get some little gifts to buy his next meal with; and he went on suffering daily. He said, "If God would but bring a turn upon my fortune so that I could make something, I would turn all his gifts to the blessing of my fellow-men; I would show the true use of riches; I would be a Christian; in the midst of my abounding prosperity, I would give a spiritual meaning to all the material gifts of God." His little was doubled, then his little became much, and his much became more, and he became,—what? He would not look at a poor man; he was ashamed to be seen of men who knew him in his low estate; he was a conceited, swaggering fool! Now the reverse in both these cases is possible. It is possible to be lifted up from the bed of affliction and become a burning, shining light in fulfilment of a vow. It is possible to get on from nothing to little, from little to much, and in the midst of abounding prosperity to be a thankful recipient of God's mercies,—a gentle little child,—made for the time being a steward of God's gifts.

Blessed are the men who have had praying mothers. The influence of that fact they cannot shake off. They may curse and swear, and go to the very boundary of the pit; nay, go into it, and we doubt whether in all their suffering they can ever shake off the influence of having had a praying mother. The mother's devotion comes up in the boy's veneration, love of right, conscientiousness, magnanimous hope, gentle courage. As with the boy and the mother, so with the girl and father. Sex is not a physiological question only. We find the sex element in disposition, in thinking, in quality of strength. Blessed are they who have had a praying ancestry. As for such as have not had praying forefathers, there is no reason why they should be lost and thrown away. God is our Father; and when father and mother forsake us, he will take us up. He will lift the beggars from the dunghill and set them among princes, and make them inherit the throne of glory.

Let no man be cast down. Let those who have had praying

mothers be charged, as by a captain of the Lord of hosts, that they go to the front of the fight, and be the most valorous men in God's camp. Let those who have been born into the world, and have had nothing but darkness and sorrow ever since they came into it, know that Jesus Christ receiveth sinners and eateth with them ; and that when he looks upon a sinner the sinner is transfigured into the son of Abraham,—as when the morning light looks upon a folded flower it opens its beautiful leaves and shows its thankfulness by telling all the secrets of its heart!

SELECTED NOTE.

It is on the mother of Samuel that our chief attention is fixed in the account of his birth. She is described as a woman of a high religious mission. Almost a Nazarite by practice (1 Sam. i. 15) and a prophetess in her gifts (1 Sam. ii. 1), she sought from God the gift of the child for which she longed with a passionate devotion of silent prayer, of which there is no other example in the Old Testament, and when the son was granted, the name which he bore, and thus first introduced into the world, expressed her sense of the urgency of her entreaty—*Samuel*, " the asked or heard of God."

Living in the great age of vows, she had before his birth dedicated him to the office of a Nazarite. As soon as he was weaned, she herself, with her husband, brought him to the tabernacle at Shiloh, where she had received the first intimation of his birth, and there solemnly consecrated him. The form of consecration was similar to that with which the irregular priesthood of Jeroboam was set apart in later times (2 Chron. xiii. 9)—a bullock of three years old (LXX.), loaves (LXX.), an ephah of flour, and a skin of wine (1 Sam. i. 24). First took place the usual sacrifices (LXX.) by Elkanah himself, then, after the introduction of the child, the special sacrifice of the bullock. Then his mother made him over to Eli (i. 25, 28), and (according to the Hebrew text, but not the LXX.) the child himself performed an act of worship.

The hymn which followed on this consecration is the first of the kind in the sacred volume. It is possible that, like many of the Psalms, it may have been enlarged in later times to suit great occasions of victory and the like. But verse 5 specially applies to this event, and verses 7 and 8 may well express the sense entertained by the prophetess of the coming revolution in the fortunes of her son and of her country.

PRAYER.

ALMIGHTY GOD, we are all thine; we are twice thine. Thou didst make us, and not we ourselves, and thou didst redeem us with the precious blood of Christ, and bring us out of a worse than Egyptian bondage. We wrestle not with flesh and blood—against these there is an answer, sure and unchangeable—but with principalities and powers, with spiritual temptations, with difficulties of the soul, with nameless forces and malignest mysteries of darkness. These are our foes; we cannot see them; we cannot touch them or name them; they are here, there, on the right hand, on the left hand, around us, above us, never sleeping, always watching. Against these thou dost call us to do battle; but thou dost call us to put on the armour which thou hast thyself provided, and being clothed in that steel of heaven, we may go on from conquering to conquer, slaying mightily and completely all evil forces and winning the Lord's battles in the Lord's great strength. Thine eye is upon us; it melts with compassion, it gleams with complacency, and if now and again it is bright with anger, we know the justice of the indignation, for we have sinned and done evil in the Lord's sight. We come to thee to find pardon, and through pardon to enjoy peace—yea, to begin the eternal Sabbath of the heavens, the calm of eternity, the peace which passeth all understanding. Thou wilt not disappoint us; if we have made any effort to come to thine house, thou wilt doubly reward us. No man can serve God for nought. If we have put ourselves to any inconvenience, thou wilt surely magnify thy grace towards us, and send a plentiful rain of blessing upon thirsty hearts. Pity us in all our littleness and weakness. Remember that our days when they are all counted are but a handful which a child might carry; and remember that we are made out of the dust of the ground, and that the dust still claims much of us. Remember the difficulty of life: its daily burden, its certain care, its sorrows, so heavy and bitter. Remember the deaths which have bereaved us, the losses which have made us poor the disappointments which have torn and stung our hearts; and then let thy mercy come to us in no few, scanty drops of pity, but in great rains of compassion, and let thy heart be moved towards us in all tenderness and grace. But why should we argue with thee, or plead with thee as if thou wert reluctant? The willingness is upon thy side; thou dost wait to be gracious. Again and again, amid all our peevish reasoning, thou dost remind us that if thou didst not spare thine only Son, but freely gavest him up for us all, how much more wilt thou with him also freely give us all things. We forget the love of the cross, and therefore we doubt the love of the providence. The Lord forgive us   Amen.

"Men abhorred the offering of the Lord.'

THE SONS OF ELI.

ELI was high-priest of the Jews when the ark of the Lord was in Shiloh. His two sons, Hophni and Phinehas, were priests of the Lord. Their office was holy, but their character was corrupt. They touched sacred things with unworthy hands. "The sons of Eli were sons of Belial; they knew not the Lord." Their administration of the priestly office was characterised by the most rapacious selfishness. Hence we read "the sin of the young men was very great before the Lord." Their evil dealings were the subject of public remark and censure. Eli himself heard of these evil dealings on every hand.

"And he said unto them, Why do ye such things? for I hear of your evil dealings by all this people. Nay, my sons; for it is no good report that I hear: ye make the Lord's people to transgress" (vv. 23, 24).

The social consequences, as might be expected, were dreadful. "Like priest, like people." The fountain was impure, and the stream was consequently defiled. "Men abhorred the offering of the Lord." Men were influenced by their leaders; the people were shocked by the priests. Forms remained; sacrifices were offered; ceremonies were observed. Yet the heart had lost its divine love; and religion, no longer the imperial force of the highest life, had become decayed and noisome. It should be observed, that this frank statement of priestly corruption is found in the book of God; it is not an enemy who says this. The inspired record is not a one-sided testimony: inspiration does not undertake to make out a case. We are plainly told in God's book that the priests became sons of Belial; that under the Urim and Thummim there were hearts agitated by the vilest passions; that mighty men sold their strength for momentary indulgence; and that wise men were caught in the snare of the fowler. It was not left for an enemy to reveal the blemishes of the nominally good; God himself tore off the mask

and probed the sore. This should never be forgotten by inquirers who love truth and yield to the claims of honour. It
will not be forgotten by men who wish to know the reality of the
case. Let it stand, therefore, first and foremost a ruling and
determining truth, that throughout God's word God himself constantly reproaches, condemns, curses all evil ; finds out, lifts up,
blesses and crowns with his approval all good. The moral tone
of the Bible must ever be the Bible's most powerful vindication.

The incident shows but too plainly the vital difference between the spiritual and the official. Hophni and Phinehas were
officially amongst the highest men of their day. They bore a
holy name, they pronounced holy words, they were clothed in
emblematic robes. Yet Hophni and Phinehas were men of
Belial. The outside was beautiful; the inside was full of corruption and death. "This people draweth nigh unto me with
their mouth, and honoureth me with their lips ; but their heart is
far from me."

Is there not a lesson here to teachers of Christian truth ? It is
possible for a man to have a pulpit, and to have no God ; to have
a Bible, and no Holy Ghost ; to be employing his lips in uttering
the eloquence of truth, when his heart has gone astray from all
that is true and beautiful and good ; at the very moment his lips
are fired by the words that ought to have converted himself, his
heart is not in his work, it is wandering far off yonder, buying
and selling and getting gain, sucking in poison where it ought to
have extracted honey, making the word of God of none effect,
and causing the people to blaspheme and alienate themselves
from the Most High !

Is there not a lesson here to professors of Christ ? We bear
the holy name, and men have a right to expect the holy deed.
We are to know a discipline that is more than decent, more than
socially irreproachable. We need instruction upon the great
question of spiritual discipline. When a man who professes to
know Christ is found drunk in the streets, we expel him from
the Church, and call that discipline ; when a man is convicted of
some heinous crime, we cut him off from the fellowship of the

Church, and call that the discipline of Christian fellowship. It is nothing of the kind; that is mere decency. There is not a club in the world that cares one iota for its own respectability that would not do the same thing. Ours is to be Christian discipline. When Christian discipline comes into play amongst the priests and the professors of Christ, when the covetous man shall be blown away by a whirlwind of righteous indignation; and the man who spoke but one unkind word shall be seen to be a murderer, and shall be driven from the circle of God's people—who then can stand? Where are Christians, if such be the rule? If an unholy thought be lust,—if the turn of an eye may be practical blasphemy,—if the momentary entertainment of an evil thought, the flash of an evil passion,—if that be held before God to be crime incipient, crime in the germ, crime in reality —who then can stand?

The accusation does not come from an enemy. We are not entitled to say, "It is a foe who speaks, therefore we heed not his calumnious words." God himself brings charges against his nominal Church. "They profess that they know God; but in works they deny him, being abominable, and disobedient, and unto every good work reprobate;" "having a form of godliness, but denying the power thereof." Unto the wicked God saith, "What hast thou to do to declare my statutes, or that thou shouldest take my covenant in thy mouth?" So the indictment comes with irresistible force, and we who best know ourselves are dumb before God.

Yet even here is a mystery,—a strange and wondrous thing. Hophni and Phinehas, officially great and spiritually corrupt; minister after minister falling, defiling his garments, and debasing his name; professor after professor pronouncing the right word with the lips, but never realising it in the life. Such is the history of the Church. In the face of all this, God still employs men to reveal the truth to other men, to enforce his claims upon their attention. Instead of in a moment of righteous anger sweeping the Church floor, so that not a footstep of man might remain upon it, and then calling the world around him, and speaking personally face to face,—he still employs men to

teach men, to "allure to brighter worlds and lead the way."
We have this treasure in earthen vessels. We are called upon
to bear testimony concerning truth,—though we are weak,
blundering, incomplete, and very foolish,—though we hardly ever
say one sentence as we ought to say it, though we preach a
noble doctrine and then throw it down by an ignoble life. Yet
God hath not withdrawn that comfort from us. He still says,
" Son, go work to-day in my vineyard." He still says to Peter
—with the scars all upon him, unhealed, and never to be taken
away, memorials of a great apostasy—" Feed my lambs, feed my
sheep." He still says to the men who forsook him and fled,
" Go ye into all the world, and preach the gospel to every
creature." It is not an indication of our weakness when we are
called to that daily continual trust, without which neither high-
priest nor doorkeeper is safe, the fervent eternal prayer, " Hold
thou me up, and I shall be safe."

The incident shows the deadly result of corruptness in
influential quarters. All quarters, indeed, are influential; yet
some are known to be more influential than others, therefore we
adopt this form of expression. The priests were sons of Belial.
What was the consequence? The people abhorred the offering
of the Lord. The minister is a bad man. What is the consequence? His character is felt through all the congregation.
Men laugh at his speech, jeer at his arguments, and return his
persuasions to his own hollow heart. We are commonly
advised to consider what is said, rather than look at the person
who says it. We should ask, What is the doctrine? not, Who
is the preacher? This advice is partly sound, and partly
fallacious,—fallacious because superficial and incomplete.

We should remember three things in connection with this
advice. First: The natural tendency of men to religious laxity
and indifference. This makes us glad of any excuse to move
further in that direction. Men are not naturally looking out
for spurs and encouragements in the way of righteousness, self-
crucifixion, and self-discipline. Their nature rather seems to say,
" Eat, drink, and be merry, for to-morrow we die." We eagerly
snatch at anything that will afford us a momentary—though we

know it to be unsound—justification of laxness, indifference, and even contempt of religious duty and service.

We should remember secondly : The effect of insincerity upon doctrine. Sincerity is itself an argument. Men who hear us, look for sincerity in us; otherwise, they have a right to say, "This man cannot teach the true doctrine, if in teaching it day by day he is continually hypocritical, insincere, unaffected by his own speech." Take some very high theory about the business, and we may be contradicted. But remember what Christian doctrine is ; then you will see that the moment it enters into the hearer's mind that the speaker is insincere, that consideration has of necessity a powerful and legitimate influence upon the doctrine. Is it possible to speak the truth with a liar's heart ? We know that we are to hear what men say who are in Moses' seat, yet not to do as they do. We know that, speaking ideally and abstractly, we ought continually to distinguish between truth and the speaker of truth, when his character is corrupt and inconsistent with his speech. At the same time there is a sense, profound and terrible, in which a man may be answering his own doctrine, overturning his own argument, and writing folly upon his own philosophy. If his lips pronounce the truth, if his heart contradict it, and his life blaspheme it, what wonder if men—who have a natural tendency towards religious indifference—should believe the life and deny the teaching!

Then we should remember thirdly : The peculiarity of moral teaching in requiring personal illustration. Men cannot understand merely theoretic morals; they must have them personified; they must have them taught by incarnation; and be illustrated in daily life. The artist may teach you to paint a beautiful picture; yet he may have no regard for moral truth. His non-regard for moral truth may not interfere, so far as you can see, with his ability and earnestness as a mere artist. You may go to learn a trade, and your chief in business may be able to teach you so completely as to give you a position in the commercial world, useful, influential, and profitable ; yet that man may tell lies every hour of his life, may break all the commandments of God, and in doing so he may not affect his ability to teach your trade, or artifice, or profession. It is not so in the Church of God. A man's character is his eloquence ; a man's spiritual reality is the argument that wins in the long run ; the soul afire with God's love ; the life that brings out in their beautiful and impressive relief God's exhortations,—these are the things that are most logical, most poetical, most pathetic, most persuasive.

The lesson is to Churches. What are we in our corporate capacity ? Are we holy ? If not we are helping to debase and ruin the world ; we have taken God's leverage to help to undo God's work ! The lesson also applies to heads of houses. If the father be the only bad character in the family, how then ? It is hard work for the sons to be fighting always against the supreme influence of the house. How if the father of the family be continually sending out of him vicious, blighting influences, corrupting young life and chilling young hope ? It applies to principals in business ; it applies to leaders of all kinds. In proportion to the volume of our being and the elevation of our position is our power to extend hurtful influences upon the circles that are round about us. The terribleness of a moral leader falling ! The awfulness of a standard-bearer dropping down ! Well may men cry, " Howl, fir tree ; for the cedar is fallen." Is there no solemn call to preachers, teachers, heads of families, principals in business, leaders of circles, great or small ? When one man falls he may jeopardise a whole community. There are men who can fall, and their falling seems to produce but very little vicious influence upon society. There are other men so eminent in position, so established in reputation, whose falling would seem to bring down the pillars of civilisation, would seem to bring down the very fabric of God's Church ! Herein is another mystery. When priests fall, and ministers play the coward and the liar, and heads of houses eat of the forbidden tree, and influential men go astray,—yet even then God interposes for the truth ; he saves in society the redeeming element, hands it on from the unworthy to the successor who may be more worthy. Thus he preserves the light of the world and the salt of the earth. So God never wants a generation to bless him ; the Redeemer has always near him some who hold his name dearest of all !

On the other hand, we cannot admit the plea that bad leaders are excuse enough for bad followers, when that plea is urged in relation to Christian teaching and life. Nor can we allow that exceptional inconsistency should vitiate the whole Church. There are some persons who are only too glad to avail themselves of this plea. The bad man will say, " Why should I care about religious truth or religious observance, when ministers themselves are false to their own doctrine ? Why should I call upon myself to be consistent and true ? " First, such a theory is inadmissible everywhere else. Why, then, should we allow it to affect the Church ? There is not a circle in the world where such a theory would be thought tenable for a moment. Why then should we apply it in the highest spiritual relations ? We go into an orchard and point to one piece of blemished fruit, and say, " Because there is a blemish upon that piece of fruit the whole orchard is decayed and corrupt." Who would believe it ? There can be found a light coin in every currency in civilisation. Suppose we took up a standard coin under weight and said, " Because this is not of the standard weight, your whole currency is defective, and, as a nation of financiers, you are not worthy of trust." Who would believe it ? We find a man who turns commerce into a species of gambling, and because so found gambling, we say, " The commerce of Britain is founded upon an illegitimate basis, and is not worthy of a moment's consideration." Would you think that sound reasoning, or a fair and noble method of dealing with such questions ? Yet this is exactly how many persons deal with the Church of God. They say, " Look at Hophni and Phinehas ; look at the minister who fell ; look at the Church officer who was expelled from Church fellowship because of his dishonourableness and untruthfulness." Because of these exceptional cases they argue that the doctrine is wrong, that every Christian exhortation is a word that ought to be unheeded.

Secondly, such a theory is instantly destroyed by the fact that Jesus Christ is the Head of the Church. We do not say, " Look at Christians." We say, " Look at Christ." It is to Christ that we appeal continually ; and in that appeal is our strength as Christian advocates or expounders of Christian truth. When a

man says, "Look at the minister," we say, "Look at the Master!"
When a man says, "What do you call this?" we say, "We call
it a copy: yonder is the original—look at that!" When we are
told that Christian professors are very unstable and inconsistent,
we say, "True; but they are not bad because of their Christianity, but because of their want of it." Find in Jesus Christ
one instance of selfishness; find in him one moment's wandering from the right way; point out in his speech one unhallowed
word or one ungenerous dishonourable expression. His life is
before you! Be just and true and manly and right! Find in
Christ's life one thing upon which you can lay your finger and
say, "This is unholy," then you may pray God's lightnings to
strike his Church and consume that which bears his name.
When will men look at Christ, and not at Christians; at the
sun, and not at the little taper? When will they look at the
Redeemer, and not at the half-educated, incomplete, struggling,
and oft-blundering Church?

Then, thirdly, such a theory is never urged but by men who
are in search of excuses for their own corruptness. Who will
undertake to repeat that on 'Change, and in the warehouse? That
is a sermon in a sentence. Such a theory is never urged but by
men who are in search of excuses for their own corruptness. A
man says, "When that one who professed so much Christianity
failed in business, I was on the point of giving up churches
and chapels altogether." Doubtless that would be virtuous on
his part. O fool, and slow of heart to believe the truth of
God! When a man who is all skin and bone, who never felt
volcanic fire in his heart,—never was led away by any dominating tyrannic passion,—hears of another kind of man straying
from the right way, he instantly almost makes up his mind—
what he is pleased to call his mind—to leave the Church. O
fool, and slow of heart! Didst thou profess the name of the
servant or the name of the Master? Didst thou enter the
Church because of the high and illustrious example of the
members of the Christian community, or because, convicted of
sin, thou didst crawl to the cross and feel the healing effect of
that falling blood? Where is reasoning—where is common-
sense—when men say they have given up their Christian pro-

fession because some Christian professors are fickle, untrue, and inconsistent ? We never yet knew a man who made much ado about Christian people's inconsistency who was not—more or less subtly, it might be, with more or less of self-concealment of purpose in the matter—seeking excuses for his own deficiencies, or seeking from his criticism of other people's vice to make his own virtue the more conspicuous.

It were nothing to kill a man,—stab him right through his heart and let him die. But when he is struggling towards light, towards God, and has to fight with all these demoniacal passions and influences round about, over which he seems to have little or no control,—when he just stumbles on the road and they point at him and say, " Ha, ha ! that is your Christianity, is it ? " that is thrice dying, that is intolerable pain ! We know we are inconsistent, we know we are selfish, we cannot boast of ourselves. Yet it hath pleased God to be more merciful to us than men are. It is better to fall into the hands of God than into the hands of men. When he smites it is that he may recover ; when he puts his sword through a man it is that he may slay, not the man, but the disease that is in him ; when he is sharpest with us there are tears in his eyes ; when he punishes us most terribly, when he takes away the one ewe lamb, and barks the fig tree, and sends a blight on the wheat-field, and turns our purposes upside down, —it is that he may save the man. When men criticise us and are harsh with us, by reason of their incompleteness, their criticism often degenerates into malice. When they point a finger at us, it does not always indicate a fault, but oftentimes a triumph over an inconsistency.

We are not to be followers of Hophni and Phinehas. The priest is not God ; the minister is not Jesus Christ ; the professor is not the Redeemer of the world. We must, therefore, insist upon the honest investigation of great principles on the one hand, and specially insist upon the calm, severe scrutiny and study of our Saviour's own personal life and ministry. We have a written revelation. To that revelation our appeal must be made ; to the law and to the testimony must be our challenge. As for those whose satire is so keen, and whose wit is so fluent when it is employed in criticism upon Christian character, wherein they do it and are able to point out something in us that is wrong, let us receive the lesson with all meekness ; they may be right, and we may learn something from an enemy.   It is lawful, according to an ancient maxim, to learn even from a foe.   Wherein their criticism is the result of malice, or brief acquaintance with our character—seeing only edges and glints of us and not the whole nature—let us remember that our sufferings are not to be compared with the sufferings of Jesus Christ.   When he was reviled he reviled not again, when he suffered he threatened not ; he gave his back to the smiters and his cheek to them that plucked off the hair. " Blessed are ye, when men shall revile you, and say all manner of evil against you falsely, for my sake.   Rejoice, and be exceeding glad : for so persecuted they the prophets which were before you."   " If any man suffer as a Christian, let him not be ashamed ; but let him glorify God on this behalf."   " If we suffer, we shall also reign with him."   What have we suffered ?   Who can show one blemish for Christ?   We may think a great deal of our little sufferings when we view them in themselves ; but when we write them out and put them in parallel columns with the sufferings of our Lord Jesus Christ, we shall be glad to draw them back again and put them away, and look upon ourselves as spoiled children.   We may try them again in another parallel column with the sufferings of the apostle Paul, and the same feeling will return, and we shall desire to change the subject.

Blessed are they that are reviled for the sake of their goodness. Not many have attained that high nobility.   We say the age of persecution is now gone.   Alas, all ages seem to have gone ; there is nothing left but insipidity.   The age of miracles— gone : the age of persecution—gone : the age of speaking with unknown tongues—gone : the age of the devil—gone !   It seems that we ought to be going too.   Presently we shall be dying of weariness,—we shall be overcome by this intolerable insipidity. The age of persecution has gone, has it ?   Why ?   Perhaps because the age of godliness has gone !

PRAYER.

ALMIGHTY GOD, it is a fearful thing to fall into thy hands! Thy throne is established in righteousness and judgment. The liar and the evil person shall not live in thy sight; thou art angry with the wicked every day; thou givest no peace unto them; thou withholdest all enduring blessings from those whose hearts go astray from righteousness. Thou dost drive the priest from priesthood, the minister from his pulpit, the head of the house from his family circle. Thou drivest out the evil-minded man, thou scourgest those who know not thy purity and thy love, thou vindicatest the righteousness of thy name by terrible judgments in the earth. We come to thee as the God of mercy as well as of judgment. We are now on praying ground; we may now plead mightily with thee for the exercise of thy pardoning mercy, lest we too be condemned and carried in the whirlwind of thy just anger; God be merciful unto us, sinners! save us in the hour of temptation; deliver us when the enemy would carry us away captive at his will; and when the great enemy of souls would come in as a flood, do thou lift up thy Spirit as a standard against him. If thou dost hold us up we shall be safe; if thou dost loose thine hand from ours, behold, we cannot stand! Have us in thy holy keeping; establish our hearts in the precepts and statutes of all thy will, and grant that, having served our day and generation with all simplicity, trust, meekness, and strength, we may be called to enter into the rest eternal as thine own being! Amen.

1 Samuel ii. 33; iii. 18.

"And all the increase of thine house shall die in the flower of their age."
"And Samuel told him every whit, and hid nothing from him."

THE HOUSE OF ELI OVERTHROWN.

WE have seen that Hophni and Phinehas were corrupt men, and that as a consequence the people abhorred the offering of the Lord. We have discoursed upon the doctrine that bad priests make bad people. We now come to the divine visitation of priestly unfaithfulness. Once and again we are permitted to see with startling vividness the Hand which rules, and in which is the rod of power. Now and again God puts aside all ministries and mediations, and shows us all the glory of his personal presence and all the wonderfulness of his irresistible power. We are glad when he retires, for no man can see God and live. Better to have the ministry of the most inexorable, faithful prophet, who never spares the word of judgment or the stroke of the rod, then stand in the unclouded and blinding blaze of the divine glory. Men prefer sunshine to lightning. They are both, indeed, rays of the divine glory; yet we feel safer under the ordinary daylight than under bolts of electric fire. Let us be thankful, then, that God comes to us through Eli, through human priests, and through man's ministry, being tempered, as it must be, by human limitations, rather than by bringing us face to face with himself, and pronouncing the word to us without minister or medium. At the same time we are made stronger, we are made tremblingly glad by occasional glimpses of his personality. Yet we are thankful that he puts a veil over his face, and communes with us by voices with which we are familiar. Hophni and Phinehas were evil-minded men; Eli was afflicted with weakness which dipped down sharply towards wickedness; and therefore God came out of his hiding-place to vindicate righteousness, to sweep the floor of his Church, and to use his great winnowing-fan.

Eli might have excited pity but for the misdirection of his amiability. There is nothing wrong in amiability, in paternal kindness, in fatherly forbearance and gentleness, within the limits of the household. Contrariwise, there is much that is beautiful and impressive and educational about such paternal administration. But no man may be amiable towards wickedness. The whole doctrine is found in that one sentence. Be amiable, kind, forbearing towards infirmity, natural defect, towards things that are of little or no consequence when compared with the verities of the eternal God. But when a man winks at an evil deed, he deserves the condemnation and wrath of God. When a man is tolerant of evil he himself becomes wicked. This is a doctrine which sometimes has severe application, and exposes a man to terrible reprisals; because people who look at comparative virtue, and not at holiness itself, always have the *tu quoque* ready for any faithful prophet, for any light-speaking and rod-using minister of God. Be ye clean that bear the vessels of the Lord! If we can keep our garments unspotted from the world we shall have proportionate power over men ; though even then there will not be wanting censorious critics who will be quick with their malicious repartee, pointing at a speck as though it were a blot which even God himself could never wash out of our life. Eli was an easy-going indulgent old man ; he was more than that. Tell us that at his own fireside his children could trifle with him, mock him, and could turn him into a family joke. Well, it was a very naughty thing for them to do. But Eli was a priest, Eli was the high-priest of the Lord ; and when a man's character sinks below his office, he involves himself in complications of evil which ultimately ruin his life. The office requiring strength and character, which is distinguished by nothing but the most senile weakness,—when they get together you have a contradiction which involves terrible moral consequences.

In dwelling upon the overthrow of the house of Eli, we will look at the subject under two divisions,—personality and doctrine. There were two persons employed in connection with this communication of terrible intelligence to the old high-priest. The first is merely described as "a man of God." So far as the page before us goes we have to deal with an anonymous communicant. Here is no great historic name; here is no illustrious reputation to sustain the man's words. He steps out of obscurity, as it were, and is known by the imperishable name, "a man of God." That is the one name that will do for all worlds, through all ages. You need not have "a man of God" described, ticketed, and detailed. When a man of God confronts you, he brings with him atmosphere and light and moral credentials which instantly show that he has been with Jesus and learned of him. There may be teachers who can analyse the character of a man of God. We prefer not to attempt any such analysis. Better let the character stand there, hear all he says, listen to his overpowering speech, and we shall soon know whether he hath learned his accent in the court of heaven. He was a terrible speaker ! Did ever mortal speech exceed in massiveness, in thunderous force, in terrific all-cleaving might, the speech which this anonymous messenger delivered to Eli :

"Wherefore the Lord God of Israel saith, I said indeed that thy house, and the house of thy father, should walk before me for ever : but now the Lord saith, Be it far from me; for them that honour me I will honour, and they that despise me shall be lightly esteemed. Behold, the days come, that I will cut off thine arm, and the arm of thy father's house, that there shall not be an old man in thine house. And thou shalt see an enemy in my habitation, in all the wealth which God shall give Israel : and there shall not be an old man in thine house for ever. And the man of thine, whom I shall not cut off from mine altar, shall be to consume thine eyes, and to grieve thine heart : and all the increase of thine house shall die in the flower of their age " (ii. 30-33).

That was a terrible speech to make to an old man whose life was all behind him, who was now tottering on the last edge ! It is a fearful thing to fall into the hands of the living God ! Ministers of God are required to come up to this point of faithfulness, now and again ; to have to say these words, terrible as lightning at midnight, right to an old man, when nobody else is there to hear,—to thunder to one man,—to shake the universe round one poor old man ! It is nothing to preach to a crowd. Our words are so distributed and divided, and, where they are unpleasant, are so handed on from one to another and finally thrown out of doors, that the speaker incurs but little danger of rousing the malice and spite of his hearers. Therefore the ministry is a poor tame thing,—a noonday luxury,—something we like by the way and care nothing for. But when the man of God comes and talks to one auditor,—and when that auditor feels, by reason of his solitude, that every syllable is meant for him alone, —you go far to test the strength of a man's character and the extent of a man's moral capacity. Eli was a priest, the speaker was a man of God. Man first, priest second ; life original, office secondary. Eli was high-priest, and the man who confronted him was a man of God. There is something deeper in the human than the sacerdotal. Robbers and thieves have come to Christ's fold, and Christ said, "My sheep would not follow them." Sometimes the sheep are wiser than the shepherd. Let us have faith in the instincts of humanity, in the general judgment of an unbiassed congregation. Let us have faith in people, in humanity ; not in ephods and mitres and staves of office,—but in that divine, living, imperishable spirit which God has put into redeemed and sanctified beings. Surely this message was enough for one day. Who can bear such thunder from the morning even until the evening ?

The next messenger that came was a little child. This is how
God educates us, by putting tutors on both sides, behind and
before. You hear a man who tells you what to you may be evil
tidings,—sharp, startling messages to your judgment and to your
conscience,—and you say, " The man is a fanatic." You walk
away, and before you have got a mile further a little child gets
up and smiles at you the same message,—says it in smiles, in
tender looks, in trembling child-like tones,—and you begin to
think there is something in it. You go further, and the
atmosphere seems to be charged with divine reproaches and
divine messages. So you go on, until the oldest, best, and
stateliest men tremble under subtle, impalpable, all-encompass-
ing, irresistible influences. There are some testimonies which
are so terrible that they cannot be believed on the spot. Some
men have such a way of speaking—piercing, crushing—that
when they are heard the auditor says, " This cannot be so ; it is
an exaggeration." So God hath appointed elsewhere child-priests,
little prophets, young ministers, unexpected interpreters of his
heart and will. When the thunder and the gentle breeze unite
in speaking the same message men begin to open their ears to it
—to cause their hearts to listen to the strange, the bitter, yet the
most needful word. Very beautiful is this part of the story
detailed,—the part, namely, which relates to Samuel, the little
child about the holy place who did not know the Lord. Samuel
had no acquaintance with God. That is a most important point
to observe. Read the exact words of the narrative :

" Now Samuel did not yet know the Lord, neither was the word of the
Lord yet revealed unto him " (iii. 7).

Still it is right to be waiting about the temple ; you never know
what you may hear. Men do not go into the temple because
they know all about God ; they enter if haply they may get any
hint about him, any initial lesson about that wondrous Being
who carries all other life in his own eternal pulse. Let no man
desist from attending the house of God ; he may some day hear
a message immediately from the Lord.

This incident brings before us some of the most solemn
moments of life. Life is not one long holiday. Life is not to

be spent upon one continuous level. There are some single moments in our life which make us old. There are some visions, which are but the flash of an eye, yet they make us old men. Look at Samuel, for the first time hearing of God. Is it not a solemn moment when we get our first notion of the infinite ? Can you recall your mental sensations or spiritual condition when you first began to feel that yonder distant, dim horizon was but a trembling, almost transparent curtain, and that just behind it, so to speak, lied God's eternity ? After such a moment as that, a man can never, if he has made right use of it, fall back into the littleness and contemptibleness of the life that thinks the world a nutshell, that calls time all duration. Some have had these solemn moments in life ; when they have heard a Voice they did not know, and from that moment have never ceased to hear it ; it has been the sub-tone of all that has reached the ear, it has been in the hum of all nature, it has been softer than softest zephyr of the spring. A man is never great until he knows all about this solemnity. The child who hears a voice, naturally thinks it is a human voice. Can any voice be so human as God's ? Thou canst not thunder with a voice like his ; thou canst not speak in so fatherly or motherly a tone either. Herein is the incarnation mystery,—God always showing his power to talk humanly, and to shoot out the lightning of his word from human lips. God has always during the history of the world been incarnating himself.

Samuel is taught that there is a voice other than Eli's. The old man has still force enough left in him to speak this wondrously beautiful word to the bewildered child, groping about in the darkness, " When thou hearest the voice again say, Speak, Lord, for thy servant heareth." That is what we are called upon to do ; to be listeners, receivers, mediums of God. Do we ever see beyond our own limited circle ? Do we know that there is a world larger than our England : that over that little thimbleful of water, which we call the sea, there are other countries ? It is a difficult thing for some Englishmen to believe that there is any other land ; very difficult for an islander to believe in a continent. Yet really we know that there are other places besides England. Are there no other spheres than the world which we call "the great globe itself"? There may be. Why then should we be compressing ourselves, minifying ourselves, and getting into the most microscopic compass? Why not pray for larger life, larger intellectual dominion, higher, sublimer moral sympathies? Why not, having infinitude around us, set ourselves as if we meant to take in as Guest and King the whole God? We shall never know what life is until we have passed this solemn moment which occurred in the history of Samuel, at the point to which we have now come. The non-religious man is not alive. How many are prepared to testify that they never knew what greatness was, what immeasurableness was, and what majesty was, until through Christ's life they had one peep into the incomprehensible eternity and infinity of God!

Now we can believe the man of God, who speaks the keen, cleaving word, or we can believe the gentle little Samuel, who comes and puts into monosyllables the thunders of the divine will. They are both the same ; only some men cannot endure the man of God—he crushes them, he is a tyrant—an imperial, dominating man, in the way of whose arm there is death! Let such be thankful that they can hear the same message—not in a less noble music or more tender strain, so far as the man's intent is concerned—from children, from other ministers and interpreters of God.

With regard to the doctrine brought out in connection with these events, it is plain in the first place, that God requires holiness in all who serve him. Why were Hophni and Phinehas dismissed with divine reproaches? Because they were wanting in original thought? We now dismiss our ministers because they are not very original. We do not learn that Hophni and Phinehas were dismissed from the priest's office because they were wanting in vitality and freshness of brain power. Why were they dismissed? Because they were behind the age? The age! Oh, what a ghost that age is to some people. We do not read that Hophni and Phinehas were dismissed because they were behind the age,—but because they were corrupt men. Corruptness cannot be atoned for by genius. Gifts are no substitute for grace. Better be the poorest, slowest, dullest thinker ; better be a man of stammering tongue, than be the most brilliant and gifted man who does not know what it is to be under the power of divine grace. Holiness, then, is the fundamental requirement in all persons who would interpret God and serve him in any department of the great ministry of his kingdom. Holiness is genius. Holiness hath keen, piercing eyes that see every filament of divine truth and holy communication to men. When the ministry is holy, when the Church is holy, when every man, high-priest and doorkeeper, is holy, then the world will begin to feel that there is something in it that is not of its own nature.

It is evident, also, in the second place, that all the covenants of God are founded upon a moral basis. " I said indeed that thy house, and the house of thy father, should walk before me for ever." There is the bond, there is the covenant of God repeated by a servant. How, then, can Eli be overthrown ? How can Hophni and Phinehas be dismissed from their office ? " But now the Lord saith, Be it far from me." Is then the Lord fickle ? Is he man that he should change, or is he the son of man that he should repent ? " Be it far from me." Why ? " For them that honour me I will honour, and they that despise me shall be lightly esteemed." Where is God's unchangeableness in the shape of trees and plants, in the order of the stars and the worlds, in any outside appointments, arrangements, and adaptations ? Where do we find the unchangeableness of God ? Only along the line of righteousness. When he speaks, he speaks upon a moral basis; all that he says is conditioned upon moral purposes. Hath he promised thee, O man, and art thou living upon that promise ? Know thou, that the promise is always secondary ; the character is primary—righteousness first. If the first archangel whom God summoned into his own solitude were to sin against him, he would dethrone him and banish him into outer darkness ! Let us look at details, at outside arrangements, and see if this is fickleness on the part of Providence, or changeableness of disposition on the part of God. Go to the first line—the great line on which all true things are built, all lasting empires and monarchies are founded—and you will find that along **the line of righteousness God never moves to the right hand**

or to the left,—on from eternity to eternity, never a break or a
deflection in the line of infinite righteousness !

In the third place, it is evident that some of the communications of God are at first very startling and terrible.
Think of little Samuel making his acquaintance with the Lord
through a speech like this ! Understand that at the beginning
Samuel did not know the Lord ; that he received from Eli instruction as to his position ; that having assumed that position, the
introductory words of the divine communication are these :—

"And the Lord said to Samuel, Behold, I will do a thing in Israel, at
which both the ears of every one that heareth it shall tingle" (iii. 11).

It is a child upon whose ear this awful message breaks ! It
would have driven some men mad ! They could not have borne
all that weight at the first ! God adapts his communications
to those to whom they are addressed. We do not all come upon
God at the same point. God's first message to man is not the
same in every case. Herein, then, there is scope for charity—
the charity that is just and noble when we are estimating the religious experience of men. You are not to say that, because others
did not hear exactly as you heard, therefore they are wrong and
you are right. When you heard God first he came to you along
the trembling pathways of the thunder, and your religion is a
sublimity. When your neighbour first knew God he heard him
with much and intense listening,—it was a still small voice that
stole in upon the ear of his soul, and his religion has always
been a tune in the minor key ; he has been perhaps somewhat
pensive, contemplative, and never quite lost the attitude of his
first listening ; he seems to be listening still, and to be afraid
lest a footfall should break the continuity of the divine message.
When another first met God he came to him through the process
of argument : the man was broken down by sheer force of
reasoning, so far as his intellectual positions were concerned ;
he saw his theories and speculations broken down, blown away,
pulverised, and scattered on the flying winds ; and his religion
has been logical, argumentative, propositional ; and whenever he
has gone to hear a minister, he has stopped the minister at every
sentence to say, "Prove it." So God comes to us in different

ways. We are not to judge one another by our own standard, but let every man show by the clearness and simplicity and nobleness of his life, whether or not he has had a communication from God.

We have spoken of holiness,—a word we can but dimly understand upon the earth. One day we shall recollect the sun as a poor pale beam that we could just see with, by using our eyes very sharply and putting our hands before us lest we should fall over something. One day we shall think of our professed sanctification as a poor morality. But as to holiness, the question is asked by many anxious hearts, How is this holiness to be had? In one way. "The blood of Jesus Christ cleanseth from all sin." There is " a fountain opened to the house of David for sin and for uncleanness." " Let the wicked forsake his way, and the unrighteous man his thought, and let him return unto the Lord, and he will abundantly pardon." That is the only answer. Some ministers of Christ have been saying that for twenty-five years, for forty years, and they can find no better thing to say. It is the same in every ministry, to whatsoever part of the great universe of truth we may go. If any man asks how to get up there, we have to point to the old way,—the Cross of Christ ; to Christ, who tasted death for every man ; to the atonement made by the Lamb of God! We want no other way. We never feel the need of any other way. When we have tried any other path, we have only had to be brought into some deeper sorrow and more bitter agony to call out after the living God to help us back again to the old way of the cross. He who walks that road finds his way to heaven!

PRAYER.

ALMIGHTY GOD, we have transgressed against thy covenant, and thy commandments have often been of none effect in our lives. We have forgotten God. We have lived in ourselves; we have been our own law; we have been our own gods. Truly, thou hast been angry with us. Thou hast scourged us until our life has become a daily pain. Thou hast impoverished us until we have seen the emptiness and vanity of our own resources. Now take us to thine heart again. Come through the dark cloud of thy judgment, and in answer to our penitence speak comfortably to our souls. We seek thee only through the covenant which thou didst make with thy dear Son. We stand behind him. Our hearts are safe in the infinite security of his righteousness and compassion. Give us joy in thy presence,—yea, fill us with the peace of God! Amen.

1 Samuel iii. 11-14.

" And the Lord said to Samuel, Behold, I will do a thing in Israel, at which both the ears of every one that heareth it shall tingle. In that day I will perform against Eli all things which I have spoken concerning his house : when I begin, I will also make an end [completing it]. For I have told him that I will judge his house for ever for the iniquity which he knoweth ; because his sons made themselves vile, and he restrained them not. And therefore I have sworn unto the house of Eli, that the iniquity of Eli's house shall not [assuredly not] be purged with sacrifice nor offering for ever " [a sentence made irrevocable by an oath].

THE CAUSES OF ELI'S OVERTHROW.

OUR last subject was the overthrow of the house of Eli. So great an event as the overthrow of a consecrated house ought not to be allowed to pass without careful inquiry into its causes. It is the more important because of a statement in the second chapter of the book that we are now studying : " I said indeed that thy house, and the house of thy father, should walk before me for ever : but now the Lord saith, Be it far from me." If we once get the notion that God's covenants are not to be faithfully carried out on his part, our moral foundations are destroyed and our confidence is shaken. For this reason, let us pause at this great breach of a covenant supposed to have been eternal, and ask how that breach came to be made. It must be noted that God himself annulled the covenant. Eli did not say that he wished for release from the bond. Eli did not complain of difficulty or incapacity. The word of rupture was spoken by God himself, thus : " But now the Lord saith, Be it far from me. Let the covenant which was made for ever between me and thee be far from me. I said the covenant was to be an everlasting covenant, and to-day I recall it. Thy house shall perish." We are shocked by such words. The conscience of man asserts a kind of right to have such words explained. Life would not be worth having but for profound and complete trust in God's honour. It were cruel on his part to lift us almost to heaven that he might dash us into the abyss of outer darkness ! The covenant was made for ever, yet God annulled it ! We pause, as earnest men having some regard for social honour, to know how an eternal covenant can be set aside. The case grows in difficulty, and, to the eye of the mere artist, it increases in dramatic interest as we call to memory the many points of excellence in the character of Eli. Can you find one vulgar sin in the venerable high-priest ? He was a man of advanced life, and therefore he had had opportunities of displaying his real quality. He was ninety-and-eight years old ; his eyes were dim, that he could not see ; he had judged Israel forty years. What of his character ? Why was he dispossessed of the priesthood ? Was he a drunkard, an adulterer, a liar, a thief, a blasphemer ? There is not a tittle of evidence to justify the faintest suspicion of the kind. Nay, more. We can give Eli still higher praise than this : for, after having carefully read his life, as it is detailed in this book, we see not why Eli might not stand most favourable comparison with many of the leading Christians of our day. We cannot see, looking at the page in the light of merely literary critics, where the great lapse was. We know not but that if Eli, as portrayed in the inspired book, were set up as the standard of determination, a great many would fall short of his lofty altitude. These considerations justify the interest of the question how Eli came to be dispossessed of the priesthood.

Look at his noble treatment of the child Samuel. He knew that Samuel was called by the Lord to occupy an official position

in holy places; he knew that Samuel was, at least in all probability, to succeed him in his sacerdotal functions. Yet what
an absence of the usual elements of rivalry ! When did he chide
the young prophet ? When did he superciliously snub the child ?
When did he flaunt all his own greatness in the eyes of the little
one, and use his power as an instrument of terror, that Samuel
might render him homage ? Did he ever nibble at the character
of Samuel ? Did he ever try to reduce the importance of
Samuel's probable position in life ? Did he point out blemish
after blemish in the child's character, and deficiency after deficiency in the child's gifts ? It is becoming in rivals to traduce
one another. If you cannot actually slay a man, yet it is per-
missible, by the rules of this honourable rivalry, to scratch him.
Yet we find in Eli's treatment of Samuel nobleness, magnanimity,
—want of all the little miserable tricks which are made use of by
men who seek to enhance their own glory by diminishing the
lustre of others.

Look at the unpriestliness of his tone when he talks to the
child. Samuel came to Eli in the hour of darkness and said,
" Thou didst call me." Eli said, " No, my child, I did not call
thee." Samuel came again, and yet again. What did Eli do,
knowing that Samuel had heard a voice more than human ?
Did Eli say to Samuel, " Pay no heed to such voice, little child.
I am the high-priest of God. If thou dost see a spectre or vision,
or hear an unearthly voice or tone, be not led away super-
stitiously by these things ; but come to me, and I will instantly
tell thee all about it, and determine what thou hast to do " ? That
would have been the talk of a priest ; that is the native accent of
a true priest. Yet Eli said to the child, " It is God that calleth
thee ; go and speak to him face to face ; stand before him and
say, Speak, Lord ; for thy servant heareth." Why, that was not
priestly at all ; that was putting a man face to face with the
Eternal, and clothing the soul with responsibilities which never
can be transferred.

Looking at this aspect of Eli's character, what reverence we feel
for the old man ! We see that he was a fine interpreter of the
supernatural section of life. He was not self-obtrusive ; he was

no mere priest; he introduced men immediately to God; he did not claim any power of exclusive or tyrannic mediation. Look, again, at the submissiveness of his tone when his doom was pronounced. When he was told that his house would be rooted up, that both his sons should die on one day, that the judgment of the Lord had set in against him and his successors, what did Eli say? Remember, he was nearly a hundred years old; his eyes were dim; for forty years he had maintained a position of supremacy. Men cannot easily throw away the traditions and the social consequence of so long-continued an elevation. Yet when the old man heard his doom, he said, "It is the Lord: let him do what seemeth good in his sight." How few could have shown the same submissiveness, the same religious homage, under circumstances so terrible! An earthquake shaking the foundations of our house,—a storm-cloud pouring out its flood upon our inheritance! Yet Eli was no vengeful priest in that hour: he was no mere self-seeker in that terrible day. Even then, when the foundations were rocking under his feet, and all the surroundings of his life were full of tempestuous and devouring elements, he said, with an old man's tremulous pathos, "It is the Lord." Equal to, "Let God be true, and every man a liar; he is Sovereign, I am servant; whatsoever the Judge of the whole earth doeth shall be done in righteousness."

Then look at the man's interest in the ark of the Lord. When that sacred box was taken out into the battlefield and was captured by the Philistines, Eli's heart trembled for the ark of God. Down to the very last, we see that Eli was an intensely religious man, from whom God withdrew his covenant, and on whom he pronounced such severe judgments as these:—

"I will cut off thine arm, and the arm of thy father's house, that there shall not be an old man in thine house. . . . And the man of thine, whom I shall not cut off from mine altar, shall be to consume thine eyes, and to grieve thine heart: and all the increase of thine house shall die in the flower of their age" (ii. 31, 33).

We would, therefore, repeat with fervour and with emphasis, that the conscience of universal man asks: "Lord of heaven and earth, is this right?" In looking at the failure of Eli as involving a moral question between the Creator and the creature, we are prepared to teach that the obligations of character must always control the obligations of covenants. All God's covenants are founded upon a moral basis. A covenant is but a form; a covenant is merely an arrangement, if it be not established upon moral conditions. There are circumstances in which God's faithfulness and God's unchangeableness are seen, not in fulfilling, but actually in the annulling, of covenants. God will never maintain the letter at the expense of the spirit. There is a pedantic morality amongst men which says, "The bond must be kept to the letter," and which cares nothing for the spirit of the engagement. God's morality is not a morality of ink and seals and witnesses. It involves life, spirit, motive, purpose. Were God to keep to the letter at the expense of the spirit, he would be no longer God. His unchangeableness is in his righteousness, not in his formality. Our confidence in him is this:—That he will set aside his oldest servants, his first-chosen men, his most princely vicegerents and interpreters,—he will utterly destroy them from the face of the earth, and hurl after them the written covenants he has made with them,—i they trifle with eternal truth, with infinite purity! To cover a corrupt life with the blessing of his approbation, simply because there is a literal covenant to be carried out, would be to deny every element which makes him God.

The answer, therefore, to the question which we put as from the conscience of universal man, is this: Eli, notwithstanding all these points of excellence in his character, is distinctly accused of moral defect. That has now to be proved. "Them that honour me I will honour, and they that despise me shall be lightly esteemed." These words were spoken to Eli by the man of God, who came to him with the divine message. These words are pointless, if they do not imply that Eli had, by some means or other, brought himself into the list of those who despise God. Then again: "I will raise me up a faithful priest." These words are out of place, if they do not clearly suggest that, to some extent or other, Eli had been unfaithful to the divine vocation. Yet again: "I will judge his house for ever for the iniquity which he knoweth—not for some iniquity of which he is unaware—I will bring up in his life iniquities which he himself has pointed out, as such; which he knows to be wickedness in my sight, and out of his own mouth I will condemn him." Now were God to keep his covenant in the face of such charges, the wicked would in time get advantage over him; the hypocrite might, in the long run, be as God in the world. God shows his Godhead in the cancelling of covenants where there has been a decay of character. Understand, this is not a business covenant; it is not a commercial bond; it is not between one man and another; it is between infinite righteousness and a human creature. We are not entitled to say that we may trifle with our human, social, commercial bonds, because there has been a lapse in character here or there. A commercial bond is a commercial bond. We are now considering covenants between God and man. These covenants cannot exist, except there be sympathy between the Maker and the creature. Moral sympathy, religious similitude : impair that, and of necessity the covenant is destroyed.

Viewed in this light, there are several impressive lessons urged by God's treatment of Eli. First of all it is clear—and it ought to be made most distinct, because of a great practical delusion which exists upon this point—that it is not enough that there be many good points in a character. Character ought not to be a mere question of points at all. Character ought not to be viewed in sections and departments, in aspects and occasional moods. Character should have about it the distinctness of wholeness, entirety. Our goodness is not to be an occasional impulse or a transitory appearance of moral conscience and moral concern for others. Out of our character there is to stream continuous and beneficent influence. We lose when we can be talked about in sections. It is no compliment when we have to take out of a character three or four good points and say to those who look on, "Observe these; whatever defects there may be in the character, do not overlook these redeeming points." When we can talk so about ourselves and about others it is not a compliment, it is a sign of incompleteness. When our moral training is perfected we shall not have points of excellence ; our whole character will be massive, indivisible, and out of it will go an influence that will constrain men to believe that we have been with God, and that we have imbibed the very spirit of his righteousness.

Eli was amiable.   A great many mistakes are made about amiability.   A man may be amiable simply through mere want of interest or force; he may be so constituted, that really he does not much care who is who, or what is what.   He may have a senile grin—some may call it a smile—for anybody and for all persons alike,—a nice old man who never says a cross word, and never has a frown upon his face.   That is not amiability Here is a man who is naturally unamiable; he looks with a discriminating eye upon men and things; he is very passionate, fiery, self-asserting.   Yet, by the grace of God, he is kept back; at times he shakes in the leash; he often seems as if he would break it and be away!   Yet God's hold upon him is such that he speaks gentle words, restrains terms of indignation and wrath, moderates his rising passion.   There,—though he cannot look very amiable, though he may have a grim face,—is the amiable man.

Eli had religious impulses.   What then?   There is a sense in which religious impulse may be but constitutional.   It is more natural for some people to pray than others.   It comes easier for some men to go to church than for others.   We must not overlook the constitutional condition.   We have heard a man say that there were two things in the world he could not tolerate; those two things were, sermons and lectures.   We do not condemn the man; it is not worth while going into a rage over such men; by his very make one could see that sermons and lectures could not tolerate him.   He would have been a mighty preacher who could have talked to such an auditor.   Eli had religious impulses; but religious impulses are not enough.   We have known a drunken man knock a Roman Catholic down because the papist said, " John Wesley is in hell."   Was the drunken man a religious character?   Certainly not; but he had religious emotions, impulses, sensibilities, and even when he was intoxicated, he would have preferred a hymn to a ribald song.   Let us clearly understand, therefore, that mere religious sensibility, religious impulse and religious susceptibility, must not be understood as proclaiming and certifying sound religiousness of character.

Eli treated Samuel without official envy or jealousy. So far so good. We commend Eli for abstinence from such interference with Samuel, and criticism of the child as would have been small and contemptible in one occupying the lofty position of the high-priest of the Jews. But absence of envy may come of mere easy good-nature. There are men in the world who do not care one pin-point who is at the head of affairs. That is not magnanimity; that is not nobleness. This is nobleness : the man who wants to be at the head of affairs himself, and feels considerable consciousness that he would be able to sustain the position; he longs for it, works for it, hopes for it day and night. Yet, there is a young man put above him, set on the chief seat, and he himself is kept down. It would be natural for that man to shake an angry hand in the face of his successful rival. Yet, by the grace of God, he says, "I bid thee God-speed." He says it perhaps with some difficulty; it does not escape him with that roundness and fervour of tone with which it would escape another man ; but he does say it—says it from the heart, and the very reluctance of the speech is a sign of its sincerity. That is the man who has, by the power of the Holy Ghost, subdued the devil of jealousy and triumphed over the fiend whose name is envy !

The second lesson that is urged upon us by this view of Eli's position is—that divine discipline is keen—intensely spiritual. We have asked, Can you point to any vulgar sin in the high-priest ? The inquiry is, Can you point out any vulgar sin in Eli ? Sin is not measurable by vulgarity. Some men seem incapable of seeing sin until it clothes itself in the most hideous forms. Forms have nothing to do with sin. Sin is sin before it takes form. Herein we see the keenness, the spirituality of divine discipline. Herein, the Church, as we have already said, fails in its purely spiritual mission. A man is expelled from the Church because he has been discovered drunk. We cannot call that Church discipline. It is simple decency, common respectability; it is not Christian discipline. Christian discipline would have applied itself to the man when he was longing for the drink ; when he was drunk in his soul, before he touched the accursed cup. A man is expelled from the Church because he has committed manslaughter. That is not Christian discipline; that is legal discipline, magisterial discipline. Society will expel him. The Church should have expelled him when he was angry without a cause ; when it was known that a bad passion had raged in his heart, and he had spoken some unkind, ignoble word. At that point,—invisible, impalpable, subtle, known only in all its significance to God, and understood only by those who understand the righteousness of law as revealed by God,—at that point Christian discipline would have interposed and asserted the law of right. The Church cannot have discipline except in its most common forms. Discipline would destroy the Church. Discipline would empty every pulpit and disband every Christian assembly if applied in all the keenness and intensity of its divine spirituality. Then let us regard the Church as an hospital; let us regard the Church as an infant school; let us regard the Church as striving after, not as having attained, the fulness of the divine idea ; and having come to that conclusion respecting the visible Church of Christ, let us have compassion on some, making a difference—let us be charitable one towards another.

See further, in this case, the terribleness of God's displeasure. " I will do a thing in Israel, at which both the ears of every one that heareth it shall tingle. I have told him that I will judge his house for ever for the iniquity which he knoweth. I have sworn unto the house of Eli, that the iniquity of Eli's house shall not be purged with sacrifice nor offering for ever." These are terrible words. Yet, if they were less terrible we should have less confidence in God. If any one could be more terrible than God, we should not worship him. The measure of his love is the measure of his wrath ; the height of his mercy is the height of his judgment. Terrible is a bad man's fate ! He cannot elude God. He may have success; but in his very success he will find a sting which will inject poison into his life, and destroy sweet, profound, refreshing rest ! He who starts to war against God, starts on a war the end of which is known from the beginning.

We would that this doctrine could follow us all through our life. We do not invite men to accept Christ because there is a terrible pain following the course of unrighteousness. That is not preaching the Gospel. We do not desire to dwell upon the punishments that befall a bad man with any wish of drawing him from his course because of those punishments. That kind of teaching we have never been able to adopt. But this we do teach distinctly, that the bad man has a painful course before him. Do not leave it on that account! The serpent shall bite you and the adder shall sting you, but do not give it up on that account! The wild beast shall shut his jaws upon you, but do not be righteous on that account! The earth will not have you, the sea will not cover you, hell will not burn you, but do not come to Christ on that account! Be a man ; "be a hero in the strife!" We do not urge that men should be good because God will lay the hand of judgment upon them. No man would turn on that account. But the way of the transgressor is hard ; he is making a hard pillow for his head. Be he high-priest or doorkeeper ; be he mighty in gift or obscure in talent,—God will not spare him. If judgment begin at the house of God, where shall the ungodly and the sinner appear ? " I the Lord am a jealous God, visiting the iniquity of the fathers upon the children unto the third and fourth generation of them that hate me." Having started the stream, you cannot dam it back !

What, then, have we to leave our study with these hard words ? No. Jehovah says : "When I say unto the wicked, Thou shalt surely die ; if he turn from his sin, and do that which is lawful and right, none of his sins that he hath committed shall be mentioned unto him : he shall surely live." So, then, our " song shall be of mercy and judgment." Penitence is the one condition on which human souls can find God : repentance towards God and faith in our Lord Jesus Christ. " If we confess our sins, he is faithful and just to forgive us our sins, and to cleanse us from all unrighteousness." " Let the wicked forsake his way, and the unrighteous man his thoughts : and let him return unto the Lord, and he will have mercy upon him ; and to our God, for he will abundantly pardon." What tuneful words—words that shine upon our life like angels sent down from heaven !

We have all sinned: "there is none righteous, no not one." Were God to set his mark upon one sin in a thousand and judge us for it, who could stand before him! But we go to Jesus Christ, God the Son, Messiah,—God; and we find our infinite security in the fulness of his righteousness, and in the worthiness of his all-prevailing mediation.

SELECTED NOTE.

Eli (*raised up*) was high-priest of the Jews when the ark was in Shiloh (1 Sam. i. 3, 9). He was the first high-priest of the line of Ithamar, Aaron's youngest son. This is deduced from 1 Chron. xxiv. 3-6. It also appears from the omission of the names of Eli and his immediate successors in the enumeration of the high-priests of Eleazar's line in 1 Chron. vi. 4-6. What occasioned this remarkable transfer is not known—most probably the incapacity or minority of the then sole representative of the elder line; for it is very evident that it was no unauthorised usurpation on the part of Eli (1 Sam. ii. 27, 28). Eli also acted as regent or civil judge of Israel after the death of Samson. This function, indeed, seems to have been intended by the theocratical constitution to devolve upon the high-priest by virtue of his office, in the absence of any person specially appointed by the divine King, to deliver and govern Israel. He is said to have judged Israel forty years (1 Sam. iv. 18). The Septuagint makes it twenty; and chronologers are divided on the matter. But the probability seems to be that the forty years comprehend the whole period of his administration as high-priest *and* judge, including, in the first half, the twenty years in which Samson is said to have judged Israel (Judg. xvi. 31), when some of his civil functions in Southern Palestine may have been in abeyance. As Eli died at the age of ninety-eight (1 Sam. iv. 15), the forty years must have commenced when he was fifty-eight years old.

Eli seems to have been a religious man; and the only fault recorded of him was an excessive easiness of temper, most unbefitting the high responsibilities of his official character. His sons, Hophni and Phinehas, whom he invested with authority, misconducted themselves so outrageously as to excite deep disgust among the people, and render the services of the tabernacle odious in their eyes. Of this misconduct Eli was aware, but contented himself with mild and ineffectual remonstrances, where his station required severe and vigorous action. For this neglect the judgment of God was at length denounced upon his house, through the young Samuel, who, under peculiar circumstances, had been attached from childhood to his person (1 Sam. ii. 29; iii. 18). Some years passed without any apparent fulfilment of this denunciation—but it came at length in one terrible crash, by which the old man's heart was broken. The Philistines had gained the upper hand over Israel, and the ark of God was taken to the field, in the confidence of victory and safety from its presence. But in the battle which followed, the ark itself was taken by the Philistines, and the two sons of Eli, who were in attendance upon it, were slain. The high-priest, then blind with age, sat by the wayside at Shiloh, awaiting tidings from the war, "for his heart trembled for the ark of God." A man of Benjamin, with his clothes rent, and with earth upon his head, brought the fatal news; and Eli heard that Israel was defeated—that his sons were slain—that the ark of God was taken--at which last word he fell heavily from his seat, and died (1 Sam. iv.).

The ultimate doom upon Eli's house was accomplished when Solomon removed Abiathar (the last high-priest of this line) from his office, and restored the line of Eleazar in the person of Zadok.

PRAYER.

ALMIGHTY GOD, thy presence overfloweth all things. All things are naked and open to thine eyes. If we take the wings of the morning and flee unto the uttermost parts of the earth, behold, thou art there! Thou art higher than all height, lower than all depth, and behold, none can take the measure of the breadth of thine infinitude. We come before thee with a song of mercy and judgment; for whilst thou art a terrible God—and it is a fearful thing to fall into thy hands—thy tender mercies are over all thy works. Thou renewest our strength in compassion; thou upholdest us by thy loving-kindness; and every day thou dost vindicate thy government to us, not by the greatness of thy power, but by the tenderness and persuasiveness of thy love. We have halted in the midst of worldly pursuits and ordinary engagements, that we might bow the knee to the God and Father of our Lord Jesus; that we might pour out our song of thankfulness, and renew our spiritual vigour by waiting patiently and lovingly upon God. May this hour refresh us exceedingly upon our earthly pilgrimage. May our strength be recovered; may our peace be augmented; may our hope be brightened; may our whole life be brought into truer harmony with thine! Dry the tears of our sorrow. Be pitiful to us by reason of our manifold infirmities. Give to us all the fulness of redeeming love, and pardon our sin, for it is great. Wash us in the precious blood of the Lord Jesus, the Lamb of God, which taketh away the sins of the world. Whom thou hast pardoned, do thou also sanctify. To this end pour out upon us the gift of the Holy Ghost, that he may reign in our understanding, control our will, purify our affections, and bring our being into entire subjection to all thy purposes. May there be nothing in us upon which thou canst not look with approval. Sanctify us in body, soul, and spirit. Abide with us; reign in our life; stablish thy kingdom in our souls; put down every rival. Reign thou whose right it is! Amen.

1 Samuel iv. 3.

" Let us fetch the ark of the covenant of the Lord out of Shiloh unto us, that, when it cometh among us, it may save us out of the hand of our enemies."

THE ARK OF GOD.*

IN order to understand the full import of these words, we must carefully study the idea which the ark of the Lord was intended to represent. The twenty-fifth chapter of the Book of Exodus gives a most minutely detailed account of the making of

* For a complete discussion, see vol. ii., p. 205.

the tabernacle. God gave Moses a special description of the proposed sanctuary. He did not consult Moses, nor did he make suggestions which Moses was to submit to the consideration of the people of Israel. God laid down the whole plan, and no more left anything to be settled by the taste of Moses than he left Noah to determine the colours of the rainbow. As he said to Job, " Where wast thou when I laid the foundations of the earth ? " so he might have said to Moses, " Where wast thou when I designed the tabernacle ? " There was not a ring, a knop, a socket, a coupling, or a pin which God himself did not specially design. Was it not like him ? Is there anywhere one sprig of moss which owes its humble beauty to any hand but his own ? As the tabernacle was built for the sake of the ark, and not the ark for the sake of the tabernacle, it becomes most important to know what the ark was, and what spiritual meaning the symbol was intended by Almighty God to signify. We read in the holy word : " Thou shalt make an ark ; thou shalt overlay it with pure gold ; thou shalt make upon it a crown of gold round about ; thou shalt put into the ark the testimony which I shall give thee ; thou shalt make a mercy seat of pure gold ; thou shalt put the mercy seat above the ark ; and in the ark thou shalt put the testimony that I shall give thee. And there will I meet thee, and I will commune with thee from above the mercy seat, from between the two cherubim which are upon the ark of the testimony, of all things which I will give thee in commandment unto the children of Israel."

The ark is called by various names. In Exodus it is called the ark of the testimony ; in Deuteronomy it is called the ark of the covenant ; in the first of Samuel it is called the ark of the Lord ; and in the same book it is called the ark of God. What was this ark ? Looked at materially, the ark of the covenant was a box or chest, fifty-four inches long, about thirty inches broad, and about thirty inches high. The box was overlaid with pure gold. The lid or cover of the ark was called the mercy seat. Upon the mercy seat were two golden cherubim, one at either end, facing each other, and covering the mercy seat with expanded wings. At the mercy seat—the lid of this box—God promised to meet Moses and commune with him. Hence, God was said to dwell between the cherubim. The ark contained the two tables of stone on which God had written the ten commandments. "I will write on the tables the words that were written on the first tables which thou brakest, and thou shalt put them in the ark." In the first of Kings we read there was nothing in the ark save the two tables of stone which Moses put there at Horeb. The ark was placed in the holy of holies ; indeed it is called in the first book of Chronicles, "the house of the mercy seat."

Let us now stand beside that box and consider its meaning, that we may be prepared to consider the text. In the box you find the commandments of God. The box is not merely in the holy house,—it is in the holiest place of the holy house. In the very midst of that box you find only the written law of the Most High. Keep that picture before you, if you would understand the spiritual significance of the symbol. As with the box in the tabernacle in the holy of holies, containing the written law of God, so with creation to-day. The great moral idea never changes. The chest is destroyed, the golden cherubim may no longer be found ; but the moral purpose, the moral intent, is the same now and for ever. Penetrate into the highest place in the universe—go higher than the clouds, higher than the sun, higher than the farthest star—pass, if you may, into the secret solitudes of God, where human strife and din are never heard—and there, at the very centre, in the great solemn heart of all systems and powers, you find,—What? The law of God! This is at once a terror and a security. The spirit of judgment quickens all creation. Out of everything there comes a fire which scorches the bad man's hand. Wherever a good man goes a blessing approves and confirms his steps. For a moment the bad man may seem to bend things according to his own will : but "the Lord shall laugh at him : for he seeth that his day is coming," when "he shall fly away as a dream, and shall not be found : yea, he shall be chased away as a vision of the night." Some men could not live but for this reflection. Life would be a constant temptation to them, unmingled with any element of mercy. It is something to know, and deeply to feel, that all things are bound together by law,—that at the heart of the universe there is a written statute and covenant. It gives steadi-

ness to life ; it defines relations, rights, consequences ; it enables
a man to view with composure all the flutter and dust of the
little day, and to draw himself forward by the power of an
endless life.   This, then, is part of the teaching of the symbolic
ark.   In the holy of holies we find the sacred chest covered with
gold, watched by the cherubim, and in that hallowed chest is
hidden the law written by the finger of God.   That law is subtle
as life.   You are assured of its presence ; you are encompassed by
a mystery which is never withdrawn for a moment ; you cannot
explain it ; you are punished when you resent it ; you are at rest
when you obey it, your very liberty is but a phase of restraint !

Happily, this is but part of the teaching of the ark.   Over the
ark there is a lid.   Very special were the instructions given
to Moses respecting it.   The lid was the mercy seat, the pro-
pitiatory.   It was there—not on the tables of stone graven with
the law of God—but on the lid, the covering of the ark, that
God promised to meet Moses.   Now see how the case stands
when you put both sides of it together.   There you have the
sovereign, unchangeable, inexorable law of God ; and over it you
have the covering of God's tender mercy.   When we look at the
law, we look at it through the mercy, because the mercy covers
it.   When the law comes to us, it comes up through the mercy,
because the mercy overlies it.   All law now comes to us through
the mediation of mercy.   "The Lord is good to all : and his
tender mercies are over all his works."   What then ?   At the
very centre of the human system we have law and mercy,
righteousness and love, sovereignty and sacrifice.   Creation says,
"My song shall be of mercy and judgment."   Society is not a
chaos ; creation is not an aggregate of unrelated fragments.
Amid all the din, confusion, stress, and upset of life, there is, at
the heart of things, a law unchanging as God,—a mercy ever
enduring, ever pitiful.

This brief sketch of the ark of the covenant, and its spiritual
significance, will enable us to follow with intelligence the varying fortunes of Israel, which have ever been associated, more
or less directly, with this ark.   We want a book written upon
the ark of the Lord.   Seek out its history ; see what becomes

of the people according to their treatment of this ark ; see how one little thing rules all things,—how the heart-beat palpitates to the extremities of the universe ! We give this counsel to youthful students :—Make this your subject,—the ark of the covenant ; its structure, its typified doctrine, its relation to the history of a nation, and the eternal principles which come out of this symbolical representation of God.

In the case before us, the Philistines had slain of the men of Israel about four thousand. When the people came into the camp, the elders of Israel said, " Wherefore hath the Lord smitten us to-day before the Philistines ? " This is an inquiry which men should always put to themselves in times of disaster and failure. " Why has God withdrawn me from the crowd and made an invalid of me, and shut me up in this shaded chamber ? Why has God sent a blight upon my wheat-fields and olive-yards, so that there should be no produce ? Why hath God barked my fig tree and taken away from me my one ewe lamb— spoiled the idol of my love ? Is there not a cause ? " So far, Israel was acting upon a principle of common sense. Every effect has its cause. Four thousand dead men of Israel are lying upon the field, slaughtered by the sword of the Philistines. Why ? Admire sagacity, common sense, wherever you find it.

But observe what a mixture is presented by the text. " Let us," said the elders of Israel, " fetch the ark of the covenant of the Lord out of Shiloh unto us, that, when it cometh among us, it may save us out of the hands of our enemies." The ark had been at Shiloh from the days of Joshua, during the ministry of all the Judges. And now suddenly the leaders of Israel, with four thousand dead men lying about them, say, " Let us fetch the ark." They brought the ark, and when the ark of the covenant came into the camp, all Israel shouted with a great shout, so that the earth rang again ! The Philistines said, " What is this ? they are bringing their god into the field ! " and the Philistines trembled. Nothwithstanding this, the Philistines gathered together their courage, came against Israel, and Israel was smitten, and the ark of God was taken.

There must be some lessons here. Learn that the formal is

useless without the spiritual. There is the ark, made as God dictated,—a sacred thing : the law is there ; the mercy seat is there. Yet Israel falls by the arms of the Philistines, and the sacred shrine is taken by the hands of the idolaters. There is nothing strange in this. The formal never can save men ; the institutional never can redeem society. A mere observance, a ceremony, a form, can never touch the dead heart of the world. This is, emphatically, the day of bringing in arks, societies, formalities, ceremonies. You have in your house an altar ; that altar will be nothing influential in your life if you have it there merely for the sake of formality. A man who cannot altogether throw away the traditions of his lifetime,—who hears, it may be, a parent's voice, saying to him in secret, again and again, "You promised me to do so and so,"—and in fulfilment of that promise he may snatch up tne ark of the covenant, the law of God, hastily read through a few verses, shut up the book, and run away,— has he read the Word of God ? He has insulted the divine testimony ! True, he opened the book, he uttered to himself the words. Yet the service was no use in his life,—it was a mere formality. God will not be trifled with. Holy words will have no holy effect, if read in that manner.

Learn that religion is not to be a mere convenience. The ark is not to be used as a magical spell. Holy things are not to be run to in extremity, and set up in order that men who are in peril may be saved. The reasoning of the Israelites was subtle, but intensely selfish. "That it may save us." That sounds like a modern expression ! To be personally saved, to be delivered out of a pressing emergency or strait—that seems to be the one object which many people have in view when identifying themselves with religious institutions, Christian observances and fellowships. We shall never have a robust, imperial piety till we get out of all these little, personal, narrow considerations, and identify ourselves with the very life of God— the infinite love of his eternal heart. We are, verily, more or less all guilty of this very thing. We have done as long as possible without the ark. We have gone a-warfare at our own charges ; we have defied the hosts of the alien in our own strength ; and when we have been worsted, overthrown, and

brought to the very brink of ruin, a lucky idea has seized us,—
we have said, " Fetch the ark!" When the ark was brought,
it was nothing but a wooden box : fetched by unworthy hands,
its inspiration and glory ceased from it. " If the light that is in
thee be darkness, how great is that darkness." Men have lived
lives of practical atheism year after year; and when there has
been a panic in the market, they have bethought themselves of
old memories, early vows, first Christian oaths ; and they have
turned pious because there was a panic barking at them like a
mad wolf,—they have begun to pray, and Heaven sent back their
voice unanswered, unblessed! We must not play with our religion. We might guarantee that every place of worship would be
filled at five o'clock in the morning and at twelve o'clock at night
under given circumstances. Let there be a plague in the city—
let men's hearts fail them for fear—let them feel that all that is
material is insecure—that nothing is real but the invisible and
the spiritual—and they will instantly flock to churches and chapels
by the thousand, and be very humble in the presence of God.
That will not do! God is not to be moved by incantations, by
decent formalities, and external reverence. He will answer
the continuous cry of the life. The man who prays without
ceasing may ever count upon the interposition of God.

We learn that the Philistines took the ark of the covenant.
But though they had captured the ark, that sacred shrine made
itself terribly felt. The Philistines took the ark to Ashdod, and
put it into the house of their god Dagon. You see there was
a good deal of religiousness in these men. They took away the
box out of the battlefield ; they unlocked the door where they
kept their pagan god, and put the box in beside him. They set
the Right beside the Wrong. What a night's work there was!
" When they of Ashdod rose on the morrow, behold, Dagon was
fallen upon his face to the earth before the ark of the Lord!"
That might have been an accident. Perhaps in going into the
house and moving the ark carelessly, they might have injured
Dagon's position, and so he might have come down, as it were,
by haphazard. So they set Dagon up again, made his position
secure and respectable, and left him in his solitude. Next
morning they came, and Dagon was fallen upon his face to

the ground before the ark of the Lord; and the head of Dagon, and both the palms of his hands, were cut off upon the threshold. A terrible night's work there was in this case! What communion hath light with darkness? What fellowship hath Christ with Belial? When Right and Wrong come face to face, there must always be a sharp collision. When the Right goes down, as it does occasionally, it will be only as the ark of the Lord went down in the case before us, to plague its very captors and throw down the idol of their hearts. Would to God we could learn this doctrine,—that in some cases success is defeat! We need to learn this lesson,—that in some cases victory is loss, and that gain stings the winner night and day.

Here let us ask young readers to consider this part of the story diligently. We know of nothing equal to it in modern writing for excitement, for that singular romantic element which always spell-binds young readers. Read the history of the ark again. The Philistines took the ark, but they wanted to get clear of it, if anybody would take it away. What! you have won the ark,—keep it. They took it from place to place, and could make nothing of it; it was a torment to them. Last of all they said, "Let us send a present along with it, and by all means get clear of it!" Aye, it will even be so with ill-gotten results; with undeserved, unrighteously attained gain, be it wealth or influence, or what it may. It will not rest with the individual; it will say, "Send me away!" Judas took the thirty pieces of silver, but they had become so hot in his hand as to boil his blood, and he said to those who had bought him: "Take them away!" But the buyers said, "No!" The bad man has a hard lot of it; when he wants to get clear of his gain, he cries and begs that somebody will relieve him of his very victories. The Lord's sword is two-edged; touch it where you like, it cuts clear away to the bone!

Learn that the false relation of things always brings torment. Be it in the family: if the heads of the house are disagreed concerning great spiritual truths and realities, there cannot be peace in the house. Be it in business: one partner is a righteous man, and another is careless about moral obligations. There cannot be peace; there may be success, sharp practice, keen fencing, and methods of doing things that look very successful; but there will be a stinging process, after all,—a sting that will pierce the heart and fill it with pain and anguish. You cannot rub right and wrong together, and make them cohere. It is so in a man's own heart. If half of the man is going one way and the other half wants to go the other way, the man's life is a most agonising, distressing struggle. Everywhere this great law is written. If it had never been spoken by Jesus, it might have been spelled out by scholars in the world's school,—"Ye cannot serve God and Mammon."

The great spiritual application and the significance of the ark is undoubtedly Jesus Christ. We have no sacred chest; we have no box covered with pure gold; no tables of stone; no manufactured seat of mercy. All the great spiritual significance and application of these things we find in Christ. What the ark was to Israel, Jesus Christ is to the Church. In Jesus Christ we find law. Some Christians find that a difficult lesson to learn. They speak of Jesus as being all love, gentleness, and compassion, tenderness exceeding, and pity infinite. He was more than that. Whenever he spoke of law, he spoke of it as the Lawgiver. "Heaven and earth shall pass away, but this law must be fulfilled." Jesus never trifled with equity, with righteousness, with probity, with moral obligation. Jesus Christ was not all mere sensibility. His was the sensibility that comes out of justice, righteousness, truth, purity, as well as tenderness, mercy, compassion. In Jesus Christ we find all the mercy of God! Observe that form of expression. By it we intend to signify that nowhere else can you find an element of mercy that is wanting in the character and spirit of Jesus Christ. He is at the head of all things. As the ark was in the tabernacle, in the holy of holies, so he is the Head over all things. He is highly exalted. All things were made by him; and without him was not anything made that was made. He was not made for creation; creation was made for him. The ark was not built for the tabernacle, but the tabernacle was built for the ark. All things are in Christ and for Christ. One day this will be seen. He must reign until he hath put all enemies under his feet. The

last enemy that shall be destroyed is Death; and in the resplendent universe there shall be everywhere life, immortality.
" He shall see of the travail of his soul, and shall be satisfied."
When he is satisfied, who shall be discontented ?   When he says,
" It is enough," who shall require any addition ?   When he who
came up from unbeginning time—God the Son, lived and died,
and rose again—suffered all Bethlehem, Gethsemane, Golgotha—
when he shall say, " I am satisfied," who shall be able to
suggest that one thing is wanting to complete the happiness of
his redeemed family ?

SELECTED NOTE.

" *Let us fetch the ark of the covenant of the Lord out of Shiloh* " (iv. 3).—We
cannot attempt to define the object of the ark. It was the depositary of the
Tables, and thus of the great document of the covenant. It seems also to have
been a protest against idolatry and materialism. The mercy-seat was the
place where God promised his presence, and he was, therefore, addressed as
dwelling between the cherubim. On this account the ark was of the utmost
sanctity, and was placed in the Holy of Holies, both of the tabernacle and of
the temple. When the Israelites were moving from one encampment to
another, the ark was to be covered by Aaron and his sons with three
coverings, and carried by the sons of Kohath (Numb. iv. 4-6, 16). Joshua
placed the tabernacle at Shiloh, and the ark does not seem to have been
removed thence until the judgeship of Eli, when the people sent for it to the
army, that they might gain success in the war with the Philistines. Yet the
Israelites were routed and the ark was taken (1 Sam. iv. 3-11). After seven
months, during which the majesty of God was shown by the plaguing of the
inhabitants of each town to which it was brought, and the breaking of the
image of Dagon, the Philistines hastened, on the advice of their priests and
diviners, to restore the ark to the Israelites. These incidents and those
of the coming of the ark to Beth-shemesh, where the people were smitten
for looking into it, show its extremely sacred character, no less than
does the death of Uzzah, when he attempted to steady it, on the journey to
Jerusalem, an event which caused David to delay bringing it in. It is
noticeable that it was carried in a cart both when sent from Ekron, and, at
first, when David brought it to Jerusalem, though after the delay on the
latter occasion, it was borne by the Levites in the ordained manner (1 Chron.
xv. 11-15; 2 Sam. vi. 13). It was then placed on Mount Zion, until Solomon
removed it to the temple. From the statement that Josiah commanded the
Levites to place the ark in the temple, and to bear it no longer on their
shoulders (2 Chron. xxxv. 3), it seems probable that Amon had taken it out
of the sanctuary, or else that the Levites had withdrawn it from the temple
then or in Manasseh's time, and the finding of the book of the Law under
Josiah favours this idea (2 Kings xxii. 8; 2 Chron. xxxiv. 14). A copy of
the Law was deposited with, or, as some suppose in the ark, and it seems
that this was the copy from which the king was required to write his own
(Deut. xvii. 18-20). But perhaps the ark was only removed while the temple
was repaired. It is generally believed that it was destroyed when the temple
was burnt by the Babylonians, and it is certain that it was not contained in
the second temple.

PRAYER.

ALMIGHTY GOD, thou settest up and thou bringest down, as servants of thy Church and ministers of thy will, whom thou pleasest, according to a counsel we cannot understand. Thou hast made the stone which the builders refused the head stone of the corner; thou hast passed over the wise and the mighty, the noble and the great, and thou hast revealed thy secret unto babes. Who can resist the call of the Lord? Who shall answer, but with all his love, the appeal and challenge of the Most High? Impress each of us with a deep sense of personal responsibility, which can be measured only by the gifts which thou hast bestowed upon us and the opportunities with which thou hast blessed us. May the servant entrusted with five talents, and the servant entrusted with but one, each do his Lord's will with simplicity, diligence, and all the homage of the soul! Save us from all uncharitableness in regard to one another; from all envy and malice; from all censoriousness and unfriendliness. May each esteem other better than himself; may the strong bear the infirmities of the weak; may the aged prophets be gentle and tender towards thy young servants; and may those who are youthful in the Church of Christ have within them sense of veneration, confidence, and respect in regard to those who have borne the burden and heat of the day. Establish us all in the counsel and service of Christ. May we love the Saviour with all our heart and soul and mind and strength. May the supreme joy of our life be to uphold the rights of his crown and to explain the mystery of his cross. Let thy blessing now descend upon us, that we may have life more abundantly, that our peace may pass understanding, that our joy may be unspeakable and full of glory. Shed light where there is darkness. Send the delivering word to souls held in the captivity of the enemy. Turn those whose faces are turned away from the living God and the eternal light. Now may our hearts lift themselves up towards their Father in praise, in thankfulness, in hope! Amen.

1 Samuel vii. 3.

"And Samuel spake unto all the house of Israel, saying, If ye do return unto the Lord with all your hearts, then put away the strange gods and Ashtaroth from among you, and prepare your hearts unto the Lord, and serve him only: and he will deliver you out of the hand of the Philistines."

SOLITARY POWER.

SAMUEL is now in full office. Eli died when the messenger told him that the Philistines had taken the ark. Up to this time we have had no express communication from Samuel him-

self. From pregnant sentences, here and there, we have known
that he has all the while been moving in the right direction.
The Lord was with Samuel, and did not suffer any of his words
to fall unto the ground. "All Israel from Dan to Beersheba
knew that Samuel was established to be a prophet of the Lord."
"And the Lord revealed himself unto Samuel in Shiloh." "And
the word of Samuel came unto all Israel." These assurances
indicate that Samuel, in his comparative obscurity, has been
steadfastly moving onward according to the purpose of God.
From this time we shall see more of him. His position in this
chapter is most conspicuous, and his deeds are most instructive.
Verily, in this case, the child was "father to the man." As
prophet of the Lord Samuel's will was supreme ;—all the main
features of the history derive their expression from the spirit
of Samuel.   There is authority in his word, there is inspiration
in his encouragement, there is death in his frown.   Under these
circumstances you see how naturally we are led to meditate
upon the profound influence of one life.   Such is the subject.
We shall develop it, by reviewing the three remarkable attitudes
in which we find Samuel in the course of this chapter.

In the first place, look at the sublime attitude which Samuel
assumed in relation to the corruption of the faith.   Samuel distinctly charged the house of Israel with having gone astray from
the living God ; solemnly, with the pathos of a godly tone, with
the solemnity of a righteous, indignant, yet pitiful heart, he said,
"You have been guilty of high crimes and misdemeanours
against the God of heaven ; you have trampled underfoot your
convictions and your traditions.   You have bowed yourselves
before the altars of forbidden gods."   Distinctly, without reservation, without anything that indicated timidity on his part, he
laid this terrible indictment against the house of Israel.   In
doing so he assumed a sublime attitude.   He stood before Israel
as a representative of the God who had been insulted, dishonoured, abandoned.   His was the only voice lifted up in the
name of the true God.   It is in such cases that men show what
stuff they are made of :—when they stand face to face with the
crowd, and say, "You are wrong;" when they mount the
popular whirlwind, and say, "Your will is moving in the wrong

direction,—it is corrupt, debased, utterly foul, and bad!" Is there a grander spectacle anywhere on the earth than to see a lonely man confronting a whole house or an entire nation, and upbraiding the whole community with a common apostasy—with a common determination to go down to darkness and death? Samuel said, "You must put away Baalim,"—a plural word, which stands for no god in particular, but for all the progeny of false gods. "You must put away Ashtaroth,"—a plural word, which signifies no goddess in particular, but the whole company of feminine idols. "That is what you must do." We find sublimity in the attitude, imperial force in the tone. How did Samuel's influence come to be so profound upon this occasion? The instant answer is, Because his influence is moral. Moral influence goes to the heart of things. He who deals with moral questions deals with the life of the world. Any other influence addresses itself to affairs of the moment; all other influences are superficial and transitory. He who repronounces God's commandments, and tells to the heart of the world God's charges, wields a moral, and therefore a profound influence. Sometimes we say that a man's intellectual influence has been profound. There is a sense in which that is perfectly possible, and may be really and gloriously true. But the heart is further in the man than the intellect. He, therefore, who purifies the heart, brings the life up to the right altitude and inspires it with the right purpose, does a work to which there is no end; it is abiding as God's eternity, lustrous in its degree as God's glory!

Herein is the supreme advantage of the Gospel. The Gospel of Jesus Christ does not come to attend to any diseases that are merely cutaneous; the Gospel of Jesus Christ does not engage to settle questions that lie merely on the surface of society; the Gospel of Christ does not undertake our local politics, and things that are little, contracted, and perishing. The Gospel of Christ lays its saving hand upon the human heart and says, " This is the sphere of my mission. I will affect all things that are superficial and local and temporary; but I shall affect them indirectly. By putting the life right, I shall put the extremities right; by making the heart as it ought to be, the whole surface of nature will become healthful and beautiful." This is the supreme advantage

of the minister of the Gospel. A true servant of the Lord
Jesus Christ has little or nothing to do, directly, with the petty,
trifling, fussy controversies of the day. It is not his business to
walk into heated committee rooms and to discuss, with all learning and profundity, transient parochial politics. The minister
of Jesus Christ addresses man as man, and by moving the heart
he moves the will; by enlightening the judgment, he elevates
the life. Having done that interior, moral, everlasting work,
there comes out of him, in all directions, the happiest influence
in relation to things that are local and perishing. We shall fall
from the great ministry, if, forgetting the universal, we give our
strength to the particular. We need men in society who stand
apart from the little fights, petty controversies, and angry contentions which seem to be part and parcel of daily life, and who
shall speak great principles, breathe a heavenly influence, and
bring to bear upon combatants of all kinds considerations which
shall survive all their misunderstandings. Regard Samuel in
this light, and you will see the sublimity of his attitude. He
stands alone ; on the other side of him is the whole house of
Israel. It would be a much easier thing for him, viewed merely
from the outside and in relation to the passing hour, to say,
" We are all brethren ; you have gone wrong, I must allow ; but
I do not think I should be harsh with you. Hail, fellows well
met! let bygones be bygones, and from this day let us enjoy
ourselves." But no man's will is merely personal when he
speaks for God. Samuel would have no right to say, " I am
setting up my little personal judgment and will against yours."
He was the medium on which the infinite heart broke into
language, and through which the infinite purpose caused itself to
be heard in all the indignation proper to its outrage, in all the
pathos becoming the infinite compassion of God ! Herein, again,
is the great influence of a moral teacher, a revealer of Christian
truth. Whenever we hear a preacher who speaks the right word,
we hear God the Father, God the Son, God the Holy Ghost ;
through his voice we hear the testimony of the angels unfallen ;
out of his words there comes the declaration of all that is
bright, pure, true, wise, in the universe of God !

Now let us look at the holy attitude which Samuel assumed

in relation to the guilt of Israel. Samuel said, "Gather all Israel
to Mizpeh, and I will pray for you unto the Lord." In the first
instance his attitude was sublime; the lonely man speaking the
charge of God to an apostate nation. In this instance his attitude
is holy. Because having charged the people in the name of God,
condemned them in the interests of righteousness, and called
them to purity of worship, he says, "If you will gather yourselves together, I will pray for you." This is the secret of great
influence: indignation,—calmness,—righteousness incorruptible
and inexorable,—devoutness that stoops to pray for the fallen, the
foul, the evil-minded, and the debased. Samuel was not borne
away by anger and fury; he did not give way even to judicial
vengeance. In the first instance he describes the corruptness of
the case, points out the right course, exhorts the people to take
that course instantly, and then he speaks these healing words:
"If ye will do these things, and gather yourselves together to
Mizpeh, I will pray unto the Lord for you." See the fulness of
the meaning of such words as these, as used by such a man, under
circumstances so distinctive and impressive! "I will pray unto
the Lord for you." Then the highest man in the Church is but
a priest, a prophet, an agent, an instrument. Not, "Gather all
Israel to Mizpeh, and there I will pronounce the word of absolu-
tion for you." Samuel lays no claim to any position, so far as
this case is concerned, but that of a suppliant who has influence
with God. That is all we can do for one another,—the work of
an instrument, the ministry of an agent. That word *all* has more
force in it than the mere monosyllable. Why, what is there
more than that? To understand the world's case,—to comprehend the terrible results of the world's apostasy,—to reproach,
rebuke, and exhort in the name of God,—and then to gather the
world we have branded with God's condemnation and pray for
it unto the God of heaven! When a man has done that he has
exhausted his resources; he has done more—he has moved
Omnipotence towards condescension and redemption!

"I will pray for you unto the Lord." Then the human needs
the divine. We never find—taking great breadths of history,
ages and centuries—that the human has been able to exist alone,
and to grow upward and onward in its atheism. We do find

hours in which atheism seems to carry everything its own way.
There are occasions in human history when God seems to be
utterly deposed, when a whole nation has got up and out-voted
God, emptied heaven, brought down the sky to the dust; but
never lifted up the dust to the sky! Observe that such periods
have been but occasional; they have always been transitory, and
in proportion to the length of their duration has there afterwards
gone up a cry to God, that he would come back again. If he
would but once show his face, the men who repudiated his existence and renounced his name "would dash their idols at his
feet, and call them gods no more." What is true in nations is
true in individuals. To any man who has not been living for
God we may say: You have not been living upward. You have
been living; you have not changed your address; people have
recognised your physical features; but you have not been going
up in the quality of your being,—your pathos has not become
tenderer, your charity has not become purer, your nobility has
not enhanced itself. This is a plain thing to say to a man's face,
but we should say it, yet not we but the whole Triune God and
all history,—when a man lives without religion—we will not say
irreligiously, as if he were profane and blasphemous, in the
ordinary sense of those terms—his life is a diminishing quantity;
he goes down in the volume and quality of his being.

Israel was gathered together to Mizpeh. The Philistines, the
enemies of the house of Israel, having heard that Israel had
gathered together to Mizpeh, the lords of the Philistines went up
against Israel. Observe, Israel was gathered at a prayer meeting. That is a modern expression, and not much in favour with
men who are "advanced." We do not know what they are
"advanced" in, and perhaps it is better on the whole not to
inquire. The Philistines went up against Israel, congregated for
a devotional purpose; and when the children of Israel heard it
they were afraid of the Philistines. And the children of Israel
said to Samuel, "Cease not to cry unto the Lord our God for us."
What became of the Philistines? The Philistines had won
many victories; they had proved their prowess in arms as against
the house of Israel; they had taken the ark of God when Israel
resorted to the formal rather than to the spiritual. Now that

Israel is getting its old heart back again, and its eyes are being turned to the heavens, what becomes of the Philistines? The Lord thundered that day upon the Philistines, and discomfited them, and they were smitten before Israel.

"And the men of Israel went out of Mizpeh, and pursued the Philistines, and smote them, until they came unto Beth-car" (v. 11).

There is a great law here. To some minds this must, of course, be sentimental. To men who have seen prayer under certain aspects and circumstances,—who have known godly persons, hard driven in life, unable to conduct a successful struggle, and yet who have been praying all the time,—this must appear to be little better than mockery. But many others have known precisely the same thing under a different class of circumstances leading to the same gracious and undeniable results. The Philistines came against a praying army. We must consider not what the praying army did in the first instance, but what God did. The Lord thundered, and the Philistines were deafened; the Lord touched the heads of the Philistinian army, and they went crazy; the Lord wielded his hand before the eyes of the Philistinian leaders, and they were blind! It is nothing to him to save whether there be many or few.

In this case it does not appear from the text that God took the rod of his lightning and utterly discomfited the Philistines. He thundered! When God's voice rolls over human life, it is either a benediction of infinite peace or a malediction no human force can turn aside. Observe when it was that Samuel said he would pray for the house of Israel. The great lesson here turns upon a point of time. When Israel returned unto the Lord with all their heart; when Israel put away the strange gods and Ashtaroth; when Israel prepared the heart unto the Lord and was ready to serve him only; when Israel had done this part, then Samuel said, "I will pray for you unto the Lord." Under other circumstances prayer would have been wasted breath. We find a great law here, which applies to the natural and the spiritual. Is there a plague in the city? Purify your sanitary arrangements, cleanse your drains, disinfect your channels, use everything that is at all likely to conduce to a good end,—then pray unto the Lord. After nature has exhausted herself, there may be something for the Lord to do, may there not? Who are we? Where did we obtain our education? Who put us up just one inch above the infinite that we might be able to say to God, "Now the people have done everything, there is nothing for thee to do"? Who are we? A man ought to have a good many certificates, credentials, and testimonials before he is able to establish a status which will justify him in suggesting that when all natural processes have been exhausted, God cannot do anything. What if God should be just one iota wiser than we are? What if after we have exhausted the resources of our skill and the efforts of our strength, God might be able to say, "See, there is one more thing to be done"? It would not be according very much to God, would it? Blessed are they who believe that after they have exhausted themselves, God can do exceeding abundantly above all that they ask or think!

Sometimes worldly people say—" Pray for us." Men have said that to us. What kind of men were they? Sometimes men who have made wrecks of themselves, who have gone as far devilward as they could get, whose hearts were like a den of unclean beasts, men who had no longer any grip of the world— the whole thing was slipping away from them—they have said to the minister whom they had previously characterised as a canting parson, "Pray for us." But one condition must be forthcoming on their part. There must be not only consciousness of loss, and consciousness that they cannot fight against God any longer, and that their next step will be into the jaws of the devil —there must be more than that. There must be self-renunciation, contrition, moral anguish, pain of the soul, repentance towards God. When these conditions are forthcoming, the servant of Christ may say, " I will pray for you unto the Lord."

In the third place, look at the exalted attitude which Samuel assumes in relation to his whole lifetime. We read in the fifteenth verse of this chapter, " Samuel judged Israel all the days of his life." Think of being able to account for all the days of a whole human history! Think of being able to write your biography in one sentence! Think of being able to do without parentheses, footnotes, reservations, apologies, and self-vindications! When we attempt to write our lives, there is so much to say that is collateral and modifying in its effect,—so much which is to explain the central line. When we have written our biography, we have seen great blank spaces—we do not know what we did then; we have seen great black patches, and we have known that these indicated service of the devil; we have seen blurred, blotched pages, with erasures and interlineations, and we have said, "This reminds us of the daily and terrible mistakes of our life." So our biographical record becomes anomalous, contradictory, irreconcilable. Here is a man whose lifetime is gathered up in one sentence. "Samuel judged Israel all the days of his life." We have seen him in his childhood, we have had glances of him as he was passing up to his mature age. To-day we see him in three impressive and remarkable attitudes. His whole history is in this sentence : He was a judge of God all his days. Think of giving a whole lifetime to God. There are those who cannot do that now. But young men may be able to give twenty, thirty, perhaps fifty years all to Christ. Fifty years in succession ; no break, no marring interruption,—half a century given to Christ ! Some grey-haired old men may be following this study. Perhaps they are not within the circle that is divine ; they may not be numbered amongst the members of the redeemed family, and now all that they can give is just the fag-end of a life. To such we would say : Death cannot be long in meeting you ! Perhaps next year only,—perhaps to-morrow. The young may die, the old must. You may only have six weeks left ; you had better give them than not give anything at all.

> "While the lamp holds out to burn,
> The vilest sinner may return."

There was a thief saved on the cross, but only one thief.

See then the profound influence which may be exerted by one life. We are dealing with Samuel, and with Samuel alone. Samuel's life is not confined to himself ; it is a radiating life, streaming out from itself and touching thousands of points in the social and national life of others. Who can tell what may be done by one man ? We shall not quote the testimony of a friend on this point, because he might be partial in his judgment. But once an enemy gave explicit testimony upon this point, and we shall accept his words just as he himself gave them. His name was Demetrius; he was an idol-maker; trade was slipping out of his fingers fast; he was not making so many gods as usual; and he spake to the people of the city in these words : " Ye see and hear, that not alone at Ephesus, but almost throughout all Asia, this Paul persuadeth and turneth away much people, saying, that they be no gods, which are made with hands." It was a valuable testimony. It was an enemy writing the report of the Church for the last year. It was the devil, reading a secretarial report of what one man had done. This Paul ! Not ten thousand Pauls, not a great army of Pauls, but one little man, with an immeasurably great soul, who was not only working mightily in Ephesus against idolatry, but throughout all Asia ! What one life can do. Let no man despise himself; do not say, " My little influence is of no avail." Every man can be intense, though only few men can be extensive in influence. The father upon the house, the head of the business in his own establishment, the friend among his friends, the mother in the nursery,—each life can have a speciality of intensity in these high matters. Whoso would wield profound, eternal influence, let him help the souls of men ; get away from things that are superficial, local, and self-contained ! Speak the truth of God, and eternity itself cannot exhaust the happy effect of that blessed influence !

PRAYER.

ALMIGHTY GOD, thy claim upon our worship is unceasing, for thy mercy, like thy majesty, endureth for ever. Thou dost never withhold thine hand from giving good gifts unto thy children. As thou hast made them in thine own image and likeness, and hast implanted within them desires which the world cannot satisfy, so thou dost especially reveal thyself unto them day by day, appeasing their hunger with bread from heaven, and quenching their thirst with water out of the river of God. Oftentimes have we said concerning thy Son, We will not have this Man to reign over us. But when we have tasted the bitterness of sin, and have been convinced of our own emptiness and helplessness, when heart and flesh have failed, when by the ministry of thy Holy Spirit we have come to understand somewhat of thine own holiness and mercy and love, our hearts' desire has been that Jesus might sit upon the throne of our love, and rule our whole life: that he might be King of kings, and Lord of lords, our Redeemer, the Mighty One of Israel. We desire to live unto the glory of God, to understand the meaning of the gift of life with which we have been blessed. Thou hast entrusted us with solemn responsibilities: enable us to understand their meaning, to feel their pressure, and to respond with all our hearts to their demands. Let thy blessing rest upon us. May thy house be unto us as the gate of heaven ; may weary souls recover their strength and tone. May desponding hearts be revived and comforted with the consolation of God. May worldly minds be given to feel that there is a world higher than the present: that round about us is the great sea of thine eternity. May we be prepared for all the future, having our hearts cleansed through the blood of Jesus Christ. We depend upon thy Holy Spirit ; we will not look unto our own resources, except as they present themselves as the gifts of God. We will rely upon thy power ; we will cry mightily unto our God! Thou wilt hear us ; thou wilt redeem our souls from all fear ; thou wilt inspire us with immortal hope ; thou wilt clothe us with adequate power. Cleanse our hearts by the precious blood of the Lord Jesus. Show to us, more and more, the meaning of the mystery of his dear cross. May we find all that is deepest and truest in our own life symbolised in that cross of Jesus. May it be the answer to our sin, the remedy of our diseases, the one hope of our wondering and anxious souls! Amen.

1 Samuel viii. 5.

"Make us a king to judge us like all the nations."

MAKING A KING.

WE have seen Israel defeated, almost destroyed, in war with the Philistines. We have seen Israel in extremity, prostrate before Almighty God, and crying unto him, in intolerable woe, for interposition in the time of torment and hopelessness. The prayer has been responded to, and Israel has been revived. A new hope has cheered the hearts of those who prayed unto the Lord of heaven. In the revival of strength Israel has become political. A new idea has occurred to the leaders of the people, namely,—that a king should be required and should be set over Israel, that Israel might be like all other nations. That seems a very reasonable request, as viewed from a certain point. It becomes us, therefore, to look at it the more carefully; because, if so-called reasonable requests be followed by the disasters which accrued upon the prayer before us, it becomes a matter of infinite moment that we should know the significance of the words we use and the full compass of the desires which we express. Truly this is a chapter of incident; the movement is rapid from beginning to end. Let us watch it; and let us gather together, so far as we may be able, the great principles with which this graphic chapter is so fully charged. The elders of Israel said unto Samuel, "Behold, thou art old, and thy sons walk not in thy ways: now make us a king to judge us like all the nations." The people of Israel, it appears, were extremely particular about the morality of other people. They had facts on their side. Samuel's sons did not walk in their father's ways, but turned aside after lucre, took bribes, and perverted judgment. When the elders of Israel saw this apostasy on the part of the sons of Samuel, they said, "Let us do away with this race of men altogether, and have a crowned head to reign over us, that we may be like the other nations of the earth." Let us then do full justice to the elders of Israel. As a matter of public notoriety, Samuel's sons were not like Samuel himself in their moral tone and in their moral example. This brings before us a sad and humiliating fact,—that the children of great men and of good men are not always worthy of their parentage. Few things can be more humiliating to a high nature, to a Christian philanthropist, than to find that his public work is undone in the very circle within which his own influence ought to have been most intense; that he, who is instrumental in doing so much good abroad, should actually have to come home to find what sin is in its utmost keenness, in its intolerable bitterness. Sometimes public men may be to blame for this in some degree. They may have to say, "Other vineyards have I kept; my own vineyard I have not kept." They may be more fitted for public teaching and public stimulus than for private utterance of truth and domestic control of life. This ought to be carefully understood before we venture to pronounce judgment upon such men, who in their own hearts feel a greater bitterness than it would be possible for us by our own mere reproaches to infuse into them. There are men who can speak to a thousand hearers, who are utterly weak and powerless when they come into the details of common life and have to teach a single child at home, and show the light of God upon the private paths of life. Others there may be who turn their public excitement into a temptation to go astray from plain, simple home duty. They have the ability; they are lacking in will. They can only show themselves upon public platforms, within great arenas of display; they are moved by public, rather than by intensely personal and moral considerations. Consequently, their own garden-wall is broken down, their own little flower-bed at home is all weed-grown, whilst they are busy with the great public fields and the great vineyards of the world. We should not speak harshly of such fathers : but if there be anything in these suggestions, and if any man should require a hint of the kind, tenderly, with self-restraint and brotherly forbearance, we would venture to say, Think of this; and, if you can improve, remember that now is the accepted time ; you cannot too soon begin the work of family cultivation.

This brings before us the equally remarkable fact, that grace is not hereditary. When we see a good man we expect his children to be like himself. But grace does not descend in the family line. The father may be an apostle, the son may be a blasphemer. There are circumstances, no doubt, in which at the very moment that the father has been preaching the gospel, his own son, whom he loved as his life, has been fulfilling some profane engagement, has been blaspheming the name of the God of his fathers! This is very mysterious, inexpressibly painful, most disheartening to the man who wants to live a simple, godly, sincere, useful life. The fact is overbearing. To the son of a godly man we would say : Your father's godliness will not save you; your father's godliness abused on your part, disregarded by you, will augment the wrath from which you shall one day suffer. It is one of many talents given to you ; and to whom much has been given, from him shall much be expected. He that had the opportunity and the privilege, and abused what he had, shall be—it is the voice of justice, common sense, and righteousness—beaten with many stripes. Why should it be thought a thing incredible, or why should it be a thing invested with tormenting mystery, that a child should not inherit the father's piety ? It is precisely the same with intellectual gifts in many cases ; it is the same with physical endowments in many instances. We find, again and again, a great man, a man of wondrous compass of mind, great and manifold ability, whose son is of a very ordinary type of intellect. It is wonderful,—but there is no occasion why we should torture it into a mystery, and look at it as one of those things which should affright us from the religious or the devotional side of life. We have not to explain these things. We may pause before them and learn much from them ; but the explanation is not with us at all.

It is important to gather all these things together in order that the case of the elders of Israel may be turned as much to their advantage as we possibly can. What our object is in thus defending them will presently appear. The elders of Israel had a case. They were concerned for the nation ; they saw the two sons of Samuel going astray from their father's paths ; they came to the man when he was old, and told him about the apostasy of his sons. They said, " Make us a king to judge us like all the nations." If ever men apparently had a simple, straightforward, common-sense case, the elders of Israel had such a case in the chapter which is now before us. Samuel heard this statement, and the thing displeased him. No man likes to see his whole life disregarded, and his tower thrown away ruthlessly. Samuel was a man in advanced life, identified vitally with the religious and political fortunes of Israel; had his hopes with regard to the future; drew out of his own life the hopes by which he was animated. Now suddenly the elders of Israel say, "We wish to dispossess all who may be supposed to have any claim upon us through your agency and instrumentality; we wish to open a new political era in Israel." No man likes to see the tower of his life thrown down in that way. We have sympathy with old ministers who have old-world notions; who view with what appears to younger men an almost ungenerous suspicion and distrust what they call new-fangled notions and methods of doing things. After all, there is a good deal of human nature and common sense in the old man's view of the changes which are proposed to him. He started from a given point; he has worked along a certain line; a man cannot disinherit and dispossess himself of all his own learning, culture, traditions, and associations, and go back again or go forward into the infancy of new and startling movements. It would be well if men could learn this more profoundly. Young Englandism and young Americanism must be very distasteful to old Samuels, high-priests, and venerable prophets. We shall show our strength by showing our moderation; we shall be most mighty when we are most yielding!

Samuel told the Lord about it. This is very startling to those who live at a far distance from God. These old men seem always to have been living, as it were, next door to him, and had but to whisper and they were heard. These little sentences come in so abruptly. We read, "And Samuel prayed unto the Lord." Not, "Samuel ordered a high ladder to be made that he might set it up against heaven, and creep up to it round by round;" but the record is "Samuel prayed unto the Lord." It is a kind of breathing process, it is ready, spontaneous as love. Samuel turned towards the elders of Israel, heard their story, then turned his face about and told God concerning the whole thing. It is a wonderful kind of life,—God always so nigh at hand. Will he not be equally nigh at hand to-day? Has he still to be sought for as if he had hidden himself beyond

the voice of the thunder, or is he nigh at hand so that a sigh
can reach him, and a whisper can stir his omnipotence into
beneficent interposition on behalf of his sorrowing, suffering
people ?   It would be a new life to us if we knew that God beset
us behind and before, laid his hand upon us, and that not a
throb of our heart escaped the ear of his love !

Samuel saw the outside of the case. Samuel saw, what we
now call, the fact of the case ; God saw the truth of it. Many
persons do not distinguish between fact and truth. There is an
infinite difference between fact and truth. Fact is the thing done,
the thing visible, the thing that has shape, and that can be
approached and touched. Truth underlies it. We must get at
the truth before we can understand the fact itself. This is ever
necessary, but specially needful where matters are complicated by
profoundly moral considerations. The Lord explained the case
to Samuel. He said, in effect, " Thou art quite mistaken ; the
matter is not as thou dost view it ; looked at from thy point, the
elders of Israel seem to have a very strong and excellent case.
But, Samuel, the elders of Israel have rejected me, they have not
rejected thee. They are only making a tool of thee ; thou art
become to them a mere convenience, or as it were a scapegoat.
They profess to be very deeply concerned about the moral apostasy
of thy sons ; they do not care one pin-point about it ; they are
extremely glad to be able to seize upon anything that will seem to
give a good colouring to their case. Samuel, Israel has cast off
its God. Is it wonderful, then, that Israel should cast off the
servant ? " What an explanation this is ! how it goes to the
root and core ! how it cleaves open the life of man, and holds up
in the sunny universe a corrupt soul, that all men may see it
and know that the heart is deceitful above all things and desperately wicked ! What a subject opens upon us here ! The great
world of excuses, social explanations, the faces which things are
made to wear, the visors and disguises which are set upon life in
order to conceal its corruption, its leprosy, its death. Truly the
word of God is sharp and powerful, sharper than any two-edged
sword ! It will not let a man alone ; it will not allow a man to
tell his own story, and go away as if he had exhausted the case.
He is permitted to state the circumstances, to make his own

advocacy of given questions, to put the question before society just as he pleases. But when he sits down, this word that searches the heart and goes through the life like a flaming fire says, "Now I will tell you what it is; you have made an excuse into a reason; you have lied, not unto me, but unto the Holy Ghost, unto God! Your case looks well. But I open thee now, I cleave through thee, I pour the sunlight through every fibre of thy leprous being, and I brand thee liar and blasphemer!" It is a fearful thing to fall into the hands of the living God!

See, for example, an individual who has a most excellent case. He goes to his minister, and says to him in a whine, which soft men may mistake for earnestness, "I really cannot remain here any longer, sir. I have seen so much inconsistency in the members of the Church; I have seen so much that has pained me; I have felt grieved at the inconsistency of professing Christians; therefore, I am going to turn over a new page, and I must withdraw from the Church." He was pained! What that poor creature carried in the way of other people's immoralities, no arithmetic can ever calculate, no poetry can ever dream! When he has told his tale, and impressed the poor minister, who believes well of everybody, in proportion as he does not know human nature, God says to him, "This is the case. That man would not care one farthing if all the Church were to prove traitorous to-morrow; that man, who has suffered so much pain, who has been so troubled about the inconsistencies of professing Christians, is now planning sin secretly in his soul; if I could show thee by taking off, fold after fold, thou wouldst see in his heart what he has never said to his wife or mother or child or friend; thou wouldst see there a determination to enjoy sin under some disguise. He wants to get clear of moral restraint, of social discipline; he wants to evade public opinion, that he may, in concealment and under such defence as secrecy may set up, enjoy sin as he has never enjoyed it before. Mark him, going away yonder, bearing the inconsistencies and immoralities of other people! He is now going to carry out the very first step of his plan—to enjoy the works of iniquity, sources of forbidden pleasure as he never partook of them before." So there are two judgments in the world. Man makes out his own case, God comes with the explanation. Man cheats man with outside appearances; afterwards God holds the light over the case. All things are naked and opened unto the eyes of him with whom we have to do!

Here is a minister of the Gospel, who says he is going to withdraw from the ministry and retire into private life. He has been so annoyed by circumstances which have arisen around him; he has been so fretted and chafed by a multitude of things, that he can no longer endure them; and now he is going to enjoy the retirement of private life. That is his statement. What does it amount to? He is going to run away because there are some difficulties in life. As if he ever could get into any sphere in this world where difficulty would not call upon him, and force its attention upon his reluctant soul! Has he told all the case? Has he not kept back part of the price? Is he not rather arranging his circumstances so that he can sin with larger license,—that he can do things in private life which he dare not do under the responsibilities of a public position? These words cut like daggers and search like fire! God forbid they should have any application to us!

The Lord told Samuel to make the people a king. "Hear them; do what they ask; hearken unto their voice: howbeit yet protest solemnly unto them, and shew them the manner of the king that shall reign over them." This is an instruction that we should do well to carry out in all life. There are times when we are pressed into certain courses; when all we can do is to protest. Sometimes when a man is weak then is he strong. The lifting, the half-lifting of a tremulous hand means—when interpreted by God's wisdom—battle, battle to the bitter end, protest, vehement opposition! It is a feeble sign: but the meaning of that poor, broken hand being lifted up is, that if the man could do that which is in his soul he would stem the torrent of the popular will and set up righteousness in the earth! The Lord instructed Samuel what to say. Here is the speech which was made to the elders of Israel:—

'And he said, This will be the manner of the king that shall reign over you: he will take your sons, and appoint them for himself, for his chariots, and to be his horsemen ; and some shall run before his chariots. And he will appoint him captains over thousands, and captains over fifties; and will set them to ear his ground, and to reap his harvest, and to make his instruments of war, and instruments of his chariots. And he will take your daughters to be confectionaries, and to be cooks, and to be bakers. And he will take your fields, and your vineyards, and your oliveyards, even the best of them, and give them to his servants. And he will take the tenth of your seed, and of your vineyards, and give to his officers, and to his servants. And he will take your menservants, and your maidservants, and your goodliest young men, and your asses, and put them to his work. He will take the tenth of your sheep : and ye shall be his servants. And ye shall cry out in that day because of your king which ye shall have chosen you; and the Lord will not hear you in that day " (viii. 11-18).

What then ?   When they heard the speech they said, " Nay ; but we will have a king over us."   Observe how men can fight their way, when so determined, through all the warnings that even God can send.   We should have supposed that the elders of Israel, in whose heads was lodged the wisdom of the people,—the men of sagacity, penetration, and self-control,—on hearing these words from the Lord's prophet would instantly have said, " Then do we repent of the sin of our request : God shall continue, if his mercy will so incline, to be our King for ever."   Instead of that, they hear the warning, they see the thunderbolts, the whole future is depicted to them in words which have not two significations.   As the result of the whole, they lift up their voices and say, " We will have a king to reign over us."   Do we condemn them ?   Let us not be ready with reproach ; nor urgent in condemnation.   We are doing a deadlier thing, it may be, than the elders of Israel did in this case.   We are told that God is angry with the wicked every day; that the wicked shall be driven into hell, and all the nations that forget God.   We are told that the liar shall have his portion in the lake which burneth with fire and brimstone, that no drunkard shall enter the kingdom of heaven, that anything that is unclean, defiled, or corrupt, shall not pass into the city of God's light ; we are told that nothing remaineth for the sinner but a fearful looking for of judgment and fiery indignation.   All the terrors of the Lord are thundered from time to time upon the people.   What is the result ?   Men can go immediately from hearing or reading the most terrific statements concerning the future of the wicked, and can throw themselves with unbridled license into all the diabolical enjoyments which stimulate but never satisfy the corrupt soul! **By so much as we** condemn Israel, we condemn the sinner.   **It may be that in pro-** nouncing the elders of Israel foolish and **criminal, we write our-** selves worthy of the condemnation of God !

Observe, man can have his way.   There **is a point at which** even God withdraws from the contest.   " My Spirit shall not always strive with man."   If we be so minded, we can force our way through all solemn warning, all pathetic entreaty, **all** earnest persuasiveness on the part of friend, wife, husband, teacher, preacher, God the Father, God the Son, and God the Holy Ghost !   We can go to hell if we will !   So do not be discouraged, you can get there !   Do not be discouraged, there is nothing before you but love, grace, mercy, tenderness, God. That is all.   There is a grim ghastly cross,—hew it down ! There is a way round it, a way through it, a way over it,—you can get there !   Fool, coward !

See the childishness of the reasoning by which they supported their case.   " That we," said the elders of Israel, " also may be like all the nations ; may be like other people."   That is what the young man says when he is hard pressed.   When he wishes to throw off family restraint, when he wishes to get away from family prayer, family reading of the Bible and domestic superintendence, he says, " I want to be as other men are ; other young men of my age have this privilege and that privilege, and I just want to be like other men."   That sounds very reasonable, but is that all ?   Be true to thyself, O young man ; do not tell lies to thyself.   If thou hast lies to tell, why not tell them aloud —tell them to other people ; why tell lies to thine own heart ? To say it is only this you want ; whereas thou knowest well, in thy heart of hearts, that it is some terrible wickedness to which thou wishest to give way.

Where the disease is vital, the remedy must be **vital too.** Nothing will reach this disease but the mediation of **God the** Son.   It is not a speck of dust which any hand can rub off.   The disease is in the heart, the poison is in the blood.   The death is in the life—this is no paradox, but an awful, grim, terrible truth.

What, then, will reach it? The blood of the Son of God, the agony of Gethsemane, the atonement of Calvary, the wondrous, unspeakable, glorious work of Jesus Christ, Son of God, God the Son! Nothing else can reach it. Every other remedy is cutaneous, is transitory. The remedy of Christ's cross, Christ's atonement, is vital, and is therefore eternal!

SELECTED NOTE.

The mustering of the Hebrews at Mizpeh on the inauguration of Samuel alarmed the Philistines, and their "lords went up against Israel." Samuel assumed the functions of the theocratic viceroy, offered a burnt-offering, and implored the immediate protection of Jehovah. He was answered with propitious thunder. A fearful storm burst upon the Philistines, who were signally defeated, and did not recruit their strength again during the administration of the prophet-judge. The grateful victor erected a stone of remembrance, and named it Ebenezer. From an incidental allusion (vii. 14) we learn, too, that about this time the Amorites, the inveterate foes of Israel, were also at peace with them—another triumph of his government. The presidency of Samuel appears to have been eminently successful. From the very brief sketch given us of his public life we infer that the administration of justice occupied no little share of his time and attention. He went from year to year in circuit to Bethel, Gilgal, and Mizpeh, places not very far distant from each other, but chosen perhaps, as Winer suggests, because they were the old scenes of worship (*Real-Wört*, sub voce).

In Samuel's old age two of his sons were appointed by him deputy-judges in Beersheba. These young men possessed not their father's integrity of spirit, but "turned aside after lucre, took bribes, and perverted judgment" (viii. 3). The advanced years of the venerable ruler himself and his approaching dissolution, the certainty that none of his family could fill his office with advantage to the country, the horror of a period of anarchy which his death might occasion, the necessity of having some one to put an end to tribal jealousies and concentrate the energies of the nation, especially as there appeared to be symptoms of renewed warlike preparations on the part of the Ammonites (xii. 12), these considerations seem to have led the elders of Israel to adopt the bold step of assembling at Ramah and soliciting Samuel "to make a king to judge them." The proposed change from a republican to a regal form of government displeased Samuel for various reasons. Besides it being a departure from the first political institute, and so far an infringement on the rights of the divine head of the theocracy, it was regarded by the regent as a virtual charge against himself, one of those examples of popular fickleness and ingratitude which the history of every realm exhibits in profusion. Jehovah comforts Samuel by saying, "They have not rejected thee, but they have rejected me." Being warned of God to accede to their request for a king, and yet to remonstrate with the people, and set before the nation the perils and tyranny of a monarchical government (viii. 10), Samuel proceeded to the election of a sovereign. Saul, son of Kish, "a choice young man and a goodly," whom he had met unexpectedly, was pointed out to him by Jehovah as the king of Israel, and by the prophet was anointed and saluted as monarch. Samuel again convened the nation at Mizpeh, again with honest zeal condemned their project, but caused the sacred lot to be taken. The lot fell on Saul. The prophet now formally introduced him to the people, who shouted in joyous acclamation, "God save the king."

PRAYER.

ALMIGHTY GOD, may the hour of worship be exceeding precious to the souls whose desire is towards thee. Come down upon us as a light above the brightness of the sun, as the cooling dew upon the parched grass, and as showers that water the earth. Bring to our memory the bitterest recollections of our sins, and then show us the cross of redemption, that our sorrow may be swallowed up in unspeakable joy. Show us thy name plainly written on every daily mercy. May our bread and our water remind us of God. May the light be a revelation, and the darkness a shield of defence. May joy be as an angel sent down from heaven, and sorrow as a cloud which shall hasten us home. Pity us in hours of weakness : save us when strong billows go over our heads. Let thy pardon be given to us, guilty helpless men, and it shall be well with us evermore. Amen.

1 Samuel x. 9.

"God gave him another heart."

SAUL.

THE threads of daily life often appear to be either loose and unrelated or hopelessly entangled. At times we seem to have nothing to do with each other. We go on our separate ways. It is only now and then that we find lines touch each other, and form figures, and see that under the apparent simplicity of daily affairs there are being wrought out strange plots, romances which no human dreamer had ever conceived, and combinations which give life new interest and enhanced importance. A man climbs a hill that he may in solitude revel in the delights of the landscape, and, lo, a little child meets him there, and the supposed accident is the turning point in his life. A traveller turns aside that he may drink of the well by the way, and, behold, the stranger who was there before him, and who would have been gone in one moment more, becomes the chief joy of his life, the ruler of his fortunes, the sovereign of his destiny. So it ever is. We know not what we do. We go, and know not how we shall return. We lie down, not knowing that the morning shall bring us a new life. We speak, and our word lifts some listening soul almost to heaven. Thus our life is a mystery ; we are strangers, yet friends. We live for many years apart, and by-and-by there comes a moment which unites us in holy confidence, giving all mysteries a meaning, and showing all difficulties to be but steps up to heaven.

The circumstances in connection with which the text is found naturally lead us into this strain of animating, yet tranquillising, reflection. The Lord had determined to grant the request of Israel for a king. Instructions to that end were given to Samuel. A certain man had lost his asses. Saul went to seek them, and in the course of his errand it was made known to him that he was to be the king of Israel. Let us study portions of the narrative, and gather some of the practical lessons with which the story is so richly charged.

"And the asses of Kish, Saul's father, were lost" (ix. 3).

This is one of what may be termed the vexatious and stupid affairs of daily life. It is apparently a most paltry statement to be found in a book which is a revelation from heaven. The asses were lost, what then ? Who cares ? Yet out of this simple circumstance there may arise events which shall startle the most indifferent reader. The asses being lost, Kish commanded his son Saul to take with him a servant, and go in pursuit. To this command Saul instantly responded ; yet this is the more remarkable, seeing that Saul is described as "a choice young man, and a goodly : and there was not among the children of Israel a goodlier person than he : from his shoulders and upward he was higher than any of the people." Smart young men ought not to be sent upon menial errands. Might not Saul have regarded the request of his father as imposing upon him a most vexatious and humiliating duty ? Contrast the majesty of his person with the contemptibleness of his errand, and say whether there be not an immeasurable disproportion. Yet Saul, so imperial in bearing, so choice and goodly in all the attributes of physical manhood, appears instantly to have obeyed the behest of his father. The filial spirit never sees anything contemptible in the paternal desire. **Men should rule their** lives not by the insignificance of the service, but by the sublimity of the one Ruler in whose hands are the laws and destinies of life. Saul might have looked at the object alone ; instead of that he looked at his father, in that look we find the secret of his obedience and alacrity. When the disciples went to seek the ass for Jesus Christ, they thought not of the meanness of the duty, but of the dignity of the Master.

"And he passed through Mount Ephraim, and passed through the land of Shalisha, but they found them not : then they passed through the land of Shalim, and there they were not : and he passed through the land of the Benjamites, but they found them not " (ix. 4).

In this verse there is nothing but the hollow sound of repeated disappointment. It emphatically describes the negative side of life. There are men to-day who are repeating this experience with most painful faithfulness. Go whither they may they find not the object of their pursuit. They climb the hill of difficulty, and, behold, their errand is lost. They speed along deep and dangerous valleys, and, lo, the object of their pursuit eludes and mocks them. They arise with the sun, they tarry until the return of the stars, their nerve is constantly on the stretch, their whole life becomes a tormenting anxiety, yet the desire of their heart is withheld from them. Their days are but repetitions of a disappointment, which is fast deepening into despair. Of how many may it be said that their experience is within the limits of this dreary verse ! Life is to us hollow, empty, and mocking. The lifting up of our hand doth but bring us weariness, and the putting forth of our strength only adds to the vexation of our spirit. Of what use is history, if an event of this kind does not renew our hope and vivify our past experience ? We are not the only men who have shivered on the dark side of life. Look at Saul, wearily wandering from place to place, inquiring, looking, hoping, yet finding all his efforts ending in disappointment ! Is there not a meaning in all this ? Is it possible that God can be taking any man along so painful and barren a road to an end which shall bring elevation and gladness ? The road to honour is often long and hard. Men have to endure the discipline of disappointment before they can bear the reward of success.

"And he said unto him, Behold now, there is in this city a man of God, and he is an honourable man ; all that he saith cometh surely to pass : now let us go thither; peradventure he can shew us our way that we should go " (ix. 6).

The great advantage of having a man of God in every city : the man of God makes his influence felt for good, and becomes honoured and trusted in matters which are not strictly religious. Two travellers have lost their way, and, behold, they inquire of a man of God ! The great principle which underlies all incidents of this kind is that in all perplexities and embarrassments the man of God shoud be the chief of earthly counsellors. There are crises in life when a man's moral influence goes for something. The man of God is sought out in trouble rather than in joy, and it is the brightest of his glories that he is willing to help those who never would have gone to him but for the stress of their difficulties. Is it not repetition to say that Samuel was an honourable man as well as a man of God ? Might not the latter title have included the former ? It undoubtedly includes all elements and attributes that are virtuous, honourable, true, and beautiful; yet there is a horrible possibility that a man may avow the name of God, and yet know nothing of the restriction and dignity of social honour. There are men in the Church whose signature stands for nothing, whose words are full of deceit, and whose covenants are but so much waste paper. A very beautiful image is this of the position of Samuel. What is the vocation of the man of God ? It is to tell other men their way ! All men are morally lost; the man of God points out the way of recovery : all men are in intellectual confusion by reason of their moral depravity ; the man of God shows the way to the light ! Ministers of the Gospel are appointed to tell men the way. This, too, is the appointment of heads of houses, conductors of educational institutions, and those who mould and lead the sentiment of the times. It should be observed that this word was spoken, not by Saul, but by his servant. The man of God was known by repute to the servant of the king, who knew and trusted the servant of the living God. Not only did he himself trust Samuel, but he commended him to the confidence of Saul. Despise no man. God's signature may be found in unexpected places. The little maid told the household the name of Elisha,— the servant told Saul of Samuel.

"Then said Saul to his servant, But, behold, if we go, what shall we bring the man? for the bread is spent in our vessels, and there is not a present to bring to the man of God : what have we?

"And the servant answered Saul again, and said, Behold, I have here at hand the fourth part of a shekel of silver : that will I give to the man of God, to tell us our way" (ix. 7, 8).

Saul was a gentleman, every whit! Eastern customs aside altogether, there was a vein of gentlemanliness in the nature of Saul. He was about to ask a favour, but a preliminary question arose in his mind. Absurd indeed is the idea of giving anything to the man of God for his services! Ask him what questions you please; exhaust his intellectual resources; drain every current of his sympathy: and when you can get no more out of him, turn your back upon him, or starve him out! The last thing you can kill in a man is true gentlemanliness. George Whitefield, when he had but a cow-heel for dinner, would have the frugal meal set out with as much care as if it had been a banquet. There are two ways of doing everything. It was but little that Saul had to give, yet he gave it of his own free will, and with all the grace of a natural king. We are not to pay mere prices for knowledge and direction in life; we are to give gifts of the heart,—such donations as are inspired by our love, though they may be limited by our poverty. It should be noted that this little arrangement was made before the lost travellers went into the presence of Samuel. It came of the spontaneous motion of their own hearts. The question was not, What dost thou charge? What shall we give thee? But a plan was laid beforehand, and Samuel was not subjected to the indignity of a commercial inquiry. Christian Churches might learn a great lesson from this example. We should then no longer see compensation given with the hand of patronage, which ought to have been bestowed with the hand of thankfulness and justice. A minister is invited to preach in a distant town ; at considerable personal inconvenience he accepts the invitation ; the greater part of two days may be consumed in discharging the service which has been requested at his hands ; and as he is about to return to his home, he is asked to name the amount of his expenses! There is no free gift; there is no offering of love; there is no working out of a plan of reward ; there is rather a desire to keep him down to the lowest possible line, and a disposition to increase public charities at the expense of personal justice. This whole thing is an abomination to Christian society. No man who works for the Churches ought ever to be asked what his expenses are ; his services should be requited on principles of the highest justice, without himself being subjected to interrogations respecting his railway and cab fares. Modern gentlemen may learn something from the ancient aristocracy.

When Saul had found his way to Samuel by the direction of the young maidens who were going out to draw water, and who, to their credit, knew the movements of the prophet, and the order of the religious engagements of the day, Samuel said to Saul, " As for thine asses that were lost three days ago, set not thy mind on them ; for they are found." A wonderful kingdom is the kingdom of God ! Though Samuel had before him the future king of Israel, and he himself was about to be deposed from his own supremacy, yet he communicated to Saul intelligence of the lost asses ! Doth anything escape the care of God ? Doth not God care for oxen ? Doth a sparrow fall to the ground without our Father's notice ? If we give the great concerns of our life into the hands of God, nothing that belongs to us shall be accounted unworthy of his notice. Mark the consideration and forethought of the prophet. Though about to dazzle the eyes of Saul with unaccustomed brilliance, yet he paid attention to the family concerns in which Saul was interested. The lesson is great to those who have hearts to understand.

"And Saul answered and said, Am not I a Benjamite, of the smallest of the tribes of Israel ? and my family the least of all the families of the tribe of Benjamin ? wherefore then speakest thou so to me ? " (ix. 21).

A man should inquire what background he has when a voice like Samuel's sounds in his ear. Saul was informed that on him was set all the desire of Israel : under such an announcement it was natural and proper that he should look to his antecedents, that, so to speak, he should gather himself up, and take correct measure of his manhood. A word of caution is needed here. Inquiry into our antecedents and resources should never be made with a fear of evading duty and difficulty. A very subtle temp-

tation assails us from this side. Spurious modesty may reduce
to the uttermost poverty and insufficiency, in order that by so
doing it may lure us from paths of difficulty and hard service.
We may speak of our loaves and fishes as if they were nothing
simply that we may save them for our own consumption. There
is a self-reduction which is actually a self-preservation. There
is a way of saying that we are unworthy which really means that
we are afraid. The inquiry should show us the disproportion
between our strength and God's call. Such a revelation will do
us good. When humility is saved from degenerating into fear, it
becomes a source of strength. Moses complained that he was a
man of slow speech; he desired that God would send his word
by some other messenger, because of his incapacity and unworthiness. Jeremiah urged in response to the call of God, that he was
but a little child. Saul declared that he was of the smallest of
the tribes of Israel, and sought to escape the duty of the hour
through a sense of personal inadequacy to fulfil its demands.
There is a medium between spurious self-depreciation and pre-
sumptuous boastfulness. That medium is reliance upon the
sufficiency of God. Whom God calls he also qualifies. He can
batter down great fortresses with any weapon which he may
choose. The web of the spider shall become as an impregnable
wall, if God so will. A little one shall utterly destroy countless
thousands, if that little one strike in the name of God.

Having had this interview with Samuel, Saul started on his
way; and we read "that when he turned his back to go from
Samuel, God gave him another heart." Observe, not increased
intelligence, not additional personal stature, not any outward sign
and proof that he was elected to be king of Israel; God gave
him another heart. The question of life is often a question of
feeling. There are many who know theologically the way of
salvation; they could answer satisfactorily many questions in
theology; they know the difference between falsehood and truth;
yet their feet are set in the broad way, and their faces are towards
the City of Destruction. What they want is another heart. Your
life requires to be set on fire with the love of God. "With the
heart man believeth unto righteousness." "My son, give me thine
heart!" We shall not be saved by the number and excellence

of our intellectual ideas, but because we have cast our whole heart at the feet of the Saviour of the world, who came to teach men the love of God.

The cry arose amongst the people, "Is Saul also amongst the prophets?" If we have to excite surprise in society, let us see to it that the surprise is awakened, not by our moral degeneracy, but by our religious elevation. If we go to the gaming-table, we shall excite surprise; if we be found on the race-course, we shall excite surprise; if we assume the leadership of bad men in bad courses, we shall excite surprise; but what of such surprise? We may, by increasing our devotion, by multiplying our beneficent labours, by courageous service in the kingdom of God, excite a surprise which shall indicate that we are no longer amongst those who live only for this world, " whose god is their belly, and who glory in their shame."

We have spoken of a king. Jesus Christ is the true King of men! Will we have him to reign over us? Are we willing to be the subjects of his immortal crown? "Choose you this day whom ye will serve!" Blessed is the man who shall run away from the camp of the alien, and set himself beside the standard of Calvary!

SELECTED NOTE.

"*Go, seek the asses*" (ix. 3).—The search appears to have been conducted without any settled plan, and among the Tartars such journeys appear to be frequent. Every one has a private mark upon his beasts, and when they stray their ownership is easily ascertained. A Tartar with a large extent of plain before him will set out at sunrise, not knowing which way to go, but choosing the direction from any chance that inclines him, this way or that. He rides on till sunset, and then dismounts, fastens his horse, and gets his supper. He carries with him in a bag six pounds of the flour of roasted millet, which is sufficient to last him thirty days. Day after day he goes on, observing the marks of all the herds he meets, and receiving information from any who, like himself, are in search of stray cattle. Very likely the search of Saul was somewhat similar.

PRAYER.

O THOU who art merciful and gracious, full of compassion and long-suffering and tenderness, thou art kind to the unthankful and to the evil! We hasten to thee with our offering of praise, inasmuch as thou hast crowned our life with loving-kindness and tender mercy and made it beautiful with continual love. We praise thee; we magnify thee; we offer thee the whole strength of our heart. We hasten to thee as men who have been mocked by the promises of the world, and who long to find satisfaction in thine infinite and unspeakable peace. We have been disappointed. The staff has been broken in our hand and pierced us. We mistook the scorpion for an egg. We have hewn out for ourselves cisterns; but they are broken cisterns, which can hold no water. Foiled, smitten, wounded, humiliated, and disgraced, we come into thy presence, knowing that in God, as revealed in the person and doctrine of Jesus Christ and made known unto us by the ministry of the Holy Ghost, we can find rest which our souls could not find elsewhere. All our springs are in thee. Thou givest us what we need. They who are in thy presence, who live in thy light, and thy love, hunger no more, neither thirst any more, neither are subjected to weariness or decay. We would live in God. We would have our being in the Eternal. We would know nothing among men but Jesus, and him crucified; and by the mystery of pain and the mystery of love, symbolised by Christ's cross, we would endure the trials of the world, and discharge the whole service of life. Meet us as sinners and pardon us! The blood of Jesus Christ, thy Son, cleanseth from all sin. May we know its cleansing, healing power! We have done the things we ought not to have done; we have withheld the testimony which it became us to deliver; we have often been timid and unfaithful; we have hesitated when we ought to have gone forward; we have compromised where we ought to have died; we have become self-seekers where we ought to have sought the crown of martyrdom; we have kept an unjust balance and an untrue weight; our measure has been false; our word has been untrue; our spirit has been worldly; our very prayers have been selfish. All this we say when we truly know ourselves, as we are revealed to ourselves by the in-dwelling, all-disclosing Spirit. God be merciful unto us, sinners, and cleanse us from all unrighteousness! Give us the hearing ear, and the understanding heart, the obedient will, the ever industrious hand in the service of Jesus Christ. When we have done our best to serve our day and generation, and the time of reckoning has come, may we find all our worth in the worthiness of the Lamb, and be accounted fit to sit with him on his throne, because in our degree we have shared the pain and shame of his crucifixion! Amen.

1 Samuel x. 24.

" God save the king."

SAUL'S KINGDOM.

WE have previously remarked upon the lowly-mindedness of Saul. The proposition which was made to him showed to his own consciousness, as he had never seen it before, how poor and even contemptible was his claim to social supremacy. " Am not I a Benjamite, of the smallest of the tribes of Israel ? and my family the least of all the families of the tribe of Benjamin ? wherefore then speakest thou so to me ? " It is well when great demands show us our own insufficiency. Sometimes they do but touch our vanity, and then they show that they are not morally great, but great only in high-sounding words,—infinite pretensions without substance or value. In solemn crises men show their quality. Loss takes a man's character to pieces fibre by fibre, and shows him what he is made of. Prosperity takes a man to the edge of a great cliff, and proves whether he be a giddy adventurer or a wise and understanding pilgrim. Sometimes we are revealed to ourselves by a tremendous shock. In an unexpected moment a kingdom is offered to us, and then we see into the hidden places of our hearts ; ambition maddens us into presumption, or modesty drives us to the Strong for strength. In the case of Saul we see proof upon proof, direct and incidental, that he was self-distrustful and diffident. When his uncle asked him what Samuel had said, " Saul said unto his uncle, He told us plainly that the asses were found : but of the matter of the kingdom of which Samuel spake he told him not." When the time came to show him forth to Israel, Saul could not be found, and the Lord himself had to tell the people that their prospective king was hidden amongst the stuff. We are now to witness the setting up of the kingdom of Israel. It is a royal day. A new epoch opens. Israel loses the distinctiveness of the theocracy, and becomes like the other nations of the earth.

Let us first of all hear the inaugural speech of Samuel.

" And Samuel called the people together unto the Lord to Mizpeh, and

said unto the children of Israel, Thus saith the Lord God of Israel, I brought
up Israel out of Egypt, and delivered you out of the hand of the Egyptians,
and out of the hand of all kingdoms, and of them that oppressed you :
" And ye have this day rejected your God, who himself saved you out of all
your adversities and your tribulations ; and ye have said unto him, Nay, but
set a king over us. Now, therefore, present yourselves before the Lord by
your tribes and by your thousands " (x. 17-19).

Here is the destruction of a great religious memory ! What is
our life when we have taken out of it all the recollections which
redeem it from irreligiousness and vanity ? Some of us would
be poor indeed, were it not for the hidden treasures of secret
memory. In our depression we remember the day of God's
deliverance. When we look onward, and see the distant horizon
filled with angry clouds, we look back, and see the way of light
along which God has conducted us ; and the pious memories of
a life which has been a succession of wonders, revive and
establish our confidence in the Holy One. The history before us
is fraught with mournful instruction to men who trifle with their
best memories. We condemn those who treat lightly what
we have done for them in their hours of darkness and sore
distress. What if we have forgotten the Egypts out of which
God has brought us, and have clamoured for some lower gift than
himself ?

It is to be observed that in this instance it was not a theoretical
but a practical, casting off of God. This is one of the great
difficulties of Christian life, and the sign which the Church makes
to the world. It is full of mystery and heart-breaking sadness.
Men retain God in their written creed, but depose him from the
throne of their life. Men who would be startled to find themselves described as atheists, yet they daily live atheistically. Israel
would have been shocked had the charge of theoretical atheism
been made against the nation ; at the same time that very nation,
so tenacious of a theoretical creed, resolutely thrust God off the
throne. We say we believe in God, yet in our daily life we
never mention his name. We are excited to indignation by the
blasphemies of atheism, yet we legislate God's Book out of our
educational institutions ! We have God, but no godliness. We
have a creed, but no life. We worship with the lips, but our
heart is dumb.

Look at the terrible possibility of God allowing men to have their own way! Israel insisted upon having a king. God said, In so insisting, you are rejecting and grieving me; yet take him and see the end! We may clamour until God's patience yields to our importunity, and he inflicts upon us the intolerable punishment of allowing us to have our own way. By this means only can some be taught the sinfulness and weakness of their own aims. Our self-sufficiency can be destroyed only through our self-gratification. Did not God allow us to carry out our will in many directions, there would linger in our hearts misgivings respecting the equity and perfectness of his government. We fix our eyes upon glittering objects in the distance ; we regard those objects as of priceless value ; we believe that their possession will elevate and satisfy our best capacities and desires. God plainly tells us that what we desire will prove to be a mockery and a torment ; yet, in spite of this revelation, we renew our entreaties, and urge our demands. At length God says, "Take that you desire." We take it, and, lo, it poisons our life, and turns our future into an intolerable terror.

We should notice solemnly the worthlessness of the success which is founded upon spiritual apostasy : Israel got a king, but Israel had first rejected God! There is a success which is but so much guilt. We get what we want, but the basis is rotten. We give up the spiritual and invisible, and imagine that we are rich because we take in exchange mountains of dust and clouds of mist. Your house is noble, commodious, and extremely inviting; a ruddy light is shining through its windows; sounds of music and delight are filling its every chamber; but what of all this, if your splendid mansion be founded on a bog ?

"God save the king" (x. 24).

In this act we see the tyrannic and fatal influence which one bad idea may exercise in a man's life. The case had been stated in a manner which ought to have caused a change of mind on the part of Israel ; yet, in the face of Samuel's distinct charge of practical atheism, Israel persisted in realising a special wish. The desire for a king became a monomania. Everything was looked at through the medium of that idea. It impaired the natural power of human judgment, it silenced every suggestion of conscience and obligation, and drove Israel headlong to the consummation of a dominant purpose. Men should be careful how they allow any single idea to rule them. It is but seldom that an isolated notion can be profoundly true. Ideas are to be compared one with another; they are to be viewed in their mutual relations, and to be modified by the deepest moral consideration. It is often only by throwing an idea into perspective that we get a true conception of its value and importance. To have a king, summed up the whole desire of Israel. This idea, instead of being a light to them, actually dazzled and blinded them by being brought too closely to their vision.

Israel was guilty of a most aggravated violation of decency in this matter. Though the people had, in the language of Samuel, rejected God, yet, in hailing their king, they appealed to the very God they had, with infinite ingratitude and recklessness, cast off! They shouted, "God save the king;" that is, they committed their king to the God whom they had denied ; they first deposed God from the government of Israel, and then asked him to bless the king whom they had set up in his stead ! Such is the contradictoriness, and such the insanity of selfish and undisciplined life. We fill up impious acts by pious ejaculations : we despise God, and then use his name in wishing blessings for others. Truly we are witnesses against ourselves !

"And Saul also went home to Gibeah ; and there went with him a band of men, whose hearts God had touched.

"But the children of Belial said, How shall this man save us ? And they despised him, and brought him no presents. But he held his peace " (x. 26, 27).

All men are made stronger by the fellowship of the good. When we are put into exceptional circumstances, either of elation or depression, we are the better for the sympathy and loving trust of "a band of men, whose hearts God has touched." The king cannot do without his subjects. Every man must have around him those in whom he has special confidence. There must be favouritism in human association. The selection of friends does not involve the development of enmity or even distrust, in relation to others. The king has his favourite counsellors; the minister has his special advisers; the general, the captain, the leader, whatsoever be his name, must have next to him a man in whose judgment he has entire confidence. It is in this way that society is consolidated. Yet even in the instance of Saul we have not only light, but shadow. The children of Belial looked upon him with an evil eye, and said, "How shall this man save us?" Is not every one of us enclosed by concentric circles? If we are God's children, there is nearest to us a circle of heavenly guardianship, of Christian defence and sympathy, and such honour as is given by God to faithful men; then farther off there is a circle of evil ones who despise us and constantly seek to upset and destroy us. Saul's conduct under such circumstances was most instructive: we read, "But he held his peace." Silence is wisdom; silence is strength. It might gratify a momentary feeling to speak angrily to the men who thus set themselves against us, but it is infinitely better to look as if we saw not, and to ponder many things in our hearts. Who are we, that we should expect to escape the criticism of the children of Belial? Such children are the contemporaries of all ages, and it is impossible for them to change the malignity of their dispositions.

Now danger came. The Ammonite laid his hand upon the sword. The people of Jabesh-Gilead were sore afraid; for Nahash encamped against them. They prayed that he would make a covenant with them; and his answer was: "On this condition will I make a covenant with you, that I may thrust out all your right eyes, and lay it for a reproach on all Israel." The leaders of Jabesh prayed for seven days' respite, that they might find if in all the coasts of Israel there was a man who had strength and skill to save them. When the condition of the people became known to Saul, the Spirit of God came upon him, and his anger was kindled greatly. The day of battle came, and the men of Jabesh "slew the Ammonites until the heat of the day: and it came to pass that they which remained were scattered, so that two of them were not left together." So much for the earnestness of one inspired man! We are but ciphers until God finds the unit to set at our head; then we who were nothing in ourselves stand up a living and mighty host. Saul could not

have done this work alone, the men of Jabesh could not have
done it alone; this is a lesson to the Church; the general and
the army are mutually necessary; the teacher and the taught in
divine things must honour one another as both being needed to
take captive the world in the name of Christ.

We admire Saul's deliverance of Jabesh-Gilead : we are touched
by every element of heroism that we find in the men of history :
it is right that we should respond to the efforts and sacrifices
made by the splendid leaders who have conducted the battles of
truth and justice to a successful issue ; but our homage to heroism
should be carried into still higher regions. We praise Saul;
shall we forget the Son of God ? "When there was no eye to
pity, and when there was no arm to save, his own eye pitied,
and his own arm brought salvation." What instance is there in
all human history to be compared with this for all that is sublime
in courage and pathetic in sacrifice ?

SELECTED NOTE.

"*And Saul also went home to Gibeah*" (x. 26).—During the time of the
Judges, when the country was almost in a state of anarchy (Judges xix. 1),
Gibeah became the scene of one of the most abominable crimes, and one of
the most awful tragedies, recorded in Jewish history. The story of the
unfortunate Levite, the siege and destruction of Gibeah, and the almost
total annihilation of the tribe of Benjamin are well known (xix.-xxi.). The
city soon rose again from its ashes, and had the honour of giving Israel its
first king. It was the native place of Saul (1 Sam. x. 26; xi. 4), and the
seat of his government during the greater part of his reign (xiv. 2 ; xxii. 6;
xxiii. 19); hence its appellation "Gibeah of Saul" (xv. 34). It was in
Gibeah the Amorites of Gideon hanged the seven descendants of Saul in
revenge for the massacre of their brethren. The city was then the scene of
that touching exhibition of maternal love and devotion, when Rizpah, the
mother of two of the victims, "took sackcloth and spread it for her upon the
rock, from the beginning of harvest, until water dropped upon them out of
heaven, and suffered neither the birds of the air to rest upon them by day,
nor the beasts of the field by night" (2 Sam. xxi.). The last reference to
Gibeah in the Bible is by Isaiah in his vision of the approach of the Assyrian
army to Jerusalem (x. 29). The city appears to have lost its place and
power at a very early period. Josephus mentions it as "a *village* named
Gabath-Saul, which signifies 'Saul's hill,' distant from Jerusalem about
thirty furlongs" (*Bell. Jud.* v. 2, 1). Jerome speaks of it as "usque ad
solum diruta" (*Opp.*, ed. Migne, i. 883). From that period, until discovered by Dr. Robinson, its very site remained unnoticed, if not unknown.

PRACTICAL ROYALTY.

1 Samuel xi.

AT this time Saul occupied a somewhat anomalous position. He had been anointed king of Israel, and all the people had shouted and said, "God save the king." It would appear from this as if Saul had really become king of Israel, and in a certain sense that was so; but in the disordered times in which the kingship was proclaimed Saul went home to Gibeah, and continued to discharge his agricultural and social duties. He was, therefore, little more than a king in name. There were certain sons of Belial indeed who despised him, and brought him no presents. They were probably princes and leading men of rival tribes, bitterly displeased because the first king of Israel had been chosen out of the insignificant tribe of Benjamin. Saul had made no great mark in history, so there was nothing so obviously great in his career as to command universal admiration and respect. In the language of modern times, he had yet his spurs to win. It is to his credit, however, that when the worthless men despised him, he had sufficient self-control to hold his peace. Such control is always associated with the highest royalty. The man who can rule his own spirit is better than he who can take a city. Sometimes silence is the last expression of power. In the eleventh chapter circumstances occur which bring Saul into the full exercise of his royal functions. Read:—

"Then Nahash the Ammonite came up, and encamped against Jabesh-gilead : and all the men of Jabesh said unto Nahash, Make a covenant with us, and we will serve thee. And Nahash the Ammonite answered them, On this condition will I make a covenant with you, that I may thrust out all your right eyes, and lay it for a reproach upon all Israel" (vv. 1, 2).

Nahash was king of the children of Ammon, and was in some indirect way related to David. The men of Jabesh-gilead had always been kind to the tribe of Benjamin, indeed they had been the only friends of Benjamin at a critical period of the history of that tribe. Now that Nahash came up and encamped against Jabesh, the inhabitants of the invaded district proposed that Nahash should make a covenant with them, and that they should serve him. The inhabitants of Jabesh-gilead were cut off from communication with the larger districts and provinces of their country, and no doubt a sense of loneliness had considerably depressed them ; they were willing, therefore, to mitigate their solitude by entering into a menial covenant with Nahash the Ammonite. It is often true in life that circumstances drive us to make approaches which are not congenial. Men are driven by stress of health or poverty, or some form of perplexity not easily to be named in words, to offer to put themselves into relations with people whom under other circumstances they would never treat with. Such facts in life we are bound to recognise. And it would betoken a poor quality of nature on our part to associate with such recognitions too severe a moral condemnation. Our common proverb is to the effect that "adversity has strange bed-fellows." The men of Jabesh-gilead, therefore, must be regarded as persons who are under oppressive circumstances, and who are willing to make the best of conditions which are very galling and humiliating. While such were the circumstances of the men of Jabesh-gilead, these circumstances developed the moral quality of the King of the Ammonites. We know what men are when we see how they treat those who are supposed to be in their power. Circumstances develop the nature of men on all sides of a controversy,—depressing some, they stimulate others to anger and revenge, or they develop cupidity and selfishness to a degree which brings infamy upon their name. It was so with Nahash the Ammonite. He was ready to make a covenant with the inhabitants of Jabesh, and this was his answer,—" On this condition will I make a covenant with you, that I may thrust out all your right eyes, and lay it for a reproach upon all Israel." There we see the true nature of the man. There indeed we see a faithful exhibition of human depravity. This kind of cruelty must not be considered as confined to Nahash ; it is the very mystery of iniquity which is found in every human heart, or if not found there, it is concealed, because circumstances constituting a sufficient temptation have not appealed to it. It is easy to fall into a mood of horror in relation to the iniquities of other men, and to suppose that when we shudder at their vices we exhibit virtues of our own. No language is too severe to condemn the barbarous cruelty of Nahash; in very deed he appears before us more like a child of hell; at the same time he only shows what we might be under circumstances of equal temptation and pressure. When we see how man can treat man, we are enabled to reason upwards, and to see how possible it is for man to treat God profanely and blasphemously. When man loves God he loves his neighbour also; but when man ceases to love his neighbour, and then passes from mere displeasure to positive and cruel hatred, it is easy for him to carry the spirit of hostility further and to include in its base action even all that is heavenly and divine. The moment we can treat a man unjustly and cruelly we have disqualified ourselves for true prayer and real communion with Heaven. Let there be no mistake about this matter. We cannot give up our philanthropy and retain our Christianity. We may be troubled in metaphysical thinking, and may sometimes depart from acknowledged lines in that high region of religious contemplation and worship, but there must not be the slightest shaking of our moral relations as between man and man, or if there is, we may justly infer that such violation of social sympathy and justice had a distinct bearing upon the reality of our religious character. The man who could issue the condition named by Nahash was simply incapable of sustaining any living relation of worship and trust to the true God.

"And the elders of Jabesh said unto him, Give us seven days' respite, that we may send messengers unto all the coasts of Israel : and then, if there be no man to save us, we will come out to thee. Then came the messengers to Gibeah of Saul, and told the tidings in the ears of the people : and all the people lifted up their voices and wept. And, behold, Saul came after the herd out of the field ; and Saul said, What aileth the people that they weep ? And they told him the tidings of the men of Jabesh. And the Spirit of God came upon Saul when he heard those tidings, and his anger was kindled greatly. And he took a yoke of oxen, and hewed them in pieces, and sent them throughout all the coasts of Israel by the hands of messengers, saying, Whosoever cometh not forth after Saul and after Samuel, so shall it be done unto his oxen. And the fear of the Lord fell on the people, and they came out with one consent. And when he numbered them in Bezek, the children of Israel were three hundred thousand, and the men of Judah thirty thousand " (vv. 3-8).

The spirit of Jabesh was not utterly quenched. The lingering fire that was in the breasts of the elders was blown into a blaze. A marvellous mystery is this, namely, how difficult it is utterly to quench and destroy the spirit of man. Even in the very midnight of despair there flames up unexpected energy. The elders of Jabesh asked for seven days in which to consider the condition which the King of Ammon had proposed. Such respite has been common in all wars claiming to be regulated at all by the spirit of civilisation. At that critical moment the messengers of Jabesh came to Gibeah of Saul. Ancient friendship urged its plea. We have seen that Jabesh and Benjamin were always on friendly terms, and now that Jabesh is in extremity it will be for Benjamin to show the reality of the historical friendship.

A very beautiful picture is presented in the fifth verse. Saul was engaged in his usual pursuits. The King of Israel was actually discharging offices with the herd in the field, attending to the wants of his cattle, and otherwise going about his business soberly and quietly. No intimation of unusual circumstances seems to have reached him. How unconscious we sometimes are of the circumstances which are nearest to us,—unconscious, that is to say, of their real import and deepest meaning ! When we think all is proceeding as usual we may be within touch of some occurrence that will determine all the remaining actions of our life. The commonplace and the marvellous often lie closely together. Why should there be any commonplace in life, in the sense of taking out of existence everything that can stimulate our best nature and build us up in the comfort of an enlarging and assured hope ? He who does his plain and simple duty, in the field and in the market-place, is best prepared for any unusual occurrences that may break in upon the monotony of his life. He who is faithful in few things shall be made ruler over many things. There is but a step from the field where the herd gathers and the throne which unites and dignifies a whole nation. The picture, then, is that of a great man attending to simple daily duties, and it will be a sad day for any people who imagine that simple daily duties are not worthy of the dignity even of the greatest man. Saul observed that the people who came near to him were in great distress :—" All the people lifted up their voices, and wept." They were at their wits' end. We shall now see whether it is true that man's extremity is God's opportunity. It is certain that the men of Jabesh can do nothing for themselves, and it is very uncertain to them whether any other man can do much for them. But they went to the greatest man known to them. Society has a right to expect great things from great men. No greater tribute could be paid to Saul than that threatened and despairing men should appeal to him in the time of their agony. The men who shouted, "God save the king," did not pay Saul so fine a tribute as the men who came to him in their extremity and asked for his sympathy and assistance. Really to pray is really to adore. This doctrine is true also in human relations; really to cast oneself upon the resources of a great man is to pay that great man the highest compliment in our power.

No sooner had Saul heard the condition proposed by the King of Ammon than he burned with anger. We can best describe a certain quality of anger by tracing it to the direct action of the Spirit of God. Truly, there is a holy indignation. We are conscious of no moral or mental shock when we read the simple terms that "the Spirit of God came upon Saul;" truly it could be no other Spirit, for depravity had reached its utmost degradation, and the terms proposed were so treasonable to everything human and right that they could only be answered justly and completely by fire directly sent from heaven. The sublime enthusiasm of Saul kindled the faith of the people. A common impression seized them that this was the man for the occasion; so " they came out with one consent." It has been pointed out that the circumstances here recorded suggested to the poet Asaph the splendid image presented in the seventy-eighth Psalm :—" Then the Lord awaked as one out of a sleep, and like a mighty man that shouteth by reason of wine." The action of Saul seems to represent the action of the Divine Being. See how one earnest man becomes an army in himself ! How true it is that great causes only need **great** leaders; and how true it is also that great leaders can only be made by the Spirit of God : they are not artificial men; they are not bound by mechanical laws and standards; they seem to be special creations and to be accountable to none but God for the outgoing and expression of their holy inspiration. A modern commentary, referring to this passage, has the following illustrative remarks :—" It was owing to some influence of a similar nature, that with scanty numbers, ill-armed, and ill-trained, the Swiss won for their land centuries of freedom on memorable fields like Laupen and Morat, though the proudest chivalry of Europe was arrayed against them. It was the same spirit which impelled the peace-loving traders of the marshes of Holland to rise as one man, and to drive out for ever from their loved strip of Fenland the hitherto invincible armies of Spain. No oppressor, though backed by the wealth and power of an empire, has ever been able to resist the smallest people in whose heart has burned the flame of the divine fire of the fear of the Lord." All these circumstances would be of little or no concern to us if they did not point to a great spiritual reality. Tremendous foes besiege us on every side. Through mind, body, and estate the great temptations come a hundred strong; yea, a thousand, multiplied by ten, yea, until their number seems to be beyond calculation. What is our defence in such time of assault ? It is the fear of the Lord, the Spirit of God, the divine energy. Where the love of God burns in the heart, or where the Spirit of the living God directs the whole energy of the life, a little one shall chase a thousand, and ten thousand shall be put to flight because of the mighty power of the indwelling Spirit. Religious rapture is a necessary element in religious education. We must sometimes become so conscious of the infinite power of God as to lose all consciousness of our own little strength, and go forth to war as if all the battalions of Heaven were placed entirely at our service.

" And they said unto the messengers that came, Thus shall ye say unto the men of Jabesh-gilead, To-morrow, by that time the sun be hot, ye shall have help. And the messengers came and shewed it to the men of Jabesh : and they were glad. Therefore the men of Jabesh said, To-morrow we will come out unto you, and ye shall do with us all that seemeth good unto you. And it was so on the morrow, that Saul put the people in three companies; and they came into the midst of the host in the morning watch, and slew the Ammonites until the heat of the day : and it came to pass, that they which

remained were scattered, so that two of them were not left together"
(vv. 9-11).

The answer returned by Saul was more than equal to the condition proposed by Ammon. A time was fixed for the combat ;
Saul put the people into three companies, and the attack ended
in the utter discomfiture of the Ammonites. God delights in
humbling the boastful and vainglorious. " He that exalteth
himself shall be abased." Presumption is always self-defeating :
it is so in business, in war, in statesmanship, and in every act
and department of rational life. " Pride goeth before destruction,
and an haughty spirit before a fall." The people who yesterday
were overborne by dismay are to-day standing upon the very
mountain of victory, and the wind seems to take delight in
blowing out the banner of triumph. When will men learn from
history that presumption is, to say the least of it, a mistake ?
" Let not him that girdeth on his harness boast himself as he
that putteth it off." Here again the spiritual interpretation is
the great lesson to which we have to take heed. It is infinitely
foolish to suppose that we can overcome diabolic assault by our
own wisdom or grace. The enemy is mightier than we are, and
his heart is full of cruelty. We must advance in the spirit of
David, saying, " I come to thee in the name of the living God."
Omnipotence can express itself through the humblest medium ;
so much so that the word of those who are faint in heart shall
become a mighty tone, having in it a mystery which cannot but
excite the fear and disable the strength of those who oppose the
best aspirations of the soul.

Notice that this war was not entered upon without preparation.
There was no rush or haste in the matter. Sometimes we proceed most swiftly when we seem to advance most slowly. There
should be a time for gathering strength together, measuring the
situation in all its dimensions, consulting divine decrees, and
putting the soul into right relations with God. After such preparation everything will go rapidly. Every stroke will be a
victory. Every arrangement will be a step in advance never to
be retraced. There must be no flutter or fear or agitation ;
otherwise the completeness of our faith will be disturbed : we
must be fully and strongly prepared by divine communion, then

the shock of war will bring with it nothing but victory to the right. The Church should be continually challenging the foe, not in a spirit of boastfulness, as if by wisdom and learning the kingdom of heaven could be set up ; but with faith, sobriety, trust in God, assurance of righteousness ; then the result will be the promotion of the dominion of truth.

"And the people said unto Samuel, Who is he that said, Shall Saul reign over us ? bring the men, that we may put them to death " (v. 12).

Now Saul is king in very deed. Popular enthusiasm had been so excited that the people wished to slay the men who had put any disloyal question regarding the sovereignty of Saul. They were quite aware that such questioning had been operating in the minds of some part of the nation, indeed they were not afraid to refer to the disloyalty when they themselves were prepared to smite it with a final blow. But here Saul shows himself to be truly royal. The man who held his peace when he was aware of what the children of Belial had said, is the same man who this day declares that not a life shall be cut off. The self-control of Saul is shown clearly in the depth of his religious feeling. Instead of taking credit to himself, and boasting loudly that he was the man who alone was qualified to be captain, he stood back, and as he retired to his proper place he said, This is the Lord's doing, not mine,—" To day the Lord hath wrought salvation in Israel " (v. 13). So long as Saul keeps in this mood, nothing can disturb the security of his throne. Men whose characters are based on strong religious foundations shall not fear the wind when it blows, or the lightning when it passeth to and fro from the east to the west ; they abide under the shadow of the Almighty : and when great distress rages in all directions they are filled with infinite and imperturbable peace. Let us remember this incident ; the recollection of it will help us in studies that are yet to follow.

Apart altogether from the history of Saul as an individual, the same great law applies to every department of human life. When a man begins to boast that he has by his own energy made himself rich, he has already opened the window through which his wealth will fly. When a man lifts his arm and boasts what its sinew has done for him, that sinew has already begun to decay.

We must live and move and have our being in God. When Herod accepted the worship of the people in the sense in which they conveyed it, as intimating that he was a deity and not a man, a most terrible fate befell him. Our strength is in our humility. Our dignity is in our communion with God. Once allow anything to come between us and the altar, between our strength and the cross from which it is derived, and instantly the vital communication is cut off, we flutter for a moment, and then die in weakness and shame.

"Then said Samuel to the people, Come, and let us go to Gilgal, and renew the kingdom there. And all the people went to Gilgal ; and there they made Saul king before the Lord in Gilgal : and there they sacrificed sacrifices of peace offerings before the Lord ; and there Saul and all the men of Israel rejoiced greatly " (vv. 14, 15).

A fit ending to a tragical process. Gilgal was a sanctuary. After great doings on the field of battle we must return to the house of prayer, we must, indeed, return to the place where we began. We should enter upon no conflict until after we have been in the sanctuary, and having completed the conflict we should return to the altar. Enter upon nothing that cannot be sanctified at holy places and by holy names There is nothing too insignificant to be associated with the most solemn acts of worship ; or if we are conscious of such insignificance, we should not undertake the affairs which admit of its application. At Gilgal the kingdom was renewed, and at Gilgal indeed the kingship of Saul was consummated. There was indeed no fresh anointing of Saul as if to repair some omission of the past ; what occurred at Gilgal was a national endorsement of what had been done popularly and partially at Mizpeh. What took place is described as having been accomplished " before the Lord,"—words which imply that the ark was in sight, or that the high-priest took part in the ceremony, having with him the mystic Urim and Thummim.

Thus Saul's private life was ended ; henceforth he was the leading figure in the history of his times. Learn the useful lesson that Saul did not thrust himself into prominence, and that even after he was anointed king of Israel he went about his usual avocations until there was something worthy of kingliness to be publicly done. Let us be rebuked in so far as we have supposed that we were released from duty until some great and critical occasion arose. Having obtained our literary prize, let us go home and take up the business of life in a quiet way. Having been greatly honoured of the people, let us not betake ourselves to a life of vanity and frivolity, but go home and discharge the duties of the household with simplicity and fidelity. Do not think that anything which nature or society requires of us is below our dignity because we have achieved this or that popular success. Then when the time of action fully comes, and greater honours still are accorded to us in the sight of all the world, let us hasten to Gilgal, the sanctuary, the chosen place of God's presence, and there thank him that we have escaped the dangers of battle, and entered upon the enjoyments of victory which he himself conferred.

SELECTED NOTE.

"*Come, and let us go to Gilgal, and renew the kingdom there*" (v. 14).— Saul was elected at Mizpeh, in a solemn assembly by the determination of the miraculous lot—a method of election not confined to the Hebrews. Previous to that election (x. 16) and subsequently, when insulted by the worthless portion of the Israelites, he showed that modesty, humility, and forbearance which seem to have characterised him till corrupted by the possession of power. The person thus set apart to discharge the royal function possessed at least those corporeal advantages which most ancient nations desiderated in their sovereigns. His person was tall and commanding, and he soon showed that his courage was not inferior to his strength (1 Sam. ix. 2 ; x. 23). His belonging to Benjamin also, the smallest of the tribes, though of distinguished bravery, prevented the mutual jealousy with which either of the two great tribes, Judah and Ephraim, would have regarded a king chosen from the other; so that his election was received with general rejoicing, and a number of men moved by the authority of Samuel (x. 26) even attached themselves to him as a body-guard, or as counsellors and assistants. In the meantime the Ammonites, whose invasion had hastened the appointment of a king, having besieged Jabesh in Gilead, and Nahash their king having proposed insulting conditions to them, the elders of that town, apparently not aware of Saul's election (xi. 3), sent messengers through the land imploring help. Saul acted with wisdom and promptitude, summoning the people *en masse* to meet him at Bezek ; and having at the head of a vast multitude totally routed the Ammonites (v. 11) and obtained a higher glory by exhibiting a new instance of clemency, whether dictated by principle or policy—"Novum imperium inchoantibus utilis clementiæ fama " (Tac. *Hist.* iv. 63), "For lowliness is young ambition's ladder,"—he and the people betook themselves, under the direction of Samuel, to Gilgal, there with solemn sacrifices to reinstal the victorious leader in his kingdom (1 Sam. xi.). Here Saul was publicly anointed, and solemnly installed in the kingdom by Samuel, who took occasion to vindicate the purity of his own administration—which he virtually transferred to Saul—to censure the people for their ingratitude and impiety, and to warn both them and Saul of the danger of disobedience to the commands of Jehovah (1 Sam. xii.).

SAMUEL'S DEFENCE.

1 Samuel xii.

IT would seem that a fitting time had now come for Samuel's retirement from his great position. We are all conscious of the fitness of certain historical occasions, so much so that we can adopt the duties which they suggest with a sense of harmony and rectitude. After the splendid victory acquired by Saul it would seem as if the dispensation of Samuel must naturally close. Blessed is he who can say, "He must increase, but I must decrease;" and still more blessed is he who looking back upon all his career can adopt the language and spirit of the veteran Samuel. In this noble speech there is no sign whatever of intellectual exhaustion or the blunting of that fine sagacity which had so long led the policy and fortune of Israel. It is better for men to retire whilst in full possession of their faculties, rather than to live themselves into the deserved contempt of their fellow-men. Still, throughout the speech there is a tone which expresses something like resentment, as if the old man would have gladly continued but for the impatience of the unruly populace. Who likes to resign a great leadership? We should consider these things in looking upon men, and their offices, and their supposed duties. Probably we do not make allowance enough for the instincts which constitute our very manhood. It is easy to stand by and to suggest to other men that they should resign their positions and abandon the fields in which they have won a hundred honours; but it is not always so easy for the man who is most deeply implicated to rise to this heroism of self-renunciation. We should be patient with our veteran leaders, our old statesmen, our well-proved teachers and guides. It is instructive to observe, however, the wonderful manner in which Providence intervenes, to show when times have arrived for the cessation of this or that function and the inauguration of a new period of rule and service. Things work together quite wonderfully in this way ; so much so that an attentive observation of their course impresses the mind with the fact that there is a Power, call it by what name we please, which centralises all things and gives them their best applications. Samuel seems to have pondered upon all the events of ·his time so wisely as to have come to the conclusion that the hour of retirement had arrived. Let us now hear his valedictory speech. Even though the king walked before Israel, Samuel was not afraid to call attention to himself. It is notable that the whole reference is distinctly of a moral quality. He seems to be anxious only to come out of the court of trial with an unstained character. He asks for no crown or sceptre or purple of a merely artificial or decorative kind ; his one desire is to be clothed with the robe of an unpolluted reputation. Truly, it is a kind of heaven which the old man claims. He would be called good, rather than great. Is there a finer picture upon earth than an old and grey-headed man who is able to challenge the world to bring a just accusation against him ? Samuel was able to descend into minute details, and to show that in so-called little things he had lived a life that was beyond suspicion. Samuel had lived in the blaze of noonday since he was a child ; indeed, he could hardly be said to have had any childhood, so early was he pressed into the public service. Now he looks up to the heavens, and asks that the people might witness against him if they had any charge to make. " Behold, here I am : witness against me before the Lord, whose ox have I taken ? or whose ass have I taken ? " (v. 3). The ox and the ass represent possessions of considerable value in that primitive age and in a country where agriculture was the principal source of revenue. A further inquiry is, " Whom have I defrauded ? whom have I oppressed ? " For many years he had been supreme judge in Israel, and now that he is about to retire from the judgeship, he gives all men liberty to speak and to testify against him if they could. Throughout the whole year nothing was more common than for judges to receive bribes, in order that their favour might be bought and a wealthy criminal might escape. On this point Samuel puts a direct inquiry :— " Of whose hand have I received any bribe to blind mine eyes therewith ? "

These are searching questions, and every man who professes to be godly ought to be able to put them to his own age. What if we have kept all the dogmas of orthodoxy and performed all the ceremonies of artificial religion, if we have not been free from the spirit of covetousness, or if we have defrauded or oppressed the helpless and the weak ? Away with the orthodoxy that is not supported by a pure morality! " Not every one that saith unto me, Lord, Lord, shall enter into the kingdom of heaven ; but he that doeth the will of my Father which is in heaven." " Wash you, make you clean ; put away the evil of your doings." These are the conditions upon which God offers communion to man ; not intellectual conditions which only a few can attain, but moral conditions which are open to the whole world. The virtue of our public men has a large influence upon the virtue of society. Where there is corruption at the head, there must of necessity be some measure of corruption in all the departments which that head rules. Like priest, like people. It is true that sometimes the nation has been in advance of the throne in the purity of its moral sentiment ; but it is also true that where the throne has been renowned for probity and beneficence a very happy influence has been exerted upon the nation at large. In this regard it is of infinite importance that men should pray for their kings, rulers, judges, and magistrates, that society in its highest places should be kept pure and healthful. Every man will have to give an account of his life, and it rests with the man himself, to a large extent, whether that account shall be good or bad. It is not every one who may be able to stand up with Samuel and make the same wide and minute challenge, with the same consciousness that exculpation will be the result of the searching criticism ; at the same time, here is a line by which we may be guided ; here is an ideal towards which we may constantly aspire.

It is further noticeable that the challenge which Samuel addresses to the people is strictly limited to themselves. There is no appeal to God to testify that Samuel has always been in his sight a **pure** and holy character, without stain or blemish. There is no pharisaic boasting, no challenge addressed to Heaven, claiming the crown on the ground of good conduct. A very wide distinction is noticeable between an appeal to society and an appeal to Heaven. Samuel was talking in his public capacity, and in his public capacity he pressed every question which he asked ; he was not engaged in the exercise of prayer, urging his respectability upon the attention of Heaven, and claiming to have been alone faithful in a faithless world. In this respect a man may adopt two distinctly different tones. Addressing his fellow-men, he may speak in a tone of superiority, moral dignity, and stainless honour ; in doing so he may in reality be magnifying God, though there may be no nominal profession of so doing ; on the other hand, when he comes face to face with God, none may hear the moaning of his discontent, or see the tears of his contrition, as he reflects upon his innumerable shortcomings and perversities. The purist and the Pharisee, therefore, must not be allowed to take encouragement from the example of Samuel, that they may boast themselves as before God. All such boasting is vain and false. Even Samuel himself may say, in the secrecy of the sanctuary, " God be merciful to me a sinner ! "

"And Samuel said unto the people, It is the Lord that advanced Moses and Aaron, and that brought your fathers up out of the land of Egypt. Now therefore stand still, that I may reason with you before the Lord of all the righteous acts of the Lord, which he did to you and to your fathers. When Jacob was come into Egypt, and your fathers cried unto the Lord, then the Lord sent Moses and Aaron, which brought forth your fathers out of Egypt, and made them dwell in this place. And when they forgat the Lord their God, he sold them into the hand of Sisera, captain of the host of Hazor, and into the hand of the Philistines, and into the hand of the king of Moab, and they fought against them. And they cried unto the Lord, and said, We have sinned, because we have forsaken the Lord, and have served Baalim and Ashtaroth : but now deliver us out of the hand of our enemies, and we will serve thee. And the Lord sent Jerubbaal, and Bedan, and Jephthah, and Samuel, and delivered you out of the hand of your enemies on every side, and ye dwelled safe. And when ye saw that Nahash the king of the children of Ammon came against you, ye said unto me, Nay ; but a king shall reign over us : when the Lord your God was your king " (vv. 6-12).

Once more we come upon an excellent practice established in olden times, namely, faithfully to recount the history of God's providence, so far as it is known in human experience. The days are never separated from one another, and treated as detailed points of time. The historians and prophets of Israel always seem to be searching for the central line of history, which indeed is the central line of purpose; hence we find continuity and cumulativeness in the statements of all the men who address the nation. Very noticeable are these speeches for their statesmanlike comprehensiveness. Every one of them begins at a well-ascertained historical point, and continues the story without omission or perversion up to the then immediate day : this is a philosophy as well as an example. We miss the whole meaning of divine providence if we look at events separately and incidentally, as we miss the whole meaning of the Bible if we read it in detached portions and texts. The providence of life is an inspired revelation of God, but it must be read in its continuity if its meaning is to be correctly and profitably seized. Not what was done yesterday, or the day before, but what was done on the earliest and on every succeeding day, is the inquiry which every man should put to himself. The expulsion of Memory from the service of the Church is an act of sacrilege. Praise is incomplete without recollection. Our hallelujah, though apparently an utterance of rapture, will be louder and sweeter in proportion to the critical accuracy and large comprehensiveness of our memory. So we find Samuel beginning at the beginning,— with Moses and Aaron, and the deliverance from Egypt, and " all the righteous acts of the Lord, which he did to you and to your fathers ; " Jacob is not forgotten, nor are any of the errors of Israel omitted, nor their consequent subjugation and cruel punishment, their bondage under the Philistines, and their sufferings under the hand of the King of Moab. On and on the great story rolls, up to the times of Jerubbaal, and Bedan, and Jephthah, and Samuel himself; nay, the very last act which they themselves had witnessed is pressed into the great body of the accumulated evidence, and then the appeal is launched upon the judgment and conscience of the people. Consider what that appeal must be to-day if we take in the whole horizon of human history ! This is literally impossible, but morally it lies within our power to make noble use of it. The world itself could not contain the books if all providential acts were minutely recorded ; but the very fact of the literal impossibleness of the exercise constitutes a direct appeal to the spiritual imagination, which in its highest moods can unite all the courses of providence, and shape them into one sublime and holy appeal. Let this be done, and the judgment will be supported, conscience will be inspired, and the heart will be excited into new enthusiasm of trust and consecration.

"Now therefore behold the king whom ye have chosen, and whom ye have desired! and, behold, the Lord hath set a king over you. If ye will fear the Lord, and serve him, and obey his voice, and not rebel against the commandment of the Lord, then shall both ye and also the king that reigneth over you continue following the Lord your God : but if ye will not obey the voice of the Lord, but rebel against the commandment of the Lord, then shall the hand of the Lord be against you, as it was against your fathers. Now therefore stand and see this great thing, which the Lord will do before your eyes. Is it not wheat harvest to day? I will call unto the Lord, and he shall send thunder and rain ; that ye may perceive and see that your wickedness is great, which ye have done in the sight of the Lord, in asking you a king. So Samuel called unto the Lord; and the Lord sent thunder and rain that day : and all the people greatly feared the Lord and Samuel. And all the people said unto Samuel, Pray for thy servants unto the Lord thy God, that we die not : for we have added unto all our sins this evil, to ask us a king. And Samuel said unto the people, Fear not: ye have done all this wickedness : yet turn not aside from following the Lord, but serve the Lord with all your heart. And turn ye not aside : for then should ye go after vain things, which cannot profit nor deliver ; for they are vain. For the Lord will not forsake his people for his great name's sake : because it hath pleased the Lord to make you his people. Moreover, as for me, God forbid that I should sin against the Lord in ceasing to pray for you: but I will teach you the good and the right way : only fear the Lord, and serve him in truth with all your heart: for consider how great things he hath done for you. But if ye shall still do wickedly, ye shall be consumed, both ye and your king " (vv. 13-25).

With this appeal the function of teacher in Israel would almost seem to cease. Samuel avails himself of the old man's right to review the course of the nation's history, and to found certain appeals upon it. A younger man might have been interrupted in this historical review and moral application; but the venerable prophet seemed to have acquired a right to make the last great speech to his people. It was a kind of farewell sermon. Nor is it weakened by mere sentiment, or turned into an occasion of self-gratulation in any impious sense. It is the speech of a judge and a great man. Samuel accepts the monarchy, and calls upon the people to behold their king, and to see in that king an answer to their own desire. Samuel does not commit himself to the absolute righteousness of this choice of a king ; but with marvellous sagacity points out that the people themselves had wished to have a king, and that God had so far granted the popular desire. But the presence of a king was not to dispossess the Lord of his throne in Israel. Samuel does not remit the nation to secondary authority, telling the people to await the decrees of the king that they may know the limits of duty and the bounds of responsibility. To Samuel's reverent mind the kingship did not displace the theocracy. In the fourteenth verse Samuel directs the attention of the people to the Lord, and calls upon them to serve him, and obey his voice, and take heed unto his commandment, and then promises them consequent reward. This is a very remarkable point in the grand appeal. Samuel clings to the eternal theocratic idea. It is God who must reign ; it is God who must be for a man or against a man ; it is God who can send forth great signs, and it is to the Lord all kings must look, if they would reign in righteousness and have honour in heaven. That such was Samuel's great conviction is proved by his performance of a miracle that day, in the sight of all the people. Even in the midst of wheat harvest he called upon the Lord to send thunder and rain, that he might himself testify that his throne was in the heavens, and that the crowning of Saul in nowise interfered with the glory of his crown and the completeness of his empire. The people themselves took a highly religious view of the occasion, and instinctively turned to Samuel that he might pray for them a kind of final prayer. This was the proper ending of a grand ministry. In putting the request to Samuel that he would pray for them, the people seemed to expunge the long record of waywardness and ingratitude. There was a turning of the heart in the right direction, and that turning was accepted as repentance and restitution.

Now comes the word of comfort, the great and holy word which is befitting for old age to speak to a new nation. A wickedness had been committed in asking for a king; still, that wickedness would be regarded as official rather than personal, if the people themselves would see to it that their hearts were kept right, and that their purpose was to serve the Lord with steadfastness of love. A distinction is made between official

mistakes and personal transgressions.   How otherwise than upon
this ground could God spare even the nations which are called
by the Christian name?   Then Samuel utters a very tender
word ; he is about to retire from the priesthood and the official
guardianship of Israel, but he says, "God forbid that I should
sin against the Lord in ceasing to pray for you" (v. 23).
There is a private ministry by which every man can help his
nation.   Who knows how many priests there are in any country,
who are obscurely, but sincerely praying to God that the land
may be saved, that war may be averted, and that the ground
may be fruitful in harvest-time?   When we resign our public
functions we may still be able to continue a private ministry.
Samuel says he will not only pray for the people : he will teach
them the good and the right way.   In the presence of the
regular authority of a royal power, surrounded by all the pomp
and show of a great soldiery, the office held by Samuel must fall
into secondary importance.   But the teacher says he will still
continue his instruction.   Though Samuel practically ceased to
be judge, he was determined to continue as a prophet.   Here is
the great function of men who have the prophetic gift.   They
cannot fight, they cannot make great proposals in the state, they
cannot attract the attention of nations, they cannot command a
field of battle ; but they can constantly teach the good and the
right way, they can protest against evil, they can rebuke injustice, they can cry shame upon oppression, they can call people
back from negligence, dissoluteness, worldliness, and hold up
evermore before the attention of the world great examples, and
turn to moral account all the events which give vividness and
significance to human history.   The world may be poor by the
loss of its kings, but it will be infinitely poorer by the removal
of its prophets.

SAUL'S EARLY EFFORTS.

1 Samuel xiii., xiv.

IN these two chapters we have an opportunity of seeing how Saul betook himself to his kingly work. He did not rush upon his office in indecent haste. We have seen that after his anointing he returned to pursue his usual avocations, and that only upon receiving a special summons from men in distress did he arise to vindicate his true position in Israel. Having overthrown Nahash the Ammonite and received a renewal of the kingdom at Gilgal, it appears that Saul rested one year, in the sense of quietly reigning over the people and carefully laying to heart the entire situation occupied by his rejoicing subjects. Who can describe the joys of the first year of assured honour and responsibility! During that period of anticipation what dreams delight the vision, what holy vows sanctify the heart, what splendid images of social and general beneficence gladden the mind! Why should not the first year be a type of all the years that are yet to come? Yet it is only a time of rest, preparation, and discipline. Saul's two years of quiet kingship saw him become at their close a most energetic and aggressive monarch. This is the danger of kingship as well as its occasional duty. Officers are bound to make work for themselves in order to justify their position. So kings may sometimes feel called upon to enter into military operations, merely to show that theirs is no nominal royalty, but a living dignity bound to demonstrate its strength and majesty. What is the use of being a king if one cannot dazzle the other nations of the earth by unimagined resources worthy of a supreme throne? Nothing is more likely to be misunderstood by rude heathenism than quietness. The undisciplined mind makes no distinction between tranquillity and cowardice. It believes in spirited policies, spectacular displays, floating banners, resounding trumpets, and flashing steel.

Apart from this the uncultured mind can see no royalty worth recognising, and the danger is that even true kings may be tempted to answer such folly in its own way, and thus to incur peril and cost to the most disastrous degree. It must be remembered that Saul was a young king, that he was in very deed the first king in Israel, wholly without experience, yet a man of like passions with all that had ever been called to lofty social position. It is easy now to criticise Saul, and to say what he should have done under the various circumstances which constituted the atmosphere of his times; but we shall display a more magnanimous judgment if we regard him as an infant king, and make large allowances for his being the first monarch in Israel. How all first men have suffered for the race! Surely, it was an awful thing to have been the first man, and a scarcely less trying thing to have been the first sovereign of any people! It would indeed be a shame to kings nowadays, and to all men of lofty office and authority, if they attempted to justify themselves by the mistakes and follies of the pioneers of history. Men in these later days should show all the virtues of their predecessors, and none of their vices, and should show the virtues themselves in their noblest proportions.

We are now face to face with the first war which Saul in his completed kingship undertook. What if it should be a record of recklessness, ambition, usurpation, and no small amount of folly? The wonder would be were it otherwise. In many instances we ought to be more surprised by the wisdom of men than by their unwisdom; yet how prone we are to point out their mistakes and accumulate them into a heavy indictment rather than to stand in amazement before their sagacity and self-control, and praise those qualifications as unexpected but most honourable characteristics. The spiritual application of this incident teaches us that every man in the Church is a soldier acting under divine leadership, or human leadership divinely appointed, and that the solemn and unchangeable duty of the great army is to make daily aggression upon the whole camp of evil. The very existence of that camp should be regarded as a challenge. There need be no waiting for formal defiance; the Christian army is justified in regarding the existence of any

form or colour of evil as a call to immediate onslaught. We fight not against men, but against their corruptions. We do not kill our brother men, we seek by divine instrumentalities to slay the evils which have debased their manhood. There must be war in the world until all evil is driven out of it. Physical carnage is incompatible with the Spirit of Christ, and is, therefore, ever to be regarded with horror and inexpressible detestation ; but the grand spiritual war is never to cease until the last black spot of wickedness is taken away from the fair robe of the moral creation.

In contrast to the energetic and aggressive monarch, we have now to look at a panic-stricken people. "When the men of Israel saw that they were in a strait (for the people were distressed) . . . as for Saul he was yet in Gilgal ; and all the people followed him trembling." It has been thought by some that the trembling refers to the Philistines ; but of this we see no proof in the narrative. The Philistines were accustomed to war. Their chariots were thirty thousand ; their horsemen were six thousand, and the people were as the sand which is on the sea shore in multitude (xiii. 5) ; it was not likely, therefore, that a people so vast and so accustomed to war under their kings and princes should be immediately struck by panic. The picture presented by Israel is remarkable for its light and shade. Look at King Saul in the first flush of royal pride and ambition, responding to what he believed to be a divine vocation, and aboundingly confident of immediate and complete success ; he was a man who regarded his own progress as the rush of a mighty wind, and looked upon his sword as the very lightning of God. But his people were unaccustomed to his leadership ; many a stout battle had Israel fought, and not a few victories had Israel won, but in this case a new element enters into the calculation. It is true that Saul had overwhelmed Nahash ; but compared with the Philistines gathered in their full strength Nahash was indeed a contemptible foe. On the other side, therefore, we have a misgiving people, faint-hearted, filled with the distracting fear which weakens all whom it agitates, and trembling with apprehension. If the case had to be argued from the condition of the people, no special sagacity would be required

to predict the result. Is it not so also in the great moral conflict of the world ? Judging by what is seen in the spirit and action of nominal Christians, who could justly regard them as men of intrepidity and invincible resoluteness ? What trembling, what hesitation, what nightmare fancies, what ghostly noises in the night, what nameless spectres have combined to make the Church afraid ! What a genius the Church has for creating fears ! How afraid the Church is of sensationalism, offending the weak, annoying the sensitive, disturbing the slumbering ! What wonder if amid all this unworthy hesitation the war should be going against the divine standard ! But we must not look at the people : our eyes must be upon the Captain of our salvation. In his heart there is no misgiving ; he must reign till he hath put all enemies under his feet ; he never turns back from the war ; his sword is always highest in the air, pointing the road to danger and to victory.

It is no injustice to say that to-day the Church is trembling in face of the scepticism, the selfishness, the cupidity, and the unspiritual philosophy, which signalise the times. Blessed are we, even in the midst of all this faint-heartedness, if we can get one glimpse of Christ as he himself presses on to the point where the fight is deadliest, and grows in strength as the battle grows in fierceness.

We now come upon one of the mistakes of Saul's first campaign. He had been ordered to go down to Gilgal before Samuel (x. 8) : "And behold, I will come down unto thee, to offer burnt offerings, and to sacrifice sacrifices of peace offerings." Saul was to wait in Gilgal seven days for the coming of the prophet. A remarkable point should be noted here, namely, that Samuel even after his valedictory address did not wholly abandon his supremacy in Israel. Saul waited as he supposed the seven days, and then in his impatience he commanded to have brought to him a burnt offering and peace offerings, and he then by his own hand, or by the hand of the priest who was with him, offered the burnt offering. Alas for Saul ! No sooner had an end been made of offering the burnt offering than behold Samuel came ; and Saul went out to meet him that he might salute him. But Samuel was an earnest man, and as such he

immediately questioned Saul as to the sacrifices. Saul justified himself on the ground that Samuel did not come within the appointed time, and as the case appeared to be urgent he ventured to command the offering of the sacrifices. Samuel was, however, within the time, for he came on the evening of the seventh day, thus testing the patience of Saul to the very extremity. But providences would be no tests did they not keep us waiting even to the last moment. Had Samuel come on the morning of the seventh day Saul's confidence would not have been subjected to a complete trial. Saul was now to be taught that to be really royal a man must first be really loyal. Obedience is the first condition of rulership. There was no need for this usurpation of the priestly office on the part of Saul. It is at this point that so many mistakes are made, that men will imagine that the cause of God is in necessity, and will rush in a spirit of usurpation to do the work which God himself has undertaken to be done by other hands. When will men learn to stand still, and in holy patience await the coming of the Lord? When will men give up the self-idolatry which supposes that unless they undertake to quicken the movements of Providence, the destinies of the universe will be imperilled? The worship of patience may be more accepted than the service of rashness. Though, however, the judgment of Heaven was pronounced against Saul, it was not intended to take immediate effect. This is a point to be often noticed in the reading of Scripture: that which we think to be imminent may be distantly perspective; but the one thing that is imminent beyond all question is the infinite displeasure of God in regard to every sinful and foolish deed. The judgment may be held back and long delayed in mercy and patience, but no evil can escape divine penalty. We are reaping every day harvests sprung from seed sown long years ago. We wonder that this or that judgment should have happened to-day, forgetting that no judgment arises, except out of a sequence which we ourselves began, the criminal misfortune being that we forget the seed-time in which we were so busy, and only see the black harvest which we are bound to cut down and appropriate.

In the fourteenth chapter we see on the part of Jonathan what may be described as a disorderly courage. Jonathan undertook to make a movement on his own part without seeking the advice or sanction of his father. We must not too hardly blame Jonathan, for if his father was a young king, he himself was a young man who had yet all his honours to win. Disorderly courage has often been crowned with successes, and has therefore presented a strong temptation to ill-controlled natures. Free lances have unquestionably done good service in many a man, physical and moral. At the same time there ought to be a great central authority in all well-conducted operations. Room should always be left for genius, and for those sudden impulses of the soul which it is sometimes impossible to distinguish from inspiration : but taking the rank and file, and looking upon the Church as a whole, it will be found that a quiet exercise ot discipline and a steady pursuit of paths of order will answer best in the great issue. In the Church, let us repeat, room should be found for all sorts of men : for the great king and the young soldier, for the flashing genius and the slow-moving mind.

This action on the part of Jonathan brought him into trouble Saul knew that some one was missing, and after going through a process of inquiry and numbering it was found that Jonathan and his armour-bearer were not present. In his eager impetuosity Saul had adjured the people saying, " Cursed be the man that eateth any food until evening, that I may be avenged on mine enemies " (xiv. 24). Jonathan was unaware of the order, so in going through a wood where there was honey upon the ground, Jonathan put forth the end of the rod that was in his hand and dipped it in an honeycomb, and put his hand to his mouth, and his eyes were enlightened. On being informed of the order of the king, Jonathan denounced the action of Saul, and in very deed it was irrational and intolerable. Afterwards when a lot was drawn between Saul and Jonathan, Jonathan was taken, and on being interrogated he confessed saying, " I did but taste a little honey with the end of the rod that was in mine hand, and lo, I must die." But the people would not have it so. The king was taught that day his first lesson as to the power of the democracy. Even kings must under some circumstances be the subjects of their people Israel was at that juncture a people to be found ready. Their appeal was nobly conceived and nobly expressed. "And the people said unto Saul, Shall Jonathan die, who hath wrought this great salvation in Israel? God forbid : as the Lord liveth, there shall not one hair of his head fall to the ground ; for he hath wrought with God this day" (xiv. 45). Trust the people. There are occasions on which the proverb is true : *Vox populi, vox Dei.* The instincts of a great people are never to be lightly treated. Saul might on this occasion indeed be secretly inclined to concur with the popular verdict, but whether he was or not, the popular verdict, in so far as it is right, must always overrule the arbitrary and oppressive decrees of kings.

We have reserved for a concluding paragraph a memorable incident recorded in the fourteenth chapter. Dealing as we now are with the early efforts of Saul, we must point out with especial vividness that in connection with this war Saul built his first altar : "And Saul built an altar unto the Lord : the same was the first altar that he built unto the Lord" (v. 35). Some have regarded this as an act kindred to the service which Samuel condemned. Whether that may be so or not in a technical sense, the fact of the altar being the "first altar" is full of beautiful significance. We read in the Gospel of John of the first miracle that Jesus did. In Genesis we have read of Abraham returning to the altar which he built at the first. What a noble vision is opened up by the very words—first altar, first miracle, first war, first victory. Some of us have not yet begun to build an altar. Some of us have not sat down for the first time at the table of the Lord. Some of us have yet to make a real beginning in life ! Behold, now is the accepted time ; behold, now is the day of salvation.

1 Samuel xv. 11.

" It repenteth me that I have set up Saul to be king : for he is turned back from following me, and hath not performed my commandments."

SAUL REJECTED.

THIS is a decisive word, and a good reason is given for its being spoken. God is said to "repent" when, for moral reasons, he sets aside arrangements which he had appointed. The change is not in God, it is in man : all the government of God is founded upon a moral basis ; when moral conditions have been impaired or disturbed, God's relation to the matter in question is of necessity changed ; and this change, justified by such reasons, could not be more conveniently or indeed more accurately expressed than by the word *repentance*.

Saul hardly begins his reign when, somehow or other, he gets wrong. He seems to be unable to take hold of anything by the right end. There is a mist before his eyes which causes him to mistake distances and proportions ; and there is a crookedness in his judgment which brings him to false conclusions whenever he tries the simplest process of reasoning. He was told to remain in Gilgal for seven days. As Samuel did not come within that period, Saul became impatient, and, by vehemence of self-will, sought to recover ground which he supposed himself to have lost. Samuel addressed him in language of terrible severity : " Thou hast done foolishly : thou hast not kept the commandment of the Lord thy God, which he commanded thee : . . . but now thy kingdom shall not continue" (xiii. 14). The anger seems to be out of proportion to the offence. Saul was impatient, and there-fore he lost his kingdom. Saul disobeyed upon a point which did not appear to be of vital importance, and therefore he was to be deposed. This was very summary ; so much so, that we feel inclined to rebel against it. We see something of the same thing in the life that is around us. Men are suddenly brought down from high and dignified positions. They are brought into desolation as in a moment ; and yet we are at a loss to see cause enough for the angry visitation of God. No doubt they have been imperfect, but so are all men : no doubt they have sinned ; but in this they have the example of the whole world to plead. The fact is, that we do not see the whole of any case. " Man looketh on the outward appearance, but the Lord looketh on the heart." This is our confidence, that every stroke of divine judgment is proportioned to the guilt upon which it falls, and, though we cannot see the proportion now, God will cause us hereafter to see that his judgments have been true and righteous altogether.

We shall now see more deeply into the character of Saul than we have yet done. We have before us a detailed account of one transaction ; sometimes into one act we put the quality of our whole character ; and one day may sometimes be taken as a condensation of an entire lifetime. There are single acts which gather up into themselves the processes of many years. One cry of anguish may tell the tragic story of a wasted life. In this case, Saul was commanded to " go and smite Amalek, and utterly destroy all that they have, and spare them not ; but slay both man and woman, infant and suckling, ox and sheep, camel and ass." Such was the commandment : what was the result ? This : " Saul and the people spared Agag, and the best of the sheep, and of the oxen, and of the fatlings, and the lambs, and all that was good, and would not utterly destroy them ; but everything that was vile and refuse, that they destroyed utterly " (xv. 3, 9).

What are the lessons with which the narrative is charged ?

1. The danger of mistaking partial for complete obedience. " Blessed be thou of the Lord : I have performed the commandment of the Lord."
   (*a*) God requires literal obedience.
   (*b*) God's language never exceeds God's meaning.
   (*c*) Conscience is seen most clearly in minute obedience.

2. The possibility of giving a religious reason for an act of disobedience. "The people spared the best of the sheep and of the oxen, to sacrifice unto the Lord thy God."

(*a*) One duty must not be performed on the ruins of another. It was a duty to sacrifice, but sacrifice must not be offered upon disobedience.

(*b*) God's commandment must not be changed by men's afterthought. Lucky ideas, sudden inspirations, and the like, mean ruin, unless well tested.

3. The danger of being seduced into disobedience by social clamour. "I have sinned: for I have transgressed the commandment of the Lord, and thy words: because I feared the people, and obeyed their voice."

(*a*) The people who tempt are not the people who can save.

(*b*) Where God has spoken distinctly, there should be no human consultation.

4. The certain withdrawment of the best influences of life, as the result of disobedience. "And Samuel came no more to see Saul until the day of his death." Parents, ministers, friends, gone!

There are some incidental points of application :

(1) Sin discovers itself: "What meaneth then this bleating of the sheep in mine ears, and the lowing of the cattle which I hear?"

(2) Sin will be punished. Four hundred years elapsed before the sword fell upon Amalek (Deut. xxv. 17, 19). Time has no effect upon moral distinctions, or moral judgments.

PRAYER.

ALMIGHTY GOD, we have no fear, because thou art on the throne. Thy power is infinite, thy mercy endureth for ever. With our whole hearts' love we say, Thy will be done. Deliver us from all self-trust. Help us to put our whole confidence in the Living One, who was, and is, and who yet will come to judge the world. May this day be to us as the Sabbath of the Lord; a time of rest and spiritual refreshment. May our souls know themselves to be near the Lord, and according to our manifold wants do thou command thy blessing to rest upon us, through Jesus Christ our Saviour. Redeem us from all worldliness, all selfishness, all debasement, all fear. Establish us in thy holy love. Lord, increase our faith. Answer the cry of our heart when we appeal to thee for the pardon of our sins. We come to thee through the appointed way; we stand beside the holy cross; we look to the one sacrifice. Fill our hearts with joy whilst we tarry at the cross. The Lord hear us, and from the hill of heaven send us answers of peace! We pray evermore in the name of God the Son. Amen.

I Samuel xvi. 12.

"Arise, anoint him: for this is he."

DAVID ANOINTED.

SAMUEL, the venerable and almost outworn prophet, would have made a mistake upon this occasion. When he looked upon Eliab, he said, "Surely the Lord's anointed is before him." It is clear, therefore, that even inspired and honoured prophets were not, in themselves, infallible. It would further appear that their inspiration was occasionally suspended. Now and again natural judgment interposed its opinion. Now and again the natural sense spoke first, without allowing the spiritual sense to lead the way. So when Samuel saw Eliab, he was struck by the natural nobleness and majesty of the young man's appearance, and said, "Surely this is the king of the Lord's choice." This notion of Samuel's is most instructive. He saw the king in Eliab's form, and he inferred that the kingliness of his stature came from the kingliness of his soul. It ought to be, surely, that outward greatness should be the expression of inward greatness;

otherwise how horrible a contradiction man may become! Evidently so. A man towering in stature, yet pining away in soul! A fine, noble, manly bearing, inspired, if inspired at all, by a spirit which has cut itself off from the divine and eternal! The man thus becomes a living lie. He becomes, too, the occasion of many mistakes on the part of others. Young men, fascinated by his outward appearance, infer that it must be safe to follow the lead of such a noble. Unsuspecting men, looking upon his openness and candour of countenance, may say, "Surely this man was made to be trusted;" others may be caught by the same reasoning, and so a man of certain form and aspect may be unconsciously misleading and seriously injuring his fellows.

Appearances ought to mean something. If a man has a noble physical appearance, that appearance ought to carry with it some moral significance. If it does not, the man himself should retire into his own heart, and ask himself a plain question or two. Did God fashion palaces for dwarfs? The man should inquire whether God intended that his outward nobleness of form and aspect should be inconsistent with his inner and better life? Ought not the natural to be the expression of the spiritual? Ought a man to have a noble head, and nothing in it—great physical power, and no power of soul—an open, beautiful countenance, yet the heart of a hypocrite or the soul of a villain? As with personal appearance, so with social appearance. Our outward figure in society ought to mean something good; something according to the measure of its greatness, and the intensity of its splendour. Shall a man live in a great house, and be surrounded by all the signs of luxury and advanced civilisation, and yet that appearance fail to denote that the inhabitant of that house and the owner of that property is a man of the noblest charity, and that what is round about him is but a poor figure and dim emblem of the reality of his spirit, and the inexhaustibleness of his love? A man ought not to feel himself at liberty to be inconsistent, to exhibit a daily discrepancy between his appearance and his reality, whether it be his personal appearance or his social appearance. If he has been gifted, either in one way or another, with great and notable outward

blessings, those gifts ought to lead him to the consideration of
questions of intellectual and moral culture ; so that the outward,
however great and impressive, may be but a feeble indication of
inward wealth, the richness of his knowledge, the depth and
truth, the purity and gentleness, of his soul !

On the other hand, there is a higher law. There is a law
which takes us clear out of the realm of appearances. All men
have not Eliab's kingliness of image, and majesty of bearing.
There are dwarfs, cripples, deformed men, men whose figure is
against them, whose outward appearance may lead people to
form the most erroneous conclusions regarding the quality and
temper of their souls. So we come for our relief and teaching to
this higher law which says, "Look not on his appearance. The
Lord seeth not as man seeth ; man looketh on the outward
appearance, but the Lord looketh on the heart." So, whilst
our subject appeals to those who are favoured with outward
beauty and external majesty, it also has a message for those
who have no such physical and external advantages. It says,
True beauty is beauty of the heart ; true greatness is greatness of
the mind ; abiding majesty is moral majesty ; what thou art in
reality, thou art in thy soul ! The bloom shall be taken off thy
cheek, the lustre shall be dimmed in thine eye ; the sap shall
be taken out of thy bodily strength : moral elements, spiritual
qualities, spiritual beauties,—these survive all wrecks, these
grow, these increase in lustre, beauty, and worth ; these, partaking of the very nature and quality of God, shall abide through
the ages of his own eternity !

Turning specially to the anointing of David, we shall regard
it in its bearing upon the divine law of election, which is so
mysteriously, yet so certainly and inexorably working amidst
the affairs of men. Looking at that law within the limits of
the present instance, two things are plain. It is plain, first,
that the law of divine election pays no regard to human prejudices.
There is, for example, a prejudice in favour of appearance.
Samuel himself was the subject of that prejudice. When a man
of towering physical stature, great breadth, and sublime aspect
came before him, he, though a spiritual man, and a specially

called prophet of the Lord, said, "Surely this kingly man must be the king of the Lord's choice." We may, too, have prejudices as respects age. We rightly say that age should speak, that a multitude of days should teach wisdom, that a man who has come to maturity, or grey hairs, has a right to a certain measure of social supremacy. There is, too, a prejudice as regards employment. We infer that because a man has been brought up in a lowly employment, therefore he is not qualified for high rule, for supreme command. Now as Samuel had the one prejudice, Jesse had the other. When Samuel asked if there was not another son, Jesse said to him, "that the youngest yet remained," pronouncing perhaps the word *youngest* so as to throw suspicion into the bare conjecture that one so young should be at all likely to ascend the throne of Israel. Not only did Jesse describe David as the youngest, but he described him also as keeping sheep. "He was but a shepherd, he watched his father's flock;" and to the mind of Jesse it seemed an impossible thing that a man could step from the shepherd's office to a royal position. Yet the Lord said of David, coming in fresh from the mountains, ruddy as the morning, strong as a youth sent down from heaven, "Arise, anoint him : for this is he;" thus setting aside human prejudices, and working according to a law which never has been sanctioned by the merely natural reason of mankind.

By calling unlikely men to the front, God humbles human judgment. No man can arise and say, "This is the Lord's chosen one," or "That ought to be the specially honoured servant of the Most High." Not the keenest, wisest, strongest of us is entitled to say who shall be sent on the Lord's errands. We are ruled by prejudices, we are oftentimes victims of appearances. We see form, not soul,—hands, not hearts. We draw conclusions from things seen and temporal. God hushes all our voices, and says, "I am the Lord; I will send by whom I will send : the work is mine, and the Master must choose the servants." So again and again we are thrown back from our most cautious reasoning, our most prudent conclusions, and God is every day in the Church and elsewhere giving our proud intellect the lie ; saying to our penetration, "Thou art blind;" saying to our judgment, "Thou art foolish, thou knowest not the measure of the case ; and when thou hast pronounced thine own opinion, thou hast but betrayed thine own incapacity and folly!"

God also keeps the world in constant expectation by calling unlikely men to do the chief of his work in society. We know not who may be called. "What I say unto one, I say unto all, Watch." We cannot tell but that the man who has been sitting on the outside, year after year, may be the very next to be called to the front, entrusted with high commissions, inspired to do the Lord's work amongst men. We ought, therefore, to live as those who are expecting messages from the Most High. At any moment he may speak to us by combinations of events which may take place with startling suddenness. He can alter our position in society, so that the man who was yesterday obscure may to-morrow be set on the very pinnacle of the social fabric, and he whose opinion was yesterday despised may rule the judgment of men to-morrow. Our life is thus redeemed from monotony, and saved from suicidal insipidity. The Lord is round about us, and at any moment he may charge us with his messages, and clothe us with his power!

By calling unlikely men to the front, God equalises the conditions of society. Suppose for one moment that all men were called from one class. What a change would take place in our social relations ! What pride would inspire some people—what despair would chill and darken others ! But God is continually working by a sovereign law, which we cannot understand, but which always vindicates its own mercifulness, as well as shows its infinite wisdom. Are the rich and the mighty and the noble always called to do the chief work in society ? Has not God sometimes gone forth that he might call the gatherer of sycamore fruit to do his work in Israel ; that he might call Elisha from the plough to speak the messages of his wisdom and love ; and that he might call great men from lowliest and obscurest positions to do some great work for him ? Thus society is equalised. One man is born to great social position ; he rules and sways. Another, born in poverty and obscurity, is called to discover, to enter upon great projects, to develop sublime schemes. Thus God equalises one aristocracy with another, and daily teaches us

that no man is to be despised ; that in the lowliest of his creatures
he can set up his temple, if he will !

See then the graciousness of the law of sovereign election. We
lay the whole stress of the emphasis in this sentence upon the
word *graciousness.* We do not speak of the majesty, the grandeur, the impressiveness, and sublimity of the law. But in this
law of sovereign election, daily at work amidst the affairs of men,
we discover infinite graciousness, beneficence, compassion. The
law has not only a sublime side, but a side which appeals to our
emotions, to our gratitude, to our confidence. God's strength is
the measure of God's love. So the Christian should say : Had I
any choice in the matter, I should prefer that God should elect to
rule according to his own counsel without ever consulting me. In
so far as I believe that he is infinite in wisdom, in power, in love,
in righteousness, in so far would I disclaim any right to participate
in his counsels, and should shrink from the responsibility of having
anything to do with determining my own life, merely as a question
of selfish calculation and policy; whilst with my whole heart would
I say to my Father in heaven, "Thy will be done !" I would
pray him to save me from consultation; I would appeal to him
not to make me a party to a decision; I would be his servant, his
agent, his son. I am but an insect born yesterday. What shall
I say to the eternal and infinite God ? I say, "Do not ask me ;
do not consult me ; thou knowest all ; let me find my liberty in
thy sovereignty ; let me find my freedom in thy rule ; what
thou doest, infinite, living One, must be best ! I will not ask to
be taken into the secret place of thy tabernacle, to be consulted ;
only fill me with thy light, and inspire me with thy love."
Thus the great law of election is not a terror, nor does it disclose
mere arbitrariness of will. It shows that there can be but one
Lord ; and in so far as we can say, "The Lord reigneth," our life
is a continual sabbath !

It is plain from this instance, in the second place, that the law
of divine election proves itself in spiritual gifts. We read, "The
Spirit of the Lord came upon David from that day forward."
The same thing we see in the case of Saul, upon whom the Spirit
of the Lord came, and of whom we read, "The Lord gave him

another heart." So it was with Joshua : "And the Lord said unto Moses, Take thee Joshua the son of Nun, a man in whom is the Spirit, and lay thine hand upon him." In like manner we read that "the Spirit of the Lord came upon Jephthah." So with Samson the strong man : "The Spirit of the Lord began to move Samson at times in the camp of Dan." It is of supreme importance that this side of the doctrine be understood ; so that the law of divine election may be saved from abuse. The law of divine election vindicates itself in spiritual expression on the part of those who are divinely elected. How is a man to show his election ? Not by pretension. The most solemn assertion on his part that he is called of God to do the work, amounts to nothing, considered in itself. A man may declare most solemnly and resolutely that he has a charge from God to reveal certain truths, to undertake certain offices, to do a specific work ; and yet his emphatic asseveration may go for nothing. How, then, is a man to prove his divine election ? Not by contemptuous treatment of other workers. Whatever be our gifts, we are not at liberty to treat with contempt those who are doing Christian work, or right work of any kind whatsoever, in Church or State, in the market-place, or in the household. The divinely elected man is a magnanimous man. He rarely has recourse to contempt ; when he is contemptuous, it is for moral, not for merely personal, reasons ; when he resorts to irony, banter, sarcasm, and contempt, it is in a spirit of righteousness—not that he enjoys the exercise, but that he sees by a vision, quickened and strengthened by God the Holy Ghost, that no other weapons could so successfully do the work to which he is called.

How, then, is a man to prove that he is called of God to do a special work, or to occupy a special position ? We answer, distinctly and emphatically, by the purity and force of his spiritual qualifications. Only so far as he has the Holy Ghost is he the elect servant, the representative of God ! What of his spirituality ? What of his calculation of things that are round about him, things seen and temporal ? what of his ideas of truth ? Is he at home in the spiritual region—has he keen, piercing insight into things,— true, living, heavenly insight into them ? By so much is he the called and crowned servant of the living God ! He must declare his election by his speech,—by its purity, spirituality, heaven-liness. When we come near him, we must feel that, though on earth, he is yet in heaven; that though he speaks the language of men, he speaks it in a tone and with an accent which he could only have learned of Jesus Christ and of God the Father! There must be something about him that is not merely physically dis-tinctive, but spiritually distinctive, separating him from all other men, and giving him a bearing and force which could only be derived from long-continued loving fellowship with the unseen, ever-living Lord! "Beloved, believe not every spirit: but try the spirits, whether they are of God." "Many shall come in my name, saying, I am Christ, and shall deceive many." "Of your own selves shall men arise, speaking perverse things to draw disciples after them." Hence we see that assertion is nothing; great, bold claim is nothing; sublimity of appearance is nothing. The whole question turns upon this: How much of the Holy Ghost is in the heart of a man, who claims to be a teacher sent from God, or a king of men?

An intelligent appreciation of this law of divine sovereign elec-tion would be attended by the happiest consequences. Life would no longer be looked upon as an irregular warfare. If we lose grasp of this doctrine life becomes a scramble; the strongest wins, the weakest is knocked to the wall; and as for the spiritual man, the soul that has not lost its sensibility, the man that has ideas of righteousness, truth, and honour—such men must be trampled in the dust. Lay hold of this doctrine, that God is at the centre, God is on the throne, marshalling all forces, and ruling all events; and how confused soever may be present appearances, we shall find a law working itself out which will justify every one who is good, vindicate every righteous claim, confound the wicked, and bear them away upon the whirlwind of divine indignation. Not only will this result follow; but responsibility will be felt to be measurable by proper limitations. All men are not equally responsible before God. Some require to be comforted upon this point, because this great question of responsibility is so heavy to carry; it troubles and overweights them till they can hardly get along at all,—so grievous is their sense of personal responsibility. Tell a man that God gives to every one a certain number of talents,—five, two, or one. Tell him that from one to whom much has been given, much will be required, and that from one to whom little has been given, little will be required ; then he begins to feel the justness, the equity, and graciousness of the living Lord. God gave us our original dowry, and from that point we must work out the sum of our responsibility. Our one talent will not be expected to be multiplied into ten ; our five talents will be expected to grow in proportion to their original number and quality. So there is righteousness at the heart of things. God's judgment-seat is a judgment-seat of light, truth, and equity ; and no man hath occasion to fear it, who has served God, and worshipped him in spirit and in truth. There will also be another result. Mutual honour will be unmingled with personal envy. We are not all equal, to begin with. God intended some to have great talents, and others to have but feeble gifts. God called some men to work at the front, and he intended other men to do a lowly, obscure, unseen work. God created yonder singing, shining poet, and God set another man down amongst the prosaic thinkers,—men who could see no further than a fact, and had little power of coming far into the empire of truth ; yet who were firm and sound within the limit and region of fact. Shall we envy the great man ? Surely not. He was made of God ; he is honoured of our Father,—we will glorify God in him. Such will be the conclusion to which we shall come, if we believe with all our heart that God is on the throne; and that he doeth in all these things, which are beyond our control, according, not only to the pleasure of his will, but the infinitude of his righteousness.

No man is elected to badness of character. God never called a man to wickedness. The whole tone of biblical teaching is against a theory so monstrous. We read of election to righteousness, of calls to high offices and noble functions, but we never read of God electing a man to hell ! As to this matter of election, we would to God that some who object to it were as common-sense in this question as they are in the daily actions of ordinary life ! We ask no higher degree of common-sense. Let us assume that a purse has been lost—a purse containing a thousand guineas ; and whoever finds it may keep it. "Ha!"

we say, " well, only one can find it ; therefore what is the use
of a thousand seeking it ?   Only one can have it ; and if I am
elected to be the man, it will come in my way." We never
heard people reasoning so with regard to an affair of that kind.
Though only one may have it, ten thousand would strive for it,
if they know the conditions.   There is a prize to be given in a
school.   It is one prize ; there are five hundred scholars in the
school.   The boys say, " Well, only one of us can get it, why
should five hundred of us be toiling and fagging for it ? " Another
boy says, " I know if I am to have the prize, I shall get it ; so I
shall read no books, and make no preparation." You would not
allow a boy to reason so.   Yet there are men who say this, " If
we are called to heaven, we'll get to heaven ; if we are elected to
be saved, we need not make any effort about it." " Thou wicked
and slothful servant : out of thine own mouth I condemn thee ; "
the whole action of thy evil life shall be thy answer on the day of
judgment, and thou shalt be condemned to an ignominious silence
because of a self-accusing conscience.

With God upon the throne, why should we be distressed by
unhappy appearances and unwelcome rumours ?   The Lord
reigneth ; that is enough.   Seated above all forms and all forces,
holding the royal sceptre, is the God and Father of our Lord
Jesus Christ.   The armies of heaven are his loving servants.   The
forces of creation are measured and controlled by his gracious
power.   Children of earth cannot go beyond the line he has
marked.   He maketh the wrath of man to praise him, and the
remainder of the wrath of men he doth restrain.   Such thoughts
bring the soul into holy quietness.   They sustain our hope when
the day is cloudiest and the night is filled with darkness.   They
rebuke our impatience and murmuring, and bid us nestle closer
to our Father's heart.   The sovereignty of the Lord is the security
of all goodness.   Destroy sovereignty and you inaugurate confusion.   What would be our poor human life, were God to leave
the throne, and allow us to go our own way, and do our own
bidding ?   Truly then we should be far away on the wild waters,
without captain or friend, and without hope of home.   Blessed
One, known to us through the great cross, leave not the throne ;
but rule us, work in us, have us in thy holy keeping !

PRAYER.

ALMIGHTY GOD, thou art always showing us thy goodness. We have said in many a song of adoring praise, "Goodness and mercy have followed us all the days of our life." Saying this, the whole earth has become the house of the Lord. We have consecrated every part of the habitable globe by songs of praise and by utterances of adoration and trust. " Behold, this is none other than the house of God," we have said, as great religious emotions have arisen in our hearts and ennobled our whole spirit by their pathos. We will now sing of judgment and mercy ; we will make mention of thy loving-kind-ness, and thy providential care shall be the subject of our song. Thou hast watched our uprising and our down-sitting, our going out and our coming in, and from the high hills thou hast sent us help every day, so that we have been lifted out of the low place, amid the cold wind and the stifling cloud, right up into bright places and into the sunlight and the music of better worlds. Thou hast disappointed our fear, as surely as thou hast exceeded our hope. We have not recognised our little prayer in thy great answer. Thou hast swallowed up our poor cry in all the bounteousness of thy great response. If our prayer was sown a little seed, thine answer has come to us as a great tree. Behold, how good thou art ! How infinite in tender-ness ! How eternal in patience ! How mighty is the delivering arm of God ! We will comfort ourselves with these words, being entitled to apply them by the grace that is in our Lord Jesus Christ, by whom alone we have come to know thee in all the loftiest and tenderest aspects of thy character. He has taught us to call thee Father, Father in heaven, and he has given to us visions of thy bounty and love which put out the brightness of the sun by their infinite glow. So we stand as children at home in the presence of the Father, and the table of his bounty, confessing our unworthiness; but whilst the confession is yet staining our lips, behold, thou art arraying us in the best robe and making our finger rich with the ring of thy love. "How good is the Lord !" our souls will say, startled into the gracious exclamation by many a sacred surprise. The high hill has been brought within easy ascent when we have come to it because of the presence of the Lord, and the rest of soul by which that presence has been testified. The stone has been rolled away from the door of the sepulchre when we have come to it ; for who can outrun the angels, and be first at the scene of battle ? Behold, thou art always first. We can but be second, for we are the creatures of thy hand, we are the sheep of thy pasture. Thou didst dwell in eternity ; thou didst come up from the infinite spaces ; by new names hast thou come down to us ; by the Lord and by Jehovah have we known thee, and then by Father —merciful, pitiful—and Redeemer revealed in thy Son. We will trust thy mercy, goodness, compassion, and love. There we feel a sense of security; there our souls fall into sweet peace; and as for the mysteries which darken around the horizon, we leave them to thee. Thou hast light enough to burn out their darkness, and to fill them with grace and glory. We will think of the past, but not too tearfully, lest we blind ourselves to its best lesson. We will call up the dead, until we know that they are more truly living than we are—a larger life, blessed with celestial liberty. We will look forward with confidence, for all our yesterdays are promises of all our to-morrows, and the Lord who has been known to us by many a name will find a new revelation for every dawning day. We will remember before thee our sick ones. Thou canst heal them with the poor health of time and the eternal health of heaven. Thou wilt remember our travelling friends, tossed on the sea, wandering in new lands, surrounded by unfamiliar associations. Their hearts are here, and yet there, with a divided attention, with a scattered and yearning love. The Lord feed them, lead them, sustain them, wherever they are, and bring them back to their desired haven with new blessings and the sense of new consecration to the living Owner of all souls. We remember the little ones, who can hardly speak their own request or tell their own necessities. We remember all classes and conditions of human life, from the lowest to the highest, from the most plebeian to the most imperial and royal, praying that all may feel themselves to be but men in the Lord's presence, and yet men even in his sight. The Lord send a fire amongst us that shall burn, but not consume. Open our mouths in blessing, in fearless, triumphant praise, and give us a deepening love, a more intense zeal for God, and a clearer view of the cross as the only answer to sin, and the only way to heaven. Amen.

<h3 style="text-align:center">1 Samuel xvii. 58.</h3>

"I am the son of thy servant Jesse the Bethlehemite."

<h2 style="text-align:center">UNDECLARED ROYALTY.</h2>

THAT is a very simple account for a man to give of himself, yet it answered the question which elicited it. Though but a stripling, David knew where to stop in his answers. On this occasion he could have startled Saul as Saul was never startled in his life, yet he held his peace! Truly, there is power in moderation; and truly, discretion is the supreme beauty of the valiant man. Notice with special care the exciting circumstances under which the answer was given. David stood before Saul with the head of the Philistine in his hand! Call up the scene! Look at the sinewy hand grasping the bleeding head of the boastful barbarian! See the flush upon the cheek of the young conqueror, then listen to the quiet answer! To be so self-controlled under such circumstances! Standing before the king, grasping the head of a man who made Israel quake, a nation looking at him, yet he speaks as if a stranger had accosted him in some peaceful retreat of the pasturage!

Now look at Saul. His position is very touching. Occasionally insane, he is to-day sober-minded and tranquil. Little does he know to whom he is speaking! David might have said, " Samuel came to my father's house in search of a king. He passed by my brethren one by one; I was sent for at length from the sheep-fold, and Samuel anointed me king of Israel. Behold in this bleeding head the first sign and pledge of my kingly power!" Instead of speaking so, he merely said, with a child's beautiful simplicity, " I am the son of thy servant Jesse the Bethlehemite."

Learn that men may be anointed long before their power is officially and publicly declared. God may have put his secret into their heart long before he puts the diadem upon their brow. We do not know to whom we are speaking. The child who looks so simple, almost insignificant, may become the man who shall render his age the greatest service, or bring upon it the most appalling ruin. You speak to the little one some gentle word, or bid him God-speed, not knowing that in after-years he may repronounce to a hushed world the convictions for which you could get no hearing, or may honour your memory by a successful vindication of its claim upon grateful regard.

Learn that God's arrangements are not extemporaneous. The men who shall succeed to all good offices are known to him from the beginning to the end. Often in our impatience we concern ourselves to know what will be done in the event of this man dying, or that—the king, the preacher, the prime minister, the commanding soldier. To us the prospect may be dark, but to God the whole course is clear; the successor is anointed, but not yet declared.

In studying the period of David's history which is comprised between his anointing and the killing of Goliath, we shall discover some qualities in David which we may well imitate.

Soon after his anointing, David became harp-player to the king.
This seems to be a descent. Are there not many apparent anti-
climaxes in life? Is this a conspicuous example of them? "Play
the harp! Why, I am king," David might have said. "Why
should I waste my time in attempting to prolong the life of the
man who is upon my throne? The sooner he dies, the sooner I
shall reign; not one soothing note will I evoke from my harp!"
Had David spoken so, he would have dropped from the high
elevation which becomes the spirit of a king. There are two
ways of looking at this harp-playing. David saw it in its right
aspect, and therefore to him it lost all its apparent humiliation.
To a mere outsider it was harp-playing; to David it was an
attempt to help a man by driving away an evil spirit. In
playing the harp David was doing a great spiritual work. He
was not trying to please the merely musical ear; he was not the
paid servant of taste; he was a spiritual minister, and as such he
was as the angel of God to the tormented man. It would help
us in our work if we looked at its spiritual rather than at its
merely outward aspect. The influence of a spiritual worker
never ceases. David's harp is being played still, and its strains
are expelling many an evil spirit. Had his work been merely so
much manipulation upon a musical instrument, his work would
have perished with his physical existence; but David played with
his soul as well as with his fingers; hence his strains linger in the
air, and find their way into our hearts when weary with much
sadness or beclouded by unusual fear. Let us remember that how
high soever be the office to which we are anointed, there is no anticlimax in our attempts to redeem men from the power of evil spirits,
or in any way, possible to us, to bring men out of the horror of
great darkness into the sweet light of hope. Are we skilled in
music? Let us help those who are sad. Have we this world's
goods? Let us seek out the poor, that they may bless us as the
messengers of God. Have we power to say beautiful words? Let
us speak to men who are weary of the common tumult which is
around them. To help a man is the honour of true kingliness.

After this engagement as harp-player, David went home to
pursue his usual avocations. How well he carried the burden
of his prospects! We see no sign of impatience. He did not

behave himself as a child who, having seen a toy, cries until it is put into his hands. David had the dignity of patience. He carried the Lord's secret in a quiet heart. Was it not a trial to him to go back to the sheepfold? Had it been so, he would have wrested the word of the Lord to his own destruction. He would then have worked from the point of his own desires rather than from the point of the divine will. In little things as well as in great, men show their temper and quality. One sign of impatience at this point would have shown that David's pride had overcome his moral strength. Who would rule, must learn to obey. Who would be master, must learn first and well the duties of a good servant. Are we conscious of superior powers? Let us show their superiority by the calmness of our patience, and by the repression of every wish that is marred by one element of selfishness.

When David came to see his fighting brethren, by the express instructions of his father Jesse, he disclosed a feature in his character in true keeping with what we have seen. When he had become acquainted with the case, he at once looked at outward circumstances in their moral bearing. Other men, including Saul himself, were talking about mere appearances. They did not see the case as it really was. Their talk, in fact, was strongly atheistic. They whispered to one another, in hot and panting breath, " Why, that staff of his is like a weaver's beam; look at his spear's head, it must weigh at least six hundred shekels of iron : I am told that the weight of his coat is five thousand shekels of brass; as for his height, it must be a span more than six cubits!" This was the talk that was proceeding when David ran into the army to salute his brethren. Is it not barbaric talk after all? It is external, mechanical, superficial. Now for another tone! David called Goliath, not a giant, not a soldier, but an uncircumcised Philistine, who had defied the armies of the living God! This is a moral tone. This is precisely the tone that was wanted in the talk of degenerate Israel! As used by David, the very word *uncircumcised* involved a moral challenge. In effect, David said : " I do not look upon his height; I ask no questions respecting the strength of his muscles, the length of his staff, the circumference of his chest, the swing of his arm; he is an uncircumcised Philistine, and has defied the armies of the living God; it is none other than God himself whom the barbarian has defied; therefore shall judgment fall upon him swiftly, and the hand of the Lord shall tear him in pieces." This tone retrieves the honour of any controversy. It brings strength with it, and hope, and dignity. Israel had fallen away from the right elevation; the contention had become one of muscle against muscle, of number against number. David said, It is a contention between light and darkness, between right and wrong, between God and the devil; to your knees, O Israel, and call upon the name of the living God!

Oh for one David in every controversy! Men lose themselves in petty details, they fight about straws, they see only the surface; David saw the spiritual bearing of all things, and redeemed a controversy from vulgarity and atheism by distinctly and lovingly pronouncing the name of God. The atheist counts the guns, the saint looks up to God; the atheist is terrified by the size of the staff, the saint is inspired by his faith in right and purity. Such a man cannot fail. If he could fail, life would be a continual mockery, and hope would be only a variety of despair. Sooner or later what is right must slay what is wrong. If we lose faith in that doctrine, we lose everything in life worth having; creation itself is unsafe:—

> "The pillared firmament is rottenness,
> And earth's base built on stubble."

The moral is the true standard of measurement. Look not at Goliath's flesh, but at his soul, and learn how soon that arm withers which is not supported by spiritual strength. Let us copy the moral tone of David! We cannot copy it mechanically; it must come out of our heart of hearts, or it will perish in the very act of its expression.

David interpreted the past so as to qualify himself for the future. When Saul doubted his ability to cope with the Philistine, David recounted some of his recollections as a shepherd: "Thy servant kept his father's sheep, and there came a lion, and a bear, and took a lamb out of the flock: and I went out after him, and smote him, and delivered it out of his mouth : and when he arose against me, I caught him by his beard, and smote him, and slew him. Thy servant slew both the lion and the bear: and this uncircumcised Philistine shall be as one of them, seeing he hath defied the armies of the living God. The Lord that delivered me out of the paw of the lion, and out of the paw of the bear, he will deliver me out of the hand of this Philistine " (vv. 34-37). The past should be our prophet. David confided in the unchangeableness of God. Forms of danger vary ; but the delivering power remains the same. Sometimes danger comes as a lion, sometimes as a bear, sometimes as a Philistine, sometimes as a devil. David did not ask what the special form was, he knew that God never changed, and that his power was the same in all cases. We know this right well ; our path is strewn with lions and bears slain in the name of the Lord, yet we are as afraid of the next lion or the next Philistine as if God had never enabled us to smite an enemy ! " Lord, increase our faith." When our theology is right, our power over circumstances will be complete, and our theology is right when the heart's whole trust is in the living Father, and our love goes out towards him through his one Son, Jesus Christ the Saviour. When our hold upon the true idea of God is lost, our life is disorganised and weakened ; when our hold of that idea is firm, we " plant our footsteps in the sea, and ride upon the storm." The great fight of life is a contention between the material and the spiritual. Goliath represents the material ; he is towering in stature, vast in strength, terrible in aspect. David represents the spiritual : he is simple, trustful, reverent ; the merely fleshly side of his power is reduced, to the lowest possible point,—he fights under the inspiration of great memories, in a deeply religious spirit, not for personal glory but for the glory of the living God.

David went to his work in the name and fear of God. " I come to thee in the name of the Lord of hosts." In that one word David disclosed the secret of his power. His mere personality ceased, and he became the minister of God. As a contest between strength and strength, the scene was simply ridiculous. Viewed materially, the Philistine was perfectly right when he disdained David, and scornfully laughed at the weapons which the stripling

produced.   Goliath showed a most justifiable contempt; as a
materialist, he could ind.ed have adopted no other tone.   David
made no boast of his weapons.   He pronounced the name of God,
and put his life in the keeping of the Most High.   It is as if David
had said, " My fall will be the fall of God ; it is not a fight between
thee and me, O strong man; it is a fight between earth and heaven ;
the victory will not be given to the weapon, but to the hand that
wields it; God shall hurl this stone at thee, thou uncircumcised
boaster, and before it thou shalt be as a helpless beast."

   In the expression, " I come to thee in the name of the Lord of
hosts," we have a watchword which may be used by true men in
all crises.   Let us use it in temptation, in times of unjust opposition, in solemn trials of strength and patience ; yes, and use it
when Death itself challenges us to the combat!   That grim monster
will one day invite us to contest.   He will call us out, that in
the open field we may try our strength together.   If we go in
our own name, we shall be worsted in the fray ; to Death itself
let us say, " I come to thee in the name of the Lord of hosts," and
death shall be swallowed up in victory.

   The application of the truths of this lesson is easy as a matter
of inference, but hard as a matter of realisation.   Some men save,
others are saved.   Such is the law of sovereignty.   This law of
sovereignty penetrates the whole scheme and fabric of life.   David
saved, Israel was saved ; activity and passivity make up the
sphere of this life.   Without any attempt at fanciful spiritualising,
we see in David the type of the one Saviour of the world, Jesus
Christ, who bruised the serpent's head, and won for us the one
victory through which we may have eternal life.   "Crown Him
Lord of all."

PRAYER.

ALMIGHTY GOD, who can bear the scourging of the rod that is in thine hand? Thou dost not willingly grieve or afflict the children of men. Thy purpose is directed by eternal love, though thy stroke be sometimes heavier than we can bear. Thou rememberest that we are dust. Our breath is in our nostrils; we hasten away like a cloud in the morning; our days are few before thee. Be merciful unto us, through Jesus Christ, our infinitely sufficient and precious Saviour, and grant that the end of all discipline may be our likeness to the beauty of his holiness. Chasten us, that we may be good, but slay us not with the sword. When we are in the furnace, be thyself our Refiner. When earthly things are plucked out of our hands, may it be that our hearts may be enriched with heavenly treasure. Lord, hear us. Son of God, come to us. Holy Spirit, dwell in us. May the holy word be to us a word of gracious explanation, lest we faint under the mysteries of thy providence. Whilst we pray, our hearts are waiting and watching at the cross. Amen.

1 Samuel xviii. 9.

"And Saul eyed David from that day and forward."

DISCIPLINE.

WE now enter upon scenes which show that long and most painful discipline is compatible with divine election to high office. David had been anointed, yet he afterwards was hunted as a beast of prey. The secret of the Lord was in his soul, yet the hand of an enemy was madly against him day and night. The inference of mere reason was obvious,—it was this: "Samuel has deceived me the old prophet has mistaken me for another man; and now through his blunder I am exposed to intolerable vexations and injuries: had God chosen me, he would have set me on a high mountain, where no evil hand could have reached me, or hidden me in a defence far away from the storm." This reasoning, as a mere intellectual effort, would have been sound and unanswerable. Yet David never uttered words so reproachful and distrustful. He accepted his ill-fortune in a spirit of wisdom, and went in and out before his enemy with a circumspection more terrible than anger. " Saul was afraid of David, because the Lord was with him." Saul himself could see the divine prese ice. There is an indefinable something about elect men which guards them without display, and announces them without ostentation.

Let us gather what instruction and comfort we can from a study of the severe discipline which David underwent immediately after victory. Remembering the undoubted anointing of David, let us see what untoward and heart-breaking experiences may befall men whom God has sealed as the special objects of his favour and the high ministers of his empire. Given, a man called of God to a great work, and qualified for its execution, to find the providences which will distinguish his course. A child might answer the easy problem : His career will be brilliant ; his path will be lined with choice flowers ; he will be courted, blessed, honoured on every hand. Look at the history of David for a contradiction of this answer. We shall find persecution, hatred, difficulty, hunger, cold, loneliness, danger upon danger ; yet he who endures them all is an anointed man—a favourite of Heaven.

The history shows four things respecting the discipline of an anointed man :—

1. That great honours are often followed by great trials.—The graciousness of this arrangement in human training. These trials not to be looked at in themselves but in their relation to the honours which went before. Imagine a garden discussing the year as if it were all winter. Look at the temptation assailing David in the fact that he alone had slain the enemy of Israel. Something was needed on the other side to chasten his feeling. Men must be taught their weakness as well as their power.

2. That great trials generally bring unexpected alleviations.— " The soul of Jonathan was knit with the soul of David, and Jonathan loved him as his own soul." " Jonathan and David made a covenant, because he loved him as his own soul. And Jonathan stripped himself of the robe that was upon him, and

gave it to David, and his garments, even to his sword and to his bow and to his girdle." The love of one true soul may keep us from despair. Love is fertile and energetic in device. See what Jonathan did. Love is more than a match for mere power. Love is most valued under such circumstances as David's. "There is a Friend that sticketh closer than a brother."

3. That no outward trials can compare in severity with the self-torment of wicked men.—We are apt to think that Saul did all the mischief, and David suffered it. That is an incomplete view of the case. Saul was himself the victim of the cruellest torment. When the women came out of all cities of Israel, singing and dancing, to meet King Saul, with tabrets, with joy, and with instruments of music, they said, " Saul hath slain his thousands, and David his ten thousands." Then there entered into Saul the cruellest of all infernal spirits, the spirit of jealousy. " Saul was very wroth, and the saying displeased him ; and he said, They have ascribed unto David ten thousands, and to me they have ascribed but thousands : and what can he have more but the kingdom ? And Saul eyed David from that day and forward." And truly, even in suffering, Saul had the worst of it. See how unjust is jealousy,—the great work of David undervalued. Saul was the slave of jealousy, and as such all his peace was destroyed. There was bitterness in his wine ; the charm of sleep had perished ; the bloom of summer had faded ; there was a cruel serpent gnawing at his heart. " The way of transgressors is hard." Let us not suppose that unjust opposition or enmity has an easy life. Better be the martyr than the persecutor, the oppressed than the oppressor. Read Saul's inner life,—anger, envy, madness, murder, evil scheming, chagrin,—hell !

4. That great trials, though calling for self-scrutiny, may not call for self-accusation.—This is a point which should be put with great delicacy, because we are too apt to exempt ourselves from self-reproach. David would be utterly at a loss to account for his treatment so far as his own behaviour was concerned ; for he had the distinct consciousness that God was with him : and as to his outward relations, it is upon record that " David behaved himself wisely in all his ways," and that Saul was afraid of him because of the wisdom of his behaviour.

The question which the tried man generally asks himself is, What have I done? Days of misery have been spent in brooding over that inquiry. The question is only good so far as it goes. It should be succeeded by another—What is God doing? Imagine the silver in the refining fire asking, What have I done? not knowing that it is being prepared to adorn the table of a king! Imagine the field asking, What have I done, that the plough should cut me up? We are strong only so far as we see a divine purpose in the discipline of our life. "Whom the Lord loveth he chasteneth, and scourgeth every son whom he receiveth." "Let patience have her perfect work." We are polished by sharp friction. We are refined by divine fire. Sorrow gives the deepest and sweetest tone to our sympathy. We should be driven mad by uninterrupted, ever-augmenting prosperity. Over every jealous soul the hand of the Lord is omnipotent. Look at Saul, and the case of David is hopeless; look beyond him, and see how by a way that he knew not the shepherd was being trained to be mighty among kings, and chief of all who sing the praises of God.

SELECTED NOTE.

"*And the women answered one another as they played, and said, Saul hath slain his thousands, and David his ten thousands*" (v. 7).—This is quite characteristic of the manners of the East. Everywhere in that part of the world the people are accustomed in this manner to hail the arrival of those who have been any time absent from them. More especially do they do so on the return of a victorious army. Multitudes then issue from the towns and villages through which they are expected to march, in order to form a triumphal procession to celebrate their valour, the principal part being composed of women and children, who band together, and, as they go along, gratify the heroes with dancing, music, and songs in honour of their martial deeds, particularly of such of the chiefs as have greatly distinguished themselves. We find this custom in Persia, Turkey, etc. Mr. Campbell, the missionary, witnessed it even in Africa. When he was leaving the city of Lattakoo, he fell in with a party of men who were returning from a distant expedition, after an absence of several months. The news of their approach had reached the town, and the women were hastening to meet them. On joining the party the females marched at their head, clapping their hands and singing with all their might, till they arrived at their homes in the town.